A HISTORY OF SOUTH AFRICA

LEONARD THOMPSON

A History of
South
Africa

FOURTH EDITION

REVISED AND UPDATED BY
LYNN BERAT

Yale UNIVERSITY PRESS
New Haven & London

First edition published 1990. Fourth edition 2014.

Preface to the Fourth Edition, Chapter 10, and
Appendix copyright © 2014 by Lynn Berat.

Copyright © 2000 by Leonard Thompson.

Yale University Press books may be purchased in quantity for educational,
business, or promotional use. For information, please e-mail sales.press@yale.edu
(U.S. office) or sales@yaleup.co.uk (U.K. office).

Printed in the United States of America.

Library of Congress Control Number: 2013953764
ISBN: 978-0-300-18935-3 (pbk.)

A catalogue record for this book is available from the British Library.

10 9 8 7 6 5 4 3 2 1

CONTENTS

v

CONTENTS

ILLUSTRATIONS

Frontispiece Nelson Mandela casts his vote in South Africa's
first all-race election, April 27, 1994. Photo:
AP/World Wide Photos.

Following page 134

1. Rock Painting, Mount Hope, Eastern Cape Province.
Reprinted from *Major Rock Paintings of Southern Africa,*
ed. Timothy Maggs (Bloomington: Indiana University Press,
1979), pl. 43. Courtesy Indiana University Press and David
Philip, Publisher, Claremont, South Africa.
2. Khoikhoi Pastoralists at Table Bay in 1706. Reprinted from
Abraham Bogaert, *Historische Rewizen Door d'oosteresche
Deelen van Asia* (Amsterdam, 1711).
3. A View in the Tswana Town of Ditakong, 1812. Reprinted
from William J. Burchell (1781–1863), *Travels in the Interior
of Southern Africa,* 2 vols. (London, 1824), facing 2:464.
4. Zulu Blacksmiths at Work, 1848. Reprinted from George
Frederick Angas (1822–1886), *The Kaffirs Illustrated*
(London, 1849), pl. 23. Photo: Yale Center for British Art,
Paul Mellon Collection.

16. South Side Staging, Kimberley Mine. Photograph by Aldham and Aldham, Grahamstown, circa 1880. Photo: Manuscripts and Archives Collection, Sterling Memorial Library, Yale University.

17. Sorting the Gravel for Diamonds. Photo: Manuscripts and Archives Collection, Sterling Memorial Library, Yale University.

18. Morning Market, Kimberley, circa 1887. Reprinted from Robert Harris, *South Africa* (Port Elizabeth, 1888). Photo: Manuscripts and Archives Collection, Sterling Memorial Library, Yale University.

19. Witwatersrand Main Reef Workings, circa 1887. Reprinted from Robert Harris, *South Africa* (Port Elizabeth, 1888). Photo: Manuscripts and Archives Collection, Sterling Memorial Library, Yale University.

20. Morning Market, Johannesburg, circa 1894. Reprinted from Photo-Publishing Co., *Photographs of South Africa* (Cape Town, 1894). Photo: Manuscripts and Archives Collection, Sterling Memorial Library, Yale University.

21. A Canteen, circa 1850. Painting by Frederick Timson I'Ons (1802–1887), reprinted from Victor De Kock, *Ons Erfenis* (Cape Town, 1960), p. 179.

22. The Conference at Block Drift, January 30, 1846. Reprinted from Henry Martens, *Scenes in the Kaffir Wars* (London, 1852–54). Photo: Yale Center for British Art, Paul Mellon Collection.

23. A British Wagon Convoy, circa 1853. Reprinted from Lt. Lumley Graham and Lt. Hugh Robinson, *Scenes in Kaffirland* (London, 1854). Photo: Yale Center for British Art, Paul Mellon Collection.

24. The Zulu War: Volunteers Burning Kraals and Driving Away Cattle. Reprinted from *Illustrated London News,* September 6, 1879, p. 217. Photo: Yale Center for British Art, Paul Mellon Collection.

25. Creating a New Colony: Hoisting the Royal Standard at Bloemfontein at the Formal Annexation of the Orange Free State. Reprinted from *Illustrated London News,* supplement, July 7, 1900, between pp. 36 and 37. Photo: Yale Center for British Art, Paul Mellon Collection.

26. The Guerrilla Warfare in South Africa: Repairing Railway Lines Cut by the Boers. Reprinted from *Illustrated London News,* January 5, 1901, p. 11. Photo: Yale Center for British Art, Paul Mellon Collection.

27. The Congress of the People, 1955. Photo: International Defence and Aid Fund (IDAF) Photographic Library, London.

MAPS

PREFACE TO THE FOURTH EDITION

South Africa is a place of stunning contrasts: extreme wealth and desperate poverty, heroic devotion to the greater good and klepto- and megalomaniacal self-interest, exceptional natural beauty and environmental desecration. It is, perhaps, not so much a "World in One Country" as the official tourism slogan once claimed, but a universe where worlds collide, always jarringly, sometimes violently. This, the fourth edition of *A History of South Africa,* includes a new chapter describing the major developments of the post-Mandela years, a time when the euphoria over the political redemption from apartheid ended and a new struggle for equality and democratic maturity began.

My thanks in this enterprise go to many friends and colleagues in South Africa, the United States, and elsewhere. My deepest gratitude goes to Sarah Miller, my editor at Yale University Press, who endured my frequent delays with equanimity and patience.

This edition is dedicated to the memory of Leonard Thompson.

Lynn Berat

PREFACE TO THE
THIRD EDITION

This edition contains two new chapters: a study of the complex political transition process in light of substantial new evidence and an original account of the new South Africa under President Nelson Mandela and his successor, Thabo Mbeki.

Once again I am deeply grateful to Lynn Berat for her knowledge and insights, her careful reading of drafts of the new chapters, and her skills in taming my extremely ill-behaved computer; also to Charles Grench, former editor in chief of Yale University Press, Laura Jones Dooley, associate managing editor, and Ali Peterson, reprints editor, for their friendship and professional skills.

PREFACE TO THE
1995 EDITION

Readers should be aware that, in South Africa as elsewhere, historians are shaped by the context in which they live and work, and that their publications in turn—especially their textbooks—influence the history of their times. During the British colonial regimes of the nineteenth century, many authors wrote in an imperialist mode. In reaction against that metropolitan bias, British colonists composed works that embodied their perspective as a dominant minority in an African milieu, often at odds with the British metropole; and by the end of the century, when British imperialism was reaching its apogee, Afrikaners were laying the foundations of an exclusive, nationalist historiography. In the segregation and apartheid years, the white regime authorized textbooks and favored other publications in the settler and Afrikaner nationalist traditions of the previous century. Today, those traditions are becoming obsolete. They have been overshadowed by counter-historiographies that, since World War II, have become increasingly rich, varied, and nuanced.

Historians writing from a critical liberal perspective began to expose the racial bias in the established historiography in the late 1920s. From the 1940s onward, their successors placed un-precedented emphasis on the historical experiences of Africans, Indi-ans, and Coloured People. By the 1970s, some scholars were creating a "radical" historiography, which was influenced by Marxism and highlighted the role of capitalism and the growth of class divisions in South Africa. Initially, a rather clear line demarcated the "liberal" and the "radical" perspectives, though each group also contained great differences—there were variations within the liberal tradition, and radicals drew on rival schools of Marxism. Recently, following the disintegration of the Soviet Union, the collapse of the communist re-gimes in eastern Europe and elsewhere, and the global movement to-ward an open economy, the perspectives have converged considerably. With some exceptions, liberals have been radicalized, radicals have been liberalized. In this book, I have drawn on the rich achievements of both streams of contemporary South African historiography.

What of the future? Because historians now live in a post–Cold War and postapartheid context, we may expect new departures in South African historiography. Historians with strong commitments to the African nationalist movement may be expected to write from that perspective, which may lead to partisan works resembling a mirror-image of Afrikaner nationalist writings. Meanwhile, scholars and bu-reaucrats are working to create and authorize school textbooks that reflect the democratic ideology of the new government, in place of the old textbooks, which emphasized the achievements of Whites and denigrated Blacks.

As a result of the racial structure of South African society, almost none of the scholars who currently hold appointments in history de-partments in South African universities are Africans and nearly all the historiography of South Africa has been written by white people. In the future, Africans will bring new perspectives, new experiences, and new linguistic skills to the study of South African history. They may be expected to explore fresh topics and produce works with dis-tinctive features. This process will be gradual. It will take time for Africans to acquire professional training and research experience and to receive appointments that provide opportunities for historical research.

We may also expect that historical themes that received scant at-tention in the past will now come to the fore. Ethnicity is a typical ex-ample. Ethnic divisions among Africans were so central to the apartheid ideology that they were taboo for most scholars not tainted by the apartheid regime. Now, the history of the politicization of ethnicity in South Africa, among Blacks as well as Whites, has become highly relevant. Women's history has already received considerable attention in South Africa, but deeper examination of the role of gender in South African history has become a high priority, owing to unresolved tensions between the ideal of gender equality and the patriarchal traditions and practices of African societies. Among many other themes that warrant closer examination in the new South Africa than previously are historical studies of African health, of African families, of African spirituality and ideology, of South African urbanization, and of the South African environment. We may look forward to works on such themes cast in long-term perspective—exploring the continuities and changes through the centuries before and since the conquest and the impact of industrial capitalism.

The scene of a variety of complex relations among diverse cultures, South Africa will always offer challenges to creative scholars. One hopes that South African historiography will remain a rich field of intellectual inquiry into the distant future. Meanwhile, this volume is a succinct survey of the present state of knowledge.

I am grateful to Lynn Berat, Leonard Doob, William Foltz, Christopher Saunders, Robert Shell, and Johann van der Vyver for valuable criticisms of a draft of chapter 8; and to Leslie Bessant, Catherine Higgs, and Sean Redding for comments on the first edition, which they have been using in their university and college classes. This edition, like the first, has benefitted greatly from the professional skills of Charles Grench and Laura Dooley of Yale University Press.

CHRONOLOGY

Millennia B.C.	Hunter-gatherers, ancestors of the Khoisan (Khoikhoi and San: "Hottentots" and "Bushmen"), living in Southern Africa
By A.D. 300	Mixed farmers, ancestors of the Bantu-speaking majority of the modern population, begin to settle south of the Limpopo River
1487	Portuguese expedition led by Bartholomeu Dias reaches Mossel Bay
1652	The Dutch East India Company founds a refreshment station at the Cape of Good Hope
1652–1795	Genesis and expansion of the Afrikaners ("Boers"); the Khoisan conquered; slaves imported from Indonesia, India, Ceylon, Madagascar (Malagasy), and Mozambique
1795	Britain takes the Cape Colony from the Dutch
1803	The Dutch (Batavian Republic) regain the Cape Colony by treaty
1806	Britain reconquers the Cape Colony

1811–12	British and colonial forces expel Africans from the territory west of the Fish River
1815	Rising of frontier Boers (later known as the Slagtersnek rebellion)
1816–28	Shaka creates the Zulu kingdom; warfare among Africans throughout much of southeastern Africa (the *Mfecane*)
1820	British settlers arrive in the Cape Colony
1828	The Cape colonial government repeals the pass laws
1834–38	Cape colonial slaves emancipated
1834–35	Xhosa defeated by British and colonial forces
1835–40	Five thousand Afrikaners (later known as voortrekkers) leave the Cape Colony with their "Coloured" clients; a movement later known as the Great Trek
1838	An Afrikaner commando defeats the Zulu army at the battle of Blood River
1843	Britain annexes Natal
1846–47	Xhosa defeated by British and colonial forces
1850–53	
1852, 1854	Britain recognizes the Transvaal and Orange Free State as independent Afrikaner republics
1856–57	The Xhosa cattle-killing
1858	Lesotho wins war versus the Orange Free State
1865–67	The Orange Free State defeats Lesotho
1867	Diamond mining begins in Griqualand West
1868	Britain annexes Lesotho ("Basutoland")
1877	Britain annexes the Transvaal
1879	British and colonial forces conquer the Zulu after losing a regiment at Isandhlwana
1880–81	Transvaal Afrikaners regain their independence
1886	Gold mining begins on the Witwatersrand

1895–96	Leander Starr Jameson leads an unsuccessful raid into the Transvaal
1897–98	Rinderpest destroys vast numbers of cattle
1898	Transvaal commandos conquer the Venda, completing the white conquest of the African population of Southern Africa
1899–1902	The War between the Whites: Britain conquers the Afrikaner republics
1904–7	Chamber of Mines imports 63,397 Chinese workers
1906–7	Britain gives parliamentary government to the former republics; only Whites enfranchised
1910	The Cape Colony, Natal, the Transvaal, and the Orange Free State join to form the Union of South Africa
1912	South African Native National Congress (NNC) founded; later becomes the African National Congress (ANC)
1913	Natives Land Act limits African landownership to the reserves; the beginning of a series of segregation laws
1914–19	As a member of the British Empire, South Africa participates in World War I
1917	Anglo American Corporation of South Africa founded
1921	Communist party of South Africa founded
1922	White strikers seize control of Johannesburg but are crushed by government troops
1936	African parliamentary voters placed on a separate roll
1939–45	South Africa participates in World War II on the Allied side
1946	70,000 to 100,000 African gold-mine workers strike for higher wages; troops drive them back to the mines
1948	The Afrikaner National party wins a general election and begins to apply its policy of apartheid
1950	The Population Registration Act classifies people by race;

	the Group Areas Act makes people reside in racially zoned areas
1950 ff.	Security legislation gives the government vast powers over people and organizations
1952	The ANC and its allies launch a passive resistance campaign
1953	The government assumes control of African education
1955	The Congress of the People adopts a Freedom Charter
1956	156 members of Congress Alliance charged with high treason
	Coloured parliamentary voters placed on a separate roll
1958–66	Verwoerd is prime minister
1959	Pan-Africanist Congress (PAC) founded
1960	African and Coloured representation in Parliament (by Whites) terminated
	Police kill 67 African anti–pass-law demonstrators at Sharpeville; the government bans African political organizations
1961	South Africa becomes a republic and leaves the British Commonwealth
1964	Nelson Mandela and other ANC and PAC leaders sentenced to life imprisonment
1966–68	Lesotho, Botswana, and Swaziland become independent states
1975–76	Mozambique and Angola become independent states
1976–77	At least 575 people die in confrontations between Africans and police in Soweto and other African townships
1976–81	South Africa grants "independence" to the Transkei, Bophuthatswana, Venda, and the Ciskei Homelands, but they are not recognized abroad

1977	The U.N. Security Council imposes a mandatory embargo on the supply of arms to South Africa
1978–84	Botha is prime minister
1979	African trade unions can register and gain access to the industrial court and the right to strike
1980	Zimbabwe (previously Rhodesia) becomes independent
1981–88	South African forces invade Angola and make hit-and-run raids into Lesotho, Mozambique, Zimbabwe, and Zambia; ANC guerrillas sabotage South African cities
1983	United Democratic Front (UDF) formed
1984	A new constitution gives Asians and Coloureds but not Africans limited participation in the central government; Botha becomes state president
1984–86	Prolonged and widespread resistance to the regime in black South African townships; violent government reactions
1985	First contacts between the government and imprisoned and exiled ANC leaders
1986	Pass laws repealed
	The government proclaims a nationwide state of emergency, detains thousands of people, and prohibits the press, radio, and television from reporting unrest
	The U.S. Congress passes the Comprehensive Anti-Apartheid Act over President Reagan's veto
1986–95	Violent conflict between Zulu supporters of Inkatha and the ANC in KwaZulu and on the Witwatersrand
1987	Three-week strike by 250,000 African mine-workers
1988	South Africa undertakes to withdraw from Angola and cooperate in U.N.-monitored independence process in Namibia
1989	De Klerk succeeds Botha, first as leader of the National party, then as president

1990	De Klerk unbans the ANC, PAC, and SACP; releases Mandela and other political prisoners
	Namibia gains independence
1990–91	1913 and 1936 Land Acts, Group Areas Act, Population Registration Act, and Separate Amenities Act repealed; political organizations unbanned; state of emergency revoked; amid widespread violence, delegates from 18 parties start formal negotiations
1992	White voters support the negotiation process in a referendum
	The ANC breaks off negotiations with the government after an Inkatha mob massacres 46
1993	Negotiations resume; de Klerk, Mandela, and leaders of 18 other parties endorse an interim constitution
1994	Governments of the Bophuthatswana and Ciskei "Homelands" collapse
	The ANC wins first nonracial election (April 27–30)
	Nelson Mandela is sworn in as president (May 10) and forms Government of National Unity
	Foreign governments lift sanctions; South Africa rejoins the British Commonwealth
	Crime escalates
1995	Racial conflict in the police force (January)
	Inauguration of the Constitutional Court (February); it abolishes the death penalty (May)
	Disturbances in universities (March)
	Inkatha withdraws from the Constituent Assembly (April)
	Inauguration of the Commission for the Restitution of Land Rights (May)
	The Truth and Reconciliation Commission starts work

1996	The Constituent Assembly enacts a permanent constitution
	The National party withdraws from the Government, leaving the Inkatha Freedom party as well as the ANC
1998	Publication of the Truth and Reconciliation Commission's report
1999	General election: the ANC wins 66 percent of the vote
	The Democratic party replaces the National party as the official opposition
	Mandela retires, succeeded by Thabo Mbeki
	Strikes by government employees, including teachers
2000	Large-scale industrial strike
	Crisis in Zimbabwe has repercussions in South Africa
	The National party merges with the Democratic party
	13th international conference on AIDS meets in Durban
2001	Promotion of Access to Information Act takes effect
	Grootboom right to housing case decided by Constitutional Court
2002	*Treatment Action Campaign* case on access to antiretroviral drugs decided by Constitutional Court
	Formation of Democratic Alliance
	African Union launched in Durban
	New Partnership for African Development created
2003	Patricia de Lille forms Independent Democrats
	Cabinet overrides Mbeki and announces antiretroviral drug rollout plan
	Enactment of Broad-Based Black Empowerment Act
2004	Mbeki elected for second term
	Law on Anti-Terrorism adopted

Jaftha v. Schoeman right to housing case decided by
Constitutional Court

2005   New National party disbands

Mbeki removes Jacob Zuma as deputy president

Zimbabwean parliamentary elections

2006   Zuma acquitted of rape charges

Judicial Service Commission rejects public inquiry into
activities of Cape judge John Hlophe

U.N. Special Envoy for AIDS in Africa says South Africa
promotes "lunatic fringe" attitude toward AIDS

2007   Scorpions indict Zuma on corruption charges

Constitutional Court judges file charges against Judge
Hlophe

Zuma defeats Mbeki for ANC presidency at ANC conference in Polokwane

2008   Power-sharing agreement in Zimbabwe

Corruption charges against Zuma dropped

Mbeki resigns

Kgalema Motlanthe inaugurated

Barbara Hogan becomes minister of health

Congress of the People (COPE) founded

2009   Zuma elected president

Zuma appoints Sandile Ngcobo as chief justice

Zuma gives World AIDS Day speech announcing policy
to distribute antiretroviral drugs widely

2010   Organization for Economic Cooperation and Development report labels South Africa one of the world's most
unequal societies

Government acknowledges that Broad-Based Black
Economic Empowerment Program has been largely a
failure

South Africa does not issue visa to Dalai Lama to attend Desmond Tutu's eightieth birthday party

2011 Activist Andries Tatane killed by police during service delivery protest

South African Human Rights Commission investigates complaints about water quality and supply

2012 ANC centenary celebrations

Marikana Massacre

Moody's downgrades South Africa

ANC conference at Mangaung, Zuma reelected ANC president

2013 Mamphela Ramphele forms Agang SA

South African troops killed in Central African Republic

Passage of Secrecy Bill

Julius Malema forms Economic Freedom Fighters

2014 Twentieth anniversary of end of white rule

CHAPTER I

The Africans

The Significance and Problems of Precolonial History

Modern Western culture is inordinately present-minded. Politicians are ignorant of the past. School curricula foreshorten the historical record by focusing on recent events. People lack a sense of their location in time and fail to perceive that contemporary society is constrained by its cultural as well as its biological inheritance.

Many historians of the white South African establishment start their history books with a brief reference to the voyage of Vasco da Gama round the Cape of Good Hope in 1497–98 and then rush on to the arrival of the first white settlers in 1652. Other historians are so committed to emphasizing the role of capitalism as the molder of modern Southern Africa that they ignore the processes that shaped society before Europeans began to intrude in the region.

The precolonial history of Southern Africa is significant in its own right, providing examples of the constraints and possibilities, achievements and setbacks of preindustrial and preliterate communities as they established their niches in a variety of environments. It is also significant as providing essential links in explaining what has followed. Indigenous Southern Africans were not a tabula rasa for white invaders or capitalists to civilize or to victimize. Over many centuries, they had been developing social forms and cultural traditions that colonialism, capitalism, and apartheid have assaulted, abused, and modified but never eradicated. One cannot understand how Africans have endured the fragmentation of their family life by migrant labor unless one has knowledge of their customary social values and networks. Nor can one fathom the vigor of black resistance to the apartheid state without knowledge of precolonial African ideas about the social and economic obligations of rulers and rights of subjects, and the basis of political legitimacy.

The precolonial inhabitants of Southern Africa, however, were not literate, and there are peculiar difficulties in reconstructing the history of preliterate societies. Archaeologists, physical anthropologists, and linguists provide us with information. So do social anthropologists who study the societies in their present condition and authors who record the traditions that have been handed down within those societies. But even when we have a rich collection of such sources, our knowledge of the history of societies in the period when they were neither literate nor in contact with literate people is patchy. The archaeological record includes only a fraction of human remains and human products. We are on shaky ground when, as we must do, we draw historical inferences from comparative linguistics and from social anthropology. We know, moreover, that people manipulate and modify traditions to suit their interests.

In unraveling the prehistory of Southern Africa, the best we can do on many crucial topics is to express approximations, probabilities, and informed conjectures derived from the available evidence. The situation improves when we reach the time when literate eyewitnesses began to produce written descriptions; but not until the nineteenth century do we have the first substantial descriptions of societies in the interior of South Africa. Those accounts, moreover, have their limitations. Alien observers are imperfect recorders and interpreters, and we cannot be sure how ancient or how recent were the things that they described. Finally, it was not until the twentieth century that many Africans themselves began to write about their past. The reader should bear these problems in mind throughout this chapter.

The Southern African Environment

Although Southern Africa is at the southern end of the Eurasian-African landmass, it was an isolated region before humanity's technological advances of the past few centuries (map 1). Ocean currents impeded regular access by sea. In the South Atlantic, the Benguela current sets in a northerly direction and retards the approach. In the southern Indian Ocean, the Mozambique current sets strongly in a southerly direction, making it difficult for sailing craft to leave the region, so that the ancient Indian Ocean trade system did not penetrate Africa south of Sofala (modern Beira).

The Southern African coastline, moreover, is punctured by few natural harbors. The best are those in the Cape peninsula and Durban. But in the Cape peninsula, Table Bay is exposed to winter gales from the northwest and False Bay to summer gales from the southeast; and a shallow bar impeded the entrance to Durban harbor until it was dredged using modern equipment. Before the sixteenth century A.D. Southern Africa was a region

1. Southern Africa in the sixteenth century

where human activity was an indigenous process, except as the arrival of people by land from further north modified it.

"Pula!" (May it rain!) is a popular greeting in Lesotho, and it is the name of the currency in Botswana. Rainfall has had a profound influence on the history of the region. In the west, the average annual rainfall is fewer than five inches, resulting in desert conditions along the coastline of Namibia and the northern Cape Province. In the east, the average rainfall reaches forty inches a year, producing subtropical vegetation along the Transkei and Natal coastlines. In between, a transitional zone receives about twenty inches of rain a year. To the east of that zone, the rainfall is sufficient for arable agriculture; to the west, it is not. One exception to this division is the Cape peninsula and its vicinity, where heavy winter rains are sufficient for intensive agriculture.

These rainfall figures are annual averages. In fact, rain varies greatly from season to season. Throughout most of the region, droughts are frequent. They vary in range and intensity. A drought might affect a very small area or last no more than a single year; but sometimes—perhaps at least once in a human generation—devastating droughts hit entire subregions and persist for as long as a decade. The climate may have been somewhat moister throughout the region during the six thousand years before about 4,000 B.C., but since then there do not seem to have been any distinctive climatic changes.

Most of the region is a plateau, ringed by an escarpment that runs parallel to the coast about a hundred miles inland and reaches its greatest height, more than ten thousand feet above sea level, in the Drakensberg range between Natal and Lesotho. No navigable waterways flow through the region, but the river valleys attracted early human occupation and provided early trade routes.

Except in the sheer desert in the far west, the region could support small, dispersed populations of hunter-gatherers with a variety of edible plants and animals. The region teemed with game—elephants, rhinoceroses, hippopotamuses, buffalo, lions, leopards, giraffes, zebras, quaggas, and numerous species of antelopes—until hunters with firearms had cleared many areas and exterminated several species, including the quaggas, by the end of the nineteenth century. Much of the region could also support domesticated animals, but tsetse flies and other bearers of diseases of cattle, sheep, and goats have made pastoralism extremely hazardous in the tropical lands of the northeast. East and north of the twenty-inch rainfall zone, arable agriculture is possible. Throughout Southern Africa, however, agriculture is constrained not only by the irregular rainfall but also by the quality of the soils, which, as in tropical Africa, are generally "poor both in mineral and organic nutrients and in structure."[1] Yet human diseases were less widespread in temperate Southern Africa than in the tropics further north.

Southern Africa possesses great mineral resources. Iron-bearing rocks were spread throughout much of the region, and rocks containing gold and copper broke surface at various points in the Limpopo river valley and the northwestern part of the Cape Province, as well as further north in Namibia, Zimbabwe, and Zambia. Preindustrial farming people mined these deposits in open stopes to a depth of several feet and extracted the minerals from the deposits; but modern industrial technology was a prerequisite for the fuller exploitation of the region's vast quantities of gold, copper, diamonds, platinum, chrome, and uranium. Gold-mining operations now penetrate two miles below the surface. It was also left to modern technology to remedy the lack of navigable waterways by constructing railroads, roads for automobiles, and, eventually, air transportation services, to enrich the soils with modern fertilizers, and to mitigate the effects of the inadequate and intermittent rainfall by building dams, reservoirs, and canals.

In the Beginning

In one respect, archaeologists have not served historians of Southern Africa well. The historians' tendency to ignore all but the most recent history has been compounded by the archaeologists' use of arcane terminology. Some of their terms are positively misleading. In particular, following precedents created in European archaeology, archaeologists of Southern Africa have used as their basic categories the terms Stone Age (which they divide into Early SA, Middle SA, and Late SA) and Iron Age.[2] Those terms are illogical, ahistorical, and inaccurate: illogical because they confuse chronological phenomena with cultural phenomena, ahistorical because their ages do not correspond with the historian's chronology, and inaccurate because they imply that, for example, every member of an Iron Age community used iron tools and weapons. They have been discarded by European and other archaeologists in favor of stages in the evolution of cultural diversity, but they linger in much work on Southern Africa.

On the evidence available at present—and there has been an escalation of sophisticated work on early humans in Southern Africa by archae-

ologists and physical anthropologists in recent years—it is probable that
the hominid predecessors of modern humans originated in various parts of
East and Southern Africa. That includes the Transvaal, where, among other
discoveries, archaeologists have found fossils that they have identified as
being in the human continuum and have dated three million or more years
ago. The earliest fossils that have been discovered anywhere in the world
that some physical anthropologists attribute to modern *Homo sapiens*
come from Klasies River mouth in the eastern Cape Province and Border
Cave on the Natal-Swaziland border, which they have tentatively dated at
more than fifty thousand years ago.[3]

Scholars now recognize that in Southern Africa as elsewhere the changes
they have identified in the shape and size of the stone tools of the hunter-
gatherers represent the development of increasingly specialized methods of
exploiting the resources of the different environments in the region. Each
group adapted its hunting methods to the climate, topography, and animal
species of its territory. The outcome of this territorial specialization was
diversity. From area to area, groups became increasingly different from one
another.

By the beginning of the Christian era, human communities had lived in
Southern Africa by hunting, fishing, and collecting edible plants for many
thousands of years. They were the ancestors of the Khoisan peoples of
modern times—the peoples white settlers called Bushmen and Hottentots.
They contributed a high proportion of the genes of the "Coloured" people,
who constitute 9 percent of the population of the modern Republic of
South Africa. What is less well known is that they also provided a smaller,
but still considerable, proportion of the genes of the Bantu-speaking Africans, who form 75 percent of the population of the republic, and that they
have provided genes to the people whom governments officially classified
as white and who amount to 13 percent of the modern population.[4]

The hunter-gatherers were small people with light brown or olive skins.
In 1811, English traveler William J. Burchell described the members of a
band who lived in isolation in the arid interior of South Africa:

They were small in stature, all below five feet; and the women still shorter;
their skin was of a sallow brown colour . . . Though small, and delicately
made, they [the men] appeared firm and hardy; and my attention was forcibly struck by the proportional smallness, and neatness of their hands and
feet . . . The women were young; their countenances had a cast of prettiness,
and, I fancied, too, of innocence; their manners were modest, though unre-
served . . . One of them wore a high cap of leather, the edge of which pro-

tected her eyes from the sun: at her back, and entirely hid excepting the head, she carried her infant, whose exceedingly small features presented to me an amusing novelty.[5]

The ways of life of these early Southern Africans varied greatly in the different environments of the region—the coastline and its immediate hinterland; the highlands rising to the escarpment; the grasslands of the eastern plateau; the area of good winter rainfall in the southwest; and the vast arid lands of the Karoo and the Kalahari and Namib deserts. Linguists demonstrate that in each area the people spoke a distinctive language but that all the languages were distantly related; all, for example, included strong click sounds that are difficult to render in the modern Western alphabet.[6] Ray Inskeep, an archaeologist, concludes that one should visualize "stable populations living in well-defined territories over long periods of time."[7]

The basic social unit was the nuclear family, but several families usually formed bands numbering between twenty and eighty people. These bands were not closed, reproducing entities. People identified with members of other bands who spoke the same language and lived in neighboring territories in the same general environment. They occupied caves or camps constructed of portable materials and moved from one watering, foraging, and hunting area to another as the seasons dictated. As in other preindustrial societies, there was a division of labor between women, who stayed close to the campsite and were responsible for childcare and most of the work of collecting edible plants, and men, who were the hunters. They were skillful in fashioning tools from wood and stone, clothing from animal hides, musical instruments from wood, catgut, and ostrich quills, and bows and arrows with tips smeared with poisons extracted from snakes or insects or plants. Their artists have left an impressive record in the rock paintings and engravings that have survived in protected places.[8]

The population probably increased slowly over the centuries but remained sparse by modern standards. Health and life expectancy varied with the environment. The principal factors were the regularity and nutritional value of the food supply and the exposure to disease. The major scourges of tropical Africa, such as malaria and yellow fever, may have affected some of the people who lived below the mountain escarpment in the eastern Transvaal and Natal. They would have been absent from the rest of Southern Africa, but in arid areas debility and undernutrition would have followed several winter seasons and periods of drought.

Harvard University expeditions have made a thorough study of a contemporary people whose name is written as !Kung and who live today near the border between northeastern Namibia and Botswana. They found that the modern !Kung live in groups that fluctuate between twenty-three and forty members during the year. The nutritious perennial mongongo nut is their staple food, providing one-third of their food supply, while other plants provide another one-third and the rest comes from hunting. They spend most of the year in poolside camps near the source of the nuts, but for a couple of months during the dry season they move to permanent water holes further from the nut trees, when some of them hike sixteen miles to collect nuts, carrying their water supply with them.[9]

Another study deals with the modern G/wi people, who live in the Kalahari Desert, where food is scarcer. The G/wi bands tend to be larger, with forty to sixty members, and they use a much larger territory than the !Kung, but they often split up into smaller family units. Plants form three-fifths of their diet, but in the early summer, the period of greatest shortage of plants and large antelopes, the men give up bow-and-arrow hunting and catch smaller game with traplines, making time to help the women with their gathering. The G/wi also eat such foods as rodents, birds, tortoises, snakes, ants, and termites, which the !Kung ignore.[10]

These studies of modern communities who still practice a hunting-gathering way of life are illustrative to a degree; but they certainly do not represent the ways of life of the many early South Africans who lived in areas with greater natural resources—the areas that have been transformed, first by the development of African farming cultures, then by the intrusion of white farmers, and eventually by the application of modern agricultural and industrial technology.[11]

The more we learn about these hunting and gathering peoples, the more we respect the skills they applied to the available resources. Inskeep sums this up well:

> The combination of food remains, environment and artifacts reveals . . . the confidence and success with which the . . . hunter and his womenfolk provided for the group. Plant fibres were spun into fine cordage which could be used as needed for traplines and bindings, or worked into fine, strong nets for catching and carrying. Wood was used with simple skill for pegs to keep things off the ground in cave or rockshelter, for arrowheads and bows, for digging sticks and tool handles. Reeds were cut for arrow-shafts or woven into mats. Time, skill and taste were brought to the fashioning of beads and pendants and objects of bone, shell, and ivory at whose use we can only

THE AFRICANS

guess. In all this we see evidence of masterly adaptation to the environment.[12]

Most modern people assume that hunter-gatherers were so incompetent and undernourished that they had to work continuously to survive. Scholars have demonstrated that that assumption is false. Describing the modern !Kung, American anthropologist Marshall Sahlins says, "They lived in a kind of material plenty because they adapted the tools of their living to materials which lay in abundance around them and which were free for anyone to take (wood, reeds, bone for weapons and implements, fibers for cordage, grass for shelters), or to materials which were at least sufficient for the needs of the population."[13] Other studies of the !Kung, as well as similar studies of modern Australian hunter-gatherers, demonstrate that their way of life involves much less work per capita than our modern "civilized" existence. In their present habitat, the !Kung spend about fifteen hours a week in hunting and gathering, and their daily per capita subsistence yield is about 2,140 calories, well above the daily requirement.[14] Hunter-gatherers had time and energy for subtle and complex aesthetic expression in rock art and in music.

Sahlins also contends that typical hunter-gatherers lived in "pristine affluence."[15] He argues that inherent in their way of life is a philosophy. Their mobility—arising from their need to leave a campsite when they had depleted the plants and game in its area—made them adopt a philosophy of limited wants. They desired no more possessions than they could carry. But lack of property had its compensations. They had a sense of living abundant lives, for the resources available to them exceeded their wants. "We are inclined to think of hunters and gatherers as *poor* because they don't have anything: perhaps better to think of them for that reason as *free*. . . . The world's most primitive people have few possessions, *but they are not poor*. Poverty is not a certain small amount of goods, nor is it just a relation between means and ends; above all it is a relation between people. Poverty is a social status. As such it is the invention of civilization."[16] There was, however, a dark side of the hunter-gatherers' way of life, and it, too, was a consequence of their mobility. People were left to die when they were too old to walk, and twins and other children were killed when they were too numerous to carry.

Inskeep provides a judicious summation of the hunter-gathering culture as it had matured in Southern Africa by the beginning of the Christian era: "We find evidence of sophisticated and successful populations employing

THE AFRICANS9

with confidence a wide range of skills to support themselves in their chosen, or inherited territories. For some there may have been hard times when food was short, but rarely would it fail completely. For others life must have come close to ideal in terms of security. With a million and a half years of experience behind him man had reached the highest points of success in the evolution of the hunting-gathering way of life in Southern Africa."[17]

The First Farmers

In the sixteenth century A.D., some people in the most arid and most mountainous parts of Southern Africa were still living as their ancestors had done, by hunting game and gathering edible plants. Elsewhere to the west of the twenty-inch rainfall zone, wherever pastures were adequate, especially in the reliable winter-rainfall area in and near the Cape peninsula, people were herding sheep and cattle. These pastoralists were genetically similar to the hunter-gatherers, and their appearance was similar, except that they were somewhat taller.

East of the twenty-inch rainfall zone lived mixed farmers—people who not only owned cattle and sheep but also grew cereal crops and used spears and digging tools with iron tips. Culturally and physically they resembled the people living as far north as the equator. Unlike both the hunter-gatherers and the pastoralists, they occupied semipermanent villages throughout the year and their political organizations were stronger and more complex. They spoke Bantu languages and had dark brown skins and robust physiques. These Bantu-speaking mixed farmers were the ancestors of the majority of the inhabitants of present-day Southern Africa.

In the course of time, Europeans called the hunter-gatherers Bushmen, the pastoralists Hottentots, and the mixed farmers Kaffirs. They used those words in a derogatory sense. When we use ethnic terms, we now refer to the hunter-gatherers as San, the pastoralists as Khoikhoi, and the Bantu-speaking mixed farmers as Africans.[18]

White scholars have not found it easy to account for the differences among these peoples. Until recently, white South Africans in particular assumed that "Bushmen," "Hottentots," and "Kaffirs" were pure racial types and that the basic process that lay behind the outcome was migration. In so doing, they were applying a model drawn from European history, with its early folk wanderings and, in the case of Britain, successive invasions by Romans, by Angles, Saxons, and Jutes, by Scandinavians, and finally by Normans. They portrayed the "Bushmen" as aboriginal hunters and gatherers who had been subjected to two great waves of migration from central Africa: first "Hottentot" pastoralists and then "Kaffir" mixed farmers.[19]

We now know that the migration model does not provide a sufficient explanation for the early history of Southern Africa. People *did* enter the region from the north, but the historical process was much more complex. There was continuity as well as change. Populations were not closed reproducing entities, equipped with unique unchanging cultures. People interacted, cooperating and copulating as well as competing and combatting, exchanging ideas and practices as well as rejecting them.

There are still many gaps in our knowledge of the processes that brought pastoralism and arable farming to Southern Africa. One problem concerns the origins of pastoralism. By the late fifteenth century, when the first Portuguese expedition rounded the Cape of Good Hope en route to India, pastoralists lived in much of the western part of Southern Africa, wherever there was enough rainfall for them to pasture their sheep and cattle, especially in the coastal lowlands from the Buffels River southward and the Fish River westward to the well-watered Cape peninsula. How and when did pastoralism reach that area?

In a book published in 1977, historian Richard Elphick weighed the evidence then available. He agreed with those who had surmised that pastoralism probably started in Southern Africa when some hunter-gatherers who lived in what is now northern Botswana acquired first sheep and later cattle from pastoral people further north. That would have sparked off a process that transformed the way of life of more and more of the aboriginal hunting and gathering peoples of the western part of Southern Africa. Social groups would have become larger than the hunting-gathering bands and also more complex, as some individuals acquired more livestock and power than others.[20]

Scholars have subsequently criticized and elaborated Elphick's informed conjectures. Linguists demonstrate that the language spoken by the pastoralists had close affinities with a language spoken by hunter-gatherers in northern Botswana, Elphick's nuclear area. Archaeologists have discovered that pastoralism began in Southern Africa several centuries before the Christian era. Several aspects of this process are still controversial, but it seems likely that, after people in tropical East Africa had begun to incorporate sheep and cattle into their economies several millennia ago, pastoralism, as an extension of the hunting-gathering way of life, was transmitted southward through the hunting-gathering communities. It may have reached South Africa as early as 2,500 years ago.[21]

Our second historical problem concerns the origins of mixed farming—arable agriculture as well as pastoralism—in the eastern part of Southern Africa south of the Limpopo River. The earliest evidence we have of this transformation shows that people were cultivating crops and using iron implements at several places in river valleys below the mountain escarpment in the eastern Transvaal and Natal in the third century A.D. The farming population gradually expanded across the escarpment and increased in numbers. By A.D. 1,000, farmers were present in much of Natal, the Cape Province east of the Kei River, the Transvaal, Swaziland, eastern Botswana, and the northeastern Orange Free State. They were living in villages where they produced pottery and metallic implements, and in most areas they integrated crop cultivation and pastoralism. After that, the mixed farming population increased rapidly and expanded into the higher areas that their predecessors had neglected. By the sixteenth century, mixed farmers occupied nearly all of the land east of the twenty-inch rainfall line in Southern Africa, except for mountainous terrain, and all were pastoralists as well as crop producers.

This transformation was part of a process of cultural transmission and gradual territorial expansion that derived ultimately from West Africa and secondarily from the area around Lake Victoria, where people began to adopt the iron-working, mixed farming way of life a few centuries before the Christian era. It accounts for the wide spread of Bantu languages and for much cultural similarity throughout sub-Saharan Africa, including, for example, a strong sense of social hierarchy.[22]

British archaeologist David Phillipson summarizes the process as revealed in the archaeological record in Southern Africa: "The archaeological sites and artifacts . . . make a marked contrast with those that had gone before, and contain the first evidence in these southerly latitudes for food-production, for settled village life, for metallurgy and . . . for the manufacture of pottery."[23] He adds: "The fact that so many important aspects of culture were introduced together over such a wide area and so rapidly makes it highly probable that the beginnings of iron-using in sub-equatorial Africa [were] brought about as a result of the physical movement of substantial numbers of people . . . . [I]t is likely that these people were speakers of Bantu languages."[24]

Their arrival was nonetheless almost certainly not a simple process of mass migration from the north and exclusion of the previous inhabitants.

There are no traditions of massive waves of migration into Southern Africa, and it seems probable that the first mixed farmers filtered into the region in small groups. Their movements are best described as a migratory drift, or a gradual territorial expansion. Throughout southeastern Africa, with its poor soils and intermittent droughts, it became customary for families, headed, for example, by energetic younger sons, to break from established village settlements and found new ones further south, or for chiefs to extend their power by placing relatives with their followers in new localities to extend their power.[25] Such events were still occurring in Lesotho and to the west of the Kei River in the early nineteenth century.[26]

Many aspects of the origins and spread of mixed farming in southeastern Africa are still unresolved. Most archaeologists emphasize the changes that took place in the farming culture toward the end of the first millennium: expansion into higher ground, greater use of pastoralism in addition to crop agriculture, and changes in pottery styles. They attribute those changes to a shift in the source of immigration from an easterly to a westerly stream.[27] Others emphasize internal dynamics, as farming communities became increasingly specialized in their various micro-environments.[28] American James Denbow, for example, has shown how herding as distinct from agriculture predominated in Botswana, on the verges of the Kalahari Desert, where the rainfall was barely sufficient for agriculture.[29]

Another unresolved question is whether the first mixed farmers to infiltrate into Southern Africa used iron or whether iron-working reached Africa south of the Limpopo later by diffusion from the north. In central Africa, agriculture and pastoralism seem to have preceded metallurgy. It seems likely, however, that by the time farmers began to infiltrate south of the Limpopo they knew how to produce iron tools and weapons.[30]

Relations between Hunters and Herders

The incorporation of domestic livestock into the economies of the aboriginal hunting and gathering people in the western part of Southern Africa profoundly affected their way of life.[31] Private property, previously associated with such small, portable possessions as clothing (made from skins) and weapons (bows and arrows), now included sheep and cattle. Gaps developed between rich and poor as some people acquired large numbers of livestock while others owned none at all. Moreover, whereas the hunter bands had been small, herders formed larger communities. Their primary social and political groups were clans, composed of people who claimed descent from a common ancestor, but several clans were often joined in loosely associated chiefdoms that Europeans have called tribes. Hereditary chiefs in consultation with their clan heads were responsible for organizing the transhumant movements of their chiefdoms and their defense against human and animal predators.

The adoption of pastoralism involved a fundamental shift in philosophy.[32] Whereas hunter-gatherers, with their mobile way of life, had no desire to accumulate property and were often affluent within their philosophy of limited needs, when they became herders they began to treat material possessions—sheep and cattle—as a form of wealth; and since the number of livestock a person might accumulate was limitless, they experienced a feeling of scarcity—a desire for more. In that sense they, unlike hunter-gatherers, were imbued with an acquisitive spirit.

The herding way of life, moreover, required more work than hunting and gathering, so that pastoralists had less time and energy to devote to aesthetic pursuits. When Europeans arrived in Southern Africa, they found that the pastoralists were not as adept in music and rock painting and engraving as the hunter-gatherers.

According to Elphick's reconstruction, the herding way of life spread by migratory drift and cultural transmission from the nuclear area in northern Botswana, where the first Southern African aborigines probably obtained livestock from herders further north. The initial direction of the expansive process would have been southward to the middle reaches of the Orange River. One segment would then have moved westward to split near the mouth of the Orange, whence some chiefdoms would have moved southward and others northward along the Atlantic coastline. The other segment may have moved southward to reach the Indian Ocean in the vicinity of the Fish River and thence westward to the Cape peninsula.

As some such process occurred, complex interactions would have taken place. In some cases, aboriginal hunters may have accommodated to the intrusion of the first herders into their territories; but, as we know from reports by literate Europeans in the eighteenth and nineteenth centuries, when the herders and their livestock seemed to threaten their control of the land and its resources, the aborigines resisted. Treating sheep and cattle as fair game, they shot them with their poisoned arrows. Symbiotic relations often developed, however. Herders provided hunters with milk in exchange for game, and this sometimes led to structured relations. Hunter clients served their herder patrons, not only providing them with meat but also defending them against human and animal aggressors and even looking after their sheep and cattle. Eventually, aboriginal individuals, and sometimes entire bands, were assimilated into the herding way of life and incorporated into the herders' clans. When Europeans began to settle in the southwestern part of the region in the seventeenth century, they found that the herding culture was dominant wherever the pastures were suitable for stock farming. The herding population was most numerous where the environment was most favorable—namely, in the lower Orange River valley and, especially, the Cape peninsula and its vicinity.

Herding had distinct advantages over hunting and gathering. The food supply was more reliable; milk was a most nutritious component of the herders' diet. That would have made them taller and stronger than their aboriginal ancestors and contemporaries. The herders, however, did not eliminate the hunting and gathering economy in their vicinity. There were always people who owned no livestock living among or near them. As a nineteenth-century observer put it:

> Nearly every tribe is found to consist of three distinct classes of persons. First, the wealthy class. Second, a portion of the poorer class disposed to reside with and serve the former, and third, the remainder of the latter class who either from disinclination to servitude or an inability to obtain it, trust for support to other means, and in pursuit of them remove from the haunts of their more settled countrymen and establish themselves in positions best adapted for the objects they have in view. It is this class which forms . . . the detached pauper population of a tribe.[33]

Following droughts, military defeats, or epidemics affecting the people or their livestock, entire communities were sometimes obliged to revert to the hunting-gathering way of life. Pastoralism, moreover, was not possible in the Kalahari Desert and the mountain escarpment. There, communities continued to practice their traditional hunting and gathering mode of life throughout the colonial period—even, in such cases as the !Kung and the G/wi, down to the present day.

Archaeologists have found no evidence that the herding way of life spread east of the twenty-inch rainfall zone. We may assume that herders would have tried to expand in that direction where, with better rainfall, the environment was more propitious. Perhaps they did so, but the evidence has not been discovered. Alternatively, by the time their eastward expansion began in earnest, it was checked by the presence of the more powerful iron-working mixed farmers.

The Mixed Farming Economy

Between the fourth century A.D. and the late eighteenth century, Bantu-speaking mixed farmers, the ancestors of most inhabitants of modern

Southern Africa, were consolidating their position in the better-watered eastern part of the region. Their numbers were growing. Along the twenty-inch rainfall zone they were creating an increasingly stable frontier with pastoralists, and east of that zone they were occupying more and more of the country suitable for agriculture and were incorporating, killing, or expelling more and more of the indigenous hunter-gatherers.

This section and the next describe the way of life of the farming societies at a time when they were still autonomous. We can draw on substantial documentary evidence from the seventeenth century onward, written by survivors of shipwrecks, explorers, traders, missionaries, and pioneer settlers who spent time in southeastern Africa before it was transformed by the rise of the Zulu kingdom and by white conquest—processes that are the subjects of later chapters.

All the mixed farming people in Southern Africa had much the same basic economy: swidden agriculture, pastoralism, and metallurgy. They also had similar cultures, including closely related Bantu languages. The farmers in the lands below the escarpment, who are known as Nguni, spoke dialects of the same language, of which the modern survivors are Xhosa in the south and Zulu in the north. Most of those on the plateau above the escarpment spoke dialects of another language, of which the modern survivors are Sotho in the south, Pedi in the east, and Tswana in the west. The two languages had a similar syntax and much common vocabulary. Farmers could and did move easily from community to community throughout southeastern Africa, and those who migrated to a new area rapidly assimilated the local culture. There were, of course, considerable differences within the region, as farmers adapted to distinctive micro-environments. Conditions in the better-watered subtropical lands below the mountain escarpment in what are now KwaZulu, the eastern Transvaal, and southern Mozambique were very different from those in the frontier zone in Botswana, where crop agriculture was rarely possible.

The mixed farming economy was more productive than the economies of both the herders and the hunter-gatherers. Besides possessing sheep and cattle, hunting the abundant game population, and gathering indigenous plants, the farmers cultivated sorghum and made, used, and traded iron tools and weapons and copper ornaments. They thus had a richer and more reliable diet and possessed stronger physiques than the hunters and herders, and they achieved denser levels of population. Moreover, whereas the hunters and herders were mobile and slept in natural or portable shelters, the farmers built stone or wattle-and-daub huts and established semi-permanent hamlets or villages; and whereas the herders' political organizations were fragile associations of semiautonomous clans, the farmers created centralized chiefdoms.

Surface deposits of high-grade iron ores, such as magnetite, were available in several parts of Southern Africa. People dug the material from the surface or mined it in open stopes. The smelting process involved high skills, because the ore had to be heated to a temperature of at least one thousand degrees centigrade. That was done by forcing air from hand-operated bellows through narrow slits in low shaft furnaces built of clay. The usable metal was then separated from the slag and brought to its desired shape by reheating and hammering.[34]

Blacksmiths were the most specialized artisans in society and were accorded high status. Eugène Casalis, a perceptive French missionary who worked in unconquered Lesotho from 1833 to 1855, reported that a blacksmith was "the principal workman, the only one whose labours amount to anything like art . . . . [A]ll acknowledge the *blacksmith* to be an exceptional character. He is more than a workman, he is the *ngaka ea tsepe,* the *doctor of iron.*"[35] Casalis described and illustrated the Sotho blacksmith's techniques and his products: spears, hatchets, two-edged knives, hoes, awls, and spatulas.[36]

Outcrops of iron were spread unevenly in Southern Africa, however. There were gaps in their incidence in the areas occupied by Bantu-speaking farmers—for example, toward the southern end of the territory of the Nguni-speaking people. Iron was thus a major trade commodity. Most farmers managed to possess iron-tipped spears, but some were obliged to use wooden digging tools.

Copper, too, was available on and near the surface in numerous localities in northern Botswana and the northern Transvaal. The people exploited this resource extensively. At Lolwe Hill in the northern Transvaal, "It has been estimated that over the centuries more than 10,000 tons of rock containing the ores were dug from its shafts and galleries, to be smelted in the myriad furnaces of the surrounding plain."[37] Throughout the region—and indeed throughout all of tropical Africa to the north—copper was in great demand. People used it almost exclusively for decorative purposes. "Copper adorned the body from head to foot and laterally to the tips of the fingers: hair ornaments, earrings, collars and necklaces, pendants, girdles and cache-sexes, bracelets, anklets, bells, amulets, crowns. Copper ornamentation is, or has been, quasi-universal in African societies."[38]

People valued iron and copper so dearly that the metals were principal commodities of trade and major targets of theft and robbery. European survivors of shipwrecks on the southeast African coast found that iron and copper items from the wrecks were in great demand. In 1689, the commander of the Dutch Cape Colony informed his superiors in Amsterdam that some survivors of the wrecked *Stavenisse* who had lived in Natal for nearly three years reported that "one may travel 200 or 300 miles through the country, without any fear of danger from the men, provided you go naked [unarmed] and without any iron or copper, for these things give inducement to the murder of those who have them."[39]

Cattle were the most prized possessions of all and the principal indicators of wealth. Ludwig Alberti, who was employed by the Dutch government as commandant of the garrison at Fort Frederick (later Port Elizabeth) between 1803 and 1806, wrote that the Xhosa, the southernmost Nguni people,

> live principally by cattle-breeding. For the well-being of the family, a sufficient number of cattle are required, whose attendance and treatment is the sole responsibility of the father of the family, in which he is assisted by his sons. The Kaffir's cattle is the foremost and practically the only subject of his care and occupation, in the possession of which he finds complete happiness. He sees to their grazing, and in the evening to their return to the stable, constructed of a jumble of thorny branches, and which adjoins his hut. He also attends to the milking of the cows and generally to everything requiring attention in cattle raising.[40]

There was a vast vocabulary concerning cattle. The Mpondo had "at least fifty-seven different terms describing cattle of different markings, as well as five terms describing the horns."[41] A man had a name for every beast he owned and composed praise songs for his favorites. Among the Basotho, there is a saying: "Dikgomo ke banka ya Mosotho" (Cattle are the bank of a Mosotho).[42]

In many areas, cattle were moved from one type of pasturage to another during the year. In the summer, the Xhosa grazed their cattle in what is now known as *sourveld*—grasses that are nutritious in their early stages of growth but then lose their protein and mineral content and become unpalatable and indigestible to animals; and in the autumn they moved them to *sweetveld,* which remains nutritious through the year. In Lesotho, when the lowlands became densely populated, cattle wintered in the lowlands but spent the summer in the mountains.[43]

The farmers practiced various types of swidden agriculture—that is, they cultivated a field for several years, then allowed it to lie fallow for a time. Whereas cattle care and ownership were a male monopoly, women did most of the agricultural work. Every married woman cultivated at least one field. The primary crop was sorghum. They also grew several varieties of millets, pumpkins, watermelons, and calabashes, and a type of tobacco; in some places they produced beans and yams. Where sufficient metal was available, they dug with iron-headed hoes with wooden shafts, but where iron was scarce they used spades made of hard wood. The Sotho-speaking people stored the grain in large baskets, the Nguni-speaking people in pits.[44]

Down to the nineteenth century, hunting was still an essential part of the mixed farmers' economy. It provided food and clothing, and it was a major sport. In about 1825, John Brownlee, a British missionary, described Xhosa hunting, which was still practiced in the customary manner:

> Though not, like the poor Bushmen, impelled to the chase to provide for their subsistence, they are passionately fond of it, as an active and animating amusement. They generally go out to hunt in large parties, and when they find game in the open fields, they endeavour to surround the animals, or drive them to some narrow pass, which is previously occupied by long files of hunters, stationed on either side, who, as the herd rushes through between, pierce them with showers of assagais [spears]. This mode is chiefly pursued with the larger sorts of antelopes. The smaller bucks they sometimes knock down with the *kirri,* or war club, which they throw with great force and expertness; birds are generally killed with the same weapon. They have also modes of catching the smaller game by gins and springs, fixed in their paths through the woods and thickets.[45]

Brownlee went on to explain how they attacked larger game: elephants, rhinoceroses, hippopotamuses, buffalo, and lions.[46]

Metals were unevenly distributed in Southern Africa. The grasslands of the southern highveld and also the southern part of the country below the escarpment were deficient in iron and copper. Many areas, moreover, were short of salt, also a desired item. Consequently, there was considerable economic specialization. At Phalaborwa in the eastern Transvaal, for example, people specialized in iron and copper production, and nearby in the same Olifants River drainage system other people specialized in the manufacture of salt from crusts formed by seepage from saline springs.[47]

Specializations such as these were the basis for complicated long-distance trade networks, which knit the region together. The Xhosa chiefdoms, for example, were linked with the Tswana chiefdoms to their north and the northern Nguni chiefdoms to their northeast, the Xhosa receiving iron and copper goods in exchange for cattle.[48] There were also trade links between the mixed farming communities and the hunters and herders, who bartered such goods as copper ornaments and tobacco for such items as meat and cattle.[49]

Nevertheless, there were no professional merchants, no marketplaces in Southern Africa, and the farmers made scarcely any use of oxen for portage. The trade was predominantly a relay trade. The mixed farmers had strong acquisitive instincts. They entered into barter transactions with people from neighboring villages as a means of increasing their prestige and their wealth by accumulating large numbers of livestock, especially cattle. The sum of such exchanges constituted the long-distance networks that moved goods from areas where they were plentiful to areas where they were in short supply.

In southeastern Africa natural hazards were less severe than in the tropics. Except for the lowveld in the northeast, the region was free of anopheles mosquitoes and, thus, of malaria. Locusts, however, frequently ravaged the crops and rains were exasperatingly irregular. Most areas experienced a drought about every eight years and some droughts were severe and widespread, resulting in famine. There was a particularly devastating drought over much of southeastern Africa during the first decade of the nineteenth century. Years later, an elderly Zulu told a white questioner that during the resulting famine "we were obliged to eat grass."[50]

The Bantu-speaking mixed farmers were generally a healthy people. This was especially true of the Nguni, whose country below the mountain escarpment was bountiful down to the late nineteenth century but is now dessicated and eroded. Ludwig Alberti found that the Xhosa "enjoy exceptional health [and] . . . very rarely suffer from infectious diseases or fatal illnesses." The men, he wrote, "are remarkable for their imposing height," and "the female is no less well-built."[51]

The farmers owed their robust health to their rich and varied diet. Except in times of drought, pestilence, or war, they drank milk (always used sour) in most seasons. They ate sorghum green during the growing season and cooked after harvest. They regularly used vegetables. They often ate meat from the hunt, and they consumed domestic cattle, sheep, and goats at frequent feasts and sacrifices. Beer brewed from sorghum was also drunk frequently.[52] This diet included an ample caloric content, as well as adequate amounts of carbohydrates for energy and calcium and other minerals essential for the functioning of the central nervous system.

Moreover, the farmers had an intimate knowledge of the medicinal effects of the plants in their vicinities and used them to mitigate the impact of illness.[53]

There is no doubt that many of the Bantu-speaking mixed farmers of Southern Africa attained a high level of material security and prosperity. In 1689, the Dutch commander of the Cape Colony interviewed the men who had survived the wreck of the *Stavenisse* and spent nearly thee years in Natal. He reported to Amsterdam that "the country is exceedingly fertile, and incredibly populous, and full of cattle, whence it is that lions and other ravenous animals are not very apt to attack men, as they find enough tame cattle to devour." He added: "In their intercourse with each other they are very civil, polite, and talkative, saluting each other, whether young or old, male or female, whenever they meet; asking whence they come, and whither they are going, what is their news, and whether they have learned any new dances or songs."[54]

Nevertheless, in comparison with farmers in other continents, the Southern African mixed farmers were not very productive. Like their counterparts in tropical Africa, they used a swidden agriculture that did not yield impressive results, and, since they accumulated as many cattle as possible, their beasts were generally thin, produced little milk, and tended to overgraze their pastures. But, as Ralph Austen points out, African agricultural methods provided insurance "by natural restoration of fertility through fallow and a scattering of plots within cultivated areas," and "a large and scattered herd is the best insurance against complete loss from [natural] . . . disasters even if individual animals are thus less well-nourished." Instead of maximizing production, African farmers minimized the risks involved in farming with a preindustrial technology.[55]

Mixed Farming Society

Unlike the hunters and herders, the mixed farmers built nonportable huts of saplings or stone, depending on what was available. Their settlements varied in size. The Nguni generally occupied small hamlets comprising extended families and their dependents; most Sotho lived in villages containing between fifty and four hundred people, including a dominant extended family, several other families, and a few dependents. In the northwest, near the limit of arable farming, numbers of villages coalesced into townlike aggregations within reach of springs or streams. When William Burchell, a British traveler, visited the Tswana town of Dithakong in 1812, it occupied "the greater part of a plain of about two miles in diameter," and he estimated its population at five thousand.[56]

The mixed farmers had a keen sense of kinship solidarity and obligations, extending far beyond the nuclear family. In 1689, the shipwrecked Dutchmen who had spent nearly three years in Natal reported, "It would be impossible to buy any slaves there, for they would not part with their children, or any of their connections for anything in the world, loving one another with a most remarkable strength of affection."[57] A century and more later, Alberti commented on "the bonds of love and friendship" among the Xhosa "and particularly in the case of blood-relations" and observed that they catered to sick relatives and respected the aged.[58]

Married men dominated farming society. The senior married man controlled his homestead. He was the owner of both the agricultural produce and the cattle. He was responsible for clearing the land for agriculture, for cattle-keeping, for building the huts, and for many crafts, including making clothes of cowhides and the pelts of wild animals. He was assisted by his unmarried sons and his clients. Boys did much of the routine work with the cattle. Women were responsible for raising the children, for planting, weeding, and harvesting the crops, for maintaining the home, for making the clay pots, and for serving the food. Catholic missionary A. T. Bryant, who was a collector of Zulu oral traditions, summed up the division of labor:

> In the Zulu social system every kraal [homestead] is self-contained and self-supporting, and by a tradition that bears the force of law, the work of the home is clearly, though far from equally divided between its male and its female inmates. It is the peculiar province of the male to provide and maintain the fabric of the kraal; of the female to provide the family and to support it, in other words, to find the food. The men function as the artisans and pastoralists; the women as the housekeepers and agriculturalists.[59]

For a woman, the daily routine was arduous. Not the least of her tasks was fetching water to the home from the nearest stream, carrying the liquid on her head in a pot. A man often had more time on his hands and would spend hours in the village center, making clothes from skins and attending to the business of village government. Women's work was neither so tedious nor so inequitable as white commentators have tended to assume, however. The women of a village or several neighboring hamlets would work together, taking each woman's field in turn; men assisted their wives when there was heavy work to be done; and from time to time a woman would make a special brew of beer and convene a working group, when up to two hundred people, men as well as women, might come together for a task such as weeding, culminating in a party when the day's work was done.[60]

Marriages were major social and economic events. Complex negotiations between the kin of the bride and the kin of the bridegroom preceded a marriage. It was accompanied by a series of exchanges of property between the two groups, including the transfer of cattle from the bridegroom's kin to the kin of the bride. This custom (Nguni *lobola;* Sotho *bohali*) cemented the relations between the two groups. It also strengthened the hold of parents over their children, since the parents received the bridewealth and usually decided whom their children should marry—though young people would often find ways to flout their parents' wishes. Wealthy men, especially chiefs, were polygynous. An exceptionally powerful chief might have as many as a hundred wives, one of whom was recognized as the "great wife" and the mother of the heir.

People owned such personal equipment as weapons, axes, hoes, mats, household utensils, clothing, and ornaments. In addition, men owned the cattle and the grain, which gave them economic power over women. There was no concept of individual land ownership, however. Land belonged to the community, not to individuals. Families could use land in the hamlet or village as building sites and kitchen gardens. During the growing season, women controlled the land they cultivated, but between the harvest and the preparation of the land for the new planting, the fields were common property; any member of the community could let his cattle forage there. The rest of the land was the property of the community as a whole throughout the year. Anyone could use it to pasture livestock, to hunt game, or to gather plants. But even with cattle and grain, the "owner" was not considered to have unqualified rights of disposal. He was meant to consult his kin and to administer the property for the benefit of his dependents.[61]

The mixed farmers were highly competitive. Skillful men built up large herds of cattle; unsuccessful men possessed none at all. The two extremes were bound by a system of clientage. A rich man would lend beasts to a poor man, who would have the responsibility for herding them and the right to consume their milk and to own a proportion of their progeny. This custom, practiced widely with local variations, saved the impoverished from starvation, took care of the most valued property of the wealthy, and spread the cattle for grazing purposes. It also made a client dependent on his patron. Indeed, society was very hierarchical. To a considerable extent, men controlled women, elders controlled youths, patrons controlled clients, and, as we shall see, chiefs controlled commoners. American anthropologist Igor Kopytoff remarks that in the farming societies through-out sub-Saharan Africa "There were seldom any equals—one was either a senior or a junior, a superior or a subordinate. . . . This inequality, how-ever, had to be instituted and maintained with circumspection, for . . . conditions also made it relatively easy for dissatisfied adherents to leave. Hence . . . the adherents had to be well-treated in everyday life—usually as quasi-kinsmen."[62]

The educational system reinforced the hierarchical principle. At or soon after reaching puberty, boys were segregated from the rest of society for as long as six months and prepared for adult life. In the form that prevailed among the Basotho, a chief would convene a *lebollo* (initiation school) when one of his sons had reached the appropriate age. This was a dramatic episode in the life of a chiefdom—the village or cluster of villages that recognized the authority of a single leader. Only the chief could authorize a lebollo and make it effective, because it was he who appointed the *mohla-bani* (distinguished warrior), the *mesuoe* (instructors), and the *thipane* (surgeon) who conducted the ceremonies. The chief also supplied the cru-cial ingredients: a bull, butterfat, and, most important of all, his *lenaka*. This was a horn, preferably a rhinoceros horn, containing a powder com-posed of a mixture of vegetable and animal materials and human flesh. The bull and the cow that produced the butterfat were meant to have been captured from a rival chiefdom, and the human flesh should have been cut from the body of an enemy who had been killed, fighting bravely.[63]

The initiation process included circumcision, various physical tests, and instruction in the customs and traditions of the chiefdoms, under rigorous discipline. When it was over, the boys were men. As the French Protestant missionary Eugène Casalis described it: "Circumcision makes the child a man. Anyone who has not experienced this rite is unequipped for war, unfitted for business, inadmissible in society. In a word he is not a Mo-sotho, he lacks the distinctive mark of his race, his father and mother disown him, his equals insult him and run away from him."[64] Another missionary observed that its objective was "to incorporate them into the nation, to attach them to the young chief who is part of the band."[65] The boys who were initiated together formed a distinct group under the lead-ership of the chief's son for whom the leballo had been convened. A chief had a group of devoted followers in his initiation-mates.

The political system was the product of the process of fission and expan-sion that had been going on ever since mixed farmers began to move into Southern Africa in the third or fourth century A.D. The effective political units were autonomous chiefdoms—territorial units under hereditary chiefs. They varied in size and population, and they changed over time. Some had less than one thousand people; a few had fifty thousand or more. Whereas small chiefdoms, comprising little more than a central hamlet or village and its immediate vicinity, were controlled directly from the center, large chiefdoms consisted of a series of "concentric 'circles' of diminishing control," from the core, where the paramount chief exercised his authority directly, to the periphery, where local subchiefs were loosely allied to the paramount.[66] Down to the nineteenth century, this regional system was maintained despite a gradual increase in population. In some cases, paramount chiefs expanded their territories by placing relatives on the periphery; in others, relatives struck out on their own to found independent polities. Chiefdoms were often named for an ancestral figure, such as Xhosa or Zulu. Sotho and Tswana chiefdoms often carried the names of the clans of the ruling family, such as *Kwena* (Crocodile), *Taung* (Lion), *Khatla* (Monkey), or *Tloung* (Elephant).

The populations of the chiefdoms were not closed entities. Besides members of a ruling lineage, they included people of different descent groups, and they frequently incorporated aliens—people who had quarreled with their original chiefs or had left drought-stricken areas. They even incorporated individuals from the aboriginal hunting communities and, in and after the sixteenth century, from European shipwrecks. For example, "There are two clans, the Lungu and Mholo, still living on the Transkei coast, who trace descent from the survivors of shipwrecks, and whose appearance and ritual practice support this claim."[67] The Western concept of tribalism, which is usually taken to refer to closed populations reproducing fixed cultural characteristics, is not applicable to African farmers.

A chief spent much of his time in the open-air meeting place near his personal hut. There, in cooperation with his councillors, who were drawn from the heads of homesteads, he regulated the affairs of his people, listening to complaints, settling disputes, and receiving visitors. He was the richest man in his territory. His subjects paid him sheep and cattle for settling their disputes, his men handed over to him any livestock they seized from neighboring chiefdoms, and he had the right to summon his people to work for him. They cultivated the fields of his senior wives, since he was expected to use their produce to entertain guests and feed the men when they were summoned to his village for political discussions or military purposes. A chief was thus rich enough to marry more wives and provide more generous hospitality than any of his subjects.[68]

Most conflicts that came to the chief arose from arguments about cattle or about women. Was that man entitled to reclaim his daughter, whose husband's family had failed to hand over the promised number of *bohali* cattle? Should that client have the right to own the calf of a cow that his patron had committed to his charge? After a case had been argued at great length by interested parties, the chief would announce his verdict. That would be based on custom, but custom could be modified to suit the occasion. In theory, the primary objective was to heal divisions in society and restore harmony rather than to punish offenders, but people guilty of disloyalty or witchcraft might be killed. In other cases, the normal penalty was a fine, shared between the chief and the successful litigant.

A chief's powers were limited by necessity as well as by custom. He had no standing army, no police force, no jail. He relied on the cooperation of his councillors—male relatives and commoners, many of whom were his initiation-mates. He also needed the respect of his people. If a chief required public support for some enterprise or had important information to communicate, he would convene a meeting of his male subjects. This custom was particularly firmly entrenched among the Basotho and Batswana. At a *pitso,* the men had considerable freedom of speech—they could, and often did, make pointed criticisms of the chief or a councillor. In the last resort, alienated subjects would vote with their feet—leaving their chiefdom and joining another, where they were nearly always welcome, because people were the most important gauge of the power and prestige of a chiefdom; or an aggrieved kinsman might build up a following and split the polity. In practice, there were great variations in the relationships between chiefs and their male subjects, and in the expansion or contraction of chiefdoms, depending on the context and the interplay of personalities. The Basotho had two sayings that summed up the underlying tension: "Morena ha a fose" (The chief can do no wrong) and "Morena ke batho" (No people, no chief).[69]

American historian Robert Harms has emphasized the powers of male commoners in African societies, pointing out that

Africa has been unique in the degree to which peasants have remained uncaptured by elites. This situation owed much to the existence of vacant land which made emigration an ever-present option to peasants who felt themselves oppressed. It is also due to the strength of kinship networks in providing vital services. . . . [The peasants] defined the limits of elite power and the framework of African political economy. They sometimes accomplished this by armed rebellion, but more commonly they would "drag their feet," "vote with their feet," and find a variety of other ways to frustrate policies emanating from higher authorities.[70]

There are no traditions of devastating warfare among the mixed farming people in Southern Africa before the nineteenth century. Their weapons were knobkerries (wooden clubs) and spears about five feet long with wooden shafts and metal blades. They would throw their spears from a distance and the enemy would usually ward them off with large cowhide shields. If they got into close combat, they would use their knobkerries. Fighting usually took the form of cattle raids. Cattle-raiding was a manly sport and a way of increasing one's wealth. Alberti noted that the Xhosa "cannot really be called a warlike people; a predominant inclination to pursue a quiet cattle-raising life is much more evident amongst them."[71] Wars of conquest were more frequent among the Tswana, since they lived in an area that was conducive to competition for control of limited water supplies. Even there, not many people died in the wars. Moreover, throughout the farming culture women and children were seldom molested and prisoners were rarely executed.

Ideology underpinned the culture of the Bantu-speaking mixed farmers. In the initiation schools, the teachers instilled respect for the elders, for chiefly authority, and for established religious beliefs and rituals. As in medieval Europe and other preindustrial societies, people sought supernatural explanations for phenomena they could not account for in material terms.[72] Ancestral spirits had powers over the material world. *Dingaka,* religious specialists, established communication with the ancestral spirits and invoked their support. In personal crises—illnesses, bereavements, domestic conflicts, material losses—individuals would sacrifice sheep or cattle to their ancestors. Alternatively, they might assume that a person had caused their calamity. Hence the concept of witchcraft:

> Evil was personified in myths of witchcraft: certain persons were believed to have innate powers which they used directly, or through familiars—hyenas, baboons, or the fabulous *tikoloshe* and lightning bird—to injure their neighbours; and other evilly disposed persons were thought to use poison. The beliefs were rooted in nightmares and the awareness of anger, lust, and envy in man. These realities were interpreted in material form—envy became a baboon sent by a poor man to suck dry the cows of his rich and stingy neighbour, and lust a demon lover. Hence the "smelling out" and torture of supposed witches and sorcerers.[73]

From time to time, an exceptional man or woman, such as Mohlomi in late eighteenth-century Lesotho, earned a reputation that extended far beyond the confines of any single chiefdom as an *ngaka* who was able to heal the sick, foretell the future, and show the people how to recover from disasters. In crises affecting a chiefdom—as during droughts—the chief would engage such a person to perform the correct sacrifices on behalf of his community.[74]

The Mixed Farmers' Relations with Hunters and Herders

With its superior technology and more diversified economy, the farming way of life gradually became dominant in the eastern part of Southern Africa wherever arable agriculture was possible. We cannot reconstruct the process in detail, but we can identify the basic dynamics of the interactions that took place.[75]

When the first mixed farmers entered a locality previously occupied by aboriginal hunting bands, they would probably have been too few in number to present a threat to the autonomy of the aborigines. In that context, mutually beneficial symbiotic relations would have developed—farmers obtaining the meat and skins of wild animals from hunters and hunters receiving grain and milk in return. We have evidence that friendly symbiotic relations persisted in the southern highveld on either side of the Caledon River as late as the eighteenth century, while that area was still being settled quite thinly by pioneer farmers.[76]

In some cases friendly symbiosis on a basis of complementarity eventually gave way to structured, differential incorporation of the hunters into plural societies under the control of the farmers. This was the nearest approach to slavery in precolonial Southern Africa. In Botswana, down to the present day, farmers control the lives of hunting aborigines.[77]

In most areas, however, as farming people built up their numbers and gained control of the land, with its springs and streams, the unincorporated hunting bands, struggling for survival, attacked the livestock of the farmers, as they were wont to attack wild game, and as hunting bands in the western part of Southern Africa had been wont to attack the sheep and cattle of the pastoralists. This interaction often degenerated into endemic warfare. White people described such a state of affairs in the eighteenth and nineteenth centuries. Alberti reported that the Xhosa lived "in constant feud" with their hunting and gathering neighbors, who persisted in robbing them of their livestock. A Xhosa, he wrote, "regards and treats these robbers as beasts of prey, follows their spoor after they have perpetrated their deed, and kills those that one can lay hold of. In the same way one also traces the whereabouts of such a robber-band, attacks them during the night-time and destroys them without the slightest forbearance and re-gardless of age or sex."[78] In 1804, German doctor Henry Lichtenstein noted that a Xhosa had told the governor of the Cape Colony that "it was impossible that a Bosjesman [Bushman: hunter-gatherer] could ever abandon his villainous ways, and it was necessary to destroy such vermin wherever they were found."[79]

At all stages, however, mixed farmers incorporated and assimilated numbers of hunter-gatherers into their societies. We know that the mixed farming chiefdoms in nineteenth-century Lesotho included people of aboriginal antecedents. Some were the children or grandchildren of hunter-gatherers who had become clients of individual farmers and gradually melded into the farming society, like clients whose parents were farmers. Chiefs themselves took such women as junior wives to acquire the ability to protect the land that was believed to be vested in the aborigines as the first inhabitants.[80]

By the time mixed farmers reached the western limit of the land where it was possible to grow crops, if not earlier, they had encountered pastoralists. The mixed farmers and the pastoralists were compatible, since both were cattle-owners, and they tended to mingle and form composite communities, with cultural and biological roots in both societies. Initially, in some cases, pastoralists incorporated mixed farming individuals and families into their polities, but sooner or later farming chiefdoms acquired control.[81] South African historian Jeffrey Peires has described the final phase of that process among the southern Nguni. During several generations starting in the late seventeenth century, the Xhosa expanded to the southwest as sons of the reigning chiefs of the Tshawe royal family split off to found new chiefdoms. Some pastoral groups joined the Xhosa voluntarily; others were incorporated through conquest. The pastoralists who were incorporated "were not expelled from their ancient homes, or relegated to a condition of hereditary servitude on the basis of their skin colour. They became Xhosa with the full rights of any other Xhosa. The limits of Xhosadom were not ethnic or geographic, but political: all persons or groups who accepted the rule of the Tshawe thereby became Xhosa."[82]

In the middle of the seventeenth century, when white people began to settle in the Cape peninsula, hunter-gatherers and pastoralists were still in sole occupation of the western part of Southern Africa. In the eastern part, the mixed farming way of life was overwhelmingly dominant with the exception of small pockets of unassimilated hunter-gatherers in the mountain escarpment, especially in the Drakensberg range, where they survived to nearly the end of the nineteenth century. In between, where the rainfall averaged about twenty inches a year, communities of mixed biological and cultural inheritance occupied a frontier zone. There, the mixed farming culture and chiefdoms were becoming increasingly dominant: the Gqunukwebe chiefdom in the south and the Tswana chiefdoms in the north.

Over the years, the mixed farmers had acquired considerable cultural and genetic influences from hunter-gatherers and pastoralists. Their Bantu languages incorporated numerous loan words from the hunters' and herders' vocabularies—notably, words with click sounds that were originally exclusive to the hunters. As one would expect, the greatest proportion of click words and hunters' and herders' genes are to be found among the mixed farming peoples nearest to the frontier zone—the Xhosa and the Tswana. Linguists estimate that one-sixth of all Xhosa words contain clicks.[83] The early history of the region has also left its mark in numerous non-Bantu names of rivers and mountains in the eastern as well as the western part of Southern Africa.

The mixed farming communities were far from static. They had many of the characteristics of a frontier society. During the first millennium A.D. a "tidal frontier" of mixed farmers had founded a series of settlements south of the Limpopo. During the second millennium, mixed farmers had been expanding from those established settlements along a myriad of "internal frontiers" into lands previously occupied, if at all, by hunter-gatherers or pastoralists. Old chiefdoms split and new chiefdoms arose, and in due course they too threw off splinter groups to form the nucleus of new chiefdoms.[84] The entire process hinged on the availability of fresh land. By the end of the eighteenth century, the population on the land east of the twenty-inch rainfall zone was reaching its limits in relation to the economic system. The precondition for the continuation of the frontier dynamics was beginning to collapse, with dire consequences, which we shall describe in chapter 3.

CHAPTER 2

The White Invaders:
The Cape Colony,
1652–1870

The hunting and herding peoples of Southern Africa remained isolated from the wider world until the end of the fifteenth century. Throughout that century, Portuguese mariners were probing further and further from Europe along the western coast of the African continent.[1] Eventually, in 1487, Bartholomeu Dias's expedition of two fifty-ton caravels rounded the Cape peninsula in a storm, anchored in Mossel Bay 170 miles further east, and sailed another 170 miles along the coast to Algoa Bay before returning to Lisbon. In 1497, five years after Christopher Columbus had crossed the Atlantic under Spanish patronage, Vasco da Gama led another Portuguese expedition that rounded the Cape, sailed along the east African coastline to Malindi (modern Mombasa), and then crossed the Indian Ocean to Calicut, India, returning to Portugal with two of his four ships after an absence of twenty-six months. These epic enterprises were longer, more hazardous, and in the short run far more rewarding than Columbus's crossings of the Atlantic Ocean. As the American historian Daniel Boorstin remarks, they "changed the course of both Western and Eastern history."[2]

During the sixteenth century, the Portuguese government sent annual fleets round the Cape of Good Hope to the Indian Ocean. They brutally destroyed the Arab shipping they encountered in the Indian Ocean and began to divert the European trade with southeast Asia from the ancient routes via the Persian Gulf and the Red Sea to the oceanic route via the Cape. During the sixteenth century, the Portuguese established fortified bases at Goa on the west coast of India, Malacca on the northern side of the strait between Malaya and Sumatra, and Ormuz, gateway to the Persian Gulf. From West Africa, they started the nefarious export of slaves to the Americas. In East Africa, they built forts at Mombasa and Mozambique. Lured by gold in what is now Zimbabwe, they created garrison towns on the Zambezi River and established trading posts in the auriferous area. They also founded *prazos* (great estates) in the Zambezi valley. By the eighteenth century, though the Portuguese had lost control of the East African interior, they were exporting slaves to Brazil and North America from the coastal fortress at Mozambique.

The Portuguese occupied no territory south of Luanda (the capital of modern Angola) and Mozambique. Their slave-trading activities just grazed the territories of the modern Republic of South Africa. Experience made them fearful of the region's navigational hazards and people. Tempestuous seas, strong currents, and perilous shoals wrecked several Portuguese ships along the coast between Mozambique and the Cape, and in 1510 Francesco d'Almeida, returning to Portugal at the end of his term as viceroy in the East, was killed with several companions in a fracas with the local inhabitants in Table Bay, at the northern end of the Cape peninsula.

By the end of the sixteenth century, Dutch, English, French, and Scandinavian merchant mariners were also beginning to use the sea route to Asia. From time to time they landed on the Cape peninsula to take in fresh water and barter sheep and cattle from the local Khoikhoi pastoralists in return for iron and copper goods. In 1620, the English government ignored a suggestion of an English ship's captain that it should annex the Cape. In 1649, however, Dutchmen who had wintered in Table Bay after losing their ship proposed that the Dutch East India Company should occupy the place. Three years later, Jan van Riebeeck arrived there as the commander of an expedition of eighty company employees. The directors had instructed him to build a fort and supply the Dutch fleets with fruit, vegetables, and meat.

The Dutch Cape Colony, 1652–1795:
Cape Town and the Arable Southwest

The seventeenth century was the Golden Age of the Dutch Republic (map 2).[3] Its merchants were the most successful businessmen in Europe; their Dutch East India Company was the world's greatest trading corporation. Founded in 1602, the company was a state outside the state. Operating under a charter from the States-General (the Dutch government), it had sovereign rights in and east of the Cape of Good Hope, and by midcentury it was the dominant European maritime power in southeast Asia. Its fleet, numbering some six thousand ships totaling at least 600,000 tons, was manned by perhaps 48,000 sailors.

Modern South Africa began as a by-product of the enterprise of these Dutch merchants. In sending Jan van Riebeeck to occupy Table Bay, the directors of the company intended the colony to serve a specific and limited role as a link between the Netherlands and their eastern empire, centered on Batavia, Java. They had no intention of creating anything more than a small fortified base, where the annual fleets bound to and from Batavia could rendezvous, take in fresh water, fruit, vegetables, and grain, and land their sick for recuperation. They did not expect the Cape station to make a profit on its own—indeed, it never did so—but they always tried to keep the costs of its administration to a minimum. Within its first decade, however, the Cape Colony began to develop a degree of autonomy and an unforeseen dynamic. By the time van Riebeeck handed over the command to his successor in 1662, the colony had become a complex, racially stratified society.[4]

Three processes contributed to this development. First, the company released some of its employees from their contracts and gave them land with the status of "free burghers." Second, the company landed slaves at the Cape and set them to work under Dutch supervision on creating the basic infrastructure for the colony—a fort, a jetty, roads, orchards, vegetable gardens, and arable fields. Third, as the Dutch settlement expanded slowly but surely from the shore of Table Bay and engrossed and enclosed land for cultivation, it did so at the expense of the local pastoralists, who had the option of withdrawing from the fresh water resources and the rich pastures of the northern part of the Cape peninsula or remaining there as servants or clients of the Dutch. All three of these processes were launched in van Riebeeck's time; all three accelerated throughout the eighteenth century. We shall discuss them separately.

In 1657, the company released nine of its employees from their contracts

2. The Cape Colony under the Dutch East India Company, 1652–1795

Elevation over 4,000 feet

Area in 1652

Additional area by 1710

Additional area bounded by 1798 frontier

Atlantic Ocean

Orange River

St. Helena Bay

Elephant River

Vaal River

Orange River

Caledon River

Orange River

Karoo

Roodezand

Berg River

Paarl

Stellenbosch

Table Bay

Cape Town

Cape of Good Hope

False Bay

Genadendal

Swellendam

Mossel Bay

Cape Agulhas

Cape St. Francis

Graaff-Reinet

Sundays River

Fish River

Algoa Bay

Kei River

Buffalo River

Keiskamma River

Indian Ocean

MI 0 100

KM 0 100

and placed them on twenty-acre landholdings at Rondebosch in the Cape peninsula six miles south of Table Bay. The directors' reasoning was strictly businesslike. These free burghers were to produce grain and vegetables and sell them to the company at fixed prices. The directors calculated that this would be more economical than continuing to have food produced exclusively by company slaves and men on the company payroll.[5]

In the years that followed, the company discharged more men at the Cape on similar conditions. It also transported a number of people from the Netherlands to the Cape as settlers, including a few orphan girls and 156 men, women, and children of French origin—Huguenots who had fled to the Netherlands after 1685, when the French government reversed its policy of tolerating Protestantism by revoking the Edict of Nantes. Until 1679, the settlement was confined to the Cape peninsula. In that year, the company began to make grants of land in the fertile valleys beyond the sandy Cape flats and below the mountains, starting at what became known as Stellenbosch, some thirty miles east of Table Bay. The company ceased to provide free transportation to settlers in 1707, by which time the colonial population included about 700 company servants and a settler community of about 2,000 men, women, and children, besides the slaves and the local pastoralists. After that, the burgher population grew partly by natural increase, partly through company servants taking their discharge in the colony, and to a small extent, as we shall see, by the manumission of slaves. In 1793, according to company records, there were 13,830 burghers (4,032 men, 2,730 women, and 7,068 children). These were miniscule numbers compared with the scale of European settlement in the Americas by that time.

Most of the settlers came from the lower and least successful classes in hierarchical Dutch or German society, since service in the company was dangerous and poorly paid. Such differences as were rooted in their European backgrounds diminished in the colonial situation, where individual initiative and practical abilities were more significant than social origins. This was also the experience of the Huguenots. The company dispersed them among the other settlers, and within a generation they were speaking Dutch rather than French.

Van Riebeeck and his successors intended that the free burghers should practice intensive agriculture on the Dutch model, but they were disappointed. Lacking adequate capital and skilled labor, the free burghers were not able to make a success of intensive agriculture, except as market gardeners in and near the village on Table Bay, which became known as Cape

Town. Many soon gave up farming altogether and became artisans and traders in Cape Town, where they catered to the needs of visiting French, English, and Scandinavian ships, as well as to the outward bound and homeward bound Dutch fleets that paused at the Cape each year. The most successful of those who remained on the land acquired large holdings and became mixed farmers, producing grain and wine but also pasturing sheep and cattle far beyond the limits of their land grants.

Initially, the company did not envisage the use of slave labor in their Cape settlement. However, van Riebeeck was soon requesting permission to follow the example of the company's settlements at Batavia and elsewhere in Asia. The die was cast in 1658, when the company imported one shipload of slaves from Dahomey and another shipload of Angolan slaves, whom it had captured from the Portuguese. After that, there was no looking back. The company-government, the senior officials, and the free burgher community all became dependent on slave labor. The Cape had become a slaveholding society.[6]

By the early eighteenth century, slavery at the Cape had acquired distinctive characteristics. First, the Cape slaves came from more diverse linguistic, religious, and social backgrounds than those in the Americas. Indeed, most of the Cape slaves were not even from Africa, which was the source of all the American slaves. A few came from Mozambique, but more from Madagascar, and more again from Indonesia, India, and Ceylon (Sri Lanka), including a large minority of Muslims. Second, from 1711 onward there were rather more slaves than free burghers in the colony. In 1793, there were 14,747 slaves (9,046 men, 3,590 women, and 2,111 children), compared with the 13,830 free burghers. Third, the augmentation of the slave population was a result of continual imports rather than natural increase. The Cape slaves never became a self-reproducing population. Until 1765, there were always more than four times as many male as female slaves, and in 1793 there were still two-and-a-half times as many men as women. Moreover, although the overall mortality rate is not known, it was usually high, especially among the company slaves. It was very high indeed during intermittent epidemics of smallpox and other diseases.

Fourth, there was nothing like the plantation system that prevailed in parts of North America, the Caribbean, and Brazil. At the Cape, privately owned slaves were distributed among numerous owners in small groups. By the third quarter of the eighteenth century, over 50 percent of the free burghers owned slaves, but few other than the most senior officials and a few successful farmers owned large numbers. The largest holding was probably that of Governor Adriaan van der Stel, who owned 169 slaves in 1706. The largest holding of a burgher was probably that of Martin Melck, who had 101 slaves in 1774. In 1750, there were 681 slave owners in the colony. Only 7 of them owned more than 50 slaves and another 25 owned between 26 and 50, whereas 385 owned fewer than 6 slaves. Finally, few Cape slaves were manumitted, and the rate of manumission declined over time, so that there was never a large community of "free blacks." The free blacks initially had the same rights as the white settlers, but the law began to discriminate against them in the 1760s, and by the 1790s they were obliged to carry passes if they wished to leave town. Though few in numbers, however, the free blacks were a significant influence in the colonial society. They moderated the congruence between race and enslavement.

The occupations of the Cape slaves varied greatly, depending on who owned them and where they lived. The company housed its slaves in a building in Cape Town, where they provided the basic labor force for public works. Company officials and burghers who lived in Cape Town employed their slaves as domestic servants, artisans, fishermen, market gardeners, and fetchers of water and wood. Rural slaves were farm laborers and domestic servants. They formed the backbone of the arable economy.

Meanwhile, the indigenous transhumant pastoralists of southwestern Africa, who called themselves Khoikhoi and whom white settlers called Hottentots, were bearing the brunt of the Dutch invasion.[7] During the century and a half following Vasco da Gama's first great voyage to India, those living in the Cape peninsula, who probably numbered between four and eight thousand, had grown accustomed to occasional visits by European seafarers. They had developed a taste for European trade goods— iron, copper, brass, and body ornaments—and become experienced and skilled in bartering them for sheep and cattle.

For the first few years after the arrival of the van Riebeeck expedition, relations were fairly cordial. Conscious of their dearth of available labor, the Dutch were concerned to consolidate their bridgehead and secure their needs peacefully. Like their predecessors, they acquired sheep and cattle in exchange for Western goods. They also cultivated friendships with three cooperative Khoikhoi, whom they called Doman, Eva, and Harry, using them as interpreters for communication with the leaders of the local communities. Tensions soon developed, however. As they witnessed the building of the fort and the planting of fruit trees, vegetables, and crops, and, more particularly, the engrossment of land by the first free burghers, it gradually dawned on the indigenous people that they were facing an unprecedented challenge. In 1659, quarrels over cattle escalated into warfare. The Khoikhoi first destroyed five settler farms and captured numerous sheep and cattle, but during 1660, using superior weaponry and tactics and exploiting the divisions among the indigenous people, the colonial government established control. It then sought to secure and limit its territorial commitment by planting a thick hedge around the settlement and building watch houses along the perimeter.

During the following generation, the settlement expanded at the expense of the pastoral communities to the north and the east of the Cape peninsula. Gaining confidence from their defeat of the peninsular people, the settlers became increasingly brutal. They branded, thrashed, and chained Khoikhoi whom they suspected of theft and placed them on Robben Island, seven miles northwest of Cape Town—an island destined to be used as a prison by successive regimes down to the present. Khoikhoi to the north of the peninsula put up the most effective resistance. War began in 1673 and continued intermittently until 1677, but once again—as would repeatedly happen throughout their conquest of South Africa—the European invaders established control with superior arms by exploiting internal divisions among the local people.

By 1713, the indigenous pastoral society of the southwestern corner of Africa was disintegrating. Whites were in control of the fertile territory below the mountain escarpment extending fifty miles north and forty miles east from Cape Town. The Khoikhoi had been unable to withstand the invasion of the Dutch East India Company and its settlers. They had lost most of their livestock—their most valued possessions: the records of the company show that between 1662 and 1713 it received 14,363 cattle and 32,808 sheep from the Khoikhoi. Their fragile political system had collapsed, and the chiefs had become pathetic clients of the company. In the 1680s, individuals and families had begun to detach themselves from their society and serve burghers as shepherds and cattleherds. The southwestern Khoikhoi were becoming a subordinate caste in the colonial society, set apart by appearance and culture from both the Whites and the slaves; technically free, but treated no better than the slaves.

Richard Elphick sums up the colonial system: "The Company and the settlers in combination . . . assaulted all five components of independence together: [they] absorbed livestock and labor from the Khoikhoi economy, subjugated Khoikhoi chiefs to Dutch overrule and their followers to Dutch law, encroached on Khoikhoi pastures, and endangered the integrity of Khoikhoi culture."[8] Then came smallpox. Brought in by a homeward bound Dutch ship in 1713, it ravaged the Khoikhoi. Not having previously experienced the disease, they had no immunity and suffered more grievously than the other inhabitants. Khoikhoi society, "already in precipitous decline, had been virtually destroyed; and the people who had lived in it had barely escaped annihilation."[9]

By that time, the settlement at the Cape was fulfilling its prescribed goal: the company's fleets were being efficiently revictualed with fresh water, wine, beef, mutton, bread, fruit, and vegetables. But the colony had also become a far more complex society than the mere refreshment station that the directors of the Dutch East India Company had envisaged in 1652, and it had developed a wholly unforeseen dynamic.

The growing town on Table Bay was a miniature Batavia—"a seaward-looking community, a caravanserai on the periphery of the global spice trade,"[10] where diverse religions, languages, and peoples jostled, and life focused on the outside world. The greatest events were the arrivals of the fleets, bringing news from Europe or Asia and a period of brisk trade. Abraham Bogaert, a Danish visitor, described the town in 1702. The castle, with its "bastions built of heavy stone and armed with large cannon" was the home of the governor and other senior officials.

> The town, lying a good musket shot to the west of the Castle, stretches from the sea to Table Mountain, and at the back touches the outermost slopes of the Lion Hill. It has wonderfully increased the number of its houses since the Company chose this place for a settlement. . . . All are built of stone. . . . They look very well from far off because of the snow-white lime with which they are plastered outside, and many shine with Dutch neatness. . . . It now boasts of a Church, built in the Dutch fashion and adorned with a fair-sized tower, in which on Sundays the Word of Truth is preached.[11]

Bogaert also described the company's garden, "the new hospital, which is tolerably extensive," and the lodge, "where the slaves of the Company live, of whom the number at times runs well into five hundred."[12]

The countryside, too, was dependent on external trade, but it was remote from the bustle of the port and dominated by its most successful landowners. The visitor of 1702 was impressed by the Stellenbosch settlement: "It is incredible how by the zeal of the Dutch this place has grown with fine dwellings, and how great a treasure of wine and grain is grown here every year."[13]

Gradations of status and wealth in the white population were infinite. The company paid meticulous regard to rank. The governors, with numerous perquisites plus a salary of two hundred guilders a month, lived in a style modeled on the patricians in the Netherlands; the common sailors and soldiers, with nine guilders a month, led spartan lives. Among the burghers, there was a small class of relatively wealthy traders and farmers, some of whose daughters married senior officials. At the other extreme was a growing class of poor Whites: landless people who were unwilling or unable to do manual labor because of the presence of slaves. They included a few army and navy deserters. In between were small traders and inn-keepers in the town, farmers hard put to make ends meet, and farm over-seers known as *knechts*.

As the population increased during the eighteenth century, the burghers became increasingly stratified. At the end of the century, the town had about 1,100 houses and there were a number of large burgher estates. In 1803, a German employed by the Batavian (Dutch) Republic described the home of Jacob Laubscher, who lived in the area of mixed arable and pastoral farming about eighty miles north of the peninsula:

> He maintained a sort of patriarchal household, of which some idea may be formed by stating that the stock of the farm consisted of eighty horses, six hundred and ninety head of horned cattle, two thousand four hundred and seventy sheep, and an immense quantity of poultry of all kinds. The family itself, including masters, servants, hottentots [Khoikhoi], and slaves, consist-ed of a hundred and five persons. . . . The quantity of corn sown upon his estate this year, including every description, amounted to sixty-one bush-els. . . . [I]t will be seen that an African farm may almost be called a State in miniature. . . . From the produce of the lands and flocks must the whole tribe be fed, so that the surplus is not so great as might be supposed at first sight.

The visitor listed items that could not be produced on the spot: "First, articles of manufacture, as cloth, linen, hats, arms; secondly of luxury, as tea, coffee, sugar, spices, &c:—thirdly of raw materials, as iron, pitch, and rosin. 'Tis only through the medium of these wants that a colonist is connected with the rest of the world; . . . excepting articles of the above description, there is scarcely anything necessary for the supply of his house-hold which is not drawn from his own premises."[14] He should have added guns, which were essential possessions of all farmers.

Except for a handful of midwives, no women were on the company payroll; but since women were always in a minority among the free popula-tion, they had exceptional opportunities for marriage and for remarriage if they outlived their first husbands. Moreover, women accumulated property, because under the prevailing Roman-Dutch law, the wife was the legal owner of half the combined estate.

Compared with contemporary European colonies in the Americas, the tiny Cape colonial population was remarkably unsophisticated. Formal educational institutions were meager. A few boys and girls were taught basic skills at several elementary schools in the town and at elementary schools of sorts attached to the churches that the company founded at Stellenbosch (1686), Drakenstein (1691), Roodezand (later Tulbagh; 1743), and Zwartland (later Malmesbury; 1745). A minister founded the only high school in the colony in 1714, but it received little support and was abandoned in 1725. Most colonists, moreover, were indifferent to religion, at least until the last few years of the eighteenth century, when a new wave of Dutch clergy spurred signs of an evangelical movement. A visitor had commented in 1714 that the clergy had made little headway among the colonists, "due in no wise to the faltering of their zeal, but to the stupidity and indolence of the burghers."[15]

Formal authority over the colony was virtually a monopoly of the Dutch officials. The governor and Council of Policy, consisting exclusively of senior officials, ruled the Cape, subject to instructions from the Council of Seventeen in Amsterdam and the governor-general in Batavia. Officials also had a majority in the judiciary (the Court of Justice) and the other administrative bodies, and the governor nominated the burgher members of those bodies. Even the religious establishment was controlled by the company. The ministers were salaried officials; the Church Council was nominated by the governor and Council of Policy, and it, too, consisted largely of officials.

The creation of a settler community led to conflicts. Competition took place between two classes of producers: the senior officials and the most successful settlers. As was common practice among servants of the Dutch East India Company, the Cape governors Simon van der Stel (1679–99), his son Willem Adriaan van der Stel (1699–1707), and their cronies used their opportunities to enrich themselves. They got possession of large blocks of the best arable land, numerous cattle ranches, and many slaves and exploited their official positions to control access to shipping and external markets. A crisis came in 1705, when Willem Adriaan van der Stel modified the wine concession to his advantage. Sixty-three free burghers signed a petition denouncing the officials and sent it to Amsterdam. The officials responded by getting 240 signatures to a counterpetition. Eventually, the directors dismissed the governor and three other senior officials, deprived them of their colonial estates, and forbade officials to own land or to trade. The local officials had been given notice that they were dependent on the goodwill of the substantial colonial farmers. Corruption was nevertheless the way of life in the Dutch East India Company. Those prohibitions had always been on the company statute book, and always ignored. Throughout the eighteenth century, as previously, Cape officials found ways to supplement their salaries in defiance of the law.[16]

The company never solved this problem. It was primarily concerned to reduce its losses in administering its colony by continuing to dominate the local economy, buying local produce low and selling imported goods high, and turning a blind eye to its servants' ways of augmenting their salaries at the expense of the local people. The resulting tensions between company interests and settler interests were only slightly ameliorated by marriages between officials and burghers' daughters. They came to a head again in the last quarter of the century, when the Netherlands had lost its economic supremacy to France and Britain and the Dutch East India Company, on the verge of bankruptcy, was in no position to satisfy the demands of the Cape burghers.

By 1778, leading Cape Town businessmen and arable farmers had accumulated considerable wealth. In that year they initiated another agitation. They sent two delegations to the Netherlands, appealing not only to the directors of the company but also to the States-General, complaining of the effects of the company's economic policies and demanding freedom to trade with foreign ships and effective political representation. The alliance between urban and rural interests, however, was fragile and soon began to fall apart. Moreover, the quarrel became embroiled in the ideological and political struggle in the Netherlands, where supporters of the status quo were confronted by "Patriots," who were influenced by the revolution in North America and the democratic ideas of the Enlightenment. The directors were conservative, and when their faction triumphed in 1787, they were able to ignore the burghers' demands.

Slavery created far the most significant division in Cape society. As in other slave societies, the relationship was rooted in the fact and threat of violence. The law that prevailed at the Cape derived from the Roman-Dutch law of the Netherlands and the statutes of Batavia. "Slaves were unable to marry; had no rights of *potestas* over their children, and were unable to make legal contracts, acquire property or leave wills. As the exclusive property of his master, a slave was obliged to obey any order that did not involve a criminal offence, and could be sold or bequeathed at will."[17]

To deter others, the company executed its major criminals in diabolical ways. Carl Peter Thunberg, a Swedish botanist, observed that

> on the 31st of July [1773] a slave was executed, who had murdered his master. The delinquent being laid on the cross and tied fast to it, first his arms and legs were burned in eight different parts with jagged tongs, made red hot; afterwards his arms and legs were broken on the wheel, and lastly, his head was cut off and fixed on a pole. The judge that tries and condemns the criminal is always present, and walks in procession to the place of execution, in order to give solemnity to the ceremony. . . . There are two gallows out of the town, one . . . on which Europeans are hanged, and the other . . . on which slaves and Hottentots are executed.[18]

The company controlled the slaves in its Cape Town lodge on military lines. The lot of women owned by the company was especially humiliating. To augment the company income, they were encouraged to prostitute themselves to sailors and were made to work alongside men on the most grueling tasks. Private slave owners were constrained by the fact that their slaves were valuable property. The condition of slaves varied with the owner's temperament, occupation, and prosperity. The relationship was characterized by paternalism, an ideology that structured and legitimized subordination and exploitation and was expressed in a blend of affection and coercion. Some of the privately owned slaves in Cape Town fared relatively well, even being allowed time to trade on their own account. In rural areas, prosperous farmers sometimes left slaves in charge of farms. Yet the threat of violence was always present, and many slave owners enforced their authority with frequent use of the whip.[19]

Many slaves made bids for freedom by absconding. Some roamed beyond the colonial frontiers and eventually joined indigenous communities. Others tried to survive as predators on colonial society. From time to time, bands of escapees lived precariously by robbing burgher homesteads from refuges on the slopes of Table Mountain and Cape Hanglip, on the eastern side of False Bay. Such escapees were fortunate if they were able to steal a gun and to have the assistance of slaves who were still in service. Sooner or later, however, colonial commandos hunted most of them down and shot or captured them, after which the Court of Justice sentenced them to death or to some other brutal punishment.[20]

Historians differ in their assessments of Cape slavery. Nigel Worden and Robert Ross stress the coercive aspects and consider that, since the slaves were derived from widely different cultures and divided in small groups among many owners, they were too atomized to form a community with a collective identity, such as existed in North America. Consequently, they contend, although male slaves greatly outnumbered male burghers in the rural areas, there were no opportunities for them to mobilize and rebel, and their only alternative to acquiescence was to abscond. That may be too clear-cut an interpretation. Robert Shell stresses the effects of the "psychological bonds which in many—but not all—cases bound the slave to his master and vice versa." He continues: "Although the slave was incorporated into the stem family, that incorporation was deliberately limited. The owners attempted to infantilize their slaves with dress, naming patterns, and ordinary language. All these measures combined to form what may be called the family means of control."[21] John Mason points out that by the nineteenth century, in spite of their disparate backgrounds, the slaves did form a self-conscious community in Cape Town and its neighborhood, where most of them lived. Escapees created organized groups on Cape Hanglip and maintained relations with slaves who remained, and many who accepted the fact of enslavement carved out a living space by resisting their masters' exactions in subtle ways—feigning illness, going slow, destroying or stealing property, and expressing their cultural autonomy in songs and dances.[22]

In slave societies, several factors may blur the distinction between slave and free, and between race and class: a shared religion, manumission, the growth of a free community of former slaves, and miscegenation. In the Cape colony, these conditions were rarely met.

"By the end of the seventeenth century, it was an accepted prerequisite of manumission that a slave should be baptised, speak good Dutch, and have a guarantor who would pay the Poor fund, which might provide relief if the freed slave became destitute."[23] The company ran an elementary school for its slave children and baptized some of them, but it neither gave special privileges to its baptized slaves nor manumitted more than a handful. The burghers baptized few slaves and manumitted an even smaller proportion than the company. As a result, the manumission rate was low: during the eighteenth century, on average, no more than one person was manumitted for every six hundred slaves each year, and the free black population was never more than 8.4 percent of the free burgher population. Only a handful of former slaves, moreover, were able to acquire capital and land and set themselves up as farmers, and as time went on nearly all of them were squeezed out. The free Blacks were therefore concentrated in the relatively fluid society of Cape Town, where they made a living as artisans, cooks,

innkeepers, fishermen, and small-scale retail traders. They formed 16 percent of the free burgher population of the Cape district in 1750 and 13
percent in 1770.[24]

Throughout the company period, there were a few marriages between
European men and freed slave women. There was also a great deal of
extramarital sexual activity across the status and color lines, nearly all of it
between white men and slave women. Visiting sailors fathered numerous
children by Cape slaves, especially in the company's lodge. Burghers also
patronized the urban slaves and had sexual relations with slave and
Khoikhoi women on the farms, where men always exceeded women in the
burgher population. The children of free fathers and slave mothers were
slaves, but many of the female children became the mistresses and, in some
cases, the manumitted legal wives of burghers. As a result of these relationships, the "black" population of the colony became considerably light-
ened, and the "white" population became somewhat darkened. It has been
estimated that approximately 7 percent of the genes of the modern Afrikaner people originated outside Europe and that this occurred mostly
during the company period.[25]

The Dutch East India Company's colony at the Cape of Good Hope had
characteristics that distinguished it from other societies. It was fulfilling its
founders' intentions to be a fortified refreshment station on the trade route
between Europe and Asia. But it was much more than a refreshment station. It was the home of a small but vital mass of people of European origin
who had become an increasingly independent force in shaping the colonial
society. They owned virtually all the productive land but did not themselves
do the manual labor. They used the labor of slaves, who were continually
being imported from Asia, Madagascar, and Mozambique, and of indigenous pastoralists, whom they had deprived of their land and livestock and
who had been decimated by smallpox. In Cape Town, a cosmopolitan
entrepôt, social relations were more fluid than in the countryside, but even
there the free blacks were too few, and the constraints on them too severe, to
blur the increasingly close coincidence between the lines of race and the
lines of class. This picture was complicated still further by events to the
north and east of the arable lands.

The Dutch Colony, 1652–1795: The Pastoral Northeast

As early as 1700, white colonists had acquired control of the land
between the Cape peninsula and the mountain escarpment, where the soil
and the reliable winter rainfall made agriculture possible. By that time, too,

virtually all the agricultural farmers were also raising cattle and sheep, at least as a sideline. Some colonists—younger sons of farmers and others who lacked sufficient land and capital for successful agriculture—were already living exclusively as pastoralists and hunters. The slave economy excluded them from other occupations. Throughout the eighteenth century, extensive pastoral farming, with hunting as a sideline, absorbed the bulk of the increase in the white population. These white pastoralists became known as *trekboers*—semi-migrant farmers.

The environment favored the trekboers. Although vast areas of arid land lay beyond the mountain escarpment, there were also areas that were suitable for sheep and cattle, where a person could make a start with relatively little capital. The indigenous pastoralists, who called themselves Khoikhoi, demoralized by the collapse of their communities in the vicinity of the Cape peninsula and, after 1712, devastated by smallpox, were unable to prevent the colonists from getting access to the streams and the springs and from gradually establishing control of the land. The result was a process of dispersal of whites from the agricultural colony: northward toward the Orange River and eastward on either side of the arid Great Karoo and Little Karoo. By the 1770s, however, trekboer expansion was checked in all directions: in the north by extreme aridity 300 miles beyond the Cape peninsula; in the northeast by hunter-gatherers based in the Sneeuberg Mountains 400 miles from the peninsula; and in the east by Bantu-speaking mixed farmers 450 miles from the peninsula, beyond Algoa Bay.[26]

The company did nothing to impede this process. In fact, needing supplies of meat and pastoral products, it adopted a system of land tenure that favored expansion. A trekboer was obliged merely to pay a small annual fee for the right to occupy a six-thousand-acre farm. In theory, he was merely a conditional lessee of a "loan farm"; in practice, he was able to treat his landholding as his outright property, which could be bought, sold, and inherited.

The trekboers supplied the southwestern Cape with sheep, cattle, and butter, but the company did scarcely anything for them. There was no government post beyond Stellenbosch until 1745, when the company founded one at Swellendam, 120 miles east of Cape Town. In 1786 it inaugurated another at Graaff-Reinet, near the northeastern limit of trekboer expansion. Stellenbosch, Swellendam, and Graaff-Reinet were district headquarters run by a *landdrost,* a salaried company employee. These local administrations were extremely sketchy. A landdrost had scarcely any salaried staff—perhaps a clerk and a soldier or two. He was obliged to rely heavily on the unpaid services of prominent trekboers known as *heemraden* and *veldkornets*. In each district, six heemraden were appointed by the government from lists prepared by the existing holders of those offices. Besides administering the affairs of the district, the landdrost and the heemraden formed a court of justice with minor civil jurisdiction. In each subdivision of a district, a veldkornet, appointed by the landdrost and heemraden, was responsible for law and order. This meant that the most substantial trekboers had a major say in the conduct of the local administration and the inside track in relations with the authorities in distant Cape Town.

As the century progressed, the trekboer families spread out thinly over a vast area. Of the 13,830 burghers in the Cape Colony in 1793, only 3,100 were in the vast eastern district of Graaff-Reinet and 1,925 in Swellendam district. Stellenbosch district, which included much of the more densely populated arable country, had 4,640 colonists, and the small Cape district, including the town, had 4,155.[27]

Transportation between the trekboer homesteads and between the trekboer country and the Cape peninsula—which contained Cape Town, the seat of government, and Table Bay and Simonstown, the only harbors in the colony that were used throughout the eighteenth century—was over rough tracks, traversed on horseback or by ox wagon. From Graaff-Reinet it took up to three months for a wagon to go to and from the Cape. Trekboers nevertheless depended on acquiring guns and gunpowder for the hunt and for protection; they also imported tea, coffee, sugar, and tobacco as essential commodities. To pay for these, they sold sheep, cattle, and butter, and in some cases elephant ivory, to Cape Town tradesmen who toured the country collecting them and drove the livestock on the hoof to the Cape. For the rest, the trekboers relied on their own resources. They were largely, but by no means wholly, a noncapitalist subsistence community, on the periphery of the market economy; and since there were no substantial villages east of Stellenbosch—Swellendam had only four houses thirty years after it had become the seat of a landdrost—there were few specialized artisans and every trekboer was a jack-of-all-trades.[28]

The further the trekboers moved from the arable southwest, the more their European material comforts and culture became diluted. Hendrik Swellengrebel, the son of a former governor of the colony, toured the colony in 1776–77 and subsequently described trekboer living conditions:

> As far as Swellendam and Mossel Bay and occasionally as far as the Zeekoei River, one finds quite respectable houses with a large room partitioned into 2 or 3, and with good doors and windows, though mostly without ceilings. For

the rest, however, and especially those at a greater distance, they are only tumble-down barns, 40 feet by 14 or 15 feet, with clay walls four feet high, and a thatched roof. These are mostly undivided; the doors are reed mats; a square hole serves as a window. The fireplace is a hole in the floor, which is usually made of clay and cowdung. There is no chimney; merely a hole in the roof to let the smoke out. The beds are separated by a Hottentot reed mat. The furniture is in keeping. I have found up to three households—children included—living together in such a dwelling. The majority, by far, of the farmers from the Overberg [beyond the mountain escarpment] come to Cape Town only once a year, because of the great distance—I have discovered that some are reckoned to live 40 "schoften" or days' journey away—and because of the difficulty of getting through the kloofs [passes] between the mountains. To cross them they need at least 24 oxen, two teams of 10 to be changed at every halt and at least 4 spares to replace animals that are crippled or fall prey to lions. Two Hottentots are necessary as well as the farmer himself. The load usually consists of 2 vats of butter (1000 lb. in all) and 400 to 500 lbs. soap.[29]

There were no schools in the trekboer areas, and the first clergyman did not arrive at Zwartland (Malmesbury), forty miles north of Cape Town, until 1745, nor at Graaff-Reinet until 1792. As far as literacy was maintained—and in many cases it was not—it was transmitted within the family. Former company employees made a living as traveling teachers, attaching themselves to trekboer families for several months at a time; but most were so incompetent that the word *Meester* (teacher) acquired a derogatory meaning.

Trekboers were more egalitarian among themselves than the burghers in Cape Town and the arable southwest. Even so, some people used the perquisites of the offices of heemraad and veldkornet to acquire more property than their fellows, and at the other extreme there were people who lacked the capital, the ability, or the will to farm independently. A few moved beyond the settled white community and lived as hunters and traders in indigenous societies. Others became *bijwoners*—tenant farmers, caring for their employers' stock in return for a share. Some bijwoners remained in an underclass; others eventually accumulated sufficient livestock to set up on their own as landowners.

This expansion involved a variety of relationships with the indigenous hunters and herders. Advancing burgher families often made use of a spring and its adjacent pastures without overt opposition and then gradually acquired exclusive control, reducing the indigenous pastoralists to various types of tenancy and clientage. An elderly Khoikhoi told Anders Sparrman, a visiting Swedish doctor and entomologist, in 1775 that "he could not forbear (though with some degree of caution and in gentle terms) making complaints of the Dutch, as unjust invaders of the Hottentot territories. For want of strength and powers, (he said) these latter were now no longer in a condition to withstand their encroachments; almost every day some Hottentot or other being obliged to remove with his cattle, whenever the pasture he was in possession of, happened to suit a colonist."[30] For their part, indigenous hunter-gatherers often raided the cattle and sheep, and sometimes the homes, of the incoming farmers. In response to that resistance, the farmers formed their one cooperative institution, the commando.

The company had initially used its own military personnel in its military operations. By the end of the seventeenth century, it had added a smattering of free burghers. From 1715 onward, commandos consisted exclusively of civilians. They were dependent on the company for their guns and ammunition and, in theory, subject to company control. In practice, they behaved independently. The main resistance came from indigenous hunter gatherers (San) and from indigenous pastoralists (Khoikhoi) who had lost their livestock. During the 1770s, indigenous bands attacked burgher property over a wide front from bases in the Sneeuwberg Mountains north of Graaff-Reinet. Large commandos, including subjected indigenous pastoralists as well as burghers, retaliated, treating their prey as vermin. In 1774, a commando of 300 men claimed to have killed 503 people; between 1786 and 1795, 2,430 were reported killed. By the end of the century, the indigenous hunting and herding peoples of the western part of South Africa had ceased to offer large-scale resistance.

With their roots in the society of Cape Town and the arable southwest, the trekboers were never a self-sufficient society. They were accustomed to using coerced slave and indigenous labor. Many continued to own slaves— in 1773, over half the burghers in Swellendam owned at least one slave. But as they moved deeper and deeper into the interior and edged more and more of the indigenous herders out of control of the land, they drew many of them into their service. The subjected pastoralists had precisely the skills that the trekboers required. For the right to continue to live on the land and to pasture a few livestock of their own, they herded the invaders' cattle and sheep, they drove their ox wagons, and they did their domestic chores. Trekboers also made use of people from the indigenous hunting and gathering communities. Commandos exterminated adult hunter-gatherers but made a point of capturing children, and before they disbanded they distributed the children as well as the cattle booty among themselves.

Beyond the trekboers north and northeast from the Cape lived people of diverse origins: displaced indigenous pastoralists and hunter-gatherers, escaped African and Asian slaves, burghers of white parentage who had committed crimes, and men and women of mixed ethnic descent. Like many trekboers, these people lived by hunting as much as stock farming. Like the trekboers, too, they were loosely linked with the Cape by trade, bartering sheep, cattle, and ivory in return for arms, ammunition, and other imported commodities. Forming fluid communities, they were penetrating and destabilizing the indigenous pastoral and mixed farming societies beyond the Orange River. By the end of the eighteenth century, some were becoming organized as chiefdoms. At first they called themselves Bastaards, but, under missionary influence, they were becoming known as Griquas.[31]

In the east the situation was still more complex. By the 1770s, the foremost eastern trekboers had reached the vicinities of Algoa Bay and Graaff-Reinet, where there were valleys with good soils and sufficient rain for extensive agriculture as well as stock farming. This desirable land was already part of the long-disputed frontier zone between indigenous pastoralists and Bantu-speaking mixed farmers, described in chapter 1. A period of intense competition for control ensued, marked by shifting alliances, cattle raids, and wars. None of the ethnic communities—Khoikhoi, Xhosa, or White—was able to establish hegemony, and the colonial government in distant Cape Town was also incapable of doing so.

People were not actuated exclusively by ethnic bonds. They had divergent identifications and conflicting concerns. Trekboers in the northern part of the district of Graaff-Reinet had a major interest in concentrating colonial resources against the aboriginal hunter-gatherers who were attacking them from their bases in the Sneeuwberg, while those in the southern part of the district were primarily concerned to secure the land they were appropriating against Xhosa attack. Xhosa chiefs were pursuing their own rivalries with one another as well as trying to cope with the intrusion of the colonists. Khoikhoi were torn between obeying their trekboer patrons and deserting them to join up with the Xhosa, which was an attractive alternative, since, as we have seen, the nearest Xhosa chiefdoms had already incorporated numerous Khoikhoi. Thus, during the first two spells of warfare in the frontier zone between the colony and the territory of the Xhosa in 1779 and 1793, people were killed, property was destroyed, sheep and cattle changed hands, but the results were indecisive.[32]

These events strained the relationship between the frontier trekboers and the colonial government, which was not seen to be offering sufficient support. Early in 1795, prominent trekboers from the southern part of the district of Graaff-Reinet drove out the landdrost and assumed control. The government soon brought them to heel, however, by cutting off their ammunition supply, demonstrating that they were dependent on their links with the Cape Town regime and the European economy.[33]

When the British captured the Cape from the Dutch later in 1795, they took over responsibility for a thinly populated, loose-knit territory. Cape Town was still the only port of entry into the region. With fifteen thousand inhabitants (including ten thousand slaves), 1,145 private houses, and such public buildings as the castle, the slave lodge, and the principal Dutch Reformed church, it was also the only real town in the colony. Stellenbosch had a mere 70 houses, Swellendam 30, and Graaff-Reinet "about a dozen mud-houses covered with thatch."[34] In the European perspective, the colony's function was still little more than the stepping-stone to Asia that it had been in the time of van Riebeeck; it yielded nothing else of significance to the metropolitan economy.

The crucial facet of the social structure of the colony was the utter dependence of the white colonists on the labor of slaves and indigenous people. In Europe, where the settler community had originated, ethnic chauvinism was already deeply embedded in the popular psyche. At the Cape, where the colonists were subject to a commercial government that practiced slavery and the slave trade, they were conditioned to life as privileged people, distinguished from their slaves and serfs by physical and cultural as well as legal and economic criteria. They were also growing apart from society in northwestern Europe, where social and economic conditions differed profoundly.

The white colonists were themselves a diverse lot. Capetonians (traders, innkeepers, and artisans), arable farmers, and remote trekboers had conflicting interests and varied cultural levels. Nevertheless, in spite of the unconventional behavior of some individuals and the fairly widespread condoning of male promiscuity with women from the subordinated classes, the colonists perceived themselves as constituting a distinct community. They often identified themselves by the label "Christian." Anders Sparrman recorded that in the 1770s all "Christians" were called "baas."[35] The distinction was essentially racial. Christianity had limited influence in South Africa during the eighteenth century. The handful of Calvinist ministers appointed by the government certainly did not challenge the norms and values that corresponded with material conditions that placed people of European descent above others.[36]

For the subordinated peoples, life in the colony was nasty, brutish, and short. The Cape slaves experienced a form of subjection that was in many respects harsher than slavery as practiced in the Americas. Extracted from diverse native cultures and dispersed in small, mixed lots among many owners, most managed to create some space for human dignity while accommodating to their lot, and a considerable minority bolted for freedom, risking starvation, capture, and fierce retribution. The indigenous pastoralists fared no better. Deprived of their means of independent subsistence, they were incorporated into a society where their masters adopted methods of control they were accustomed to applying to slaves.

This stratified and violent society was a linguistic Babel. Some colonists were holding to the Dutch of the Netherlands, the official language of the colony. Some indigenous people were still speaking their native languages. A few slaves were able to use their languages of origin, whereas Portuguese Creole had become a common means of communication among the Asian slaves. A simplified form of Dutch, which dropped certain inflections and vocabulary items, modified the vowel sounds, and incorporated loan words from the other languages, however, was becoming the dominant lingua franca. This dialect, which originated as a medium of oral communication between burghers and slaves, would become a distinct language—Afrikaans—which, with English and nine African languages, would be recognized as official languages in postapartheid South Africa.[37]

The British Cape Colony, 1795–1870

During the European turmoil sparked off by the French Revolution, Great Britain became the dominant sea power and occupied the Cape peninsula to prevent it from falling into the hands of the French. A British expedition easily forced the capitulation of Dutch officials in 1795, and although the Dutch—then constituted as the Batavian Republic—regained the Cape under the terms of the Treaty of Amiens in 1803, they were ousted again in January 1806. British sovereignty over the colony was confirmed in the eyes of Europe, but, of course, without any consultation with black or white South Africans, in the peace settlement of 1814.

In the British perspective of that era, South Africa was still significant for the single reason that had previously concerned the Dutch. The Cape peninsula was a stepping-stone to Asia, where the English East India Company was conducting a highly profitable trade, primarily in India. Like the Dutch before them, the British had no vital material interest in South Africa beyond the peninsula. But appended to that strategic prize was a complex, violent, and largely anarchic society scattered over a vast hinterland.[38]

Down to the late 1860s, when South Africa's vast mineral wealth began to be revealed, the region produced little of significance to the British economy. Its exports included wine, which was produced in the southwestern part of the colony and did well on the British market between 1811 and 1826, when it was benefiting from a preferential tariff, but declined after Britain reduced the preference. Wool became the mainstay of pastoral farmers in the central and eastern part of the colony by the 1840s. Elephant ivory and animal hides were acquired by hunters and traders in the interior. Total exports, however, were a fraction of Britain's external trade.[39]

Consequently, only a tiny proportion of the emigrants who left the British Isles before 1870 settled in Southern Africa; only a minute proportion of British overseas investment was placed there; and the British government provided the colony with a minimal administrative establishment and repeatedly ordered it to restrict expenditure. The contrast with economic growth in North America in that period is remarkable. By 1870, the United States had a population of over 32 million people of European descent and nearly 53,000 miles of railroad, but in all of Southern Africa there were no more than 70 miles of rail and 250,000 white people.

Possession of the colony nevertheless evoked demands that the British government could not ignore. Some form of law and order was needed in the anarchic eastern frontier zone. There, during the first British occupation of the Cape, Xhosa farming people overran the country far to the west of the official boundary line at the Fish River; trekboers, accustomed to taking the law into their own hands, staged short-lived rebellions; groups of Khoikhoi were trying to maintain some degree of autonomy; and two newly arrived radical white missionaries of the London Missionary Society (an interdenominational Protestant organization) were espousing the cause of the Khoikhoi and the Xhosa.[40] In Britain, military, commercial, and evangelical interests interpreted these events in different ways and brought conflicting pressures to bear on the bureaucrats and politicians responsible.[41]

Until the 1850s, when steam began to replace sail, ships took about three months each way between England and Cape Town, and the Cape was not connected with London by submarine cable until 1870.[42] Thus, although the British government could set general lines of policy, dismiss obstructive officials, and impose overriding laws, the colonial authorities inexorably had a wide latitude of action. They could, for example, refrain from effectively enforcing London's dictates.

Until the first elected legislative body was created in 1853, senior officials responsible to the British government dominated the government of the Cape Colony. Indeed, until 1825 the governor himself possessed autocratic powers. The governors of this period were military officers drawn from the landed aristocracy. Lieutenant-General Sir John Cradock (1811–14) was the younger son of the Earl of Cadogan. His successor, Lieutenant-General Lord Charles Somerset (1814–26), second son of the Duke of Beaufort, drew an annual salary of £10,000 and spent £28,000 of public money on his country residence at Newlands, thereby consuming an inordinate proportion of the local revenue. Both men were deeply conservative Tories. Unlike their Dutch predecessors, they identified with the substantial local landowners—the wine and grain farmers of the southwestern part of the colony—and accepted with little question the structure of society that they inherited from the Dutch.[43]

When they first occupied the Cape Colony, the British regarded themselves as temporary custodians and had no intention of tampering with the status quo. The Batavian Republic regime, also, was too short-lived to have enduring effects.[44] After 1806, however, the British made several changes. First, they tried to establish British control in the turbulent eastern frontier zone. In 1809, Colonel Richard Collins was appointed as a commissioner to examine the situation in that area. After a three-month tour, Collins produced a blueprint for the handling of relations between the colony and the Xhosa. The two societies should be kept absolutely separate from one another until the Whites were powerful enough to dominate the region. "All intercourse between the settlers and the Caffres should be scrupulously prevented, until the former shall have increased considerably in numbers, and are also much more advanced in arts and industry." A military force, meanwhile, should clear the Xhosa out of the land west of the colonial boundary at the Fish River, and beyond that to the Keiskamma. Finally, up to six thousand people should be imported from Europe to form a close settlement on small agricultural farms along the right bank of the Fish; the colony was to be "fully protected by this formidable barrier."[45]

Step by step, the government tried to carry out this blueprint. In 1811 and 1812, in a campaign that set the precedent for the piecemeal conquest of all the black farming people of Southern Africa, British regular troops, assisted by colonial commandos and Khoikhoi units, ruthlessly expelled the Xhosa inhabitants from the land through to the Fish River, burning crops and villages and making off with thousands of head of cattle. Concluding his report on these achievements to his superiors in London, Governor Cradock said, "I am happy to add that in the course of this service there has not been shed more Kaffir blood than would seem to be necessary to impress on the minds of these savages a proper degree of terror and respect."[46] The government then forbade further contacts between colonists and Xhosa across the Fish River. In 1819, the Xhosa made a desperate attempt to regain their land, but British forces and their colonial allies drove them back beyond the Keiskamma in another brutal campaign.[47]

In 1820, British politics changed the destiny of the Cape Colony. The chancellor of the Exchequer had persuaded Parliament to vote £50,000 to transport settlers from the British Isles to the region and set them up as agricultural farmers on lots of about one hundred acres. This unusual grant was a political decision in response to unemployment and social unrest in Britain. Historian Jeffrey Peires calls it a "political manoeuvre by a Tory Government, desperate to demonstrate public concern for the unemployed in order to stave off pressures for more radical reform."[48] The Colonial Office in London administered the grant, choosing nearly four thousand men, women, and children from among eighty thousand applicants. They reached their destination in 1820, accompanied by another thousand who came at their own expense. The immigrants were a mixture of people from England, Wales, Scotland, and Ireland. Most were from the lower middle classes—neither very rich nor very poor. The majority had no farming experience at all but were urban artisans.[49]

The 1820 Settlers, as they became known, did not prosper as the government intended. The soil of the area west of the Fish River where they were located was ill-suited to intensive agriculture. Within a few years more than half of them had abandoned their lots and became merchants and artisans in the military post at Grahamstown, or in the settlement on Algoa Bay called Port Elizabeth, or in other colonial villages. Others took to trading with the African farming communities beyond the frontier—a practice that became legal in 1828. Some who stayed on the land eventually prospered by increasing the size of their holdings and producing wool for the market with merino sheep.[50] What the 1820 Settlers did not realize was that the British government had placed them on land claimed by Africans—Xhosa communities who had been the victims of white aggression in the clearances of 1811–12 and 1817–19.

The 1820 Settlers and subsequent immigrants from Britain introduced further complexity into an already complicated colonial society. With their different language, traditions, religious affiliations, and experiences, they were culturally distinct from the earlier settlers. They were the first white immigrants who did not assimilate with them. Deep into the twentieth century, except among the elite of the southwestern part of the colony, social mixing was rare and intermarriages were few. The British immigrants expressed the distinction by calling the earlier settlers *Boers,* meaning farmers, and the term came to have derogatory overtones. During the Dutch period, Dutch-speakers themselves had begun to use the word *Afrikaner,* alongside *Christian* and *European.* We shall employ the word *Afrikaner,* which gradually gained in popularity and became the universally recognized label in the twentieth century.

White South Africans thus acquired an ethnic problem analogous to the Anglo-French problem of Canada. But the demographic proportions were—and have remained—decisively different. In the colonies that became Canada, British settlers soon outnumbered the French Canadians. In greater South Africa, Afrikaners have always formed at least 55 percent of the white population.

There was another difference between the two cases. In Canada, the Whites became overwhelmingly more numerous than the native population at an early stage, whereas in South Africa the white population never amounted to more than about 20 percent of the total. This disparity mitigated the tensions between the white communities. Although they were expressly forbidden to own slaves, the British settlers, like the Afrikaners, had an interest in acquiring and controlling indigenous labor. Like many Afrikaners, too, they experienced the insecurity of life in an exposed frontier zone that Africans considered to be their rightful property. The result was that the British settlers became involved in intermittent warfare, defending and expanding their territory (1834, 1846, 1850). The racism that was part of nineteenth-century British culture became accentuated by their experiences in their new milieu.[51]

In Great Britain, meanwhile, the dislocations of the industrial revolution were giving rise to reform impulses that had a strong impact on British politics. The reform movement was essentially a middle-class movement with both moral and material roots. It was linked with progressive capitalism influenced by the market ideas of Adam Smith, whose *Wealth of Nations* was published in 1776, and with evangelical religion, which was prominent among the nonestablishment Protestants, especially the

Wesleyan-Methodists. Its thrust was directed at reducing political corruption, which had become endemic during the eighteenth century; eliminating the curbs on trade that had been created by the dense network of mercantilist monopolies; and freeing the labor market from its preindustrial constraints. Hence, the struggle for parliamentary reform, leading to the Act of 1832, which increased the number of voters and reduced inequalities among the electoral divisions; the battle for the reduction of protective tariffs, culminating in the repeal of the Corn Laws in 1846; and the agitation first to put an end to the slave trade, then to "ameliorate" the institution of slavery, and finally to outlaw it.[52]

When Parliament banned British participation in the slave trade in 1807, it deprived the Cape colonial farmers of their customary influx of fresh supplies of labor. They responded by increasing the work load of their slaves and by agitating for greater control of the services of the indigenous Khoikhoi people. After the Napoleonic Wars, however, critics were revealing and denouncing the excesses of plantation slavery in the British West Indies, and businessmen who suffered from competition from the products of the slave estates joined in the attacks. In response, the British government tried to gain leverage over the behavior of slaveowners and to eliminate their worst abuses of power. In 1823 it ordered Governor Somerset to apply to the Cape Colony a law it had imposed on Trinidad, prescribing minimum standards of food and clothing and maximum hours of work and punishments. Somerset grudgingly consented; sympathizing as he did with the slave-owning class, however, he turned a blind eye when the local administrators—landdrosts, heemraden, and veldkornets, composed almost to a man of slave owners—gave no more than token enforcement of the law. Faced with similar obstruction in the Caribbean, the British government tightened the requirements and devised effective reporting procedures in successive orders to the governors of the Cape Colony as well as the British West Indies.[53]

By the late 1820s, laws limited the right of owners to punish their slaves and ordered them to record punishments in special books for inspection by local officials. There was also a Guardian of Slaves (renamed Protector of Slaves in 1830), who was responsible for administering the amelioration program. Although these regulations, too, were incompletely enforced, they undermined the authority system. Slave owners resented the unwonted interference in their customary powers, and slaves became restless and receptive to rumors that local officials and farmers were blocking fundamental change. The only substantial slave revolt in the history of the

Cape Colony took place in 1808, the year after the abolition of the slave trade. Over three hundred slaves and Khoikhoi from the grain-producing area north of Cape Town marched on the Cape peninsula but were easily defeated by the militia on the outskirts of town. In 1825 a slave named Galant created another stir. Galant had repeatedly but unavailingly tried to persuade the landdrost at Worcester, sixty miles northeast of Cape Town, to stop his owner, Willem van der Merwe, from flogging him. Eventually, "when the freedom of the slaves I had so frequently heard of came into my head," Galant mobilized his fellow slaves and Khoi servants. They seized some guns and ammunition, took over the farmstead, and killed van der Merwe, as well as his wife, who had hidden, in vain, in the brick oven. However, a commando quickly crushed the rebels.[54]

In 1833, the reformed British Parliament abandoned the attempt to ameliorate the institution of slavery and passed a law emancipating the slaves in the British Empire and providing some compensation for the slave owners' loss of property. After a transitional period during which the former slaves were apprenticed to their former owners, they became legally free in 1838. By that time, the concept of freedom had been given a new meaning in the Cape Colony as a result of a struggle concerning the Khoikhoi.

During the reactionary period after 1807, the colonial government systematically defined the status of the "Hottentots" for the first time. In 1809, the governor issued a proclamation that sought to safeguard them against such abuses as wage deductions and withholdings but also applied legal constraints that had previously been used to control slaves. A "Hottentot" was to have a fixed "place of abode," registered at the landdrost's office, from which he was not to move without a pass signed by his employer, veldkornet, or landdrost. Three years later, a further proclamation provided that a Khoikhoi child who had been maintained by his parents' employer up to the age of eight years should be apprenticed to him for a further ten years—a provision that had the effect of binding the parents, too. Because few Khoikhoi still possessed land inside the colony and because the mission stations and the Cape Regiment had places for only a small proportion of the Khoikhoi population, these laws bound most of them to compulsory servitude to white landowners.[55]

Whereas the British antislavery movement was directed primarily at the Caribbean islands and only secondarily at the Cape, evangelical missionaries had been generating a radical critique of the status of the Khoikhoi. The first missionaries to the Khoikhoi were German Moravians who worked briefly at Genadendal, forty miles east of Stellenbosch, between 1737 and 1743 and refounded that mission in 1792. The Moravians concentrated on improving the material conditions of their charges rather than on trying to influence the structure of the colonial society. It was the London Missionary Society (LMS)—a new, interdenominational organization, predominantly Congregational—that brought into the heart of the Cape Colony a radical evangelicalism, which the historian Andrew Ross defines as "the belief that social and political issues were central to the concerns of a Christian." Doctor J. T. van der Kemp, a former lieutenant in the Dutch dragoons, went to South Africa as an LMS missionary in 1797, married a young Khoikhoi woman with whom he had four children, and founded a mission he called Bethelsdorp near Algoa Bay (modern Port Elizabeth) in the disputed eastern frontier zone in 1803. Bethelsdorp was a haven for Khoikhoi who left the white farms. There, van der Kemp discovered and denounced the exploitation that they were suffering at the hands of white farmers and officials. Van der Kemp died in 1811. His colleague James Read survived him but was unable to sustain many of the charges he brought against individual farmers before the colonial circuit court in 1812.

In 1819, a far more effective and equally radical personality appeared on the scene. John Philip, a director of the LMS, was sent to the Cape by his fellow directors to supervise the work of the mission in South Africa. The son of a Scottish handloom weaver, Philip projected into the South African situation his experience of life in Scotland during a period when the condition of skilled workers was improving. Education, Christianity, and freedom from preindustrial constraints were a recipe for welfare for all South Africans, Boers and British, slaves and Khoikhoi. As a radical evangelical, Philip was committed to fighting for the liberation of oppressed classes.[56] He identified initially with the cause of the British settlers, chairing a committee that assisted distressed colonists and joining in their criticisms of Governor Somerset. But in 1821 he found correspondence at Bethelsdorp that convinced him that the circuit court had been wrong in throwing out most of the charges against the farmers. He also discovered that the local landdrost, Jacob Cuyler, had used his office both to acquire land and Khoikhoi labor and to obstruct justice.[57]

Having failed to obtain local redress, in 1826 Philip went to England, where he lobbied the Anti-Slavery Society with the argument that the fate of the Khoikhoi "was bound up with the fate of the slaves" and wrote a long, passionate polemic, exposing the injustices experienced by the Khoikhoi.

"I found them," he wrote in the Preface to his *Researches in South Africa,* "in the most oppressed condition of any people under any civilized government known to us upon earth. . . . The Hottentot has a right to a fair price for his labour; to an exemption from cruelty and oppression; to choose the place of his abode, and to enjoy the society of his children; and no one can deprive him of those rights without violating the laws of nature and of nations."[58] Philip's mission was fruitful. On July 15, 1828, the House of Commons passed a motion that the colonial government was to be told to "secure to all the natives of South Africa, the same freedom and protection as are enjoyed by other free people of that Colony whether English or Dutch."[59]

That motion proved to be redundant. Seeing the writing on the wall, the Cape governor had consulted Landdrost Andries Stockenstrom, whose Swedish father had come to the Cape Colony in the service of the Dutch and who was sympathetic to the Khoikhoi cause. On July 17, 1828, the governor promulgated Ordinance 50, which repealed the previous Khoikhoi legislation and made "Hottentots and other free people of colour" equal before the law with Whites. The 50th Ordinance met with strident protests from Afrikaners and British settlers, and a Vagrancy Ordinance was drafted that would have turned the clock back by compelling the Khoikhoi, and also the former slaves at the end of their period of apprenticeship, "to earn an honest livelihood." Before he left England, however, Philip had ensured that the 50th Ordinance should not be amended without British consent. The British government accordingly disallowed the draft Vagrancy Ordinance, and on emancipation the slaves stepped into the legal status won by the Khoikhoi in 1828.[60]

The freedom acquired by the Khoikhoi and the former slaves, however, was limited. The 50th Ordinance freed them from overtly discriminatory legislation; it did nothing to assist them to overcome their poverty, which was the result of the entrenched domination of the economy by the white population. In a preindustrial and predominantly rural context, land ownership is an essential basis for individual and group autonomy. By 1828, Whites were the legal owners of nearly all the productive land in the colony, and the emancipated Khoikhoi—and, later on, the emancipated slaves—had few alternatives but to continue to work for white people.

One option was service in the Cape Regiment. Khoikhoi units had formed part of the Dutch garrison in the Cape peninsula, fighting courageously against the British invaders in 1795 and again in 1806. Khoikhoi also participated regularly in commandos against hunter-gatherers. The

British continued both practices. In 1799, a Khoikhoi detachment took part in the suppression of the Afrikaner rebellion in the eastern frontier zone. After 1806, the Cape Regiment—later known as the Cape Mounted Rifles—with white officers and Khoikhoi other ranks to the level of sergeant, fought, and fought well, in all the frontier wars against Africans and in several skirmishes against Afrikaners, until it was disbanded in 1870. The regiment's enrollment varied between two hundred and eight hundred. The conditions of service were not good enough to make it popular among the Khoikhoi, and white farmers always opposed and often obstructed recruiting them on the grounds that it deprived Whites of labor.[61]

Another option was residence on a mission station. By the 1830s, seven such institutions in the colony were catering for Khoikhoi—five Moravian and two LMS. Each station comprised up to ten thousand acres and provided homes for up to twelve hundred people. In material terms, the most successful was Genadendal, which the Moravians conducted in a strong paternalist spirit. The LMS missionaries were less demanding and their stations were less prosperous. The location of Bethelsdorp, moreover, was ill-chosen. It had no arable land and the able-bodied inhabitants were obliged to go out to work while using the station as their base. John Philip improved the condition of the LMS stations in the 1820s, supervising the construction of substantial buildings and watercourses.

In spite of doctrinal differences, both societies provided their charges with some insulation from the civil society and some training in skills of value to them in making the transition to colonial life. Even so, they were constrained by their own lack of financial resources, as well as by the power of the colonial society in which they were embedded. As Richard Elphick and V. C. Malherbe put it: "Mission life gave a few Khoikhoi a measure of financial independence, but the shortage of suitable land on the overcrowded stations meant that most remained poor with no option but to hire themselves periodically to the farmers, or to enlist in the Regiment."[62]

For the people of Khoikhoi and slave antecedents, these options were palliatives rather than cures. Although they were not technically enslaved, lacking land and political power, most of them were effectively enserfed to the white colonists. In the Cape Colony, the white settlers had repeatedly demonstrated a determination to achieve and maintain a near monopoly of the productive land. In 1799, for example, the Dutch authorities had granted land on the Gamtoos River in the frontier zone to a band of Khoikhoi under David Stuurman; but in 1809, when Stuurman refused to surrender two Khoikhoi whose employer had not allowed them to leave his farm although they had completed their contracts, Landdrost Cuyler seized Stuurman by deceit and had him condemned to work in irons on Robben Island for the rest of his life. Stuurman's settlement was broken up and Cuyler obtained the land as his personal possession.[63]

That was a precedent for what happened on a larger scale after 1828. In 1829, Andries Stockenstrom, who had been promoted to the rank of commissioner-general of the eastern part of the colony, set aside about four hundred square miles of fertile land that had formerly been occupied by Xhosa, on the upper reaches of the Kat River as a settlement for Khoikhoi. At first things went well. By 1833, there were 2,114 settlers—Khoikhoi and people of mixed descent. They owned 2,444 head of cattle, 4,996 sheep, and 250 horses and produced wheat, barley, and fruit. They had dug fifty-five irrigation channels and built a dozen stone houses as well as wattle-and-daub cottages.[64]

However, Xhosa farmers raided their livestock from across the border and filtered back into the area with or without their permission, and they were joined by groups of Mfengu—Africans who had fled southward from the expanding Zulu empire. The settlement also bore the brunt of the frontier wars of 1834–35, 1846–47, and 1850–53. In the first two of those wars, the Kat River Khoikhoi provided loyal and courageous service to the colony. In 1847, for example, the British commanding general said that nine hundred of the one thousand male adults in the settlement were on active service, compared with "not more than three per cent of the adult population . . . of any other Division of the Colony."[65] On each occasion, the Khoikhoi of the Kat River lost most of their livestock, their crops were destroyed, and many of their houses were burnt down.

Unlike the British 1820 Settlers, the Kat River people eventually became the victims of racism and official hostility. By 1847, Stockenstrom was out of office, and in that year the colonial government appointed T. J. Biddulph as magistrate in Kat River. Biddulph was an 1820 Settler and so was his successor, J. H. Bowker. Both held their subjects in utter contempt, calling them inferiors and wastrels and their settlement "the abode of idleness and imposture."[66] When some Khoikhoi managed to make a living by felling timber and taking it to market, Biddulph killed their business by quadrupling the license fee on timber. Not surprisingly, during the 1850–53 frontier war some of the Kat River people, including men like Andries Botha who had led loyal Khoikhoi forces in the previous wars with distinction, sided with the Xhosa. Thereafter, the government yielded to the clamor among the British immigrants for the opening up of the fertile Kat River valley to white settlement. Whites began to pour into the area. With official support and relatively easy access to capital, they gradually edged the Khoikhoi people out of their landholdings.[67]

As the collapse of the Kat River settlement shows, the land issue was intimately bound up with the question of political power. By the mid-nineteenth century, Great Britain was making its final breaks with its mercantilist heritage. The protective tariff on grain went in 1846, and with it the very idea of running a formal empire as a closed economy. In that heyday of British industrial power, British businessmen, confident in their capacity to outproduce, out-trade, and out-finance foreigners, were questioning the rationale for colonial dependency. Why should their tax money go to administering and policing overseas territories, when their inhabitants would choose to import British manufactures for their needs and to seek British markets for their produce, even if formal political ties were lacking? Businessmen did not govern England; but the Whig faction of the landed aristocracy and gentry who still controlled the British political system met them halfway. Their approach to the colonial question "was fashioned, not by a calculated appraisal of economic interests, but by a desire to give British communities overseas the fullest possible control over their internal affairs that circumstances permitted."[68]

This approach was echoed by British colonists in North America, Australia, and New Zealand, who were involved in various conflicts with their metropolitan officials and nominated councils. Accordingly, by midcentury the British government was devolving increased power to those settler communities. Canada, whose elective assemblies dated back to 1791, set the pace, advancing from locally elected legislative bodies ("representative government") toward legislative control over the executive ("responsible government"). Australia and New Zealand followed suit. In all those cases, the settlers outnumbered the aborigines and nearly all of them came from Britain.

How was the Cape Colony to fit into the imperial picture? Was it to be treated as another Canada? Or like India, where the British government of the mid-nineteenth century had no intention of creating elective institutions, since the Indian people vastly outnumbered the tiny pockets of white settlers? Hesitatingly, Britain opted for the Canadian model. Inside the colony, 1820 Settlers, alienated by Somerset's autocracy and confident that they could handle their racial problems more effectively than British governors, initiated the demand for "British institutions." The British government made the first cautious concessions in 1825 and 1834, first obliging the governor to act in consultation with a council composed of the other senior officials, and then increasing the power of the council and enlarging it to include a number of nominated colonists as well as officials. The effects were shown in the Masters and Servants Ordinance of 1841, which began to undermine the 50th Ordinance. Even so, colonists were not satisfied with this constitutional arrangement, which left great power in the hands of officials responsible to London. It broke down completely in 1849, when a British attempt to offload a shipload of British convicts on the Cape Colony evoked a rare response of indignant cooperation between all sections of the white population—British and Afrikaner, western and eastern, rich and poor. The government was obliged to yield. The Cape did not follow the Australian colonies into becoming a dumping ground for British convicts.

By then, the British government had already asked the local officials to suggest a constitutional framework for representative institutions. As consultations continued at the Cape, the anticonvict coalition fell apart, and ethnic, racial, and class cleavages took over. The ethnic cleavage impelled the leading British merchants, professional people, and farmers, who had the wealth but not the numbers, to opt for high property qualifications for the franchise and for membership in parliament; Afrikaners, who had superior numbers but were mostly quite poor, preferred low qualifications. The racial cleavage prompted many white colonists, both British and Afrikaner, to desire high qualifications, whereas a few influential white liberals, such as Andries Stockenstrom, the former landdrost, and John Fairbairn, editor of the Cape Town *Commercial Advertiser,* favored qualifications that would bring some of the Khoikhoi and former slaves into the political system.

When the final draft was prepared at the Cape for submission to London, Acting Governor Charles Darling and Attorney-General William Porter opted for a liberal solution. In 1853 the British government thus provided the Cape Colony with a bicameral parliament empowered to legislate on domestic matters subject to a British veto, while the executive branch continued to be filled by officials responsible to London. The parliamentary franchise was open to any male adult inhabitant, irrespective of race or ethnicity, who occupied property valued at £25 or who earned either a salary of £50 or a salary of £25 if board and lodging were provided.[69]

In principle, this constitution was a victory for the liberal point of view. It was, indeed, significant that the principle of nonracialism was incorporated in the constitution. In practice, however, Cape politics were always dominated by the white population. Handicapped by poverty and by white control of the press and of the machinery to register voters and conduct elections, people who were not white never amounted to more than 15 percent of the colonial electorate and never produced a member of the colonial parliament. Their impotence was soon demonstrated. In 1856, the Cape parliament passed the Masters and Servants Act, which made breach of contract a criminal offense and obliged magistrates to impose imprisonment without the option of a fine on workers who refused to work or used insulting language to employers.[70]

The British government raised no questions about this act. By 1856, the tide of philanthropism had receded in Britain. Indeed, in responding to the evangelical pressures during the previous decades, the British government had never contemplated transforming the underlying structure of colonial society. Slavery was to end and the Khoikhoi were to be freed from the most blatant abuses, but the white colonists were to continue to have the use of their labor. The most advanced evangelicals of the day, including John Philip, did not look much further. Philip, like other Europeans of his time, did not believe that Khoikhoi would ever be the economic and social equals of Whites. With his doctrine of moral and material improvement, moreover, he was looking to a free market to produce a humane outcome. The notion that the state itself should actively assist the subordinate classes to achieve prosperity and substantial equality was not in his repertoire.[71] After emancipation in the Cape Colony, as later in the United States, the forms were the forms of freedom, but the facts were still the facts of exploitation.

Emancipation gave the Khoikhoi and the former slaves the same legal status, and officials soon began to refer to them comprehensively as the Cape Coloured People. The term has stuck. In twentieth-century South Africa, the Coloured People became one of the four main racial categories recognized by the South African government, as distinct from the ruling class, which was deemed to be White; from the Bantu-speaking Africans, who formed the majority of the population; and from Asians, who had begun to be imported from India to Natal as indentured laborers in the 1860s.

In fact, biological and cultural differences among the Coloured People were immense. Those who lived in Cape Town had a long tradition of urban life. Most were of slave origin, and they included a cohesive Muslim community. As we have seen, the Cape Town slaves had been able to acquire skills as artisans (builders, carpenters, smiths, tailors, and cobblers), as well as domestic servants and laborers. The greater the distance from the town, the larger the proportion of Khoikhoi among the Coloured People and the more severe their subjection. By 1870, the traditional culture and social networks of the Khoikhoi had been destroyed by the process of conquest and subjection. Scattered as they were in small groups under white control, they had no means of contesting the new order.

Under favorable circumstances, the people who became known as Coloured People might have been expected to merge socially and biologically with the Afrikaners. There had always been considerable cohabitation across the color line, and the Afrikaner community had incorporated many individuals of mixed descent. Afrikaner race consciousness, however, was strong enough to limit that process. In 1857, social pressures caused the synod of the Dutch Reformed church of the colony to authorize the separation of Coloured from white congregations, which led to the creation of a distinct and subordinate mission church for Coloured People. By 1861, moreover, Coloured children were effectively banned from the public schools. Those who received any formal education did so in mission institutions, which transmitted little secular knowledge. In spite of the nonracial terminology of the 1853 constitution, the white rulers of the Cape Colony were treating the Coloured People as a distinct and inferior community, dependent on white employers.[72]

The first official census of the Cape Colony (which was subject to a large margin of error) was taken in 1865, on the eve of the mineral discoveries that would transform the entire Southern African region. The population was reported to comprise about 180,000 "Europeans," 200,000 "Hottentots" and "Others" (that is, Coloured People), and 100,000 "Kafirs"— people of African farming stock who were becoming the main labor force in the eastern districts.[73]

With a few breaks, the colonial economy had been expanding continually since the time of van Riebeeck. Contrary to earlier views, which accepted burgher polemics against the Dutch East India Company at face value, Peter van Duin and Robert Ross have shown that this was true throughout the Dutch period: "All major sectors of the Cape's agrarian economy, namely the production of wheat and wine and the ranching of sheep and cattle, underwent continual, if relatively gradual expansion . . . in response to a steady expansion of the market, both external and, particularly, local."[74]

Expansion continued under the British. After 1820, the pastoral districts became the source of a large production of wool from merino sheep imported by British officers. Between 1860 and 1869, wool accounted for 73 percent of all exports from the colony. The economic infrastructure also became more complex. After a pause following the 1820 settlement, British immigration resumed with government assistance. The colonial government also improved the roads, inaugurated a postal and a telegraph service, and started to build a railway from Cape Town to Stellenbosch and down the Cape peninsula to Wynberg. Two banks, incorporated in London, amalgamated many of the small, local banks that had sprung up since the 1820s and established branches throughout the region. Foreign trade was dominated by Great Britain. In 1865, Britain provided 80 percent of the imports, which were valued at £2,103,000, and absorbed 85 percent of the exports, which were valued at £2,218,000. The colony was still essentially rural. The largest towns were Cape Town, with 28,000 inhabitants, and Port Elizabeth with 9,000.[75] There was also a widespread network of small towns—local markets and merchant centers.

In the seventeenth and eighteenth centuries, the legal practices of the Dutch, notably the institution of slavery, had led to the development of a racial order. Under the British, the racial order had adapted to the transition from formal slavery to formal freedom. In the coming century the racial order would also survive and adapt to the advent of industrialization and urbanization—a striking example of the durability of deeprooted social structures.

Even so, many Afrikaners, especially those in the eastern districts, found it difficult to accept these and other changes. In 1815, when a few impoverished trekboers had fomented a rebellion, the substantial farmers had joined with the British forces in suppressing them.[76] During the 1830s, however, anti-British feeling was widespread among all classes of eastern Afrikaners, and by 1840 some six thousand men, women, and children—about 9 percent of the total white population of the Colony—had left their homes with their wagons, cattle, sheep, and all movable property. They took with them perhaps five thousand Coloured servants, most of whom were of Khoikhoi descent, though some were former slaves who had become apprentices in 1834. The Afrikaner migrants—later known as *voortrekkers* (pioneers)—were escaping from an alien government whose policies they had come to detest and hoping to find some Promised Land where they might make their own arrangements with one another, with their servants, and with the other inhabitants.[77]

Since 1806, the world the Afrikaners had known had been transformed.

Their customary vent for population increase by expansion was blocked by Africans in the east and by the aridity of the land in the north. In 1813, moreover, the government stopped letting people occupy land in the old easy way, by paying a nominal fee for the use of six thousand acres. Instead, a quitrent system, intended to promote more intensive farming practices, made land ownership more legally secure but more expensive.[78]

Under the British regime, the autonomy that the farmers had enjoyed under the Dutch East India Company was ending. Whereas the company's colonial state had been extremely weak beyond the vicinity of Cape Town and Stellenbosch, the British gradually asserted control over the entire colony, and in so doing emphasized British culture and institutions. From 1811 on, judges of the colonial court went annually on circuit to the various district headquarters to hear criminal as well as civil cases. The pace of administrative change quickened after the arrival of the 1820 Settlers, who pressed for anglicization. Previously, the British had preserved the Dutch system of district administration, under landdrosts appointed by the central government and heemraden and veldkornets drawn from the farming population. By 1834, the powers of the veldkornets had been curtailed, and the landdrosts and heemraden had been replaced by magistrates without local affiliations. In place of the amateur (and sometimes corrupt) bench of Dutch officials, moreover, the government appointed qualified lawyers from Britain to the Court of Justice and introduced British legal procedures.

There were also cultural changes. The government continued to support the Dutch Reformed church but asserted supervision over it. Moreover, although English was a foreign language for the Afrikaner population, by the 1830s it alone was authorized for use in government offices, law courts, and public schools.

It was in this changing institutional and cultural environment that Afrikaners experienced the dislocations that were inevitable short-term consequences of emancipation. Initially, many newly emancipated Khoikhoi and slaves left the farms, hoping to enjoy their freedom. Some crowded into the mission stations, others squatted on Crown lands or moved to the towns and villages, and for a time, many roamed the countryside, trying to live by pilfering. As a result, white farmers were not only short of labor but also the victims of social unrest; hence their demand for a law against vagrancy and their disgust when the British government disallowed it.

Afrikaners experienced further setbacks. Many who lived near the Xhosa frontier lost livestock and other property during the invasion of

December 1834 and were outraged in 1836, when London reversed the postwar plans of the governor to annex more land from the Africans and make it available for white settlement. Many former slave owners were disappointed financially when they learned that the British government was providing as compensation only about one-third of the assessed value of their slaves. Moreover, claims had to be proved in London, with the result that agents purchased the claims at a reduced rate and the owners eventually received no more than one-fifth of their slaves' assessed value.

Many of these changes affected farmers in the western as well as the eastern districts. Indeed, far more slaves were held in the west than the east. Nevertheless, although eastern farmers had used far more Khoikhoi than slave laborers, most of them had possessed at least one slave, and they rather than the westerners were most deeply affected by the other events. The west was a more stable region. Its white population was more sedentary and more fully integrated into the market economy. Under the British, many substantial townsmen and wine and grain farmers became involved in the social life emanating from government house, whereas eastern Afrikaners of all classes were alienated from the British regime and regarded it as responsible for all their misfortunes. As a result, nearly all the Afrikaners who left the colony were easterners. About one quarter of the Afrikaner inhabitants of the eastern districts took part in the remarkable exodus that historians call the Great Trek.[79]

Piet Retief, one of the emigrant leaders, informed the *Grahamstown Journal* that they were leaving because of "the turbulent and dishonest conduct of vagrants," because of the losses they had sustained through the emancipation of their slaves, and because of "the plunder which we have endured from the Caffres and other coloured classes." He added a complaint of the sort that would recur again and again, down to the late twentieth century: "We complain of the unjustifiable odium which has been cast upon us by interested and dishonest persons, under the cloak of religion [that is, the missionaries], whose testimony is believed in England, to the exclusion of all evidence in our favour; and we can foresee, as a result of this prejudice, nothing but the total ruin of our country."[80]

CHAPTER 3

African Wars and White Invaders: Southeast Africa, 1770–1870

White invaders and their diseases destroyed most of the hunting and herding societies in the western part of Southern Africa during the regime of the Dutch East India Company. They did so to such an extent that, with the exception of a few bands of hunters who still eke out an existence in arid, isolated terrain in Namibia and Botswana that Whites have not coveted, the only descendants of the aboriginal Khoisan are the so-called Cape Coloured People—an amalgam of people of diverse origins who possess few of the cultural traits of their precolonial ancestors.

White people did not begin to invade the eastern part of southern Africa—the terrain of the Bantu-speaking mixed farmers whose background was described in chapter 1—until the late eighteenth century. Most of the mixed-farming communities were scarcely affected by European colonization before the 1830s. In the early stages of contact in each successive chiefdom, Africans welcomed and assisted the intruders, despite their pale skins and strange clothing: hunters, who shot game, especially elephants for their ivory; traders, who bartered their imported beads, metal wares, clothing, and groceries in exchange for ivory, hides, and cattle; missionaries, who expounded novel religious ideas; and pastoral farmers with large herds of cattle and flocks of sheep. However, in African culture visitors should report to the chief on their arrival; they should ask his permission to carry out their activities; and, if they remain, they should expect to be incorporated in the chiefdom. In particular, if a chief allowed a visitor to pasture his cattle and sheep in a given locality in his domain, he was doing no more than giving the visitor the right to use the land; he could withdraw this right at any time. Some white people complied with those norms. Others did not and, as their numbers increased, became more demanding and more arrogant. White farmers, for example. claimed to own the land they had been permitted to use, whereas the idea that a person could have property rights in land did not exist in African culture. The time finally came when a chief and his councillors realized that they were confronted with a threat to their autonomy. Then, some accommodated, others resisted.

In the ensuing conflicts, neither side was monolithic. The interests of white hunters, traders, missionaries, and farmers did not coincide. The goals of the British government and its colonial officials were different from those of British settlers, and often quite antithetical to those of Afrikaners. Among Africans, there were tensions among chiefs and commoners; among rival members of ruling families; between chiefdom and chiefdom; and among established communities and refugees from other areas. In the last resort, however, Whites were able to exploit the cleavages in African society more successfully than Africans could exploit the cleavages in white society. When they considered that racial hegemony was at stake, Whites did not obstruct one another; whereas Africans never created a united front and Whites were able to use African allies in every conflict.

Whites also possessed great technological advantages. Their firearms were far more effective than African spears; and although there were always traders who were willing to make a profit by selling guns to Africans, most of the guns they dispensed were poor-quality, obsolescent models, grossly inferior to those used by the British army and the colonists.[1] Even where Africans gained the upper hand in the opening stages of a conflict, they lost it as time went on. They lacked the equipment to capture fortified positions or laagers composed of circles of wagons, and when Africans resorted to guerrilla tactics the invaders forced them into submission by attacking their food supplies. Time after time, Afrikaner commandos and British regiments brought Africans to their knees by systematically destroying their homes, crops, and grain reserves, seizing their livestock, and turning their women and children into refugees. With their superior economy, which can accumulate and store wealth in a variety of forms, they were able to feed themselves from commissariats carried in ox-drawn wagons.

Some white settlers predicted that the African societies would disintegrate as the Khoisan in the southwestern part of Southern Africa and the aboriginal Indians in North America were doing. They were wrong. Unlike the Khoisan and the American Indians, the African farmers were already conditioned to the diseases brought from Europe. Smallpox and measles, which took a heavy toll of the Khoisan and the American Indians, do not seem to have affected the African farmers much more severely than they affected the white settlers.[2] The African farming societies, moreover, were far more populous, their economy was far more complex, their social networks were far more resilient, and their political systems were far more durable than those of the Khoisan. They were thus able to resist the invaders more effectively than the hunters and herders had done. Furthermore, even though they, too, were eventually subjected and the world they had known vanished for ever, they did not disintegrate. They maintained their cohesion as organized communities. They adapted their culture and their social, economic, and political institutions to the new order. They occupied substantial blocks of their ancestral land. What is more, they continued to be far more numerous than the white invaders.

In 1870, the outcome in southeast Africa was still in doubt. Whites had made their presence felt as far north as the Limpopo River, had defeated many of the farming communities in a series of separate campaigns, had assumed ownership of much of the best land in the territories they called the Ciskei, Natal, the Orange Free State, and the Transvaal, and had drawn many of the indigenous inhabitants of the region into the labor market. But the white settlers were few in number, their polities were frail, and their pockets of settlement were bordered by autonomous African polities, including the Tswana chiefdoms in the northwest, the Venda in the northern Transvaal, and the Pedi, the Swazi, the Zulu, and the Mpondo in the east.

In this chapter we follow these events down to 1870, when the white impact intensified dramatically as a result of the discovery of the world's greatest deposits of diamonds, soon to be followed by gold, in the heart of southern Africa. Since there were great variations over time and place, we shall deal in sequence with each major community, starting with the Xhosa, who were the first farming people to bear the brunt of invasion.

The Xhosa

Afrikaner trekboers moving eastward from the Cape began to overlap with the westernmost Xhosa settlements in the land between the Bushmans River and the Fish River in the last quarter of the eighteenth century. That was the beginning of a century of interaction that culminated in the conquest of all the Xhosa (map 3).[3] The process was profoundly influenced by cleavages among Xhosa political factions. During the seventeenth century, a single lineage had dominated most of the Xhosa chiefdoms, but following the death of its head in about 1750 the lineage split into two rival sections, one of which split again in 1782. Thereafter, there were three major divisions: the Gcaleka centered east of the Kei River; the Ngqika between the Kei and the Fish; and the Ndlambe in the area known as the Zuurveld, west of the Fish. The Ndlambes shared the Zuurveld with several other Xhosa-speaking chiefdoms, including the Gqunukhwebe, who had incorporated numerous people of Khoikhoi origin.

In the first three conflicts—1779–81, 1793, and 1799—the Zuurveld Xhosa held their ground. Indeed, in the third war they benefited from a period of exceptional weakness in the colonial state. Trekboers were rebelling against the new British government of the Cape Colony, and some of their Khoikhoi servants absconded and joined the Xhosa. By 1800, the Xhosa and their allies had destroyed white farmsteads as far west as the Gamtoos River and were in firm control of the Zuurveld. The tide turned in 1811 and 1812 when, as we have seen, acting on the recommendations of Colonel Collins, the colonial government mustered a large force of regular troops and Afrikaner and Coloured auxiliaries who drove the Xhosa men, women, and children beyond the Fish River.[4]

The government then tried to make the Fish River an absolute barrier between the colony and the Xhosa territory, impermeable to Whites and Blacks. In pursuit of this goal, it entered into cordial relations with the chief Ngqika, treating him as the supreme chief of all the Xhosa (whereas the Gcaleka chief had that status in Xhosa custom) and holding him responsible for preventing his people from raiding cattle across the border. The result was that Ngqika's prestige plummeted, many of his followers deserted him, and the Gcaleka and the Ndlambe combined their forces and overwhelmed the Ngqika in a pitched battle in 1818. Confident in their

3. Xhosa land losses, 1795–1850

strength, the Xhosa allies invaded the colony in 1819 and made a frontal
attack on the new garrison town of Grahamstown in the heart of the
Zuurveld. After barely surviving that attack, the colonial forces gained the
upper hand. The government then annexed the territory between the Fish
and the Keiskamma, indicating that it was to be a "neutral belt," keeping

Whites and Africans apart. Ngqika died in 1829. Some of his contemporaries regarded him as a collaborator, but he is honored in modern Xhosa tradition as a leader who stood up to the white invaders.[5]

During the 1820s, newcomers arrived on both sides of the border to accelerate the erosion of Xhosa autonomy. On the colonial side, the 1820 Settlers from Britain took occupation of the Zuurveld and soon persuaded the government to abandon its effort to prevent people from crossing the border. By the end of the decade, British traders and missionaries were purveying new commodities and new ideas throughout Xhosaland, and several hundred Xhosa were sampling life in the colony by working for a few months at a time for white farmers. Meanwhile, thousands of African refugees were flooding into Xhosaland from Natal. Known as Mfengu, they had, as we shall see, been dislodged from their homes by the Zulu army. The Mfengu were accepted by the Xhosa, but since they arrived without property and had no local kin they had low status in Xhosa society. Consequently, the Mfengu were particularly susceptible to the ideas and practices of the traders and missionaries and prone to be disloyal to their Xhosa patrons.[6]

By the 1830s, relations between Blacks and Whites were deteriorating. There was cattle rustling both ways across the frontier. Government officials and British settlers humiliated African chiefs in the presence of their followers. Colonial forces expelled Africans whom the government had allowed to settle in part of the "neutral belt." White traders, with access to capital and supplies of Western commodities, eliminated Xhosa competitors and formed cartels to change the terms of trade to their advantage. By December 1834, Xhosa resentment was so general that, with few exceptions, the chiefs cooperated in organizing a massive invasion of the colony. Absorbing the lesson of their failure to capture Grahamstown in 1819, they attacked on a wide front and waged a skillful guerrilla war, forcing most of the British settlers to abandon their farms. Eventually, however, an imperial force carried out a destructive expedition into the heart of Xhosa territory across the Kei River. The Gcaleka chief Hintsa, who was generally recognized to be the senior of all the Xhosa chiefs, was tricked into captivity and shot dead when he tried to escape; and many Mfengu deserted their patrons and joined the colonial forces. In September 1835, the surviving chiefs capitulated.[7]

Egged on by inflammatory settler pressures for the ejection of the Xhosa, the British governor then announced peace terms to assembled Xhosa chiefs. All the land between the Keiskamma and the Kei was to be annexed as the province of Queen Adelaide. A fire-eating colonel named Harry Smith began to administer it, intent on imposing British civilization upon its inhabitants. This new order had scarcely begun, however, when, responding to the still influential humanitarian lobby, the British colonial secretary ordered the abandonment of the province and appointed Andries Stockenstrom as lieutenant-governor of the eastern districts.[8]

Stockenstrom, who had held official appointments in the frontier zone since 1808, sought to pacify the frontier by making treaties with the Xhosa chiefs and holding the colonists responsible for organizing the protection of their property. The system did not work. The chiefs had never had autocratic powers, and by 1836, some of the Xhosa people, battered and impoverished by the wars and the land losses, were taking to banditry. Moreover, the government did not provide funds to police the border and the settlers themselves could not do it. The settlers never favored the system. They had hoped to get hold of more land in Queen Adelaide and raised a clamor for its reannexation.[9]

The tenuous peace collapsed after Stockenstrom was superseded by men who lacked the will to check the settlers. In 1846, war broke out again. In white circles it was known as the War of the Axe, because it was sparked by an incident in which a Xhosa band released a man who had been arrested for stealing an ax and killed the Khoikhoi prisoner who had been hand-cuffed to the accused. The Xhosa—assisted this time by allies from the neighboring Thembu chiefdoms—drove the colonial forces back beyond the Keiskamma River, but once again the troops concentrated on destroying their homes, cattle, crops, and grain reserves. With their women and children facing mass starvation, the chiefs sued for peace.[10]

In 1847, Sir Harry Smith—the man responsible for killing Hintsa—became governor of the Cape Colony, and on 23 December he paraded his troops in the presence of two thousand Africans. Sitting on horseback, he read out a proclamation reannexing the land between the Keiskamma and the Kei as a separate colony, called British Kaffraria. Then, according to one report, he called the chiefs forward and required them to kiss his feet. Two weeks later, the report continues, he assembled the chiefs again and, after lecturing them, told them to look at a wagon that he had loaded with gunpowder. The gallant governor then gave the order "Fire!" whereupon the wagon exploded into a thousand pieces. "That is what I will do to you," Smith is reported to have said, "if you do not behave yourselves."[11] Whether or not apocryphal, these stories celebrate the importance of technological superiority.

Smith strengthened the human barrier against the Xhosa by settling Mfengu and white military veterans in the fertile land between the Fish and the Keiskamma. British Kaffraria east of the Keiskamma he ruled autocratically, placing white magistrates over the chiefs. He interfered drastically in domestic Xhosa politics—for example, by deposing Sandile, the senior Ngqika chief, and proclaiming the son of a British missionary as regent in his stead. Deeply humiliated, in December 1850 the Ngqika chiefs and councillors initiated yet another round of military resistance. In this, they were encouraged by a prophet, Mlanjeni, who had been influenced by Christianity. Mlanjeni claimed that "he had been to Heaven and had talked to God who was displeased with the white man for having killed his Son . . . God would help the black man against the white . . . a stick from the plumbago plant would make them invulnerable."[12]

Mlanjeni's War, as it became called, continued for more than two years. The Ngqika were joined by many other Xhosa, by numerous Thembu, and by Khoikhoi rebels from the Kat River settlement, making a total of about 20,000 fighting men. The colonial government mustered nearly as many, including Mfengu, Gqunukhwebe, colonial volunteers, a few Khoikhoi, and 8,600 British regular troops. At the outset, as in previous conflicts, the Xhosa took the offensive, destroying the military villages along the Cape colonial frontier and forcing colonists to abandon their farms deep inside the colony. But, as in every previous war since the Zuurveld was cleared in 1811–12, the imperial forces eventually prevailed by systematically destroying Xhosa food supplies.[13]

Further forced removals and relocations followed that war. "Loyal" Africans were given relatively generous landholdings, whereas the Ngqika were confined to a small tract of land, and much of the new colony of British Kaffraria was thrown open to white settlement. Assuming office in December 1854, Governor Sir George Grey, a high-minded soldier who, unlike the egregious Harry Smith, had serious intellectual interests but also possessed the unquestioning cultural arrogance of the ruling class of Victorian Britain, presided over a program inspired by his recent dealings with the Maori in New Zealand. The chiefs became salaried officials, responsible to white magistrates. Their people were to be "civilized." Missions, schools, and hospitals would wean them from "barbarism"; employment on beneficial public works—roads and irrigation ditches—would teach them the dignity of wage labor; and, with white settlements interspersed among their landholdings, they would profit from the example of civilized people.[14]

No sooner was peace restored than a lethal cattle disease, lung sickness (bovine pleuropneumonia), arrived from Europe and spread rapidly, intensifying the anguish of the battered, impoverished, and humiliated Xhosa. They responded by trying to control the movements of infected beasts and by holding individuals responsible for these calamities and executing them as witches. But to no avail. All chiefdoms were affected; some lost more than 80 percent of their cattle—their most valuable possessions.[15]

Conquest and lung sickness turned the Xhosa world upside down. People wondered how they could account for these unprecedented events and how they should respond. They naturally sought answers in their indigenous concepts of witchcraft, pollution, sacrifice, and the powers of the ancestors; but they also adapted concepts of sin and the resurrection from the teachings of the missionaries. If they erased the pollution that had caused the calamities by a massive sacrifice of the remaining cattle and the grain, they might eradicate witchcraft and their ancestors might return and restore "a happy state of things."[16]

Several prophets gave expression to these ideas—most notably, a sixteen-year-old girl named Nongqawuse, who lived in the country of the Gcaleka Xhosa, four miles east of the Kei River. Nongqawuse declared that when she and another girl were in the fields scaring away the birds from the corn, two men appeared and said they had died long ago:

> You are to tell the people that the whole community is about to rise again from the dead. Then go on to say to them all the cattle living now must be slaughtered, for they are reared with defiled hands, as the people handle witchcraft. Say to them there must be no ploughing of lands, rather must the people dig deep pits (granaries), erect new huts, set up wide, strongly built cattlefolds, make milksacks, and weave doors from buta roots. The people must give up witchcraft on their own, not waiting until they are exposed by the witchdoctors. You are to tell them that these are the words of their chiefs.[17]

Later, she had more visions. On one occasion, she reported that "there was another chief . . . [whose] name was Grey, otherwise known as Satan. All those who did not slaughter their cattle would become subjects of the chief named Satan."[18]

Nongqawuse convinced her uncle, Mhlakaza, that her visions were authentic. Mhlakaza was the head of her homestead and a councillor of the Gcaleka chief Sarhili. News of Nongqawuse's visions spread throughout the country, causing immense excitement. The news was hotly debated at every level. The community was split in two. Father fell out with son, brother with brother, chief with subjects. Nongqawuse's converts were known as *amathamba,* "soft" believers, who submitted to the common will and accepted the truth of the prophecy; those who rejected the prophecy were known as *amagogotya,* "hard" unbelievers, who pursued their own individual interests.[19]

Chief Sarhili was skeptical at first, but after going to Mhlakaza's homestead to investigate, he became convinced that the prophecy was authentic and threw his immense prestige behind the movement. Most Gcaleka chiefs followed suit, and the movement spread across the Kei river, where Sandile, the principal Ngqika chief, eventually participated. It stopped short of the Mfengu. According to one tradition, the ancestors had no message for the Mfengu.[20]

A sensitive historian of these events, J. B. Peires, considers that "the believer/unbeliever divide followed no clear pattern of kinship, age, gender, or social class." He also considers that the believers were engaged in "a popular mass movement of a truly national character, uniting both chiefs and commoners . . . in a communal defence of their way of life." Peires adds: "The 'soft' party of believers saw themselves as properly loyal and submissive adherents of the old order, who put their nation first in giving up their cattle for the good of all. They viewed the *amagogotya* as selfish and even despicable 'cowards who fear hunger.' The unbelievers probably thought of themselves as sensible men, who realized that one could not eat grass, but their unbelief was probably sustained by a deep unwillingness to slaughter their cattle."[21]

A mass slaughter of cattle and destruction of grain ensued. The frenzy rose to a crescendo at the new moon on February 18, 1857, when the prophecy was to have been fulfilled; and again on successive dates designated in revised prophecies. The scale of the catastrophe was appalling. It is estimated that the people destroyed 400,000 head of cattle and that at least 40,000 Xhosa died of starvation. By the end of January 1858 another 33,000 had moved inside the Cape Colony to become laborers on farms or in the towns and villages as far away as Cape Town.[22]

Throughout most of 1857 social relations bordered on anarchy, as amathamba plundered amagogotya for food. Sir George Grey took advantage of the occasion to relegate the British Kaffrarian chiefs to the sidelines, while real power was exercised by magistrates and their African assistants. He also used the opportunity created by the depopulation of the territory to make more land available in British Kaffraria for white settlement, notably for a group of German immigrants.[23]

On January 1, 1866, British Kaffraria was incorporated in the Cape Colony, which then included all the land west of the Kei River between the mountain escarpment and the Indian Ocean. The African inhabitants of that area, which later became known as the Ciskei, were Mfengu and the remnants of the Gqunukhwebe, Ndlambe, and Ngqika chiefdoms. The invaders had deprived them of the land their ancestors had occupied west of the Fish River and had confined them to small landholdings between the Fish and the Kei. These were insufficient for their subsistence, so they were obliged to provide the main labor force for the white farmers and the white inhabitants of the towns and villages in the eastern districts of the Cape Colony. The British government, however, had halted plans for white settlement in what became known as the Transkei, where the Gcaleka Xhosa and the Thembu were still nominally independent people.

Repeated military defeats, lung sickness, and the cattle-killing had profoundly affected the religious beliefs and social aspirations of the Xhosa, especially those living in the Ciskei. Tiyo Soga, a Xhosa commoner back from Britain with a Scottish education, a Scottish wife, and the status of minister of the Presbyterian church, was to be a forerunner in the process of evangelization. Soga showed his fellow Xhosa how they might adapt to their condition as conquered people in a capitalist economy. In 1861, in words that foreshadowed the doctrines of Booker T. Washington in the United States, he wrote: "The country of the Kafirs is now forfeited and the greater part of it has been given out in grants to European farmers. I see plainly that unless the rising generation is trained to some of the useful arts, nothing else will raise our people, and they must be grooms, drivers of wagons, hewers of wood, or general servants. But let our youth be taught trades, to earn money, and they will increase and purchase land." Soga added a most prescient statement: "When a people are not land-proprietors, they are of no consequence in this country and are tenants on mere sufferance."[24]

The Zulu Kingdom and the Mfecane

Until the late eighteenth century the Bantu-speaking mixed farmers south of the Limpopo River lived in small chiefdoms. By the 1830s, when white people began to invade southeastern Africa beyond the Fish River in substantial numbers, however, society throughout the region had been drastically transformed. The nucleus of change lay in northern Nguni country. There, in the country between the mountain escarpment and the

Indian Ocean, the Zulu kingdom had incorporated all the northern Nguni chiefdoms. The royal family and its Ntungwa clan constituted a new ruling class. They controlled a standing army of conscripted warriors and exacted tribute from the commoners. Moreover, in a process known as the *Mfecane* (Zulu) or *Difaqane* (Sesotho), meaning time of troubles, emigrant bands from modern KwaZulu had created new kingdoms as far north as modern Malawi, Zambia, and Tanzania. The Mfengu, who arrived among the Xhosa and became allied with the Cape Colony, were among the refugees displaced by these events (map 4).[25]

This transformation was in essence an internal process within the mixed farming society in southeastern Africa. By the last quarter of the eighteenth century, the relation between the population level and the environment was changing. Previously, the society had been expansive and the scale of political organization had remained small in spite of the tendency of the population to increase, because members of ruling families had frequently split from their chiefdoms with their followers and founded new chiefdoms between or beyond existing settlements. Gradually, however, the population of the region had been increasing to a level where that expansive process was no longer possible. Farmers were reaching the limits of land with arable potential on the verge of the Kalahari Desert in the northwest and in the rugged mountains at the southern end of the highveld. Throughout southeastern Africa, as the possibilities for further expansion diminished, competition for land and water supplies grew more acute.[26]

Changing climatic conditions exacerbated the crisis. Rainfall decreased significantly throughout the region during the first three decades of the nineteenth century, with an exceptionally severe drought between 1800 and 1807, followed by another between 1820 and 1823.[27] The problem was especially serious in the northern Nguni area. There, the terrain is marked by steep hills and deep valleys, which create widely different environments within short distances, and it was necessary for people to move their cattle seasonally from one type of pasture to another. As the land filled up, pastures began to deteriorate through overstocking and people began to interfere with the customary movements of cattle. By the end of the eighteenth century, strong chiefdoms were subduing their neighbors and incorporating them into loosely structured kingdoms.[28] Then came the first great drought of the century, which people remembered as the time when "we were obliged to eat grass."[29]

By the 1810s, there were two rival kingdoms in the area: the Ndwandwe kingdom, led by Zwide, and the Mthethwa kingdom, led by Dingiswayo,

4. Shaka's Zulu Kingdom and the Mfecane Wars, 1817–1828

who created a standing army composed of age regiments. The two king-doms clashed repeatedly and with unprecedented ferocity. The outcome of the crisis was shaped very largely by Shaka. The eldest son of Senzanga-kona, the chief of the small Zulu chiefdom, Shaka was illegitimate, since his father never married his mother, Nandi. Rejected by his father, Shaka grew up among his mother's relatives. In Zulu tradition, he was "a tall man, dark, with a large nose, and was ugly," and "he spoke with an impedi-ment."[30]

When he was about twenty-two, Shaka joined the army of Dingiswayo, king of the Mthethwa, where he acquired a reputation as a brave warrior and a man of original ideas and became commander of his regiment. When Senzangakona died in about 1816, Dingiswayo helped Shaka succeed to the Zulu chieftaincy over the heads of his numerous legitimate half-broth-ers. Shaka then equipped the Zulu warriors with short stabbing spears in addition to the traditional long spears and trained them to fight in close combat. A year or two later, the Ndwandwe captured and killed Din-giswayo. The Mthethwa kingdom then disintegrated and Shaka's Zulu conquered and incorporated its chiefdoms. In 1818, the Zulu defeated the Ndwandwe in a decisive battle at the Mhlatuse River and became the dominant power throughout northern Nguni territory. By the mid-1820s, Shaka's Zulu had established control over most territory from the Pongola River in the north to beyond the Tugela River in the south and from the mountain escarpment to the sea.[31]

The transformation of the northern Nguni was accentuated by external factors. Some historians believe that foreign trade was crucial in the rise of the Zulu kingdom. Traders from the Portuguese settlement on Delagoa Bay were increasingly active in this period, bartering beads, brass, and other imported commodities for ivory and cattle. Creating competition for con-trol of the trade route, they probably intensified the conflicts and the centralizing process.[32] The available evidence, including the recorded oral traditions of the African informants, however, does not seem to warrant the conclusion that the trade was sufficient to have been the primary cause of the transformation.

One historian has gone so far as to assert that external forces—white slave traders and white colonists and their Coloured allies—bore most of the responsibility for the transformations in southeastern Africa. Accord-ing to him, the export trade in slaves from Delagoa Bay precipitated the changes among the northern Nguni, and Griquas and Whites from the

Cape Colony were the principal disrupters of the African chiefdoms in the modern Transvaal and Orange Free State. The first claim is palpably false: scarcely any slaves were being exported from Delagoa Bay before 1823; subsequently there was a rise in slave exports, but that was a result, not a cause, of the warfare in the area. The second claim draws attention to a previously underestimated factor: Griquas did cause considerable havoc in some parts of the highveld; nevertheless, the main agents of that disruption were Nguni emigrants from modern KwaZulu.[33]

The Zulu kingdom was the end product of radical changes in northern Nguni society that had begun in the late eighteenth century. It was a militarized state, made and maintained by a conscript army of about forty thousand warriors. Instead of the initiation system, which had integrated young men into the discipline of their particular chiefdoms, men were removed from civil society at about the age of puberty and assigned to age regiments, living in barracks scattered throughout the country. During their period of service they were denied contact with women and subjected to intense discipline. They were employed on public works for the state, but their most conspicuous duties were military. In warfare, their standard tactic was to encircle the enemy and then, in close combat, to cause havoc with short stabbing spears. They celebrated a victory by seizing booty, principally in cattle, and, sometimes, by massacring women and children. Survivors were incorporated into the Zulu kingdom under chiefs whose tenure depended on their loyalty.

In earlier times, there had been no standing armies, women and children were seldom killed, and defeated chiefdoms were rarely incorporated. Men, women, and children had lived in their homesteads throughout their lives and had forfeited only a relatively modest amount of their produce to their chiefs. Under Shaka, grain and cattle flowed in larger quantities to the royal residence and the regimental barracks; and, with a high proportion of their mature men absent, women had greater responsibility for rural production and for managing the homestead.

To foster loyalty to the state, Shaka and his councillors drew on the customary Nguni festivals. They assembled the entire army at the royal barracks for the annual first-fruits ceremony and before and after major military expeditions, when they used spectacular displays and magical devices to instill a corporate morale. The traditions of the Zulu royal lineage became the traditions of the kingdom; the Zulu dialect became the language of the kingdom; and every inhabitant, whatever his origins, became a Zulu, owing allegiance to Shaka. Nevertheless, as Carolyn Hamilton, drawing on Zulu evidence, points out, "The process of centralization was far from smooth. . . . . There were . . . great inequalities within the Zulu kingdom, deep-seated divisions and considerable disaffection. . . . [O]utbreaks of rebellion . . . prompted continued coercive responses from the Zulu authorities. These included merciless campaigns and stern sentences for individual rebels. . . . The Zulu authorities fostered this image through carefully managed displays of despotism and brutal justice at the court, using terror as a basis for absolute rule across a huge kingdom."

During the 1820s, the Zulu kingdom became increasingly predatory. Shaka sent the army on annual campaigns, disrupting local chiefdoms to the north and the south, destroying their food supplies, seizing their cattle. Tensions within the royal family came to a head on September 24, 1828. While the army was away on a campaign to the north, Shaka's personal servant and two of his half-brothers assassinated him. One of those half-brothers, Dingane, eliminated his rivals and succeeded to the kingship, maintaining Shaka's domestic and external policies, though he lacked Shaka's originality and panache.[34]

Meanwhile, militant bands of people who had been driven from their homes by the Ndwandwe, the Mthethwa, and the Zulu created the widespread havoc throughout southeastern Africa that became known as the *Mfecane*. By the early 1830s, organized community life had virtually ended in some areas—notably, in modern Natal, south of the Zulu kingdom, and in much of the modern Orange Free State between the Vaal and the Caledon river valleys, where the only human beings were small groups of survivors trying to eke out a living on mountaintops or in bush country. Settlements were abandoned, livestock were destroyed, fields ceased to be cultivated, and in several places the landscape was littered with human bones. Demoralized survivors wandered round singly or in small groups, contriving to live on game or veld plants. Some even resorted to cannibalism—the final sign of society's collapse. A self-proclaimed former cannibal later told a missionary: "Many preferred to die of hunger; but others were deceived by the more intrepid ones, who would say to their friends . . . : *here is some rock rabbit meat, recover your strength*; however, it was human flesh. Once they had tasted it, they found that it was excellent. . . . Our heart did fret inside us; but we were getting used to that type of life, and the horror we had felt at first was soon replaced by habit."[35]

By that time, a rival Nguni kingdom controlled much of the central highveld. In about 1821, one of Shaka's allies, a chief named Mzilikazi, fled over the escarpment to the highveld with a small band of warriors. There, they became known as *Ndebele* (Nguni) or *Matabele* (Sotho). Using Zulu military methods, they carved out a state between the Vaal and the Limpopo rivers, conquering several Sotho and Tswana chiefdoms and incorporating many of their people as subordinates, exacting tribute from others, and, like the Zulu, sending impis out to terrorize more distant communities.[36]

Other states were developing on the periphery of the areas dominated by the Zulu and the Ndebele. Several militant bands of refugees from the northern Nguni area, enthused with similar zeal for conquest, struggled to establish themselves in modern Mozambique. The most successful were those led by Soshangane, who created the Gaza kingdom there and drove out others led by Zwangendaba and Nxaba, who eventually carved out new chieftaincies for themselves in parts of modern Malawi, Zambia, and Tanzania. Similarly, a Sotho community known as the Kololo, harrassed by the Ndebele, fled northward from the highveld and eventually founded a kingdom in modern Zambia. In mountainous territory northwest of the Zulu, meanwhile, an Nguni chief named Sobhuza, who had been driven out of land near the Pongola River by Zwide's Ndwandwe, absorbed several Sotho as well as Nguni communities and created a durable kingdom that became known as Swaziland after Sobhuza's son and heir, Mswati.[37]

Perhaps the most significant of the new states was Lesotho. Its leader was Moshoeshoe, the senior son of a Sotho village headman, who gathered the survivors of the wars in the Caledon River valley. Besides Sotho, who had belonged to numerous different chiefdoms before the invasions began, they included people who had arrived in the area as members of invading Nguni bands. From headquarters on a flat-topped mesalike mountain named Thaba Bosiu, the Basotho warriors warded off attacks by a series of aggressors, including an Ndebele impi and Griqua raiders.

Lesotho differed fundamentally from the Zulu kingdom. It was the scene of postwar reconstruction on pacific rather than coercive principles. Although Moshoeshoe placed his sons and other relatives over chiefs of other lineages, he never created a standing army, he remained on easy, familiar terms with all and sundry, he encouraged his people to debate public questions freely in public meetings, and he tolerated a great deal of local autonomy. "Peace," he said, "is like the rain which makes the grass grow, while war is like the wind which dries it up."[38] With its humane leader and its central position in southern Africa, Lesotho played an important role throughout the next half-century.

In transforming the farming society of southeastern Africa, the Mfecane wrought great suffering. Thousands died violent deaths. Thousands more were uprooted from their homes. Village communities and chiefdoms were eliminated. A century later, Solomon Tshekisho Plaatje, a Motswana, started his novel *Mhudi* with tragic incidents in the Mfecane. Yet, in Thomas Mokopu Mofolo's well-known novel *Chaka,* written in Sesotho and translated into English, German, French, and Italian, and in an epic poem by Mazisi Kunene, the name of Shaka has passed into African literature and the consciousness of modern Africans as a symbol of African heroism and power.[39]

Besides the destruction, the immediate consequences of the wars were twofold. First, thousands of Basotho and Batswana from the highveld, as well as Mfengu and Xhosa from the coastal area, poured into the Cape Colony in search of subsistence, which they were able to obtain by working for white colonists. Second, the wars provided Whites with unprecedented opportunities to expand into the eastern part of southern Africa. In much of the central highveld, the population was sparse throughout the 1830s. The surviving inhabitants, fearing further disruptions, tended to conceal themselves from intruders, which gave white travelers the impression that the area was uninhabited and unclaimed. In fact, however, the rulers of the newly created Zulu, Ndebele, Swazi, and Sotho kingdoms assumed that, jointly, they had dominion over the entire region, though they contested its distribution among themselves. In particular, Dingane and Mzilikazi continued to send impis through the sparsely occupied southern highveld.

The Afrikaner Great Trek, 1836–1854

By the mid-1830s dissatisfaction among the Afrikaner inhabitants of the eastern districts of the Cape colony was widespread.[40] The 50th Ordinance of 1828 and the British parliamentary act of 1833 were depriving Afrikaners of their customary controls over labor. They had lost property in the frontier wars, culminating in the Xhosa invasion of December 1834. Above all, the British government seemed to be influenced by evangelicals who were challenging their engrained racial assumptions and practices with no sensitivity to their predicament.

During the early 1830s, some bold spirits among the Afrikaner population began to canvass the idea of trekking out beyond the colony and running their own affairs in their own way beyond British colonial limits. By 1836, reconnaissance expeditions had revealed a crucial consequence of the Mfecane—the existence of fertile and apparently unpopulated land in two localities: on the highveld beyond the Orange River and below the escarpment south of the Tugela River. During the next few years, several large, organized groups trekked out of the colony with their wagons, cattle and sheep, and personal possessions (map 5). By 1840, about six thousand Afrikaner men, women, and children had migrated—about one-tenth of the white population of the Cape Colony. Most of them were pastoral farmers from the eastern districts, which lost about one-fifth of their white population. Accustomed to mobility, they had the skills necessary for the migration. They took with them about as many Khoikhoi servants and former slaves—the unregarded members of their movement.

In the statement that Piet Retief sent to the *Grahamstown Journal* to explain their decision, he said that they hoped that the British government would "allow us to govern ourselves without its interference in future." He added: "We are resolved, wherever we go, that we will uphold the just principles of liberty; but, whilst we will take care that no one shall be held in a state of slavery, it is our determination to maintain such regulations as may suppress crime, and preserve proper relations between master and servant."[41] That is to say, they intended to recreate the social and economic structure of the eighteenth-century Cape Colony, but—to ward off British reprisals—they disclaimed the practice of overt slavery. Retief's niece, Anna Steenkamp, made this clear in her memoirs. Referring to the emancipation of the slaves she wrote: "It is not so much their freedom that drove us to such lengths, as their being placed on an equal footing with Christians, contrary to the laws of God and the natural distinction of race and religion, so that it was intolerable for any decent Christian to bow down beneath such a yoke; wherefore we rather withdrew in order thus to preserve our doctrines in purity."[42]

During 1836, the first large groups of emigrants spread out on the grasslands on either side of the Vaal River, unaware of the power of Mzilikazi's Ndebele kingdom and its aggressive strategy from its headquarters 120 miles west of modern Pretoria. The Ndebele, who had been attacked by Zulu impis and Griqua commandos from the south, decided to eliminate these new intruders who approached from the same direction. In October an Ndebele force of about 5,000 warriors launched an attack on

5. The Afrikaner Great Trek, 1836–1854

emigrants near the Vaal River, who lost their livestock but saved most of their skins by lashing their wagons together in a circle to form a laager, which the Ndebele were unable to penetrate. During 1837, strengthened by new arrivals from the colony, the emigrants went on the offensive with mounted commandos. In January, they destroyed an Ndebele settlement, killing 400 people and regaining their livestock. In October, a commando about 330 strong attacked the Ndebele headquarters and sent the entire community fleeing northward across the Limpopo into modern Zimbabwe, where they eventually carved out a new "Matabeleland" at the expense of the Shona inhabitants.[43]

The emigrants, meanwhile, had tried to organize themselves into a coherent community. That was not easy. They had left the Cape Colony in a series of trek parties, each of which was organized by a prestigious man and consisted of his kinsfolk, neighbors, and dependents. North of the Orange, those parties tended to amalgamate into larger groups under conspicuous leaders—Andries Hendrik Potgieter, Gerrit Maritz, Piet Retief, and Piet Uys—but the leaders quarreled and their followers took up their quarrels. Tensions were exacerbated when some of the men elected Retief as governor and chief commandant, and Maritz as president and judge. Potgieter and Uys, given no office, were aggrieved. There were also policy differences. Should there be personal rule or should control be vested in an elected body? Should they ignore Britain or negotiate for independence? Where should they found their permanent settlements?[44]

Those rivalries led to a split. Potgieter's people made their new homes in the highveld, while most of the others preferred Natal, with its better rainfall and its potential harbor. In October 1837, Retief went ahead with a small party to negotiate with a few British men who had been trading at Port Natal (modern Durban) to forestall British intervention, and with Dingane to ask for a grant of land and to prevent a Zulu attack. He found that the traders would welcome the emigrants, believing that their presence would increase their security. Dingane prevaricated, telling Retief to show his good faith by recapturing some cattle that had been stolen by a Sotho chief, Sekonyela, who lived back across the mountains on the plateau. Retief complied. He tricked Sekonyela into giving up the cattle, and in February 1838 he returned to Dingane's headquarters with a cavalcade of seventy emigrants and thirty Coloured servants.

By that time, most of the emigrants were already trekking across the mountains with their wagons and their livestock and settling on the fringe of Zulu territory. Moreover, Retief had sent Dingane a message boasting of the emigrants' victory over Mzilikazi's people. Pondering these events, the Zulu king and his councillors concluded that the emigrants were threatening their vital interests. They decided to make a preemptive strike to end white settlement in their vicinity. On February 6, 1838, after Dingane may have put his mark to a treaty purporting to cede the land between the Tugela and the Mzimvubu rivers, he lured Retief's party, unarmed, to a final beer drink, where his warriors clubbed them to death. Zulu impis then attacked the emigrants' encampments around the sources of the Tugela River, killing 40 more white men, 56 white women, 185 white children, and over 200 Coloured servants and capturing about 35,000 cattle and sheep.[45]

During the next few months, the Zulu seemed to be masters of Natal. In December, however, having received reinforcements from the Cape Colony, the emigrants mustered a powerful commando, five hundred strong. Led by Andries Pretorius, it trekked with fifty-seven wagons toward the heart of the Zulu kingdom. Every white member of the commando possessed at least one gun, and the expedition also had two small cannons. As they advanced, they formed a laager at night by lashing their wagons together. On 15 December, they laagered in a strong defensive position on the banks of the Ncome River. The next day, a vast Zulu army—perhaps ten thousand strong—launched a series of attacks. The Zulu displayed the utmost courage in the face of devastating fire from the emigrants' guns and cannons. Eventually, they retreated, leaving about three thousand dead around the laager. The commando lost not one member. Blood River, as Whites call the Ncome battle, was a classic example of the superiority of controlled fire, by resolute men from a defensive position, over Africans armed with spears, however numerous and however brave.[46]

In response to that decisive defeat, the Zulu kingdom split—a process that was typical of Nguni political culture. Dingane's brother, Mpande, opted for collaboration with the invader. In 1839 his regiments, accompanied by a commando of Afrikaner emigrants, defeated Dingane's forces and sent the king fleeing northward, where he was killed by the Swazi. Mpande then acquired control of the Zulu kingdom in the area north of the Tugela River.

Following up their victory, most of the emigrants settled in Natal, spreading out wherever good pastures and perennial water were found. By 1842, a community of some six thousand men, women, and children had laid claim to almost all of the fertile land between the Tugela and the Mzimkhulu. A committee drew up a constitution, creating a Volksraad (peoples' council) of twenty-four men, with legislative, executive, and judicial authority. The Volksraad in turn appointed a military commandant and sketched out a scheme of local administration under landdrosts, heemraden, and veldkornets, as in the Cape Colony before the British innovations. That, however, remained a blueprint rather than a reality. The embryonic Natal Republic lacked capital and administrative personnel and was hampered by further quarrels among would-be leaders.

In the emigrants' efforts at statemaking, one crucial issue went without question: they limited citizenship to the members of their community of Dutch-speaking people of European descent who had quit the Cape Colony to found an independent state.[47] Other people of European origin were to be treated with suspicion, but if they gave proof of their loyalty a few might safely be absorbed. Their community, however, was not a complete society. It was the dominant part of a society that included servants of African, Asian, and mixed descent. Those they assumed to be of a separate species. Indeed, they often referred to them as *skepsels* (creatures) rather than *mense* (people). That was what custom prescribed, self-interest demanded, and (for those who were religious) what God ordained. That was how it had always been and always must be in South Africa.[48]

To satisfy their labor needs, the commandos against Dingane did as commandos had been wont to do in the Cape Colony: they seized African children. After the defeat of Dingane, however, thousands of Africans flooded into Natal. Many of them were returning from what are now Pondoland and East Griqualand to the home areas from which Shaka had ejected them. By 1843, it was estimated that the African population of the republic had increased from ten thousand to fifty thousand; and still the influx continued. Greatly outnumbered, the emigrants were not able to establish their version of law and order. Not for the last time in South African history, a white minority was faced with the problem of reconciling its need for security with its dependence on the labor of conquered peoples. In December 1840, Pretorius led a commando with African allies southward to intimidate the nearest African chiefdoms in that direction, and during 1841, the Volksraad decreed that not more than five African families should live on one farm and that "surplus" Africans should be removed to the south. Although the emigrants lacked the means to give effect to that decision, it was the beginning of the end for their Natal Republic.[49]

The British authorities learned of those developments with mixed feelings. During the second quarter of the nineteenth century, British politicians were averse to incurring the cost of further territorial expansion, since the British navy was unchallenged and British commerce was capable of dominating competitors in foreign markets. Moreover, Southern Africa, with its small white population and its powerful African kingdoms, still had few attractions for British enterprise. Before Afrikaners began to emigrate from the Cape Colony the British government had rejected several requests from Natal traders and Cape merchants to annex Natal. The initial activities of the emigrants did not alter the government's mind.

Events in Natal did eventually lead to a change, however. Chief Faku of the Mpondo, threatened by Pretorius's southern sweep, appealed through his Wesleyan missionary for British protection; and the British colonial secretary came to the conclusion that if the emigrants were not brought under control, they might acquire protection from a rival European state and cause widespread disorder among the African population, thereby destroying the prospect of stability on the eastern frontier of the Cape Colony. That strategic impulse coincided with pressures from commercial and evangelical organizations.[50] Accordingly, in 1842 a small British force occupied the harbor, and in the following year a special commissioner exacted a submission from members of the Volksraad in their Pietermaritzburg headquarters, bringing Natal into the British Empire. He included a stipulation "that there shall not be in the eye of the law any distinction of colour, origin, race, or creed; but that the protection of the law, in letter and in substance, shall be extended impartially to all alike."[51] As that stipulation indicated, the evangelical lobby was still effective in British politics in the early 1840s.

After the British annexation, nearly all the emigrants trekked back from Natal across the Drakensberg to the highveld, where they founded several distinct settlements at places chosen for the availability of water, timber, pasture, and good soil. The Potgieters, anxious to make a complete break with the British, were trying to establish a viable settlement below the escarpment northeast of the Vaal River, from which they could open up a regular line of communication with the outside world via the Portuguese settlement on Delagoa Bay. They were not successful. The lowlands of the eastern Transvaal and the Limpopo River valley were breeding grounds for anopheles mosquitoes and tsetse flies, which took a heavy toll of the emigrants and their cattle.[52] Other emigrants, including Pretorius and his followers, made their new homes in the western highveld, around Potchefstroom. Still others settled south of the Vaal River.

The emigrants considered the highveld grasslands they were occupying to be theirs by right of conquest from Mzilikazi's Ndebele. After the

Ndebele fled, however, Sotho and Tswana people whom they had recently displaced percolated back to their home areas, and Sotho and Tswana polities that the emigrants had confined to the periphery of the highveld began to expand. Mobilized and concentrated, the emigrants, with their guns, horses, and wagons, had been more than a match for the Ndebele; but when they then dispersed to reestablish themselves as pastoral farmers, they encountered conditions like those in Natal. They lacked the means to control the growing African population in their midst, let alone the African polities that surrounded them.

The entire highveld region became a scene of divided loyalties and endemic conflict. The area between the Vaal and the Orange rivers was particularly confused. Besides the scattered emigrants, there were people of mixed descent, known as Griquas, who had been pushed out of the Cape Colony, a number of white farmers still loyal to the colonial government, and, by far the most numerous, Tswana and Sotho peoples regrouping from the disasters of the Difaqane.[53]

To compound matters, each population suffered internal cleavages. The Potgieters and the Pretoriuses were at odds with one another and with other emigrant factions. The western Griqua state of Andries Waterboer was rivaled by an eastern Griqua state under Adam Kok. Moshoeshoe's kingdom of Lesotho was struggling to establish control over the fertile grasslands north of the Caledon River and to incorporate their Sotho and Tswana inhabitants. Conflicts among these peoples were exacerbated by rivalries among several European missionary societies that were active in the area and espoused the cause of the leaders they regarded as their clients: the London Missionary Society, which worked among the Griqua; the Paris Evangelical Society, which had stations in Moshoeshoe's Lesotho; and the Wesleyan Missionary Society, active among Moshoeshoe's African rivals.[54]

Great Britain gradually got sucked into the area because of initiatives taken by a succession of Cape colonial governors who hoped to stabilize the northern frontier of the colony by establishing client states. In 1834, Governor Sir Benjamin D'Urban had made a treaty with the West Griqua chief, Andries Waterboer. In 1843, Governor Sir George Napier made treaties with Adam Kok of the East Griqua and Moshoeshoe of Lesotho, giving them small salaries in return for their commitment to maintain order in their territories and defining Moshoeshoe's territory in terms that accepted his contention that he was the overlord of most of the lesser African chiefdoms north of the Caledon River. The next governor, Sir

Peregrine Maitland, went a step further. He amended Kok's treaty to allow emigrants to acquire land in the northern part of his territory.

Sir Harry Smith—the epitome of British military arrogance and naïveté—took the final step. In 1848, having annexed Xhosa territory between the Keiskamma and the Kei rivers and having misled both Pretorius and Moshoeshoe about his intentions, he issued a proclamation annexing the entire area between the Orange and the Vaal rivers, for the "protection and preservation of the just and hereditary rights of all the Native Chiefs" and "the rule and government of Her Majesty's subjects, their interests and welfare."[55] That area, which became known as the Orange River Sovereignty, included not only numerous emigrants but also nearly all of Lesotho. The British government reluctantly accepted Smith's fait accompli, noting his assurance that the territory would be financially self-supporting. The attempt to raise a local revenue in fact produced no more than £12,000 a year, with the result that only a handful of officials and a puny military detachment were stationed there.[56]

Major Henry Warden, the British administrator of the sovereignty, made a bad situation worse. Succumbing to pressures from emigrants and Wesleyan missionaries, he imposed new internal boundaries that treated the lesser African chiefdoms as independent from Moshoeshoe. But in 1851, when Warden patched together a force of emigrants and Africans to give effect to this decision, Moshoeshoe's Basotho won a convincing victory at Viervoet.[57]

The British government then started to withdraw from the highveld. First, it recalled Smith and sent out two commissioners, who negotiated an agreement with Pretorius, granting independence to the emigrants in the territory north of the Vaal River (January 17, 1852). Next, Smith's successor, General Sir George Cathcart, warned London that to rule the sovereignty effectively would require a permanent garrison of two thousand troops and a greatly increased civil establishment, which he knew the British government would not provide. But before abandoning the territory, Cathcart believed that, as a matter of honor, Moshoeshoe should be humiliated. In December 1852, he led a military expedition into Lesotho. His troops captured over four thousand head of cattle, but the people resisted fiercely, killing thirty-eight British soldiers. On the night of December 20, Moshoeshoe sent Cathcart a skillfully phrased face-saving message: "I entreat pace from you—you have shown you power,—you have chastised,—let it be enough I pray you; and let me no longer be considered an enemy to the Queen."[58] The next day, Cathcart decided to withdraw, rather than attempt to assault the stronghold of Thaba Bosiu. The British government then empowered another special commissioner to negotiate a withdrawal from the sovereignty with men who would accept the responsibility for governing the territory. That was done on February 23, 1854.

In those two agreements, known as the Sand River and Bloemfontein conventions, the emigrants achieved their major political goal—independence from Britain. That was not all. Both conventions stated that the new governments would not allow slavery in their territories. They also said that the new governments would be permitted to buy ammunition in the British colonies, but the Sand River Convention added that "all trade in ammunition with the native tribes is prohibited both by the British Government and the emigrant farmers on both sides of the Vaal River."[59] The Bloemfontein Convention declared, moreover, that the British government had no alliances with any "Native Chiefs or tribes" north of the Orange River except Adam Kok and that "Her Majesty's Government has no wish or intention to enter hereafter into any treaties which may be injurious or prejudicial to the interests of the Orange River Government."[60] In London, the philanthropic lobby was in decline and the cabinet had concluded that jostling communities in the Southern African interior lacked the resources to warrant the cost of administration. The pendulum had swung hard over since the early 1840s, from a declared policy of protecting black Southern Africans from disruption by turbulent British subjects, to a policy that amounted to an alliance with independent white communities against their black neighbors.

The emigrants were free and independent. When Afrikaners began self-consciously to fashion a national historical tradition toward the end of the nineteenth century, they referred to the emigrants as Voortrekkers, and their movement as the Great Trek. In 1854, however, they were still poor, scattered, disunited, politically inexperienced, and virtually surrounded by Africans.

The British Colony of Natal, 1843–1870

After the British conquest, Natal became a second focus of British political authority in Southern Africa.[61] While most of the Afrikaners were trekking back across the Drakensberg Mountains to the highveld, settlers were arriving from Britain. Five thousand men, women, and children arrived in the years 1849–51 under a scheme initiated by an adventurer named Joseph Byrne. They were mostly middle-class people who had been able to deposit a small capital sum in return for transport to Natal and possession of twenty acres of land per head. Their early experiences in Natal were similar to those of the 1820 Settlers in the Cape Colony. Most failed to make good as farmers and returned to England, tried their luck on the highveld, or settled in the port town of Durban, which was named for the former Cape governor, or the inland capital, Pietermaritzburg, which had been named for the trek leaders Piet Retief and Gerrit Maritz. By 1870, the white population had reached eighteen thousand—fifteen thousand British settlers and three thousand Afrikaners.[62]

The white population of Natal was engulfed and surrounded by vast and increasing numbers of Africans. The influx reached flood proportions during a series of disturbances in the Zulu kingdom, where Mpande continued to enroll young Zulu men in age regiments. Initially he was successful in reestablishing the unity of the state, but in the 1850s factions formed around two of his sons, Cetshwayo and Mbuyazi, who were rivals for the succession to the monarchy. In 1856, Cetshwayo defeated his rival in a massive battle at Ndondakusuka on the Tugela River, and thousands of people who had belonged to the Mbuyazi faction fled across the river to Natal. By 1870, the African population of the colony was estimated to be fifteen times as numerous as the white population.

Facing the problem that had been the nemesis of the Afrikaner republic, the Natal colonial government tried to place the Africans in reserves (which it called *locations*), leaving the rest of the colony available for white settlement. By 1864, there were forty-two locations, with an area of 2 million acres, and twenty-one mission reserves, with 175,000 acres, out of the total colonial area of 12.5 million acres. In terms of colonial law, the rest of the colony was either owned by Whites or held by the government as unassigned Crown lands. At least half of the African population, however, lived not in the reserves at all but on Crown lands or on land owned by Whites, to whom they paid rent. Until the 1870s the white landowners were making more money from "Kaffir farming" than from their efforts to produce agricultural or pastoral products for the market. The colonial state, too, exacted a substantial revenue from the Africans in the form of direct taxation and customs duties on imported commodities that they consumed.

The official responsible for controlling the African population was Theophilus Shepstone. Brought up in the eastern frontier region of the Cape Colony as the son of a Wesleyan missionary, he spoke the Nguni languages well. A convinced and skillful paternalist, he improvised a method of

African control similar to what the British would later apply in colonial tropical Africa and call *indirect rule*. The key was the use of African chiefs as subordinate officials, made responsible, in the last resort, not to their own people but to the colonial government. Shepstone recognized the existing chiefs in communities that had survived the turmoil of the Mfecane; in other cases, he appointed men as chiefs. He also imposed a dual legal system: customary African law, as codified by him, prevailed among Africans; but the colonial Roman Dutch law, taken over from the Cape Colony, applied among Whites and in relations between Africans and Whites.[63]

Shepstone had ideas of "civilizing" the Africans with a program of Western education and economic development, but financial constraints prevented him from carrying that out. From the beginning, the senior officials appointed by the British government to administer the colony relied on the support of the white population, and the white population, searching for security and prosperity in an isolated and alien milieu, became unequivocally racist. The bars to empathy were potent, for the settlers were ignorant of the history, the language, the social institutions, and the moral norms of the Africans around them; yet they took Africans into their service, only to become disappointed with their performance as laborers. The dominant impressions settlers had of Africans were consciousness of difference, fear of numbers, and chagrin at instrumental deficiencies. They regarded the nonracial clause in the 1843 annexation agreement as "utterly inapplicable," because Natal was "a white settlement," and its Africans were "foreigners."[64]

In 1856, following the 1853 precedent in the Cape Colony, the British government provided Natal with a constitution under which appointed officials controlled the executive but were a minority in the legislature, where the majority was elected by the tiny white population. Not surprisingly, the elected members used their powers to foster the sectional interests of their constituents. They passed laws to ensure that Africans should not acquire the franchise, and egged on by a vigorous press, they put continuous pressure on the senior officials both to ensure that the requisite number of Africans turned out to work for Whites and to block the allocation of public funds for African interests. In effect, no more public money was made available for that purpose than the five thousand pounds a year expressly set aside in the constitution—and sometimes not even that much was actually spent on Africans, even though Africans were paying ten thousand pounds a year and more to the colonial treasury, in the form of a tax of seven shillings on every one of their domestic buildings or huts.[65]

In the absence of state support, missionaries were the only white people who tried to help Natal Africans to adapt to the colonial situation. As has been mentioned, missionaries got control of 175,000 acres of land in Natal. The most effective were members of the American Board of Commissioners for Foreign Missions, who began to arrive in 1835. By 1851, the ABCFM had eleven stations and six outstations in Natal. Africans received them enthusiastically at first, because the Shakan wars had disrupted their society and discredited their methods of coping with disasters. The missionaries opened elementary schools and medical dispensaries; in some cases, they mediated on behalf of their protégés with the civil authorities. They even made a number of converts, especially among fringe members of African communities. That was the beginning of a process that was producing a new class of Africans who eagerly adopted Western practices, taking English names, learning the English language, wearing imported clothes, buying land from white settlers, and absorbing Christian ideas of social and political justice. By the 1860s, many Africans had become quite prosperous peasants, producing maize for export to Cape Town or wool for the local market.[66]

White colonists, meanwhile, had not been prospering as farmers, and they complained that Shepstone's system of African management made it difficult for them to obtain an adequate supply of cheap labor. One group of white settlers' labor needs were especially ill-served: landowners who were finding that the subtropical coastal zone was suited to the production of sugar but that they could not attract sufficient African laborers to do the arduous labor demanded—labor for which, unlike stock farming or grain production, the Africans had no previous experience. First, the planters tried to persuade the colonial government to break up the locations and "release" the required African labor. When that failed, they turned to British India, which was already exporting labor to Mauritius and the British West Indies to remedy the labor shortage that followed Britain's emancipation of the slaves in 1833. Under laws and regulations of the Indian and Natal governments, Indians began to arrive in Natal in 1860. They were contracted to serve employers on stipulated conditions for five years. At the end of that time they were free to branch out on their own, and after another five years they were entitled either to a free return passage to India or to a small grant of land in Natal. Since the laws provided that at least twenty-five women should accompany every hundred men transported to Natal, it was inevitable that a permanent Indian population in the colony would emerge.

Between 1860 and 1866, six thousand Indians arrived in Natal from Madras and Calcutta. In terms of caste, language, and religion they were heterogeneous; although most were low-caste Hindus, some were Hindus of higher castes, 12 percent were Muslims, and 5 percent were Christians. As they completed their five years' indentured service, some remained on the coastal estates as laborers; others became semiskilled workers—artisans, cooks, house servants, tailors, or washermen; still others acquired small landholdings and grew fruit and vegetables for sale in Durban or Pietermaritzburg; some became shopkeepers; and a few moved to other parts of Southern Africa. In 1870, when the first Indians became entitled to a return passage to India, nearly all elected to stay—an example most of their successors would follow. A third major community had been established in the colony. The system continued until 1911 and resulted in the creation of a sizeable Indian population, one that would eventually outnumber the Whites in Natal.[67]

By 1870, there were three distinct communities in Natal, distinguished by history, culture, and wealth and power in the colonial situation. The Africans, numbering more than a quarter million, had experienced two drastic changes in fifty years: the rise of the Zulu kingdom, which had removed most of them from Natal, and the creation of the white colony, which had given them some security on limited acreage. Many Africans still had a partial autonomy in the locations, many others were labor tenants or rent payers on white property, a few were landowners, and others were occasional wage laborers. All were experiencing the effects of white power and influence, which limited the authority of chiefs, imposed taxes, created new material needs, eroded customary values, and insinuated new ones. The Whites, newcomers to Natal, numbered about eighteen thousand, owned most of the land, controlled the legislative branch of government, exerted great influence over the executive branch, and steadfastly ignored the nonracial principle set out in the annexation proclamation. The six thousand Indians, more recent arrivals still, were beginning to exploit opportunities that, though limited, were greater than those available to most people in India.

The Highveld, 1854–1870

After Britain relinquished political claims over the emigrant Afrikaners on the highveld, that region continued to be a scene of complex interactions among numerous peoples and polities. Africans were trying to recuperate from the Mfecane disruptions, to regain control of their land, and to preserve their political autonomy vis-à-vis the Whites; Afrikaners were trying to assert hegemony over the region and to safeguard their own autonomy from imperial Britain. The highveld was still peripheral to the capitalist global economy. Communications were primitive. Mails, if any, were entrusted to itinerant traders or African runners. Roads were tracks worn by wagons, horses, and pedestrians. Money was scarce. Nevertheless, increasing numbers of missionaries and traders were penetrating the territory from the Cape Colony and Natal, and the dominant trends were the growth of linkages between the diverse communities, the diffusion of a money economy, the dissemination of Western, especially Christian, ideas, and the enhancement of white power. The outcome, however, was far from certain in 1870.[68]

The Afrikaner population of the region gradually increased, reaching about fifty thousand in 1870. Families were large, and newcomers filtered in from the Cape Colony. They were still uniformly committed to the stockfarming and hunting way of life. Aliens, mainly English-speaking people from the Cape Colony or Great Britain, formed small clusters of traders, clergy, and artisans in such villages as Bloemfontein and Potchefstroom, while manual labor was left to Coloured people and Africans. Like the Africans, the wealth of the Afrikaners was in cattle; but unlike the Africans, Afrikaners owned their land individually. The land in the territories under white control rapidly passed into private hands. Since there was very little currency in circulation, these embryonic states were unable to raise substantial revenues and often paid officials in land grants rather than cash. As a result, able and ambitious men who were elected as local administrators and military officers were able to accumulate vast holdings and become a distinctly superior class. Piet Joubert, the future commandant-general of the Transvaal republic, who started his public career as a veldkornet, or local official, had acquired over a dozen farms by 1871; so had Paul Kruger, the future president.[69] In addition, commercial companies based in the British colonies acquired vast holdings in the republics. Most of the land was not used productively. Afrikaners ran their cattle or sheep over parts of their holdings, but acquired their grain from African producers, and the companies were absentee landlords who did scarcely anything to develop their properties.

The Afrikaners south of the Vaal River fashioned a more stable society than those further north. In 1854, the year of their independence, they adopted a constitution that was an amalgam of the old Cape colonial system of local administration, the legislative system that had existed in the Natal Republic, and several ingredients taken over from the United States Constitution, of which an immigrant from the Netherlands had a copy. Their Orange Free State was a unitary republic. The legislature was a unicameral Volksraad whose members were elected by male citizens—white men (not necessarily Afrikaners) who had lived in the republic for six months—provided they had registered for military service. Executive power was in the hands of a president, directly elected for five years, and an executive council composed of officials and Volksraad nominees. Local administration was in the hands of landdrosts appointed by the government and locally elected veldkornets and commandants. American influence was evident in provisions guaranteeing equality before the law, personal freedom, and freedom of the press; prohibiting the Volksraad from legislating against peaceful assembly and petition; and making the entire constitution extremely rigid by requiring the support of three-quarters of the members of the Volksraad in three successive annual sessions for constitutional amendments.[70]

The state-making process north of the Vaal was entirely different. Not until 1860 did the various factions unite behind a constitution, and the document itself, with 232 articles, was wordy, ambiguous, unsystematic, and a curious mixture of substance and triviality. The institutions it created were similar to those in the Orange Free State. The qualifications for citizenship were nowhere defined, but they were implied in Article 9: "The people are not prepared to allow any equality of the non-white with the white inhabitants, either in Church or State." The internal sovereignty issue, moreover, was obscured. The Volksraad was "the supreme authority and the legislative power of the country," but "any matter discussed [there] shall be decided by three-fourths of the votes recorded," while other articles implied that sovereignty was vested in the white population as a whole.[71]

In practice, after a shaky start when a mob ousted the first president, the Orange Free State constitutional framework was a success and the citizens and officeholders developed a respect for law. Among the Afrikaners north of the Vaal, by contrast, political authority depended on the mobilization and application of force uninhibited by constitutional formulas. There, factionalism led to intermittent civil warfare in the early 1860s and contributed to the British annexation of the state in 1877.

Some highveld Africans first viewed the incoming Afrikaners as liberators and assisted them in driving the Ndebele out of the Transvaal, but they soon found that they had exchanged one oppressor for another. As their strength increased, Afrikaners vigorously sought to recreate the relationships that had existed before the British reforms in the Cape Colony. Africans who lived on white farms—which in many cases were located on the lands of their ancestors—did so under a variety of conditions, ranging from providing labor services to paying rent in cattle or sheep. To satisfy the white demand for labor, commandos raided neighboring African chiefdoms to capture male children and train them as servants. They called them apprentices to avoid the charge of slavery and to minimize the risk of British intervention. Anglo-Irish immigrant J. M. Orpen, who served for a while in the 1850s as a landdrost in the Orange Free State, recorded ample details of this traffic.[72] In the Transvaal it was more devastating still. In their search for security, moreover, both republics prohibited Africans from possessing firearms and required them to carry passes when traveling. All such laws were enforced unevenly. The outcome in each time and place hinged on such contingencies as the relative density of the white and the black populations and the energy of the veldkornets and the African chiefs.[73]

The Africans living in chiefdoms and kingdoms around the periphery of the republics were subjected to intermittent attacks by commandos. Quickly appreciating the value of firearms, they made great efforts to arm themselves. Many traders made handsome profits by supplying arms in defiance of republican and colonial laws. The republican Afrikaners tried to stop this illegal trade by punishing gunrunners severely. In an episode that became notorious, a Transvaal commando once destroyed the property of David Livingstone, the missionary and explorer, when Livingstone was absent from his mission station, on the grounds that he had been arming the Kwena chief Sechele or repairing his guns.[74] The mob that ousted Josias Hoffman, the first president of the Orange Free State, in 1855 did so because he had given the Lesotho king Moshoeshoe a small keg of gunpowder as a diplomatic gesture.[75] But the trade continued; in fact, traders could not transport sufficient arms to the African territories to meet the demand. The shortfall was met by Africans traveling to the Cape Colony or Natal, working there for white people for several months, and receiving payment in cattle or sheep, which they bartered with colonial traders for guns and ammunition. To defend themselves while traveling through republican territory, Africans formed bands of a hundred or more. Peter Delius has shown that Pedi from homes in the eastern highveld used Lesotho as a staging post. In defiance of the Sand River and Bloemfontein conventions and republican and colonial laws, the Sotho, the Pedi, the

Tswana, and the Venda thus managed to equip themselves with firearms and ammunition. Although their guns were generally obsolescent models in European terms and they often ran short of ammunition, Africans increased their capacity to resist the invaders.[76]

The Tswana occupied open terrain between the Transvaal republic and the Kalahari Desert. Divided among half a dozen major chiefdoms that had a history of conflict between one another and were also rent by internal rivalries, they never succeeded in cooperating against their successive invaders. Instead, under Afrikaner republican pressures, several chiefdoms split into two or more entities, some of which were incorporated in the Transvaal republic, others of which preserved their autonomy on the edge of the desert. Searching for allies against republican aggression, the Tswana were particularly susceptible to missionary influences. Several of their chiefs converted to Christianity and tried to enforce their missionaries' social prescriptions, outlawing such customs as the payment of bridewealth and the convening of initiation schools—actions that created yet another line of cleavage in a sorely divided society.[77]

The medley of Bantu-speaking communities that occupied the northeastern highveld was more favored by the terrain. During the 1840s and 1850s, white prospectors, hunters, and adventurers of many nationalities were attracted to the area because it was a rich source of elephant ivory, and a settled population became established there. Tsetse flies and mosquitoes, however, decimated the settlers in the lowlands, whereas the Soutpansberg provided defensible mountain refuges for Venda chiefdoms close by. In 1867, Paul Kruger's punitive expedition of four hundred men to the area was repulsed by the Venda and by disease, and the settlement collapsed.[78]

During the 1850s, the Pedi chief Sekwati checked Afrikaner expansion in the fertile and disease-free eastern Transvaal by creating a loose-knit kingdom centered on a defensible mountain stronghold. After Sekwati's death in 1861, however, the kingdom was rent by a civil war rooted in rivalry between two of his sons— a setback that was typical of the mixed-farming societies of Southern Africa. This cleavage, accentuated by a bitter religious controversy resulting from the activities of German Protestant missionaries, prevented the Pedi from consolidating their state and maintaining a united front against Afrikaner aggression. Even so, most Pedi remained autonomous throughout the 1860s.[79]

The most dramatic events of the 1850s and 1860s were played out in and near the Caledon River valley (map 6). There, the Sotho occupied terrain similar to the country of the Pedi: a fertile valley and defensible mountains.

Legend:

Land over 6,000 feet

▲ Mountain

Moshoeshoe's territory as recognized by Sir George Napier in 1843

British Colony of Basutoland

○ Paris Missionary Society Mission

△ Wesleyan Missionary Society Mission

+ Roman Catholic station

6. Basotho land losses, 1843–1870

Harrismith

Ladysmith

Mont aux Sources

Botha Botha

Thabana Ntlenyana

Caledon

THABA BOSIU ○

+ ROMA

▲ Thaba Bosiu

MORIJA ○

Orange River

Caledon River

Aliwal North (Buffel's Vlei)

MILES

KILOMETERS

0   100

0   100

Philippolis

Colesberg

Orange River

Pretoria

Johannesburg

Durban

Port Elizabeth

Bloemfontein

THABA 'NCHU △

Thaba 'Nchu ▲

Cape Town

Orange River

In addition, the Sotho had one exceptional boon: the skillful leadership of Moshoeshoe, who had been creating the kingdom of Lesotho out of the debris of the Mfecane. During the 1850s, Lesotho conquered and absorbed the rival southern Sotho chiefdom of Sekonyela and several other communities that had been clients of the short-lived British administration. Conflict with the Orange Free State was inevitable. The British had shed responsibility for the region without attempting to consult Moshoeshoe or settling his boundary with the Orange Free State. The Afrikaners and Sotho thus jostled one another for control of the land and raided each others' cattle. Open warfare broke out in 1858, when Afrikaner commandos invaded Lesotho from both north and south, capturing cattle and ravaging villages and mission stations, and converging on Thaba Bosiu. There, they faltered. Mustering some ten thousand men, all mounted on horses and equipped with firearms, the Sotho defended their fortress and raided Afrikaner farms, seizing livestock and burning homesteads as the Afrikaners had been doing to them. White morale collapsed. The commandos disbanded, leaving Moshoeshoe the victor.

When war broke out again in 1865, the relative strengths of the contestants had changed. Moshoeshoe, nearly eighty years old, was losing control over his sons, who were intriguing for the succession and indulging in uncoordinated raids. The Orange Free State, meanwhile, had grown in population and had acquired an able president in J. H. Brand. This time, the Free State commandos destroyed Sotho property so relentlessly that Molapo, Moshoeshoe's second son, whom Moshoeshoe had placed as his chief in the northern part of the kingdom, surrendered, and Moshoeshoe himself signed a treaty ceding much of the kingdom. But hostilities continued. The Free State was on the verge of achieving a complete victory over a demoralized and famished enemy when, dramatically, Sir Philip Wodehouse, governor of the Cape Colony and British high commissioner for South Africa, annexed Lesotho.[80]

Moshoeshoe had been appealing for British protection since the early 1860s, in the belief that Britain had less interest than his aggressive neighbors in exploiting his people. For their part, British officials doubted the wisdom of the conventions soon after they were signed. In 1857, High Commissioner Grey checked a movement toward the unification of the two republics by threatening to cut off their ammunition supplies. In reasoning similar to that which had led to the British annexation of Natal, he argued that a united highveld republic might create disturbances along the colonial frontiers. Wodehouse agreed with that analysis. Sympathetic to the Sotho in their distress, he thought that the convention policy had produced divisions, conflicts, and poverty. As the dominant power in Southern Africa, Britain should resume its responsibilities and, as a first step, take Moshoeshoe's people under protection. In December 1867, the British cabinet accepted that argument and instructed Wodehouse to incorporate Lesotho in the colony of Natal; but Wodehouse, finding that the Sotho chiefs were strongly opposed to rule by Natal and its arrogant administrator, Theophilus Shepstone, annexed Lesotho as the separate British colony of Basutoland, on March 12, 1868. Faced with a threat to prohibit the supply of arms and ammunition, the Free State government reluctantly accepted Wodehouse's decision.[81]

In February 1869, Wodehouse and Free State commissioners settled the Basutoland boundary without consulting the Basotho. Basutoland was to consist of the land between the Caledon River and the mountain escarpment, minus a triangle between the lower Caledon and its junction with the Orange. Stripped of the fertile area north of the Caledon, the Sotho were confined to a small proportion of the arable lands that their ancestors had occupied before the Mfecane and far less than Governor Napier had recognized as coming under Moshoeshoe's sway in 1843. The Sotho were profoundly disappointed with that outcome. They still refer to the lost lands as "the conquered territory" (map 6).[82]

By the time the agreement was signed, Moshoeshoe was ailing, and he died on Thaba Bosiu on March 11, 1870. He had experienced all the crucial changes that had taken place on the highveld—from the comparative stability of his youth, through the anarchy of the Mfecane, to the intrusion of French missionaries, Afrikaner farmers, and British officials. More skillfully than other Africans 'confronted with similar problems, he had managed to create a kingdom out of chaos and to steer that kingdom through manifold dangers to what was probably the best destiny open to it in the changed world of the late nineteenth century.[83]

In December 1867, the British cabinet thought they were authorizing the resumption of responsibilities in the interior because to fail to do so would risk further instability, with repercussions throughout the region. They were not doing it because they believed the area had great economic promise. But in that very month a prospector named Carl Mauch was in Pretoria claiming to have found gold in Tswana country, and a stone was on exhibition in Cape Town that had been identified as a diamond.

In 1870, Southern Africa was occupied by numerous small agrarian societies, loosely linked by the dynamic forces of settler expansionism and merchant capitalism originating in northwestern Europe. In spite of its temperate climate, the entire region had attracted a minute proportion of Europe's emigrants, capital investment, and overseas trade. It contained only about 250,000 people regarded as white; more than a hundred times as many lived in the United States. Most members of the white population depended on numerous imported commodities—not only clothing, hardware, guns, and gunpowder but such foodstuffs as coffee, tea, flour, and sugar. Even so, the total value of imports was only about £3 million a year. Exports—mostly in the form of wool and ostrich feathers from the eastern districts of the Cape Colony—amounted to rather less than that. In 1870, furthermore, the annual revenues of the four white states amounted to only about £750,000—nearly three-quarters of that being the Cape Colonial revenue. Cape Town, in the extreme southwestern corner, with nearly 50,000 inhabitants (about half of them white), was the only town of more than 30,000. Durban and Pietermaritzburg had fewer than 7,000 inhabitants each; the highveld towns were smaller still. In the entire region, there were only 70 miles of railroad track; there were 38,000 in the United States.

Nevertheless, by 1870 the region was poised to take advantage of the mineral discoveries. Cape Town and its suburbs had a wide range of small-scale industries—steam flour mills, coach and wagon builders, cabinet makers, saddlers, leather and soap manufacturers. Elsewhere, in numerous small towns entrepreneurs and artisans were gaining industrial experience. There were wool-washing establishments throughout the Cape Colony, notably at Uitenhage; sugar mills on the Natal coast; tanneries near Bloemfontein. In addition, the banking industry was overcoming its teething troubles. There were many small, local banks, and one institution, the Standard Bank of British South Africa, with headquarters in London and a capital of nearly £2 million, had branches in Natal and the Orange Free State, as well as the Cape Colony.

Wherever Afrikaners had settled, they tolerated scarcely any social interaction with black people except as masters with servants. Indeed, they went a long way toward preserving the patriarchal relationships that had originated in the seventeenth century, minus the overt practice of slavery. The British settlers in the Cape Colony and Natal, and in the towns and villages in the republics, had rapidly complied with the established mores.

In spite of their setbacks as a result of the Mfecane and white expansion, the African peoples of the region were proving to be remarkably resilient. They showed no signs of disintegrating like the aboriginal peoples of North America and Australia. In 1870, they were probably more than ten times as numerous as the Whites in the area covered by the modern Republic of

South Africa. Independent African territories formed a semicircle around the colonies and republics, stretching from the Tswana chiefdoms in the northwest, through the Venda in the north, to the Swazi, Zulu, and Mpondo in the east. The colonial and republican states were fragile entities. There were large areas within the boundaries they proclaimed where they had little influence. In the Transvaal, in Natal, and in the Transkei many African communities still had effective control over their own lives. Numerous Africans, moreover, were adapting to the opportunities as well as the constraints created by the invaders. Although some were being reduced to serflike status, most were keeping control of enough of their ancestral land to feed themselves and produce a surplus of grain for consumption by Whites.

Great Britain, unchallenged by European rivals, dominated the external trade of the region. In spite of the ambitions of their creators, the Afrikaner states were inexorably part of the informal British Empire. As the Orange Free State had discovered, the British had a powerful lever in the threat to apply sanctions against the flow of arms and ammunition. The Transvaalers had tried but failed to open up an outlet to the sea on Delagoa Bay; and victory, even had they succeeded, would have been pyrrhic, since Portugal was a virtual client of Great Britain.

In 1870, South Africa was an imbroglio of peoples of disparate African, Asian, and European origins and cultures. Unresolved conflicts over land and labor were accentuated by different ideological assumptions and by contradictory perceptions that created tensions in each community. Whites were dependent on the services of black laborers but (with some exceptions in the Cape Colony) were determined to exclude Blacks from participation in their social and political systems. Africans were striving to preserve their freedom but were becoming dependent on manufactured commodities and interested in Western technology and Western religion. The imperial power was spending little money in the region but was committed to maintaining control of the sea route via the Cape of Good Hope and to exercising some responsibility for the stability of the region. The mineral discoveries accentuated these tensions and inaugurated a new phase of South African history.

CHAPTER 4

Diamonds, Gold, and British Imperialism, 1870–1910

After 1870, the rate of change in many parts of Southern Africa accelerated dramatically under the impact of both external and internal forces. The peak of British imperialism coincided with the identification and exploitation of prolific deposits of diamonds and gold in the Southern African interior.

By the end of the century, Southern Africa had become, for the first time, a significant contributor to the world economy. Most of the capital invested in the mining industries came from overseas, and a high proportion of the profits were absorbed in Britain, continental Europe, and North America. Nevertheless, the mineral discoveries stimulated major developments inside Southern Africa. Deep in the interior, Kimberley, the city of diamonds, and Johannesburg, the city of gold, sprang up on land that had been sparsely populated. Johannesburg, on the Witwatersrand (White Waters Ridge) in the Transvaal, attracted Africans from as far north as modern Tanzania and people of European descent from North America, Australia, continental Europe, and, particularly, Great Britain and grew to contain the largest concentration of people in the entire region. Coal mines, dynamite factories, and several smaller industrial establishments produced commodities required by the core mining industries, but the dominance of mining resulted in policies favoring cheap imports rather than protective tariffs to foster local textile and clothing industries. African and white farmers supplied grain and meat to the new markets. The governments of the Cape Colony and Natal vied with each other to share in the new wealth by improving their port facilities and constructing railroads to Kimberley and Johannesburg.

While these things were happening, Whites were also conquering African communities that had previously preserved their independence in Southern Africa. Throughout the region, Whites were incorporating Africans into a capitalist, white-dominated economy. Many Africans were obliged to pay rent, or to surrender a share of their produce, or to provide labor services for the right to live on land that white people had appropriated. In areas where the land was still in African hands, the white governments were obliging chiefs and headmen to acquiesce in the presence of recruiters of labor for the mines as well as magistrates, whose duties included the collection of taxes. Some African families were enjoying increasing prosperity by producing food for the urban markets, but other families were experiencing periodic separation as the men traveled to mining towns or white farms to work for several months at a time, leaving the women with greatly extended responsibilities for the household economy. By 1900, moreover, a few Africans were living permanently in the towns and becoming the nucleus of an urban proletariat.[1]

These events were accentuating differences among the inhabitants of Southern Africa. The primary division was still the racial cleavage that had been present in Southern Africa since the beginning of white settlement, slave importation, and Khoikhoi incorporation in the seventeenth century (chapter 2). This division was enhanced by the racist ideology that was now pervasive among Europeans and North Americans, as well as white South Africans, and it was becoming more rigid than ever. White men maintained an absolute monopoly of formal political power in the Transvaal and Orange Free State republics and a virtual monopoly in the colony of Natal. Even in the Cape Colony no black person ever became a member of the parliament or cabinet, and laws were passed to check the increase of the black members of the electorate, who never numbered more than 15 percent of the total.

Perhaps the most fateful process of the period was the struggle that led to the racial structure of preindustrial, colonial South African society being applied in the mining industries. This was done by splitting the labor force between white workers, with skilled or supervisory roles, opportunities for advancement, high wages, and relatively good living conditions, and black workers, devoid of the means to exercise skilled or supervisory roles, poorly paid, and subjected to harsh living conditions in all-male compounds. A precedent was thus established for structuring industry on racial lines throughout the region.[2]

There were also deepening secondary divisions inside each racial category. Most of the descendants of the seventeenth- and eighteenth-century settlers identified themselves as Afrikaners, with their distinct language, religious affiliation, historical consciousness, and social networks, whereas nearly all of the nineteenth-century white immigrants (most of whom came from Britain) kept aloof from Afrikaners, despised their language and culture, and underestimated their achievements. Nearly all Afrikaners, moreover, continued to live and work in a rural environment, whereas most immigrants were townspeople.

Neither the Afrikaners nor the immigrants were homogeneous communities. Among the Afrikaners there were well-to-do people—long-established wine farming families in the southwestern Cape Colony, wool farmers in the Cape interior, and grain and cattle farmers in the republics—but there were also increasingly numerous Afrikaners who owned no land, were unequipped to compete with white immigrants in the towns, and were becoming known as Poor Whites. Among the nineteenth-century immigrants, those who settled in Southern Africa before 1870 did not readily identify with the subsequent rush of people to Kimberley and Johannesburg. English-speaking lawyers, merchants, tradespeople, skilled workers, and semiliterate proletarians jostled and competed among themselves and with immigrants from the Continent in the older towns—Cape Town, Port Elizabeth, Durban, and Pietermaritzburg—as well as in the mining cities. A few superrich mining magnates commuted between Southern Africa and England, where they made a splash in high society.

Although people of British origin were a majority among the Whites in Natal and on the Witwatersrand, Afrikaners formed more than half the white population in the region as a whole. Moreover, whereas there was a balanced ratio of men, women, and children in the Afrikaner population, men predominated among the immigrants. Johannesburg, in particular, had a huge male adult majority in its white as well as its black population.[3]

Black South Africans, too, had varied affiliations. The people whom Whites grouped together as "Coloured" differed greatly among themselves. Their ancestors included indigenous Khoisan people and slaves from Indonesia, Madagascar, and tropical Africa. They ranged from culturally deprived farm laborers to skilled urban craftspeople. Some were Christians, others Muslims. Moreover, although there were small Coloured communities in the Witwatersrand and in Natal, most Coloureds still lived in the western part of South Africa and had no contact with Africans.

Most Africans still identified with specific chiefdoms, which had a history of conflict with neighbors, especially during the Mfecane wars. Nevertheless, "tribalism," as the Whites called it, was less rigid than Whites believed. African social and political communities had always been flexible. In the late nineteenth century and afterwards, Africans continued to move from one chiefdom to another and chiefs willingly incorporated newcomers. Conquest and industrialization intensified social divisions among Africans. Mission-educated clergy and teachers, and successful peasants, formed a new hierarchy in competition with the old hierarchy of chiefs.

To compound the diversity of the Southern African population still further, the Natal government continued to import laborers from India to such an extent that by the end of the century there were more Indians than Whites in Natal. It was on behalf of the Indian traders that a young London-trained barrister, Mohandas Gandhi, went to South Africa in 1893. In the next twenty-one years, Gandhi led several campaigns against unjust laws in South Africa. Although he did not achieve decisive results there, the technique of passive resistance that he developed in Natal and the Transvaal would have profound effects on the British Raj in India, after he returned home in 1914.[4]

Great Britain was deeply involved in all these transformations. During the mid-nineteenth century, Britain had been by far the most urbanized and industrialized country in the world, and British merchants had been able to penetrate overseas markets without serious competition from foreigners and without the need to invoke the state to support them with protective tariffs or territorial annexations. After 1870, however, other countries were becoming industrialized, notably Germany and the United States, and they were eroding the economic preeminence on which British global strength had rested. In an international environment that was strikingly different from the free-trading Western world of the midcentury, European states were playing an increasingly active role at home and abroad. Competition intensified among them and developed into an arms race that eventually tore Europe apart.[5]

The British government was put on the defensive by the decline of its relative power and the rise of economic and military competition, especially from Germany. In the last three decades of the century, successive British administrations tried to find a policy that would prevent rivals from encroaching on territories hitherto dominated by British trade and capital, such as those in the Southern African interior. As the mineral wealth of the region became revealed, some British politicians and businesspeople came to regard its control as a matter of national importance. The increase in the British political commitment in Southern Africa was modified by tactical differences between the political parties. Under Disraeli and his successors, the Conservative or Unionist party took a strong imperialist line, whereas Gladstone's Liberal party split from top to bottom over the question of territorial expansion.

In the 1870s local circumstances rather than international competition prompted Britain to annex first the diamond fields (1871) and then the Transvaal republic (1877) and to conquer the Zulu kingdom, the most powerful African state in Southern Africa (1879). When the Transvaal Afrikaners rebelled and defeated the British forces in the region, in 1881, however, a Liberal administration granted them a qualified independence rather than incur the cost of reconquest. International competition influenced British policy more profoundly after the mid-1880s, when Germany annexed South West Africa (Namibia), as well as Togoland, Cameroon, and Tanganyika, and dominated an international conference in Berlin that set the ground rules for a general "scramble" for African territories. By 1890, moreover, the Witwatersrand gold fields had transformed the Transvaal from a backwater into the economic hub of Southern Africa.

Even so, until 1895 British administrations generally relied on settler communities to sustain their interests in the region. Although the government authorized the annexation of the Transvaal in 1877, it did so in the hope that annexation would pave the way for the amalgamation of all the territories in Southern Africa into a federal state within the British Empire. In 1889, it empowered a commercial company dominated by Cecil Rhodes—prime minister of the Cape Colony and the most powerful man in the diamond- and gold-mining industries—to annex and administer territories north of the Limpopo. It was not until the strategy of delegation of imperial responsibilities backfired with the ignominious failure of Rhodes's attempt to supplant the government of the Transvaal republic in an attempted coup known as the Jameson Raid—a classic piece of naive adventurism—that the British government assumed direct responsibility for preventing the Transvaal from slipping out of the imperial network. British pressures culminated in the South African War, 1899–1902, Britain's greatest war since the Napoleonic Wars.

Britain eventually conquered the republics and annexed them as British colonies but did not use its victory to modify the racial structure of Southern African society. On the contrary, the war ended in a treaty that guaranteed that black people would not participate in parliamentary elections in the new colonies when they were given representative institutions. In 1907, the British honored that agreement, and three years later the Cape Colony, Natal, the Transvaal, and the Orange Free State joined to form the Union of South Africa, which, from the day of its birth, was dominated by its white inhabitants.[6]

Diamonds, Gold, and the Mining Cities

Africans had worked outcrops of copper, iron, and gold in various parts of Southern Africa for over a millennium. By the 1860s, Whites, too, had been extracting small outcrops of copper in the northwestern Cape Colony and of gold in the eastern Transvaal. There was flurry of excitement in 1867 when alluvial diamonds were found near the confluence of the Vaal and the Harts rivers in arid country west of Bloemfontein. By late 1870, five thousand people were there, Whites and Blacks, using picks and shovels to extract promising soil and hand sieves to sift it, and forming a rugged gambling, boozing, and whoring society like that of the mining camps in North America. A few lucky ones were finding diamonds, which they sold to local representatives of European merchants. A year later, the supply was petering out, and the episode would have been yet another brief incident had not more diamonds been discovered on sparsely populated land several miles from the river valleys. By 1872, twenty thousand Whites and thirty thousand Blacks had converged on the area. Within a few years, geologists realized that the "dry diggings" were the outcrops of diamondiferous pipes that extended far below the surface and contained the largest concentration of gem diamonds yet discovered. Kimberley, the diamond city, was born 550 miles from Cape Town and 350 miles from the nearest coastline at East London.

Profound technical problems had to be overcome before those bountiful resources could be fully exploited. Initially, as in the alluvial fields, individual diggers acquired small claims and worked the surface with pick and shovel, helped, perhaps, by three or four assistants. Most of the diggers were white; nearly all their assistants, black. By the end of 1872, four mines were taking shape and many of the claims were subdivided into tiny plots. On the Kimberley mine, the most productive of the four, there were no fewer than 1,700 properties, one of which, for example, measured seven feet by thirty and was sold for fifteen hundred pounds. As their excavations deepened, the miners erected an elaborate haulage system with pulleys and wires and wooden staging to remove the excavated ground. Chaos resulted. Collapsed roadways, mounds of earth, and floodwaters made more than half the mine unworkable.

Concentration and mechanization gradually overcame these problems. Steam traction replaced man and animal power, and underground shafts and tunnels eventually replaced open mining. As advanced technology took over, small properties and individual diggers were superseded by larger holdings and highly capitalized organizations. The mid-1880s were years of mutually destructive cutthroat competition among those companies.[7]

As the competition developed, a few individuals, most of them youthful immigrants from Europe, struggled to the top and amassed great wealth. There was Barney Barnato, born in 1852, the son of a London publican and grandson of a rabbi, who arrived in Kimberley in 1873 with "a little cash and forty boxes of cheap cigars,"[8] set himself up as a dealer in diamonds, and step by step, by fair means and foul, acquired more shares in the Kimberley mine than anyone else. There was Alfred Beit, born in 1853, son of a Hamburg merchant, a shy and socially unobtrusive man who was sent to Southern Africa in 1875 to buy diamonds for a German firm and became the brains behind the amalgamation of plots and the development of deep-level mining. And there was Cecil Rhodes, younger son of an English country parson, who went to Natal for his health in 1869 at age sixteen and then alternated between Kimberley and Oxford University, where he imbibed grandiose visions of imperial expansion and graduated in 1881, already a multimillionaire.[9]

By May 1887, Rhodes had acquired practical control of De Beers, the second most productive of the four mines, but Barnato and Beit, as well as Rhodes, still had large holdings in the Kimberley mine. Within the next year, however, Rhodes's De Beers Consolidated Mines acquired control of the Kimberley mine by entering into partnership with Beit, getting financial backing from the Rothschilds of London, and cajoling Barnato to cooperate. De Beers thus acquired a monopoly of the diamond production of the area.

Politics had affected this outcome. Four authorities initially claimed sovereignty over the diamond fields: the two Afrikaner republics (the Transvaal and the Orange Free State), the southernmost Tswana chiefdom, and the Griqua chiefdom of Nicholas, son of Andries Waterboer. The strongest white claim to the dry diggings was that of the Orange Free State, since the area included farms that had been recognized not only by the Orange Free State government but also, in some cases, by the British officials who had ruled the area between 1848 and 1854. Nevertheless, in 1871 the British high commissioner proclaimed the annexation of the territory which became known as Griqualand West, after a British arbitrator had ruled in favor of Waterboer and Waterboer had been persuaded to request British protection. The British government failed to provide for an efficient local administration, however, and thus its officials depended on the cooperation of the local white population: first the diggers' committees and later the major industrialists. The industrialists' grip tightened after 1880, when Griqualand West was incorporated in the Cape Colony. They established control over the parliamentary representation of the area, and in 1890, Cecil Rhodes, by then the dominant figure in the diamond industry, became prime minister of the Cape Colony.[10]

Throughout those years, the financial basis of the diamond industry was insecure. Marketing was one major problem. The value of gem diamonds is set by fashion rather than utility. In the late nineteenth century, it swung abruptly with the state of the capitalist world economy. It was actually in danger of collapsing as South African stones flooded the market and as production costs rose during the installation of expensive capital equipment. The viability of the industry thus came to depend largely on control of the marketing of the diamonds. Market control followed quickly on the consolidation of the production process, however. In 1895, a syndicate of London merchants contracted to buy De Beers's output for the next eighteen months for £5.4 million which was the start of a continuing pattern of long-term contracts. The industry was stabilized by cooperation and eventual merger between a monopoly producer and a monopoly marketer.

Labor management was another major determinant of the viability of the industry. During the formative years, struggles between the companies and the workers, and among different classes of workers, were intense. The outcome was significant for the future of South Africa. It came in two stages. First, white populism created a color bar in Kimberley. Initially, a few African and Coloured men as well as white men controlled claims and competed for unskilled labor. In 1872 an all-white diggers' committee drew up a set of rules designed to adapt the established racial order of South Africa to the urban and industrial context, by eliminating black diggers and making Blacks liable to be searched without a warrant and to receive as many as fifty lashes if found to be in possession of diamonds they could not account for.[11]

The British officials declined to endorse such overtly racial rules, but the high commissioner issued proclamations that had much the same effect without being overtly racial. Any black person was de facto excluded from owning diamond claims or trading in diamonds and was liable to imprisonment or corporal punishment if found "in precincts of the camp without a pass signed by his master or by a magistrate."[12] These proclamations were intended to appease the antislavery lobby in Britain. Color-blind in form, in practice they applied exclusively to blacks and divided ownership and production of diamonds by color.

As the individual digger phase passed, mining personnel became structured into a complex hierarchy. The machines were worked by skilled immigrants from overseas, including men from Cornwall, England, where the tin-mining industry was in decline. At the other extreme, a mass of people was recruited to do the manual labor, especially the heavy and dangerous work underground, from the African societies of Southern Africa. In between, there were overseers of the African labor—white South Africans drawn largely from the erstwhile digger population. The skilled operatives, being scarce, commanded high wages, and the overseers, being white men in a colonial society already structured on racial lines, were able to carve out an intermediate and sheltered niche for themselves; but the manual laborers, drawn from societies with no previous experience of industrial labor and having no say in the colonial political system, got short shrift. Step by step, the working class was split into two strata, white and black: the white, privileged, well paid, and free; the black, unprivileged, poorly paid, and unfree.

This great and historic racial cleavage was preserved and reinforced by drastic differences in living conditions. In Kimberley, white workers were free to live in the town with their families. During the 1870s, however, Africans became required to carry passes and to live in segregated parts of the town, or, if they were mineworkers, to live in all-male compounds attached to the mines. After 1885, moreover, the African mineworkers were not allowed outside the compounds throughout the duration of their contracts. The stated reason for this was to prevent them from stealing diamonds. Diamonds were entering the market illegally, and illicit diamond buying was a serious threat to the industry. But compounding also gave the companies inordinate control over their African workers, as well as economies of scale in lodging and feeding them.

Africans in Kimberley were subject to summary justice and the indignity of being stripped for intimate body searches for diamonds. Their annual mortality rate reached 8 percent in the late 1870s. In most years, pneumonia was the principal killer, but in 1883, when smallpox broke out in Kimberley, the industry tried to hush it up until more than five hundred people had died of the disease. Conditions in the compounds were especially inhumane. There, African men, accustomed to living with their families in a rural environment, were cooped up in confined quarters under tight discipline without any women for the duration of their contracts—six months or a year. The migrant labor system also had serious social and economic effects on the home areas of the migrants. Family life was disrupted for long periods, and women became responsible for the economic and social management of households.

The mining companies dominated Kimberley and overrode the merchants and traders on most issues when interests clashed. At one stage, the companies even planned to make white as well as black workers live in compounds and submit to intimate body searches for diamonds, but that was too great a departure from colonial norms, and the companies desisted in the face of opposition from the local tradespeople as well as the white workers. Since as white men they had the vote, white workers were able to realize a common interest with capitalism in entrenching a racial division in the first industrial city in South Africa. That was a momentous precedent for the structure of urban life and industry throughout the region. The arrangements in Kimberley foreshadowed later refinements of urban segregation, labor control, and all-male hostels for migrant black workers.

In 1886, at a time when the diamond industry was approaching its mature form, gold was discovered thirty miles south of Pretoria, the capital of the South African Republic. The deposits were uniquely rich. Outcrops of reefs containing gold stretched forty miles east and west along the Witwatersrand, the watershed between the Limpopo and the Orange river systems. The reefs dipped below the surface to the south, and their gold content was regular and reliable, though low grade in comparison with the Australian and Canadian goldfields.[13]

Kimberley was a natural precedent for the Witwatersrand. Men such as Rhodes, Beit, and Barnato who had made fortunes in Kimberley extended their scope to the Rand, as the Witwatersrand became known, and invested their profits there. White workers who were redundant in Kimberley as a result of the economies effected by consolidation brought their skills there. Within a decade, however, immigrants from Britain and Europe and people from the coastal colonies were flocking to the area and the Rand, with Johannesburg at its center, had far surpassed Kimberley, to become the site of the greatest industrial complex in Southern Africa and the largest gold-mining operations in the world. The MacArthur-Forrest process had solved the problem of extracting the gold from the complex conglomerate, and the industry was committed to mining at deep levels. By 1899, the industry, in which £60 million had been invested, was producing 27.55 percent of the world's output of gold, Johannesburg had 75,000 white residents, and the gold-mining companies were employing 100,000 Africans.

On the Witwatersrand, the individual digger was soon eliminated. Capital and large-scale organization were required to extract the gold from the ore and to mine below the surface. By 1888, joint-stock companies were buying out small claim-holders along the line of the outcrops and purchasing from the Afrikaner pastoral farmers the bare land above the dipping reefs to the south. In the following year, mining industrialists formed the Witwatersrand Chamber of Mines to advance their common interests. The amalgamation process continued, but it stopped short of unifying the gold-mining industry. In 1899, the 124 companies were divided among nine groups controlled by European finance houses.

The gold-mining industry followed the Kimberley precedent of a racially split labor force. Since the international gold standard set a fixed ceiling price for gold, labor costs were the crucial variable in determining profitability. The industry had a strong incentive to keep the proportion of expensive white operators as low as possible, to exploit African labor as fully as possible, and to prevent the two sections of the labor force from combining. Two factors prevented the industry from being completely successful in the nineteenth century. One was internal: the mining companies and groups competed with one another, especially in the recruitment and treatment of labor. The other was external: the Afrikaner government of the republic, representing farmers who relied on African labor and to whom Johannesburg was a den of iniquity and also, as we shall see, a threat to the survival of their state, had material, cultural, and political interests that were poles apart from those of the industrialists.

Racial segregation and discrimination were nevertheless the hallmarks of the industry. On the Rand, as in Kimberley, African men who had homes in the rural areas left their families for several months at a time to earn money on the mines. As in Kimberley, they lived in all-male compounds owned and controlled by the companies, under severe discipline imposed by African foremen responsible to white managers. They were clustered together, as many as fifty to a room, where they slept without beds in double-decker concrete bunks. Although, unlike their fellows in Kimberley, the African gold-miners were permitted to go outside their compounds when off-duty during the day, they had neither the money nor the leisure time to derive much benefit from that theoretical advantage. White workers earned about eight times as much as Africans and were free from supervision of their living arrangements. The mines even provided them with heavily subsidized housing.

When disputes arose, the Transvaal government as well as the industrialists favored the Whites. In 1889, for example, white workers struck with some success to protect their skilled positions and their rights to organize and to have some control over their working conditions, and in the 1890s the state created color bars for particular mining tasks, setting a limit to the upgrading of African workers. By contrast, in 1890, when African workers resorted to violence they were ruthlessly suppressed. Moreover, in 1895 the Transvaal legislature, the Volksraad, enacted a Pass Law, drafted by the leaders of the mining industry, that gave employers greater control over the movements of their African laborers. On entering the Witwatersrand, an African had to get a pass authorizing him to seek employment for three days, and when he found work his employer took possession of the pass and kept it until he was discharged. If he was found without a pass, he was liable to be arrested. In practice, the Transvaal government lacked the means to enforce such a law consistently, but it was an ominous harbinger for the future.

In a set of stimulating essays, the historian Charles van Onselen has shown how, on the Witwatersrand, Africans were not the only people who were trying "to find a place of dignity and security within a capitalist world that encroached on them all too quickly." In the early years of the gold-mining industry, landless Afrikaners as well as Africans settled on the Witwatersrand and organized small businesses. For example, Afrikaners became cabdrivers and brickmakers, while Zulus created a laundry service. By the mid-1890s, however, most Afrikaner and African entrepreneurs were being crushed out of business by industrial enterprises run by the mining companies, swelling the ranks of the poor Whites, as well as the poor Blacks. The arrival of railroads from the Cape colonial ports in 1892, Delagoa Bay in 1894, and Durban in 1895 terminated the role of the Afrikaner transport riders, who had originally provided a vital service to the mining industry and the Witwatersrand population.[14]

The Conquest Completed

Accelerated by the growth of the mining industries, two major political processes transformed Southern Africa in the last three decades of the nineteenth century. British regiments, colonial militia, and Afrikaner commandos completed the conquest of the African inhabitants, and, in a major war, the British army conquered the Afrikaner republics.

The African societies of Southern Africa experienced intensified pressures after 1870. Although they differed in many other respects, white farmers and businesspeople, traders and missionaries, and government officials had a common interest in subjecting the Africans, appropriating their land, harnessing their labor, dominating their markets, and winning their hearts and minds. By the end of the century, they had completed the process of conquest that had begun in the time of van Riebeeck. All the indigenous peoples of Southern Africa were incorporated in states under white domination.[15]

Virtually all the Whites in the region, in common with their contemporaries in Europe and the Americas, regarded themselves as belonging to a superior, Christian, civilized race and believed that, as such, they were justified in appropriating native land, controlling native labor, and subordinating native authorities. So dominant was this assumption that Whites did not permit their serious internal differences—Boer versus Briton, farmer versus townsfolk, employer versus worker—to retard the conquest. In critical situations Whites assisted one another against Africans, and Whites who had benefited from African patrons betrayed them. In 1879, Paul Kruger, who would soon lead Afrikaner commandos against the British occupation force in the Transvaal, gave the British military sound advice on how to cope with the Zulu, and John Dunn, the son of one of the early British traders in Natal, who had become wealthy and powerful as a client of the Zulu king Cetshwayo, went over to the side of the Whites as soon as the imperial army invaded his country.

The Africans, by contrast, were unable to unite in self-defense. It would have been extremely difficult for Africans to create large-scale combinations against the invaders, because by 1870 they occupied distinct territorial clusters that were separated by wedges of white settlement. Moreover, the Africans, as well as the Whites, had serious internal cleavages. The political culture of the African farming societies in Southern Africa had involved frequent power struggles between segments led by members of their ruling families—father versus son, brother versus brother. Recent strife, including the Mfecane wars, had set chiefdom against chiefdom, lineage against lineage, and chief against commoner. When African chiefs and their councillors were confronted with white expansionists, they had to make critical choices along the spectrum from outright physical resistance to outright cooperation, and in some circumstances cooperation was a logical option.

Whites, assisted by black allies, dealt with the African societies piecemeal. Whenever fighting occurred, white access to superior technology, in transportation as well as arms, more than offset the Africans' numerical advantage. The longer a conflict lasted, the more likely the Whites' victory, since white forces, sustained from commissariats borne by ox wagons from the nearest railhead, would destroy the food supplies of their enemies. To crown it all, in 1896–97, when the last indigenous community in South Africa (the Venda) was about to be conquered, a tragedy struck the entire region. An acute infectious disease known as rinderpest swept through from the north and destroyed up to 90 percent of the Africans' cattle, which had been their principal form of wealth.[16]

The course of events varied from case to case. Traders and speculators, drawing African polities into the international capitalist network, eroded some of them, notably the Swazi, to such an extent that they collapsed without offering physical resistance. Other Africans, such as the Zulu, fought desperately before they succumbed to superior force, but even in such cases economic penetration and internal cleavages contributed to the outcome.

Consider the Zulu case.[17] The Zulu kingdom had survived the assassination of its founder, Shaka, in 1828 and defeat by Afrikaner voortrekkers a decade later, but it was subject to endemic factionalism. In customary Nguni fashion, rival members of the royal family built up segments that competed for power and wealth—a process that led to civil war in 1856. The authority of the monarchy was also challenged by interests associated with representatives of pre-Shakan chiefdoms. By that time, furthermore, Afrikaner farmers were infiltrating Zulu territory from the Transvaal republic in the north; so were British traders from the colony of

Natal in the south. John Dunn attached himself to Cetshwayo, the victor in the civil war, and became the most powerful and wealthy man along the Natal border in the southern part of the kingdom, where he accumulated forty-six Zulu wives, ten thousand followers, and vast herds of cattle.

After the death of Dingane's successor, Mpande, in 1872, Cetshwayo strengthened the central government of the kingdom and based his foreign policy on an alliance with Natal, represented by the powerful secretary of native affairs, Theophilus Shepstone, as a safeguard against Afrikaner expansion from the Transvaal. Dunn supplied Cetshwayo with firearms, helped him to funnel African labor from the Tsonga chiefdoms in Mozambique to Natal, and served as his de facto foreign minister and private secretary.

In 1877, the foundations of Zulu security began to crumble. Acting as an agent of the British government, Shepstone annexed the Transvaal as a British colony and became its administrator. Then, seeking to win the support of the Afrikaner population by assuaging their hunger for land and to satisfy the ambitions of Natal traders and British missionaries and imperialists, Shepstone threw his erstwhile Zulu allies to the wind. He espoused Transvaal territorial claims against the Zulu and persuaded the British high commissioner that the kingdom, with its powerful military organization, was the major obstacle to peace and order in Southern Africa.

In December 1878, disregarding the report of a boundary commission appointed by the Natal government rejecting the Transvaal claim to Zulu territory, the high commissioner peremptorily demanded that Cetshwayo should disband his army within thirty days. Cetshwayo's response was to mobilize about thirty thousand men. On January 11, 1879, a British force of seven thousand British regulars, about as many Natal African levies, and a thousand colonial volunteers invaded Zululand. Ignoring the advice of no less a person than Paul Kruger, the British commander failed to order entrenchments around his camps and reconnaissance in depth ahead of the line of march. Sixteen hundred British soldiers spent the night of January 21 unprotected, beside the hill Isandhlwana. Early the next morning, a Zulu army took them unawares and slaughtered nearly every one of them, in the greatest disaster to British arms since the Crimean War. However, a British outpost warded off a Zulu attack at Rorke's Drift on the Natal frontier, and, after reinforcements had arrived, the war gradually drew to its inexorable conclusion, culminating in July with the destruction of the Zulu capital at Ulundi. John Dunn, followed by several leading Zulu chiefs, had defected to the British at the start, but it was technological factors that were decisive. The Zulu never made effective use of their guns, while lumbering ox-wagon trains replenished the invaders' supplies of food and ammunition.[18]

The military campaign was not the end of the Zulu kingdom. Having defeated the army, the British set Zulu against Zulu, preventing a revival of Zulu power without cost to Britain. They abolished the monarchy, banished Cetshwayo to Cape Town, and divided Zululand into thirteen separate territories under thirteen appointed chiefs—members of the royal family, descendants of pre-Shakan chiefs, and the inimitable John Dunn. Chaos resulted. John William Colenso, an Anglican bishop, espoused the cause of Cetshwayo, with the result that Cetshwayo was permitted to plead his case in Britain and then to return to Zululand with limited powers. But it was a truncated Zululand: a substantial area in the north was placed under a distant relative of Cetshwayo named Zibhebhu and another in the south was administered from Natal.

Civil war followed between the conservative, royalist party led by Cetshwayo and the reform-minded party of Zibhebhu. Zibhebhu initially gained the upper hand: his men burned Ulundi for the second time, and Cetshwayo fled and died under British protection. The councillors of Cetshwayo's fifteen-year-old son, Dinuzulu, then made a deal with Afrikaners who had been infiltrating the country. During 1884, the Afrikaners carved a ministate, the New Republic, out of the northern third of the former Zulu kingdom, and with their help the royalist faction defeated Zibhebhu's forces. In 1887, the Transvaal incorporated the New Republic and Britain annexed the rest of Zululand, divided it into districts, appointed magistrates, and began to collect a hut tax. Dinuzulu and his councillors tried to prevent the magistrates from usurping the powers of the chiefs, but it was too late. Dinuzulu was arrested, convicted of treason, and exiled to Saint Helena, and when he was allowed to return it was only as a local headman. By that time, Zululand had been incorporated in Natal, where white farmers and speculators were agitating for Zulu territory. The government appointed a land commission that marked out a number of reserves for the Zulu and threw the rest of the country open to white settlement, leaving only about one-third of the former kingdom in Zulu hands (1902–4). Before the war of 1879, Shepstone had expressed the hope that Cetshwayo's warriors would be "changed to labourers working for wages." His wish was granted.[19]

The Zulu story is one illustration of the process of subordination of

Africans in the last decades of the nineteenth century. There were, however, great regional differences in the rate and the extent of the erosion of African political, economic, and cultural autonomy. The key variables were the structure and the dynamics of each African society and the degree to which each had resources that attracted Whites.

Other Nguni societies were also profoundly transformed by the end of the nineteenth century. After the colonists got control of the executive branch of the Cape colonial government in 1872, in a series of steps they annexed the territories between the Kei River and the Natal border, which became known as the Transkei. Many of the Xhosa and Thembu inhabitants, whose morale had been broken by the cattle-killing disaster in 1856, offered little physical resistance. Between 1877 and 1881, however, others, including the main Xhosa chiefs Sandile and Sarhili, did defy the government, only to be suppressed by Whites and their Mfengu allies. The hundred years' war between the Whites and the Xhosa and Thembu had ended at last. Cape colonial expansion to the east culminated in 1894 with the peaceful incorporation of the Mpondo, who had been weakened by civil war between conservatives and modernizers (similar to the cleavage in Zululand) following the death of their paramount chief.[20]

Within the Transkei, the government took one area from the Africans and allotted it to Griquas—people of mixed descent who migrated there from the middle Orange area, which was being overrun by Afrikaners—calling it Griqualand East. The Griqua, however, gradually lost their land to white settlers in Griqualand East, as they had previously done in Griqualand West. The rest of the land in the Transkei remained in African hands, whereas in the Ciskei to the west of the Kei River a mixture of Whites and Africans held land.

During the last three decades of the nineteenth century, magistrates, traders, and missionaries multiplied among the southern Nguni. Raising taxes and enforcing the law, magistrates undermined the authority of the chiefs. Selling imported foods, clothing, and agricultural implements and buying African produce, traders provided basic instruments of a market economy. Offering practical assistance as well as a literary education and a contemporary Christian, European world view, missionaries assisted Africans to adapt to conquest. All those innovations created fresh divisions in the population, between the chiefs and those commoners who had acquired new forms of wealth and new skills. Many Xhosa, and still more Mfengu, seized the new opportunities and produced a surplus of wool and grain for the market or earned wages as clerical assistants to the magistrates, traders, and missionaries. Among the Mpondo, in contrast, the chiefs were able to exert some control over the activities of traders until their country was annexed in 1894. Some Mpondo chiefs themselves even produced grain and cattle for the market, using communal land and labor, but the dominant trend was for production to be decentralized to the homestead level. By the end of the century, however, the rinderpest, population increase, and the heavy hand of the colonial state were reining in all the southern Nguni peasantry, and the men were finding it increasingly necessary to leave home to earn wages on colonial farms or in the mines.[21]

Circumstances differed in Natal, where Shepstone had left the chiefs in charge of the African population subject to his ultimate control, but by the end of the century there was a similar trend toward impoverishment. In the early days of white settlement, the Natal Africans had access to sufficient land for their needs, and traders and missionaries provided them with means to market their surplus produce and to acquire a literary education. Nevertheless, the white settlers showed their power in 1873, when they raised such an outcry after a chief named Langalibalele had resisted arrest on a trumped-up charge that he was deposed and banished and his people's land confiscated. After 1893, when the settlers gained control over the executive branch of the Natal government, they placed increasingly severe demands on the Africans. By the end of the century, the African population had grown to a stage where it was running short of fertile land, while Whites were becoming increasingly involved in commercial farming. This conjuncture, in combination with the rinderpest and taxation, paved the way for a rebellious outburst in 1906, which was ruthlessly suppressed by the Natal forces.[22]

The southernmost Tswana societies had the misfortune to occupy land in the vicinity of Kimberley, where they bore the brunt of the forces generated by the diamond-mining industry, as well as experiencing pressures both from merchants using long-established trade routes from the Cape to the north and from Afrikaner farmers expanding in a westerly direction from the original settlements in the Transvaal republic. Step by step, they were subjected and impoverished. Much of their land lay inside the boundaries of Griqualand West, as annexed by Britain in 1871. After 1880, when it was incorporated in the Cape Colony, the colonial government corralled the African inhabitants into reserves, thereby freeing land for white speculators. De Beers acquired no fewer than 400,000 acres. Transvaal farmers meanwhile were penetrating the territory between Griqualand West and the Molopo River, playing off one set of southern Tswana chiefs against another. In 1885 Britain annexed most of that territory, and in 1895 Britain transferred it to the Cape Colony. Twice—in 1878 and 1896–97—some of the southern Tswana rebelled against white domination, but to no avail. Then the rinderpest struck the area. By century's end, the southern Tswana had lost most of their land and nearly all their cattle, and they were among the most indigent and dependent people in Southern Africa.[23]

The Tswana who lived north of the Molopo River were less disastrously disrupted. By the mid-1880s, British traders and missionaries and imperialists such as Cecil Rhodes were urging the British government to prevent the area from falling into the hands of the Transvaalers, which would have given them a link with the newly annexed German colony of South West Africa (now Namibia). Some of the Tswana chiefs, too, asked for British protection as security against Transvaal expansion. Accordingly, in 1885 Britain proclaimed a protectorate, without encountering Tswana opposition. In theory, protectorate status meant that the chiefs retained control over internal affairs. In practice, a symbiotic relationship developed between the chiefs and the British officials. The chiefs used the officials to strengthen their position against internal rivals and factions. Indeed, the northern Tswana retained exclusive control over most of their land, except for a strip along the eastern border for a railroad to the Zambezi and beyond. In 1896–97, however, the northern Tswana were hit especially hard by the rinderpest. After that, they, like other African societies in the region, were obliged to send out some of their young men to work in the mines.[24]

The Sotho, who were separated from Griqualand West by the Orange Free State, became closely integrated into the regional economy as suppliers of grain and labor to the diamond-mining industry, but they continued to experience political turmoil. They suffered internally from intense rivalries among the chiefs, notably among Moshoeshoe's sons and grandsons. Moreover, Great Britain, which had annexed "Basutoland" in 1868, incorporated it in the Cape Colony in 1871, and the colonial government proceeded to appoint magistrates with instructions to undermine the authority of the chiefs, as they were doing in Xhosa country. Resentment by the chiefs led to a popular uprising in 1880, when the colonial prime minister announced that the government would increase taxation and enforce a law for the disarmament of the Sotho. Using guerrilla tactics honed in their wars against the Orange Free State, some 23,000 armed and mounted Sotho warriors outmaneuvered the government's poorly led amalgam of white, Coloured, and African police, volunteers, and conscripts. Eventually, the colonial government suspended the disarmament legislation and implored Britain to reassume responsibility for Basutoland, which Britain did in 1884.

British administrators then worked closely with the royal family, notably Letsie and Lerotholi, Moshoeshoe's senior son and grandson. That policy restored domestic peace, but at the cost of reducing the customary checks on abuse of power by the chiefs. Moreover, by the end of the century, the Sotho population had increased to a level where it was eroding the narrow belt of arable land between the Caledon River and the mountains, and it could no longer produce a surplus. The Sotho had their homes in a rural society devoid of white settlers, but their major source of wealth was in the form of wages they earned by working for white people elsewhere.[25]

In the eastern highveld, two African communities stood in the way of white ambitions: the Pedi and the Swazi, who occupied fertile but rugged country along the mountain escarpment north of the Zulu. In the 1850s, an able leader named Sekwati brought the Pedi together after they had been shattered during the Mfecane. His hold over the subordinate chiefs was always fragile, however, and during the 1860s, three alien forces threatened the cohesion of the Pedi: Swazi invaders from the southeast; Afrikaner infiltrators from the southwest; and German resident missionaries— Lutherans who, more completely than missionaries of other denominations, regarded themselves as agents of white culture and allies of the Afrikaner farmers. Young Pedi men, moreover, were accustomed to going to work for white farmers, and after 1870 they became the principal laborers on the diamond mines. The pressures then intensified. Subordinate chiefs tried to establish autonomy by playing off Afrikaners against the monarchy. In 1876, Thomas François Burgers, president of the Transvaal, invaded Pedi country unsuccessfully with an army of 2,000 burghers, 2,400 Swazi warriors, and 600 Transvaal Africans. That rebuff contributed to Afrikaner acquiescence in the proclamation of British rule the following year. In 1879, however, having defeated the Zulu, the British overwhelmed the Pedi with a massive invasion force, including 8,000 Swazi and 3,000 Transvaal Africans. Under white domination, the Pedi state then fell apart.[26]

The Swazi state that emerged from the Mfecane was a ruling aristocracy of Nguni conquerors superimposed on an indigenous Sotho population. By 1870, the aristocracy had unified the country, employing a dense network of dynastic marriages, the national symbolism of an elaborate annual first-fruits festival, and a military organization on the Zulu model that cut across ethnic and regional ties. The Swazi rulers maintained good relations with the Transvaal and with Natal, because the Zulu had tried to destroy the state in the time of Shaka and Dingane and continued to threaten it under Mpande and Cetshwayo. After the defeat of the Zulu in 1879, however, white stock-farmers, gold prospectors, and adventurers of all sorts pestered the Swazi king Mbandzeni and his councillors with gifts ranging from greyhounds to champagne, and promises of more to come, if the Swazi would only sign the documents they thrust at him; the Swazi got into the habit of putting their crosses to documents and enjoying the proceeds without understanding their significance. By the time of his death in 1889, Mbandzeni had signed away almost the entire resources of his kingdom, actual and potential: the land, the minerals, and the right to create and operate industries, customs duties, licenses, railroads, telegraphs, and postal services. Finally, a superconcession gave the holder the right to collect all the king's revenues, including his concession revenues, for an income of twelve thousand pounds a year.

By that time, the Transvaal government was determined to annex Swaziland, as a step toward fulfilling the old voortrekker ambition to get access to the sea. Transvaal and British representatives then settled the fate of Swaziland in a series of negotiations without consulting the Swazi. In 1895, the Transvaal assumed control of Swaziland, but the British blocked the Transvaal from the sea by annexing the coastal strip. Seven years later, having conquered the Afrikaner republics, the British detached Swaziland from the Transvaal and treated it as a separate colony, like Basutoland. Unlike Basutoland, however, when a commission had sorted out the conflicting claims, Whites became the legal owners of nearly two-thirds of the land in the Swazi kingdom.[27]

In the northern Transvaal, the Venda had held together in the face of early Afrikaner encroachments by occupying the Soutpansberg Mountains. In 1867 they had repulsed a commando led by Paul Kruger and caused the Afrikaners to evacuate their settlements in the area. During the 1880s, however, Afrikaners began to reoccupy the vicinity, and in 1898 a force of four thousand Whites, with Swazi and Tsonga allies, stormed the main Venda stronghold.[28]

In spite of their losses in the Mfecane and the wars of conquest, Africans continued to constitute a vast majority of the population of the entire region, and of every part of it east of the twenty-inch rainfall line. This is the great and fundamental difference between the outcome of the conquest of the indigenous peoples in North America and South Africa. The Native

Americans were reduced to a tiny proportion of the population of North America and were confined to scattered reservations forming a minute proportion of the land area. The indigenous Africans had experienced havoc and losses, but survivors still occupied substantial parts of their ancestral land. A struggle ensued as Africans strove to maintain control over their lives while Whites tried to consummate their political victory with economic success; or, rather, a series of struggles, for the relationships between Whites and Blacks varied immensely from place to place.

In some areas, Africans still exclusively occupied the land, except for the sites of white traders, missionaries, and administrative officials. That was the case in all of Basutoland, in most of Bechuanaland and the Transkei, in much of Zululand and Swaziland, and in the reservations in the Ciskei and Natal; also in scattered areas in the Afrikaner republics, especially in the arc of land around the white settlements in the Transvaal. There, African communities were struggling to continue to produce enough food for subsistence. Where possible, especially among the Xhosa and the Basotho, innovative families were seizing the opportunity to produce a surplus for the market in such towns as Kimberley and Johannesburg, but they were experiencing increasing constraints by the end of the century.

The experience of the Sotho illustrates this process. Ever since the 1830s, when Afrikaner stock farmers began to settle on the highveld, the Sotho had been their major suppliers of grain, and during the 1870s the Sotho responded vigorously to the new market opportunities in Kimberley, but the tide began to turn in the 1890s. The burgeoning population of Basutoland was beginning to bear heavily on the arable land left to it within the boundaries set in 1870. The arrival of the railroad from the ports to Bloemfontein, Kimberley, and Johannesburg led to the importation of grain from the United States, Argentina, and Australia, which could be marketed more cheaply than grain could be transported by ox wagon from the farms. At the same time, white landowners in the Orange Free State were turning increasingly from pastoralism to crop production, the republican government was imposing a tariff against Basotho grain, and the diamond- and gold-mining industries were vigorously recruiting Sotho labor. By 1900, the colony of Basutoland was set on its tragic course from its nineteenth-century role as the granary of the Orange Free State to its twentieth-century role as an impoverished labor reserve for white South Africa.[29]

In the rest of the region, where white people had effective legal claims to the land, far from expelling the Africans, they were trying to harness their productive capacities, in various ways and with varied success. As yet, few

Africans had completely lost control of the means of production. "Kaffir-farming," as Whites called it, was commonly practiced by absentee owners, such as mining companies and mining capitalists, who invested some of their profits in land and exacted rent from the African occupants. The republican governments tried to reduce this practice by prohibiting more than five African families from residing on a farm, but rarely were they able to enforce such laws. Elsewhere, there were many types of sharecropping arrangements, in terms of which the African tenants had effective control of the means of production—land, plows, and draft oxen—but gave about half of their produce and some labor services to the legal owner, who might be an absentee individual or corporation but more commonly lived on the farm. In some cases, Africans paid rent for their use of part of a farm by providing labor for the white farmer. These categories were neither clear-cut nor static. Many farms contained both sharecroppers and labor tenants. Relationships were fluid and ambiguous; both sides were continuously probing and testing them.

These processes increased the social differences among both the conquerors and the conquered. There were losers as well as gainers among the Whites, and gainers as well as losers among the Africans. Before the end of the century, there was a distinct class of Poor Whites—Afrikaners who, now that the frontiers had closed, were no longer able to live by rearing cattle, hunting, and transport riding and had failed to make good as arable farmers. There was also a rising class of modestly prosperous African peasant farmers, many of whom had had a mission education and were imbued with the Victorian spirit of improvement.

In 1896–97, the rinderpest carried off most of the cattle of the entire region, and in 1899, a three years' war broke out among the Whites—a war that disrupted many African communities, as well as Afrikaners throughout the Orange Free State and the Transvaal.[30]

British Imperialism and the South African War

Before 1896, the affairs of Southern Africa never held the attention of the British public and government for more than brief, intermittent episodes, occasioned by startling news of defeats by the Zulu or the Transvaalers, or of vast finds of diamonds or gold. The British cabinet was far more concerned with domestic problems, the Irish question, or the intricacies of European diplomacy. British officials in South Africa were thus able to exercise great latitude, subject to supervision from London that varied with the energy and personality of the colonial secretary.

Insofar as British politicians gave a thought to the future of South Africa, they placed it in the same category as Canada—a region dominated by white settlers of foreign and British origin who had joined to form a federal British dominion in 1867. Following that precedent, the British colonies and Afrikaner republics in South Africa, from the Cape to the Limpopo and perhaps beyond, should amalgamate in a self-governing, white-controlled state under the Crown. Such a state should be strong enough to keep internal law and order and to incorporate the African communities; the Royal Navy would protect it from foreign aggression; British merchants would dominate its foreign trade; and the British government would control its foreign political relations. Also, some politicians would add, the British government should have a say in its treatment of its African inhabitants.

How was this to be achieved? One way was to give the Cape Colony self-government and have it engross the other states in the region. That method was tried. The Cape Colony acquired responsible government in 1872, but the colony was too weak and its white inhabitants too divided for it to become the instrument of such a policy. Until 1880, the colonial government refused to incorporate Griqualand West, and although it took over Basutoland in 1871, it soon lost control of the Basotho people, so that Britain had to resume responsibility for that territory in 1884.

Meanwhile, in 1875 Lord Carnarvon, an unusually activist colonial secretary serving in Benjamin Disraeli's Conservative ministry, had set in motion a series of events that he intended to culminate in a Canadian solution.[31] He started by writing a dispatch to the high commissioner in Cape Town, proposing a conference of representatives of the white communities in Southern Africa to discuss native questions, the control of the arms trade, and, perhaps, confederation. The South African responses were not auspicious. The Cape colonial cabinet—the first under responsible government—resented what it construed as imperial interference. In the Orange Free State, the voortrekker spirit had been reinforced by the well-grounded belief that Britain had manipulated the arbitration process that had led to including the Kimberley diamond fields in Griqualand West. In the Transvaal, Afrikaner morale was low because of the weakness of the economy and the unpopularity of the president, Thomas François Burgers. When he interviewed Burgers in London, Carnarvon nevertheless deduced that he would support confederation under British auspices, which was foolish because that would have amounted to political suicide by Burgers.

Rebuffed by the Cape colonial government and, so he thought, deceived by the president of the Transvaal, Carnarvon convened a conference in London after trying to conciliate President Brand of the Orange Free State by granting him ninety thousand pounds' compensation for the loss of the diamond fields. The conference achieved nothing significant. The Cape and the Transvaal were not represented; Shepstone, a nonelected official, represented Natal; and President Brand was present to make sure that confederation was not discussed.

Foiled in diplomacy, Carnarvon resorted to more dramatic methods. Using propaganda to exploit missionary charges that the Transvaal practiced slavery, the concerns of British merchants, traders, and bankers about the security of their investments in the Transvaal, and reports about the Pedi defeat of a Transvaal commando, Carnarvon entrusted Shepstone with the task of annexing the republic, preferably with the consent of its Afrikaner citizens. In January 1877, Shepstone entered the Transvaal with a small police escort and settled in Pretoria. There he played a skillful waiting game. Interviewing leading citizens, he exploited their fears of the Zulu, their factionalism, and their dislike of President Burgers and demanded that the Volksraad make financial and administrative reforms. When it had done so, he declared that the reforms were not good enough. The Volksraad eventually adjourned, and so demoralized were the citizens that on April 12, 1877, Shepstone was able peacefully to proclaim the Transvaal a British colony.

In Pretoria, nobody resisted annexation, but in its final session the Executive Council of the republic appointed a delegation led by Paul Kruger, the senior military officer of the republic, to go to London and protest. Refused an audience by Carnarvon, the delegation returned to the Transvaal, organized petitions against the annexation signed by 6,591 Transvaalers, and traveled back to England, where Carnarvon's successor in the Colonial Office declined to reopen the question. British officials, meanwhile, had mismanaged the affairs of the Transvaal, alienating their Afrikaner subjects and failing to create an effective coalition in support of their administration. In defeating the Zulu and the Pedi, moreover, the British had alleviated Afrikaner fears of African military power. Consequently, late in 1880, when a Transvaal farmer refused to pay his taxes, his action precipitated an armed rising. Commandos quickly cut off the imperial garrisons in the Transvaal and invaded Natal, where they inflicted a

1. Aboriginal hunters have left Southern Africa a rich legacy of rock paintings and rock engravings. This painting is at Mount Hope, 140 miles northeast of Port Elizabeth, in the frontier zone between hunters (San) and African mixed farmers. Evidently a fight is on between the smaller hunters who use bows and arrows and the larger farmers who carry spears and shields.

CABO ☆ GOEDE HOOP.

2. In 1706, transhument pastoralists (whom Whites called Hottentots and who called themselves Khoikhoi) still occupied the north shore of Table Bay for part of the year. The Danish artist shows an elephant hunt in progress on the left. In the distance, ships ride at anchor off Cape Town, the young Dutch colonial capital, which nestles beneath the Devil's Peak, Table Mountain, and the Lion's Head.

3. The Tswana people—African mixed farmers—lived in large townships. This scene is in Dithakong (near modern Kuruman), which was the seat of the Tlhaping chiefdom. William Burchell, a British naturalist-artist, spent several weeks there in 1812. The town, he said, occupied "the greater part of a plain of about two miles in diameter." Burchell estimated that it had five thousand inhabitants or more.

4. African blacksmiths made hoes, spears, and knives. George French Angas painted a Zulu smithy in 1848. The principal blacksmith works a pair of leather bellows. The bellows are connected by elands' horns with a clay tube that is thrust into a charcoal fire, where a white heat is kept up while the iron softens. The blacksmith's assistant removes the heated lumps of iron with a pair of forceps to a flat stone, where another man beats it into shape.

5. African women made a beer of fermented millet for use on festive occasions. Angas illustrated the process in a Zulu homestead at the Tugela River. "The large earthen jars over the fire contain the beer which, after boiling, is set aside for some days to ferment. One woman is stirring the millet with a calabash spoon, while another is testing its quality in a little cup; a third woman is advancing with a basket of millet on her head, and a fourth is pouring out the liquor in waterproof baskets."

6. Willem Adriaan van der Stel, governor of the Cape Colony, became a wealthy landowner. This is a modern, romanticized rendering of his great estate, Vergelegen, thirty miles east of Cape Town. The governor and his cronies are overseeing the slaves alongside the elegant homestead. Van der Stel fell foul of the settlers and was recalled in 1705.

7. George French Angas made this painting of Cape Town in 1847, when its population numbered 21,000. "Nothing," he wrote, "can exceed the beauty of the scenery in the environs of Cape Town" — "a thriving and flourishing place [with] . . . a gay and cheerful aspect."

8. Genadendal, seventy miles east of Cape Town, was the principal Moravian mission station in South Africa. Angas noted that it had a "Hottentot" population of 2,837 and contained "268 solid houses, and 266 huts and reed buildings, all the work of the Christian Hottentots." The German staff of about ten families included cutlers, cabinetmakers, tanners, and teachers.

9. In the mid-nineteenth century, white pastoralists (*trekboers*) and their servants were still living nomadic lives in the arid Cape colonial interior. This farmer and his wife occupy the tented wagon while their servants make do in the open. One of them is knee-haltering the riding horses; the draft oxen are out to pasture.

10. Ox-wagon travel in roadless, mountainous country was no easy thing. On their Great Trek in 1838, Afrikaner *voortrekkers* crossed the Drakensberg Mountains from the highveld to Natal with nearly a thousand wagons. Although men held onto thongs fastened to the sides, several wagons crashed on the precipitous slopes.

11. The first significant number of British settlers—some 5,000—reached South Africa in 1820. Thomas Baines shows them arriving in Algoa Bay, where they founded the town of Port Elizabeth.

12. Baines found traveling conditions difficult. In April 1848, his oxen got into a chaotic tangle while he was trying to cross a small stream. "The wagon stuck with its disselboom or pole so elevated that the after-oxen could not apply their strength, and turning refractory, they were kicked, lashed, dragged, and twisted by the tail, beaten, cursed and remonstrated with, as if language were actually intelligible to them."

13. In 1847, Baines described Grahamstown, the center of the British settlement, as containing "six thousand persons, of whom one fourth were coloured, and houses to the number of seven hundred and fifty."

14. During the 1860s, white hunters were taking a heavy toll of the elephant population of the Transvaal and neighboring areas. It was estimated that more than fifty-three tons of ivory were exported annually from the Transvaal. Much of it found its way overseas via the market in Grahamstown in the eastern Cape Colony.

15 and 16 (*overleaf*). Soon after Whites discovered diamonds in South Africa in 1867, the diggings began to penetrate the surface. Artists showed the chaos that ensued as individuals and small companies tried to work their holdings independently.

Gradually, amalgamations took place, and by the mid-1890s Cecil Rhodes and his associates dominated the mines. De Beers Consolidated Mines controls the diamond industry to the present day.

17. Gravel sorting was a delicate step in the process of recovering diamonds. To prevent thefts, the companies confined African workers in closed compounds and subjected them to intimate body searches before permitting them to leave. White workers successfully resisted attempts to impose similar controls over them.

18. By the mid-1880s, Kimberley, two hundred miles from the coast, was a bustling city of twenty thousand inhabitants. It had modern shops, a library, a hospital, a posh club for the elite, and even electric light. Wagons brought produce to the market square, where auctioneers sold it in lots.

19. In 1885, gold was discovered on the Witwatersrand. Here is the beginning of work on the surface of the main reef—a reef that has yielded the richest supply of gold the world has known. Today, mines operate at twelve thousand feet below the surface.

20. By the early 1890s, Johannesburg had surpassed Kimberley as the greatest city in the South African interior, the principal magnet for investment, and the main goal of railroad construction from the ports.

21. Grahamstown (founded 1812) and Kingwilliamstown (1847) were bases for military operations against the Xhosa. Frederick l'Ons captured the spirit of the campfollowers in this lively painting.

22. On 30 January 1846, Col. John Hare, a British colonial official, met the Xhosa chief Sandile in Xhosa territory, 110 miles northeast of Port Elizabeth. Sandile had three thousand armed followers; Hare deployed three British regiments and the Cape Mounted Rifles. The negotiations were not a success. War between the British and the Xhosa, waged intermittently since 1811, broke out again two months later.

23. By March 1853, the British had cleared Xhosa warriors from their mountain fastnesses and had destroyed the homestead of Sarhili, senior chief of all the Xhosa.

24. In January 1879, the Zulu annihilated an invading British regiment at Isandhlwana, but British forces and colonial volunteers then destroyed the Zulu capital, pulverized the army, banished the king, and divided the Zulu people among thirteen chiefdoms.

25 and 26. In the last quarter of 1899, Afrikaner commandos defeated British forces in Natal and the Cape Colony and besieged Ladysmith, Kimberley, and Mafeking. During 1900 the British relieved the besieged cities, captured Bloemfontein, Johannesburg, and Pretoria, and formally annexed both Boer republics. They then assumed that the "Boer War" was virtually over. They were wrong. Commandos resorted to guerrilla warfare and held out until 31 May 1902. They repeatedly broke the railway network that linked the coast with the interior.

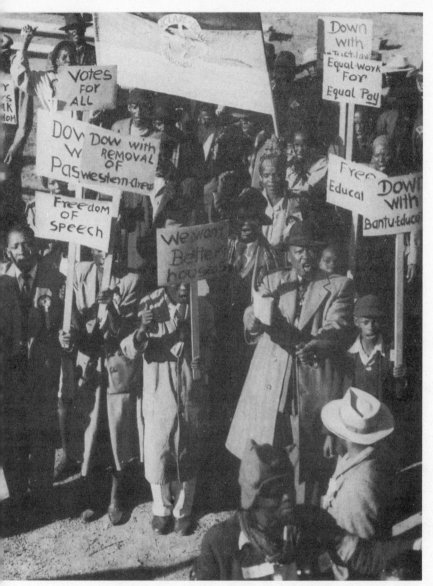

27. In 1955, 3,000 delegates from all over South Africa—320 Indians, 230 Coloured People, 112 Whites, and about 2,300 Africans—met in an open space near Johannesburg. There they adopted a Freedom Charter, which became the basic policy statement of the African National Congress. Police broke the meeting up on the second day.

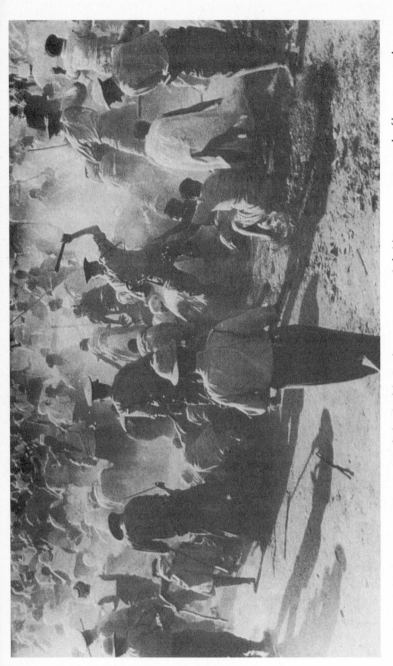

28. The sjambok (whip) was a major weapon in the hands of the South African police. In June 1959, at Cato Manor near Durban, police used sjamboks to beat African women who were protesting the government's decision to create a monopoly of beer canteens, thus depriving the women of a customary source of income.

29. In the 1950s, the government destroyed Sophiatown, an African township four miles west of Johannesburg that had been the center of African resistance to apartheid.

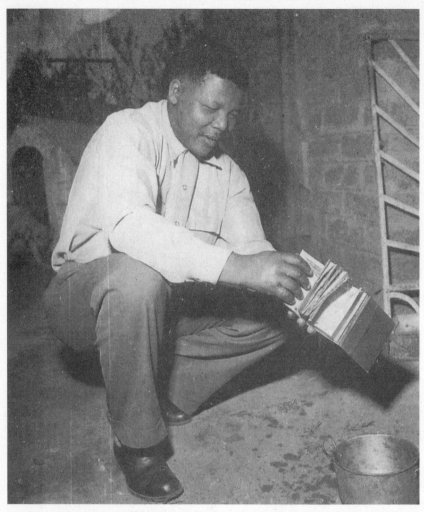

30. Nelson Mandela set an example for other Africans by burning his "pass" in 1959. Mandela became president of the African National Congress after the death of Albert Luthuli in 1967, but he would spend most of his life as a political prisoner.

31. On South African farms, white landowners live in modern houses, their black laborers in sordid shacks and cottages.

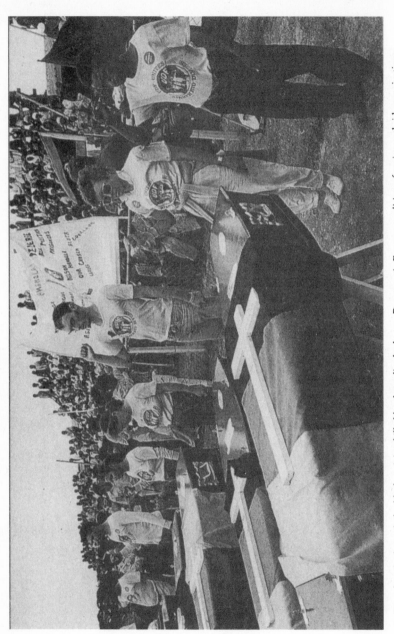

32. By 1985, the funerals for black activists killed by the police had become occasions for political demonstrations by the United Democratic Front, a coalition of anti-apartheid organizations.

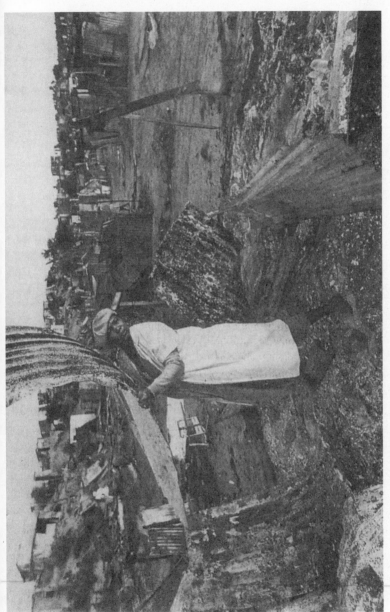

33. In 1986, the police and African collaborators destroyed Crossroads, a vast African shantytown near Cape Town.

34. Havoc in the Cape peninsula in 1988!

35. An elderly couple on the way to vote on April 27, 1994, passes a long line of voters. Thousands waited for hours to cast their ballots in the country's first nonracial election.

36. President Nelson Mandela receives the five volumes of the Truth and Reconciliation Commission Final Report from Commission Chairman Archbishop Desmond Tutu in Pretoria on October 29, 1998. Mandela acknowledged that the TRC alone could not heal the nation.

37. President Jacob Zuma (center left) and Deputy President Kgalema Motlanthe (center right) cut the cake at the ANC centenary celebrations at Mangaung on January 8, 2012.

38. Police check bodies on the ground after the Marikana Massacre of August 16, 2012. The incident caused international outrage.

series of defeats on ineptly led British forces. The brief war culminated in February 1881, when a commando stormed Majuba Mountain in broad daylight and virtually annihilated the 280 British soldiers on the summit.

William Gladstone's Liberal ministry, which had succeeded the Conservatives the previous year, resisted the popular clamor for revenge, and in August 1881 British commissioners signed a convention giving the Transvaal "complete self-government, subject to the Suzerainty of Her Majesty"—a reservation with no precise meaning. That ended the forward movement that Carnarvon had initiated.

During the ensuing years, Afrikaners adapted in different ways to their changing environments. In the Cape Colony, where most Afrikaners still lived, they were exposed to two distinct paradigms, idealistic and pragmatic. The idealistic paradigm was set out by S. J. du Toit, a rural *predikant* (Dutch Reformed minister), who created the nucleus of an exclusive ethnic mythology for Afrikaners in a newspaper, *Die Afrikaanse patriot,* and a book *Die geskiedenis van ons land in die taal van ons volk* (The history of our country in the language of our people). Afrikaners, according to du Toit, were a distinct people, occupying a distinct fatherland and endowed by God with the destiny to rule South Africa and civilize its heathen inhabitants. This was the first time that an Afrikaner intellectual had adopted the concept of a chosen people. Du Toit's writings were accessible to his public because he wrote in simple Afrikaans, the language of common speech, as distinct from the stilted High Dutch of the Reformed churches and previous publications in South Africa.[32]

The pan-Afrikaner nationalist ideology initiated by du Toit would ultimately triumph in a fateful general election in 1948, but it did not dominate Afrikaner political institutions in the nineteenth century. Although du Toit launched a political organization, the Afrikaner Bond, to give effect to his principles, Presidents Brand and Kruger snuffed it out from the republics, where they were concentrating on consolidating their separate state identities, and the Bond was captured by advocates of a different paradigm in the Cape Colony, led by Jan Hofmeyr. Hofmeyr, a Cape Town journalist, was a pragmatic man. He operated within the colonial system to achieve reforms for his people. He tolerated the British connection, provided it was not onerous, he worked for harmony between the Afrikaner and the British elements in the colonial population by removing Afrikaner grievances, and he looked ultimately to the unification of South Africa on that basis.[33]

Holding those opinions, Hofmeyr brought the Bond into a political alliance with Cecil Rhodes, one of the most remarkable products of the imperial epoch. Rhodes was determined to use the wealth he was accumulating in the mining industries to promote the expansion of the British Empire in Africa from its base in the Cape Colony along the road to the north through the Tswana chiefdoms, the territories of the Shona and the Ndebele, and onward through the East African highlands to the Nile valley. This was not an unduly original idea, for social Darwinism and Anglo-Saxon racism were the main ingredients in the political fantasies of many of England's ruling classes in the Victorian age, but Rhodes had exceptional ambition and exceptional means to fulfill it. First, he was rich; second, he was a persuasive talker and a skillful negotiator.

Rhodes, the British imperialist, and Hofmeyr, the Afrikaner colonialist, found many points of agreement. Both wished to foster cooperation between Boer and Briton; to resist British interference in the internal affairs of South Africa; to prevent Africans from dominating South African political systems; and to work toward a South African union, with the British link retained for trade and defense. Based on that alliance, Rhodes, a member of the Cape parliament since 1881, became prime minister of the Cape Colony in 1890, on the understanding that he would promote the interests of the colonial Afrikaner farmers and that Hofmeyr would support his plans for expansion beyond the Limpopo.

The government of the restored Transvaal republic, meanwhile, was having to accommodate the boisterous, volatile mining community in its midst. The gold-mining industry was both a boon and a potential cancer: a boon because it remedied the financial weakness that had contributed to the collapse of the state in 1877, a potential cancer because it was alien and dangerous. The Witwatersrand attracted a massive influx of white men from overseas, as well as from other parts of South Africa. By 1896, the 44,000 white alien men, who became known as *Uitlanders,* may have outnumbered the Afrikaner males in the Transvaal. They were a heterogeneous mixture of English, Irish, Scots, continental Europeans, Australians, and North Americans; of artisans, engineers, lawyers, businesspeople, and unskilled workers. Most Uitlanders nevertheless spoke English, and English was the lingua franca of the gold-mining industry. A deep cultural gulf stretched between all those urban, individualistic, raucous Uitlanders and the rural, socially integrated Calvinist Afrikaners.[34]

The restored Transvaal republic was managed by an elective Volksraad and president. The citizens elected a formidable man as president on four successive occasions. Born in 1825, Paul Kruger had been a boy in the Great Trek and had risen to fame as a commando leader and an opponent of the British annexation. Foreigners underestimated him—misled by his rough style and fundamentalist beliefs. Kruger's book was the Bible. His earth was so irrevocably flat that when an American told him he had sailed round the world, Kruger called him a liar.[35] But he was an extremely skillful politician and an effective representative of his people. The burgers heartily approved of his simple manner and shared his political objectives: to maintain the independence of the republic and to keep it under their control.

Alarmed by the political implications of the foreign immigration, the Volksraad took steps to ensure that Uitlanders should not get control of the State, by limiting the franchise for presidential and Volksraad elections to those white men who, besides being naturalized citizens, had lived in the republic for fourteen years. The Volksraad also created a separate body for which naturalized male citizens could vote two years after arrival, but that body had limited powers and the Volksraad remained the sole sovereign legislature.

The rulers of the Transvaal could not possibly satisfy the expectations of the immigrants from developed industrial countries. Uitlanders complained of high living costs, bureaucratic inefficiency and corruption, and the effects of the government's granting monopolies to friendly companies for the supply of dynamite, water, and railroad transport to the Witwatersrand. But they were not an oppressed community. Few Uitlanders identified with the Transvaal by becoming citizens, and fewer still were really concerned about the franchise.

The magnates who dominated the mining industry were of varied national and class origins and sympathies, and were responsible to boards located in different European cities. Some made quick profits at minimal cost from the surface deposits; others, when it became known that the gold-bearing reefs extended deep below the surface, made heavy investments for the long term. In spite of these differences, by 1895 the managements of most of the companies—French, German, and British—had come to the conclusion that the republican government was an obstruction. Similarly, the American engineers who predominated in many of the companies came to identify "Britain with economic opportunity and the Boers with economic restriction" and to favor "a British take-over of the Transvaal in the interests of economic development."[36]

The British government and Cecil Rhodes thwarted the Transvaal's attempts to expand. In 1885, as we have seen, Britain checked its expansion to the west by proclaiming a protectorate over "Bechuanaland" (modern Botswana). In 1889, Rhodes's agents having extracted a concession from Lobengula, Mzilikazi's successor as king of the Ndebele, the British government granted Rhodes's British South Africa Company a charter, empowering it to exercise political and administrative rights under the Crown in a vaguely defined area north of the Limpopo. Two years later, a British South Africa Company force from the Cape Colony occupied the land north of the Limpopo River that became known as Rhodesia (modern Zimbabwe).[37]

Kruger devoted his principal thrust to the east, where, like Hendrik Potgieter before him, he sought to free the republic from British commercial domination by getting independent access to the Indian Ocean. Although the Transvaal did manage to incorporate Swaziland in 1895, Great Britain closed the coastal gap by annexing the strip between Zululand and the Portuguese colony of Mozambique. The British had hemmed the Transvaal in politically, "as it were in a kraal."[38]

Even so, by 1895 the Transvaal was loosening the British stranglehold. It was channeling the bulk of its foreign trade through the Mozambique port of Lourenço Marques (now Maputo) at Delagoa Bay, by controlling the Delagoa Bay railroad and giving it preferential rates over the lines from the Cape Colony and Natal. The Transvaal government had also entered into diplomatic relations with Germany, which supported its refusal to enter into a customs union with the British colonies. In fact, in annexing South West Africa and encouraging the Transvaal, the German government had no intention of challenging British supremacy in the region. Trying to coerce Britain into an alliance, it was using the region as a pawn in European diplomacy. But Rhodes and the British government could not be sure of this.[39]

By that time, British politicians were becoming alarmed about the political dynamics in Southern Africa. The relative decline of British industrial power relative to other Western states; the aggressive diplomacy of Germany; the rise of popular chauvinism in Britain—all these factors coincided with the realization that the Witwatersrand discoveries were the greatest known source of gold in the world. After the Conservatives replaced the Liberals in a general election in June 1895, the problem of the Transvaal republic rose to the top of the political agenda. Lord Salisbury, the aging prime minister, appointed a Birmingham industrialist, Joseph Chamberlain, as secretary of state for the colonies and gave him a great deal of latitude. Chamberlain was a new phenomenon in British politics—self-confident, aggressive, and an avowed imperialist.[40]

Chamberlain proceeded to facilitate a plot that Rhodes was hatching to force the Transvaal into the British Empire. In Johannesburg, a reform committee was to mobilize the Uitlanders, capture Johannesburg, and proclaim a provisional government. Leander Starr Jameson, a Scottish medical doctor who had been a close associate of Rhodes since he had migrated to Southern Africa in 1878, would assist them from Bechuanaland with British South Africa Company police. The high commissioner would then go to Pretoria to arbitrate, and the Transvaal would become a British colony. The reality was far different. The Johannesburg conspirators bickered among themselves and did not command a mass following. Learning of this, Rhodes tried to stop Jameson, but Jameson ignored his order and invaded the republic with a motley force of five hundred company police. The reform committee then belatedly tried to assume control of Johannesburg but also entered into negotiations with Kruger. On January 2, 1896, Jameson surrendered to Transvaal commandos twenty-five miles short of Johannesburg and the reform committee capitulated. From the point of view of Chamberlain, Rhodes, and the reform committee, the worst had happened—a compromising fiasco; from the point of view of Kruger, the best—the tortoise had stuck out its head and he had chopped it off.[41]

The Jameson Raid accentuated the polarizing processes in Southern Africa. In the Transvaal, Kruger commuted the death sentences imposed on the five reform committee ringleaders into fines of £25,000 and handed over the members of the invading force to British authorities. He then imported large stocks of arms from Europe, curbed the political activities of the Uitlanders, dismissed his chief justice, who had challenged the validity of Volksraad legislation, tightened his alliance with his sister republic, the Orange Free State, and won an immense majority in the 1898 presidential election. In the Cape Colony, the white electorate split along ethnic lines, and the Afrikaner Bond narrowly won a bitterly contested election in 1898. In Britain, Chamberlain managed to cover up his complicity in the raid by dexterous use of his official position.

The raid having failed, Chamberlain concluded that direct British action was necessary to check the growth of Afrikaner power in Southern Africa. Initially, he was confident that strong and relentless diplomatic pressure on the Transvaal government would suffice, but he made two errors of judgment. First, he exaggerated Afrikaner solidarity and the threat to British

interests in Southern Africa. In fact, there were class, regional, and ideological differences among the Afrikaners. The governments of the Orange Free
State and the Cape Colony were moderating influences on the Transvaal,
where younger members of the government, including State Attorney Jan
Christian Smuts, who had been born in the Cape Colony and had had a
brilliant career at Cambridge University, were trying to purge it of its worst
abuses. Second, Chamberlain underestimated both the Transvaalers' determination to sustain their independence and the military self-confidence
they had gained through their victories over British forces in 1881.

In 1897, Chamberlain appointed Sir Alfred Milner as high commissioner in South Africa. Milner, a talented man who had swept the prizes as
a student at Balliol College, Oxford, and had been a senior member of the
British administration in Egypt, had an authoritarian personality. He believed that the "British race" had a moral right to rule other people—
Asians, Africans, and Afrikaners. He was also keenly aware of the relative
decline of British power and the global significance of the Transvaal gold-
mining industry. From his perspective, it was his duty to check the cen-
trifugal forces in South Africa, "the weakest link in the imperial chain."[42]

Milner made little attempt to comprehend the interests and motivations
either of the members of the governments of the Cape Colony and the
Orange Free State or of the Afrikaner reformers in the Transvaal, who were
fundamentally well disposed toward Britain and extremely eager to preserve the peace.[43] Instead, he encouraged the jingoistic elements on the
Witwatersrand to agitate for radical reform. They responded by producing
a petition with over 21,000 signatures, calling for British intervention, and
when the Transvaal government tried to settle the Uitlander problem by
direct negotiations with leaders of the mining industry, they were sabo-
taged by Milner's confidant, Percy Fitzpatrick, the head of intelligence for
Wernher, Beit, the largest gold-mining company. In May 1899, Milner sent
Chamberlain a telegram declaring that "the case for intervention is overwhelming," since "thousands of British subjects [were being] kept permanently in the position of helots."[44]

The Cape colonial government tried desperately to ward off a conflict.
Although Milner decided to meet Kruger, however, he did so only to
demand that he should give the vote to all Uitlanders who had lived in the
republic for five years, and he broke off the discussion when Kruger was
unwilling to go that far. In a final effort, Smuts agreed to accept Milner's
conference demands, provided that Britain would refrain from further

interference in the internal affairs of the republic; but Chamberlain rejected that condition.[45]

In September, having persuaded the British cabinet to accept the prospect of war, Chamberlain drafted an ultimatum and reinforcements sailed for South Africa. By that time, the Transvaal and Orange Free State governments were convinced that Britain was determined to destroy Transvaal independence. To strike before the reinforcements arrived, Kruger issued his own ultimatum, which expired on October 11, 1899. Thus Britain went to war to reestablish British hegemony throughout Southern Africa, the republics to preserve their independence.

Commentators have offered different economic explanations for the origins of this war. An analysis was initiated by J. A. Hobson and generalized by Lenin, who made imperialism and consequent warfare the inexorable product of "the highest stage of capitalism." Others have identified chauvinistic British public opinion, or the ideas and actions of Joseph Chamberlain or Alfred Milner, as the crucial independent variable. Modern scholarship points to a more complex explanation for this flagrant outburst of British imperialism. At a time of growing economic and military competition from European rivals, especially Germany, powerful British interests were concerned to prevent a region of great, newly discovered material resources from escaping Britain's century-old hegemony. In that context, British political culture enabled members of the ruling class to maneuver Great Britain into war in the belief that brute force would solve the problem.[46]

War, Peace, and the Transfer of Power

When the South African War began—the Boer War, as the British called it, the Second War of Freedom to Afrikaners—the British expected an easy victory.[47] Although the Transvaal government had imported substantial stocks of artillery and rifles from Europe, once the fighting began they could not replenish their arms, because the Royal Navy controlled the seas and the Portuguese government agreed to forbid the passage of military equipment through Mozambique. Moreover, although North American and European public opinion was largely pro-Boer, no foreign government assisted the republics. There was also a potential numerical disparity. The republics could muster no more than 88,000 fighting men during the war, including 12,000 Cape colonists, and although there were only 20,000

British troops in South Africa at the outset, by the end of the war about 450,000 men in uniform had served on the British side—365,000 British, 53,000 South African colonists, and 31,000 from Canada, Australia, and New Zealand.

Nevertheless, the republics held the British Empire at bay for two and a half years. Most of their men had been bred to the horse and the rifle and had seen commando service against Africans. Expert horsemen and marksmen, they could live off the country, whereas a large proportion of the British troops were tied down in communication and commissariat services. Their loose, democratic commando organization was admirably suited to the needs of a rural people defending their home terrain, whereas the British army was weakened by its textbook orthodoxy, its rigid separation of officers and men, and relatively poor horsemanship and marksmanship. The republican Afrikaners, moreover, believed passionately in the justice of their cause, whereas British Tommies had far less incentive to sacrifice.

The fighting fell into three unequal phases. Republican commandos first took the offensive in three directions—southeastward into Natal, and south and southwestward into the Cape Colony—and in December they repulsed British attacks on all three fronts. But then they lost the initiative and got bogged down in sieges of British forces in Ladysmith (Natal) and Kimberley and Mafeking (northwestern Cape).

The second phase, the year 1900, was marked by British victories. The British relieved the besieged towns, turned back the republican advances, captured four thousand men, occupied Bloemfontein, Johannesburg, and Pretoria, drove the aged President Kruger into exile via Lourenço Marques (Maputo), and gained control of the entire railway network. In December, the British proclaimed the annexation of the two republics under the names Transvaal and Orange River Colony, and Commander-in-Chief Lord Roberts returned to England, confident that the war was virtually over.

But Roberts miscalculated. The republics resorted to guerrilla warfare. Living off the land, and organized in small, mobile commandos, the Afrikaners seized British supplies, cut railroad tracks, overwhelmed small British units, and eroded the fringe of larger columns. Some commandos penetrated deep inside the Cape Colony, where they tried, not very successfully, to whip up Afrikaner support. To crush this resistance, Roberts's successor, Lord Kitchener, adopted the scorched earth policy that imperial troops and Afrikaner commandos had been accustomed to using against Africans. He burned Afrikaner crops and destroyed thirty thousand farmsteads. He exiled captured commandos to Saint Helena, Bermuda, and Ceylon and removed the civilian population to camps, where they suffered great hardships under inefficient administrators. Nearly 28,000 Afrikaner civilians, most of them children, died of dysentery, measles, and other diseases in the camps. The British also built eight thousand blockhouses at one-and-a-half-mile intervals along the railway lines and elsewhere, linked them with 3,700 miles of barbed-wire fences, and made a series of sweeps within the perimeters of the fenced areas.

These methods gradually undermined the fighting capacity of the republics. By 1902, eroded by deaths, captures, and desertions, their field strength had declined to about 22,000 men, most of whom were undernourished, ill-clad, exhausted, and dispirited. President Kruger had gone to Europe, where he would die in 1904 without ever having revisited his native land. The gold mines were in production again. Africans were occupying abandoned farms and collaborating with the British forces. Many Afrikaners had surrendered voluntarily and resumed farming operations, and 1,800 Afrikaners, most of them members of the landless class, had gone over to the British side.

Britain and the republics had claimed that the war was among Whites only and denied that they were using Blacks for military purposes. In fact, both sides made extensive use of black labor, and Africans as well as Afrikaners suffered from the scorched earth policy. Peter Warwick has shown that "at least 10,000 and possibly as many as 30,000 Blacks" had fought with the British army and that "almost 116,000 Africans had been removed to concentration camps, in which over 14,000 refugees lost their lives."[48]

On May 31, 1902, what became known as the Peace of Vereeniging was signed in Pretoria, after its terms had been accepted, fifty-four to six, by representatives of the commandos at Vereeniging in the southern Transvaal. As high commissioner, Milner had the major say in drafting the terms. He was determined to translate the military victory into durable British supremacy throughout Southern Africa. He planned to rule the former republics autocratically, without popular participation, until he had denationalized the Afrikaners and swamped them with British settlers. When that was done, and not before then, it would be safe and expedient to introduce representative institutions. Finally, he planned that the anglicized former republics should join the Cape Colony and Natal in a self-governing dominion that would be a source of economic as well as political strength to Great Britain.[49]

Milner thus made sure that the treaty included no concessions to Afrikaner demands that might undermine his plans. In response to the demand for cultural autonomy, the treaty stopped short of making Dutch an official language in the new colonies, though it stated that Dutch would be taught in the schools where the parents desired it and would be allowed in the courts where necessary for the better administration of justice. In response to political demands, the treaty set no date for institutional changes, saying merely that military administration would be succeeded by civil government "at the earliest possible date" and that "as soon as circumstances permit, representative institutions, leading up to self-government, will be introduced."[50] The Peace of Vereeniging also included one major concession to Afrikaner and British colonial sentiment: "The question of granting the franchise to natives will not be decided until after the introduction of self-government."[51] That was a momentous commitment. The white inhabitants of the Transvaal and the Orange River Colony were themselves to decide whether to enfranchise their black fellow subjects. It was a forgone conclusion that they would exclude the Blacks, since the republics had never allowed Blacks to vote. That outcome was in harmony with Milner's prescription for the role of Blacks in Southern Africa. "The *ultimate* end," he had written in November 1899, "is a self-governing white Community, supported by *well-treated* and *justly-governed* black labour from Cape Town to Zambesi."[52]

Africans in the former republics had reason to expect that their lives would improve under British administration, since British propaganda had repeatedly criticized the republican governments for their treatment of Africans. Those hopes quickly subsided. In the rural areas, where Africans had carried out a "rebellion from below" during the war, the Milner regime reestablished Afrikaner landowners and made Africans' lives harsher than before the war. In the towns, too, Africans' conditions worsened, especially in the gold-mining industry, which Milner nourished as a magnet for white immigration, a source of profit for investors and taxation for government, and a catalyst for the region's economy. He tightened the pass laws to restrict the mobility of African laborers, while the mining companies cut Africans' wages and stopped competing for their labor by combining to form a Witwatersrand Native Labor Association (WNLA). When Africans walked off their jobs, the government responded with force; when Africans failed to come to the mines on the prescribed terms in the required numbers, the government arranged for laborers to be imported from China. By 1907, 63,000 Chinese had arrived, contracted for unskilled and semiskilled mine work at low wages. In combination, the government, the WNLA, and the Chinese laborers made the gold-mining industry profitable to investors and the state by undermining the bargaining power of Africans.[53]

In white ethnic terms, Milner's grand design did not succeed. He failed to create the conditions he had considered essential before it would be safe to establish self-government in the former republics. The British population of the coastal colonies and the Transvaal did increase considerably during Milner's regime, and British merchants and companies bought up significant quantities of land. Yet there was no mass British immigration to the towns, and fewer than three thousand British settlers—men, women, and children—were established on the land under his subsidized scheme. Milner failed swamping the Afrikaners with people of British descent. As before, Afrikaners formed well over 50 percent of the white population of Southern Africa. Only in Natal was there a clear British majority among the Whites.

Nor were the Afrikaners denationalized. Far from destroying Afrikaner nationalism, Chamberlain and Milner, Roberts and Kitchener were the greatest recruiting agents it ever had. The Jameson Raid, coercive diplomacy, military conquest, concentration camps, and bureaucratic reconstruction gave Afrikaner nationalism a powerful stimulus. Most Afrikaners in the former republics retained an indelible conviction that their cause had been just; so did the ten thousand colonial Afrikaners who had joined or assisted the commandos. Up and down Southern Africa, Dutch Reformed clergy used their great influence to unite their people and keep them true to their Calvinist religion and their culture. In the Transvaal in 1905, two former commando leaders—Louis Botha, a progressive landowner, and Jan Smuts, the Cape-born and British-educated man who had served the Kruger government before the war—denounced the Milner regime in general and its decision to import Chinese labor in particular, and appealed to *bittereinders, handsuppers,* and National Scouts (those who resisted to the end, those who surrendered, and those who fought for the British) to unite in support of a new political movement, Het Volk (The People). In the Orange River Colony, Abraham Fischer and J. B. M. Hertzog founded a similar organization, the Orangia Unie (Orange Union).[54] Cleavages would soon open among these leaders and their followers, but so long as Milner was high commissioner they pulled together in demanding self-government.

While Afrikaners were moving closer together, South Africans of British origin remained deeply divided. Milner's obsession with "race" had made him miscalculate their political behavior. He failed to realize that most of them subordinated their ethnic sentiments to their economic interests, which differed vastly. In his haste to revive and expand the gold-mining industry, Milner sided so blatantly with management that he alienated many British artisans, professionals, and businesspeople.

By 1905, when Milner left South Africa, the political pendulum had turned in Britain. The jingoistic spirit that had added the word *mafficking* to the English vocabulary, when a mob celebrated the lifting of the siege of Mafeking on May 17, 1900, had been dissipated by the knowledge that the war had claimed the lives of 22,000 imperial soldiers and cost the British taxpayers £200 million. The internal strains in the Unionist party were accentuated in 1903 when Chamberlain resigned from the cabinet to campaign for a high imperial tariff to knit the empire together as a closed economic bloc.

During the war, the Liberal party had been divided. Liberal imperialists had supported the government, pro-Boers had opposed it, and a central group led by Sir Henry Campbell-Bannerman had endorsed the war in principle but denounced the resort to what he called "methods of barbarism" in the treatment of civilians. The Liberals later converged on the center, criticizing Milner's reconstruction program, especially the importation of Chinese labor, and in a general election in January 1906 they won a majority of eighty-four over all other parties in the House of Commons.

Campbell-Bannerman's government was no less anxious than its predecessor to preserve British interests in South Africa, but it differed profoundly about the means. The Unionists' resort to force had been counterproductive; it had alienated the Afrikaners. As British historian Bernard Porter has said, the Liberals appeased the Whites at the expense of the Africans because they realized that the imperial connection depended on the help of colonial collaborators, and they believed that "in South Africa collaboration had to be with the white communities," including the Afrikaners, who constituted the majority among the Whites. They were following their predecessors in classing South Africa in the same category as the other great British colonies of European settlement—Canada, Australia, and New Zealand—rather than placing South Africa with Britain's Asian and tropical African dependencies, where the European population was a much smaller proportion of the whole.[55]

Accordingly, the government decided to grant Het Volk's request for self-government in the Transvaal, but on terms that would honor the Vereeniging commitment to confine the franchise to white men and also, it hoped, ensure an initial electoral victory for the British element. First, it appointed a committee that, after visiting South Africa, submitted a secret report with specific recommendations to this effect, regarding "British supremacy as vital and essential."[56] The government then promulgated a constitution for the Transvaal that created an executive cabinet responsible to an elected parliament, in which each electoral division contained the same number of voters (which favored the British element, with its high proportion of single men), as distinct from the same number of white inhabitants (which would have favored the Afrikaners, with their large families).

The British government miscalculated the outcome of the election, however. On February 20, 1907, many British working-class Transvaalers voted not for the Progressives, the true-blue party led by mining magnates, but for the Transvaal National Association, led by English-speaking professional men who had made an electoral pact with Het Volk, whereas the Afrikaners were solid for Het Volk, which won thirty-seven of the sixty-nine seats in the new parliament. Thus, five years after they had been forcefully incorporated in the British Empire, Transvaal Afrikaners regained control of the territory as a self-governing British colony. Nine months later, the Orangia Unie won a still more sweeping victory under a similar constitution in the Orange River Colony, where Afrikaners greatly outnumbered those of British descent. In February 1908, an election was held in the Cape Colony, where the South African party, led by John X. Merriman, an anti-imperialist son of an Anglican priest, came into power with the support of the Afrikaner Bond. That left Natal, with its British electoral majority, as the only South African government sympathetic to British imperialism.

Once in office, Botha and Smuts found it expedient to work in harmony with the powerful gold-mining industry and to accept the overtures of the British Liberal government. They described their policy as one of "conciliation," which involved reconciling the differences among Afrikaners and between Afrikaners and British Transvaalers. Although they repatriated the Chinese laborers, they allayed the fears of the industrialists by siding with them in labor disputes, and although Afrikaner conservatives suspected their motives, Botha and Smuts managed to maintain control of the Het Volk.[57]

Botha and Smuts also discovered powerful incentives to join the Transvaal in a political union with the other self-governing South African colonies. The existing system of trade relations in the region, which were regulated by a customs union and railway agreements that had been negotiated by Milner, was on the verge of collapse. The customs union was threatened because the coastal colonies relied heavily on tariffs for revenue, whereas the inland colonies were more interested in reducing the cost of imported goods. There was also intense competition among the state railways for the trade from the ports to the interior, and Portugal was threatening to stop sending Mozambican laborers to the gold mines if the colonies imposed differential rates to offset Lourenço Marques's advantage as the closest port to the Witwatersrand.[58]

Events in Natal, where Africans outnumbered Whites by ten to one, were another factor that led many white South Africans to favor a political union. In 1906, the Natal militia suppressed an African rebellion led by Bambatha, a former chief whom the government had deposed, with a loss of thirty white men and some three thousand Zulu; and in the following year the Natal government remobilized the militia and arrested Dinuzulu, the head of the Zulu royal house, on the grounds that he had been behind the rebellion and was plotting further resistance. By 1908, a government commission had revealed that the Natal Africans had substantial grievances, including insensitive administration and economic hardship. Later, when Dinuzulu's trial for treason was completed, the presiding judge concluded that there was no evidence that he had formented rebellion before or after 1906. The result was that Whites in Natal were unsure of their capacity to control a distinct state, whereas Whites in the other colonies feared the consequences if Natal was left to its own devices.[59]

The idea of South African federation or unification was not new. It was central to the imperialist philosophy. As we have seen, Lord Carnarvon and his officials bungled an attempt to give effect to it in the 1870s. Subsequently, Rhodes and Milner regarded it as their mission to create a vast British state extending northward from the Cape to the Zambezi or even further. After Milner left Southern Africa, a group of bright young men whom he had brought out from England to assist in administering the new colonies and who became known as the Milner Kindergarten hoped to salvage his work. They wrote a memorandum for public consumption, stressing the attractions of unification to white South Africans.[60]

South African unity was also a goal of many thoughtful Afrikaners, but with the opposite intent—that it should weaken not strengthen imperial influence. Before the war it had been beyond the bounds of practical pol-

itics, but after Het Volk and the Orangia Unie assumed office in the Transvaal and Orange River Colony and the South African party did so in the
Cape Colony, anti-imperialists throughout Southern Africa could look to
unification as a means of solving their trade squabbles, consolidating the
white South African communities, and eliminating imperial interference.
Accordingly, in May 1908 an intercolonial conference patched up the
railway and customs agreements and recommended that the four parliaments appoint delegates to a national convention to prepare a constitution
for a united South Africa (map 7).

The convention assembled in Durban in October 1908. There were
thirty delegates with voting rights: twelve from the Cape Colony, eight
from the Transvaal, and five each from the Orange River Colony and
Natal. All, needless to say, were male and white. Fourteen were Afrikaners,
sixteen were of British origin. Jan Smuts arrived with a well-thought-out
constitutional scheme that he had cleared with the Progressive and Het
Volk members of the Transvaal delegation, as well as with the leaders of the
ruling parties in the Orange River Colony and the Cape Colony. Conse-

7. Southern Africa in 1908

quently, in spite of some heated debates, the convention moved fairly rapidly toward consensus. In February 1909 the delegates signed a draft constitution, and in May they amended it in the light of modifications recommended by the colonial parliaments. The document was then approved unanimously by the parliaments of the former republics, with two dissentients in the Cape parliament, and by a three-to-one majority in a referendum of the voters in Natal.[61]

The constitution contained four major principles that have profoundly affected the course of South African history. First and foremost, it followed the British model, creating a unitary state with parliamentary sovereignty. It included no substantial concessions to Natal's demands for federalism. The four colonies became the provinces of the Union of South Africa, but the central government was legally supreme over all local institutions. Moreover, powers were not divided within the center. As in Great Britain, the executive was responsible to a majority in the lower house of parliament, named the House of Assembly; the Senate, the upper house, was indirectly elected and weaker in several respects; and there was no bill of rights. In addition, with two exceptions to be noted, laws amending the constitution could be enacted in the same way as other laws—by simple majorities in both houses of parliament. The judiciary thus had scarcely any scope for testing the validity of acts of parliament. That institutional system of winner take all, devoid of checks on the legal competence of a majority party, was to have momentous consequences.

Second, the convention had to cope with the fact that the franchise laws of the four colonies differed substantially. In the Transvaal and Orange Free State, as we have seen, all white men, and none but white men, were entitled to vote in parliamentary elections or to become members of parliament. In Natal, where the colonial government had whittled away the political rights of blacks, white men could vote provided they satisfied quite low economic criteria, but law and practice excluded all but a few Africans, Indians, and Coloureds. In the Cape Colony, although Rhodes's administration had diminished the black proportion of the total vote in the 1890s, the franchise laws were still nonracial in form. There, any man could vote or become a member of parliament, regardless of race, provided that he was at least barely literate and that he either earned fifty pounds a year or occupied a house and land worth seventy-five pounds, outside the communal land in the African reserves. In fact, however, no black man ever sat in the Cape colonial parliament, and in 1909, 85 percent of the registered voters were Whites, 10 percent Coloured, and 5 percent Africans.[62] That problem caused passionate debates in the convention. Some Cape delegates, who had black as well as white constituents, proposed a uniform franchise on the Cape colonial model, but the other three delegations remained adamantly opposed to that proposal. The outcome was a compromise: membership in parliament was confined to white men, and the franchise laws of each colony remained in force in each province, but, to protect the rights of Blacks in the Cape province, any bill altering those laws would require the support of two-thirds of both houses of parliament in a joint sitting.

Third, the constitution provided that at regular intervals judicial commissions were to divide the country into electoral divisions for the lower house of parliament and that each division was to contain the same number of voters, although the commissions could vary that number 15 percent either way from the average to take into account several factors, including "sparsity or density of population." In practice, delimitation commissions would attach great weight to that factor, to the advantage of parties that represented rural voters. It would be crucial in 1948, when it enabled D. F. Malan's National party to form a government and institute its policy of apartheid.

Fourth, the constitution made both English and Dutch the official languages of the country. Discerning the crucial importance of language to the survival of Afrikaner culture and identity in the face of the forces of anglicization, J. B. M. Hertzog had recently piloted a bill through the Orange Free State parliament to place the Dutch and English languages on the same footing in the white public schools of that colony. In the convention, Hertzog and ex-president M. T. Steyn made it clear that they would have no truck with unification unless the constitution included a strong safeguard for the Dutch language. The language clause, and the clause protecting the Cape nonracial franchise, were the two rigid elements in the constitution. Neither could be amended without the approval of two-thirds of both houses of Parliament sitting together.

The constitution also included provisions under which the British government might at some unspecified date incorporate Southern Rhodesia, Basutoland, Bechuanaland Protectorate, and Swaziland into the new Union. Three Southern Rhodesians were present at the convention, without the right to vote. The British South Africa Company, which still controlled its territory under a royal charter, wished to see whether the new South African government supported its interests before deciding whether it should join the Union. Many white Rhodesians, moreover, being pre dominantly of British stock, were loath to be placed in a state with an Afrikaner political majority. Several convention delegates had hoped to incorporate the other three territories forthwith, but the British government, which administered them in cooperation with their African chiefs, informed the convention that this was not possible, since the chiefs did not wish to be placed under the control of white South Africans. As we shall see, these provisions never went into operation.

Having completed their work in South Africa, the four colonial governments sent delegates to London, since only the imperial parliament had the legal authority to give effect to their decisions. Members of the Western-educated black elite in Southern Africa—clergy, journalists, teachers—and a handful of white sympathizers had also sent a deputation to London to agitate for the removal of the color bars from the constitution.[63] They were supported by the *Manchester Guardian* and several prominent individuals. However, though most members of Parliament preferred that the constitution should not contain a color bar, nearly all realized that it was politically impracticable to attempt to alter the wishes of the four self-governing colonies. Indeed, the crucial decision had been made in 1902. The political color bars in the Transvaal and Orange River Colony constitutions, and the color bars in the draft South African constitution, were natural consequences of Milner's decision to appease the fighting men of the republics at the expense of the black population.

Both major British parties were extremely anxious for a solution to the South African problem. Among the 670 members of the House of Commons, a few Liberal backbenchers, Irish nationalists, and Labour members fought the color bars, but no amendment received more than fifty-seven votes. In the House of Lords no amendment was pressed to a vote. The South Africa Act (1909), as enacted by Parliament, was substantially the same as the document produced in South Africa. Prime Minister H. H. Asquith summed up the dominant mood—one of regret covered with a strong dose of wishful thinking: "Any control or interference from outside . . . is in the very worst interests of the natives themselves. . . . I anticipate that, as one of the incidental advantages which the Union of South Africa is going to bring about, it will prove to be a harbinger of a native policy . . . more enlightened than that which has been pursued by some communities in the past."[64]

On May 31, 1910, eight years to the day since he had lain down his arms as a leader of the military forces of the Afrikaner republics, Louis Botha became prime minister of a British dominion with a population of 4 million Africans, 500,000 Coloureds, 150,000 Indians, and 1,275,000 Whites. That outcome was not what Milner had encouraged British South Africans to expect; nor was it what had been expected by the many black South Africans who had supported the British cause in the war.

CHAPTER 5

The Segregation Era,
1910–1948

The material expectations of the founders of the Union of South Africa were fulfilled. Between 1910 and 1948, the economy weathered the Great Depression, and the national income of the country increased more than three times in real terms.[1] The gold-mining industry made a major contribution to the national budget and provided enough foreign exchange for essential imports, especially heavy machinery and fuel oil. White farmers precariously held their own with massive state support, and manufacturing expanded prodigiously after 1933.[2] The country produced plenty of coal but no oil, and to sustain its economic growth, it needed large inputs of foreign capital and technology. In other respects, the economy was nearly self-sufficient by 1948.

During the same period, the white population consolidated its control over the state, strengthening its grip on the black population and eliminating the British government's legal power to intervene in South African affairs. Politics under the constitution was dominated by the question of relations between the two segments of the white population—Afrikaners and English-speakers. Should they forget the past, reconcile their differences, and work together to form a single white South African "nation," or should each ethnic community struggle to control the political system as a means of advancing its particular interests? Though this question was usually posed in ethnic terms, it also had a class basis. In the early twentieth century, people of British origin virtually monopolized the entrepreneurial, managerial, and skilled positions in every sector of the economy except agriculture, whereas many Afrikaners were impoverished. Known as Poor Whites, they were being driven off the land as agriculture became capitalized, and they were finding it difficult to adapt to the urban economy, except as unskilled workers, where they were liable to encounter competition from Blacks. In practice, no government could afford to ignore the needs of the Afrikaners, since they formed more than 55 percent of the electorate. By 1948, as a result of industrial growth, pervasive color bars, and state aid, white poverty was being phased out and individual Afrikaners were getting a foothold in top positions throughout the economy.[3]

That was the period when colonialism and segregation, reinforced by racist assumptions, prevailed elsewhere in Africa and also in much of Asia and the Caribbean, and racist ideas and practices were widespread in the United States. In South Africa, though Whites were embroiled in internal quarrels, they dominated every sector of the capitalist economy and did so with the use of cheap black labor. The categories Race and Class coincided closely: with few exceptions, black people, however able, were subordinate to white people, however feeble. Blacks did the manual work in the white household and the mining stope, the arable field, and the factory floor. Many Africans in the agricultural areas outside the reserves were being transformed from renters and sharecroppers into tenant and wage laborers.[4] Land shortage, population increase, and taxation were impoverishing the families in the African reserves, many of which could survive only by sending the men out to work for Whites for months at a time. Yet most Whites spoke no African language and never set foot in an African reserve. They assumed that all Africans had adequate homes in the reserves and that they came out to work merely to supplement viable domestic economies.

In the cities, a few European socialists tried to mold black and white workers into a single, self-conscious working class. They failed. The mining industries maintained the split between well-paid Whites (with access to political power) and poorly paid Blacks (without such access) that had emerged in Kimberley and Johannesburg in the late nineteenth century, and the manufacturing industries applied the same principle. White gold miners' annual cash earnings were 11.7 times the cash wages of black gold miners in 1911, and 14.7 times in 1951. In manufacturing, where there was widespread employment of white women at low wages, the differential was 5.3 in 1916 and 4.4 in 1948.[5] In 1946, white income per head in South Africa was more than ten times that of Africans, six times that of Asians, and five times that of Coloureds.[6] The material gap between the two white ethnic communities was closing, but the gap between Whites and Blacks was as wide as ever and more rigid than ever.

Black South Africans adopted a variety of strategies to cope with their problems. Most were preoccupied with day-to-day survival. In the reserves, for example, where families were split by the periodic absence of men, women were assuming the full burden of maintaining the domestic economy as well as bringing up the children. Christian missionaries were having a profound impact on the African and Coloured populations, however. Evangelization increased rapidly after the conquest, and by 1951, according to the census of that year, 59 percent of the Africans and 91 percent of the Coloureds were Christians.[7] Most missionaries came to South Africa from Europe or North America and did not fully share the interests and prejudices of the white South African population. Because the government failed to provide education for them, those Africans who received a modern education did so in missionary schools, such as Lovedale in the Ciskei, Adams College in Natal, and Morija in Basutoland, and in the South African Native College, which was founded at Fort Hare in the Ciskei in 1916 and was largely controlled by missionaries. There, they encountered a relatively liberal Western tradition.

Africans who had received a missionary education—clerks, teachers, clergy, and small businesspeople—periodically tried to harness the resentments of the black masses to counter white hegemony. In 1912, Africans founded a nationwide organization that became known as the African National Congress. It survived official obstruction and was destined to become a formidable instrument of resistance in the second half of the century.[8] In the late 1920s, the Industrial and Commercial Workers' Union of South Africa grew to be a massive rural movement of national liberation, with a membership of at least 150,000 before it fell apart in the face of official repression and internal conflict.[9] By 1948, urban African workers had experimented with various forms of trade unions, even though the law excluded them from the formal collective bargaining process.[10] Some African Christians adopted a different response. They broke away from white churches and formed religious communities where African leaders acted without white intervention and where Christianity was adapted to African culture.[11]

The tensions in the system intensified during World War II, when South Africa participated on the side of Great Britain and its allies, to the dismay of numerous Afrikaners. Under wartime conditions, the economy expanded and diversified particularly rapidly, drawing more and more Africans into the urban labor market. Yielding to arguments that migrant labor, pass laws, and job color bars were inefficient as well as unjust, the government bent the job color bar, allowed black wages to rise at a faster rate than white wages, and temporarily relaxed the pass laws. It also recognized that Africans were a permanent part of the urban population and toyed with the idea of recognizing African trade unions. In those circumstances, a radical Afrikaner party managed to mobilize sufficient ethnic support to win a narrow victory in a general election in 1948.[12]

White Politics, 1910–1939

During the years 1910 to 1939, the successive South African administrations were all concerned to consolidate white power in the new state.[13] In spite of a rural uprising by aggrieved Afrikaners during World War I, militant strikes by white workers, one of which escalated into a bloody confrontation on the Witwatersrand, and intermittent resistance by Blacks, the reach of the state increased steadily and scarcely anyone questioned its legitimacy. When Whites talked about "the racial question," they were referring to the ethnic cleavage between Afrikaners and English-speaking white South Africans. They vented much of their political energy in internal squabbles over symbols—postage stamps, anthems, and flags. Insofar as they differed over "native policy," it was in the search for the most effective means to advance their own material interests and ensure their security.

The general election of 1910 was won by the South African party led by Louis Botha and Jan Smuts, the former republican guerrillas who had come into power in the Transvaal in 1907. Botha, a progressive farmer with vast landholdings, and Smuts, an able and ambitious Cambridge-educated intellectual, had reached the conclusion that it was sound policy to come to terms with the gold-mining industry as the most powerful economic enterprise in the country and to build a coalition from both ethnic sections of the white South African population. Since rabid imperialism was out of favor in Westminster, they also accepted South Africa's membership in the British Empire and nudged Westminster in the direction of greater autonomy for South Africa and the other white dominions—Canada, Australia, and New Zealand.

The outcome was ironic. Although Parliament enacted laws in the interests of white workers and farmers, by 1919, when Botha died and Smuts succeeded him, the erstwhile fighters for liberation from British imperialism were losing Afrikaner votes and becoming dependent on the support of British South Africans. The Union of South Africa's electoral arithmetic meant that a distinctly British party had no chance of winning an election. South Africans of British origin were fewer than Afrikaners and had widely divergent occupational, class, and regional interests. As the 1907 Transvaal election had shown, mining magnates like George Farrar and Percy FitzPatrick could not win the support of the British working-class colonists, who had founded aggressive trade unions and a Labour party in the Transvaal. A similar class division existed among the British in the Cape Province and in Natal, the one province with a British electoral majority. Moreover, as we have seen, the formula written into the constitution for the division of the country into unequal electoral divisions favored the rural, that is to say the Afrikaner voters. From the beginning, Jameson, Farrar, and FitzPatrick, the leaders of the Unionist party, found it expedient to establish cordial relations with Botha and Smuts, with a view to influencing their policy; and in 1921 the South African party absorbed the remnants of the Unionists.

Botha and Smuts, meanwhile, were losing control over much of the Afrikaner electorate, which resented their policy of reconciliation. James Barry Munnik Hertzog, the Orange Free State leader who had already crossed swords with Smuts for his failure to give Dutch equality with English in the Transvaal schools, joined Botha's cabinet in 1910 with misgivings. He soon quarreled with his colleagues, and in January 1914, he founded a new National party, committed to protecting the cultural and economic interests of Afrikaners and dissociating South Africa from the empire. Hertzog's support came mainly from lower-class Afrikaners—marginal farmers who resented exploitation by rich landholders and people who had been dislodged from the land and were hard put to make ends meet in the towns. Afrikaner intellectuals, insecure in the face of anglicization and urbanization, also supported Hertzog; so did some lawyers, businesspeople, and successful farmers in the western part of the Cape Province.

World War I sharpened this division. When Britain declared war on Germany in August 1914, Botha and his colleagues accepted the fact that South Africa, like the other self-governing British dominions, was automatically involved, since it was not a sovereign state. But that was not all. Botha and Smuts also acted on a British request that South African forces should conquer the German protectorate of South West Africa, personally commanding South African troops in an operation that gave South Africa control of that territory. Their decision prompted a number of Afrikaners in the former republics, who had hoped to use Britain's distractions as an opportunity to regain their independence, to raise an armed rebellion. The government quickly and firmly suppressed the uprising, and Smuts went on to a remarkable wartime career, commanding imperial forces in a prolonged campaign against the Germans in East Africa, serving as a member of the British Imperial War Cabinet in London, and contributing to the creation of the League of Nations at Versailles. Having entered on the world stage, Smuts became largely preoccupied with international rather than local affairs. As Afrikaner nationalists saw it, he had sold out to imperial interests.[14]

The government also lost the support of working-class Whites by intervening in a series of industrial disputes on the Witwatersrand. By 1922, three-quarters of the white workers in the Witwatersrand gold-mining industry were South African-born, but British immigrants still controlled the Mineworkers' Union. Conditions of work and the racial composition of the work force continued to be explosive issues. Mineowners, though they did not favor complete replacement of Whites by Blacks, were at moments of financial difficulty keen to expand the functions of lower-cost black workers. White workers in general favored the expansion of protected employment for themselves.

Following a series of strikes by white miners about conditions of work and about black competition in 1907, 1913, and 1914, mineowners agreed to reserve some semiskilled work for Whites. After World War I, however, the industry faced an acute financial problem. It was a period of high inflation. Moreover, mining was taking place at ever-greater depths, the ore was of low grade, and the price of gold was low. One factor stood out in the industry's balance sheets: the cost of white labor. The wages of white workers were fifteen times those of black workers, who could easily have performed the semiskilled operations. The Chamber of Mines thus decided to break its agreement and replace some of the highly paid white workers with Africans. The Whites went on strike in January, and the impasse continued until March. Miners formed armed commandos, one of which used the slogan, "Workers of the World Unite, and Fight for a White South Africa." Smuts eventually came down heavily on the side of the owners, declaring martial law and deploying military aircraft, artillery, tanks, armored cars, and machine guns. When the dust settled, 687 people were injured and 153 were dead—4 of them executed. For the South African party, the political costs were high. Hertzog's Nationalists formed an electoral pact with the Labour party and won the general election of 1924.[15]

Between 1924 and 1933 the Hertzog administration passed more legislation in favor of the white population, especially of the Afrikaners, and acquired greater economic and political autonomy for South Africa. It made further capital available to white farmers through the Land Bank and through marketing controls and guaranteed prices for farm produce. It created a state corporation for the manufacture of steel. It protected white industrial workers from black competition and enfranchised white (but not black) women, thereby reducing the black proportion of the voters in the Cape Province from 20 to 10 percent. By promoting bilingualism, it opened up the civil service to Afrikaners.

The government also fulfilled a major Afrikaner cultural goal. As we have seen, the South Africa Act made English and Dutch the official languages of the country, although Afrikaans, the spoken language of Afrikaners, had deviated considerably from its Dutch roots. By 1925, however, the Bible had been translated into Afrikaans, there was an Afrikaans dictionary, and there was a substantial literature in Afrikaans. In that year a constitutional amendment replaced Dutch with Afrikaans as an official language.[16] The opposition did not dispute that change, but differences over the design of a national flag caused a prolonged and bitter ethnic conflict. Parliament eventually created a hybrid flag that incorporated the Union Jack and the flags of the Afrikaner republics.[17]

In 1926, largely at Hertzog's instigation, an imperial conference attended by the prime ministers of Great Britain and the self-governing British dominions devised a subtle formula that described the dominions as "autonomous communities within the British Empire . . . though united by a common allegiance to the Crown."[18] Five years later, the British Parliament passed the Statute of Westminster, which gave legal effect to that declaration. The South African government, meanwhile, like the governments of Canada and Australia, had begun to act independently in international affairs, placing diplomats in major foreign capitals and separating the office of governor-general (head of state) from that of the British representative in South Africa. Hertzog, like Smuts before him, also tried, but failed, to persuade Britain to allow South Africa to incorporate Basutoland, Bechuanaland Protectorate, and Swaziland.[19]

The Great Depression led to a realignment of political parties. After the collapse of Wall Street in October 1929, South African exports plummeted. Australia, the major wool-producing country in the Commonwealth, followed Britain in devaluing its currency, leaving the South African pound worth twice as much as the Australian, and making it almost impossible to market South African wool. Nevertheless, the Hertzog administration adhered doggedly to the gold standard, causing distress among its main supporters, the farmers, until it finally devalued the South African pound in December 1932. By then, the South African economy had been greatly damaged. Negotiations then took place between the leaders of the two major parties. In March 1933, they formed a coalition government, with Hertzog as prime minister and Smuts as deputy prime minister. In an election later that year, the coalition parties won all but 14 of 158 seats in Parliament, and in December 1934, they merged to form the United party. By that time, the Labour party, rent by disputes over the government's labor legislation, had splintered, some of Smuts's former followers in Natal had founded a British ethnic party, the Dominion party, and a group of Afrikaners, led by D. F. Malan, a Dutch Reformed minister and newspaper editor, had left Hertzog's camp and founded the Purified National party.[20]

Until 1939, the United party maintained the drive to national autonomy and white hegemony initiated by its predecessors. The Status of the Union Act (1934) reinforced the Statute of Westminster, providing that acts of the British Parliament would no longer be valid in South Africa unless they were also enacted by the South African Parliament and that the governor-general should act exclusively on the advice of his South African ministers. The Natives Representation Act (1936) drastically weakened the political rights of Cape Province Africans, removing those who were qualified to vote from the ordinary voters' rolls and giving them instead the right to elect three white people to represent them in the House of Assembly, the dominant house of Parliament. It also gave Africans in all four provinces the right to elect indirectly a total of four white senators, and created a Natives Representative Council with advisory powers.[21] The white members of the House of Assembly and Senate whom the Africans then elected spoke up for their constituents in Parliament but did not significantly stem the trend toward segregation and discrimination.[22]

The Dominion party was confined to Natal and of little account on the national stage. The Purified National party was a different matter. It addressed its appeal to an Afrikaner population that was experiencing a rapid rate of urbanization and benefiting from state provision of compulsory white education. During the late 1930s, it built up its strength with the support of a plethora of Afrikaner cultural and economic organizations. At the center of those organizations was the Afrikaner Broederbond (Brotherhood), a secret society of the Afrikaner elite—farmers, businesspeople, clergy, teachers, and academics. With the assistance of the Broederbond, the Purified National party achieved a propaganda coup in 1938, when it captured control of the organization of the centennial celebrations of the Great Trek. The celebrations culminated in a ceremony laying the foundation stone of a monument to the voortrekkers on a hill outside Pretoria. There, orators painted the voortrekkers in heroic hues, giving them the qualities necessary to promote the nationalist cause. They were profoundly religious. They were adamantly opposed to the mixing of the races. They stood for Afrikaner solidarity in the face of alien Western influences. "God," said the Reverend T. F. Dreyer, "has willed that we must be a separate, independent people."[23]

Even so, the United party seemed to be in firm command of the state apparatus. The economy was booming. The standard of living of nearly all white South Africans was improving. White poverty was decreasing. In the election of 1938 the United party won 111 seats in the House of Assembly, Malan's Purified Nationalists won only 27, and the Dominion party won 8. But there was a cloud on the horizon. Though Smuts's supporters had welcomed Hertzog's insistence on making South Africa's national sovereignty foolproof, they had different views as to how the government should exercise its sovereignty after Hitler's Third Reich had absorbed Austria, conquered Czechoslovakia, and invaded Poland. When Britain declared war on Germany on September 3, 1939, the United party split. A passionate debate ensued in the South African Parliament. Hertzog's people were for strict neutrality, Smuts's for joining Britain. When the vote was taken, Smuts's motion for a South African declaration of war against Germany was carried by 80 votes to 67. That evening, the governor-general refused Hertzog's request to dissolve Parliament and hold a general election. Hertzog resigned as prime minister, Smuts succeeded him at the head of a truncated United party, and South Africa went to war as an ally of Britain.[24]

Segregation and Discrimination, 1910–1939

By 1910, Whites had conquered the indigenous inhabitants of South Africa. The people whom Whites grouped together as the Coloured People, whose ancestors included the indigenous hunting and herding inhabitants of the western part of Southern Africa, owned scarcely any land; but many Bantu-speaking African farmers were still able to practice subsistence farming, modified but not destroyed by their conquerors, in reserves proclaimed by the colonial governments or on land they bought from Whites.[25] During the ensuing years, however, the new state applied a comprehensive program of racial segregation and discrimination and gained control over the African peasantry. Laws limited land ownership by Africans to demarcated reserves, transformed Blacks who lived in rural areas outside the African reserves into wage or tenant laborers for white farmers, and ensured white dominance in the industrial cities and rural townships. Although the government was unable to enforce these laws to the letter, they played a crucial role in expanding the capitalist order under white control and reducing the black population to a proletarian status in that order.

Three years after the inauguration of the Union, without consulting any Africans, Louis Botha's South African party administration, under strong pressure from its rural supporters, enacted a crucial law. The Natives Land Act (1913) prohibited Africans from purchasing or leasing land outside the reserves from people who were not Africans. It also prohibited sharecropping in the Orange Free State. The act listed areas totaling about 22 million acres, or about 7 percent of the area of the Union of South Africa, as constituting the reserves and recommended that they should be substantially increased.[26] Three years later, a commission appointed in terms of the act recommended that about 18 million more acres should be added to the area set aside under the Natives Land Act, but those recommendations met with a storm of protest from Whites and were not enacted.[27] In 1936, fresh legislation created the South African Native Trust, managed by Whites, and empowered it to buy more land for Africans from funds provided by Parliament. By 1939, the trust's purchases had brought the augmented African reserves to 11.7 percent of the area of South Africa.[28]

Those African areas, which were destined to be treated as the Homelands of all the African inhabitants of South Africa in the apartheid era (chapter 6), were scattered throughout the eastern half of the country. The Transkei was the only substantial bloc of African territory in South Africa. Elsewhere, even in Zululand, Whites had acquired legal title to much of the best land during and after the conquest, whereas the republican governments of the Orange Free State and the Transvaal had set aside relatively little land for the exclusive use of Africans.

The land thus proclaimed as African formed a small proportion of the territory that African mixed farmers had occupied before the Mfecane and the white conquest. By the 1920s, some of it was already carrying such a heavy concentration of people and livestock that the original vegetation was disappearing, streams and waterholes were drying up, and soil erosion was spreading. In the years that followed, the African reserves continued to deteriorate. The state network of railways and roads served the white farmers but neglected the reserves, and the government provided massive assistance to white farmers but scarcely any to Africans.

After 1910, the people in the reserves became unable to produce enough food to feed themselves and to pay the taxes imposed by the municipal, provincial, and central governments, which, after 1925, included a poll tax of one pound paid by all African men aged eighteen years or more and a local tax of ten shillings per dwelling in a reserve.[29] African farming gradually collapsed. Prosperous peasants, who had been producing a substantial surplus for the market, were wiped out.[30] The quality of life declined for all Africans in the reserves. Over one-fifth of the children died within their first year of life. Undernutrition was common. The government left African education to the missionary societies, whose resources were very limited, and although it contributed more after 1925, in 1939 fewer than 30 percent of African children were receiving any schooling at all to equip them to adapt to the new order.[31]

The reserves were being transformed into reservoirs of cheap, unskilled labor for white farmers and industrialists. In 1936, 447,000 Africans out of an officially estimated population of 3,410,000 were temporarily absent from the reserves. Only a tiny proportion of these absentees were female, and nearly all the males were between fifteen and fifty years old. By that time, almost every African man with a home in a reserve went out to work on a white farm or in a white town at some stage in his life. The wages he earned, though small, became an essential part of the economy of his rural household.[32]

The South African economy thus developed unique characteristics. The regime professed to be applying a policy of racial segregation. It was a complex segregation that met white economic needs by making a high proportion of the subject people both labor for Whites and provide for their own maintenance.

Besides dividing the country into white-owned and African-owned land, the Natives Land Act contained clauses designed to reduce all Africans in the white-owned rural areas into tenant and wage laborers. It prohibited Africans from paying rent to absentee landlords or from having the use of part of a white farm and sharing the produce with the owner. The government could not fully enforce those clauses, however. In the Transvaal and Natal, powerful absentee landlords, including mining companies, continued to exact rent from African tenants, and in all four provinces, farmers continued to allow Africans to use part of their land and to make sharecropping arrangements with them. Moreover, a judicial decision made the act inoperative in the Cape Province, since the prohibition on Africans purchasing land outside the reserves would have prevented them from satisfying the property qualification for the franchise, which was protected in the constitution.[33] The act caused the greatest hardship in the Orange Free State, where many farmers evicted Africans from their land immediately after the act was passed. Sol Plaatje, the secretary of the recently created African National Congress, described their experiences in *Native Life in South Africa:*

> Some readers may think perhaps that I have taken the Colonial Parliament rather severely to task. But, . . . if you see your countrymen and countrywomen driven from home, their homes broken up, with no hopes of redress, on the mandate of a Government to which they had loyally paid taxation without representation—driven from their homes, because they do not want to become servants . . . , you would, I think, likewise find it very difficult to maintain a level head or wield a temperate pen.[34]

White farmers paid their African workers lower wages than they could earn in the mining or manufacturing industries. Even so, many Africans preferred to stay on the farms, where, unlike urban workers, they had access to the land and lived as family units. If they tried to leave, however, some farmers tied them to the farm by using their control of local authorities to prevent Africans from getting "passes" to work in towns, by whipping workers who broke their contracts, and by placing Africans in debt.[35] Most farm laborers were isolated from both the reserves and the towns and thereby were deprived of wider traditional as well as modern social networks and cultural opportunities. At best, their lives were ameliorated by paternalist farmers; at worst, they were victims of systematic exploitation.

Before World War II, white farmers were just beginning to mechanize their operations. In 1937, they still owned more animal-drawn wagons than automobiles, trucks, and tractors combined.[36] Even so, the volume and value of their produce doubled between the wars. Not only did the government make it possible for them to use coerced black labor; it also provided them with massive financial assistance. Between 1911 and 1936, the government spent £112 million on agriculture, in the form of direct assistance and subsidies, tariff protection, research, administration, and the dissemination of information. In addition, the state railways charged exceptionally low rates on farm produce. Nearly all of this assistance went to white farmers; scarcely any went to Africans in the reserves.[37]

More and more South Africans, meanwhile, were moving to the cities, especially Johannesburg, Cape Town, Durban, Pretoria, and Port Elizabeth. Most were Whites who were squeezed out by the increasing commercialization of agriculture and Africans who could not survive in the reserves. By 1936, according to the official census of that year, the urban population numbered more than 3 million and comprised 31 percent of the total population. Of this, about 1.3 million were classified as White, 1.1 million as African, 400,000 as Coloured, and 200,000 as Asian. Sixty-five percent of the White population of South Africa, 44 percent of the Coloured, 66 percent of the Asian, and 17 percent of the African population were in the towns. Johannesburg, the largest city, had 519,000 inhabitants: 258,000 Whites, 229,000 Africans, 22,000 Coloureds, and 10,000 Asians.[38]

The government tried to limit the flow of Africans into the cities with a complex accumulation of pass laws. The origin of those laws goes back to the eighteenth century, when slaves were obliged to carry documents signed by their masters when they were absent from their masters' homes. Some pass laws were designed to ensure that white farmers should not lose their African laborers. It was unlawful, for example, for Africans to leave the farms where they were employed without a pass (Document of Identification) provided by the farmer. Others were designed to prevent Africans from living in towns except as laborers for Whites. By 1930 in the Transvaal, for example, an African entering a proclaimed urban area was obliged to report to an official within twenty-four hours and obtain a permit to seek work. The official would issue a permit only if his other passes were in order. The permit was valid for six days. If the African failed to produce it on demand by an official, he would be jailed or expelled from the town. The attempt to enforce such laws created a vast class of lawbreakers. In 1930, 42,000 Africans were convicted for pass law offenses in the Transvaal.[39] Nevertheless, despite the enactment of still tougher curbs in 1937, the African population of the towns continued to increase.

The gold-mining industry continued to be the backbone of the South African economy. After 1933, the rise in the price of gold made it practicable to mine a large tonnage of low-grade ore. On the eve of World War II, the industry was producing one-fifth of the country's net income, contributing more than two-fifths of the revenue, accounting for three-quarters of the exports, and providing the nucleus for a rapid growth of manufacturing industry.

In 1939, the gold mines employed 364,000 workers: 43,000 Whites and 321,400 Africans. After 1910, the industry continued to attract skilled operatives from overseas, but most of the white miners were South African-born. The industry drew African workers from a wide region within and beyond the borders of South Africa and avoided competition among the mining companies by joining in a monopsony. The Native Recruiting Corporation ran a network of recruiting stations in South Africa, Basutoland, southern Bechuanaland, and Swaziland. The Witwatersrand Native Labour Association operated in Mozambique and, after 1933, in Nyasaland, Tanganyika, Northern Rhodesia, northern Bechuanaland, South West Africa, and Angola. By 1936, 52 percent of the African mine workers came from within South Africa (39 percent from the Cape Province) and 48 from outside the country, especially from Mozambique (28 percent) and Basutoland (15 percent).[40]

Soon after the foundation of the Union of South Africa, the state gave legal effect to color bars that had previously existed in the mining industry, in custom if not in law. In 1911, the government prohibited strikes by African mine workers and issued regulations under a Mines and Works Act to give white workers a monopoly of skilled operations. On that basis, mine labor continued to be split on a hierarchical, racial basis. The all-white Mine Workers' Union, founded in 1902, was a formidable force. It won relative security of long-term employment for its members and the continuation of a vast gap between their wages and those of African workers. After 1920, the gap was never less than eleven to one in cash wages, or ten to one when allowance is made for the food that the companies supplied to the African workers. Furthermore, by 1939 white miners were receiving paid leave and pensions, which Africans did not receive, and far larger disability payments than those for Africans.[41]

In 1922, as we have seen, the mining companies tried to offset the high cost of white labor by reducing the proportion of white workers from 1 White to 8.2 Africans to 1 to 11.4. But, although the Smuts government used military force to overcome white resistance, the votes of white workers brought Hertzog's Afrikaner Nationalist party into power in alliance with white labor in 1924. The proportion of white workers employed in the gold mines increased thereafter, reaching 1 white to 7.5 Africans in 1939, even though the wage gap gave the companies a strong inducement to decrease the proportion of Whites. The mineowners had learned that in a country where Whites had votes and (except to a limited extent in the Cape Province) Blacks had none, it was not politically possible to replace some of its expensive white labor with Africans.[42]

Labor in the South African gold mines is arduous, unhealthy, and dangerous. The heat is intense. The stopes are so narrow that men work at the rock-face in a crouching position. Between 1933 and 1966, 19,000 gold-miners, 93 percent of them Africans, died as a result of accidents.[43] Many Africans miners contracted diseases on the mines. During 1931, the Miners' Pthisis Medical Bureau classified 1,370 African miners as suffering from tuberculosis or lung diseases, or both, caused by mining.[44] Living conditions were appalling. Down to World War II and beyond, only 1 percent of African mine workers were legally eligible for family housing. The rest were housed, as in the past, in single-sex compounds with between three and six thousand men to a compound. Those built before World War I housed between sixty and ninety men to a dormitory; those built during the 1930s, about twenty. Beds were not supplied. Men either slept on the short concrete bunks or made or bought wooden beds designed to fit them. The food, though nutritious, was unattractive and monotonous. Most mines had no dining rooms and men ate outside or in their dormitories.[45]

The mines were run on military lines. The officers—the shift bosses and compound managers—were white; the noncommissioned officers—the underground "boss-boys" and compound "indunas"—as well as the mass of laborers, were black. No women were allowed in the compounds.[46]

The state used its power to apply racial discrimination in manufacturing industries and public works. For this purpose, the Hertzog government invented a convenient euphemism. Instead of admitting that he was discriminating on grounds of race, Hertzog said he was discriminating in favor of "persons whose standard of living conforms to the standard generally recognised as tolerable from the usual European standpoint," as contrasted with "persons whose aim is restricted to the bare requirements of the necessities of life as understood by barbarous and undeveloped peoples."

To stimulate growth, he provided manufacturing industries with tariff protection, provided that they maintained a satisfactory ratio between "civilised" and "uncivilised" workers in each industry. Furthermore, the wages of "civilised" workers, including those engaged in unskilled work, were set at higher rates than those of "uncivilised" workers.[47]

Laws governing apprenticeship and industrial bargaining further buttressed the racial structure of industry. The Apprenticeship Act (1922) gave unionized white workers a secure position by setting educational qualifications for apprenticeship in numerous trades. That made it impossible for most Africans to be apprenticed, since they lacked the means to meet the prescribed educational level.[48] The Industrial Conciliation Act (1924) and its successors set up machinery for the prevention and settlement of disputes but excluded Africans from the definition of "employees." That meant that white workers negotiated with employers the conditions of employment for themselves and for the African workers. Africans, debarred from participation, fell under state legislation.[49]

Those decisions created pervasive racial discrimination in manufacturing and public works, as in the mining industry. Poverty among Whites was reduced at the expense of the black population, by giving Whites sheltered employment at uncompetitive wages in public works and in such state enterprises as the railroads. In manufacturing as in mining, moreover, the gap between skilled and unskilled wages was higher than in other industrializing countries, and Whites monopolized the skilled positions. In 1939, white workers earned 5.3 times as much as African workers in manufacturing and construction in South Africa.[50] Government officials knew of these disparities. The secretary for labour wrote in his annual report for 1938 that "the unskilled, and for the most part inarticulate section of the employees did not secure that share of the increased prosperity of industry to which they were in equity entitled."[51]

In addition to attempting to check the urbanization of Africans, the government tried to segregate Africans within the urban areas. By 1910, there were laws in the Cape Colony, Natal, and the Transvaal authorizing the colonial governments to create and control urban "locations" for Africans, but many townships, especially the large cities, had areas where Whites and Blacks lived alongside one another. As the urban population increased, so did slums, crime, and disease. In 1918, there was a severe influenza epidemic. Five years later, the Smuts government enacted the Natives (Urban Areas) Act, which empowered an urban authority, subject to the approval of the government, to establish an African location. The government could then order all Africans in that town, except domestic servants, to reside in the location. The location was to be administered by a superintendent, assisted by an African advisory council, and employers were to be responsible for providing housing for their employees. When the act had been applied to a town, the urban authority was empowered to expel Africans if they did not carry registered service contracts or permits to seek work. An amendment of 1930 specifically empowered an urban authority to remove "surplus females." This law was applied seriatim to most of the towns in the country, but the process was slow. By 1932, it had been applied to fifty-one towns in the country, including Cape Town and Pretoria, but was not yet fully in force in Johannesburg, Durban, or Port Elizabeth.[52]

Over the years, South African towns acquired a characteristic dual form. The largest and most conspicuous part was a spacious modern town, consisting of a business sector where people of all races worked during the day and suburbs of detached houses, ranging from opulent to mediocre, owned by white families and served by black domestics. Separated from the modern town was a black location, where mud, clapboard, or corrugated iron buildings, with earth latrines, stood on tiny plots of land and were served by water from infrequent taps along the unpaved paths and roads. With various anomalies, the same principle applied in a hundred or more country villages. There were modifications in Durban and Pietermaritzburg, which contained districts where Indian and white shops and households intermingled. In Cape Town, Whites and Coloureds lived alongside one another in several districts, and District Six, abutting on the business center, was long-established as the home of Coloured People.

Black Adaptation and Resistance, 1910–1939

Before World War II, the subject peoples lacked the means to oppose the growth of the power of the South African state. Whites had a virtual monopoly of military weapons and training. The Defence Act of 1912 created an all-white Active Citizen Force. In World War I, black South Africans served in campaigns in South West Africa, East Africa, and Europe, and 5,635 Blacks lost their lives. Most, notably the 21,000 African members of the South African Native Labour Contingent in France, were employed as unarmed laborers. The exception was the Cape Corps, which consisted of white officers and Coloured other ranks and was organized as a combatant unit 18,000 strong in the East African campaign. White South

Africans deeply resented the arming of the Coloured batallions, however, and at war's end the government disbanded all the black units and failed to recognize their services.[53]

Black South African resistance to the racial order was impeded not only by Blacks' lack of access to firearms but also by their cultural and historical differences. Indian and Coloured South Africans had little in common with one another or with Africans, and were themselves disunited. Indians, amounting to 2 percent of the population of nearly ten million in 1936, were concentrated in Natal and the southern Transvaal and were first- and second-generation South Africans. Most were Hindus, the product of the process that had brought indentured laborers to Natal between 1860 and 1911. There was also a conspicuous minority of traders, mostly Muslims, who had come to South Africa independently; some of these had built up large businesses. Most Indians did not identify with the other subject peoples. Gandhi's movement won minor concessions for the Indian population but fought no battles on behalf of the Africans.[54]

The Coloured People—8 percent of the population—were concentrated in the Cape Province. They were exceptionally diverse by ethnic, cultural, and economic criteria. Members of the Cape Town Coloured elite, Muslims and Christians, were facing the fact that their status was deteriorating. Before Union, there had been no legal discrimination against Coloured People in the Cape Colony, and they had looked forward to a future of equal treatment and opportunity. After Union, legal discrimination against Coloured People as well as Africans increased in the northern provinces and extended to the Cape Province in the form of official regulations and administrative actions that made it difficult for Coloured People to compete with Whites in public service as well as private industry. The large Coloured underclasses, including illiterate, poorly paid farm laborers, had exceptionally high rates of illegitimacy, crime, and alcoholism, and many shared white fears and prejudices about Africans.[55]

The Africans—69 percent of the population of the Union of South Africa, according to the census of 1936—had different histories, experiences, and interests. In the reserves and adjacent British and Portuguese territories, Africans continued to live in homesteads or villages and to acknowledge the political authority of chiefs and headmen. Nevertheless, white magistrates, traders, missionaries, and recruiting agents were transforming their culture and their social and economic relations. As we have seen, labor migrancy was becoming a central feature of the political economy of the region, since few Africans were able to produce enough to feed themselves and pay their taxes. African families were being disrupted. Women were assuming some of the responsibilities of household heads previously reserved to men. With their wages, young men were acting independently of their seniors, buying cattle for their own bridewealth, forming their own associations, and establishing their own homesteads, creating tensions between the generations.

In the reserves, the ultimate authority in a district was the white magistrate, but he had little physical force at his disposal. He relied on the cooperation of the chiefs, who continued to settle disputes among Africans and to control the distribution of land but also tolerated the collection of taxes and received a small salary. A chief was therefore caught in the middle. He was legally responsible to the state but socially dependent on the support of the community. As Shula Marks has demonstrated in the case of Solomon ka Dinuzulu, the Zulu king who died in 1934, a chief held an ambiguous position; to be successful, he had to be a shrewd reinterpreter of tradition and a skillful manipulator of people, white as well as black.[56]

Missionaries presided over "an enormous benevolent empire" that reached into every African reserve community. In 1928, forty-eight missionary organizations were operating in the Union of South Africa. They employed over 1,700 white missionaries, teachers, doctors, and nurses and over 30,000 African clergy, lay preachers, and teachers.[57] Receiving grants-in-aid from the provincial governments, the missions ran virtually the only institutions where Africans could acquire the literary skills necessary for effective participation in the industrializing economy. In 1935, they registered 342,181 African pupils. Over half of them were in the elementary Standards, and most of the rest were in Standards 1 to 6. Only 1,581 Africans were in Standards 7 and 8, and a mere 193 were in Standards 9 and 10, which culminated in the matriculation, or school-leaving, examination and corresponded with the eleventh and twelfth grades in the United States.[58]

Most teachers in the mission schools were Africans, who, being underqualified and poorly paid, could provide no more than a rudimentary elementary education. Some were responsible for as many as eighty pupils. Several high schools, however, were staffed by relatively competent people—notably, Adams College in Natal (American Board of Foreign Missions), St. Peter's in the Transvaal (Anglican), and Healdtown (Methodist) and, above all, Lovedale (United Free church of Scotland) in the eastern Cape Province. At the top of the system was the South African Native

College at Fort Hare in the Ciskei, which was founded by the Methodist, Anglican, and Scottish missions with government support in 1916. By 1940, Fort Hare had 195 students, primarily Africans but some Coloureds and Indians. Even so, because they were preparing students for public examinations controlled by white South African educators, students in this system were obliged to conform to officially prescribed syllabuses. The history syllabuses and textbooks, in particular, expressing the dominant assumptions of the period, treated the history of South Africa as the record of white settlement and had no empathy with African culture, the African side of conflicts, or the condition of Africans since the conquest. In his memoirs, Z. K. Matthews, an African who became a lawyer and received a master's degree from Yale University, recalled his time as a student at Lovedale and Fort Hare:

> Our history, as we had absorbed it from the tales and talk of our elders, bore no resemblance to South African history as it has been written by European scholars, or as it is taught in South African schools, and as it was taught to us at Fort Hare. . . . The syllabus for matriculation emphasized South African history, so . . . we struggled through the white man's version of the so-called Kaffir Wars, the Great Trek, the struggles for control of South Africa . . . and . . . we had to give back in our examination papers the answers the white man expected.[59]

Africans who lived on white farms had exceptionally bitter experiences. "Unskilled and easily replaceable," as well as "isolated and illiterate," they were "grouped in tiny clusters, and separated by vast distances and wretched poverty from others, even within the same district."[60] Their main concern was to retain the use of the land they regarded as rightfully theirs. But white landowners, operating in adverse market conditions and coping with droughts and pests, were themselves hard pressed to make a living and were trying to do so by squeezing the utmost from their "volk," expelling those who were surplus to their needs, converting the rest into laborers, and paying them as little as possible.

Following the white conquest, new cleavages meshed with old in the African societies. One can distinguish four main tendencies.[61] The African masses were largely concerned with their immediate situation, whether they resided in the reserves, on white farms, or in towns or were migrant laborers moving between the reserves and the white areas. Their grievances were specific, and with few exceptions, they held fast to traditional African values. Whatever their situation, they relied heavily on their extensive kinship networks. Poor or incapacitated people received food and shelter from relatives. African women were especially resilient in the responsibilities that were thrust on them.

Second, the chiefs and headmen more or less reluctantly, and more or less skillfully, adapted to the loss of their autonomy and to their ambiguous roles in the white state. Third, a small, relatively prosperous educated elite monopolized the salaried jobs—high school teachers, ministers in the mission churches, official interpreters. They tended to accept the premise of liberal ideology, with its distinction between barbarism and civilization, and to see themselves as the modernizers of African society. Finally, many people had a little education but failed to get or to hold salaried jobs. They were particularly frustrated, alienated from traditional society but excluded from the benefits of modernization. Many joined independent churches and espoused an Africanist ideology, with modern as well as traditional elements.

In the reserves, Africans used a variety of stratagems to improve their lot. William Beinart and Colin Bundy have demonstrated in eight case studies from the Transkei that "peasants/migrants were trying to defend their rights to land, their ownership of cattle and other resources, and their ability to affect local political processes."[62] Before 1939, these were the main forms of political expression for most Africans. Though their successes were few and their links with national movements sporadic, they exemplified the vitality of local political life and their deep-seated desire to control their lives.

Three political organizations strove to improve the lot of the subordinated peoples on the national scale: a Coloured organization, the African Political Organization (APO), founded in 1902; an Indian organization, the South African Indian Congress (SAIC), which was founded in 1923, and the South African Native National Congress (later known as the African National Congress, or ANC), founded in 1912.[63]

The leaders of those three organizations were Western-oriented middle-class people, the products of the best schools available. They aimed to realize the promise inherent in the Cape colonial tradition, first by gaining full equality with Whites for the middle classes they represented, and later by extending the benefits to the masses of their people. The precedent they had in mind was the step-by-step extension of the parliamentary franchise to all classes in England. They sought by rational argument and pressure within the framework of the constitution to persuade the white electorate to reverse the discriminatory tide.

The founders of the ANC, Pixley ka Isaka Seme, Alfred Mangena, Richard Msimang, and George Montsioa, were mission-educated Christians who had qualified as lawyers in England. Seme, for example, had grown up on the American mission station in Natal, attended Mount Hermon School in Massachusetts, received a bachelor's degree from Columbia University, studied law at Oxford University, and been called to the British bar in 1910. In his keynote address to the founding conference of the ANC in Bloemfontein, Seme said that "in the land of their birth, Africans are treated as hewers of wood and drawers of water." He added: "The white people of this country have formed what is known as the Union of South Africa—a union in which we have no voice in the making of laws and no part in their administration. We have called you therefore to this Conference so that we can together devise ways and means of forming our national union for the purpose of creating national unity and defending our rights and privileges."[64] In the spirit of the black American educator Booker T. Washington, the ANC constitution proclaimed "loyalty to all lawfully constituted authorities" and stressed "the educational, social, economic and political elevation of the native people in South Africa."[65]

Down to 1939 and beyond, the ANC remained under the control of lawyers, clergy, and journalists, who tried to elicit white support to redress African grievances "by constitutional means." Most of the time they adhered scrupulously to those cautious methods and modest objectives, lobbying sympathetic white missionaries, journalists, and politicians and protesting each installment of discriminatory legislation from the Natives Land Act of 1913 through the Representation of Natives Act of 1936. In 1914, they sent a fruitless delegation to England; in 1919, they sent another to Versailles to try to influence the peacemakers on their behalf.

The Coloured and Indian organizations were under similar middle-class leadership and pursued corresponding goals for their people. Abdullah Abdurahman, president of the APO from 1905 until his death in 1940, was a doctor trained at Glasgow University; the leaders of the SAIC were such men as P. R. Pather, an estate and financial agent, and Abdulla Ismail Kajee, a businessman. The APO made some not very successful efforts to cooperate with African leaders, but the SAIC concerned itself exclusively with the interests of the Indian population.[66]

In the 1920s and 1930s, members of all three organizations worked with such white liberals as Edgar Brookes, who represented Africans as a senator under the legislation of 1936. In and after 1921, liberals established a number of joint councils, where small groups of Whites, Africans, Coloureds, and Asians met to discuss racial problems, and in 1919, they founded the South African Institute of Race Relations, which collected and published information about the effects of segregation and discrimination. Few white South Africans, however, were susceptible to the influence of those bodies. Most Whites were determined to maintain their own privileges and power. The ANC, APO, and SAIC thus won no substantial victories; nor did they mobilize the black masses. By the 1930s, indeed, they were moribund.

Sporadic attempts were made to create more radical movements. The most spectacular such organization was founded by Clements Kadalie, a mission-educated African from Nyasaland (modern Malawi).[67] In 1919, Kadalie formed a small trade union among Coloured dockworkers in Cape Town; by 1928, it had swollen into a nationwide Industrial and Commercial Workers Union (ICU), claiming a membership of more than 150,000 Africans, 15,000 Coloureds, and 250 Whites. By then, it was primarily a rural movement, tapping, especially, African sharecroppers' and tenant laborers' land hunger and exasperation as white landowners were squeezing them while they themselves were struggling for economic survival.

The ICU organizers were frustrated Africans who had had a few years of missionary education but had not fulfilled the expectations of upward mobility engendered in their schools. They regarded the leaders of the ANC as "good boys" who were tied to the apron strings of white liberals. Drawing ideas from the independent churches, from Marxism, and from the back-to-Africa movement of Marcus Garvey, they galvanized rural audiences with strong rhetoric, including promises of land repossession and national liberation. In the Transkei there were echoes of the millennial beliefs that had led to the cattle-killing in 1857: "Ama Melika"—the Afro-Americans—were coming with ships and planes to liberate South Africa and destroy all Whites and black nonbelievers.[68] Incidents occurred from the eastern Cape to the northern Transvaal. Africans refused to work, deserted, stole livestock, destroyed property.

White farmers and the government acted ruthlessly to suppress the ICU, harassing organizers and evicting "trouble-makers." The ICU leaders, moreover, proclaimed grandiose goals but failed to design realistic programs of action, became corrupt and quarrelsome, and lost touch with the masses. Kadalie himself drew a salary of thirty pounds a month, at least sixty times that of many farm laborers; some Africans came to regard him as "a great cheat."[69] The movement disintegrated into numerous uncoordinated segments and petered out in the early 1930s. "It all ended up in speeches," according to a former tenant laborer in the Transvaal.[70]

In 1921, meanwhile, a small group of white intellectuals had founded the South African Communist party. It was the only political organization in South Africa that recruited members from all racial groups and had a multiracial executive. But, like other Communist parties outside the Soviet Union, it was subject to directives from Moscow, notably in 1928, when the Communist International ordered it to cease giving priority to the class struggle and to adopt the slogan and analysis of an "independent South African Native republic" or "black republic," which threw the party into turmoil and led to schisms. The Communist party never gained a wide following. Its membership peaked at about three thousand in 1930 and then declined. Nevertheless, it exerted a considerable influence on the ICU, and by 1939, it was beginning to attract several of the younger and more frustrated members of the ANC, APO, and SAIC.[71]

World War II and the Triumph of Afrikaner Nationalism

During World War II, South African forces fought in East and North Africa and in Italy. At war's end, 218,260 South Africans were in uniform: 135,171 white men, 12,878 white women, 27,583 Coloured men, and 42,627 African men. All were volunteers. The Coloured and African men were distributed among the white detachments as laborers and transport drivers. A few were trained in South Africa as gunners, but the white reaction was intense. Nationalist party leader D. F. Malan railed in Parliament against the employment of "Kaffir soldiers," and they were not used in combat. Even so, of the 5,500 South Africans who were killed in World War II, more than a quarter were black.[72]

South Africa also made significant strategic and economic contributions to the Allied cause. After the Axis closed the Mediterranean to Allied shipping in 1941, the sea route via the Cape of Good Hope became vital for supplying the Allied forces in North Africa as well as Asia. Durban and Cape Town provisioned the vast number of ships on passage to and from Egypt, and South African factories suppled them with munitions, food, clothing, and cigarettes. South Africa was also a major source of strategic minerals for the Allies, notably gold, platinum, and uranium; the products of the Iron and Steel Industrial Corporation (ISCOR), a state corporation created by the government in 1928, rose to 866,107 metric tons in 1945.[73]

Gold-mining remained the greatest South African industry. In 1946, it employed 370,959 people (42,624 Whites and 328,335 Blacks) and sold £102 million worth of gold. But whereas the gold-mining industry entered a period of slight decline after 1941, coal-mining and the manufacturing industries continued the rapid expansion that had begun in 1933. Between 1938–39 and 1945–46 the number of employees in the coal-mining industry increased by 50 percent to 51,643 and in manufacturing by 60 percent to 379,022. In particular, the garment industry nearly doubled in those years; by the end of the war it was employing 60,856 people and producing goods worth £42 million.[74]

This expansion drew more and more people into the towns. By 1946, 76 percent of the white population, 70 percent of the Indians, 62 percent of the Coloureds, and 24 percent of the Africans were in towns. The African figure was the most significant. There were more Africans than Whites in the towns by 1946. Moreover, whereas 55 percent of the Africans who were in towns at the time of the census of 1911 were male migrant laborers, serving short-term contracts in the gold, diamond, and coal mines, at the time of the census of 1946 only 21 percent of the urban Africans were employed by those industries. Large number of Africans, including African women, like Whites, Coloureds, and Asians, were settling permanently in the towns.[75] The most pregnant social process in South Africa in the first half of the twentieth century was this massive relocation of Africans, pushed out from the impoverished reserves and the gradually mechanizing white farms and pulled into the towns by the prospect of jobs in the burgeoning manufacturing and service industries. Economic forces were counteracting government policies that had aimed to keep Africans out of the towns, except as migrant laborers with domicile in the reserves.[76]

The government tried but failed to stop increased African settlement in the towns. And because neither the government, nor the urban authorities, nor industry provided housing for the influx, the Africans built shacks of sacks, wood, corrugated iron, and cardboard on the outskirts of the towns and improvised their own methods of social control. This squatting movement was especially effective outside Johannesburg. During the second half of the 1940s, between sixty thousand and ninety thousand Africans settled in squatter camps there, mainly in the area beyond the city's southwestern borders that later became know as Soweto. As Oriel Monongoaha, one of the squatter leaders, put it: "The Government is beaten, because even the Government of England could not stop the people from squatting. The Government was like a man who has a cornfield which is invaded by birds. He chases the birds from one part of the field and they alight in another part of the field. . . . We squatters are the birds. The Government sends its policemen to chase us away and we move off and occupy another spot."[77]

As more and more Africans became committed to urban life, they created a vigorous proletarian culture. The towns and squatter camps were violent places, seething with discontent. To survive in adverse circumstances, many people made a precarious living in the informal economy. Women ran *shebeens,* centers of liquor, fun, and sex; boys sold newspapers; gangs stole and fought. In Peter Abraham's novel *Mine Boy* (1946), a woman gives advice to a newcomer from the country: "In the city it is like this: all the time you are fighting. Fighting. Fighting! When you are asleep and when you are awake. And you look only after yourself. If you do not you are finished. If you are soft everyone will spit in your face. They will rob you and cheat you and betray you. So to live here you must be hard, hard as a stone. And money is your best friend. With money you can bribe a policeman. With money you can buy somebody to go to jail for you. That is how it is, Xuma."[78]

Rises in the cost of living exceeded any increases in the wages of those who had jobs. By 1945, food was particularly expensive as a result of a prolonged drought. The state itself continued to apply its Civilised Labour policy, providing sheltered employment for Whites and paying its unskilled white laborers more than twice as much as its unskilled African laborers.[79]

To cope with their predicament, Africans formed trade unions and organized numerous boycotts and strikes, although the Industrial Conciliation Act excluded Africans from participation in the collective bargaining process and the government made strikes illegal. By 1945, the Council of Non-European Trade Unions claimed a strength of 158,000 members in 119 unions, amounting to 40 percent of African employees in commerce and manufacturing.[80] The inhabitants of Alexandra, a township in the northeastern part of Johannesburg, repeatedly and successfully boycotted the buses that took them to work when the companies tried to raise the fares. For ten days in 1943, for example, 20,000 boycotters got up at three in the morning and walked to work, returning home at nine in the evening.[81]

The crucial terrain for labor relations was, as ever, the mining industries. Between 1939 and 1948, police or departmental inspectors reported over a hundred gold and coal mine disturbances to the Native Affairs Department. The largest was a four-day strike called by the African Mineworkers Union on the Witwatersrand in August 1946, when 74,000 workers brought eight gold mines to a standstill, after the Chamber of Mines had refused to accept the reformist recommendations of a government commission. The union demanded a minimum wage of ten shillings a day, family housing, paid leave, and better food. The government reacted brutally. It arrested strike leaders, drove men underground at bayonet point, killed 12 men, and injured more than 1,200. The Chamber of Mines then announced that the "Gold Mining Industry considers that trade-unionism as practised by Europeans is still beyond the understanding of the tribal Native. . . . A trade union organisation . . . would not only be useless, but detrimental to the ordinary mine Native in his present stage of development." The chamber's victory broke the African Mineworkers Union and seriously weakened the Council of Non-European Trade Unions.[82]

Between 1939 and 1948, the racial division among South African workers became sharper than before. This was largely because the wartime expansion involved changes in the structure of manufacturing industries. Before the war, for example, the Transvaal garment industry provided employment for many Afrikaner women who had moved from the farms to the towns. During the war, however, the expansion of the garment industry led to the employment of increasing numbers of Coloured and African women. Solly Sachs, an energetic socialist leader of the Garment Workers' Union, and several remarkable Afrikaner women, tried to maintain workers' solidarity across the color line, but by 1948 the Garment Workers Union had split into two racially defined branches, and segregation notices had gone up in entrances, elevators, and offices.[83]

The Smuts administration maintained the segregation system set out in the Representation of Natives Act (1936), the Native Trust and Land Act (1936), and the Native Laws Amendment Act (1937). Nevertheless, there was much uncertainty about the future. A small but articulate white intelligentsia concentrated at the University of the Witwatersrand and the Institute of Race Relations pressed for increased wages for black workers, the recognition of African trade unions, and the abolition of the pass laws. Commercial and industrial businesspeople saw a need for a stabilized work force rather than the migrant laborers used in the gold mines. A few senior officials who were aware of the miserable conditions of Africans' lives believed that the laborers posed dangers for the white population. In Parliament, the Africans' white representatives who were elected under the legislation of 1936 continuously pressed for reforms. Prime Minister Smuts's ablest cabinet colleague, J. H. Hofmeyr, who became deputy prime minister and heir apparent, gave them intermittent encouragement. He once declared in Parliament, "I take my stand on the ultimate removal of the colour bar from our constitution."[84] Smuts himself raised liberal hopes in 1942, when he admitted that he could not stop Africans from flocking to the towns and announced that "segregation has fallen on evil days."[85]

International events added to domestic pressures for reform. The propaganda of the Allies during the war against Nazism, including the Atlantic Charter, was antiracist. During 1942, the Japanese victories raised the possibility of a Japanese invasion of South Africa and with it the need to conciliate the black masses. And after the war ended, Smuts himself took part in drafting the Charter of the United Nations, the Dutch and the French failed to regain control of their eastern empires, and in 1947 the British government withdrew from India.

In response to those domestic pressures and external developments, the government appointed numerous committees and commissions, staffed by reform-minded white people, to investigate the racial problems of the country and to plan for the future. In their reports they criticized specific hardships experienced by black South Africans but cast their recommendations within the established segregation framework. One report exposed the appalling conditions in the reserves and denounced the system of migrant labor as "morally, socially, and economically wrong" and looked forward to "its ultimate disappearance."[86] Others, influenced by contemporary thought in Britain, proposed that welfare services should be created for all South Africans, on a segregated basis. Particularly significant was the report, issued in February 1948, of a commission chaired by Justice H. A. Fagan. It concluded that the trend toward urbanization was irreversible and recommended that the pass laws be eased and that the migrant stream be directed into the most useful channels by a national system of labor bureaus.[87]

Government and private industry actually made a few concessions to their reformist critics. They eased the job color bar, extended the industrial training facilities for Africans, raised black factory wages by a larger proportion than white wages, made Africans eligible for small old age and disability pensions, and increased the grant for African education and freed it from its dependence on African taxes. In 1942, they even relaxed the pass laws.[88]

But those reforms were mere palliatives. In 1946, the government was still paying more than twenty times as much per capita for white education as for black education. In 1942, moreover, Smuts removed from the cabinet Deneys Reitz, the minister who had been responsible for easing the application of the pass laws, and from the end of 1943 Reitz's successor was enforcing them as rigorously as ever. Smuts never wavered in his belief that Africans were an inferior people; his was at best a paternalist attitude. Like most contemporary white people in Europe and North America, as well as South Africa, he could not imagine that Africans themselves were capable of improving their own status and living conditions. "Of course," Smuts confided to a correspondent, "everybody [meaning, every white person] in this country is agreed that European and African should live apart and preserve their respective cultures."[89] Hofmeyr, too, never overcame his white South African fear of social mixing.[90] Even the parliamentary representatives of Africans, committed though they were to reform, had virtually no close social contacts with Africans and stopped short of recommending universal suffrage or social equality.

By the end of the war, a new generation of black leaders, faced by the growing gulf between African realities and African expectations, was seeking more effective methods of resistance. In 1943, the annual conference of the ANC adopted a statement, *Africans' Claims in South Africa,* which cited the Atlantic Charter and set out a bill of rights calling for the abolition of all discriminatory legislation, redistribution of the land, African participation in collective bargaining, and universal adult suffrage. That year a group of young professional Africans founded a youth league as a pressure group in the ANC, stressing the need for African self-reliance and unity. Graduates of the best missionary high schools in South Africa and of the Native College at Fort Hare, they included Nelson Mandela, Oliver Tambo, and Walter Sisulu. In 1945 and 1947, ANC delegates attended pan-African meetings in Manchester, England, and Dakar, Senegal, where they met such African nationalists as Léopold Sédar Senghor of Senegal, Jomo Kenyatta of Kenya, and Kwame Nkrumah of the Gold Coast (Ghana), who would soon become rulers of independent states. Nevertheless, in 1948 the ANC still had fewer than six thousand members, and it had no fully developed plan of action when white South Africans went to the polls in a general election.[91]

By that time, the Smuts government had finally lost the confidence of the older Africans who controlled the Natives Representative Council, created by the legislation of 1936. The councillors had become increasingly frustrated. They had taken their assignment seriously, but the government had continued to ignore their advice. In August 1946, when the council assembled in Pretoria for its regular session, the white chairman refused to make a statement about the massive strike of African miners that was taking place nearby on the Witwatersrand. The council then passed resolu-

tions denouncing the shooting of strikers, calling the government's maintenance of discriminatory laws and practices "the antithesis and negation of
the letter and spirit of the Atlantic Charter and the United Nations
Charter," and demanding the abolition of all discriminatory legislation.[92]

In November 1946, Hofmeyr, acting prime minister in the absence
of Smuts, who was attending a session of the United Nations, addressed
a final meeting of the council. He defended the government's racial policies and said that the removal of discriminatory laws "would not be in
the interests of the Native peoples, since experience has shown that the
average Native has not reached a stage in his development when he can
retain the ownership of land under conditions of free competition."[93]
The chairman of the council's caucus was Professor Z. K. Matthews, head
of the African Studies Department at the South African Native College.
In dignified language, Matthews replied to Hofmeyr's speech. It had,
he said, "raised no hope for the future as far as the African people are
concerned."[94] The council then adjourned, never to meet again. The ANC,
at its annual conference in December, 1946, endorsed the council's
decision.

By 1939, Afrikaners still dominated the agricultural sector of the economy, but more than half of the Afrikaner people were living in towns, where
they were struggling to establish themselves in an English-dominated milieu. They were concentrated in the lowest-level white occupations: unskilled laborers, miners and factory workers, teachers and junior civil
servants. Only a few were beginning to enter the professions or compete
with the English ascendancy in trade and business. In South Africa the
average English-speaking White was twice as wealthy as the average
Afrikaner.[95]

For many Afrikaners, ethnic identity was more important than occupational and class differences. The Broederbond, the Federasie van Afrikaanse Kultuurverenigings (Federation of Afrikaner Cultural Associations), the Afrikaner churches, the Reddingsdaadbond (Rescue Association), and the National party combined to mobilize Afrikaner cultural,
economic, and political power.

The outbreak of war caused deep splits among Afrikaners. The predominant feeling was one of profound dismay that the country should
again be allied to Britain in a European war. But Afrikaners reacted in
different ways. Thousands of young Afrikaners joined the army; indeed,
more than half of the white men in South Africa's armed forces were

Afrikaners, predominantly men of rural origins who had settled in the towns but had failed to prosper in their new environment.

Other Afrikaners tried to exploit the opportunities created by the German victories. German radio broadcasts in Afrikaans were beamed to South Africa. Afrikaner intellectuals who had studied in German universities, such as Nicholaas Diederichs (later president of the Republic of South Africa) and Piet Meyer (subsequently chairman of the South African Broadcasting Corporation), wrote articles, pamphlets, and books and spoke to enthusiastic audiences, using ideas from German national socialism. A certain J. Albert Coetzee started a pamphlet with the statement, "The history of South Africa is really the history of the origin of a new nation—of how, from different European nations, groups, and individuals it was separated, cut off, differentiated and specialized to form a new *volksgroep*, with its own calling and destiny, with its own traditions, with its own soul and with its own body."[96] The lexicon included explicit racism. In *Rasse en Rasvermenging* (Races and Race Mixing), G. Eloff described distinct white, black, and yellow races, each with its spiritual as well as biological characteristics: "The preservation of the pure race tradition of the *Boerevolk* must be protected at all costs in all possible ways as a holy pledge entrusted to us by our ancestors as part of God's plan with our People. Any movement, school, or individual who sins against this must be dealt with as a racial criminal by the effective authorities."[97]

A militant organization known as the Ossewa Brandwag (Oxwagon Sentinel) welcomed the spate of German successes and resorted to sabotage but did not threaten the state. Malan meanwhile retained control of the National party, which absorbed some of the men who had followed Hertzog out of the United party and ejected others, including Hertzog himself. The National party adhered to constitutional methods and, as the prospects of a German victory dwindled, won the whole-hearted allegiance of the Broederbond and the other Afrikaner cultural and economic organizations. Although the ruling coalition composed of the United party, the Labour party, and the anglophile Dominion party won 105 seats in the general election of 1943, the National party, with 43 seats, emerged as the parliamentary opposition.[98]

As the election of 1948 approached, the National party, assisted by the plethora of local branches of Afrikaner organizations, formed an effective alliance of the principal rural and urban classes of Afrikaners, appealing to their ethnic and racial attitudes, as well as their material interests. It attacked the British link, which had led to the involvement in two world wars and the alliance with communist Russia. It denounced Smuts as a British toady, pointing out that, in spite of his obsession with global politics, he had not deterred the United Nations from refusing to allow South Africa to incorporate South West Africa, nor had he stopped the United Nations from rebuking South Africa for limiting the rights of Indian traders in Natal and the Transvaal. It criticized the government for its liberal reforms and for its failure to stop both the flow of Africans into the towns and the outburst of African industrial strikes.[99]

Afrikaners were deeply worried about the state of race relations. Nearly all believed that the state should do more to maintain white supremacy and the "purity" of the white "race." They differed as to how that should be done. Farmers and businesspeople wanted unimpeded access to African labor, combined with stringent government controls over its allocation and discipline. By contrast, Afrikaner workers wanted greater protection from African competition—an attitude that harmonized with the ideas of intellectuals who were developing a blueprint for complete economic as well as political segregation of South African society.[100] Professor of Sociology at the University of Pretoria G. S. Cronje systematized those ideas in 'n Tuiste vir die Nageslag (A Home for Posterity), in which he argued that the only way to ensure the long-term survival of the Afrikaner people was to separate the races into completely distinct territories in South Africa and make the Whites do without black labor.[101] Cronje's book was the subject of earnest debate in Afrikaner cultural circles, including the South African Bureau of Racial Affairs, which Afrikaners founded in opposition to the liberal South African Institute of Race Relations. The Afrikaans press and the Afrikaner churches also publicized the ideal of absolute racial separation.

In 1946, the National party appointed a committee, chaired by Paul Sauer, a senior party politician, to prepare a policy statement on the racial problem. The Sauer report treated Indians as an alien, unassimilable element in South Africa. It recommended the rigorous segregation of the Coloured People, the consolidation of the African reserves, the removal of missionary control of African education, and the abolition of the Natives Representative Council and the representation of Africans in Parliament. On several crucial matters, however, the report was an inconsistent, contradictory hybrid of two competing ideas. It set out complete economic segregation of Africans in their reserves as an ultimate goal but qualified it by stressing the need to satisfy white farming and manufacturing interests. Everything possible should be done to deter the exodus of Africans from the farm. Labor bureaus should be created to harness African labor to meet the demands of both rural and urban employers. And the migrant system should be extended, not reduced. Urban African workers should not be accompanied by their families.[102] The label given to this policy was *Apartheid*, a coined word that Afrikaner intellectuals had begun to use in the 1930s.[103] It means, simply, Apartness.

In comparison with its opponents' preparation for the election, the United party campaign was feeble. Smuts, at seventy-eight, was tired and out of touch. Apart from Hofmeyr, the other members of the cabinet were inefficient and complacent. Unlike the Sauer report, the Fagan report was unclear and alarming to many Whites. In accepting Africans, including African women, as a permanent element in the urban population and in rejecting influx control, it aroused racial fears. The National party's election propaganda repeatedly pilloried Hofmeyr, Smuts's deputy, characterizing him as an extreme liberal under whom the South African population would be bastardized if he became prime minister.[104]

When the votes were counted, the National party had won seventy seats, mainly rural, and the United party had won sixty-five seats, mainly urban. Ironically, the United party would have won the election if the rural electoral divisions had not contained fewer voters than the urban divisions, as laid down in the constitution for which Smuts had been primarily responsible. Malan then formed a government in alliance with the Afrikaner party, a Hertzogite rump, which he soon absorbed. Afrikaners, skillfully mobilized, had peacefully won political control of a country in which they formed no more than 12 percent of the population.

On June 1, 1948, Malan arrived in Pretoria by train to receive a tumultuous welcome. "In the past," he said, "we felt like strangers in our own country, but today South Africa belongs to us once more. For the first time since Union, South Africa is our own. May God grant that it always remains our own."[105]

CHAPTER 6

The Apartheid Era
1948–1978

After its initial victory in 1948, the National party consolidated its power. In that year it created new parliamentary seats for representatives of white voters in South West Africa (six in the House of Assembly and four in the Senate) who were elected to support the government. Then, step by step, it eliminated every vestige of black participation in the central political system. In 1956, after a long political and legal struggle, it dealt the Coloured votes in the Cape Province, most of whom had supported the United party, the same blow as the Hertzog government had dealt the African voters in 1936: it placed them on a separate roll and gave them the right to elect Whites to represent them in Parliament. Fourteen years later, it abolished the parliamentary seats of the white representatives of both African and Coloured voters.[1]

For three decades, the National party had the support of the overwhelming majority of the Afrikaner people. In the election of 1966, it also began to win substantial support from English-speaking Whites, who were attracted by the government's determination to maintain control in the face of increasing black unrest and foreign criticism. It won successive elections by increasing majorities. The United party never recovered from its defeat in 1948. Once in 1959 its leaders actually tried to outbid the Nationalists in racism by rejecting the purchase of more land for Africans, whereupon its relatively liberal members broke ranks and founded the Progressive party. In 1977, a shadow of its former self, the United party dissolved. In the general election that year, the Nationalists won 134 seats in the House of Assembly, whereas the major opposition, the Progressive Federal party, won a mere 17 seats.

The National party used its control of the government to fulfill Afrikaner ethnic goals as well as white racial goals. It achieved a major ethnic objective in 1961 when, after obtaining a narrow majority in a referendum of the white electorate, the government transformed South Africa into a republic, thereby completing the process of disengagement from Great Britain. The government had intended to follow the precedent whereby India remained a member of the British Commonwealth when it became a republic. At a conference of Commonwealth countries, however, the African members, supported by Canada as well as India, sharply criticized apartheid, and South Africa then withdrew from that loose association.

The government meanwhile Afrikanerized every state institution, appointing Afrikaners to senior as well as junior positions in the civil service, army, police, and state corporations. Medical and legal professional associations, too, came increasingly under Afrikaner control. The government also assisted Afrikaners to close the economic gap between themselves and English-speaking white South Africans. It directed official business to Afrikaner banks and allotted valuable state contracts to Afrikaners. Afrikaner businesspeople channeled Afrikaner capital into ethnic banks, investment houses, insurance companies, and publishing houses. By 1976, Afrikaner entrepreneurs had obtained a firm foothold in mining, manufacturing, commerce, and finance—all previously exclusive preserves of English-speakers. Whereas in 1946 the average Afrikaner's income had been 47 percent that of an English-speaking white South African, in 1976 it had risen to 71 percent and continued to rise thereafter.[2]

The political successes of the National party were due in part to the rising standard of living of white South Africans of all classes. Except for recessions in the early 1960s and the late 1970s, the South African economy was buoyant. The value of South African output at 1970 prices grew from R 4,434 million in 1950 to R 15,474 million in 1979.[3] The Whites were the principal beneficiaries. White farmers, most of whom were Afrikaners, received massive state support. They mechanized their farms and trebled their output, while the government assisted them to obtain and keep black wage laborers and to eliminate the vestiges of black occupation of white land as sharecroppers or renters.

The Nationalist government also gave fierce expression to its determination to maintain white supremacy in postwar South Africa. Much of its early legislation coordinated and extended the racial laws of the segregation era and tightened up the administration of those laws. The term *apartheid,* however, soon developed from a political slogan into a drastic, systematic program of social engineering. The man largely responsible for that development was Hendrik Frensch Verwoerd.

Verwoerd was born in the Netherlands in 1901 and migrated to South Africa in 1903 with his pro-Boer Dutch parents. Brought up in Cape Town, Southern Rhodesia, and the Orange Free State, he identified passionately with the Afrikaners. In private life he was charming; in public affairs, dogmatic, intolerant, domineering, and xenophobic. After acquiring a doctorate in psychology at Stellenbosch, the premier Afrikaner university, and spending 1927 visiting German universities, he became professor of applied psychology at Stellenbosch. In the mid-1930s, he promoted the cause of the Poor Whites and opposed Jewish immigration from Nazi Germany. In 1937, he became founding editor of *Die Transvaler,* created with nationalist funds for the express purpose of rallying Transvaal Afrikaners to the party. By 1948, he was widely known as a fiery republican. Malan then made him an appointed senator and in 1950 minister of native affairs. He was prime minister of South Africa from 1958 until September 6, 1966, when, as he was about to make a major speech in Parliament, a deranged attendant stabbed him to death.[4]

During Verwoerd's premiership, apartheid became the most notorious form of racial domination that the postwar world has known. The cabinet, with enthusiastic support from the rank-and-file members of the National party, tried to plug every gap in the segregation order. The process continued under Verwoerd's successor, B. J. Vorster, prime minister from 1966 to 1978. The Smuts government had interned Vorster during World War II because he was a general in the extraparliamentary Ossewa Brandwag (Oxwagon Sentinel), which opposed South Africa's participation in the war. Since 1962, he had been minister of justice in Verwoerd's cabinet.

Apartheid

The National party government applied apartheid in a plethora of laws and executive actions.[5] At the heart of the apartheid system were four ideas. First, the population of South Africa comprised four "racial groups"— White, Coloured, Indian, and African—each with its own inherent culture. Second, Whites, as the civilized race, were entitled to have absolute control over the state. Third, white interests should prevail over black interests; the state was not obliged to provide equal facilities for the subordinate races. Fourth, the white racial group formed a single nation, with Afrikaans- and English-speaking components, while Africans belonged to several (eventually ten) distinct nations or potential nations—a formula that made the white nation the largest in the country.

Soon after coming to power in 1948, the government began to give effect to those ideas. The Population Registration Act (1950) provided the machinery to designate the racial category of every person. Its application led to the breaking up of homes; for example, where one parent was classified White and the other was classified Coloured. The Prohibition of Mixed Marriages Act (1949) and the Immorality Act (1950) created legal boundaries between the races by making marriage and sexual relations illegal across the color line. In 1953, after a court had ruled that segregation was not lawful if public facilities for different racial groups were not equal (as in waiting rooms at railroad stations), Parliament passed the Reservation of Separate Amenities Act to legalize such inequality.

As mentioned above, the National party used its majority in Parliament to eliminate the voting rights of Coloured and African people. During the 1950s, when the Nationalist party's majority in Parliament was still short of two-thirds, it enforced its will by a stratagem that circumvented the Constitution by packing the Senate (the upper house of Parliament) and the Appellate Division of the Supreme Court—South Africa's highest court. In 1951, it passed an act by the ordinary legislative procedure (that is, by simple majorities in each house, sitting separately) to remove Coloured voters from the common electoral rolls. The Appellate Division ruled that the law was invalid, because the Constitution required such an act to be passed by a two-thirds majority of both houses in a joint sitting. Parliament then passed another act by the ordinary procedure, purporting to transform Parliament into a High Court with the power to review and override such judgments of the Appellate Division. The Appellate Division ruled, however, that that act, too, was invalid, on the ground that the High Court was Parliament under another name. Foiled in that maneuver, in 1955 Parliament passed two more acts by the ordinary procedure: one adding sufficient nominated members to the Senate to give the government a two-thirds majority in a joint sitting, the other increasing the number of appellate judges from five to eleven. Finally, in 1956, a new act to revalidate the act of 1951 and deny the courts the power to inquire into its validity received a two-thirds majority in a joint sitting (thanks to the packed Senate), and the enlarged Appellate Division agreed that the act was valid. The government had used a blend of legalism and cunning to remove Coloured voters from the common roll.[6]

The government also transformed the administration of the African population. In 1951, it abolished the only official countrywide African institution, the Natives Representative Council. Then it grouped the reserves into eight (eventually ten) territories. Each such territory became a "homeland" for a potential African "nation," administered under white tutelage by a set of Bantu authorities, consisting mainly of hereditary chiefs. In its Homeland, an African "nation" was to "develop along its own lines," with all the rights that were denied it in the rest of the country. The legislative framework, foreshadowed by Verwoerd, was completed in 1971, when the Bantu Homelands Constitution Act empowered the government to grant independence to any Homeland.[7] Government propaganda likened this process to the contemporaneous decolonization of the European empires in tropical Africa (map 8).

The Transkei was the pacesetter for this process. The government made it "self-governing" in 1963 and "independent" in 1976. Bophuthatswana followed in 1977, Venda in 1979, and Ciskei in 1981. As they became "independent," their citizens were deprived of their South African citizenship. The Pretoria government also ensured that collaborative chiefs such as the Matanzima brothers in the Transkei controlled all the Homelands. KwaZulu, the most populous Homeland, was a partial exception. There, Chief Mangosuthu Buthelezi created a powerful political organization, Inkatha, refused to accept "independence" on the South African government's terms, and developed an ambiguous relationship with Pretoria.[8]

Although the South African economy burgeoned in the 1950s and 1960s, the Homelands remained economic backwaters. Nearly every Homeland consisted of several pieces of land, separated by white-owned farms. Bophuthatswana had nineteen fragments, some hundreds of miles apart; KwaZulu comprised twenty-nine major and forty-one minor fragments. Verwoerd forbade white capitalists from investing directly in the

8. The African "Homelands" of South Africa

Homelands, and the governments of the Homelands depended on sub-sidies from Pretoria. Under apartheid the condition of the Homelands continued to deteriorate. They could provide full subsistence to a smaller and smaller proportion of the African people. Consequently, the economic incentives for Africans to leave the Homelands, either as migrant laborers or permanently, grew more powerful than ever. The African people relied on wage labor in the great industrial complexes of the southern Transvaal and the Durban, Port Elizabeth, and Cape Town areas. Moreover, no foreign country recognized the sovereignty of the "independent" Homelands.

Apartheid included rigid and increasingly sophisticated controls over all black South Africans. The government tried to herd into the Homelands nearly all Africans, except those whom white employers needed as laborers. In 1967, the Department of Bantu Administration and Development stated this policy quite bluntly in a general circular: "It is accepted Government policy that the Bantu are only temporarily resident in the European areas of the Republic for as long as they offer their labour there. As soon as they become, for one reason or another, no longer fit for work or superfluous in the labour market, they are expected to return to their country of origin or the territory of the national unit where they fit ethnically if they were not born and bred in their homeland."[9] To give effect to this policy in the towns, the government intensified its predecessors' attempts to limit the influx of rural Africans by prohibiting them from visiting an urban area for more than seventy-two hours without a special permit and by authorizing officials to arrest any African who could not produce the requisite documents. Every year, more than 100,000 Africans were arrested under the pass laws; the number peaked at 381,858 in the year 1975–76.[10] The government also removed African squatters from unauthorized camps near the cities, placing those who were employed in segregated townships, and sending the rest either to the Homelands or to farms where the white owners required their labor.

The government also began to eliminate "black spots" in the countryside—that is to say, land owned or occupied by Africans in the white areas. And since white farming was becoming largely commercial and mechanized, Africans lost their last land rights on white farms and many Blacks became redundant to the labor needs of farmers. The "surplus" Africans were expelled from the white rural areas, and, because they could not enter the towns, most were obliged to resettle in the Homelands, even if they had never been there before. In several cases, the government started new townships alongside existing urban complexes and treated them as parts of Homelands, as in Mdantsane in the Ciskei outside East London and Umlazi in KwaZulu outside Durban. In other cases, displaced people were congregated so densely in Homelands, far from the existing urban complexes, that they formed new townships. In 1980, in the tiny Sotho

Homeland called QwaQwa, 157,620 Africans were trying to survive on 239 square miles.[11]

In the cities outside the Homelands, the government transferred large numbers of Coloureds and Indians, as well as Africans, from land they had previously occupied to new segregated satellite townships. Under the Group Areas Act (1950) and its many subsequent amendments, the government divided urban areas into zones where members of one specified race alone could live and work. In many cases, areas that had previously been occupied by Blacks were zoned for exclusive white occupation. Of the numerous removals effected under this act, one of the most notorious was Sophiatown, four miles west of Johannesburg center. Sophiatown was one of the few townships where Africans had owned land since before the Urban Areas Act (1923) put an end to African purchases. In 1955, the government removed the African inhabitants to Meadowlands, twelve miles from the city. Sophiatown was rezoned for Whites and renamed Triomf (Triumph). Another notorious removal was District Six, adjacent to the center of Cape Town, which had been the home of a vibrant Coloured community since at least the early nineteenth century. The homes were razed and the inhabitants relocated to the sandy, wind-swept Cape flats. In Durban, many Indians also suffered severely, losing homes and businesses in areas zoned for Whites.[12]

The government claimed that these removals were voluntary. In fact, it intimidated the victims and when they resisted used force. An African woman who had been moved to a Homeland told an interviewer: "When they came to us, they came with guns and police. . . . They did not say anything, they just threw our belongings in [the government trucks] . . . . We did not know, we still do not know this place. . . . And when we came here, they dumped our things, just dumped our things so that we are still here. What can we do now, we can do nothing. We can do nothing. What can we do?"[13]

One cannot know for sure how many Blacks were uprooted by those measures. The number was certainly vast. The Surplus People Project, which made a thorough study of the removals, estimated that 3,548,900 people were removed between 1960 and 1983: 1,702,400 from the towns, 1,129,000 from farms, 614,000 from black spots, and 103,500 from strategic and developmental areas.[14]

The removals resulted in a great intensification of the overpopulation problem in the Homelands. At the time of the 1950 census, 39.7 percent of the African population of South Africa lived in the areas that became

Homelands; in 1980, 52.7 percent was there. The Homeland population increased by 69 percent between 1970 and 1980, by which time the density of population in the Homelands was 23.8 per square mile, compared with 9.1 for all of South Africa, including the Homelands. In spite of all those removals, the African population of the towns continued to increase rapidly under apartheid, and so did the Coloured and Asian urban populations. By 1980, the towns were occupied overwhelmingly by Blacks. Their 4 million white inhabitants were greatly outnumbered by 6.9 million Africans, 2 million Coloureds, and 700,000 Indians.[15]

By that time, the black urban settlements of the war years had expanded into vast "townships" adjacent to the major white "cities"—Johannesburg, Durban, Port Elizabeth, Pretoria, and even Cape Town where previously few Africans had lived. Hundreds of thousands of Africans had been born and bred in the towns, and nearly as many African women as men were living there. Still the government persisted in treating all urban Africans as visitors whose real homes were in the Homelands and whose real leaders were "tribal" chiefs. Moreover, the material gap between employed Africans and employed Whites increased significantly between 1948 and 1970, by which time white manufacturing and construction workers were earning six times as much as Africans and white mineworkers were earning no less than twenty-one times as much as Africans. In 1971 the real wages of African mineworkers were less than they had been in 1911. During the 1970s, African wages began to rise in response to competition among employers for experienced workers and vigorous African trade union activity—even though African trade unionism was illegal. The gap was down to 4.4 in manufacturing and construction and 5.5 in mining by 1982.[16] But wage rates do not provide a complete picture of the condition of the Africans. Unemployment, always high among black South Africans, increased during the 1970s. South African economist Charles Simkins estimated that African unemployment almost doubled from 1.2 million to 2.3 million between 1960 and 1977, by which time perhaps 26 percent of Africans were unemployed.[17] Consequently, Blacks experienced high levels of poverty, undernutrition, and disease, especially tuberculosis.

The government also intensified its control of the educational system. Although it treated Whites as a single entity in politics, in defense of Afrikaans culture it insisted on separation between Afrikaners and other Whites in the public schools. Building on the policy that J. B. M. Hertzog had initiated in the Orange Free State, the government maintained parallel sets of white public schools throughout the country and made it compulsory for a white child to attend a public school that used the language of the child's home—Afrikaans or English.

Previously, as we have seen, the government had left African education almost entirely to the mission institutions, whose capacity to meet the needs of the large African population was constrained by lack of funds, despite increasing public subsidies. This was unsatisfactory to the Nationalist government. It considered that the mission schools were transmitting dangerous, alien ideas to their African students and turning them, in Verwoerd's words, into Black Englishmen. As the economy expanded and became more sophisticated, moreover, industry required more literate workers than the mission schools could produce. Under the Bantu Education Act (1953) the central government thus assumed control of public African education from the provincial administrations, made it virtually impossible for nongovernmental schools to continue, and proceeded to expand African education while controlling it firmly. During the 1960s, the government also assumed control over the education of Coloured and Asian children. Verwoerd was frank on the subject of African education: "Native education should be controlled in such a way that it should be in accord with the policy of the state. . . . If the native in South Africa today in any kind of school in existence is being taught to expect that he will live his adult life under a policy of equal rights, he is making a big mistake. . . . There is no place for him in the European community above the level of certain forms of labour."[18]

Under government control, the number of black children at school increased considerably. By 1979, 3,484,329 African children in the entire country including the Homelands (21.41 percent of the African population of the country) were officially listed as attending school. Substantial differences remained in the quality of education provided for different "races," however. Education was compulsory for white but not black children. White children had excellent school buildings and equipment; black children, distinctly inferior facilities. Most African children were in the pre-primary and the primary classes. In 1978, when there were five times as many African children as white children in South Africa, only 12,014 Africans passed the matriculation examination or its equivalent (similar to American graduation from high school), whereas three times as many Whites did so. The government spent ten times as much per capita on white students as on African students, and African classes were more than twice as large as white ones. Moreover, most teachers in African schools were far less qualified than the teachers in white schools; African teachers were paid less than Whites even when they did have the same qualifications; and they had to teach African schoolchildren from textbooks and to prepare for examinations that expressed the government's racial views. The white schools were also superior to the Coloured and Indian schools, though to a lesser extent.[19]

The government imposed segregation in higher education as well. When the National party came to power in 1948, there were in South Africa four English-language universities, four Afrikaans-medium universities, one bilingual correspondence university, and the small South African Native College at Fort Hare. Though autonomous, all were largely dependent on government subsidies. The Afrikaans-medium universities and English-medium Rhodes University admitted white students only. Twelve percent of the students at the University of Cape Town and 6 percent of the students at the University of the Witwatersrand were black and were taught in integrated classes; 21 percent of the students in the University of Natal were black and were taught in segregated classes.[20]

In 1959, brushing aside large-scale student and faculty opposition in the English-medium universities, Parliament passed the Extension of University Education Act, which prohibited the established universities from accepting black students except with the special permission of a cabinet minister and led to the foundation of three segregated colleges under tight official control for Coloured, Indian, and Zulu students and another one for African students in the Transvaal. At the same time, the government took over the South African Native College at Fort Hare, fired the principal and seven senior staff members, and made it a college for Xhosa students, subjecting it to the same controls as the other black colleges. By 1978, nearly 150,000 students were enrolled in universities in South Africa, 80 percent of them White.[21]

From 1948 on, "Whites Only" notices appeared in every conceivable place. Laws and regulations confirmed or imposed segregation for taxis, ambulances, hearses, buses, trains, elevators, benches, lavatories, parks, church halls, town halls, cinemas, theaters, cafes, restaurants, and hotels, as well as schools and universities. It was also official policy to prevent interracial contacts in sport: no integrated teams and no competitions between teams of different races in South Africa, and no integrated teams representing South Africa abroad. Although no legislation was specifically designed to give effect to this policy, the government was able to keep sports segregated under other legislation, such as the Group Areas Act.[22] Verwoerd even tried to prohibit Blacks from attending church services in white areas and moderated his demands only when Geoffrey Clayton, Anglican archbishop of Cape Town, died of a heart attack after signing a letter saying he could not counsel members of his church to obey such legislation.[23]

The government also established tight controls over the communications media. The South African Broadcasting Corporation (SABC), a public corporation controlled by government appointees, had a monopoly on radio broadcasting and on television when it began to operate in South Africa in 1976. Chaired by Piet J. Meyer, who had been interned as an Ossewa Brandwag leader during World War II, the SABC became an instrument of official propaganda. Other government-appointed bodies exercised wide powers of censorship. In 1977, for example, they banned 1,246 publications, 41 periodicals, and 44 films. Most of those banned publications were books and pamphlets dealing with such radical opposition movements as the African National Congress, so that it became difficult for South Africans to find out what opposition movements were doing and thinking.[24]

The impact of the Nationalist regime on the mentality of Afrikaners was profound. Their language was unique, and most Afrikaners experienced little but the Nationalist world perspective from cradle to grave: at home, in Afrikaans-language schools and universities, in Dutch Reformed churchs, in social groups, on radio and television, and in books and newspapers. In particular, their schools imbued them with a political mythology derived from a historiography that distorted the past for nationalist purposes. For example, it made heroes out of the border ruffians who were responsible for the Slagtersnek rebellion in 1815, and it associated God with the victory of the Afrikaner commando over the Zulu at the battle of Blood River on December 16, 1838.[25]

The Nationalist government inherited a substantial coercive apparatus from its predecessors. It expanded that apparatus prodigiously.[26] Among its first punitive laws was the Suppression of Communism Act (1950), which defined communism in sweeping terms and gave the minister of justice summary powers over anyone who in his opinion was likely to further any of the aims of communism. The minister could "ban" a person and prevent him or her from joining specified organizations, communicating with another banned person, or publishing anything at all; or he could confine the person to his or her house without the right to receive visitors.

The minister did not have to give reasons for his decision, and the victim had no legal means of challenging it.

The repressive legislation escalated from the mid-1950s onward. The catalog includes the Riotous Assemblies Act (1956), the Unlawful Organizations Act (1960), the Sabotage Act (1962), the General Law Amendment Act (1966), the Terrorism Act (1967), and the Internal Security Act (1976). That mass of legislation gave the police vast powers to arrest people without trial and hold them indefinitely in solitary confinement, without revealing their identities and without giving them access to anyone except government officials. The government could ban any organization, prohibit the holding of meetings of any sort, and prevent organizations from receiving funds from abroad. There were also laws giving the government special powers over Africans, such as the Bantu Laws Amendment Act (1964), which empowered the government to expel any African from any of the towns or the white farming areas at any time. The Public Safety Act (1953) included a provision that empowered the government to declare a state of emergency in any or every part of the country and to rule by proclamation, if it considered that the safety of the public or the maintenance of public order was seriously threatened and that the ordinary law was inadequate to preserve it. Most of those repressive laws barred the courts from inquiring into the ways in which officials used their delegated powers. Although some judges sought to protect individuals by finding humane interpretations in the laws, their capacity to do so was very limited.

To administer the laws of apartheid, the bureaucracy grew enormously. By 1977, about 540,000 Whites were employed in the public sector (including the central, provincial, and homeland governments, the local authorities, the statutory public bodies, the railways and harbors service, and the postal service), and Afrikaners occupied more than 90 percent of the top positions. The vast majority of the white bureaucrats were ardent supporters of apartheid. Most of the black bureaucrats, numbering about 820,000, were reliable servants of the regime on which they depended for their livelihood.[27]

To enforce the laws of apartheid, the government had powerful resources. Few black civilians were licensed to carry firearms, whereas most white men and many white women possessed firearms and were experienced in using them. The South African police force was well trained and equipped. In 1978, it had 35,000 members (55 percent of them white) and 31,000 reserves. The police force included a security branch, which was responsible for interrogating political suspects and frequently resorted to torture.[28]

Whereas the police were relatively few in proportion to the population, the Nationalist government embarked on a massive program of military expansion. In 1978, defense absorbed nearly 21 percent of the budget and 5.1 percent of the gross national product. By that time, every young white man was subject to two years' compulsory military service, and the active duty defense force comprised 16,600 permanent members (about 5,000 of whom were black) and 38,400 white conscripts. There were also 255,000 white citizen reserves. The police and the army, navy, and air force were well armed. ARMSCOR, a state corporation, and its subsidiaries manufactured a high proportion of the country's military needs, including armored cars, mortars, guns, bombs, mines, fighter aircraft, missiles, and tear gas and napalm. Local production was supplemented by military hardware and technology imported from Europe, the United States, Israel, and Taiwan. The flow continued, mainly from Taiwan and Israel, despite the international arms embargo imposed by the United Nations in 1977. The South African armed forces were far the most powerful and disciplined in Africa south of the Sahara.[29]

Apartheid Society

South Africa in the apartheid era was unique. It became increasingly distinctive from other countries as decolonization and desegregation spread elsewhere. South Africa was a partly industrialized society with deep divisions based on legally prescribed biological criteria. As the economy expanded, industry absorbed more and more black workers, but racial categories continued to define the primary social cleavages.

Possessing privileged access to high-level jobs and high wages, white South Africans were as prosperous as the middle and upper classes in Europe and North America. Characteristically, they owned cars and lived in substantial houses or apartments in segregated suburbs, with black servants. The state provided them with excellent public services: schools and hospitals; parks and playing fields; buses and trains; roads, water, electricity, telephones, drainage, and sewerage. Social custom, reinforced by the official radio and television and the controlled press, sheltered them from knowing how their black compatriots lived.[30] Few Whites ever saw an African, a Coloured, or an Asian home. Fewer still spoke an African language. Wherever White encountered Black, White was boss and Black was servant. Indeed, Whites were conditioned to regard apartheid society as normal, its critics as communists or communist-sympathizers.

Public services for Blacks were characteristically inadequate or nonexistent. In the Homelands, women still walked miles every day to fetch water and firewood; in the towns, people crowded into single-sex compounds, leaky houses, or improvised shacks. Schools, hospitals, and public transport for Blacks were sharply inferior. Electricity, running water, public telephones, sewage systems, parks, and playing fields were rare.

Besides their common lot as victims of apartheid, Blacks had varied experiences. Black residents of the cities, the white farming areas, and the African Homelands had vastly different lives. The government accentuated black ethnic differences, favoring Coloureds and Indians over Africans and encouraging internal ethnic divisions among Africans. The government also promoted class divisions among Blacks. It supported collaborators and provided relative security of urban residence for some Africans, whereas it kept African laborers tied to white farms and made it illegal for Africans to leave their Homelands, except as temporary migrant workers.

There is a story to be told by social historians of the ways in which black people not only survived under apartheid but also created their own social and economic worlds.[31] In the urban ghettos, Africans mingled, regardless of ethnicity. For example, they ignored the government's attempt to carve up the townships into ethnic divisions; they married across ethnic lines; and members of the younger generation identified themselves as Africans (or even, comprehensively, as Blacks, thus including Coloureds and Indians) rather than as Xhosa, Zulu, Sotho, Pedi, or Tswana. The story will also emphasize the achievements of African women, who were particularly insecure, since the law codified the inferior status that they had had in precolonial custom and applied it to the very different circumstances of a capitalist state. Under apartheid, African women, many of them heads of households as a result of the persistence of male migrant labor, held the fabric of African society together.[32]

Social historians will also record the experiences of African children under apartheid. In a report for the United Nations Children's Fund, Francis Wilson, an economic historian, and Mamphela Ramphele, a doctor, drew attention to the fact that "children may be socialized into vandalism or find themselves having to adopt violent measures as a matter of survival and, in the process, losing any sense of right and wrong. The impact on children's minds and values of the physical violence that they witness and experience, not least at the hands of the police, is a matter of grave concern." Wilson and Ramphele also emphasized "the widespread disorganization of family life due to the migratory labour system" and the political, economic, and social powerlessness experienced by a large proportion of black South African men, which engenders a frustrated rage that all too often manifests itself in domestic violence, particularly against women.[33]

These generalizations can be illustrated in the fields of wealth and health. As we have seen, under apartheid there were huge differentials in the wage rates of white and black workers, and although those began to narrow in the 1970s, they remained high, and black unemployment rose to extraordinary levels. Economic inequality has existed everywhere in the modern world, but nowhere was it as great and as systematic as in apartheid South Africa. A University of Cape Town economist stated in 1980 that of ninety countries surveyed by the World Bank, South Africa had the most inequitable distribution of income. Estimates by the World Bank and the Ford Foundation showed that the top 10 percent of the population received 58 percent of the national income and the lowest 40 percent received 6 percent.[34]

The Second Carnegie Inquiry into Poverty and Development in South Africa revealed that nearly two-thirds of the African population had incomes below the Minimum Living Level (MLL), defined as the lowest sum on which a household could possibly live in South African social circumstances. African conditions were worst in the places where the government had relocated the largest number of displaced people—notably, QwaQwa, with a population density of 777 per square mile in 1980. Throughout the Homelands, the land was eroded, people were deriving little income from agriculture, and over four-fifths of the people lived below the MLL. In the white farming areas, most black men, women, and children worked for a pittance. In the cities, the wages of some employed Africans were actually below the MLL, and unemployment was high and rising. There was also a vast shortage of housing for Blacks. In Soweto, with a population of over one million by 1978, seventeen to twenty people were living in a typical four-room house; in Crossroads, outside Cape Town, there were more than six people to a bed.[35]

Under apartheid, there were intense contrasts in the health of the different sections of the South African population. White South Africans, like Europeans and North Americans, had a low infant mortality rate (14.9 per thousand live births in 1978) and a long life expectancy (64.5 years for males and 72.3 years for females in 1969–71). Their diseases were those of

202

the industrialized countries—including the highest rate of coronary heart disease in the world—and they enjoyed some of the highest standards of health care in the world. Ninety-eight percent of the medical budget was spent on curative rather than preventive services, and most of it was consumed by white patients. Doctor Christiaan Barnard performed the world's first heart transplant operation at Groot Schuur Hospital in Cape Town in 1968, and there were many transplants in later years, almost exclusively for white recipients. Medical education concentrated on the problems of the white population. The vast majority of doctors were white, and the medical schools were not substantially changing the balance. At the end of 1980, 657 white, 52 African, 62 Indian, and 18 Coloured medical students qualified as doctors.[36]

The government did not keep detailed medical statistics for Africans. In urban areas, black infant mortality rates and life expectancies improved substantially during the 1960s and 1970s, but there was no discernible improvement in the Homelands. The official estimate of the African infant mortality rate in South Africa as a whole in 1974 was 100 to 110 per 1,000, which was worse than every country in Africa except Upper Volta (now Burkina Faso) and Sierra Leone. In South Africa as a whole, the Coloured infant mortality rate was 80.6 per 1,000 and the Indian rate was 25.3 per 1,000 in 1978. Mortality rates for both African and Coloured children aged one to four years old were thirteen times as high as for Whites. The principal cause of these exceptional infant and child mortality rates was inadequate nutrition. An Institute of Race Relations survey revealed in 1978 that 50 percent of all the two- to three-year-old children in the Ciskei were undernourished and that one in ten Ciskeian urban children and one in six Ciskeian rural children had kwashiorkor (a severe protein deficiency disease) and/or marasmus (a wasting disease ultimately induced by contaminated food and water). Official life expectancy figures for Africans were not available in the apartheid period, but official estimates (almost certainly overestimates) put them at 51.2 for males and 58.9 for females in 1965–70.[37]

The principal African diseases were those common in third world countries: pneumonia, gastroenteritis, and tuberculosis (TB). Apart from kwashiorkor, TB, which is closely associated with poor socioeconomic conditions, was the most important cause of severe morbidity and death for the African population. According to official statistics, in 1979 there were 45,000 reported cases of TB in South Africa, 78.5 percent of them African, 18.5 percent Coloured, 1.5 percent Indian, and 1.5 percent White. Unofficial estimates are much higher. The head of the Community Health Department at the South African medical school for Africans said that in 1982, 110,000 people had active TB in South Africa, while about 10 million had it in dormant form, and that 82 percent of these were Africans. Moreover, though TB was decreasing among Whites (whose children were routinely inoculated against it), it was increasing among Blacks. Other infectious diseases included typhoid fever (more than three thousand cases reported annually), typhus, measles (which was often fatal among undernourished children), and rheumatic fever. Venereal diseases were prevalent. There were also epidemics of cholera, polio, and bubonic plague, while trachoma was endemic in the northern Transvaal. Many mine workers suffered disabling injuries or contracted lung diseases. In all these cases, the incidence was higher among Africans than among Coloureds and Asians, and far higher than among Whites.[38]

Apartheid society was also ridden with mental stress and violence. Suicides were exceptionally frequent among white South Africans.[39] Murder was a frequent cause of death among Africans and Coloureds.[40] South African society was very different from the benign picture produced by the government's information services and presented by official guides to foreign visitors.

Adaptation and Resistance to Apartheid

There were always some members of the enfranchised population of South Africa who sought to arouse the conscience of their fellow Whites against apartheid. They focused on the gulf between the theory of apartheid (separate freedoms) and its practice (discrimination and inequality) and on the brutality of the apartheid state—the pass laws, forced removals, house arrests, and detentions without trial.[41]

Soon after the election of 1948, leaders of all the white South African churches except the Dutch Reformed churches issued statements criticizing apartheid. In following years, many clergy came into conflict with the government. In 1968, the South African Council of Churches labeled apartheid a pseudo-gospel in conflict with Christian principles.[42] Initially, nearly all the Afrikaner clergy were united in support of apartheid. But in 1962, C. F. Beyers Naudé, a leading Broederbonder and former moderator of the principal Dutch Reformed church in the Transvaal, broke ranks and founded the Christian Institute, which brought black and white Christians of various denominations together, launched a Study Project on Christianity in Apartheid Society (SPROCAS), and espoused increasingly radical responses to official policies. The government banned Naudé and the institute in 1977, but by that time apartheid was a controversial issue within the Dutch Reformed churches, and in 1978 a group of Afrikaner clergy produced a radical critique of apartheid.[43]

The English-medium universities, especially the Universities of Cape Town and the Witwatersrand, were foci of opposition to apartheid. The National Union of South African Students (NUSAS), founded in 1924, organized a series of spectacular demonstrations in 1959 against the closure of the established universities to black students and in 1966 arranged for a visit by Sen. Robert Kennedy, who denounced apartheid in rousing speeches. In 1973, the government banned eight NUSAS leaders on the ground that they endangered internal security, and the following year it prohibited NUSAS from receiving funds from abroad. Nevertheless, NUSAS continued to introduce fresh generations of white (predominantly English-speaking) students to critical thinking about South African politics and society. In the late 1970s, NUSAS organized conferences on the theme "education for an African future."[44]

Apartheid also brought into being a women's organization, the Black Sash. The white, mainly English-speaking, middle-class members of the Black Sash devised a skillful method of embarrassing Nationalist politicians and attracting media attention. Wearing white dresses with black sashes, they stood silently with heads bowed in places where politicians were due to pass, such as the entrance to Parliament buildings. The government banned such demonstrations in 1976, but the Black Sash remained in existence, running offices that gave legal advice to Africans who fell foul of the apartheid laws.[45]

Authors, too, were exposing the effects of apartheid. Alan Paton, who in 1947 had written the best-selling *Cry, the Beloved Country*, calling for humane race relations, published a series of pungent criticisms of apartheid in the 1950s and 1960s. "God save us all," he wrote, "from the South Africa of the Group Areas Act, which knows no reason, justice, or mercy."[46] By the 1970s, such authors as André Brink, Nadine Gordimer, J. M. Coetzee, and Athol Fugard were demonstrating the destructive effects of South African racism in perceptive novels and plays. Other white critics included lawyers who deplored the disregard for human rights and the rule of law; historians who recalled that apartheid was an attempt to reverse the process of economic integration that had operated in South Africa for over three hundred years; and an archaeologist who declared, "Science provides no evidence that any single one of the assumptions underlying South Africa's racial legislation is justified."[47] Furthermore, the "Native Representatives" who sat in Parliament until that form of representation was abolished in 1960 and Helen Suzman, the only Progressive party member of Parliament from 1961 to 1974, vigorously opposed every racially oppressive bill.[48]

Nevertheless, before the late 1970s no powerful economic interest was fundamentally opposed to apartheid. White industrial workers benefited from an economic system that gave them a virtual monopoly not only of skilled jobs and high wages but also of workers' legal participation in the industrial bargaining process. White bureaucrats depended on a system that provided them with sheltered employment. Farmers, too, had reason to be satisfied with a government that gave them generous subsidies and ensured their supply of cheap black labor, and then helped them to dispose of it when there was a surplus.

The relation between mining and industrial capitalism and apartheid is a highly controversial subject. Some have argued that capitalism was inexorably opposed to apartheid and that economic growth was bound to erode and destroy it; others have charged capitalists with being the real creators and sustainers of apartheid.[49] Each argument draws attention to one part of the complex reality. On the one hand, it was white South African politicians, organized in an ethnic party that excluded most major capitalists, who devised and enforced apartheid. On the other hand, though apartheid imposed costs on the different sectors of business, it also benefited all of them, and although they criticized specific actions of the government, all sectors accommodated apartheid before 1978.

The behavior of Harry Oppenheimer, the South African financial giant, was most ambiguous. In 1957, he succeeded his father as head of the great global "empire" that included the Anglo American Corporation and De Beers Consolidated Mines. "It controlled forty percent of South Africa's gold, eighty percent of the world's diamonds, a sixth of the world's copper and it was the country's largest producer of coal."[50] He subsidized the Progressive party, which was launched in 1959, recommended the incorporation of educated Africans into the political system, and through the Urban Foundation, established in 1976, contributed to welfare projects in African urban areas. Yet he had no respect for African culture and, though admitting that the migrant labor system was bad in principle, treated it as essential for the gold-mining industry.

The behavior of manufacturing industrialists, too, was most equivocal.

As manufacturing became more diversified and sophisticated, it was increasingly hampered by the small size of the domestic market for its products, by the shortage of skilled workers, and by the inefficiency of black workers through their lack of education. By the late 1960s, not only the Federated Chamber of Industries, which represented the English-speaking manufacturers, but also the Afrikaanse Handelsinstituut, the organization of Afrikaner businesspeople, were criticizing aspects of influx control, the industrial color bar, and the black educational system as obstacles to the creation of a skilled black work force. Nevertheless, manufacturing was expanding and making substantial profits throughout the period in spite of the constraints imposed by apartheid. Industry, moreover, had relatively little influence in government circles, compared with mining, agriculture, and white labor, and its leaders, like other white South Africans, believed in white supremacy. Consequently, although they pressed for economic reforms within the apartheid framework, even the manufacturing industrialists stopped short of working for changes in the political system before 1978.[51]

Lacking substantial support from the other side of the color line, black South Africans continued to face immense odds in coping with their erstwhile conquerors. Poor, unarmed, and insecure, most experienced life as a continuous struggle for survival. For many Africans, success involved adapting to apartheid by circumventing the law, living in the informal economy, or acquiring a powerful patron—a chief or a white person. Other Africans found a niche in the formal economy as teachers, nurses, or industrial workers. Such people ceased to be marginal. They formed the nucleus of an African middle class and an African working class.[52]

Needled by the increasing brutality of the government and inspired by contemporary events in tropical Africa and other parts of the world, black leaders gradually transcended their regional, ethnic, and class divisions and devised more effective means of mobilizing the masses and confronting the regime. Soon after the National party came to power, a new generation took control of the African National Congress, spurred by the wartime protests in Johannesburg and the miners' strike of 1946. In 1949, the annual conference elected three members of the Youth League to the national executive: Walter Sisulu (b. 1912), Oliver Tambo (b. 1917), and Nelson Mandela (b. 1918). All three were from the Transkei and had attended mission schools. Both Tambo and Mandela had been expelled from Fort Hare, but they had later qualified as lawyers by correspondence at the University of South Africa and shared a practice in Johannesburg. Mandela was the dominant personality in the group. A member of the Thembu ruling family in the Transkei, he was a man of powerful physique, commanding bearing, sharp intelligence, and deep commitment to the cause of African liberation. Three years later, the conference elected Albert Lutuli as president-general of the ANC. Born in about 1898, Lutuli bridged the old and new elites. He was the elected chief of a small Zulu community in Natal, a teacher at Adams College (the leading African high school in Natal), a polished orator in English and in Zulu, a devout Christian, and a man of impeccable moral character.[53]

In 1952, the ANC and the South African Indian Congress, which had undergone a similar change of leadership, launched a passive resistance campaign that attracted wide support. Large numbers of volunteers defied discriminatory laws and eight thousand were arrested. The ANC called off that campaign early in 1953, however, after rioting had broken out in Port Elizabeth, East London, Cape Town, and Johannesburg and Parliament had enacted severe penalties for civil disobedience.[54]

In 1955, the ANC formed a coalition representing a broad spectrum of South African society to organize a campaign designed to enlist the participation of the black masses and win the sympathy of the outside world. With the cooperation of the South African Indian Congress, the South African Coloured People's Organisation, the small, predominantly white Congress of Democrats, and the multiracial South African Congress of Trade Unions, the ANC convened a Congress of the People. On June 26, 1955, 3,000 delegates (over 2,000 Africans, 320 Indians, 230 Coloureds, and 112 Whites) met in an open space at Kliptown near Johannesburg and adopted a Freedom Charter before the crowd was broken up by the police.[55]

The Freedom Charter was destined to endure as the basic policy statement of the ANC. It was drafted by a small committee, including white members of the Congress of Democrats, after numerous individuals and committees in various parts of the country had submitted lists of grievances. The charter started with the ringing assertion that "South Africa belongs to all who live in it, black and white, and that no government can justly claim authority unless it is based on the will of the people." It then set out a list of basic rights and freedoms, derived largely from ideas then current in liberal circles in Britain, continental Europe, and the United States: equality before the law; freedom of movement, assembly, religion, speech, and the press; the right to vote and to work, with equal pay for equal work, a forty-hour work week, a minimum wage, annual leave, and unemployment benefits; free medical care and free, compulsory, and equal education. The Freedom Charter also included some socialist ideas: "The mineral wealth beneath the soil, the banks and monopoly industry shall be transferred to the ownership of the people as a whole," and "Restriction of land ownership on a racial basis shall be ended, and all the land re-divided amongst those who work it." But it made a concession to advocates of group rights: "There shall be equal status in the bodies of the state, in the courts, and in the schools for all national groups and races."[56] Critics noted the inconsistencies in the document. Liberals as well as government supporters raised the specter of communism; radicals deplored the concession to "national groups."

The government responded by enacting further repressive legislation, and in December 1956 it arrested 156 people and charged them with high treason, in the form of a conspiracy to overthrow the state by violence and replace it with a state based on communism. The court was not persuaded that any of the accused had planned to use violence, but the trial dragged on, preoccupying the leadership, until March 1961, when the last thirty were found not guilty.

Though the ANC and its allies in the Congress movement were all male-dominated organizations, Lilian Ngoyi and other women had formed the Federation of South African Women, which organized protests against the decision of the government to extend the pass laws to African women. The demonstrations culminated on August 9, 1956, when 20,000 African women assembled outside the Union Buildings—the national administrative headquarters in Pretoria—delivered a petition to the empty prime minister's office, and stood in silence for thirty minutes. Two years later the police arrested two thousand African women for refusing to accept passes. Nevertheless, the government stood by its decision and from 1961 African women were obliged by law to carry passes. Other protests were reactions against specific local events. African men and women in the townships around Johannesburg and Pretoria, for example, boycotted the bus company for raising the fares and walked up to twenty miles a day to and from their work between January and April 1957.[57]

Failure to modify government policy caused frustration and divisions of opinion among politically conscious black South Africans. Whereas Lutuli, Mandela, and their colleagues continued to work for a reconciliation between the races in South Africa, others contended that the alliance with the white-dominated Congress of Democrats had impeded the ANC, as shown by what they regarded as a concession to white interests in the Freedom Charter. They wanted a purely African movement, dedicated to the emancipation of the African population. An African journalist struck a popular note when he wrote: "The masses do not hate an abstraction like 'oppression' or 'capitalism'. . . . They make these things concrete and hate the oppressor—in South Africa the White man."[58] With such forces behind him, Robert Sobukwe emerged as an alternative to the Lutuli-Mandela leadership. Sobukwe, a powerful orator, was born in Graaff-Reinet in the eastern Cape Province in 1924. He was educated at Fort Hare and was a Bantu language instructor at the University of the Witwatersrand. He did not hold the extreme views of some of his followers. Ultimately, according to Sobukwe, Whites might become genuine Africans; but since they benefited from the existing social order, they could not yet identify with the African cause.[59]

Failing to gain control of the ANC, the Africanists under Sobukwe broke away in 1959 and founded the Pan-Africanist Congress (PAC). On March 21, 1960, upstaging the ANC, they launched a campaign against the pass laws. Large numbers of Africans assembled at police stations without passes, inviting arrest in the hope of clogging the machinery of justice. At the police station at Sharpeville, near Johannesburg, the police opened fire, killing 67 Africans and wounding 186, most of whom were shot in the back. In the following weeks there were widespread work stoppages, and disturbances in various parts of the country. In Cape Town, on March 30, a crowd of Africans, estimated at between 15,000 and 30,000, marched in orderly procession to the center of the city, near Parliament, which was in session; but the police assured their leader, a twenty-three-year-old university student named Philip Kgosana, that the minister of justice would receive him that evening if he would persuade the people to return home. He told them to go, and they did so. That evening, when Kgosana reported, the police arrested him.[60]

As the disturbances mounted, the government struck back fiercely. It declared a state of emergency, mobilized the army reserves, outlawed the ANC and the PAC, and arrested 98 Whites, 90 Indians, 36 Coloureds, and 11,279 Africans. The police jailed another 6,800 people, including the PAC leaders, as well as beating hundreds of Africans and compelled them to return to work. These measures broke up the campaign. They also deprived Africans of the last chance of organizing lawful, peaceful, countrywide opposition to apartheid and forced the ANC leaders underground to reconsider their strategy and goals.

The year 1960 was a watershed in modern South African history. Previously, nearly every ANC leader had been deeply committed to nonviolence. But nonviolent methods had achieved nothing except a series of defeats at the hands of a violent state. In those circumstances, the ANC concluded, and the PAC agreed, that South Africa was not like India, where passive resistance had persuaded the British to quit. As Mandela put it in 1964, when he was on trial for sabotage after his eventual arrest: "We of the ANC had always stood for a non-racial democracy, and we shrank from any policy which might drive the races further apart than they already were. But the hard facts were that fifty years of non-violence had brought the African people nothing but more and more repressive legislation, and fewer and fewer rights . . . . [I]t would be unrealistic and wrong for African leaders to continue preaching non-violence at a time when the Government met our peaceful demands with force."[61]

The first attempts to meet state violence with revolutionary violence were not successful. Umkhonto we Sizwe (The Spear of the Nation, the militant wing of the ANC), Poqo (Pure, the militant wing of the PAC), and the African Resistance Movement (a multiracial organization consisting mainly of young white professionals and students) made over two hundred bomb attacks on post offices and other government buildings and on railroad and electrical installations near the main industrial centers. The government succeeded in breaking the three organizations, however. The police forces achieved a major coup in July 1963, when they arrested seventeen Umkhonto leaders in a house near Johannesburg. By the end of 1964, the first phase of violent resistance was over, and for another decade the country was quiescent. Mandela and Sisulu were serving life sentences on Robben Island four miles from Cape Town. Sobukwe, too, was jailed on Robben Island until 1969, when the government released him but kept him politically impotent by banning him; he lived in Kimberley until his death in 1978. Tambo escaped the net and settled in Lusaka, Zambia, where he became acting president-general of the ANC after the death of Lutuli in 1967.

Quiescence did not mean acquiescence. Three significant developments fueled a spirit of resistance until it broke out in massive confrontations in 1976. First, there was a vigorous movement in the arts. During the late 1950s and early 1960s, the Johannesburg magazine *Drum* was a vehicle for black criticism of apartheid. During the late 1960s and early 1970s, copies of books that were published overseas, such as Bloke Modisane's *Blame Me on History* and Alex La Guma's *A Walk in the Night,* and the poetry of

Dennis Brutus, evaded the censors and brought a strong liberationist message to the townships. A popular black theater movement made a strong impact on the Witwatersrand and in Durban. As Nomsisi Kraai wrote in the newsletter of the People's Experimental Theatre, "Black theatre is a dialogue of confrontation, confrontation with the Black situation."[62]

Second, the rapid growth of the economy, involving a vast increase in the number of black semiskilled as well as unskilled workers, led to the development of class consciousness among black workers and the creation of an effective black trade union movement, despite its exclusion from the formal bargaining process. The year 1973 marked the beginning of a wave of strikes with demands for higher wages and improved working conditions.[63]

Third, the government's attempt to mold the minds of young black people through tight control over their education boomeranged. Black students were profoundly frustrated by the conditions in their schools and colleges. In 1968 Steve Biko, a twenty-two-year-old student, led a secession from the white-controlled National Union of South African Students to found the exclusively black South African Students Organisation (SASO). SASO declared that all the victims of white racism should unite and cease to depend on white organizations that claimed to work for their benefit. As Biko wrote in 1971:

> Black consciousness is in essence the realisation by the black man of the need to rally together with his brothers around the cause of their subjection—the blackness of their skin—and to operate as a group in order to rid themselves of the shackles that bind them to perpetual servitude. It seeks to demonstrate the lie that black is an aberration from the "normal" which is white. . . . It seeks to infuse the black community with a new-found pride in themselves, their efforts, their value systems, their culture, their religion and their outlook to life. The interrelationship between the consciousness of self and the emancipatory programme is of paramount importance. Blacks no longer seek to reform the system because so doing implies acceptance of the major points around which the system revolves. Blacks are out to completely transform the system and to make of it what they wish.[64]

The ideology of Black Consciousness penetrated the urban schools. On June 16, 1976, thousands of black schoolchildren in Soweto demonstrated against the government's insistence that half of their subjects be taught in Afrikaans—as they saw it, the language of the oppressor. The protests became nationwide after the police shot and killed a thirteen-year-old African student during the demonstration. The government reacted brutally. By February 1977, according to an official commission of inquiry, at least 575 people had been killed, including 494 Africans, 75 Coloureds, 5 Whites, and 1 Indian. Of the victims, 134 were under age eighteen. During 1977, the government also banned SASO and all its affiliated organizations and jailed numerous black leaders. Police arrested and killed Steve Biko. He died from brain damage caused by injuries to his skull. After inflicting the injuries, police transported Biko naked in the back of a van for 750 miles on the night before he died.[65]

After those events, thousands of young black South Africans fled the country and received military training in camps in Tanzania and Angola. The militant wings of the ANC and the PAC planned to infiltrate trained men and women into South Africa from the north, attack police stations, explode bombs in public places, deposit caches of arms, and, ultimately, launch a guerrilla war.

South Africa in the World

The postwar world was quite a different place from the imperialist world of the 1930s. While apartheid was taking root in South Africa, political power was flowing in the opposite direction in the rest of Africa.[66] In 1957, following the decolonization of its Asian territories, Britain transferred power to African nationalists in the Gold Coast (Ghana), soon to be followed by the other British territories in West Africa—Sierra Leone, Nigeria, and the Gambia. In 1960, the French relinquished political control over their two federations of colonies in west and central Africa, and the Belgians withdrew from the Congo (Zaire), their vast territory in central Africa.

By that time, African nationalism had swept eastward and southward into the British territories where there were significant pockets of white settlers. Early in 1960, Prime Minister Harold Macmillan of Britain toured tropical Africa and then visited South Africa. On February 3, in the Parliament in Cape Town, he spoke of "the wind of change" that was sweeping over the continent and made it clear that Britain would not support South Africa if it tried to resist African nationalism. Over the next four years, the British transferred power to local nationalist parties in Tanganyika (Tanzania), Uganda, Kenya, Malawi, and Northern Rhodesia (Zambia). In 1965, the white settler government of Rhodesia postponed a similar outcome by asserting sovereignty over the colony and making a unilateral declaration of independence. No country recognized Rhodesian independence, however, and local Africans resorted to guerrilla warfare against the regime.[67] Between 1966 and 1968 Britain transferred power to Africans in three other neighbors of South Africa—Basutoland (Lesotho), Bechuana-land Protectorate (Botswana), and Swaziland. Successive governments in Pretoria had tried to persuade London to allow South Africa to incorpo-rate those three territories, as had been envisaged by the South Africa Act of 1909. But after 1961, when South Africa became a republic and left the Commonwealth, incorporation was no longer possible.[68]

African nationalism continued to transform the Southern African re-gion. In 1974, African resistance to Portuguese colonialism led to a coup in Lisbon, and the following year Angola and Mozambique gained indepen-dence.[69] By 1978, the white settler regime in Rhodesia was barely surviv-ing a fierce civil war and international sanctions, and South Africa was controlling Namibia only by defying the United Nations.

The United Nations differed from its predecessor, the League of Na-tions. Whereas the European powers had dominated the League of Na-tions, which the United States never joined, the Soviet Union and China, as well as France, Britain, and the United States, had permanent seats and vetoes in the U.N. Security Council, and other countries, including third world countries, served in turn on the Security Council and formed a majority in the General Assembly.[70] From 1952 onward, the General As-sembly passed annual resolutions condemning apartheid. Then, as the number of independent Asian and African states increased, each with a seat in the General Assembly, the United Nations devoted more and more attention to racism in South Africa. By 1967, the General Assembly had created both a Special Committee on Apartheid and a Unit on Apartheid, which issued a stream of publications exposing and denouncing the effects of South Africa's racial policies. The General Assembly also declared that South Africa's mandate over South West Africa (Namibia) was terminated and established a U.N. Council for Namibia. In 1971, the International Court of Justice gave an advisory opinion to the effect that South Africa's control of Namibia was illegal.[71] Two years later, the General Assembly declared apartheid to be "a crime against humanity." In 1977, after South Africa's police were known to have killed Steve Biko and its government had suppressed numerous antiapartheid movements, the Security Council unanimously voted a mandatory arms embargo against South Africa. That was the first time the United Nations had done that to a member state.

In 1963, meanwhile, independent African states founded the Organiza-tion of African Unity (OAU), which set up a Liberation Committee with headquarters in Dar es Salaam, Tanzania. The Liberation Committee established camps for refugees from South Africa and provided them with education and military training. But although the new African regimes earnestly desired to eradicate apartheid, they lacked the means to do so. They were weak regimes, preoccupied with survival. Singly or in combination, they could not match South Africa's military power. In varying degrees all of South Africa's neighbors were economically dependent on South Africa. Lesotho was exceptionally vulnerable. Entirely surrounded by South Africa, its main source of income came from the wages its people earned in white South African mines and factories and on white South African farms. Even Zambia imported food from South Africa and exported half of its copper—the source of 95 percent of its export earnings—via South African railroads and South African ports.[72]

Down to 1978, international opposition to apartheid, though strong in rhetoric, was weak in substance. The South African government mustered an effective response to the challenges resulting from changes in the world order. The response included skillfully formulated ideological components. As decolonization swept through tropical Africa, Verwoerd presented his Homelands policy as an analogous process. In 1961, he told a London audience:

> We do not only seek and fight for a solution which will mean our survival as a white race, but we seek a solution which will ensure survival and full development—political and economic—to each of the other racial groups. . . . We want each of our population groups to control and to govern themselves, as is the case with other Nations. . . . In the transition stage the guardian must teach and guide his ward. That is our policy of separate development. South Africa will proceed in all honesty and fairness to secure peace, prosperity and justice for all, by means of political independence coupled with economic interdependence.[73]

Above all, South African foreign propaganda was well tuned to the cold war fears and prejudices of Europeans and Americans. It portrayed South Africa as a stable, civilized, and indispensable member of the "free world" in its unremitting struggle against international communism. Moscow's aim was world domination. The imperial powers were leaving tropical Africa open to communist infiltration. The ANC was a communist organization, directed by Moscow. Communists were responsible for the uprisings of 1960 and 1976–77.[74] For domestic consumption, this formula was accompanied by the assurance that the interests of the white population were the first priority of the government. "Our motto," said Verwoerd, "is to maintain white supremacy for all time to come over our own people and our own country, by force if necessary."[75]

How real was the "communist menace"? The Soviet Union and its Eastern European satellites, especially East Germany, did indeed champion the interests of the third world against Western imperialism. They supplied arms to resistance movements in colonial Angola, Mozambique, and Rhodesia. In Rhodesia, however, the Soviets supported the weaker of the two African movements, whereas its communist rival, China, supported Robert Mugabe's Zimbabwe African National Union (ZANU), which triumphed in the election held on the eve of the independence of what had been Rhodesia in 1980.

When the Portuguese left Angola in 1975, the Soviet Union armed and transported Cuban troops to help the Popular Movement for the Liberation of Angola (MPLA) consolidate its control over rival African nationalist organizations and to resist an invasion launched by the South African army in collusion with the United States. The Soviet Union and its allies also had close links with the ANC. They provided education and military training for South African refugees, and they were the main suppliers of arms for the military wing of the ANC that began to infiltrate guerrillas into South Africa in the late 1970s. Moreover, the ANC included communists in its ranks and among its leaders.

Yet Southern Africa never had high priority on the Soviet agenda. Moscow was mainly concerned with preserving its hegemony in Eastern Europe, defending its border with China, and increasing its influence in Southeast Asia and the Horn of Africa. It was not practicable for Moscow to risk a military confrontation with the Western powers in distant Southern Africa. The level of Soviet trade with Southern Africa was insignificant; so was the level of its aid to the black Southern African states. The ANC, moreover, was an open organization and its top leaders—Nelson Mandela and Oliver Tambo—were not communists. At minimal cost, the Soviet Union was deriving advantages from the equivocation of the Western powers in the face of the rampant racism and discriminatory state capitalism of South Africa. Pretoria's rhetoric against communism was a skillful attempt to divert attention from the domestic causes of black resistance in South Africa. Black South Africans needed no foreign indoctrination to oppose apartheid.[76]

The South African regime also benefited from material factors. After World War II, technological developments were drawing the world together and the capitalist world economy was becoming increasingly integrated. South Africa possessed a distinctive place in it as the producer of a wide range of valuable minerals, which accounted for about three-quarters of South Africa's foreign exchange earnings. In 1979, according to the U.S. Bureau of Mines, besides producing 60 percent of the world's annual supply of gold, South Africa produced significant quantities of four minerals that were essential for Western industry and defense: 47 percent of the world's platinum group of metals (which are used as catalytic agents for refining petroleum and for reducing automobile emissions) and 33 percent of the world's chromium, 21 percent of the world's manganese, and 42 percent of the world's vanadium (some of which are indispensable in the production of steel). South Africa was known to contain vast reserves of all those minerals. And South Africa was still the world's major producer of gem diamonds and a producer of significant quantities of asbestos, coal, copper, iron, nickel, phosphates, silver, uranium, and zinc.[77]

The South African economy was extremely attractive to American and European business and defense interests. In 1948, Britain, the former colonial power, had far the largest foreign stake in the South African economy, but in the 1950s and, particularly, during the boom years of the 1960s and early 1970s, American and continental European trade and investments grew spectacularly. By 1978, the United States had surpassed Britain as South Africa's principal trading partner and the Japanese as well as the Europeans were trading with South Africa on an increasing scale. By then, too, $26.3 billion of foreign capital was invested in South Africa. About 40 percent of the total was British capital, 20 percent was American, and 10 percent was West German, while the Swiss and the French contributed about 5 percent each. About 40 percent of the total consisted of direct investment in the South African subsidiaries or affiliates of American companies, such as Ford, General Motors, Mobil, and Caltex Oil, and 60 percent of the total consisted of indirect investment—American and European bank loans, and shares in South African gold-mining and other stock. The returns on foreign investment were high. American returns averaged over 15 percent in 1970–74, declined to 9 percent in 1975, and rose again to 14 percent in 1976–78.[78]

The South African economy was not autarchic. It was vulnerable in three respects. First, it required considerable infusions of foreign capital. Second, except in mining, South Africa did not possess the latest technology and needed to import heavy machinery and electronic and transportation equipment. Third, South Africa produced no natural oil. Nevertheless, except for brief periods after the disturbances following the

Sharpeville killings in 1960 and the Soweto uprising in 1976, the United States and Western Europe provided the necessary capital and equipment, and although the Organization of Petroleum Exporting Countries (OPEC) imposed an oil embargo on South Africa in 1973, it was unable to enforce it, and most of South Africa's oil came from Iran until the fall of Reza Shah Pahlavi in 1979. To reduce its dependence on imports, the government meanwhile created a stockpile of petroleum products, and by 1978 it was producing more than 10 percent of South Africa's domestic consumption of gasoline in two large oil-from-coal plants created by a state corporation, the South African Coal, Oil and Gas Corporation (SASOL).[79]

In those circumstances, powerful interests in the United States and Western Europe were loath to disturb the status quo in South Africa. With their cold war perspective they were prone to exaggerate the communist menace, and with their business perspective they tended to assume that economic growth was bound to erode apartheid.

Great Britain had especially close ties with South Africa, even after 1961, when South Africa became a republic and left the Commonwealth. Tens of thousands of white South Africans were born in Britain, hundreds of thousands had relatives and close friends there, and the culture of English-speaking white South Africans was oriented toward Britain. The South African economy also meant far more to Britain than to any other country. In 1978, Britain was responsible for about 40 percent of all foreign investment in South Africa and a considerable share of the trade. About 10 percent of British overseas direct investment was in South Africa, and British banks—Standard Chartered and Barclays International—controlled 60 percent of South African bank deposits. Some South African émigrés, white as well as black, organized a vigorous antiapartheid movement in Britain, but from 1965 until 1980 Britain's concern in Southern Africa was focused on the Rhodesian problem, since white Rhodesia's unilateral declaration of independence was an act of rebellion. British administrations, Conservative as well as Labour, joined in the antiapartheid rhetoric, but even Labour vetoed resolutions for sanctions in the Security Council, except in 1977, when Britain abstained on the resolution for an arms embargo against South Africa.[80] South Africa's other major European trading partners—West Germany, France, and Switzerland—were also disinclined to risk their growing trade and investments in South Africa by taking action against apartheid.[81]

Relations between South Africa and the United States became more important as British power ebbed.[82] The South African economy meant far less to the United States than to Britain and accounted for only about 1 percent of American foreign trade and investment. Nevertheless, some sectors of American business were profitably involved in South Africa, and the Pentagon deemed it essential to have access to South Africa's strategic minerals. Although few South Africans had American origins, as the civil rights movement registered gains in the United States, black American leaders began to identify with black South Africans and to lobby against apartheid.

Under Dwight D. Eisenhower (1953–61), the United States continued to treat South Africa as an ally regardless of its racial policies. The Pentagon and the Central Intelligence Agency (CIA) had contacts with South Africa's military and security services. As a producer of uranium, South Africa became a member of the International Atomic Energy Board and joined the United States in nuclear research, and an American firm built South Africa's first nuclear reactor. The adverse effects of the Sharpeville episode of 1960 were short-lived. The United States voted for U.N. condemnation of apartheid, but business quickly resumed as usual, and that December the National Aeronautics and Space Administration (NASA) obtained an agreement to set up three tracking stations in South Africa. The Kennedy and Johnson administrations (1961–69) were more critical of apartheid and committed the United States to stop selling arms to South Africa, but they continued to reject proposals for economic sanctions, and the implications for South Africa of Lyndon Johnson's support for civil rights at home were overshadowed by the Vietnam War.

Under Richard Nixon and Gerald Ford (1969–77) there was a distinct tilt away from the antiapartheid lobby and the relatively liberal Africa Bureau in the State Department toward the Pentagon and big business. In 1969, Henry Kissinger, Nixon's national security adviser, ordered a review of American policies throughout the world. The administration chose the second of five options outlined in the Southern African review, National Security Study Memorandum 39, which reasoned,

> The whites are here [that is, in Southern Africa] to stay and the only way that constructive change can come about is through them. There is no hope for the blacks to gain the political rights they seek through violence, which will only lead to chaos and increased opportunities for the communists. We can, through selective relaxation of our stance toward the white regimes, encourage some modification of their current racial and colonial policies and through more substantial economic assistance to the black states . . . help to draw the two groups together and exert some influence on both for peaceful

change. Our tangible interests form a basis for our contacts in the region, and these can be maintained at an acceptable political cost.[83]

That memorandum led to increased official contacts with white South African officials, pro–South African U.N. votes, and the appointment of an ambassador to South Africa who showed minimal concern for the lot of black South Africans and was reported to have gone hunting on Robben Island with political prisoners as beaters.[84]

The Carter administration (1977–81) tilted in the opposite direction. It considered South Africa to be a liability to the Western alliance rather than an ally. It believed that the future lay with black nationalists and that the United States had an interest in coming to terms with them. Vice-President Walter Mondale would even tell Prime Minister John Vorster that America supported the principle of majority rule with universal suffrage—the ANC formula—one person, one vote.

CHAPTER 7

Apartheid in Crisis, 1978–1989

By 1978, the apartheid state was in trouble. South Africa's economic boom of the 1960s and early 1970s had been followed by a sharp recession. The administration of the complex network of apartheid laws was proving to be extremely costly. Inflation was running at over 10 percent. The increase in the gross domestic product was scarcely keeping up with the increase in the population, and many white people were becoming poorer. There was also a shortage of the skilled labor needed to run private industry and the bureaucracy. That shortage was accentuated by the fact that in 1977, for the first time, there was a net white emigration from South Africa—largely of professionals and men and women with much-needed managerial and industrial experience. Moreover, the black population was increasing at a far greater rate than the white population and demographers were forecasting a rapid decline in the white proportion of the total population of South Africa. It had already dropped from its peak of 21 percent to 16 percent and was expected to fall to 10 percent early in the twenty-first century.[1]

In other respects, too, the illusions of the Verwoerd era were shattered. The "decolonization" process, which Verwoerd had intended to assuage foreign criticism and provide Africans with the means to "develop along their own lines in their own areas," had failed on both counts. No foreign government recognized the independence of the Transkei or Bophuthatswana, which the government had declared to be independent states in 1976 and 1977, and the economic integration of the entire country was not arrested. The client rulers of the Homelands were becoming an embarrassment. Utterly dependent on Pretoria for subsidies and protection, most of them were corrupt, inefficient, and authoritarian. Their territories were decaying and their inhabitants were struggling to survive by sending family members out to work in the white cities and on the white farms. As workers and consumers, black people were developing economic and political muscle in the heart of "white" South Africa, and their children had come to loathe the regime and its institutions. Young Indians and Coloureds as well as Africans regarded the regime as illegitimate. They were not deferential toward Whites; they were defiant.[2]

The South African government also faced a transformed world order. Instead of being at the southern end of a continent controlled by Europeans, in a world dominated by Europeans and North Americans, South Africa had become an isolated anomaly. Except for Rhodesia and Namibia, its neighbors were no longer European colonies but black states. The white minority in Rhodesia was losing its war against African guerrillas. The United Nations had declared South Africa's control of Namibia illegal and in 1978 devised a program to liberate that territory.[3]

In 1977 the United Nations had passed a mandatory embargo on the sale of arms to South Africa. By 1978 the civil rights movement had made significant gains in the United States and racist opinions were no longer acceptable in American politics. Racial discrimination had been eliminated from American law and, to a considerable extent, from American practice, and black American activists were beginning to espouse the cause of black South Africans.[4]

Indeed, whereas the structure of South African society had been compatible with the structure of the societies in tropical Africa, the Caribbean, much of Asia, and the United States before World War II, that was no longer the case. Since 1948, systematic racism had become the bedrock of

South Africa's law and practice. The ways had parted between South Africa and the rest of the world.[5]

In those circumstances, Afrikaners were divided as to what should be done. Afrikaner solidarity, which had been the key to the electoral successes of the National party in the 1960s, was collapsing. Ironically, economic success was eroding the Afrikaner nationalist movement. Whereas in the previous decade the overwhelming majority of Afrikaners had placed ethnic above class interests, by the late 1970s Afrikaner class divisions had become more marked and more potent. Eighty-eight percent of Afrikaners were urban, 70 percent of those in white-collar jobs. Prosperous professionals, businesspeople, and absentee landowners had replaced the old rural and cultural elites in control of the National party and the Broederbond. They talked about reforming apartheid by making carefully crafted changes to appease foreign and domestic critics and at the same time to strengthen white supremacy by creating further divisions among the subject peoples. But they were encountering opposition from Afrikaners on both flanks.[6]

On the right, Afrikaner urban workers and marginal farmers who relied on apartheid's defenses against black competition and the numerous bureaucrats who lived by administering the apartheid laws feared the consequences of extending effective political rights to Blacks. They were determined to preserve the Verwoerdian system with the utmost rigor. On the left, some Afrikaner clergy and intellectuals—the very class that had produced the apartheid ideology in the first place—and several Afrikaner business leaders were beginning to realize that apartheid was both immoral and inexpedient and were starting to strive for substantial changes.

In 1978, the National party itself was tainted by scandal. It was revealed that members of the government had misappropriated public funds intended for secret propaganda purposes. The taint extended to senior cabinet ministers and even to Prime Minister John Vorster, who had succeeded Verwoerd in 1966. On September 28, Vorster resigned and the parliamentary members of the party elected Pieter Willem Botha as their leader and hence as Vorster's successor.[7]

Botha, who was born in 1916, was intelligent, determined, hot-tempered, and domineering. A politician through and through, he was a National party organizer at the age of twenty, a member of the Sauer commission that provided the party with its racial agenda in 1946, and a member of Parliament for George, an eastern Cape constituency, since the Nationalist triumph in 1948. As minister of defense since 1966, he had built the South African army into the most formidable military machine in Africa. He claimed that the international community was waging a "total onslaught" against South Africa and gave the military a major say in the government. The State Security Council, which had been created in 1972, had rarely met under Vorster. Under Botha, it became more powerful than the cabinet. Botha chaired the council, which included the minister of defense (Gen. Magnus Malan, the former head of the Defence Force), five other cabinet officers, and the heads of the Defence Force, the police, and the intelligence services.[8]

Reforming Apartheid

The policy of the Botha administration was a complex attempt to adapt to changing circumstances without sacrificing Afrikaner power. It included efforts to neutralize South Africa's neighbors, to scrap apartheid symbols and practices that were not essential to the maintenance of white supremacy, to draw English-speaking citizens into the party, to win the cooperation of big business, to intensify the ethnic and class cleavages among the subject peoples, and to suppress domestic dissidents.

The government's domestic reforms resulted from investigations made by special commissions of inquiry and by the President's Council—a sixty-one-member body appointed by the president with a large white majority and a few Coloureds and Indians but no Africans. The first significant change concerned labor relations and was a response both to the rash of industrial strikes that had occurred since 1973 and to the need of manufacturing industry for settled and compliant labor. By 1979, there were twenty-seven—illegal—democratically organized African trade unions, with African working-class leaders and significant support from key white activists. A commission chaired by Professor N. Wiehahn recommended that African workers be brought under control by legislation. Job reservation should be abolished, all trade unions (including African) should register, and each union should be free to prescribe membership qualifications as it saw fit. During 1979, Parliament passed the proposed legislation. Unions were to apply for registration, and all registered unions were to have access to the industrial court and the right to strike after a thirty-day notification period. In the same year, Parliament passed further legislation as a result of the recommendations of a commission chaired by Dr. P. J.

Riekert, making it a criminal offense, subject to a large fine, for employers to hire Africans who did not possess residential rights in the cities.[9]

By 1986, African trade unions had a dues-paying membership of over a million, spread between two national federations: the Congress of South African Trade Unions (COSATU) and the Council of Unions of South Africa-Azanian Confederation of Trade Unions (CUSA-AZACTU), which was imbued with a black consciousness philosophy. Besides their demands for wage increases, which met with considerable success, these unions gave Africans experience in democratic organization and became sources of worker power. The government's intention to control the African trade unions by legalizing them had backfired. By 1986, both federations were politically militant. African unions had become a central force in the struggle for power in South Africa.[10]

The next major change was constitutional. Following prolonged debates in the President's Council and the all-white Parliament, and a two-to-one majority in a referendum of white voters, a new constitution came into force in 1984. The new Parliament consisted of three uniracial chambers: a House of Assembly, comprising 178 white people elected by Whites; a House of Representatives of 85 Coloureds elected by Coloureds; and a House of Delegates of 45 Indians elected by Indians. Accordingly, when joint sessions were held Whites held a distinct majority. A multiracial cabinet drawn from the three chambers became responsible for "general affairs," such as taxation, foreign affairs, defense, state security, law and order, commerce and industry, and African affairs. Uniracial ministers' councils became responsible for "own affairs," such as education, health, and local government. The State President, elected by a college of 50 White, 25 Coloured, and 13 Indian members of Parliament, appointed the members of the cabinet and the ministers' councils. He could dissolve Parliament at any time. He was empowered to decide which were "general" and which were "own" affairs, and he was responsible for "the control and administration of black [that is, African] affairs."[11]

For the first time, the Nationalist government had addressed the question of power by including Blacks in the political process. But the new constitution was inadequate on three counts. First, the primary official groupings of South Africans continued to be racial. Second, Whites continued to be dominant under the new constitution, since they could always outvote the Coloureds and Indians on important questions. Third, the Africans—75 percent of the population of South Africa (including the

Homelands)—had no say in the new dispensation. The other significant feature of the new constitution was that it introduced a strong presidential system in place of the previous Westminster model of cabinet government.

Duly elected state president, P. W. Botha appointed a cabinet in which members of his National party were in charge of all the departments responsible for "general affairs." The cabinet included one Coloured and one Indian member, but neither had a departmental portfolio. This cumbersome arrangement did not succeed in winning the hearts or minds of most Coloured and Indian people, who showed their discontent by refraining from participating. Only 61 percent of the Coloured adults and 57 percent of the Indian adults bothered to register, and only 30 percent of registered Coloureds and 20 percent of registered Indians voted in the election.[12] The new constitution, moreover, accentuated the alienation of the African population from the regime, and it compounded the costs and the confusion of government by adding still more departments of education, health, and welfare to those already existing in South Africa and its ten Homelands.

The government also made a fresh effort to deal with the problem of African urbanization. By the early 1980s, it recognized that some Africans, referred to as "urban insiders," were legally entitled to live permanently in the metropolitan areas, but it was still trying to apply the pass laws to prevent Africans domiciled in the Homelands from coming to the cities except as migrant workers on temporary contracts. In 1984, for example, officials arrested 238,894 Africans for pass law offenses. Even so, they were unable to stem the tide. The reason was obvious. The Homelands could not sustain their populations. For their inhabitants, it was a matter of survival. As one African worker said, "The countryside is pushing you into the cities to survive; the cities are pushing you in the countryside to die."[13]

In 1986, accepting this reality, the government repealed no fewer than thirty-four legislative enactments that had constituted the pass laws. It announced a policy of "orderly urbanization." It still hoped—vainly, as it proved—that orderly urbanization would be promoted by the Natives Land Act (1913) and the Group Areas Act (1950) and its amendments, which confined Africans to specific zones in towns, by the lack of housing and other amenities in those zones and by the ceiling on urban employment. The concession applied, moreover, only to Africans who were South African citizens. Citizens of the "independent Homelands," which by then included Venda and the Ciskei, as well as the Transkei and Bophuthatswana, were regarded as aliens in South Africa, and employers were not to hire them without special official permission.[14]

The government had also come to realize that the geographical framework of the Verwoerd era did not correspond with economic realities. It planned to create new institutions, cutting across the Homeland boundaries, by dividing South Africa into four metropolitan regions (the Pretoria-Witwatersrand-Vereeniging triangle, Port Elizabeth, Durban-Pinetown, and Cape Town) and four development regions centered on such cities as Bloemfontein. The regional institutions would parallel the institutions at the national level, except that Africans were to be included. Each region was to have a multiracial Regional Services Council for general affairs and uniracial councils for own affairs. The government also replaced the provincial councils with executive committees responsible for general affairs. Although Africans were to be included in these new bodies, however, the councils would be undemocratic: their members would be appointed by the government or indirectly elected.[15]

By June 1986, the government had also eliminated some segregation laws. It had repealed the bans on multiracial political parties and interracial sex and marriage. It had stopped reserving by law particular categories of jobs for white workers. It had opened up the business centers in the cities to black traders. It had desegregated some classes of hotels, restaurants, trains, buses, and public facilities and had permitted sports contests to take place between teams of different races. It was also turning a blind eye to black occupation of apartments and houses in parts of Johannesburg and Cape Town that were zoned under the Group Areas Act for exclusive white occupation. Year after year, the government had also increased the funds for black education. During the early 1980s, moreover, industry had raised the level of black wages (although by 1986 black real wages had stabilized as a result of inflation). From time to time, government spokespeople had also made a number of reassuring statements for African consumption. On one occasion, Botha himself said that South Africa had outgrown apartheid and that Africans would be incorporated into the decision-making process at the national level.[16]

The reform process had distinct limits. School education remained strictly segregated, and in 1986 the government was still spending more than seven times as much to educate a white child as to educate an African child,[17] and similar disparities remained in health and welfare services. Although some black people in the townships were well-to-do, the vast majority of Blacks were poor, and several million (3.5 million by one estimate) were unemployed and destitute. The Land Act and the Group Areas Act still excluded Africans from land ownership outside the Homelands and the African townships. Moreover, in spite of assurances to the contrary, the government was continuing to remove African communities from their homes. It was also destroying squatter camps that Africans had formed on the outskirts of Cape Town and Port Elizabeth.[18] The army as well as the police was being used to control the townships. Thousands of people were being detained in solitary confinement, without being brought to trial and without the knowledge of their families, friends, or lawyers. In addition, in spite of much vague official talk about including Africans in national decision-making, President Botha and his colleagues were adamant about retaining the racial structure of government institutions and rejected any suggestion that Africans should participate equally with Whites.

Domestic Resistance, 1978–1986

Whereas in 1960 and 1961 the government had successfully reimposed its version of law and order for the next decade and more by arresting dissidents and banning their organizations, similar actions in 1976 and 1977 failed to have the same effect. Black resistance soon became more formidable than before. After the Soweto uprising, a protest culture pervaded the black population of South Africa. Students and workers, children and adults, men and women, the educated and the uneducated became involved in efforts to liberate the country from apartheid. Poets, novelists, dramatists, photographers, and painters conveyed the resistance message to vast audiences. A new journal, *Staffrider,* published much of their work. Children scrawled antiapartheid graffiti on walls. Crowds wore the ANC colors and sang ANC songs at funerals. Indeed, with relatively few exceptions, the government failed to drive wedges between urban "insiders" and "outsiders," or between middle-class and proletarian Blacks, or between Africans and Coloureds and Asians; nor did it deter an increasing number of young Whites from identifying with the resistance.[19]

In August 1983, a thousand delegates of all races, representing 575 organizations—trade unions, sporting bodies, community groups, and women's and youth organizations—founded the United Democratic Front (UDF) to coordinate internal opposition to apartheid. The conference declared that it aimed to create a united democratic South Africa, free of

Homelands and group areas and based on the will of the people. It provided continuity by endorsing the Freedom Charter and including prominent former-ANC members as participants. It recognized the need for "unity in struggle through which all democrats, regardless of race, religion or colour shall take part together."[20]

During the next three years, there was vigorous resistance to the apartheid regime in every city and nearly every Homeland in the country. In 1983 and 1984, workers domiciled in the Ciskei boycotted the commuter buses that carried them to East London. Bus companies were boycotted when they tried to increase fares on the Witwatersrand. The Coloured and Asian elections of 1984 were marked by widespread violence. In the Pretoria-Witwatersrand-Vereeniging triangle, bloody demonstrations ensued when the African councils that the government had established increased rents, which formed their principal source of revenue. By year's end, official statistics reported 175 people killed in such incidents, including four black councillors killed by enraged crowds. There was also an unprecedented number of strikes, including a major strike by black miners. Moreover, the government reported fifty-eight incidents of sabotage against state departments, petrol depots, power installations, and railroad lines, and twenty-six attacks on police.[21]

The year 1985 was still more disturbed. School boycotts and bus boycotts often led to violence. There were worker stayaways, clashes between township residents and security forces, and attacks on black police and councillors. Rural disturbances included resistance to a government decision to transfer an African community from the Bophuthatswana Homeland to the KwaNdebele Homeland for political purposes. The number of recorded insurgency attacks rose to 136, the recorded death toll in political violence to 879. There were also 390 strikes involving 240,000 workers. The protests continued into 1986. By that time, the formal machinery of local government had broken down in parts of the black townships. Fearing for their lives, many black councillors had resigned and informal groups had assumed control.[22]

There was also a great deal of violence among black South Africans. Circumstances varied from place to place. In some locations, rival gangs, brutalized by the conditions in which they lived and only loosely associated with the national political struggle, fought for mastery. In others, government officials cultivated and gave surreptitious assistance to vigilante mobs, as in the destruction of the Crossroads settlement near Cape Town.[23]

Organizations affiliated with the UDF commanded the allegiance of most political activists, including people who had formerly been inspired by the Black Consciousness movement. Some, however, disagreed with the UDF's inclusive policy and adhered to the original Black Consciousness line that Whites could not be trusted to cooperate with Africans. They were in a distinct minority. More significant was Inkatha, a movement founded in 1928 and led by Chief Mangosuthu Buthelezi, head of the KwaZulu administration, since 1975. Buthelezi claimed that Inkatha was a national liberation movement, and initially he seemed to reach an accommodation with the black nationalists. But it soon became clear that Inkatha was an ethnic movement. It drew on the Zulu military tradition, derived its main support among rural Zulu, and was divisive in the black resistance to apartheid. In parts of Natal and KwaZulu, Inkatha gangs and Zulu supporters of the UDF had violent confrontations. Buthelezi was tolerated by the South African government and was popular in conservative circles overseas, since he opposed sanctions and spoke out strongly for the capitalist system. The UDF was more heterogeneous and included people who were for as well as against sanctions, and socialists as well as capitalists.[24]

The government claimed that the UDF was a surrogate for the banned ANC. Although that was an exaggeration, the ANC acquired great prestige during the 1980s. The UDF respected its policies, as embodied in the Freedom Charter, and most UDF supporters treated the ANC as the prospective government of South Africa and the imprisoned Nelson Mandela as their prospective president.

South Africa's Foreign Relations, 1978–1986

The Botha government used South Africa's economic superiority to dominate the neighboring countries and prevent them from providing sanctuary for militant refugees. South Africa's economic leverage over the region was formidable (map 9). The South African Customs Union integrated Lesotho, Botswana, and Swaziland into the South African economy. The giant Anglo American Corporation of South Africa and its subsidiaries had substantial interests in Botswana, Zimbabwe, and Zambia, as well as Namibia. South African railroads and ports dominated commodity transport throughout the region. South Africa controlled the supply of oil and electricity to its neighbors. South Africa also employed 280,000 migrant workers from other countries in the region in 1984, and miners' remittances to them amounted to R 538 million in 1983. In 1980, in an

9. Modern Southern Africa

effort to reduce their dependence on South Africa, Angola, Botswana, Lesotho, Malawi, Mozambique, Swaziland, Tanzania, Zambia, and Zimbabwe founded a Southern African Development Coordination Conference, but they were unable to make substantial progress toward their goal.[25]

South Africa also used its military superiority to restrain neighboring governments from pursuing antiapartheid policies. Between 1981 and 1983, South African commandos raided or carried out undercover operations against every one of its neighbors. In addition, the South African armed forces continued to occupy Namibia, and South Africa intervened substantially in both of the former Portuguese territories. It cooperated with the National Union for the Total Independence of Angola (UNITA), which was also supplied with arms by the United States, in its civil war against the government of Angola; and it provided arms and financial and technical assistance to the Mozambique National Resistance (M.N.R. or RENAMO), a motley collection of ex-Portuguese colonials and local chiefs and peasants who were wreaking widespread havoc in Mozambique. So destructive was this activity that in 1984, in the Nkomati Accord (an agreement signed on the banks of the Komati River), Mozambique undertook not to assist the ANC, while South Africa promised to stop aiding RENAMO. In the same year, South Africa promised to remove its troops from Angola. But South Africa did not honor those commitments; it continued to aid both UNITA and RENAMO.[26]

The Botha government was fortunate in the shifts in domestic politics in London and Washington. Margaret Thatcher became prime minister of Britain in 1979, and although her government then presided over the negotiations that led to the transfer of power in Zimbabwe, she was adamantly opposed to sanctions against South Africa. In ensuing years, Thatcher rejected demands by other members of the Commonwealth that Britain should join them in taking strong economic measures against apartheid. The Reagan administration, too, opposed sanctions and ignored the increasingly popular antiapartheid lobby in the United States. Chester Crocker, Ronald Reagan's able assistant secretary of state for African affairs, devoted most of his time and energy to a prolonged diplomatic effort to remove Cuban troops from Angola in exchange for implementation of the U.N. plan for the liberation of Namibia from South African control. Accepting the premise of National Security Study Memorandum 39, that the only way for meaningful change to come about in South Africa was through the Whites, he formulated a policy of "constructive engagement" toward South Africa, which amounted to encouraging the South African government to reform apartheid and refraining from making contacts with antiapartheid organizations, such as the ANC.[27]

Nevertheless, by 1986 foreign countries were beginning to exert substantial pressure on the South African government. As violence erupted in South African townships night after night, millions of television sets in tens of countries showed South African police and soldiers beating and shooting unarmed Blacks. The government stopped journalists from reporting such incidents in November 1985, but by then South Africa had become a major focus of public attention.

Margaret Thatcher tried hard to prevent Britain and the Commonwealth countries from taking joint measures against apartheid. Early in 1986, however, seven senior Commonwealth politicians, led by Malcolm Fraser, a former prime minister of Australia, and Gen. Olusegun Obasanjo, a former head of the Nigerian government, visited South Africa. The other members were from Barbados, Britain, Canada, India, and Tanzania. A Commonwealth conference had instructed them "to promote . . . a political dialogue aimed at replacing apartheid by popular government." After meeting a wide range of South Africans, from President Botha to Nelson Mandela, on March 13 they made a proposal to the South African government. The government should remove the military from the townships, provide for freedom of assembly and discussion, suspend detention without trial, release Mandela and other political prisoners and detainees, unban the ANC and the PAC, and permit normal political activity; for its part, the ANC should enter into negotiations with the government and suspend violence, which Mandela had agreed to do. On May 19, 1986, the mission came to an abrupt end. On that day South African forces attacked alleged ANC bases in Zimbabwe, Botswana, and Zambia—all Commonwealth members. The Commonwealth group then left South Africa and issued a report deploring the conditions in the country, condemning the government, and predicting full-fledged guerrilla warfare unless the cycle of violence was broken.[28]

In the United States, meanwhile, antiapartheid protests had developed a powerful momentum. Randall Robinson, the executive director of Trans-Africa, a black lobbying organization, built a coalition of clergy, students, trade unionists, and civil rights leaders. In the two years since November 1984, six thousand Americans, including eighteen members of Congress, had been arrested while picketing the South African embassy and consulates. Many state and city governments and universities sold their investments in companies that did business in South Africa, and American companies themselves began to withdraw from their South African enterprises—forty in 1985, another fifty in 1986. In July 1985, Chase Manhattan bank created a financial crisis in South Africa when it refused to roll over its short-term loans and other banks followed suit.

The question of punitive economic sanctions against South Africa was hotly debated throughout the United States. Opponents of sanctions argued that economic progress would eventually erode apartheid, that sanctions would hurt Blacks more than Whites, and that Botha's reform policy was moving South Africa in the right direction. Supporters of sanctions replied that segregation and apartheid had developed in a century of economic growth, that many black South Africans supported sanctions, and that Botha was unrelenting in his refusal to give Africans an effective say in the political system.[29]

Accepting Pretoria's propaganda at face value, President Reagan remained ill-informed about the situation in South Africa and prejudiced in favor of the white population. South Africa, he said in 1985, has "eliminated the segregation we once had in our own country."[30] By September 1985, however, American public opinion was so aroused that, to preempt more vigorous action by Congress, Reagan issued an executive order imposing limited sanctions against South Africa. But the momentum grew. In October 1986, Congress passed the Comprehensive Anti-Apartheid Act over the president's veto, banning new investments and bank loans, ending South African air links with the United States, prohibiting a range of South African imports, and threatening to cut off military aid to allies suspected of breaching the international arms embargo against South Africa.

In South Africa, meanwhile, the government's reforms, combined with widespread black resistance, evoked a political backlash among white bureaucrats who lived by administering apartheid, semiskilled workers threatened by black competition, and ideologues steeped in racist simplicities. The Conservative party, led by Andries Treurnicht, a former cabinet minister, was cutting into the government's majorities in by-elections on a platform of strict Verwoerdian apartheid. Still further to the right was the Herstigte Nasionale party (Reestablished National party), and beyond that, the Afrikaner Weerstand Beweging (Afrikaner Resistance Movement), an extraparliamentary group, used swastika-like symbols and broke up government meetings.[31]

The government's problems were compounded by a deteriorating economic situation, engendered in large part by the political uncertainty and the withdrawal of foreign investment. The annual rate of inflation rose from 11 percent in 1983 to 13.25 percent in 1984, 16.2 percent in 1985, and 18.6 percent in 1986. Real growth per capita declined in 1985 and 1986. Unemployment was rising continuously.[32]

In those circumstances, National party members were tugging the government in different directions. Doves wanted to keep trying to appease the West. Hawks prevailed on May 19, 1986, when the military raids on neighboring states ended negotiations with the Commonwealth group.

Thereafter the reform program ground to a halt. Botha himself realized that foreigners would never be satisfied unless he gave the franchise to Africans. That he was not willing to do.

Between July 20, 1985, and March 7, 1986, the government applied a state of emergency in many parts of the country. On June 12, 1986, it proclaimed what became an annually renewed, indefinite, nationwide state of emergency and arrested hundreds of antiapartheid activists. The emergency regulations gave every police officer broad powers of arrest, detention, and interrogation, without a warrant; they empowered the police commissioner to ban any meeting; and they prohibited all coverage of unrest by television and radio reporters and severely curtailed newspaper coverage. The government had resorted to legalized tyranny.[33]

The State of Emergency

In proclaiming the state of emergency, the Botha government's primary objective was to reestablish control over the republic, especially over the African townships. The government also continued to pursue two other goals: the durable pacification of South Africa and hegemony over South Africa's neighbors. But none of those goals was fully attainable; moreover, they were mutually incompatible. First, the use of emergency powers in the search for domestic control reduced the manifestations of resistance but did not remove its underlying causes. Second, the government's reform program created a backlash within the white electorate but stopped short of giving Africans—the majority of the population—a substantial say in government, which alone might have achieved durable pacification. Third, the employment of emergency powers at home and the use of South Africa's economic and military strength to overawe its neighbors provoked increased economic pressures from the industrialized countries, with serious consequences for the national economy.

To reestablish control of the black population, the government resorted to bannings, arrests, detentions, and treason trials. Police interrogators tortured victims, and unidentified persons who were widely believed to be members of the security police assassinated antiapartheid activists inside and outside South Africa. The South African Defence Force said that South Africa was in a state of war and deployed 5,000 to 8,000 soldiers in the townships to augment the police. On February 12, 1987, Adriaan Vlok, minister of law and order, admitted that 13,300 people, a high proportion of whom were children, had been detained under the emergency regulations; unofficial estimates ran as high as 29,000. On March 2, 1987, Vlok also admitted that 43 people had died in police custody and that 263 people detained since the beginning of the state of emergency had been hospitalized. In 1988, a study by doctors of the National Medical and Dental Association revealed that about 78 percent of a test group of 131 detainees had been mentally abused through interrogation, threats, or humiliation. During that year the government banned more than thirty organizations, including the UDF and AZAPO, and severely curtailed the activities of COSATU, the largest and most militant black trade union federation.[34]

These events were largely unreported because of draconian restrictions on the communications media.[35] In 1987, however, the International Commission of Jurists sent four Western European lawyers to South Africa. In May 1988, they reported that "an undemocratic government has extended the executive power of the state so as to undermine the rule of law and destroy basic human rights. . . . We have found that the government has allowed intimidation of suspects and accused persons, and interference with legal processes by the security forces . . . to take place on a large scale and in a variety of ways. . . . We stress particularly the widespread use of torture and violence, even against children, which is habitually denied by the government and thus goes unpunished, though plainly illegal."[36]

South African forces also continued to invade neighboring countries. According to a report by a British Commonwealth committee, South Africa's destabilizing tactics between 1980 and 1989 led to the deaths of one million people, made a further three million homeless, and caused $35 billion worth of damage to the economies of neighboring states. This included raids into every one of its neighbors, massive support for RENAMO in Mozambique in spite of Botha's promise to the contrary, large-scale military invasions of Angola, and continued military occupation of Namibia. In February 1988, moreover, a South African force intervened to thwart a coup against the government of the "independent" homeland of Bophuthatswana.[37]

From time to time, President Botha and his colleagues made vague promises of domestic reform. In August 1988, Chris Heunis, minister of constitutional development and planning, declared that "the road of reform we have chosen is irreversible." In the same month, a government spokesman said that equal political rights for all was the ultimate aim of government planning.[38] On the vital question of political empowerment, however, the best the government could offer Africans was thirty out of fifty-nine seats in a National Council that would have had merely advisory powers. Twelve of those African seats, moreover, were to have been held by representatives of the nonindependent homeland governments, and the other eighteen seats were to have been occupied by Africans elected indirectly by the councillors who succeeded in the township elections in October 1988. African nationalist leaders and several homeland leaders promptly condemned the proposal. No Black of "caliber or representativeness" would sit on the National Council, said Chief Mangosuthu Buthelezi of KwaZulu. That idea, like its predecessors, was stillborn.[39]

Botha and his colleagues, thinking in racial categories, could not contemplate giving Africans an effective say in national politics because they feared that it would lead to rule by the African majority and that the consequences would be calamitous for the white population. President Botha made his meaning clear on August 18, 1988, when, addressing the National party's annual congress in Durban, he said, "As far as I'm concerned, I'm not even considering the possibility of black majority government in South Africa."[40]

The government made a great effort to acquire legitimacy for the township administrations, the existing African councillors having been totally discredited. But African nationalists boycotted the municipal elections that were held on a segregated basis in October 1988. Only 905 out of 1,839 seats for black councillors were contested, and in 183 wards there were no nominations at all. In the contested wards, only 25 percent of the registered voters cast their ballots—that is, 3 percent of the African population of South Africa (including all ten Homelands).[41]

While the government was trying to create institutions Africans could respect, it was losing ground among the white electorate. In the general election for the House of Assembly on May 6, 1987, the National party share of the vote fell to 52 percent (from 57 percent in 1981). Although that still gave the National party a commanding majority with 133 seats in the House of Assembly, the Conservative party, which stood for a reversion to strict Verwoerdian apartheid, polled 26 percent of the vote and won twenty-three seats, displacing the Progressive Federal party, which won only 14 percent of the vote and twenty seats, as the official parliamentary opposition.[42] The swing to the right in white politics continued in the elections in white municipalities in October 1988, when the Conservative party won control of most of the small towns in the Transvaal and nearly got a majority in Pretoria.[43] In the same period, unidentified persons destroyed the headquarters of four major antiapartheid organizations—

COSATU, the Southern African Catholic Bishops' Conference, the South African Council of Churches, and the Black Sash. In February 1988, several hundred armed members of the extra-parliamentary Afrikaner Weerstand Beweging marched through the streets of Pretoria to the Union Buildings and presented a petition calling on the government to create a "traditional Boer state" without Blacks.[44]

While white opinion was swinging to the right, black opinion was moving in the opposite direction. The government's attempt to co-opt significant elements in the Coloured and Indian communities by providing them with Houses in the tricameral Parliament was not a success. Since the new constitution had been inaugurated in 1984, many Coloureds and Indians had denounced those who participated, and in 1987, Allan Hendrickse, the leader of the party that controlled the Coloured House, resigned from the cabinet. In 1988, both the Coloured and the Indian houses blocked the government's attempt to enact legislation that would have imposed heavy penalties for violations of the residential segregation in the Group Areas Act.[45]

Official attempts to appease Africans were no more successful. Oupa Thando Mthimkulu expressed the feelings of many people in the townships in his poem about the Soweto uprising:

> Nineteen seventy-six
> You stand accused of deaths
> Imprisonment
> Exiles
> and detentions.
> You lost the battle
> You
> were not revolutionary
> Enough
> We do not boast about you
> Year of fire, year of ash.[46]

Township residents often clashed with police and soldiers, who were present in strength. There was also a spate of sabotage in South Africa, most of it attributed to the ANC. Between June 1986 and September 1988, more than a hundred explosions caused 31 deaths and 565 injuries in streets, restaurants, cinemas, shopping centers, and sports complexes in the major cities.[47]

Black workers contributed to the resistance. The government plan to control the trade unions by legalizing and registering them backfired. In

1987, there were 1,148 strikes—an unprecedented number. Most serious was a strike by the National Union of Mineworkers, led by Cyril Ramaphosa, when more than half of the country's 500,000 miners took part in a stoppage that lasted three weeks, during which 9 miners were killed and up to 300 were injured. Although they failed to achieve more than the 23 percent wage increase the Chamber of Mines had offered, they did receive improved death and holiday benefits.[48]

Because most secular antiapartheid leaders were in exile, in prison, or banned, clergy were thrust into the fore of the struggle against apartheid. Especially prominent were Desmond Tutu, Anglican archbishop of Cape Town, who was awarded the Nobel Peace Prize in 1984; Allan Boesak, moderator of the Dutch Reformed Mission church and president of the World Alliance of Reformed Churches; and Beyers Naude, general secretary of the South African Council of Churches from 1985 to 1987, and his successor in that office, Frank Chikane. In June 1988, they and twenty-two other clergy, representing sixteen denominations, openly defied the state of emergency regulations by calling on all Christians to boycott the elections of October 26 for segregated municipal councils. "The truth cannot be bound by unjust laws," they declared. "By involving themselves in the elections, Christians would be participating in their oppression or the oppression of others." No elections could be free and fair under the emergency because "the structures of the constitutional system in South Africa are based on racial and ethnic identity."[49]

The government, meanwhile, was suffering setbacks abroad. In spite of its claim to be recognized as "the regional power" in Southern Africa, the financial and human costs of intervening in Angola and administering Namibia proved excessive. In 1988, the army incurred losses in engagements with well-equipped Cuban and Angolan troops in southern Angola, and on December 22, South Africa signed an accord with Cuba and Angola through the mediation of the United States and the cooperation of the Soviet Union. There was to be a phased withdrawal of 52,000 Cuban troops from Angola and of South African troops from Namibia. A U.N. peace-keeping force was to monitor an election for a constituent assembly, and Namibia was to become independent during 1990, in accordance with the provisions of U.N. Security Council Resolution 435 of 1978. South Africa also undertook to stop assisting UNITA in Angola. South Africa did derive two substantial benefits from the agreement. The ANC was obliged to close its Angolan bases, and South Africa was not debarred from exercising sovereignty over Walvis Bay during the transition. Walvis Bay, an enclave on the Namibian coast, was the only effective port for Namibia, but it had been annexed to the Cape Colony in 1884 and had been treated as part of South Africa since 1910.[50] Nevertheless, by 1989, it was evident that the policies of the Botha government were bankrupt.

The time had come for negotiations.

CHAPTER 8

The Political Transition, 1989–1994

Between 1989 and 1994, South Africans surprised the world. Although the country was wracked by unprecedented violence and teetered on the brink of civil war, black and white politicians put an end to more than three hundred years of white domination and fashioned a nonracial constitution, which effectively transferred political power from the white minority to the black majority. May 10, 1994, the day the presidency of South Africa passed from an Afrikaner who led the party of white supremacy to the leader of an African nationalist movement, was the culmination of one of the finest achievements of the twentieth century.[1]

The Background to Negotiations

In the mid- and late 1980s, while the government was trying to establish control of the African townships under a state of emergency, ineluctable processes were undermining the regime's long-term prospects. One was demographic. According to official census reports, the white population of South Africa (including the Homelands) dropped from its peak of 21 percent of the total in 1936 to 15 percent in 1985. In 1988, officials estimated that by the year 2005 Whites would form only 10 percent of the population. (In fact, it sank to that level by 1999.) Moreover, the African surge to the cities, propelled by the rapid increase of the African population and the persistent deterioration of the Homelands, was continuing unabated. Even though most newcomers were living in shacks without electricity or water, the African population of the townships doubled from 5.2 million to 10.6 million between 1951 and 1980. Demographers foresaw that by the year 2000, Africans would outnumber Whites by five to one in the urban areas.[2]

Second, the economy was structurally unsound, and South Africa was in a deep recession. The apartheid state was an extravagance, with three parliamentary chambers, fourteen departments of education, health, and welfare (one for each "race" at the national level, one for each province, and one for each Homeland), large military and security establishments, and financially dependent Homelands. Isolated by sanctions, the South African economy was inefficient. The country did not make good use of its human resources: Whites, however mediocre their talents, had a near monopoly on middle- and upper-level jobs in the bureaucracy and in the private sector. South African products were not competitive with those of the developing countries of Asia, Latin America, and eastern Europe, because South African trade unions had forced wages far above those of such countries. Nor were South African–manufactured products competitive with those of Japan, the United States, Canada, and western European countries, because of low productivity and poor quality. In addition, sanctions and a spate of disinvestments from South Africa were beginning to bite. In particular, South Africa lacked access to foreign capital. As Gerhard de Kock, governor of the South African Reserve Bank, said in 1988: "In the present international political climate the capital account remains the Achilles heel of South Africa's balance of payments."[3] World Bank figures showed that South Africa's growth rate was among the lowest in the world. The gross domestic product per capita at constant 1985 prices decreased by 1.1 percent in the period 1980 to 1987. The Bank for International Settlements reported that South Africa's inflation rate, which was about 15 percent in the period 1980 to 1987 with a slight decrease in

1988, was the third highest among industrialized nations, surpassed only by those of Turkey and Israel.[4]

Third, despite the government's segregation dogma and its Homelands fantasy, white and black South Africans were inextricably interdependent. Africans, no longer self-sufficient peasants, were obliged to seek employment, and Whites needed African labor. The cumulative economic power of black people as consumers, workers, and entrepreneurs was becoming increasingly significant. In 1985, Whites had about 55.5 percent of the disposable income (income from all sources after taxation), Africans had 31.8 percent, Coloureds 8.8 percent, and Indians 3.9 percent; and the black share was rising.[5] By 1990, substantial numbers of Blacks were reaching the middle level of employment in industry, and a few had reached the managerial level. Others were prospering in the informal economy. Africans dominated the transport services in the townships, for example. There were about 80,000 unlicensed African-owned taxis, and 45,000 African operators belonged to the South African Bus and Taxi Association.[6]

Furthermore, by the end of 1989 profound changes in the wider world were contributing to the demise of apartheid. The Soviet Union was beginning to disintegrate, the communist regimes in eastern Europe were collapsing, and the Berlin Wall had fallen. Moreover, capitalist and communist governments were cooperating in freeing Namibia from South African control—the South-West African People's Organization won a U.N.-sponsored election in November 1989 and became the government of an independent Namibia in March 1990. These events had two complementary effects. They deprived the liberation movement of its main sources of support. They also made nonsense of the government's claim to be protecting South Africans from a communist onslaught. In the Western-dominated post–Cold War world, both sides in the South African conflict had an interest in solving their problems peacefully and democratically. The domestic situation pointed in the same direction. It was becoming increasingly evident that the South African government could not maintain white supremacy indefinitely; but it was also apparent that the liberation movement could not overthrow the regime. Either side could damage the other, neither could win total victory. Furthermore, the longer the conflict continued, the worse the damage would be to all South Africans.

By the mid-1980s, many influential Whites were facing up to these realities. Since the ANC was the most popular and most effective of the banned black political organizations—the prospects of its principal rival, the Pan Africanist Congress, were blighted by poor leadership—white business people, intellectuals, clergy, and sports administrators made pilgrimages to open dialogues with the ANC leadership in exile. In September 1985, a group of businessmen, led by no less a figure than Gavin Relly, Harry Oppenheimer's successor as chairman of the giant Anglo American Corporation, met with ANC president Oliver Tambo in Zambia. In 1986, Pieter de Lange, chairman of the elite Afrikaner Broederbond, had a long discussion with Thabo Mbeki, the ANC information director, after attending a Ford Foundation conference in Long Island, New York. In August 1987, sixty-one white South Africans, most of them Afrikaners, led by Frederik van Zyl Slabbert, founder of the Institute for a Democratic Alternative for South Africa and a former leader of the Progressive Federal party, went to Dakar, Senegal, where they held three days of talks with seventeen members of the ANC. In meetings such as these, Mbeki, a suave and intelligent graduate of Sussex University with the style of a stereotypical English gentleman, put the white participants at ease, and both sides grew to realize that they had a common interest in seeking a peaceful solution to the conflict in South Africa. The Dakar session culminated in a joint communiqué expressing unanimous support for a negotiated settlement. Mbeki praised Slabbert as an Afrikaner pioneer and stressed that both sides were agreed on "the kind of democratic, non-racial South Africa we want."[7]

Not only reform-minded Whites were facing up to the prospect of fundamental change in South Africa. The demands by the Afrikaner Weerstand Beweging (AWB; Afrikaner Resistance Movement) and other rightwing Afrikaner groups that a white state be carved out of South Africa were evidence that fatalism was infecting the entire white population.[8]

Meanwhile, even as the Botha government was trying to manage the situation by brute force, it also secretly began to contact ANC leaders, exploring alternative ways of controlling the country and trying to discover and exploit the ANC's internal divisions. Aware that Mandela, through sheer force of intellect and personality, had become the leader of the black political prisoners and that his name was a rallying call at home and abroad for liberation, the government hoped to persuade Mandela to accept his freedom on condition that he abstain from politics, or renounce revolutionary ideas and become the head of a "moderate" African movement, including the Homeland politicians. For these purposes, it moved him from Robben Island to Pollsmoor prison in the Cape peninsula. Initially, he was accompanied there by Walter Sisulu and three other prisoners, but in 1985 he was placed alone in a different part of the prison, without access to colleagues. Mandela rejected several offers of conditional freedom and had no intention of becoming a moderate, but, believing that it would be possible to negotiate an end to apartheid, he wrote to justice minister Kobie Coetsee and requested an interview. In 1988, after they had several sessions, the government appointed a committee comprising Coetsee, two senior prison officers, and Neil Barnard, the director of National Intelligence, to hold a series of meetings with Mandela. The committee urged Mandela to renounce the ANC's commitment to the armed struggle, its alliance with the Communist party, and its goal of majority rule. Although he refused to do as they asked, his realism and his stress on reconciliation between Whites and Blacks in a postapartheid South Africa made a deep impression on the committee.[9]

In December 1988, recognizing that Mandela would probably become the head of a transformed South Africa, the government moved him to a comfortable house on the grounds of the Victor Verster prison near Paarl, about forty miles from Cape Town, where he was treated as an honored guest rather than a prisoner and could entertain visitors. Three months later, Mandela sent President Botha a ten-page memorandum that went to the heart of the matter. "I now consider it necessary in the national interest for the African National Congress and the government to meet urgently to negotiate an effective political settlement." Responding to the Coetsee committee's demands, he said that armed struggle was "a legitimate form of self-defense against a morally repugnant system of government"; cooperation with the Communist party was "strictly limited to the struggle against racial oppression"; and "white South Africa will simply have to accept that there will never be peace and stability in the country until the principle [of majority rule] is fully applied." Mandela also set out his preconditions for the suspense of the armed struggle and the opening of formal negotiations: the government should legalize the ANC, release political prisoners, end the state of emergency, and withdraw its troops from the townships. But he realized that "two central issues would have to be addressed" in the negotiations: "the ANC's demand for majority rule in a unitary state" and "the concerns of white South Africans over this demand. The most crucial task which will face the government and the ANC will be to reconcile these two positions."[10] As journalist Patti Waldmeir comments, that Mandela memorandum contained "the eventual deal in outline."[11]

The members of the ANC executive in exile were not fully informed about Mandela's dealings with government officials, but they, too, had been having a series of secret meetings with prominent Afrikaners. At a private house in England they discussed the future of South Africa and developed considerable social rapport across the color line.[12] Yet they were deeply divided about the desirability of having formal discussions with the government. In August 1989, meeting in Zimbabwe, they issued a cautious document known as the Harare Declaration. It might be possible to "end apartheid through negotiations," they said, if the Pretoria regime was prepared to negotiate "genuinely and seriously." But first the government would have to do five things: lift the state of emergency and remove the troops from the townships, end the restrictions on political activity, legalize all political organizations, release all political prisoners, and stop all political executions. There was no suggestion of concessions to the white population.[13]

Botha could not bring himself to negotiate with Africans, however, and in July 1989, when he eventually invited Mandela to the presidential residence in Cape Town, he did no more than indulge in small talk. But Botha's leadership days were numbered: he had a stroke in January 1989, in February he resigned as National party leader, and in August he lost the post of state president following a revolt by his cabinet, whose members resented his autocratic ways.

As Botha's successor, the National party parliamentary caucus chose Frederik Willem de Klerk. De Klerk was the son and grandson of National party politicians. He was deeply committed to Afrikaner cultural and political nationalism, and he was regarded as a conservative member of Botha's cabinet. He was, however, twenty years younger than Botha, and like many other Afrikaners of his generation, he realized that in its current form apartheid was not workable; it was necessary to respond to the domestic and foreign pressures by taking more drastic action than the tentative reforms adopted by Botha. His older brother, Professor Willem de Klerk, believes that soon after his election he underwent "a political conversion"; others have called it a "religious conversion."[14] After reviewing the situation, the new president concluded that the best hope for his people was to negotiate a settlement from a position of strength, while his government was still the dominant force in the country, and he persuaded his cabinet to approve of a remarkably radical initiative.[15] On February 2, 1990, he announced in parliament the lifting of the ban on the ANC, the Pan Africanist Congress (PAC), and the South African Communist party

(SACP); the removal of restrictions on thirty-three domestic organizations, including the United Democratic Front and the Congress of South African Trade Unions; the freeing of political prisoners who had been incarcerated for nonviolent actions; and the suspension of capital punishment. That speech went a long way toward meeting the preconditions for negotiations set by Mandela and the Harare Declaration. It was de Klerk's great moment in history.[16]

Nine days later, Mandela was released unconditionally after twenty-seven years in jail. Soon afterward he began a series of foreign travels to become acquainted with the contemporary world. He went first to Lusaka to meet his ANC friends in exile, then to England and the United States. He was treated as a hero everywhere. In New York, he had a triumphant ticker-tape parade down Broadway in a forty-car motorcade; in Washington he addressed both houses of Congress, where he received a standing ovation.[17] De Klerk, too, visited Europe and the United States, where he received a warm welcome from politicians and businesspeople.[18]

Talks about Talks

Before they could start negotiations on substantial issues, the parties had to agree upon a format—who should participate and what should the agenda be? This took nearly two years. Leaders of the white establishment and the black resistance had to get to know each other and create a minimum of mutual trust before they could sit down together and thrash out the terms of a new political and constitutional order. Moreover, on both sides of the color line there were people who wished to torpedo the peaceful, negotiated change process. White South Africans—especially Afrikaners—had been molded by years of racist propaganda to abominate the very idea of black empowerment. The Conservative party, which won 30 percent of the vote for the white legislature in a general election in 1989, as well as several organizations still further to the right, vehemently opposed negotiations with Blacks; and so did elements in the army, the police, and the bureaucracy. Africans, too, were deeply divided on the issue. Many, especially former guerrillas who had spent years training to seize control of South Africa by force, were profoundly suspicious of Mandela and shocked by his independent discussions with the government.

De Klerk met Mandela for the first time a month before he released him from prison. Although they disagreed about the way to solve South Africa's problems, the meeting went reasonably well, and in his first speech as a free man, Mandela called de Klerk a man of integrity—a phrase that would come back to haunt him.[19] Relations between them began to sour as early as March 26, 1990, when police, in one of many clashes with township residents, opened fire and killed eleven demonstrators at Sebokeng, thirty miles south of Johannesburg.[20] Mandela then called off further meetings for a while, but on May 2, 3, and 4, about a dozen ANC leaders met their government counterparts for three days of talks at the president's official residence near Cape Town. This was a get-to-know session, which went some way toward easing their personal relationships.[21] The government then canceled the state of emergency, repealed the remaining apartheid laws, released most of its political prisoners, and allowed the exiles to return to South Africa with immunity from prosecution. In response, after a heated debate in the ANC executive council, Mandela announced that he was suspending the armed struggle on the advice of none other than Joe Slovo, the former head of the military wing of the ANC—the white man who was the symbol of evil communism to white South Africa.[22]

But suspicions soon revived because there were loose cannons in both camps. In 1988, the ANC leadership in exile had authorized a group of ANC militants, led by Mac Maharaj, an Indian member of the ANC executive and former Robben Island friend of Mandela, to create an underground revolutionary network inside South Africa. This operation, known as Vula (the opening), did not achieve much, and Mandela probably knew nothing about it. But in July 1990 the police uncovered it, arrested Maharaj, and unearthed a mass of Vula documents, from which de Klerk concluded that even then, while Mandela and his colleagues were talking peace, they were still following a hidden agenda to overthrow the state by force.[23]

The anti-ANC dirty tricks were much more serious. Throughout the years 1990 to 1994, deadly physical struggles for power were taking place alongside the negotiations for a peaceful settlement. In 1989, according to the South African Institute of Race Relations, 1,403 people died of political violence in South Africa. That was a record number, but it was only a prelude to what followed. There were 3,699 political killings in 1990; 2,706 in 1991; 3,347 in 1992; 3,794 in 1993; and 2,476 in 1994.[24] It was the South African state, in the form of the government, the civil service, and the security forces, that was largely responsible for the killings. Ever since at least 1948, the state had been a gross perpetrator of human rights violations in South Africa, and it continued to be so during de Klerk's presidency. Elements in the police, the army, and the security forces continued to kidnap, torture, and assassinate political opponents. De Klerk always denied that his government was behind the violence and insisted that he did everything he could to stop it; but Mandela came to the conclusion that a government-related Third Force was responsible for extensive attacks on ANC supporters, and his trust in de Klerk evaporated.[25] News of the abuses began to appear in the press in July 1991, and over the next three years a commission headed by Judge Richard Goldstone issued a series of reports increasingly critical of government agencies. However, the full extent of the criminal activities was not revealed until after the change of regime, when Mandela appointed a Truth and Reconciliation Commission, chaired by Archbishop Desmond Tutu.[26] In 1998, after three years' work and thousands of interviews the commission reported that "a network of security and ex-security force operatives . . . fomented, initiated, facilitated and engaged in violence, which resulted in gross violations of human rights, including random and targeted killings."[27]

The KwaZulu Homeland and the province of Natal, which included Durban, South Africa's major seaport, were a main focus of the vendetta against the ANC by government agents. Chief Mangosuthu Buthelezi, an ambitious, mercurial character, was prime minister of KwaZulu and head of Inkatha, which was originally a cultural movement but which became more and more political until 1990, when it was renamed the Inkatha Freedom party (IFP). Supported by conservative chiefs and largely illiterate peasants, he ran KwaZulu as a one-party state with gross violations of human rights, while most urban and better-educated Zulus supported the ANC. The two sides fought for control of territory. Buthelezi had previously been an active member of the ANC, which had encouraged him to form Inkatha; but he had broken with the ANC executive in exile in 1979, when it denounced him as a government collaborator for outspokenly advocating capitalism, opposing sanctions against South Africa, and presiding over an apartheid institution, the Zulu Homeland.[28] Thereafter, Buthelezi identified himself as a Zulu nationalist, in contrast to the broad South African nationalism of the ANC. After the unbanning of the ANC, the struggle that had begun in KwaZulu and Natal in the 1980s intensified dramatically. Buthelezi resented being excluded from the ANC's meetings with the government and feared that Zulu interests would be ignored. Like other Homeland leaders, he hoped to retain power by making KwaZulu a sovereign state or, at least, a member of a loosely federal South Africa.[29]

Buthelezi and the government therefore had a common interest: both wished to undermine the ANC. South African army and police units provided valuable assistance to the IFP in the form of money, training, weapons, and personnel, and collaborated with the homeland government in covert activities against the ANC. Supporters of the ANC replied in kind. IFP "hit squads" and ANC "self-defense units" fought one another in rival villages, killing men, women, and children, and burning their homes. Although most of the victims were ANC supporters, a large minority were IFP supporters. Mandela tried to calm the situation in KwaZulu but without success, largely because local ANC warlords prevented him from dealing directly with Buthelezi until it was too late to be effective.[30]

In 1990, political violence escalated in the Johannesburg area as well as in KwaZulu and Natal. There were struggles between rival political factions for control of the townships. In many cases, police turned a blind eye to IFP aggressors, or actually assisted them. Zulu male migrant workers, housed in squalid hostels, started a series of brutal attacks on township residents, killing many and destroying their homes. South African police planned and participated in some of those attacks. Also, gangs of unidentified people murdered passengers on trains commuting to and from Soweto. The Truth and Reconciliation Commission later found that members of the South African army's special forces had collaborated with IFP people in planning those massacres.[31]

The odds against a peaceful settlement in South Africa were increased by confusion within the ANC, which had enormous problems. The ANC members—700,000 according to Mandela—were an amalgamation of people who agreed in hating apartheid but who had very different experiences. Some, like Mandela, had been in prison for years. Others had been in exile—many had trained for guerrilla warfare in the former Soviet Union, eastern Europe, and tropical Africa. Most had remained inside South Africa and had been active in the United Democratic Front (UDF) and the Congress of South African Trade Unions (COSATU). Opinions differed sharply between those who favored negotiations with the government and those who feared that negotiations would result in a sell-out of black interests and clung to the vain hope that they could overthrow the regime by force. There were also ideological differences between the substantial number of dedicated communists in the ANC and those who were more open-minded about the structure of a future South Africa. Mandela was not a communist, but he was influenced by Marxist literature and communist friends. He was widely distrusted by many ANC members because of his secret discussions with the government, which took place without consultation with his fellow prisoners or with the exiled leadership in Lusaka.[32] Moreover, his prestige (as well as his peace of mind) suffered because of the errant behavior of his wife, Winnie. He was deeply loyal to her because the government had grossly ill-treated her during his long imprisonment, but she had become an arrogant and violent woman. In June 1991, after a four-month, much-publicized trial, a judge called her an "unblushing liar," found her guilty of kidnapping and assault, and sentenced her to six years in jail.[33] (In June 1993, the Supreme Court confirmed the kidnapping charge, removed the assault charge, and reduced the punishment to a two-year suspended sentence and a fine.)

In July 1991, the ANC held its first conference in South Africa in thirty years. Ever since it had been banned in 1961, a tight clique of about thirty-five people had laid down policy for the ANC. In a highly contentious atmosphere, the 2,244 delegates, who had been elected by ANC branches inside and outside South Africa, met to transform a once secret, illegal movement into a mass political party with a broader and more democratic management. Since Oliver Tambo, who had held the ANC together during the later apartheid years, was not a candidate (he had had a stroke and died in 1993), there was no possible rival to Mandela; the delegates elected him president, although many of them still had reservations. For secretary-general they rejected Alfred Nzo, Mandela's candidate and a senior member of the ANC in exile, in favor of Cyril Ramaphosa, who had built COSATU into a powerful opponent of apartheid and had become a conspicuous leader of the United Democratic Front. They also elected a sixty-six-member National Executive Committee (NEC), which included numerous men and women who had been active in the UDF and were virtually unknown to the formerly imprisoned or exiled members. Thereafter Mandela was the unchallenged head of the ANC, but he had to be careful to work in cooperation with the NEC.[34]

Meanwhile, as the violence escalated in KwaZulu and the Witwatersrand townships, relations between Mandela, de Klerk, and Buthelezi degenerated. On September 14, 1991, concerned South African church, business, and civic leaders tried to stem the chaos by holding a conference at the Carlton Hotel in Johannesburg, where the three leaders and heads of other parties signed a code of conduct, which prohibited all parties from intimidating, threatening, or killing each other's members. But Buthelezi misjudged the situation and ruined the conference. To demonstrate his strength, he bussed in two thousand armed Zulu warriors, who paraded outside the hotel, and at the signing ceremony he refused to shake hands with Mandela and de Klerk. Afterward, de Klerk tried to make excuses for Buthelezi's behavior, but Mandela disagreed and publicly lambasted de Klerk.[35] Nevertheless, both de Klerk and Mandela were determined to get substantial negotiations going, and they met privately several times to work out ways and means. Following these meetings, in late November leaders of twenty political organizations laid down ground rules for the talks. A Convention for a Democratic South Africa (CODESA), composed of twelve-member delegations from every participating party, was to meet under the chairmanship of two judges (one Afrikaner, the other Indian). CODESA was to write an interim constitution, in terms of which elections would be held for a Constituent Assembly, which would write a final constitution in accordance with principles laid down in the interim document.

Constitution-making

CODESA opened on December 20, 1991, in the World Trade Centre outside Johannesburg. It was strikingly different from the National Convention of 1908–9, when thirty white men created the Union of South Africa out of four British colonies, with a flexible constitution that enabled the white minority to establish a system of racial domination. CODESA comprised nearly three hundred delegates, most of them Africans, many of them women. There were delegations from the government, from eight political parties, and from the ten Homelands. But CODESA was boycotted by parties on both extremes that hoped to wreck the negotiation process: the Pan Africanist Congress (PAC) and Azanian People's Organization (AZAPO) on the African side, and the Conservative party and others still further to the right on the white side. Buthelezi allowed an IFP delegation to take part, but declined to do so himself.[36]

In the plenary session on the first day, seventeen of the delegations endorsed a crucially important document—a Declaration of Intent setting out the basic components of an interim constitution.[37] It was to provide for universal suffrage, a bill of rights including civil and political rights, an independent judiciary with the power to declare legislation invalid, the elimination of the Homeland governments, and the incorporation of their territories into a new set of provinces. The IFP and Bophuthatswana delegations wished to retain the autonomy of their Homelands and refused to sign. The day ended in an explosion between the two principals: de Klerk made a bitter attack on the ANC and an outraged Mandela responded in kind.[38]

Although de Klerk and his colleagues endorsed the Declaration of Intent, they aimed to protect the interests of the white population by setting up constitutional obstacles to prevent white domination from being followed by black domination. Whereas in the past the National party had used its parliamentary majority to steamroll racist laws through parliament, now, facing the prospect that the ANC would become the majority party, it sought to curb it. Drawing on the work of Arend Lijphart, an American political scientist, the National party contended that political power in the new South Africa should be shared. Leaders of the two or three most successful parties should take turns as president. The cabinet should include members of those parties, and cabinet and parliamentary decisions should require the support of two-thirds or more of their total memberships. The bill of rights should protect racial and ethnic groups as well as individuals. Power should also be divided between the central and provincial governments, and the entire constitution should be extremely difficult to amend. De Klerk seems to have believed that, with the resources of the state behind him, he and his colleagues would be able to include enough of those obstacles in the constitution to preserve substantial power in white hands.[39]

They were greatly mistaken. The ANC, confident that it would win most of the seats in the new parliament, was adamant that the new constitution should create a unitary state with minimal checks on the power of the majority to impose its will. Moreover, Mandela was psychologically and intellectually stronger than de Klerk, and in the committees where the day-to-day work of CODESA was done, Cyril Ramaphosa, the chief ANC negotiator and former trade union bargainer, was more effective than Tertius Delport, his government counterpart. Mandela's determination that the Whites should not be able to prevent the ANC from dominating the new South Africa was bolstered by his knowledge that if he yielded too much he would play into the hands of his ANC critics. But, as he had shown in the memorandum he sent to President Botha from jail, he was also realistic in his awareness that the ANC would have to placate the Whites, who dominated the economy and controlled the police, the army, and the bureaucracy, by giving them some sense of participation and security in the new South Africa.[40]

In spite of their fundamental differences and their increasing dislike for each other, de Klerk and Mandela were bonded in a common commitment to the peace process.[41] But de Klerk had to secure his own power base. Therefore, in March 1992, after losing two by-elections to the Conservative party, he held a referendum of the white electorate. The result was resounding support for the peace process. Eighty-seven percent of those eligible did vote, and 68.7 percent of those who voted endorsed "the continuation of the reform process that the state president started on February 2 1990 and which is aimed at a new constitution through negotiations."[42] That result emboldened de Klerk to toughen his stand in CODESA; however, on May 26, when he insisted that the new constitution should place more limits on the power of the majority than the ANC could possibly accept, CODESA broke down.

Four months of heightened conflict throughout the country followed the failure of CODESA. There was a particularly bloody episode on June 17, 1992, when Zulu hostel dwellers at Boipatong, forty miles south of Johannesburg, made a vicious attack on a neighboring shack settlement and killed forty-five people, mainly women and children. Three days later, de Klerk courageously tried to appease the residents of Boipatong, but his convoy was driven out by an angry mob and police opened fire, killing three and wounding many more.[43] Mandela then suspended all talks with the government, and fighting escalated in KwaZulu and Natal, where both sides committed atrocities. The ANC was running a campaign of "rolling mass action," which culminated in August when several million workers went on strike and Mandela led fifty thousand followers though the streets of Pretoria to the government buildings. But that was not enough for the ANC radicals, who believed that events justified their demands for a resumed armed struggle. They managed to persuade a majority of the ANC's executive committee to campaign to bring down the governments of three Homelands—the Ciskei, Bophuthatswana, and KwaZulu—starting with the Ciskei. On September 7, Ronnie Kasrils, a former chief of intelligence of the guerrilla forces and member of the Vula operation, led seventy thousand marchers from Kingwilliamstown to nearby Bisho, the Ciskei capital; but the Ciskei police opened fire and routed them, killing twenty-eight. Mandela, who had consented to the project with reluctance, then called a halt to mass action and reprimanded Kasrils.[44]

By that time, South Africa verged on anarchy. As bloodshed mounted, the economy slumped, Western governments pressured all parties to cooperate in finding a peaceful solution, and de Klerk and Mandela both came to the conclusion that it was essential to get the negotiations back on track. The decline in their personal relationship made that difficult, but Cyril Ramaphosa and Roelf Meyer, the government's new principal negotiator, had been meeting quietly throughout the crisis and persuaded the two leaders to talk with each other. On September 26, when they met, Mandela and de Klerk signed a Record of Understanding that incorporated Mandela's demands. The hostels would be fenced, IFP members would be prohibited from publicly carrying axes, knobkerries, sharpened metal sticks, and spears (which they called their traditional weapons), and the remaining ANC prisoners (including convicted criminals) would be released. Martin Meredith, a biographer of Mandela, believes that this was the moment when the government lost control of the transition process and Mandela gained a psychological ascendancy over de Klerk that he never lost.[45] Although de Klerk endorsed that Record of Understanding, he still hoped to get a white veto in the constitution, but Mandela made it clear that that was not possible. It was Joe Slovo who paved the way to a solution of the problem of satisfying the National party without sacrificing the long-term interests of the ANC. Realizing that an ANC-dominated regime would not be able to govern effectively without the cooperation of Whites, he suggested in an article in the fall 1992 issue of the *African Communist* that the constitution should contain "sunset clauses." After heated debates, the ANC executive committee agreed that the interim constitution should honor the existing contracts of civil servants, judges, police, and military personnel, and provide for a period of compulsory power-sharing in the cabinet.[46]

By the time the government and the ANC resumed negotiations, the government's authority had eroded. In his frequent foreign travels, Mandela had clearly won the battle for external support. At home, the white right was gaining on the National party in the polls and several cabinet ministers had resigned. Moreover, the Goldstone commission's latest report said that it had uncovered a secret operation set up in 1991 by the Department of Military Intelligence to discredit the ANC, and Lieutenant-General Pierre Steyn, the army chief of staff, had discovered evidence of military intelligence involvement in train massacres, assassinations, and gun smuggling.[47] Negotiations between the two major parties went well enough for a new Multiparty Forum to be convened on April 1, 1993. This body included all the major political organizations in the country except the IFP and the Conservative party, which continued to oppose the process. Throughout its sessions, there was ferocious fighting among Africans in KwaZulu, Natal, and the Johannesburg area. Buthelezi threatened civil war if his demands were not met and joined the white right to form a Freedom Alliance to struggle for a federal constitution. The AWB, trying desperately to derail the proceedings, was responsible for two conspicuous events. First, on April 10, an AWB member shot and killed Chris Hani, the popular and able young general secretary of the Communist party, outside his home in a Johannesburg suburb. Mandela stopped that event from triggering riots serious enough to destroy the peace process by making a dignified appeal for calm on national television. He pointed out that the assassin was a Polish immigrant and the eyewitness who made the report that led to his arrest was an Afrikaner woman. In that crisis it was Mandela, not de Klerk, who had shown himself to be the real leader of South Africa.[48] The second episode was bizarre. On June 25, hundreds of AWB men, led by Eugene TerreBlanche, drove an armored car through the glass windows of the World Trade Centre while the Multiparty Forum was in session. They shouted abuse at the delegates, assaulted them, occupied their seats, and urinated on the floor.[49]

In spite of those distractions, the Multiparty Forum delegates toiled slowly but surely to create the interim constitution. Delegates and advisers of the small Democratic party—the party led by well-educated liberal white professionals—played a major part in the drafting process. On June 3, 1993, the Forum set a date—April 27, 1994—for the election of the new legislature. On November 17, de Klerk reluctantly yielded to Mandela yet another time and consented that decisions in the cabinet would not require a special majority; the next day a plenary session approved the interim constitution. In December the old white-dominated South African parliament passed the necessary legislation to ratify the document, thus providing legal continuity between the old regime and the new. Parliament also created a multiparty Transitional Executive Council, which became the de facto government of South Africa until the election, and an Independent Electoral Commission, which was responsible for organizing the election.[50]

In his autobiography, de Klerk states that in his closing speech to the Multiparty Forum he said, "We have shown that it was possible for people with widely differing views and beliefs to reach basic and sound agreements through compromise, through reasoned debate and through negotiation. I added that the transitional constitution was the distillation of the dreams of generations of disenfranchised South Africans. It offered a reasonable assurance of continuing security for those who traditionally had had the vote. . . . It satisfied all of us sufficiently to meet our most pressing concerns and hopes."[51]

The ANC was delighted with the outcome. Its major concessions—the sunset clauses—would gain the cooperation of Whites during a transitional period, but their effects would be only temporary. In the long run, the ANC expected to have unfettered legal power to implement its program. Slovo called it "a famous victory," as indeed it was.[52] It was also a vindication of Mandela's vision and persistence in concentrating on the negotiation process and ignoring the cries of ANC hotheads for the continuation of an armed struggle that was unlikely to achieve victory in the foreseeable future.

The Interim Constitution

Under the terms of the interim constitution, the legislature it created was to enact a final constitution in 1996.[53] However, the interim document included a set of basic constitutional principles and made them binding on the new legislature. It therefore became a precedent that the final constitution would follow in most respects. The document was long and detailed, filling 222 printed pages that were complex enough to be unintelligible to most South Africans. It was a liberal democratic constitution, including ideas borrowed from western Europe and the United States, modified by South African experience. The entire constitution was rigid: amendments required a two-thirds majority in a joint sitting of both houses of parliament. A Constitutional Court was to judge the constitutionality of laws and executive actions. South Africa was divided into nine provinces, which incorporated the former Homelands as well as the four former provinces (map 10). Although the powers of the provinces were considerable, they stopped short of federalism as it exists in the United States.

The document contained several peculiar features. First, there was an elaborate Bill of Rights, including economic rights as well as the classic civil and political rights; but many of the economic rights could not possibly be enforced at law, as in a clause that gave children the right to security, rudimentary nutrition, and basic health services. Second, as a result of Slovo's initiative, civil servants, judges, police, and military personnel could hold their jobs until they reached retirement age, and there was a form of compulsory power-sharing until 1999, when the election was to be held under the final constitution. A minority party that won 20 percent of the vote could designate a deputy president, and parties that won 5 percent of the vote were entitled to cabinet seats. Third, party bosses acquired exceptional powers. Under a list system of proportional representation, they prepared the list of candidates for their party. If members of parlia-

10. South Africa's postapartheid provinces

ment resigned from their party or were dismissed by it, they lost their seats, which were automatically filled by the next persons on the party list. Fourth, "traditional authorities" (chiefs) were empowered to apply customary African law in their communities, even though customary law was often in conflict with the Bill of Rights; for example, it subordinated women to male control, whereas the Bill of Rights guaranteed women equality with men. Fifth, in a provision not equaled anywhere else in the world, there were no fewer than eleven official languages: English, Afrikaans, and nine African languages, including isiZulu, isiXhosa, and Sesotho. In practice, English was already becoming the principal language of business and administration. Finally, several sections of the interim constitution, including those dealing with human rights, land restitution, customary law, and the powers of the provinces, were ambiguous and would need to be fleshed out by political action or resolved by the Constitutional Court.

The Election of 1994

Between the completion of the interim constitution on November 18, 1993, and the election in late April 1994, South Africa continued to teeter on the brink of civil war. The National party and the ANC, which had brokered the constitution, and the other political parties that had been involved in the negotiations and had endorsed the document were committed to taking part in the election; but on February 12, the deadline for registering to participate, the Conservative party, the IFP, the ruling parties in the Ciskei and Bophuthatswana, the PAC, and the radical Azanian People's Organisation (AZAPO) failed to do so. The PAC and AZAPO still favored the armed struggle and believed that the ANC had given too much to the Whites; but although they made a few murderous attacks on Whites, such as when the PAC's military wing fired on the congregation in a church in a Cape Town suburb, killing twelve people and injuring fifty-six, neither of them had enough resources or members to threaten the peace process. The Ciskei and Bophuthatswana leaders wanted to hold on to the powers they had acquired under apartheid, but unlike KwaZulu, they were pawns of the South African government and were unpopular with their own people.

The serious challenges to the peace process came from the IFP and the white right. The IFP resented its failure to succeed in the negotiations and demanded that KwaZulu should be virtually independent. It probably had the support of a majority of the Zulu people who, in all, amounted to 22 percent of the population of South Africa. For several years it had been acquiring funds, arms, and military training from rogue elements in the South African government. The white right denounced de Klerk as a traitor. The Conservative party and several more extreme parties coalesced into a Volksfront led by Constand Viljoen, a former head of the South African army, who would play a vital role in the events leading up to the election. Like his colleagues, Viljoen found it difficult to abandon his engrained racist assumptions, feared that the ANC would wreck the country, and was furious with de Klerk and his colleagues for negotiating away white supremacy. The Volksfront was formidable because its members were accustomed to military discipline, owned modern firearms, and permeated the senior ranks of the army, the police, and the bureaucracy. In October 1993, moreover, the Volksfront joined in an unlikely alliance with the IFP and the governments of the Ciskei and Bophuthatswana. They demanded that South Africa should be a loose confederation of sovereign states, including the Homelands and a Volkstaat for Afrikaners. Violence between the ANC and IFP rose to unprecedented levels on the Witwatersrand and in KwaZulu and Natal, while far right Whites broadcast racist propaganda from an illegal radio station and bombed ANC offices.[54]

Realizing that it would be disastrous if any substantial organization refused to take part in the election, both Mandela and de Klerk tried hard to win over the standouts. Ever since he left prison in February 1990, Mandela had repeatedly tried to befriend Buthelezi and persuade him to cooperate in founding a nonracial, united South Africa. Moreover, in August 1993, soon after the creation of the Volksfront, Mandela had made contact with Viljoen and other senior generals, and by the end of 1993 he and Mbeki had succeeded in gaining Viljoen's respect by showing that they had sympathy for Afrikaners and understood their fears for the future. On February 16, as the crisis deepened, Mandela announced a series of concessions. There would be wider powers for the provinces and more protection for both Zulu and Afrikaans culture; KwaZulu would be joined to Natal province with the name KwaZulu/Natal; and members of the new parliament who wanted a Volkstaat would be able to elect a council to explore that possibility. Since Buthelezi still did not yield, Mandela went to Durban on March 1 to meet him and make an impassioned speech for peace: "I will go down on my knees," he said, "to beg those who want to drag our country into bloodshed and to persuade them not to do so."[55] De Klerk, too, held a series of meetings with Buthelezi and the Zulu king, Goodwill Zwelethini, but to no avail.[56] Buthelezi still refused to participate in the election; but Viljoen decided to keep the election option open by announcing the formation of a new party—the Freedom Front party—and registering it just before midnight on March 4, the extended deadline set by the Independent Electoral Commission.[57]

A week later, the opposition from the right and its associated Homelands collapsed. Lucas Mangope, the dictator of Bophuthatswana, insisted that his Homeland should maintain the "independence" it had been given by the apartheid regime and banned the ANC from campaigning there. But the overwhelming majority of the inhabitants of the territory, including most of the civil servants and many members of the security forces, resented Mangope's autocratic leadership and wished to be part of the new South Africa. When they rose in rebellion, Mangope appealed to the Volksfront for help, and Viljoen mobilized a private army of four thousand men, telling the AWB leaders that he did not want them to participate. On March 11, however, a ragtag group of AWB men drove their cars to Mmabatho, the capital of Bophuthatswana, shooting randomly at African men, women, and children in the streets. The local army then rebelled and forced the raiders to retreat ignominiously. Three AWB men, who had been shooting through the window of their Mercedes, were stopped by gunfire and a Bophuthatswana policeman shot them to death in full view of television cameras. The South African government then assumed direct control of the territory and Mandela was wildly applauded at a mass rally in Mmabatho. Soon afterward, the equally unpopular Ciskei government also surrendered its independence, in the face of striking civil servants and looming mutiny in the police and army. Those events thoroughly discredited the Volksfront and its allies. Viljoen, supported by a substantial section of the Conservative party leadership, took the final step toward participation in the election by registering the names of his Freedom Front candidates, which left the IFP and a greatly weakened Conservative party as the only significant holdouts. The Conservative party could then be ignored, but not the IFP, which controlled a large territory and millions of potential voters.[58]

In March and early April, violence escalated to even higher levels in KwaZulu and the Johannesburg area. Nigerian reporter Dele Olojede described the tragic situation in a typical war-torn township—Umlazi, just south of Durban—in a New York newspaper on March 27: "The township, a collection of mud huts and red-brick matchbox homes scattered over the slopes of conical hills, is a virtual chessboard of exclusive ANC- or Inkatha-controlled neighborhoods. Thrown into the mix is an assortment of warlords, gangsters, and thugs who enforce political codes that allow anything but plurality. Mere valleys—or sometimes a collection of burnt-out huts—divide the territories."[59] On March 28, the IFP staged a massive demonstration in Johannesburg. Thousands of Zulus, armed with their "traditional weapons," marched through the city center. Snipers shot at them on the way, and when they reached Shell House, the ANC headquarters, the ANC security officers opened fire. By day's end fifty-three people, mostly IFP demonstrators, lay dead.[60]

Mandela, de Klerk, the Independent Electoral Commission (IEC), and the Transitional Executive Council worked hard to end the strife and bring Buthelezi into the fold. The IEC extended the deadline for registering for the election, and de Klerk recalled the old parliament to make several amendments to the interim constitution, increasing the range of issues on which the provinces would be able to legislate and permitting the provinces to devise their own constitutions. But Buthelezi continued his brinkmanship, supported by his nephew, King Goodwill Zwelethini, who declared that all of the territory ruled by Shaka in his prime in the 1820s should be reconstituted as an independent Zulu kingdom. Mandela and de Klerk made a final effort to satisfy the IFP on April 8, when they met Buthelezi and Zwelethini at Skukuza in South Africa's largest game reserve, the Kruger National Park. If the IFP would come into the election, they would suspend the deadline for registration and Zwelethini would be recognized as the constitutional monarch of the new KwaZulu/Natal province, with his own police and a secure stipend. Buthelezi rejected the offer. The ANC and the National party then decided to proceed with the election without the IFP and to subdue the IFP by force. On March 31, de Klerk declared a state of emergency in Natal and ordered troops to concentrate there. In a last desperate effort, Buthelezi persuaded Mandela and de Klerk to allow a foreign group of seven members to mediate, headed by Henry Kissinger, the former U.S. secretary of state, and Lord Carrington, Britain's former foreign secretary; but because the two sides disagreed about their terms of reference, most of the foreigners returned home within forty-eight hours without achieving anything. However, Washington Okumu, a Kenyan member of the group and an old friend of Buthelezi, met Buthelezi at the Johannesburg airport, where Okumu pointed out that if the IFP stayed out it would be isolated and defeated in a bloodbath. Buthelezi then decided to compete in the election—a decision that was eased by an agreement he concluded with de Klerk and Mandela (which was kept secret at the time) transferring three million acres of KwaZulu land to the Zulu monarch, so that he would not fall under the financial control of the new national government. Buthelezi registered his party on April 19, a mere week before the election, and the electoral commission made last-minute arrangements to include the IFP by adding an IFP sticker at the bottom of the ballot sheets.[61]

Meanwhile, the election campaign developed into a personal contest between de Klerk and Mandela. De Klerk aimed to capture the white vote; he explained that the Conservative party's vision of an Afrikaner Volkstaat was unrealistic because Whites were a minority in every district in South Africa. Since the National party had transformed itself into a multiracial party, de Klerk also expected to attract Coloured voters, who spoke Afrikaans and shared white fears of Africans. He claimed that it was he who had been responsible for the end of apartheid and that only the National party had the knowledge and experience to run a government. He was optimistic because he seemed to assume that the ANC would not be able to mount an effective campaign.[62] Once again, de Klerk underestimated his opponents. The ANC managed to create quite a sophisticated electoral machine, and drawing on the advice of Americans who had assisted Bill Clinton in his 1992 presidential campaign in the United States, it held numerous peoples' forums, where leaders listened to groups of potential voters. It also published a Reconstruction and Development Program, which set out plans to improve the quality of life for the African masses by creating jobs, redistributing land, providing low-cost housing, extending the supply of electricity and clean water, and improving education. Mandela was an indefatigable and highly successful canvasser among Africans (although he spoke extremely slowly), but he also took great pains to reassure the white, Coloured, and Indian minorities, emphasizing his goal of reconciliation between the races.[63]

The election was unexpectedly peaceful. To cope with the crowds, it took place over four days, April 26 to 29. Television viewers throughout the world saw long lines of Africans waiting patiently, often for many hours, to get to the polling stations and cast their votes. For former voteless people, it was the experience of a lifetime; for some it took on the aura of a religious experience. Nevertheless, by the standards of western democracies, it was seriously flawed, and not only in KwaZulu, where the IFP had only a week to prepare. That was not surprising. There was no voters' roll or accurate census of African areas, and there was a huge shortage of buildings suitable as polling stations and people qualified to operate them. Many areas were so completely dominated by one party that rivals had not been able to campaign there and people were too scared to vote against the tide. Although the IEC itself was not well led and contained many inexperienced and inefficient workers, it did try to overcome these deficiencies. Inevitably, though, there was much confusion as nearly twenty million people (estimated to be 86 percent of the electorate), many of them illiterate, sought to vote. In many cases, people voted more than once, pirate polling stations were set up, underage youths were permitted to vote, ballot papers did not arrive in time, partisan officials stuffed ballot boxes with returns supporting their party, boxes were tampered with after leaving the polling stations, and counting procedures were corrupt.[64]

On May 6, when the IEC eventually announced the results, the National party and the Democratic party denounced them, and the European Union's observer mission declared that the election "fell short of what South Africans as well as foreigners expected." However, the IEC, the

Commonwealth, and the Organization of African Unity observers as-serted that the election was substantially free and fair. There had, un-doubtedly, been many errors in the process, including bargaining between the ANC and the IFP about the KwaZulu/Natal figures. Yet the gross offi-cial figures were quite close to the pre-election polls and were probably a reasonably accurate reflection of reality. The ANC had won 62.65 percent of the votes and 252 seats in the National Assembly, the National party 20.39 percent of the votes and 82 seats, and the IFP 10.54 percent of the votes and 43 seats. Mandela was elected president and Mbeki first deputy president, and under the sunset clauses de Klerk became second deputy president. The National party obtained 5 other cabinet positions and the IFP won 3 seats in the cabinet. The ANC became the majority party in seven of the nine provinces. In the western Cape, more than a million Coloured people, who shared with Afrikaners their language, religion, culture, and many of their genes, joined Whites to give the victory to the National party, while in KwaZulu/Natal the IFP won a clear victory over the ANC. All the other parties did abysmally. Viljoen's Freedom Front won only 2.17 percent of the vote (9 national assembly seats), the Democratic party won only 1.73 percent (7 seats), and the PAC only 1.25 percent (5 seats). In large measure, the election was a racial and ethnic census. The National party had wide support from Coloureds as well as Whites, but the ANC and PAC were overwhelmingly African, the IFP was overwhelmingly Zulu, and the Freedom Front and the Democratic parties were overwhelmingly white.[65]

On May 10, 1994, three hundred and forty-two years after the Dutch East India Company formed a settlement at the Cape of Good Hope, lead-ing to the importation of slaves from Asia and tropical Africa and the con-quest of his people, Nelson Mandela took the presidential oath in the pres-ence of the secretary-general of the United Nations, forty-five heads of state, and delegations from the United States, Russia, China, Japan, Ger-many, and Great Britain. Reconciliation was the dominant theme of his in-augural address. "Out of the experience of an extraordinary human disas-ter that lasted too long, must be born a society of which all humanity will be proud. . . . Never, never, and never again shall it be that this beautiful land will again experience the oppression of one by another."[66] Mandela also paid a cordial tribute to his old rival, de Klerk, who was sworn in as second deputy president. De Klerk had started the process with a won-drous break with the past, but it was Mandela who then called the shots and whose vision of a free South Africa triumphed.[67]

CHAPTER 9

The New South Africa, 1994–1999

The Legacy of Apartheid

As the euphoria that marked the election and the inauguration died down, it became apparent that in South Africa, as in many other countries, although the creation of a democratic constitution was a vital step forward, it was merely a skeleton that might or might not lead to the growth of a democratic society. The tasks that confronted the new government were awesome. The country was racked by the cumulative effects of colonialism, apartheid, and urbanization. According to the United Nations Human Development Program, in 1994 the level of human development in South Africa ranked ninetieth out of 175 countries, behind Thailand, Malaysia, Brazil, and Cuba, but ahead of the Philippines and Indonesia.[1] The judiciary, bureaucracy, army, police force, and municipal administrations were all dominated by white men who had been brought up in a racist milieu and had been trained to serve the apartheid state. The country had one of the greatest gaps in the world between rich and poor, and although new multiracial classes were forming, the gap marked primarily a division between races. The most accurate measure of these differences was provided by a detailed census that was held in 1996—before substantial changes had taken place since the transfer of political power. That census revealed the enormity of the problem. Most white South Africans were well-to-do, well educated, and well housed. Most Africans, like most people of tropical Africa, were poor, badly educated, and ill housed. The conditions of the Coloured and Indian members of the population were in between those of Whites and Africans.[2]

The Mandela government inherited a particularly intractable education situation: nineteen separate education departments—one for each race and one for each Homeland, and so on; immense disparities between the buildings and the equipment in schools created for Whites and those created for Blacks; a dearth of qualified teachers; and the inordinate cost of raising the "black" schools to anything like the level of the "white" schools. Moreover, the established syllabi and textbooks were devised under the apartheid regime, and there was an imbalance between the focus on the humanities and the national need for industrial skills. The higher education system had similar disparities and imbalances. The universities that the apartheid government created for African students were grossly inadequate. In 1994, 24 percent of the adult African population had no schooling at all, 37 percent had attended only primary school, 22 percent had some secondary education, and only 6 percent had some higher education. Africans had gained the dignity of full citizenship, but most of them were not equipped to prosper in the country where they now formed the political majority.[3]

South Africa had an inordinate number of marginalized people. Illegal immigrants swarmed into the country—most of them refugees from the civil war in Mozambique. Although the previous government had returned thousands of "illegal aliens" to their countries of origin—88,575 in 1992—vast numbers remained, and the influx continued. Police estimated that in 1993 there were more than one million illegal immigrants in South Africa, but the number was probably more than three million. Furthermore, at least eleven thousand members of the ANC's military wing, Umkhonto we Sizwe, had returned to South Africa by the end of 1993. Most of the illegal immigrants and former guerrillas had no preparation for civilian life.[4] According to the 1996 census, 46 percent of the African population, more than fourteen million people, were under twenty years old. Many of these young people were raised in families with high rates of divorce, teenage pregnancy, and children born outside of marriage. With that background, millions of youths were socialized in lawless gangs, which contributed to the rampant crime that was a hallmark of the society.[5]

South Africa was an exceptionally violent society. Whereas in previous generations Whites had a near monopoly of firearms, by 1994 South Africans of all races owned modern weapons, including AK-47 assault rifles, most of which, like the illegal immigrants, came from Mozambique.[6] According to the South African Institute of Race Relations, the annual murder rate per one hundred thousand people in 1990–91 was four in France and Germany, ten in the United States, and fifteen in the Netherlands. In South Africa it was ninety-eight. South Africa was also the unchallenged leader in the rates of rape and serious assault.[7] Cape Town and Johannesburg vied for the title of murder capital of the world. In 1994, Tony Leon, the leader of the Democratic party, asserted that in Cape Town only one in ten murderers was caught and that only one in a hundred of those who were caught went to trial. Throughout the country carjackings were commonplace, and competition between rival African taxi companies erupted into shooting wars in all the major cities. Industrial strikes also led to bloodshed. Africans murdered Whites on isolated farms in the north, but Africans were both the victims and the perpetrators of most violent crimes.[8] Property was also in jeopardy in some areas. Vacationers and shoppers returned to find squatters occupying their houses, and the police did nothing about it.[9] In 1995, police reported that at least 278 crime syndicates were operating in South Africa.[10] Such were the conditions that the Mandela government inherited.

To cope effectively with these problems South Africa needed a robust economy, but the economy that the Mandela government took over was not in good shape. The recession that began in 1988 continued through 1992, and although recovery started in 1993, the gross domestic product per head was still far below the 1988 level. The inflation rate hovered around 10 percent overall (the cost of food rose at a far higher rate), foreign reserves had shrunk to an abysmal low, and personal taxes were already very high. South Africa did have excellent economic potential: valuable mineral resources, a well-developed infrastructure, sound financial institutions, and skills and experience in engineering, the legal and medical professions, and business management. But apartheid had distorted and damaged South Africa's potential. As a result of economic sanctions, South Africa had pursued increasingly isolationist economic policies, and confidence in the country's future had been undermined. Structural flaws, such as protective tariffs and high wages in relationship to productivity, meant that South African products were not competitive in international markets. Professional and managerial skills were almost all in white hands, because successive generations of black citizens had been denied access to education and training. The high level of black unemployment perpetuated poverty and crime. Finally, following the collapse of the Soviet Union, changes in the global political economy, which emphasized deregulation, liberalization, and privatization, imposed harsh constraints on the new regime.[11]

The Polity

Soon after his inauguration, Mandela completed the Government of National Unity in terms of the interim constitution. As his first deputy president, he appointed Thabo Mbeki rather than Cyril Ramaphosa, the former trade union leader who had been a highly successful ANC negotiator in 1993 and early 1994. That made Mbeki, aged fifty-one, heir-apparent to the seventy-six-year-old president. Son of a veteran ANC and Communist party stalwart and Robben Island prisoner, Mbeki had been in exile since 1961. After completing a master's degree in economics at Sussex University in England and undergoing military training in the Soviet Union, Mbeki became Oliver Tambo's right-hand man in the ANC in exile. He is a gifted, hard-working, energetic man, at ease with educated people, but he lacks Mandela's liberation-struggle credentials and common touch. His collected essays, *Africa: The Time Has Come,* reveal a man repulsed by racism, intensely proud of being an African, and imbued with a vision of a South African democracy, an African Renaissance, and a global system purged of capitalist excess.[12] De Klerk, as leader of the National party, assumed office as second deputy president.

In accordance with their share of the vote in the election, eighteen ANC members, six National party members, and three Inkatha Freedom party (IFP) members formed the rest of the cabinet. Two of the cabinet ministers were women. Mandela placed ANC colleagues in most of the important portfolios; but he gave the National party finance, where experience was paramount, in order to send cooperative signals to the business community. The result was a truly multiracial cabinet. Including the president and his two deputies, the cabinet contained sixteen Africans, eight Whites (two of them ANC members), and six Indians or Coloureds. Especially significant appointments were those of Buthelezi as minister of home affairs; Joe Modise, former commander of the ANC guerrilla force Umkhonto we Sizwe, as minister of defense; and Joe Slovo as minister of housing. It was also an inexperienced cabinet. As Mandela himself admitted, many ANC members were "men and women who have been taken literally from the bush and without previous training . . . have been asked to run the government of such a highly developed country as South Africa."[13]

In the following years, the ANC consolidated its power and appointed supporters to crucial offices. In 1996, it had the upper hand over an increasingly demoralized National party in the negotiations leading to the enactment of a permanent constitution. This document replaced the 1994 interim document and was enacted by both houses of the national parliament sitting together as a Constituent Assembly. The constitution was approved by an overwhelming majority of 421 to 2, with 10 abstentions.[14] It had been the subject of extended public debate, in which the National party and the IFP tried unsuccessfully to obtain greater powers for the provinces. When Buthelezi saw that he was not getting his way, he repeated the tactic he had used previously and withdrew from the negotiations. In most respects, the permanent constitution resembled its forerunner. It replaced the Senate with a National Council of Provinces, which comprised delegates appointed by the provincial legislatures and whose decisions could be overridden by the National Assembly; it permitted the central parliament to override provincial legislation except in such matters as abattoirs, libraries, museums, and provincial planning; it extended the Bill of Rights chapter to include rights of "access" to housing, health care, food, water, and social security (which, in practice, were aspirations rather than justiciable rights); and it provided for the appointment of a Human Rights Commission, a Commission for Gender Equality, an Electoral Commission, and an independent broadcasting authority. In an important decision, the permanent constitution ceased to make it obligatory for the dominant party to include members of other parties in the central or provincial cabinets after the next election, which was to take place in 1999.

De Klerk by that time had become dissatisfied with his role as a member of the government. The National party was caught between its responsibility to support the government, of which it was a part, and its need to defend itself from criticisms by its caucus and electorate. The ANC, with huge majorities in parliament and cabinet, had no compelling reason to compromise on important issues. Moreover, de Klerk's personal relations with Mandela were abysmal. Mandela was convinced that de Klerk had been responsible for the Third Force and distrusted him. On several occasions, the president denounced him in cabinet, and in September 1995 a photographer caught the two of them in a heated dispute in a Johannesburg parking lot. For de Klerk, the new constitution was the final straw because it had no provision for power-sharing beyond the 1999 election. He convened the Executive Council of the National party and persuaded a very divided meeting that the party should withdraw from the government. The result was that the National party began to disintegrate. Several leaders retired from politics; de Klerk himself retired in August 1997. Soon afterward, he divorced his wife, married a wealthy Greek woman, and spent most of his time in London.[15] Mandela placed ANC members in the cabinet seats vacated by the National party. Buthelezi and his two IFP colleagues remained in the cabinet, and relations between Mandela and Buthelezi improved. The ANC-IFP conflicts decreased in KwaZulu-Natal and Gauteng (the province that includes Johannesburg and Pretoria), and Mandela gratified Buthelezi by naming him acting president when both he and Mbeki were out of the country.[16]

To its immense credit, the Mandela government transmitted to its successor a stable, democratic political system. It had respected the constitution and the rule of law. For example, in 1996, the Constitutional Court rejected the first draft of the permanent constitution on the ground that several clauses did not comply with the thirty-four principles laid down by the interim constitution. The Constituent Assembly then submitted a revised document, and the court certified it as valid. In 1998, furthermore, the Pretoria High Court ordered the president to justify his appointment of a committee of inquiry into alleged racism and corruption in the South African Rugby Union. Mandela complied. He was subjected to a severe cross-examination, and the judge, a white man, ruled against him; but Mandela's action was eventually upheld on appeal by the Constitutional Court.[17]

South Africa, however, was a one-party democracy. The ANC's closest rival in the 1999 election (see below), the Democratic party, won less than 10 percent of the vote. Other African states, such as South Africa's neighbor Zimbabwe, that had once been one-party democracies had ended up as one-party dictatorships; and already there were signs of disrespect for the rights of opposition parties. Stanley Uys, a former political editor of the Johannesburg Sunday Times, noted that at the ANC's December 1997 conference, Mandela himself "challenged the right of opposition parties to oppose his government in the style that would be commonplace in democracies."[18] The ANC, moreover, had significant centralizing tendencies. But there were strong checks on abuse of power by the ANC: a free press, a vigorous civil society, and powerful business and trade union organizations. Indeed, as political scientist David Welsh said, "South Africa's stability rests upon a tacit trade-off between the political power of the majority as represented by the ANC and the economic and social power of the minority."[19]

Deracializing State Institutions

The established Supreme Court of South Africa, with appellate and provincial divisions (renamed the Supreme Court of Appeals and the High Court in 1996), remained in place under Chief Justice Michael Corbett until that year, when he was succeeded by Ismail Mahomed. White male judges, some of them unsympathetic to the new regime, continued to dominate the judiciary; there were very few black or female lawyers, and the tenure of existing judges was protected by the sunset clause in the interim constitution. As late as 1998, only about 30 out of 275 judges were not white.[20] Even the new Constitutional Court, whose members Mandela appointed after extensive consultations, comprised seven Whites (including the president, Arthur Chaskalson, who, like Mahomed, had been prominent in defending people prosecuted by the apartheid regime), as well as three Africans and one Asian. Two were women—one black, one white. Five came from the liberal wing of the existing bench, one was a Transkei judge, and the other five were professors or practicing lawyers.[21]

The bureaucracy inherited by the new regime was a vast, unwieldy, and largely inefficient public service of two million people who had been accustomed to operating the apartheid system and who, like the judges, were protected by the sunset clause. It was dominated by male Afrikaners, many of whom had no sympathy for the goals of the new regime. The Mandela government eliminated many of the obsolete departments, deployed their personnel out of "useless jobs" into essential services, announced its intention to make the bureaucracy "reflect the country's make-up in terms of race and gender over a period of five years," and advertised eleven thousand affirmative action positions. At its conference in December 1994, the ANC noted that "until we transform the state machinery as a whole into a loyal instrument of democracy, transfer of power to the people will not be complete."[22] But that was not possible without making the bureaucracy still more inefficient than it had been, because, as a result of the appalling deficiencies of black education under apartheid, there was a dearth of suitably qualified black South Africans. The government did manage to place reasonably well-educated supporters in the most senior posts, but most middle- and lower-level posts were held by Whites. Consequently, the bureaucracy did not become an efficient instrument for the implementation of the wishes of the new government.

The restructuring of the army was another formidable task. The government had a constitutional commitment to create a new South African National Defence Force (SANDF) from the 65,000 regular soldiers and sailors of the old South African Defence Force (SADF), members of Umkhonto we Sizwe (ANC guerrillas, estimated to number 27,000), the Azanian People's Liberation Army (APLA; the PAC guerrillas estimated to number 6,000), and the approximately 10,000 members of the defense forces of the four "independent" Homelands. This was a merger of very dissimilar entities, most of which had been on opposite sides in the conflict between defenders and opponents of apartheid. The SADF was a well-equipped, disciplined, standing army, navy, and air force, which had been trained to enforce apartheid, whereas the guerrillas and Homeland units were ill-equipped and poorly disciplined troops who had been committed to overthrowing the apartheid state.[23]

Anticipating this problem, Joe Modise, the commander of Umkhonto we Sizwe who became Mandela's minister of defense, and General Piet Meiring, a former commander of South African military operations in South West Africa (Namibia) who became the initial chief of the SANDF, had begun in 1993 to plan the merger. After the inauguration, they cooperated to obtain an increase of 10 percent in the security budget (thereby destroying the expectation of a substantial financial dividend from the end of apartheid) and to train the guerrillas as modern soldiers. They also won over seven former guerrilla leaders by appointing them as generals in the new army. But two serious problems arose. The guerrillas were not satisfied with their treatment, and in October 1994 many of them went absent without leave from their main training camp on the eighth day of a boycott over pay and status. It took a special visit by Mandela and the firing of 2,221 deserters to restore order.[24] Second, the army, especially the military intelligence service, still included covert units that continued to oppose democratic change. As stated in the newsletter *Africa Confidential,* they had "a vested interest in destabilization. It is their job."[25] Nevertheless, by May 1997 there were 77,882 uniformed members in the SANDF, including 9,388 officers, of whom 8,033 were members of the former SADF, 1,079 were from Umkhonto we Sizwe, and 306 were from the APLA.[26] Racial tensions persisted, however, within the armed forces throughout the Mandela presidency and beyond.

The police force was probably the most venal state institution inherited by the Mandela government.[27] Its primary function had been to maintain white supremacy, and it was notorious for torturing and even murdering its victims. Many police were deeply corrupt and lacked the most basic skills needed for conventional police work. Mandela's minister of security and safety, thirty-five-year-old Sidney Mufamadi, a founding member of COSATU and the UDF, took over 130,000 police divided among eleven different agencies. Two-thirds of its members were black, but nearly all of the officers were white. From those materials he created a single national South African Police Service led initially by a white commissioner, General George Fivaz. But there was no significant improvement in the quality of the police force. Many members were still functionally illiterate. Morale was low, especially among the African members of the force, who were highly unpopular as the enforcers of apartheid. In 1997, a typical year in this respect, 232 police were murdered and more than 118 committed suicide. In 1996, moreover, 15,236 members of the police were charged with crimes including assault, murder, rape, and reckless or negligent driving, and 210 deaths occurred in police custody.[28]

The nine provincial governments—consisting of elected legislatures, premiers elected by the legislatures, and executive councils appointed by the premier—gradually assumed the powers that were allotted to them in the interim constitution and that were slightly amended by the permanent document. However, the provincial governments were inefficient. They had a weak revenue base, they inherited sterile, corrupt bureaucracies, and several of them were run by incompetent people; most of the better-educated ANC and IFP politicians had won seats in the National Assembly. They were also dogged by allegations of fraud, nepotism, lack of discipline, and misgovernment. In August 1997, the director general of public service and administration reported that three provincial administrations were on the verge of collapse (the Eastern Cape, KwaZulu-Natal, and the Northern Province), that four others were experiencing serious difficulties, and that only Gauteng and the Western Cape were functioning relatively well. The central government had to bail out the provinces because they had huge deficits and were hopelessly in debt.[29]

A lower tier comprised elected local government institutions. Their main responsibilities were health and sanitation services, public transportation, and local roads. But in most cases the municipal councils, too, lacked managerial capacity and an adequate revenue base. By 1998, 71 percent of consumers regularly paid their taxes and services charges, including electricity, but the rest did not, and the debt to municipalities mounted to nearly ten million rand.[30] In the cities, the previously segregated local governments were gradually integrated into large metropolitan units run by elected councils. In African rural areas—the former Homelands—local government was a hybrid, because chiefs ("traditional authorities") were empowered to apply customary law subject to the terms of the constitution. Attempts were made to meld the chiefs into the municipality system, but many rural Africans still honored customary law, which subordinated women to men and gave chiefs control of the allocation of tribal land. However, educated, urbanized Africans questioned how long the traditional authorities should survive.[31]

Truth and Reconciliation

As the first president of the new South Africa, Nelson Mandela made it his highest priority to lay the foundations of a united nation while respecting the cultures of its different racial and ethnic elements. He was particularly concerned with conciliating the most dangerous minority, the Afrikaners, who had been close to wrecking the negotiations on the eve of the 1994 election. For this purpose, he committed a series of highly publicized symbolic acts. He visited in their homes ex-President Botha and the widow of Hendrik Verwoerd, the principal architect of apartheid. He had General Johan Willemse, the former Robben Island commander, to dinner. He even took lunch with Percy Yutar, who had prosecuted him and got him sentenced to life imprisonment, and he joined the Sunday congregation in an Afrikaner church. In his most successful gesture, he identified with the South African rugby team, who were all Afrikaners except for one Coloured man, by walking onto the field wearing the Springbok jersey after South Africa won the World Cup against New Zealand; the largely Afrikaner crowd cheered him wildly.[32]

Mandela also set in motion an ambitious attempt to make South Africans come to terms with their past. Unless the crimes of apartheid were addressed, he said, they would "live with us like a festering sore."[33] This became the most contentious episode of his presidency. During the negotiations leading to the 1994 election, the National party had wanted to be given a general amnesty for apartheid. The ANC refused, but eventually de Klerk and Mandela agreed that a commission should be appointed with the power to grant amnesties to individuals, on condition that they revealed the truth and could prove that their actions were politically motivated. After looking at precedents in eastern European and Latin American states that had recently rejected authoritarian regimes, parliament created a Truth and Reconciliation Commission (TRC). Its mandate was to deal with gross human rights violations committed since March 1, 1960 (the month of the Sharpeville massacre). Unlike some of the foreign precedents, the TRC was to meet in public and was empowered to subpoena witnesses and to grant individual amnesties on the above conditions.[34] Instead of appointing a legal body, such as the Constitutional Court, to perform this task, Mandela selected seventeen commissioners from candidates nominated by nongovernmental organizations. Most of them were chosen because of their roles in opposing apartheid. Nine were men, eight were women. Ethnically, it was a diverse group of two Afrikaners, four English-speaking Whites, two Indians, two Coloureds, and seven Africans. Mandela persuaded Archbishop Desmond Tutu to accept the chairmanship. Recipient of the 1994 Nobel Peace Prize, Tutu was a man of the utmost integrity, but his appointment and that of three other clergy, including the vice chairperson, gave the TRC an overridingly emotional and religious tone rather than a legal one, even though six of the commissioners were lawyers.[35]

The TRC was divided into three committees: one dealt with gross human rights violations, another with amnesty, and the third with reparations for victims. Provided with a large budget, much of it from foreign donors (including $1.4 million from USAID), the commission set up an elaborate organization, with four regional offices and a large number of employees who took more than twenty thousand statements from victims of political violence. Starting in December 1995, the commission worked for more than two years and held more than fifty public hearings around the country. More than seven thousand individuals applied for amnesty, but by the time the TRC report went to press in 1998, the amnesty committee had granted only about 150 amnesties, and it still had another two thousand applications to deal with.[36]

The commission started by hearing victims of human rights abuses tell their stories, which were more horrific than anyone had imagined and fully vindicated Mandela's suspicions that some sort of Third Force had been operating under Presidents Botha and de Klerk. Most of these statements highlighted the callous brutality of the police and military forces, including murders and exceptionally cruel methods of torture.[37]

The amnesty committee managed to break through the denial of responsibility by the National party politicians and their senior police and military officers. This began when Colonel Eugene de Kock, who had been found guilty of six murders and given two life sentences, applied to the amnesty committee for mitigation of sentence. He admitted many crimes, including helping to blow up the headquarters of the South African Council of Churches in Johannesburg, but he insisted that his orders had come from police generals who in turn had received their instructions from cabinet ministers. That was followed by a flood of confessions by other agents of the National party regime, and in virtually every case they fingered the top police and the cabinet, including former Presidents Botha and de Klerk. When ex-ministers Pik Botha and Adriaan Vlok applied for amnesty, they, too, said that Botha and de Klerk had given orders to kill.[38]

The TRC subpoenaed Botha and de Klerk. Botha refused to comply; everything he did was in defense of South Africa against international communism, and he would never apologize for apartheid: "I've said many times that the word apartheid means good neighborliness."[39] Unlike Botha, de Klerk sent two written submissions and accepted his invitation to attend the commission. He gave a half-hearted apology for apartheid but insisted that he had never authorized and had not even been aware of the brutal activities of the police and military units. De Klerk never budged from that position, and the exasperated commissioners were convinced that he was lying.[40] Buthelezi also accepted the commission's invitation, but he used the occasion to denounce the TRC and put all the blame for violence on the ANC. In their report, the commissioners found that Botha and Buthelezi were responsible for gross violations of human rights and that de Klerk was an accessory to such violations.[41]

Although white supremacists linked to the former government had been responsible for a vast majority of the violence reported to the TRC, the liberation forces, too, had committed a substantial number of grave abuses—exploding bombs in public places, planting land mines, murdering collaborative councillors and policemen (some by "necklacing"—placing a tire filled with kerosene around the victim's neck and setting the tire on fire), and torturing and killing suspected spies in the guerrilla camps in Angola. Thabo Mbeki admitted to the commission that some such events had taken place, and he said that the ANC accepted responsibility for attacks carried out by its members; but he insisted that all such actions should be condoned because the ANC had been involved in a just war of liberation, which distinguished them from atrocities committed by the apartheid state. The commission, led by chairman Tutu, would have none of that. When the ANC demanded a blanket amnesty, he threatened to resign if that was granted, and the ANC relented. The TRC endorsed the United Nations resolution that apartheid was a crime against humanity, but it drew a distinction between a "just war" and "just means" and found the ANC guilty of gross violations of human rights. In his introduction to the TRC report, Tutu explained that "a gross violation is a gross violation, whoever commits it and for whatever reason. There is this legal equivalence between all perpetrators. Their political affiliation is irrelevant." Nevertheless, the committee granted amnesty to thirty-seven ANC politicians, including Mbeki.[42]

From the beginning, the TRC was the recipient of much white criticism. Whites denounced the law creating the commission and the anti-apartheid background of most of its members. Then, as African victims poured out accounts of their sufferings, most Whites bitterly opposed the entire process. This grew to a crescendo of hatred in the Afrikaans press after the commission cross-examined de Klerk and granted amnesty to the thirty-seven ANC leaders. When the TRC held hearings in Afrikaner strongholds like Ladybrand in the Orange Free State, residents insulted the commissioners and refused to serve black members in the restaurants or threw them out.[43] Moreover, one of the two Afrikaner commissioners resigned, and although the other signed the TRC report, he attached a dissenting minority report.[44] Many Africans, too, were outraged that the TRC criticized crimes committed by the liberation forces as severely as apartheid crimes.[45]

Before its report was published, the TRC, in accordance with its legal obligations, sent summaries of its findings to two hundred individuals and organizations it had criticized. Their reactions were unanimously hostile. De Klerk demanded changes in the findings against him, and when the TRC refused, he obtained an interdict from the Cape provincial division of the High Court, forcing the commission to remove the passage pending a further court hearing. Mbeki accused the commission of criminalizing the anti-apartheid struggle and applied to the High Court to stop publication, whereupon an outraged Tutu gave a series of press interviews. "We can't assume," he said, "that yesterday's oppressed will not become tomorrow's oppressors. We have seen it happen all over the world, and we shouldn't be surprised it if happens here."[46] However, the court threw out the ANC's application, and three hours later Tutu presented the report to Mandela, who accepted it graciously, "with all its imperfections." But Mbeki described the report as "wrong and misguided," the National party called it "flawed and divisive," and Buthelezi insisted that his hands were clean.[47]

The TRC discovered and revealed a great deal of information about the heinous behavior of agents of the apartheid regime, even though the National party tried to thwart it by destroying masses of incriminating documents. The commission also showed that some ANC operatives, too, had committed serious crimes. But the TRC did not advance the cause of racial reconciliation. Indeed, in the short run it had the opposite effect, accentuating the racial divisions in South African society. Nor did the TRC bring justice to the victims of political violence. Many killers and torturers walked free for talking about their crimes, and victims received little compensation from the reparation committee. Notwithstanding the noble efforts of many South Africans, including Nelson Mandela and Desmond Tutu, race continued to be the basic line of division in South African society, with class becoming increasingly significant among blacks.[48] The political parties were overwhelmingly racial or ethnic in membership: Africans in the ANC, Zulus in the IFP, Whites and Coloureds in the Democratic party and the National party; and most South Africans still socialized exclusively with members of their own "race," as they had under colonialism and apartheid. This was largely because of economics—the persisting gulf between the prosperity of most Whites and the abject poverty of most Blacks.

The Economy

Besides reconciliation, the Mandela government had two major goals: to create growth and to improve the quality of life for the majority of the citizens—the victims of apartheid. Both goals were desirable; moreover, if successful they would support each other. Economic growth would generate the means to pay for programs to improve the lives of the poor, and a population provided with better living conditions would create unprecedented wealth. Nevertheless, if both goals were pursued simultaneously from the beginning of the new regime, they would not be compatible. In order to promote growth, the government needed to attract massive infusions of foreign investments and postpone spending substantial resources on welfare. That would be a difficult and risky policy. It would involve opening South Africa to the global market and exposing South African industry to foreign competition. This would oblige industry to stand firm against demands for higher wages, to slim the workforce, and to make greater use of high technology; and this, in turn, would increase the already vast numbers of the unemployed. If the Mandela government, however, had concentrated on improving the living conditions of the masses, it would have rapidly exhausted its financial resources and neglected the structural reforms that were essential for growth.[49]

Understandably, the Mandela government tried to do both things at once. During the run-up to the 1994 election, the ANC issued a Reconstruction and Development Program (RDP), which became the official policy of the government of national unity. Government and the private sector were to cooperate in creating jobs through public works; three hundred thousand houses were to be built each year; all South Africans were to have access to clean water, sanitation, and electricity; health, education, and welfare services were to be improved; and 30 percent of the land was to be redistributed to Blacks. This ambitious program aroused great expectations that could not possibly be fulfilled.[50] The government also tried to make the economy grow rapidly. For this purpose, since there seemed to be no rational alternative in the globalizing post–Cold War world, the ANC pursued capitalist policies—even though it had been imbued by its Soviet sponsors with a belief in a command economy, and the South African Communist party was still an integral part of the ANC. The government began to open South Africa to the world economy, reducing trade tariffs and easing currency convertibility for foreign residents and companies. The international community was delighted and welcomed South Africa back into the fold. The government also enhanced its esteem by dismantling the nuclear weapons that its predecessor had secretly created. The United Nations restored the credentials that South Africa lost in 1992: the Security Council and the United States and other countries lifted their sanctions, South Africa rejoined the British Commonwealth, which it had left in 1961, and South African rugby and cricket teams went on international tours again.[51]

Mandela launched a campaign to attract investment capital from foreign businesses, governments, and international agencies. He devoted much time and energy to this cause. He traveled repeatedly to Europe and the United States, where he was feted as a hero. In October 1994, he addressed the United Nations General Assembly and both houses of Congress. "We cannot rest," he told the United Nations, "while millions of our people suffer the pain and indignity of poverty in all its forms. The success of South Africa's democracy depends on our ability to change the material conditions of life of our people so that they not only have the vote, but bread and work as well."[52]

The response was considerable but far short of what South Africans hoped for. Between 1995 and 1997, the principal sources of direct foreign investment in South Africa were the United States and, surprisingly, Malaysia, followed by Germany, the United Kingdom, and Japan.[53] But most government contributors offered grants to South Africa for specific projects, and private investors remained cautious, deterred by South Africa's culture of violence; its burst of strikes; its unionized, highly paid, unskilled labor force; and lingering doubts about the government's long-term commitment to capitalism. Investors typically bought shares in long-established companies, reacquired control of subsidiaries from which they had withdrawn in the era of sanctions, and arranged to market goods that had been manufactured in their own countries; but they did not invest much capital in new enterprises or create many new jobs. Moreover, some of the funds promised by foreign governments for development were not claimed for many months—through bureaucratic bungling.[54]

By 1996, it was evident that the economy was not growing at a rate sufficient to fund the RDP program. After the declines in 1990–93, the gross domestic product per head grew by only 0.6 percent in 1994, 1.2 percent in 1995, and 1.0 percent in 1996, when it was still far below the 1981 level. In 1996, gold production fell to its lowest level in forty years, the rand declined by 21 percent against the U.S. dollar, and unemployment reached a shocking level. According to the Central Statistical Service, in 1995 29 percent of those aged fifteen and above were unemployed, another 12 percent were employed in the informal sector, and only 59 percent had jobs in the formal sector. This burden fell heavily on those who lacked skills and were not white: 37 percent of Africans aged fifteen and above, 22 percent of Coloureds, and 15 percent of Asians were unemployed; but only 6 percent of Whites were unemployed, an excellent level in industrial societies.[55] At the other end of the labor market, there was a serious dearth of skills and a consequential decline in efficiency in both the private and the public sectors. In 1994 and 1995, South Africa sustained a net loss of more than 1,700 people in professional occupations, and further losses occurred throughout the Mandela presidency, while many Africans were appointed to jobs for which they did not have appropriate education or training.[56] This combination of massive black unemployment and the unskilling of the labor force was the great economic challenge confronting South Africa. Meanwhile, the RDP was falling far short of its targets.

In response to these problems, Mandela abolished the RDP ministry in March 1996, and three months later the government adopted a new policy, labeled Growth, Employment, and Redistribution (GEAR), which focused on growth rather than on trying, at the same time, to make major, immediate improvements to the lives of the poor. GEAR, as Jesmond Blumenfeld explains, contained "the conventional world-wide policy wisdom of the 1980s and 1990s: improved macroeconomic balance, increased openness to international flows of goods and capital, and greater liberalization of markets." It committed the government to new investment incentives, further tariff reductions, a drastic decrease in public sector employment, and budgetary reforms; and it set targets for 2000, including a GDP annual growth rate of 6 percent and the creation of 1.3 million new formal sector jobs.[57]

Those expectations, too, were not fulfilled. The government was not able to apply the new policy effectively, due to a lack of administrative skills and also because it could not overcome trade union protection of the high level of unskilled and semi-skilled wages. The result was that investors preferred capital-intensive projects in South Africa or placed their capital elsewhere. Furthermore, the global financial crisis that started in Southeast Asia had serious spillover effects in South Africa; there was a general decline in investment in countries like South Africa, and Malaysia, which had invested heavily in South Africa before the crisis, ceased to do so. The annual growth rate of the GDP actually declined from 3.2 percent in 1996, to 1.9 percent in 1997, to near zero in 1998; and early in 1999 the economy was in recession again. The dollar value of the rand dropped by 17 percent in 1998; unemployment continued to increase; public services continued to deteriorate; more professional people emigrated; and Anglo American and South African breweries transferred their headquarters to London.[58] According to the World Competitiveness Yearbook of the Swiss Institute for Management Development, South Africa ranked forty-second out of forty-seven countries—behind Brazil, Thailand, the Philippines, and the People's Republic of China. In 1999, the Harvard Institute for International Development placed South Africa forty-seventh out of fifty-nine countries—last in terms of labor practices, such as firing and hiring of workers, labor relations, and work ethic.[59]

GEAR meant that the interests of big business coincided with state policy, but it caused strains in the relationship between the ANC and its political allies—the South African Communist party (SACP), which supplied a
substantial proportion of the ANC leadership, and COSATU, the trade union
federation that had been the strongest element in the anti-apartheid movement. Under GEAR the government was, indeed, closer to big business than
to its allies. Both COSATU and the SACP criticized GEAR from the outset.
COSATU threatened to terminate its alliance with the ANC and form a separate party pledged to support labor and eradicate poverty; but there was
no sign of a COSATU or SACP secession. The affiliates of COSATU amounted
to only 1.5 million members, and the SACP claimed a membership of just
75,000. Both organizations needed the ANC more than the ANC needed
them; and their leaders knew where their bread was buttered. Consequently, both allies supported the ANC in the 1999 election.[60] As American
political scientist Thomas Koelble stated, "The ANC glue, the solidarity
against racism, colonialism, and apartheid, and Mandela's charisma, is
likely to work against breakaway parties" for years to come.[61]

The Quality of Life of the Majority of the People

It was inevitable that no quick fix could alleviate the sufferings of the
victims of apartheid. The government did receive kudos from Africans for
symbolic changes. These began shortly before the 1994 election, when the
Transitional Executive Council, expressing the result of negotiations
among the major parties, unveiled a new South African flag that replaced
the British and Boer symbols in favor of a colorful geometrical design. In
May 1995, the government approved a new national anthem, which began with the Nguni and Sotho versions of the popular ANC hymn "Nkosi
Sikelel' iAfrika" (God Bless Africa), continued with the opening lines of
the Afrikaans anthem "Die Stem van Suid Afrika" (The Voice of South
Africa), and ended with an English except from "The Call of South
Africa." The government also began the process of renaming places; for
example, the province that included Pretoria and Johannesburg was
named Gauteng. The government also introduced new public holidays.[62]

Improving the material conditions of the victims of apartheid was another matter. As a result of the disappointing performance of the economy,
there was never enough money for South Africans to achieve the goals set
out in the Reconstruction and Development Program and GEAR. The
Mandela government managed to increase the annual budgetary alloca-

tions for welfare services and some progress was made. Least successful was the RDP's lavish promise to return land to the more than one million Africans who had been forcibly removed. Of 63,000 claims for restitution, by June 1999 only 231 had been granted, and another 215 households had shared ten million rand as compensation.[63] After a slow start, the RDP commitment to provide a million state-subsidized houses was within reach. By March 1999, 747,717 had been built, amounting to 75 percent of the target, but many of them were very rudimentary buildings.[64] Likewise, by late 1997, 82 percent of urban households and 32 percent of rural households had electricity, but 41 percent of all South African households still had no electricity; and 3.5 million people were supplied with water between 1994 and 1999, which still left 12 million people without piped water in their homes.[65] There was also a substantial increase in the supply of telephones.[66] Even so, according to the government's 1998 Report on Social and Economic Development in South Africa, about 19 million people (just under half of the population) lived below the official poverty line of 353 rand (U.S. $60) per month; 72 percent of the poor lived in rural areas; and although poverty was not confined to one racial group, it was concentrated among Africans, of whom 61 percent were poor.[67] But there was a significant development in the class structure of South Africa. Under apartheid the black middle class was very small and politically impotent, but during the Mandela presidency, as a result of the transfer of political power, there was a rapid growth of a new, prosperous, black elite, composed largely of Africans. ANC and IFP politicians dominated the central and regional executives and legislatures and were appointed to senior posts in the bureaucracy. Blacks, especially Africans, also benefited from affirmative action in the business world. Virtually any African, Indian, or Coloured adult who had managed to acquire a decent education was assured of a well-paid job, to such an extent that universities had great difficulty recruiting black faculty members.

By the end of the Mandela presidency, the health of South Africans was blighted by major setbacks. The government did provide access to health care for thousands of people who had never had it before by shifting limited resources from expensive city hospitals to clinics in the rural periphery, where doctors were extremely scarce. There was, however, a serious deterioration in the quality of the public hospitals, including Baragwanath, a large hospital in Soweto built for Africans in the apartheid era. In May 1999, deputy president Thabo Mbeki visited Baragwanath and was told that the place was crippled by crime and corruption. Nurses said that drugs, food, crockery, and essential equipment were frequently stolen; thieves seized the property of patients who died; and nurses were afraid to work at night "as they are threatened inside the hospital by gun-wielding thugs." A month later, four senior doctors reported that the health services in Gauteng province were on the verge of collapse from a shortage of staff and money.[68] By that time, South Africa was in the early stages of a medical catastrophe. The diseases of the AIDS-related complex, which in Africa are spread mainly by heterosexual contact and contaminated blood, were killing more people in East and Southern Africa than had been killed by all the wars in the region, and they were already wreaking havoc in South Africa. According to official estimates, 3.6 million South Africans were HIV positive in 1999, and the number was increasing by more than half a million a year. A quarter of a million South Africans would die of AIDS each year by 2002, rising to half a million by 2007. UN-AIDS estimated that life expectancy in South Africa would fall from 68 years in 1998 to 48 in 2010. On account of AIDS, South Africa dropped thirteen places in the United Nations Development Program's Human Development Index, from 89 in 1998 to 101 in 1999.[69] As the scourge inexorably intensified, it was beginning to affect every aspect of life in South Africa. For example, a vast number of AIDS orphans were being drawn into crime as their way to survival.[70] The health of South Africans was also adversely affected by high levels of air and water pollution. The leaded exhaust fumes of the heavy urban traffic, combined with factory emissions and the smoke of coal and kerosene fires, created dangerous levels of air pollution in the cities; open-cast coal mines were heavy air polluters in Mpumalanga, and the vast dumps of treated rock from the gold mines contaminated water supplies. Environmental questions had always ranked low on the political agenda in South Africa, and no appreciable improvement took place during the Mandela presidency.

Under a weak education minister, little progress was made in coping with the education mess. Although the system was formally desegregated, there continued to be a vast disparity in quality, and despite many overlaps, the quality of education still corresponded closely with race. Schools ranged from expensive private establishments, attended by whites and the new black elite, to former white public schools with mixed student bodies, to schools that catered to the vast majority of the black population and continued to be almost exclusively black. The national and provincial education departments received a fair share of the budget, but not all poor children attended school, because the government could not fulfill its commitment to provide free education for all South Africans. A culture of learning was not restored in the black schools, where it had been lost during the struggle against apartheid. Students were unruly and intimidated their teachers, 26 percent of whom were un- or underqualified in 1998, and many teachers were lazy, incompetent, and often drunk or drugged. Morale among teachers was very low, and fewer and fewer South Africans were choosing the teaching profession—South Africa was facing a serious shortage of teachers.[71] In 1998, only 49 percent of the 551,000 candidates passed the South African school-leaving examination ("senior certificate"), and only 13 percent did so with sufficient credits to qualify for admission to university. These figures represented a decline since 1994, when 58 percent of the half million candidates passed the senior certificate, and 18 percent did so with university entrance qualifications. The African rate was especially low.[72] African students were particularly weak in mathematics and the sciences; as one academic report noted, "Scientific literacy levels [still] reflected the hierarchy of inequality of apartheid education policies"—a poor preparation for life in the twenty-first century.[73]

The universities were in no better shape than the schools. By 1999, with racially open admissions, African students formed not only a distinct majority in colleges founded for Coloured and Indian students but also increasingly large minorities in formerly all-white institutions. The universities founded for Africans were still attended almost exclusively by Africans, and these were in serious trouble. After serious confrontations, the government removed students who refused or were unable to pay the fees, but students, professors, and administrators were dissatisfied, and the quality of the degrees was dubious. Since few Africans were qualified for university appointments, and those who were found much better-paid jobs in business or politics, the professors were still overwhelmingly white. The top administrators were Africans, some of them incompetent and corrupt. By 1999, six African universities had incurred huge deficits and accumulated student debts totaling more than $40 million, and their enrollments were declining. Although erstwhile all-white schools continued to receive the bulk of state funds for higher education, the government cut their subsidies quite deeply, prodded them to admit more and more black students, and encouraged them to emphasize such practical subjects as accounting. These universities had to lower their entrance qualifications and shrink their humanities departments—a process enhanced by the step-by-step removal of history as a subject in school syllabi.[74] No wonder that when the energetic Kader Asmal, the new minister of education in the Mbeki cabinet, had studied the total educational picture in South Africa, he told reporters that "the educational condition of the majority of people in this country amounts to a national emergency. It will not be an exaggeration to say that there is a crisis at each level of the system."[75]

The Mandela government did not succeed in reducing the appallingly high crime rate inherited from the apartheid regime. Surveys indicated that in 1998, 83 percent of the total South African population believed that the government had little or no control over crime; 43 percent of the black population and 56 percent of the white population felt unsafe. Half of the South African population did not believe in the official crime statistics, which are derived from data provided by the notoriously unpopular and inefficient police, if only because of widespread underreporting.[76] Even so, the official figures are awesome. According to these figures, whereas the murder rate per 100,000 decreased 7.3 percent between 1994 and 1998 (largely because of the decline of political killings), the attempted murder rate increased by 7.8 percent, robbery with aggravating circumstances increased by 4 percent, rape (including attempts) increased by 16 percent, assault with intent to commit grievous bodily harm rose by 11 percent, and residential housebreaking by 17 percent.[77] Throughout the Mandela presidency, South Africa had indubitably the highest rape rate in the world—49,280 women were reported to have been raped in 1998. This shameful preeminence was related to the male chauvinist element in South African culture. South Africa also had one of the five highest rates of other violent crimes; in 1998, for example, the official South African murder rate was 58.5 per 100,000, nearly ten times the U.S. rate of 6.3 murders per 100,000.[78]

There was also a high level of corruption in the new South Africa.[79] Some of it was inherited from the apartheid regime, but much of it was unprecedented. A few examples illustrate the range of political corruption. In the central government, police and other officials stole pensions from the dead and issued duplicate pensions, ran a scam in driving licenses, extorted money from people they had arrested illegally, and colluded with syndicates in stealing and marketing a million cars a year. Political corruption was even more widespread in the provincial and municipal governments. In Gauteng, school examination papers were for sale, and there was massive fraud in the Department of Housing and Land. In Mpumalanga province, political notables were endemically corrupt; in June 1999, the premier, Ndaweni Mahlangu, said that it was "politically correct" for politicians to lie. A KwaZulu/Natal department paid four million rand to ghost workers, and in another department a single official stole one million rand. White officials were responsible for some of these excesses, but as political scientist Tom Lodge explained, most transgressions were due to the absorption into the burgeoning political class of the new black elite, comprising "cadres and governors . . . with recent experience of extreme poverty."[80] Political scientists Heribert Adam, Frederik van Zyl Slabbert, and Kogila Moodley were scathing in their criticism of members of the new black political and business elite: "The state is perceived as a source of enrichment. . . . The extraordinary gap between elite remuneration and bottom income erodes cohesion and solidarity in favor of everyone for himself and herself by all means available. . . . Comparative extreme inequality remains South Africa's ticking time bomb."[81] In 1998, the government tried to cope with this problem by appointing Judge William Heath to head a Special Investigating Unit, which recovered, saved, or prevented the loss of 1.3 billion rand by March 12, 1999; but that was only the tip of the iceberg.[82]

Exit Mandela

On February 5, 1999, as his presidency drew to a close, Mandela delivered in parliament a somber review of the state of South Africa.[83] His government, he said, had laid solid foundations for the future. The judiciary made no one, not even the president, above the law. "Equality, the right to vote in free and fair elections and freedom of speech" were now taken for granted. "Though we might differ on method, it has become a national passion to pronounce commitment to a better life for all." Fresh water, electricity, and telephones were supplied to many more people, even though targets were not met; many school classrooms were built or repaired, adult education was expanding, and a recent meeting of representatives of government, labor, business, and local communities created "a splendid partnership between business and government."

But, said Mandela, "The long walk is not yet over. The prize of a better life has yet to be won." Racism survives in the new South Africa; full reconciliation was not to be expected before the remnants of apartheid attitudes and practices were dismantled. "Turning the tide against crime cannot be expected overnight," but "we can and shall break out of this bog. There is hope." There was hope, too, that the economy would improve and unemployment would decrease: "Our fundamentals are robust."

In words that white South Africans could not use without being branded as racist, Mandela denounced corruption by the new black elite, especially in local government. "All of this," he said, "was spawned by apartheid," but, he added, "it is also a reality of the present that among the new cadres in various levels of government, you will find individuals who are as corrupt as—if not more than—those they found in government. When a leader in a provincial legislature siphons off resources meant to fund service by legislators to the people; when employees of a government institution defraud it for their own enrichment; then we must admit that we are a sick society." Nevertheless, he concluded, "We dare to hope for a brighter future, because we are prepared to work for it. The steady progress of the past few years has laid the foundation for greater achievements. But the reality is that we can do much, much better."

Mandela had prepared for a peaceful succession to the presidency. In 1997 he yielded the leadership of the ANC to his first deputy president, the energetic Thabo Mbeki, and he delegated most of the day-to-day administration to Mbeki. When the election was held in June 1999, the ANC won more than 66 percent of the vote, and a reinvigorated Democratic party replaced the National party as the official parliamentary opposition. The ANC retained control of seven provinces, but the IFP again won a majority in KwaZulu/Natal, and in the Western Cape the National party formed a coalition government with the Democratic party. Parliament then elected Mbeki as president, and Mandela, universally admired as one of the greatest people of the twentieth century, retired into private life, though not into obscurity. He continued to play an active role in global affairs; for example, he helped pacify Rwanda and Burundi.[84]

We should not forget the enormity of the task that the new regime undertook in 1994—the task of transforming a society that had been molded by colonialism and then dominated with ruthless thoroughness by a racist minority, into a nonracial, democratic society. Bear in mind that before 1994 Africans had been almost totally excluded from the authoritative political system. No African had ever been a member of parliament, and the small number of Africans who had been entitled to vote in the Cape Colony lost that right under apartheid. It would, however, be unrealistic to ignore the fact that in some crucial aspects conditions worsened in South Africa after the transfer of political power, but it would also be unrealistic to underestimate the achievements of the new regime. It restored dignity to black South Africans; it pacified a country that was on the brink of civil war; it entrenched a democratic constitutional order and maintained the rule of law; it adapted to the existence of an outspoken (though relatively small) political opposition and acquiesced (though grudgingly) in the presence of a relatively free press; and it provided millions of people, who had never had them before, with electricity, piped water, telephones, and adequate housing. Except for the AIDS pandemic, which was tearing all of Southern Africa apart, the major problems that afflicted South Africa—poverty, crime, the weak economy, and the education mess—were mutually reinforcing and had deep roots in the past. They could not possibly have been solved in six years. Moreover, in spite of the gravity of the situation, South Africa in 2000 was richer, more stable, more peaceful, and more humane than any country in mainland tropical Africa. The 2000 edition of the United Nations Human Development Report, based on 1998 data, ranked South Africa 103 out of 174 states. That was disappointing in the global context, but much better than any other country in mainland sub-Saharan Africa. The closest were Swaziland, Namibia, and Botswana, all neighbors of South Africa, followed by oil-producing Gabon. Nigeria, South Africa's principal rival for leadership in sub-Saharan Africa, ranked 155.[85]

Nothing is preordained in human history. In 1999 it was still conceivable that the dreams of Nelson Mandela, Thabo Mbeki, and millions of other South Africans would eventually, in some fashion, triumph.

CHAPTER 10

Beyond
the New South Africa,
1999–2014

LYNN BERAT

By the time Mandela left office, he had become a secular saint. After all, against what often had seemed like impossible odds, he had given the world the miracle of the new South Africa, vibrant, democratic, and determined to overcome its tragic past. There was euphoria in the land, and, as he was in office for only five years, the people who had waited so long for liberation were prepared to hold on a little longer for the economic gains that would fulfill the promise of the nation's stunning political achievement. While expectations were high for Thabo Mbeki, the ANC's golden prince, it would be difficult for anyone, no matter how competent, to maintain the level of unity and enthusiasm of the Mandela years. The task of nation-building is a difficult, messy business, and the more time that elapsed, the clearer it became that the ANC's dream of "a better life for all" would be hard to realize. Mbeki's seemed increasingly to be an "imperial presidency," as the media called it. His unceremonious ejection from government would, after a brief, constitutionally appropriate interlude under the much respected Kgalema Motlanthe, bring to power Jacob Zuma, often portrayed as a man of the people—

albeit one with an unusual gift for scandal. With his populist tendencies, Zuma was the perfect foil to Mbeki's heavy-handed remoteness, but, in politics as in life, image and reality are not always consonant. Zuma's leadership was tainted by growing corruption and bureaucratic bungling that made the prize of economic liberation recede ever further from the people's grasp.

The Presidency of Thabo Mbeki

Mbeki's First Term: The Polity

The international community welcomed Thabo Mbeki's election. Widely known in diplomatic circles from his days as an ANC exile and his years as Mandela's deputy president, he had a reputation as a capable intellectual. More than a year before he became president, he had caused excitement with his talk of an African Renaissance in which South Africa would be an active partner in bringing development and prosperity to the African continent.[1] Mbeki appointed as deputy president Jacob Zuma, a long-time ANC activist with no formal education who since December 1997 had been deputy president of the ANC. Unlike Mbeki, Zuma had spent ten years on Robben Island before following Mbeki's path into exile. Also unlike Mbeki and the majority of the ANC leaders, he was a Zulu, and his appointment may have helped mute the common criticism that the ANC elite was dominated by a Xhosa clique, derisively referred to in politics and the media as the Xhosa Nostra.

With the exception of Zuma, who had not served in the Mandela presidency, Mbeki's government represented continuity. All the former ministers who were available remained in the cabinet, except one white man and one African who had been a critic.[2] On June 16, 1999, in his inaugural address, Mbeki spoke eloquently of expanding the frontiers of human dignity and sounded a balance between continuity and change.[3] Nine days later, in his first state of the nation speech to both houses of Parliament, Mbeki reprised these themes in a thorough statement of his government's determination to cope with the many problems facing the country.[4] He did not mention reconciliation, which had been among Mandela's top priorities, and whereas Mandela had been a rather relaxed administrator, Mbeki signaled that he would be active in the day-to-day work of government. His February 4, 2000, state of the nation speech also made no mention of reconciliation. Rather, after congratulatory remarks about the country's achievements on the tenth anniversary of de Klerk's momentous release of Mandela, Mbeki announced a "common national offensive against all forms of inequality and discrimination."[5] The following year South Africa would host the International Conference against Racism.

Mbeki's early presidential actions illustrated the contrast between Mandela and Mbeki discernible from the speeches. As there was now no danger of a white counterrevolution, Mbeki emphasized implementation of the affirmative action policy to reduce the political, economic, and cultural power of the white minority. For instance, when Dr. Chris Stals stepped down as governor of the South African Reserve Bank in August 1999, Mbeki appointed as his successor the ANC economist Tito Mboweni.[6] Mbeki also concentrated a great deal of power in his own hands. He appointed his old friend Essop Pahad, with the rank of cabinet minister, to his presidential office, which absorbed the office of the deputy president (whose significance was thereby greatly reduced) and which became responsible for coordinating the work of the ministries. Mbeki would dominate the cabinet and would make all major official decisions.[7] The opposition alleged he was becoming a dictator, but he replied that centralization was essential for efficiency.[8] Both at home and abroad, he frequently decried "global apartheid,"[9] a phrase he used for the disparities between the small number of rich countries compared to the much larger number of poor states.[10] Yet despite the elegant rhetoric, on a personal level many found him cerebral and remote. He also rapidly gained a reputation for intolerance, and it appeared that a chosen route for his consolidation of power was the thwarting of criticism.

In February 2000, Parliament passed the Promotion of Access to Information Act (PAIA), which took effect in March 2001.[11] Its purpose was to "foster a culture of transparency and accountability in public and private bodies by giving effect to the right of access to information." Under the act, any person could demand records from government bodies without giving a reason, and individuals and government agencies could obtain certain records in the possession of private organizations.[12] The South African Human Rights Commission (SAHRC), appointed by the government under the constitution, was to have administrative oversight. Despite a number of cases where applicants went to court to gain access to documents and the court ruled in their favor, in 2003, the Open Democracy Advice Centre found improper or inconsistent implementation of the act, partly due to a lack of funding for the SAHRC and partly because of poor record keeping on behalf of government departments.[13]

Beyond PAIA, the government was not especially fond of free access to information. In 2000, it made a submission to the SAHRC in which it accused the media of being "ashamedly racist."[14] The SAHRC itself made a series of attacks on the press. Labeling journalists racist when they criticized the government, it intimidated them by issuing subpoenas to, among many others, the editor and staff of the *Mail and Guardian,* which had been a conspicuous critic of the white government in the apartheid era and continued to expose corruption in the new regime; whereupon Sheena Duncan, who had been a courageous leader of the antiapartheid Black Sash organization, resigned from the commission, declaring it was "violating the rights it was established to protect."[15]

The Judiciary

Mbeki showed a distaste for judicial independence when decisions interfered with government policy making. The courts, increasingly reflecting the country's racial demography, had a significant political role, especially in interpreting the constitution. As early as 1998, the Constitutional Court had addressed the government's commitment to socioeconomic rights.[16] Some lower courts also considered the matter. Mbeki expressed his displeasure with such activism in a July 2003 address to a judicial symposium, in which he clashed with Chief Justice Arthur Chaskalson and indicated that he favored judicial deference to the executive and legislative branches.[17]

The Opposition

After the 1999 election, when Mbeki continued to include Buthelezi and two other IFP members in his cabinet, the ANC's relations with the IFP mellowed; there was even talk of a merger between them. The ANC's dealings with its tripartite alliance partners—the SACP and COSATU—were complicated. In response to the government's economic policies, communist politicians left the SACP in droves to become staunch capitalists.[18] The government's relations with COSATU became increasingly strained, but COSATU continued to provide political support to the ANC on the basis of solidarity.[19] Meanwhile, the PAC and other black organizations still offered no serious challenge to the ANC.

There was a process of consolidation among the ANC's adversaries. The National party had become the official opposition when it withdrew from the government in 1998 and, in a symbolic break with the past, rechristened itself the New National Party (NNP) that December.[20] After being superseded as the official opposition in the 1999 elections by the Democratic Party (DP), which itself won less than 10 percent of the vote, the NNP, with diminishing support and just 28 seats in Parliament, gradually withered away. Many of its members switched to the DP, and in May 2000 its survivors formed an alliance with that party, which had moved to the right to become the political home of most Whites, as well as many Coloureds and Indians, but had scarcely any African support.[21] In August, the DP, the NNP, and the Federal Alliance formed the Democratic Alliance.[22] The NNP withdrew the next year, and, in an ironic end for the party of apartheid, it then made a pact with the ANC.[23] In 2005, after years of declining popularity, it disbanded.[24] Meanwhile, in 2003, Patricia de Lille, a former trade unionist and PAC member of Parliament, crossed the floor to found the Independent Democrats (ID), whose power base would be largely in the Northern and Western Cape.[25]

Mbeki's Second Term: The Polity

By the time of Mbeki's second presidential campaign, his supporters said Mbeki had grown into his role, seeming more at ease and even kissing babies on the campaign trail. He secured his second five-year term with a huge ANC victory at the polls.[26] In his April 2004 inaugural address, he delighted in South Africa's ten years of non-racial democracy.[27] In his state of the nation speech the following February, he gave details of various programs he said would make South Africa "a winning nation" in "the renewal of Africa and the creation of a better world."[28] Political conflict would interfere with Mbeki's goal.

Access to information remained difficult, and attacks on press freedom continued. Compliance with PAIA fell.[29] The 2004 Law on Anti-Terrorism allowed the government to prevent reporting on the security forces, prisons, and mental institutions.[30] In 2005, the *Mail and Guardian* began to receive gag orders compelling it to stop running stories on various corruption scandals. In 2006, Deputy President Zuma sued the *Sunday Times* political cartoonist and former antiapartheid activist Jonathan Shapiro, known by his pen name Zapiro, and several South African newspapers for millions for damage to reputation, a tactic he would use repeatedly in the years to come. Zuma objected to cartoons of himself with the moniker Showerhead, a reference to his testimony in his trial for rape of an HIV-positive family friend, testimony widely ridiculed in a South Africa devastated by AIDS, in which he claimed he had guarded against the disease by taking a shower after the encounter.[31] Zuma eventually was acquitted.[32] In 2007, the ANC sought to censor all Showerhead cartoons. The next year, Zuma called for damages for defamation over another Zapiro cartoon, known as "The Rape of Lady Justice." It depicted Lady Justice being held down by ANC, ANCYL, SACP, and COSATU leaders as Zuma prepared to rape her.[33]

Zuma's problems did not lie just with the press. A bitter rivalry arose between Zuma and Mbeki. As deputy president, Zuma became embroiled in corruption scandals beginning in 2003. The director of public prosecutions charged Schabir Shaik, Zuma's financial adviser who had bankrolled him since 1990, with corruption and fraud for buying influence in order to procure lucrative contracts, including arms sales, for companies in which he had a major interest.[34] Shaik's trial revealed that he had spent large sums on Zuma's residence in Nkandla, KwaZulu-Natal. He had also solicited a bribe of R500,000 per annum in exchange for Zuma's support for the giant defense contractor Thomson SC.[35] A Durban High Court judgment against Shaik on June 2, 2005, asserted that the many payments to Zuma "can only have generated a sense of obligation in the recipient."[36] Twelve days later, amid ongoing media coverage, Mbeki removed Zuma from the deputy presidency.[37] Zuma then resigned from Parliament.

Once the Shaik trial concluded, the National Prosecuting Authority (NPA) charged Zuma with corruption. For procedural reasons the court struck the case from the roll, but the outcome meant that Zuma could be recharged. In December 2007, the NPA's investigative team known as the Scorpions indicted Zuma for racketeering, money laundering, corruption, and fraud.[38] A sentence to a prison term of more than a year would have made Zuma ineligible to be elected president.

After Zuma's dismissal, the Mbeki-Zuma friction intensified. Mbeki said he would not seek to have the constitution amended in order to serve a third term but he hoped to continue to lead the ANC. This would have been contrary to ANC custom, begun with Mandela, that the president of the ANC was also the president or president-in-waiting of South Africa. Zuma, following precedent, expected to become ANC president at the ANC's fifty-second national conference, held at Polokwane in December 2007. There, the rift between Mbeki and Zuma supporters exposed the ANC factionalism between the neoliberal economic moderation of Mbeki and the populist, left-wing, pro-CPSA and pro-COSATU politics of Zuma. It also highlighted the split between the Xhosa represented by Mbeki and the Zulu represented by Zuma. In the end, Zuma carried the voting and became ANC president.[39] The corruption charges he still faced, however, threatened to destroy his political career.

On September 12, 2008, Pietermartizburg High Court judge Chris Nicholson found the charges unlawful on procedural grounds. He set off a whirlwind when he commented that he believed the recharging of Zuma, coming after Mbeki had lost to Zuma at Polokwane, had been politically motivated.[40] Not only did the ruling open the way for Zuma to run for president in the 2009 election, it also prompted the ANC National Executive Committee (NEC) to withdraw its support of Mbeki, effectively recalling him. Mbeki was incensed. He appealed unsuccessfully to the Constitutional Court.[41] Mbeki announced, and Parliament accepted, his resignation, effective September 25.[42] On January 12, 2009, too late to save Mbeki's presidency, the Supreme Court of Appeal deputy judge president would find that Nicholson's improper influence allegations "overstepped the limits of [the court's] authority."[43]

Mbeki's departure necessitated the appointment of an interim president until the next presidential elections, scheduled for April 2009. Those constitutionally eligible were the deputy president, the speaker of Parliament, or any member of Parliament chosen by that body.[44] Zuma, on behalf of the ANC, suggested Member of Parliament (MP) Kgalema Motlanthe.[45] The 59-year-old was a lifelong ANC member who had spent ten years on Robben Island. He had been elected ANC secretary general at the ANC's Mafikeng conference in December 1997 and deputy president a decade later at Polokwane, where he defeated Mbeki's candidate. Widely respected within the party, he had a low-key manner and no independent power base to threaten Zuma's. In May 2008, Motlanthe had become an MP. Two months later, under pressure from the newly dominant Zuma faction, Mbeki added Motlanthe to his cabinet, a move widely viewed as an effort to ensure a smooth transition to a Zuma government. On September 25, Parliament duly elected Motlanthe the third president of postapartheid South Africa and its first Tswana leader.[46] Thereafter, various high-ranking Mbeki stalwarts announced their resignations.

The Judiciary

The Mbeki-Zuma affair highlighted the prominence of the judiciary in South African life. In Mbeki's second term, the judiciary continued to refine its stance on socioeconomic rights. In 2004 and 2005, the Constitutional Court was at odds with the government.[47] Then, in 2008, after a three-year hiatus, the court issued five rulings on socioeconomic rights in cases concerning access to water, electricity, adequate housing, and basic sanitation.[48] While the court extended the meaning of socioeconomic rights by expanding the list of entitlements, it limited its involvement in policy making by deferentially adopting a weak reasonableness standard for judging government behavior.

For their part, Mbeki, in a retreat from his 2003 attack, and the ANC affirmed the value of judicial independence both in the ANC's 2005 Statement of the National Executive Committee[49] and in Mbeki's address at the ceremony to mark Chaskalson's retirement and the installation of Chief Justice Pius Langa that June.[50] Despite the high-minded language at that event, scandal was bringing the judiciary into disrepute, a dangerous development threatening the democratic order. Particularly notable was a polarizing episode involving Cape judge John Hlophe. In 2005 and 2006, there were four allegations of misconduct by Hlophe, including financial impropriety and racism, which the Judicial Service Commission (JSC) referred for investigation.[51]

In October 2007, in a divided vote, the JSC concluded, largely on the basis of technicalities,[52] that there was not enough evidence for a public inquiry to be held.[53] The decision caused a brawl. Johann Kriegler, the former head of the Independent Electoral Commission at the time of South Africa's first nonracial elections and later a Constitutional and Appeals Court judge, attacked Hlophe in the *Sunday Times*,[54] as did nine senior members of the Cape Bar Council in the *Cape Times*, asserting that Hlophe was "unfit for the Bench" and calling upon him to resign.[55] A number of University of Cape Town law professors were in accord.[56] Conversely, the Black Lawyers' Association's judicial committee chairman Dumisa Ntsebeza assailed Kriegler's "unsolicited attack" on Hlophe, and, derivatively, on the JSC.[57]

The next year, Hlophe was at the center of a controversy about judicial and prosecutorial independence. At the end of May, the Constitutional Court filed a complaint against Hlophe, with the JSC alleging he had tried to influence improperly "one or more cases," including the Zuma corruption case.[58] The ANC secretary general Gwede Mantashe called the Constitutional Court's behavior "counterrevolutionary." Subsequently, the Johannesburg High Court decided that the Constitutional Court had violated Hlophe's rights by filing its complaint publicly.[59] The judges' and jurists' travails did not enhance South Africa's image abroad, the very image Mbeki so assiduously tried to cultivate.

Mbeki's Foreign Policy

Just as domestically Mbeki's lofty pronouncements clashed with the reality of a not easily transformed South Africa, so too did the complexities of international affairs compromise Mbeki's vision of "build[ing] a global movement of human solidarity."[60] Mbeki devoted much time and energy to foreign affairs—critics said too much, in light of the domestic situation. He was so often away that the media sometimes referred to him as the president who most frequently visited South Africa. In 2004 alone, he made twenty-two African trips. He championed democracy and the rule of law, but, with his experience in dealing with members of the National party in the apartheid era, he preferred quiet diplomacy to public denunciation of African despots. Via his travels, he gained recognition as an effective spokesman not only for South Africa but also for all of sub-Saharan Africa and for developing countries everywhere, as he campaigned for debt relief, foreign investment, poverty reduction, and reform of the International Monetary Fund, the World Bank, and the U.N. Security Council. He kept the country at the forefront of global issues when South Africa hosted the World Conference against Racism and the World Summit on Sustainable Development.

Mbeki worked hard to create rapport with African governments, notably the new civilian government of Nigeria; he helped Mozambique cope with a catastrophic flood; he established cordial relations with Western leaders, especially President Clinton and Prime Minister Blair; and, building on Mandela's 1998 recognition of China at the expense of the country's apartheid-era ally Taiwan, he signed a controversial trade agreement with the Chinese president Jiang Zemin.[61] He also joined in a continent-wide effort led by intellectuals to give substance to the idea of an African Renaissance.[62] In 2002, he was a major figure in establishing the African Union (AU), which replaced the moribund Organization of African Unity, and in the creation of the union's Constitutive Act, replete with multiple human rights provisions.[63] Later, in a politically astute move much like New York's offer to host the United Nations after World War II, South Africa became the permanent home of the AU's legislature, the Pan African Parliament.[64] Mbeki also was instrumental in establishing the AU's development initiative, the New Partnership for Africa's Development (NEPAD), replete with an African Peer Review Mechanism.[65] In cooperation with the United Nations, the government sent peacekeeping missions to Burundi and the Democratic Republic of the Congo. Mbeki became a key figure in peace talks in those countries as well as in Rwanda and Côte d'Ivoire. Indeed, Mbeki, with his talk of an African Renaissance and years of diplomatic experience, frequently called for African political disputes to be resolved by African players and for Africa to end its reliance on foreign aid and the political toadying by African governments that accompanied it.

Under Mandela, South Africa's foreign policy had a strong human rights component, befitting a country acclaimed for its astonishing transition to majority rule. Mandela frequently gave speeches on human rights. He had also intervened in Nigeria regarding the execution of activist Ken Saro-Wiwa and had openly criticized the regime of Nigerian dictator Sani Abacha. In contrast, Mbeki's twin desires to effectuate his African Renaissance and to grow the economy, largely through access to foreign markets, soon led to what can at best be described as a realpolitik approach and at worst a rejection of Mandela's human rights strategy. Thus, South Africa voted against U.N. resolutions condemning human rights violators in countries such as Iran, Myanmar, and Zimbabwe, and in so doing destroyed, as the *Economist* put it, the country's reputation as "a beacon of human rights."[66]

Beginning in 2000, the human rights aspects of Mbeki's foreign policy faced a severe test from events in South Africa's most important neighbor, Zimbabwe. President Mugabe had a good start but had degenerated into an autocrat and was largely responsible for wrecking the country's economy. In the run-up to parliamentary elections, which he seemed likely to lose, Mugabe unleashed violence against his opponents and encouraged impoverished young men, led by veterans of the war against the white regime of Ian Smith, forcibly to occupy farms that had been owned by and occupied by Whites since the colonial conquest at the end of the nineteenth century.[67] As the crisis developed, Nelson Mandela denounced Mugabe, but Mbeki praised him for leading the fight for African freedom in Zimbabwe.[68]

As Mugabe's authoritarian kleptocracy brought Zimbabwe ever closer to perdition, Mbeki did not condemn him. In 2002, during Zimbabwe's presidential elections, the OAU and representatives from African countries, including Nigeria, Namibia, and South Africa, were unwilling to rebuke an African leader, especially one who had been a freedom fighter. The local Zimbabwean Election Support Network, Western governments, and official observer delegations from the Commonwealth and Norway blasted the elections, which they believed had occurred in a climate of fear.[69] Zimbabwe's 2005 parliamentary elections, which Mugabe's ZANU-PF won handily, revealed the same split in international opinion.[70]

Zimbabwe's presidential elections in 2008 were even more controversial.[71] No election results appeared for over a month, and all during this period human rights groups documented growing anti-opposition violence by Mugabe supporters, especially militias, and the police. While Zimbabwe remained in political limbo, Mbeki met with Mugabe, with whom he was photographed smiling and holding hands, and insisted there was no crisis.[72] Media criticism was harsh. The *Mail and Guardian* attributed his failure to act forcefully to "misplaced loyalty or crippling deference."[73] The *Washington Post* characterized him as a "bankrupt democrat" with a "perverse and immoral [foreign] policy."[74]

Before the results appeared,[75] ZANU-inspired violence spiraled upward, and barely five days before a June 27 runoff, Morgan Tsvangirai of the opposition Movement for Democratic Change withdrew out of fear for his supporters' safety.[76] With Tsvangirai gone, Mugabe won easily. His victory did not calm international controversy, with the

AU at odds with the United States and the European Union,[77] which were at odds with the Russians and the Chinese.[78] With Mbeki again serving as mediator, on September 11, just days before he left office, there was a power-sharing deal between Mugabe and Tsvangirai.[79] Despite the fanfare accompanying the signing of the Mbeki-brokered agreement a few days later in Harare, implementation would be problematic. Zimbabwe remained a deeply troubled state—as, in its own way, was South Africa.

The Economy

Mbeki reaffirmed his belief that sustained and rapid economic growth was the answer to South Africa's economic problems and that it was to be achieved through persisting with GEAR.[80] In practice, all his government did, like its predecessor, was try to streamline the public services, limit the size of wage increases, privatize the parastatals, and diminish the power of labor over business. COSATU opposed those efforts, which were throwing thousands of workers out of their jobs. It also claimed that the government was doing little to alleviate the poverty of the African masses. In July and again in August 1999, teachers and other public servants went on strike, and in May 2000 perhaps half of South Africa's industrial force ceased work for a day, protesting that half a million jobs had been lost since the ANC came to power.[81] Although the government stood firm against the demands, as the May 2000 strike approached, the populist sector of the ANC persuaded the leadership to reverse course and claim to support the strikers.[82]

Indeed, the economy remained in poor shape through the first year of Mbeki's presidency as more unskilled people lost their jobs, more skilled people emigrated, foreign investment declined, and the rand continued to drop sharply in value against the U.S. dollar.[83] On June 30, 2000, the South African Bureau for Economic Research reported that consumer confidence in all racial and economic groups fell 16 points (from +3 to −13) in the second quarter, bringing the index to its lowest since 1993, with Blacks pessimistic for the first time since the 1994 elections.[84]

By the time he gave the first state of the nation speech of his second term in February 2005, Mbeki was more sanguine.[85] The previous year the government had laid out a Program of Action to enhance economic development. Now, Mbeki quoted approvingly from a Rand Merchant Bank report that found accelerated growth in 2004 reaching an annual rate of 5.6 percent in the third quarter. He said this trend had begun in September 1999 and represented the longest period of expansion since the close of World War II. At the end of 2007, the government was claiming real progress against poverty. Minister of Finance Trevor Manuel said those in poverty had "dropped steadily from 52.1% in 1999 to 47% in 2004 and to 43.2% by March this year."[86] University of Cape Town researchers later debunked the claim.

In his February 2008 state of the nation address, Mbeki launched the "War on Poverty."[87] In July, he said the program would focus on the most deprived areas. The next month, Deputy President Phumzile Mlambo-Ngcuka's office became the national "war room on poverty." Little would happen.

The Quality of Life of the Majority of the People

In this economic climate, the social trends of the Mandela period accelerated. The gap between the rich (including the new black elite) and the poor (who were overwhelmingly African) continued to widen. Educated, skilled people were in such demand that they had no difficulty finding jobs with high and rapidly rising salaries, whereas half or more of the uneducated and unskilled were unemployed, and the wages of those who did have jobs were largely stagnant.[88] To alleviate abject poverty, the budget included handouts in the form of pensions, housing subsidies, and child care benefits, but many of these grants did not reach their targets because of bureaucratic incompetence and corruption. The government also expanded Black Economic Empowerment (BEE), the cornerstone of economic affirmative action, dating to the Mandela years. BEE, which emphasized black equity ownership and management in corporations, had benefited only those with high-level ANC ties, the so-called black elite. In 2003, the government sought to create a new class of black small businesspeople through a Broad-Based Black Economic Empowerment program[89] (B-BBEE but usually still referred to as BEE). It, too, would prove unsuccessful, because fledgling companies suffered from a lack of skills and from difficulties acquiring capital.[90]

Meanwhile, South Africa subscribed to the U. N. Millennium Development Goals (MDG) promulgated in 2000.[91] The eight goals for the world's countries to reach by 2015 included reducing extreme poverty, decreasing infant mortality by two-thirds, and achieving universal primary education. By the time of Mbeki's second term, ten years into the new dispensation, it was apparent that South Africa would not realize its ambitions. Desmond Tutu, by then Anglican archbishop emeritus of Cape Town, criticized Mbeki for policies that promoted the interests of the small African elite, called tenderpreneurs because they had amassed fortunes through the BEE program that had given them access to government contracts known as tenders.[92]

Mbeki and the ANC used the party mouthpiece ANC *Today* to respond. The ANC sought to marginalize Tutu, who, it noted, had never joined the ANC, as an "icon" of "white elites."[93] Mbeki insisted that valuable discussion occurred both inside the ANC and outside it in public forums. Curiously, he supported his faith in intraparty debate by extolling the slogan "let a hundred flowers bloom." This was a reference to the Chinese Communist party's abortive "let a hundred flowers bloom" campaign of 1956–57, during which Chairman Mao Zedong encouraged open debate and then brutally punished critics of the regime.[94] Tutu answered the attacks by saying he would pray for Mbeki and the ANC, just as he had prayed for apartheid government leaders.[95]

By the time Mbeki left office, South Africa, with its extreme differences between the rich and the poor, was on its way to becoming the most unequal society on earth. The long economic expansion Mbeki had praised had brought not only a decline in poverty but also a marked rise in inequality. The Organization for Economic Cooperation and Development (OECD) found that the high level of overall income inequality had further accentuated the country's Gini coefficient, the standard measurement of income inequality, which increased markedly between 1993 and 2008.[96] More and more, income was concentrated in the top decile of the population.

Inequality between the races fell slowly but remained significant, and there was growing intraracial inequality. Among Africans there were the fabulously wealthy tenderpreneurs and a growing middle class whose affluence was in marked contradistinction to the desperate poverty of the masses.[97] Among Whites, particularly Afrikaners, there was the reemergence of the white poverty that apartheid had eliminated.[98] Although real incomes had risen, the poor were overwhelmingly African, and, as under apartheid, Africans generally were much poorer than Coloureds, who were much poorer than Indians, who were much poorer than Whites.

A Crisis in Electricity

Among the many development issues, the government could not solve the problem of electricity, which was largely the result of official policies. In January 2008, the government announced there would be electricity rationing, known as rolling blackouts.[99] By the end of the month, the lack of supply was so serious that the world's largest gold and platinum mining companies, which were responsible for much of South Africa's foreign exchange, had to cease operations.[100] ESKOM, the parastatal electricity supply company, which said its directors had failed to heed its own predictions of a dire situation in reports going back as far as 2003, apologized.[101] The government did likewise. Mbeki made the crisis a major subject of his 2008 state of the nation speech, in which he reiterated the apologies.[102] He acknowledged that for a decade the government had not responded to ESKOM warnings about the coming crisis.[103]

In the national debate about electrification, two major economic policies received particular opprobrium. First, bypassing established large companies, BEE had awarded coal supply tenders to often undependable small and medium-size tenderpreneurs.[104] Second, Mbeki's government had offered cheap electricity as an enticement to energy-intensive industrial investment in fields such as aluminum smelting.[105] The government, having stressed South Africa's desirability as an international investment destination, could not now be seen to violate the sanctity of contract. Moreover, any cessation in supply to the aluminum industries would have repercussions for the government by adversely impacting the companies' refineries and bauxite mines outside South Africa. Thus, the government was bound to have the rest of the country suffer electricity disruptions. Mbeki ignored allegations of flawed government economic policy and announced a national energy conservation initiative to complement ESKOM's building program.[106]

Water

Water supply was similarly problematic. South Africa is one of the few countries in the world whose constitution enshrines the basic right to sufficient water.[107] For millions, however, that right remained unrealized. In 1990, about 15 million people did not have potable water, and more than 20 million were without adequate sanitation services.[108] After apartheid, the numbers of those with access to an improved water source rose gradually. In his 2004 state of the nation speech, Mbeki insisted that everyone would have running water within five years.[109] Success was elusive.

For those with water, the quality of the water and its delivery seemed to be highly variable, although data were poor.[110] In 2008, the Department of Water Affairs announced an incentive-based water quality regulation plan known as "Blue Drop"[111] to certify municipal providers. The World Health Organization welcomed the unique initiative.[112] A considerable public relations campaign followed. Observers claimed that behind the hype, water quality was declining and pollution, especially from the mining industry, soon would render about one-third of the water in strategic storage undrinkable.

Housing

As with water, housing for all proved difficult to attain. While Department of Housing records showed an increase in the provision of housing from 1994 to 1998, there was a decrease during Mbeki's first term.[113] By July 2001, the government failed to meet its target of one million houses a year. The backlog grew from 1.5 million in 1994 to 2.4 million a decade later. Although the National Housing Code of 2000 promised "sustainable housing and a sustainable urban environment,"[114] squatter camps—informal settlements in South African parlance—which had grown dramatically in the last years of apartheid, mushroomed. Protests were frequent. Activists used the constitutional right to housing to challenge the government. The Constitutional Court's 2000 landmark decision in *Grootboom* received international attention for its ruling that the government could not remove Mrs. Grootboom and several hundred other squatters from a Cape Town sportsground until it provided them with a decent alternative.[115]

For low-income families who wished to purchase a low-cost home, the government relied on a housing subsidy program.[116] Depending upon how far below the threshold their earnings were, those eligible received either a full or a partial subsidy. Although annual budgetary allocations rose steadily during the Mbeki years, it was not enough to meet demand. In Gauteng province, which included Johannesburg and Pretoria, there was a waiting list with 500,000 names.[117] In Cape Town, there was a list with 120,000 names.[118] With a population containing a very high percentage of children and young adults, who would require their own accommodation once they started families, demographics were not in South Africa's favor regarding unmet and projected housing needs.

Particularly dismaying to activists was the government's eviction of squatters from central urban areas and sending them to low-cost housing developments, typically on the outskirts of cities.[119] The practice was redolent of the apartheid government's policy of forced removals, which had brought the wholesale destruction of thriving urban communities, most notably Sophiatown in Johannesburg in the 1950s and District Six in Cape Town in the 1960s. Then, the government had justified its actions on the grounds of improving health and preventing crime. Now, in a public relations disaster, the eviction policy relied on the apartheid-era National Building Regulations and Buildings Standards Act and the very rhetoric about health and crime used during apartheid.[120] Critics said the official reasons masked the government's ambition to remove urban squatters to make way for urban renewal programs readying South Africa for its duties as the host country of the 2010 Soccer World Cup[121] and to attract tax-paying businesses to redeveloped, high-value, urban real estate. The few attempts to place low-cost housing in or close to the city had engendered hostility from middle- and upper-middle-class homeowners who felt that the proximity of such housing would diminish the value of their property.[122]

While government efforts initially focused on free or low-cost home ownership, in August 2004, it added a R160 million Social Housing Program to provide government-owned housing for the poor, not unlike the public housing projects in American and Western European cities.[123] The next month, Housing Minister Lindiwe Sisulu unveiled the Comprehensive Housing Plan for the Development of Integrated Sustainable Human Settlements, which aimed to create low-cost housing, medium-density accommodation, and rental housing.[124] She committed the government to slum eradication by 2014, a year before the MDG deadline.

Corruption and low-quality construction complicated matters.

There were widespread allegations of fraud and inefficiency in the subsidy program. In 2006, an Auditor-General's report found hundreds of millions in irregular allocations of housing subsidies between 1994 and 2004.[125] Two years later, in July 2008, an Auditor-General's report on low-cost housing in six provinces found that years after they took occupancy many residents had still not received deeds to their property.[126] Worse, many of the already constructed houses, built hastily and poorly, were deteriorating rapidly. More than three-quarters of these structures had serious defects or were substandard. One Democratic Alliance MP noted that "for many who moved from informal settlements to low-cost housing, the houses that were provided to them were no better than the houses from which they had moved."[127] In the end, it seemed the government often had neither the capacity nor the will to effect change. The government even ignored the Constitutional Court's *Grootboom* ruling. No houses were ever built for the victorious plaintiffs, and Mrs. Grootboom was living in a shack when she died in 2008.[128]

Health Care and AIDS

In 1995, when he was deputy president, Mbeki, speaking in Cape Town at the International Conference for People Living with HIV and AIDS, held for the first time in Africa, recognized that AIDS was a serious problem in the country.[129] When he assumed the presidency, South Africa's health care system ranked 151 in "attainment" and 175 in "efficiency" out of 191 countries listed in the World Health Organization's World Health Report, 2000.[130] It came under international scrutiny that year, by which time more South Africans were infected with HIV than the inhabitants of any other country—about 4.2 million people or 20 percent of the adult population—and at least one in two fifteen-year-old South Africans seemed destined to die of AIDS. Previously, the South African authorities had failed to make adequate preparations for the pandemic as it approached from the north; indeed, in 1999 more than a third of the AIDS budget was left unspent; but in 2000, as the crisis deepened into an overwhelming national catastrophe, the president himself became involved. Shocked by the fact that drugs used to treat AIDS patients in rich countries were far too expensive for general consumption in poor ones, he encouraged local firms to produce alternative drugs; his spokesman claimed that the drug AZT widely recommended for HIV-positive mothers was toxic and part of a conspiracy to kill Africans. The government also introduced a law permitting the sale of less expensive locally made generic medications and in April successfully defended a legal challenge by transnational companies seeking to invalidate it.[131] The prominent AIDS advocacy group Treatment Action Campaign (TAC) and its supporters believed that Mbeki intended to offer a program using inexpensive antiretroviral drugs (ARVs). They praised him, but their approbation quickly turned to dismay. The minister of health stopped government clinics and hospitals from using reasonably priced drugs that had seemed to be successful in Uganda and elsewhere in reducing the risk of transmitting HIV infections from pregnant women to their unborn children, a process known as mother to child transmission (MTCT). Relying on the constitution's socioeconomic guarantee of a right to health, TAC and its allies sued to overturn the minister's decision. In 2002, in the landmark *Treatment Action Campaign v. Minister of Health,* the Constitutional Court ordered the government to ensure the availability of the ARV nevirapine to pregnant women.[132]

By then, Mbeki had become embroiled in the scientific controversy about the cause of AIDS by appointing an AIDS advisory panel that included several members of the tiny minority of specialists, commonly known as AIDS dissenters or denialists, who disputed the widely accepted theory that HIV causes AIDS.[133] Their views fit nicely with Mbeki's idea that poverty was a major contributor to the AIDS/HIV pandemic. Thus, he said that poverty should be addressed in lieu of a singular focus on AIDS itself. In reply, 5,000 scholars, including several Nobel Prize winners, publicly reaffirmed the HIV theory,[134] and at the Thirteenth International AIDS Conference, held in Durban in July 2000, Mbeki drew much criticism for confusing South Africans and distracting the health services from addressing the epidemic. Mbeki was undeterred. He preferred the poverty explanation to what he regarded as the Western racist underpinnings of AIDS theory replete with old stereotypes of African promiscuity.[135] Mbeki took an extreme position in a 100-page paper he wrote in 2001 and circulated anonymously to the ANC leadership. Echoing the remarks Mbeki made at the University of Fort Hare earlier in the year, it argued that the HIV/AIDS thesis was part of "centuries old white racist beliefs and concepts about Africans."[136] Although in 2003 Mbeki's cabinet overruled him and the government approved a plan to make ARVs universally available, by 2005 not even half of those eligible received the drug regimen.[137]

Making matters worse and holding South Africa up to global ridicule was Mbeki's minister of health, Manto Shabalala-Msimang. She had spent 28 years in exile. Now she defended the government's position on AIDS with the argument that South Africa could not afford ARVs. In 2002, it became clear that cost was not paramount when Tshabalala-Msimang blocked U.S. funding to assist in the distribution of ARVs in her native KwaZulu-Natal. Tshabalala-Msimang's views on the treatment of HIV/AIDS drew international condemnation, especially her advocacy of beetroot, garlic, lemon, and African potatoes. These, she said, "are absolutely critical—first of all to have a beautiful face and beautiful skin—but they also protect you from disease."[138] The media mocked her as Dr. Beetroot, and in August 2006 the U.N. special envoy for AIDS in Africa said South Africa promoted a "lunatic fringe" attitude.[139] By that time, life expectancy had fallen to 49 years, thanks to AIDS-related fatalities, which—with 4.2 million infected by the virus—saw deaths nearly double between 1999 and 2005.[140] Despite the uproar, Mbeki never removed Shabalala-Msimang as minister.

Education

After describing South African education as in crisis soon after he assumed office, Minister of Education Kader Asmal periodically made positive forecasts. In January 2000, he vowed to improve the matriculation pass rate by 5 percent a year, and in February he promised to break the back of illiteracy within five years.[141] Instead, the crisis deepened. The education department continued to make unsuccessful changes in school curricula, there was still a desperate shortage of qualified teachers, especially in mathematics and the sciences, and conditions in many schools remained chaotic. The leaders of the Congress of South African Students (COSAS) refused to relinquish the powers they had exercised in the apartheid era, and by June 2000 students around the country were disrupting classes and defying the government. Many schools in Alexandra were reportedly controlled by gun-toting youths. In July 2000, a UNESCO study found that grade 4 South African pupils had among the worst numeracy, literacy, and life skills in Africa. That was a dreadful augury for the future of a country where a dearth of skills was already one of its greatest weaknesses.[142]

Government-funded higher education continued to decline. The schools were not producing enough people qualified for university entry. In 1999, of the half-million students who took the final school exam, only 272,000 passed; of those, only 69,800 obtained the exemption that allowed entry into higher education and only 20,000 passed advanced mathematics. Moreover, not all who were qualified entered the government-funded universities and technikons, because by 2000 there were numerous private colleges, which concentrated on providing job-oriented training and attracted increasing numbers of students. As the government restructured the universities to shift the emphasis away from the humanities, faculty morale at the formerly white universities fell to an all-time low,[143] and the historically black universities struggled with financial problems and student unrest.

Ever-larger infusions of capital into the education system marked Mbeki's presidency. The 2007 budget provided for R16 billion for education, with R13.3 of that going to higher education. In addition, there was another R88.7 billion in education money in the year's provincial education budgets.[144] The financial outlays were not used effectively enough to meet the country's growing need for an educated population. In 2007, Education Minister Naledi Pandor told Parliament that neither the legacy of apartheid nor inadequate resources sufficed as explanations for continued failures.

As for tertiary education, by 2006, only one in ten South Africans had any type of tertiary qualification. There had, however, been strides toward racial and gender equity. Three out of five of the nearly 750,000 university students were African, while only a quarter were white, a reversal of the apartheid proportions, while 14 percent were Coloured or Indian. Fifty percent of students were female. Overall enrollment figures also increased. The gross enrollment rate for 20- to 24-year-olds rose from 13 percent in 2000 to 16 percent in 2006, but graduation rates were low.[145]

A 2008 OECD survey of South African education found that low graduation rates meant that higher education was not able to yield the "high quality human capital needed to propel and sustain" social and economic development.[146] The low retention rates were a function of student lack of preparedness. Also unprepared were the large numbers of junior faculty members who had been hired by universities in an effort to change the ethnic profile of academics, who, under apartheid, were almost all white. The report recognized that the government had engaged in restructuring to make tertiary education "more accessible, equitable, integrated, rational and manageable." In practice, this meant that through mergers the government had reduced the number of public institutions from 36 to 23, and the comprehensive universities were "in a state of disarray."

Crime

There was little, if any, abatement of crime. For example, in June 2000 a group of workers went on a rampage in the Helen Joseph Hospital in Johannesburg, trashing the hospital, breaking property, and throwing patients out of wheelchairs in protest against the arrest of several colleagues for intimidation and assault. White-collar crime was also thriving. For example, three South African Airways pilots and four other people appeared to have bought and sold license examination papers, and the chief of civil aviation himself bought a dubious pilot's license.[147] An American medical journalist described her visit to South Africa in May 2000. "Everyone I met warned me to be careful. . . . The sense of suspicion and paranoia seemed to me to pervade even the fancy shopping malls, tourist beaches, and expensive hotels."[148]

In September 2004, early in Mbeki's second term, the official annual crime statistics indicated that most types of crime had diminished in the previous year.[149] However, many in the media attacked the validity of the statistics. Among these was journalist Charlene Smith, who had become a major voice opposing violence against women since she herself had been raped. She claimed that South Africa had the world's highest rate of rape.[150] In what had already become a familiar retort by the ANC in general and by this president in particular, Mbeki said the detractors, including Smith, were white racists who wanted the country to fail.[151] Mbeki also castigated the *Citizen* newspaper and other critics as pessimists who were suspicious of black rule.

In January 2007, the African Peer Review Mechanism (APRM), which Mbeki had been instrumental in creating, released a draft report on South Africa.[152] It found that with approximately 50 people a day being killed, South Africa's murder rate was the second highest in the world. It also noted that despite a falling rate of serious crime, rape and violent robberies were more frequent.[153] Mbeki's reaction was to claim to an interviewer that people's fear of crime was exaggerated.[154] Similarly, when the final APRM report appeared at the end of the year and indicated that the level of violent crime was unacceptably high, Mbeki lashed out at the panel's acceptance of "a populist view."[155] His indignation did nothing to quell anxiety among the citizenry, whose fears often took the form of xenophobia directed at the large numbers of illegal immigrants from elsewhere on the continent. The newcomers often received blame for South Africa's crime, unemployment, and housing shortages. Passions exploded in May 2008 when riots rocked many townships, particularly in Gauteng, leaving 42 dead, hundreds injured, and thousands homeless.[156] Prominent among the victims were Zimbabwean economic refugees from Mugabe's failed state. Widespread criticism of Mbeki's inattention to the issue of illegal immigration followed.[157] Mbeki said he would set up an official investigation of the riots. He also, in a first for post-apartheid South Africa, authorized the use of military force against the rioters.

Corruption

Perhaps more than riots, growing corruption greatly diminished South Africa's prospects for eradicating poverty. Surveys found that more than half the population believed that corruption was common among government officials. Nearly half of the population thought civil servants were crooked, and a third felt the same about managers of private businesses. Mbeki was quick to dismiss allegations of official corruption as racist, and in December 2006 he criticized as anti-black newspapers that published stories about ANC and government corruption.[158] In April 2007, speaking at the Fifth Global Forum on Fighting Corruption and Protecting Integrity, held in Sandton, Mbeki acknowledged that corruption was antithetical to democracy and development, but still he returned to the notion that Westerners viewed corruption as "peculiarly African . . . something to do with the biological character of the African."[159] In the end, it was this obsession with racism that crippled Mbeki's ability to deal with many pressing social issues. It was also one that led many South Africans to welcome his departure from office.

The Interregnum of Kgalema Motlanthe

Motlanthe's caretaker presidency was marked mostly by continuity rather than change. In his first speech to Parliament, in September 2008, Motlanthe indicated that he would follow the established ANC path and not "reinvent policy."[160] His cabinet by and large reflected his desire for stability. Motlanthe reappointed Minister of Finance Trevor Manuel after Manuel tendered his resignation, a move regarded as indicative of Motlanthe's intention not to alter South Africa's economic course. There were, however, two major cabinet changes that signaled new policy directions. First, Motlanthe appointed Nathi Mthethwa as minister of safety and security and promised to address the issue of rampant crime. Second, he moved controversial health minister Manto Tshabalala-Msimang to the post of minister in the presidency and in her place appointed MP Barbara Hogan, a longtime ANC activist who had spent eight years in Pretoria Central Prison in the apartheid era. Hogan, reportedly a close friend of Motlanthe's, had been a vocal critic of Mbeki's AIDS policy.

Hogan acted quickly to reverse Mbeki's policies. In mid-October she announced to an international AIDS vaccine conference, "We know HIV causes AIDS."[161] In November, a study by Harvard researchers estimated that had South Africa provided antiretroviral drugs to those with HIV, including drugs for pregnant women to prevent MTCT, the premature deaths of some 365,000 people could have been prevented.[162] Hogan's response was, "The era of denialism is over completely in South Africa." She sought to provide every HIV-positive pregnant woman with the ARV nevirapine. Her work received international recognition, and in April 2009 *Time* magazine named her one of the world's 100 most influential people.[163]

Motlanthe was, however, ensnared in controversy surrounding his December 2008 decision not to reinstate the national director of public prosecutions, Vusi Pikoli. Mbeki had suspended Pikoli in 2007 to protect Commissioner of Police Jackie Selebi from an arrest warrant obtained by Pikoli. The government then established a commission of inquiry into Pikoli's fitness to serve, known as the Ginwala Commission for its head, Frene Ginwala, chancellor of the University of KwaZulu-Natal and former speaker of the National Assembly. The commission's report, issued in November 2008, was generally favorable to Pikoli,[164] and when Motlanthe, said to be bowing to

ANC pressure, ignored its recommendation to reinstate Pikoli, the opposition and the media vilified the president.

The episode was not part of a pattern of scandal of the type that beset the flamboyant Zuma. The Zuma camp worried that Motlanthe would eclipse him when the quiet, scholarly interim president carried out various changes that gained him considerable respect among members of the ANC, the parliamentary opposition, and the public, who gave him extremely high approval ratings.[165] Motlanthe created emergency teams to cushion job losses, pushed for racial and political reconciliation, and offered international solutions to the worldwide financial crisis. His foreign policy, however, was controversial. He praised Mbeki's leadership on Zimbabwe, and regarding the Dalai Lama he went even further than Mbeki, who, under Chinese pressure, had refused to meet with the spiritual leader during a 1999 visit. With South Africa now China's top African trading partner,[166] after the government repeatedly delayed granting him a visa the Dalai Lama withdrew from a peace conference sponsored by South African soccer officials to draw attention to the following year's World Cup, the first to be held in Africa. His fellow Nobel Prize winners Anglican archbishop emeritus Desmond Tutu and former president F. W. de Klerk announced they would boycott the event, as did members of the Nobel Committee; the Nobel Institute's director found it "disappointing that South Africa, which has received so much solidarity from the world, doesn't want to give that solidarity to others."[167]

Motlanthe's presidency was perhaps most notable for the crisis in the ANC that Mbeki's resignation had provoked. On October 8, 2008, just two weeks after Motlanthe took office, the pro-Mbeki Minister of Defense Mosiuoa Lekota announced that he had served the ANC with "divorce papers."[168] He said there would be a national convention to discuss the ANC's future and the possible creation of a new political organization.[169] This prompted various well-known Mbeki supporters in the ANC to leave the party, and thousands of rank-and-file members to burn their membership cards publicly. The incipient movement held a convention in Sandton on November 1, attended by more than 5,000 people and representatives of other political parties, with the exception of the ANC.[170] By November 15, the new party had chosen the name Congress of the People (COPE), an obvious reference to the 1955 Congress of the People at Kliptown, which had adopted the Freedom Charter that had so informed the antiapartheid struggle. This was not lost on the ANC, which sued unsuccessfully for an interdict preventing COPE from using the name on the grounds that the ANC itself was affiliated with the 1955 gathering.

The formal launch of the party occurred at a three-day conference in December, at which Lekota became president.[171] Thereafter, he was joined by various former ANC luminaries, including Mbeki's nonagenarian mother. The platform was one of multiracialism and multiculturalism in government, promoting the free market and eschewing any connection to Marxism.[172] Most significant was the position on electoral reform. COPE sought to abolish pure proportional representation whereby voters choose a party, not individual candidates. Instead, candidates would be elected directly by their constituents and could be removed only by the courts, thus increasing individual accountability and diminishing the grip of party machines.

The Democratic Alliance (DA), the United Democratic Movement, and the IFP all welcomed the new party and its potential to dilute the ANC's dominance. Even before the party's official launch, COPE candidates, running as independents, won 10 of 27 wards in the Western Cape municipal by-elections, while the ANC carried only three.[173] The new party contested the 2009 general elections with the Rev. Mvume Dandala, a Methodist with impeccable theological credentials, as its presidential candidate, and won 7.42 percent of the vote.[174] It also took the leadership of the opposition in the legislatures of the Eastern Cape, Free State, Limpopo, and Northern Cape, and won representation in all nine provinces. The strengthening of contrary voices would characterize the Zuma years.

The Presidency of Jacob Zuma: 100 Years of Struggle and Beyond

The Polity

The April 2009 national elections, the fourth since the end of apartheid, were peaceful. As expected, the ANC won a decisive victory, but to the delight of the opposition it took 65.9 percent of the vote, just short of the two-thirds majority necessary for the ANC to amend the constitution unilaterally. Still, it had 264 seats in the 400-seat National Assembly and clear majorities in eight of the nine provinces.[175] The DA retained its status as the largest opposition party, winning 67

National Assembly seats and outright control of Western Cape province. COPE won 30 seats, and the IFP got 18. Zuma was easily elected president by the National Assembly the following month with 277 of the 400 votes.[176]

Zuma inherited a country that had done much to overcome its apartheid past. Officials pointed to statistics showing a decrease in poverty and hunger, lower unemployment, and greater access to housing, water, health care, and education. Zuma's inaugural address praised Mandela, Mbeki, and Motlanthe for their leadership and extolled South Africa's achievements.[177] He said the country had to "forge a partnership for reconstruction, development and progress . . . enriched by democratic debate that values diverse views and accommodates dissent." There would be "unfettered free expression," including freedom to protest, free media, and a strengthened democracy to check the abuse of power.

This ringing endorsement of free expression would clash with a more sinister reality. After surviving the negative publicity associated with the scandal of the rape and arms deal corruption trials as well as the challenge to his anointment as ANC president at Polokwane, Zuma displayed a greater intolerance than Mbeki for dissent from within the ANC and in the larger society. Free speech issues came to the fore in a new and sustained way. In 2009, civil liberties groups were "dismayed"[178] when the Film and Publications Amendment Act, meant to guard against child pornography and hate speech, adopted the use of tacit or prepublication censorship.[179]

The next year, there began the publication of *New Age,* a paper owned by the fabulously wealthy Gupta family, which had close ties to Zuma.[180] The government endorsed *New Age* as "supportive." In June 2011, the same month in which Zapiro published another controversial cartoon, the government said that the cabinet had approved a R1 million advertising budget that would be directed toward newspapers that helped spread the government's message. In November, presidential spokesman Mac Maharaj threatened the *Mail and Guardian* with criminal prosecution after it ran a story about Maharaj's alleged involvement in the arms deal corruption scandal of the late 1990s. He then filed criminal complaints against the two journalists who wrote the story, claiming they had stolen records from the government's investigation.[181] The *Mail and Guardian* censored most of the story because of a 1988 law prohibiting the unauthorized disclosure of a suspect's testimony in a prosecutorial investigation.

Zuma continued to use lawsuits as vehicles to attack his critics. As deputy president he had sued newspapers, a radio station, and Zapiro. In 2010, he asked for millions for defamation and injury to his dignity in a suit against Zapiro and Avusa, the parent company of the *Sunday Times*, where Zapiro's work had appeared.[182] In 2011, Zapiro stirred controversy again, with a cartoon published in the *Mail and Guardian*. It showed Zuma about to rape Freedom of Speech. Like its predecessors, it drew condemnation from the ANC, but the *Mail and Guardian*'s editor said he found it ironic that the ANC was so upset over a cartoon about free speech.[183]

The most controversial of all the cartoons appeared in July 2012 when Zapiro drew the president as an erect penis and ridiculed his efforts at racial reconciliation. The cartoon's publication in the *Mail and Guardian* came just weeks after the ANC went to court seeking the removal from a Johannesburg art gallery of a painting by a white South African artist showing Zuma in the pose struck by Lenin in a Soviet propaganda poster but with his genitals exposed. Besides the court case, the ANC encouraged street protests over the painting. The gallery had taken it down after two men defaced it.[184] Now, the ANC's position was that Zapiro's latest effort was racist and dehumanized Zuma in the same way apartheid treated all blacks.[185] Zuma brought suit over the cartoon but eventually dropped the case because, his office said, even though it was an affront, the president wanted to avoid a precedent that might limit free speech. Zuma's critics said the cartoon merely reflected Zuma's personal behavior; Zuma, married six times, calls himself a traditionalist and has four wives and 20 or more children, some from his well-known extramarital affairs.

More ominous than the wrangling over the cartoons and the painting was the Protection of State Information Bill, popularly called the Secrecy Bill,[186] whose purpose was to replace the apartheid-era Protection of Information Act of 1982. First introduced in 2010, the bill was to regulate the classification and dissemination of state information, balancing state interests with transparency and freedom of expression. It gave the government the authority to classify information using vague criteria and to restrict the disclosure of information so classified. There was no "public interest" defense, and penalties included lengthy prison terms for violators. It engendered unprecedented shrieking from the media, the opposition, and Right2Know, a coalition of some 400 civil society and community groups. COSATU and the Nelson Mandela Foundation were among the critics. Demonstrations were frequent in Cape Town, Johannesburg, and Durban. The bill also drew international attention from the Committee for the Protection of Journalists, Human Rights Watch, and the U.N. Human Rights Commission.[187]

The ANC reacted by criticizing the "vitriol, vilification, name-calling . . . and blatant lies" about the bill.[188] The minister of state security, Siyabonga Cwele, even claimed in Parliament that the bill's opponents were local proxies for foreign spies. The bill passed the National Assembly in November 2011 by a vote of 229 to 107, with two abstentions.[189] The abstainers were both ANC members, and the party immediately referred them to its disciplinary committee. The National Council of the Provinces (NCOP) passed it a year later with amendments favoring press freedoms.[190] Incongruously, in April, just in time for the nineteenth anniversary of South Africa's first democratic elections, the National Assembly passed the bill, voting 190 for and 75 against, with one abstention.[191] In a heated debate before the voting, some ANC MPs insisted that various opposition members were "foreign intelligence agents" or "foreign spies."[192] Zuma would still have to sign the bill. The DA, COSATU, and the Right2Know Campaign said they would use the legal system to attack the law's constitutionality. Internationally, the controversy had already damaged South Africa's reputation as an open society. The Reporters Without Borders 2013 World Freedom Index dropped South Africa ten spots to fifty-third, part of a pattern of slippage that placed it beyond the list of freest countries.[193]

By the time the ANC held its 2012 national conference in Mangaung, at the end of its centennial year, which had begun with great fanfare and self-congratulations,[194] the party, in the absence of a unifying apartheid enemy, began to show fissures even more pronounced than those that had led to Mbeki's removal. Before Mangaung, Motlanthe had indirectly criticized the party as well as Zuma and his followers. In 2009, he had attacked the corruption attendant to "the sins of incumbency."[195] Now, in an assault on the Zuma camp, Motlanthe, whose name was floated as a possible ANC presidential candidate,[196] lambasted Zuma's web of political patronage.[197] He also decried the authoritarianism in the organization, particularly in its electoral practices, which he likened to SACP and COSATU rubber-stamping that nullified any need for elections in the first place.

Unlike Zuma, Motlanthe did not campaign actively, but his name was put forward for three positions—president, vice president, and member of the NEC. Eventually he ran only for the presidency and withdrew his name first from the vice presidential slot, which was won by Cyril Ramaphosa, the antiapartheid trade union lawyer and activist who had gradually withdrawn from politics after his disappointment that Thabo Mbeki and not he had become Mandela's deputy president. Ramaphosa had spent the intervening years becoming a tenderpreneur billionaire and one of South Africa's richest men. Given the pattern of the ANC vice president becoming the ANC president and then the country's president, speculation began immediately about a Ramaphosa presidency. Some in the media described him as "the best president South Africa never had,"[198] but others cautioned that his business interests and presence on the boards of many of South Africa's largest companies likely had led him far from his populist past.

In what the press called the Mangaung Massacre, by a three-to-one margin Zuma trounced Motlanthe, who then withdrew from consideration for an NEC position. Zuma's faction swept the NEC places, too.[199] Motlanthe's political career was not the only victim. Several prominent ANC leaders who had backed Zuma against Mbeki five years before at Polokwane found themselves purged from the party leadership. Zuma, reveling in his consolidation of power, humiliated his opponents by wondering aloud "how it must be to be outside the ANC."

Zuma and the newly anointed set about making authoritarian changes to the ANC constitution. While the ANC had justifiably expelled Julius Malema, president of the ANC Youth League (ANCYL), earlier in the year because he had displayed racist behavior divisive for the nation as well as the party, now the ANC sought to stop even measured dissent. There would be disciplinary action against any ANC member, officer, or public representative bringing or possibly bringing the ANC into disrepute. Zuma criticized members who publicly challenged its decisions, particularly via the judicial system. There were intense attacks on the media and those ANC members who used the media to express dissent. On the last day of the conference, the

SACP general secretary Blade Nzimande condemned the press. Rama-phosa, given the chance to showcase himself, read the conference declaration at the closing session. He praised Zuma effusively and then extolled Nzimande's speech.

In mid-March 2013, at the ANC's NEC meeting in Irene, outside Pretoria, there was blood still to be drawn over Mangaung. The NEC voted to disband the Limpopo Provincial Executive Committee (PEC) and remove the Limpopo premier, as they had not supported Zuma's presidential bid. The NEC also disbanded the ANCYL NEC.[200] There was perhaps a fear of history repeating itself. After all, it had been the young Mandela, Sisulu, and Tambo generation that once had taken control of the ANC after dissatisfaction with the tactics of their elders. Zuma praised the NEC decisions.[201]

Nevertheless, there was fighting aplenty, and not just at the very top. There were frequent physical attacks and assassinations by ANC members involved in power struggles. Graft was ubiquitous. The *Los Angeles Times* described an ANC transition from "liberators to ex-ploiters."[202] Known as Nkandlagate, the scandal surrounding the use of R30 million in state money to renovate Zuma's private residence at Nkandla reinforced the ANC's image as a gigantic sponge. The govern-ment justified the vast expense by relying on an obscure apartheid-era security law that said the president's personal dwelling was a "national keypoint." Thus, the improvements were for security purposes and the public had no right to know how the government used the mon-eys. Many high-ranking ANC members of the government defended Zuma. One minister argued that critics did not understand African values and lifestyles. Mac Maharaj, Zuma's spokesman, said that calling the walled residence a compound was racist. This prompted political analyst Justice Malala to respond incredulously, "Racism? Is this what the ANC has been reduced to? When looting takes place in front of our eyes, the only argument the presidential spokesman can make is that this is racism?"[203]

The scandal continued in 2013 when the minister of public works and his deputy told Parliament's Standing Committee on Public Ac-counts that total Nkandla spending had increased by R2 million, to R208 million. While the department insisted all improvements were security related and could not be discussed publicly, there were wide-spread reports of an elevator being installed, various upgrades, and a snack shop run by one of Zuma's wives.[204] Eventually, in July, after continued pressure on the government, reporters from the *Mail and Guardian*'s Centre for Investigative Journalism, amaBhungane, managed to use PAIA to get the government to release thousands of pages of Nkandla files.[205] The documents revealed Zuma's complicity in a hugely corrupt procurement process.[206]

In April 2013, the Gupta family, publishers of *New Age* and the employers of at least two of Zuma's children in very high-paying jobs, became the subject of a scandal, pejoratively called Guptagate. The family held a decadent four-day-long wedding at the Sun City entertainment complex's garish Palace of the Lost City, which they rented for exclusive use. A national uproar followed the revelation that the family had landed 200 private wedding guests from India in a private plane at the military Waterkloof Air Force Base. The affair sparked allegations of Zuma's abuse of the national patrimony for private purposes, which he and a subsequent official report on the incident denied.[207] The press and many private citizens were skeptical. It seemed the marriage that deeply concerned many South Africans was not the Guptas' but that between government officials and their capitalist partners.

Zuma had problems beyond accusations of financial chicanery and abuse of official powers. There were multiple examples of thuggery by his security detail, including police misconduct. Zuma also displayed a gift for offensive remarks. Before his election he upset gays and children's rights advocates. As president, in 2010, he insulted the British. The next year he offended Christians. In 2012, he made a series of objectionable comments. At the ANC centennial celebrations in January, he sang the antiwhite "Shoot the Boer," the very thing for which ANCYL leader Julius Malema had been convicted of hate speech. During Women's Month he told a television interviewer that women must marry and have children. Three weeks later, speaking to the National Assembly, he shared his unorthodox perspective on democracy by declaring minority groups had "less [*sic*] rights."[208] In December, he managed to distress animal lovers by insisting that owning a dog was un-African, as it was part of white culture. Further angering Christians and the political opposition was Zuma's assertion that the ANC governed by divine right. Already in 2004 and 2007 Zuma had expressed the belief that the ANC would remain in power indefinitely by using what many Christians felt was blasphemous language about the Second Coming. In May 2008, he insisted that the ANC "will rule until Jesus comes back,"[209] language he would repeat at a political rally the next year. By 2011, this language had become acceptable among the members of the ANC leadership.

The Judiciary

Zuma's dealings with the judiciary also stirred controversy. In August 2009, he nominated Sandile Ngcobo as chief justice. The DA, COPE, the IFP, and the ID criticized Zuma for not consulting them properly in advance. They expressed a preference for the more experienced deputy chief justice Dikgang Moseneke and urged Zuma to reconsider.[210] He ignored them, and on October 1 Ngcobo, who was close to mandatory retirement age, was confirmed.[211] In 2011, Zuma sought to extend Ngcobo's term for an additional five years. There was a furor. Three legal justice groups challenged the constitutionality of the law Zuma had relied upon, claiming that the president had exceeded his powers.[212] Before the court ruled, Ngcobo withdrew in order to preserve the integrity of the office of chief justice.[213]

Ngcobo's retirement brought an even more disputed candidate to fill the position, Constitutional Court judge Mogoeng Mogoeng, nominated by Zuma in August 2011. Well-known jurists, including the judges of the Constitutional Court, COSATU, gay rights organizations, and women's groups all rose in opposition. Critics noted that Mogoeng, an ordained minister, belonged to a church that was vehemently opposed to homosexuality.[214] Particularly worrisome were a number of egregious rape cases in which Mokoeng had given light sentences.[215] The ANC was particularly unhappy with the Constitutional Court's opposition. The ANC secretary general Gwede Mantashe said the judges threatened the stability of the government and their resistance was racist.[216]

Shortly thereafter, on November 1, 2011, Zuma gave a speech to both houses of Parliament to bid farewell to Ngcobo and to welcome Mogoeng. Zuma expressed a truncated view of the judicial role antithetical to that enshrined in the constitution and objected to judicial involvement in policy formulation.[217] He affirmed the position he had taken earlier in the year at an Access to Justice Conference.[218] Later, in 2012, the minister of justice and constitutional development released a discussion document on the transformation of the judicial system. Meanwhile, there was a row over reverse discrimination in judicial appointments and the role of the JSC. By October 2012, there had been a huge change from the apartheid era in the composition of the judiciary, with Blacks now outnumbering Whites and the presence of many women.[219] Nevertheless, prominent lawyer and JSC member Izak Smuts wrote a memo claiming that for transformation's sake, the JSC unfairly passed over for appointment or promotion highly qualified candidates who were not African, especially white males.[220] He then raised the elephant-in-the-room issue of the rationale for having such a "largely unaccountable judicial appointment authority" in a democracy, and resigned. The media obtained the memo—some said it was leaked or that Smuts had distributed it before the JSC could discuss it—which renewed the public debate about the judiciary's role and composition.

At the Eighteenth Commonwealth Law Conference held in Cape Town in April 2013, Mogoeng dismissed Smuts's arguments, insisting that "the surest way to weaken, and ultimately destroy, democracy is to weaken the country's legal profession and delegitimise its judiciary"[221] If criticism was tantamount to delegitimization, it was already too late. Freedom Under Law announced it would bring legal action against the JSC over the question of reconciling the constitutional provisions on judicial appointments, which required candidates to be fit, proper, and appropriately qualified, with those that demanded racial and gender equity.[222]

The rights of women also formed part of an ongoing debate about the role of traditional courts. Self-styled traditionalists in the ANC, including Zuma, wanted to confer judicial powers on hereditary chiefs.[223] Assemblies of chiefs and tribal elders would become courts of the first instance for 14 million rural people, a huge voting bloc Zuma wanted to control. These traditional courts would use customary law, which, contrary to the constitution, typically gave women a subordinate status. Another concern was untoward influence over voting. In Zimbabwe, Mugabe had relied on a chiefly system to limit the number of registered voters, ferreting out those thought to oppose the ruling party.

The Opposition

The political commentator Justice Malala expressed the views of many when he described Zuma as "the worst leader the ANC has ever had. He's a lost cause. He merely fights to save his own skin and to stay out of jail."[224] Certainly, impatience with the scandal-ridden Zuma government to effect positive change invigorated a growing opposition. The DA in particular benefited. In the 2009 national elections, when it ended its campaign with a "Stop Zuma" pitch, it garnered more than a million new votes, obtaining just under 3 million votes or 16.7 percent of the total, a huge transformation from its 1.7 percent showing in 1994.[225] Thus, it was the only party to grow in each of the three most recent elections. It had kept the ANC below the two-thirds majority needed to change the constitution, become the first party to win a majority in the Western Cape since democratic elections first began in 1994, increased its numbers in Parliament from 47 to 67, and added ten more seats in the National Council of the Provinces. The DA's showing also improved in eight of the nine provinces, taking its seats in provincial legislatures from 51 in 2004 to 65 in 2009. The May 2011 municipal elections—with relatively high voter turnout—saw the ANC win 62 percent of the vote and the DA win just under 24 percent, including outright control of Cape Town and 11 of 24 municipalities in the Western Cape. The ANC won the vast majority of municipalities in every other province. The IFP took slightly more than 3.5 percent, and COPE just over 2 percent.

Meanwhile, in order to present a greater challenge to the ANC, in August 2010, the DA and the ID announced an antigovernment alliance in which, by design, the ID would cease to exist in 2014.[226] There also was periodic speculation that Mbeki would return to politics. Since his resignation, he had concentrated mostly on the Thabo Mbeki Foundation, aimed at promoting the African Renaissance. Although he had never endorsed COPE, he had not been active in the ANC either. Now Mbeki appeared to thunderous applause at the ANC's centenary celebrations in early 2012. In his Oliver Tambo Memorial Lecture at the University of Fort Hare in October, also part of centenary celebrations, he took a swipe at Zuma, saying the country "should be led by people who conduct themselves by always and practically keeping with moral practices informed by commitment to serve the people."[227]

Zuma's February 2013 speech at the opening of Parliament further united the opposition. Although he emphasized development, many of the projects he mentioned had been in progress for years.[228]

He addressed the numerous recent, horrific sexual attacks on women but did not propose any major new campaign. He also claimed the government was doing its utmost to fight corruption. Many political analysts and the opposition parties condemned the speech as extremely weak and lacking in leadership. Already, several parties had been offering a series of talks under the banner of the Multiparty Forum—a name redolent of the Multiparty Negotiating Forum that had approved South Africa's interim constitution—examining the possibility of forming a coalition to contest the 2014 national elections. Just before Zuma's address, eight of these parties, including the DA, the IFP, and COPE, held a press conference at which they expressed "extreme disappointment" in the speech, which they said "delivered no hope."[229] In advance of the press conference, the ANC issued a press release alleging the independent political parties "are once again being hoodwinked into an unholy alliance with the Democratic Alliance (DA)." It said there was a "gullible troop of opposition leaders not aware that they served as useful idiots in the DA's scheme to influence the internal leadership election process of the ANC in Mangaung." Zuma followed this theme during the parliamentary debate that, in South African custom, came days after his speech. He characterized opposition unity as a blurring of views, which, in a democracy, was "a problem."[230]

There was further political excitement just days later when, after months of speculation, Mamphela Ramphele made a major announcement.[231] Steve Biko's former Black Consciousness partner as well as a doctor and anthropologist who had been the vice-chancellor of the University of Cape Town and managing director of the World Bank but never a member of the ANC, she had become a successful businesswoman. Speaking for symbolic appeal at the old Women's Gaol on Constitution Hill in Johannesburg, Ramphele said she was forming Agang SA or, in its English translation, Build SA, whose purpose was to "focus on rekindling hope that building the country of our dreams is possible in our lifetime." Agang would become a full-fledged party in June with plans to contest the 2014 national elections. While the opposition parties' reaction generally was favorable, there was discussion in the media, just as there had been with Ramaphosa's ascension as Zuma's heir apparent at Mangaung, as to whether Ramphele's ties to big business—she resigned from positions on the boards of some of South Africa's largest and sometimes labor unfriendly companies before the Agang SA launch—would cloud her judgment.

The ANC looked for conspiracies. Secretary-General Mantashe declared, in anachronistic language straight out of the Cold War, "We are hoping against hope that it is not an American initiative aimed at destabilising our country. . . . We are very much alive to concerns by Western powers that liberation movements in Africa are too powerful."[232] Also inclined toward left-wing hyperbole was Julius Malema, the disgraced former head of the ANCYL who had had his possessions and multimillion rand real estate auctioned to satisfy R16 million in debts to the South African Revenue Service. He also was facing money-related criminal charges he insisted were trumped up by Zuma. In June, he launched—like Ramphele from Constitution Hill—the Economic Freedom Fighters (EFF).[233] Distinguishing EFF from Agang and other opposition parties, he said it would "move away from a discourse of reconciliation to one of justice." Its "anti-capitalist and anti-imperialist ideology" included land appropriation and nationalization of mines without compensation as nonnegotiable. Whites would be "forced to share." Malema styled himself commander in chief and, using outmoded leftist liberation struggle terminology, members called each other comrade. With his history of capitalist excess, Malema might have been better suited to the title poseur in chief, but his message was likely to appeal to some of the poorest, least educated, and most marginalized citizens.

Zuma's Foreign Policy

Zuma initially gave hope to human rights advocates. In a shift from Mbeki's opposition to an International Criminal Court indictment of Sudanese president Omar al-Bashir for war crimes in Darfur, the government announced that, his invitation notwithstanding, if Bashir attended Zuma's inauguration, he would be arrested.[234] In a symbolic change of perspective, the Department of Foreign Affairs became the Department of International Relations and Cooperation (DIRCO) because, the rhetoric went, relations and cooperation signified engagement, not just presence.[235]

Beginning in July 2009, however, the AU took a series of actions favoring Bashir and Libyan leader Muammar Gaddafi.[236] South Africa did not comment, a silence many construed as approbation born of a desire not to offend other African countries. Moreover, by not objecting to these decisions, the country violated its International Criminal Court treaty obligations. On Libya, it supported U.N. Security Council resolutions; it voted for a no-fly zone although it opposed NATO incursions. It refused to do the same regarding Syria. Zuma's special adviser on foreign relations said "global politics" determined South Africa's decision; its biggest trading partner, China, also had not supported sanctioning Syria.[237]

The Zuma government displayed a lack of concern about human rights violations close to home as well. In 2011, the South African Reserve Bank said it would extend a R2 billion loan to Swaziland guaranteed by the South African government despite Swaziland's failure to abide by a 2004 bilateral agreement requiring it to implement various human rights guarantees. The DIRCO minister defended this move because the government had a policy of "non-interference in the internal affairs of a sovereign state, and especially a neighbouring state, [which] would not make it possible for South Africa to attempt to bring about political change in any country unilaterally."[238] Meanwhile, despite its new emphasis on cooperation, under Zuma, as under Mbeki, South Africa failed to ratify many major international human rights instruments[239] and, since Mandela's presidency, had frequently ignored its reporting responsibilities in compliance with treaties to which it was a signatory.[240]

A highly contentious foreign policy episode involved the proposed 2010 visit of the Dalai Lama to attend Archbishop Emeritus Desmond Tutu's eightieth birthday celebrations. South Africa, presumably keen to please China, with which Zuma had greatly expanded relations, repeatedly delayed issuing the Dalai Lama a visa until he withdrew. Tutu blasted the regime as "worse than the apartheid government," saying it had betrayed the liberation struggle and the constitution.[241] When the Supreme Court of Appeal heard an urgent application from COPE and Inkatha and determined that the minister of home affairs had "unreasonably delayed her decision,[242] Tutu proclaimed the ruling a "credit to South Africa's judicial system"; he said he looked forward to inviting the Dalai Lama to his ninetieth birthday festivities.[243]

The behavior of the Zuma government could be termed inconsistent and, less charitably, a rejection of Mandela's human rights–based policy, something not altogether surprising given the domestic move toward authoritarianism and disdain for democratic rights.[244] In October 2011, Zuma, in an address on aspects of foreign policy, said little about human rights.[245] Under the terms of a bilateral agreement, he did send 400 SANDF troops to the Central African Republic to support its president by training the military and, very likely, to protect South African mining interests. After thirteen soldiers died trying unsuccessfully to prevent the fall of Bangui to a rebel coalition, the parliamentary opposition, which had not been briefed, was shocked.[246] The lack of communication led to allegations that the ANC viewed the armed forces as its exclusive domain.

Zuma, who had assumed Mbeki's role of regional mediator, also came under attack for following Mbeki's quiet diplomacy stance on Zimbabwe.[247] Since the Mbeki-brokered election accord, the country had continued to struggle. Local groups and international observers reported that typical violence, thuggery, and fraud accompanied special voting in mid-July 2013 for the police and military officers who would serve during the upcoming elections. When Lindiwe Zulu, Zuma's international relations adviser, questioned Zimbabwe's ability to have free and fair elections, Mugabe attacked her as "a stupid, idiotic street woman," in other words, a dumb prostitute.[248] To the astonishment of women's groups in particular, instead of assailing Mugabe, Zuma said his officials had made "unauthorized . . . regrettable and unfortunate" statements.

The Economy

The global financial crisis of 2007–8 negatively affected South Africa. Coupled with the virtual cessation of economic growth after 2008, foreign direct investment dropped dramatically from R74.4 billion in 2008 to R11.4 billion in 2010.[249] The country was unlikely to meet its 2015 MDG employment target. With a sluggish economy and a growing young population, many predicted unemployment rates, officially pegged at around 20 percent but estimated by outside observers to be between 40 and 50 percent, to continue to be among the highest in the world.[250]

In 2010 high levels of poverty in the majority of the population led to a U.N. Development Program's Millennium Development Goals country report classification as a low-income country.[251] Data from the National Income Dynamics Study found 47 percent of South Africans living below the poverty line—56 percent of Africans, 27 percent of Coloureds, 9 percent of Indians, and just 2 percent of whites. The U.N. Development Program's Human Development Index (HDI) ranked South Africa 110 out of 169 countries in 2010.[252] The HDI's Human Poverty Index (HPI) placed South Africa 85 out of 135 countries. Whereas under apartheid poverty in South Africa was largely a function of race, now it was increasingly defined by inequality within population groups as the gap between rich and poor in each grew markedly.

In February 2010, the OECD found that South Africa was one of the world's most unequal societies.[253] While interrace inequality was still high, it was diminishing slowly, but intrarace inequality prevented overall inequality figures from declining. The change in the country's ethnic composition, with a rising African population and a declining white one, meant that intra-African income distribution was all the more important in determining inequality. The OECD acknowledged that the government had improved access to housing, electricity, water, and sanitation. It had also reduced poverty via social assistance grants—the poorest 20 percent got two-thirds of their income this way—instead of expanding the labor market, even though the years studied, 1993 to 2008, represented South Africa's longest-ever period of economic growth. Thus, it was not economic achievement but social welfare that had caused the relative improvement in poverty levels. The report questioned the viability of grants as a means of ending economic inequality, especially as the economy slowed. It noted that because many of the unemployed were school leavers, the longer-term goal should have been to help them enter the labor force and remain there. Expanded educational opportunities had not helped alleviate poverty because the system did not give people skills required by the labor market.

B-BBEE also had not achieved a greater distribution of wealth and was mostly perceived as a failure.[254] It had, after all, created a class of African millionaires and billionaires, often disparagingly called the "usual suspects."[255] These included possible president-in-waiting Cyril Ramaphosa; Ramaphosa's brother-in-law Patrice Motsepe, with a fortune estimated at R14.2 billion; and Minister of Human Settlements Tokyo Sexwale. A 2011 University of Cape Town study maintained that of the richest 10 percent, nearly 40 percent were black, whereas this group had been almost entirely white under apartheid; 29 percent of the absolute wealthiest also were black.[256]

By 2012, Euromonitor International found that the Gini Index showed South Africa with the highest income inequality in the world,[257] in a category with such deeply divided countries as Brazil and South Africa's neighbor and former pseudo-colony Namibia. Extreme income inequality had been relatively constant between 1990 and 2011 while the income gap between rich and poor had widened. The middle class had grown by 6.5 percent to 4.7 million between 2006 and 2011 but still was not even 10 percent of the population. Helping to create these huge disparities in wealth was a corruption pandemic. Seemingly, no government department—national, provincial, or local—from the presidency to the most remote rural office was untouched. By one estimate, by 2013 approximately one-tenth of South Africa's annual GDP, some $50 billion, was lost to corruption and graft, money that otherwise could have been used to help right the country's many economic wrongs.[258] Even the minister of finance, Pravin Gordhan, admitted that corruption was "becoming a cultural problem."[259]

These unresolved problems had prompted Moody's, the credit rating agency, to downgrade South Africa in 2012, citing "long-standing, socio-economic challenges," including "the fractiousness of the environment," a negative investment climate worsened by problems with transportation, electricity, and other infrastructure, high labor costs and low productivity, high unemployment, and the persistent gap between the rich and the poor. Labor troubles were also a factor, especially the violent events at Marikana.[260]

While the Moody's rating was a blow, the government placed much hope in trade and investment, particularly in its ever-growing relationship with China, which had become a significant investor in the economy.[261] China also was one of South Africa's partners in a trade association of emerging national economies known as BRICS, an acronym for its members Brazil, Russia, India, China, and South Africa.[262] In 2011, BRICS established the Forum, an independent international organization fostering commercial, political, and cultural cooperation among member states. In March 2013, at the fifth BRICS summit, in Durban, members announced they would create a world financial institution to rival the Western-led International Monetary Fund.[263] The South African business community was unimpressed. In April, the Chamber of Commerce and Industry's monthly Business Confidence Index showed business confidence at its lowest level in thirteen years.[264]

Labor Unrest

Labor unrest continued. It was a legacy of the last years of the antiapartheid struggle when COSATU and its affiliate, the National Union of Mineworkers (NUM), gained exceptional political influence. Labor and the economy became victims of their success. The widespread use of strikes often yielded wages higher than in other developing countries. This made South Africa less attractive to foreign investment and its attendant job creation in a world where capital is highly mobile and seeks the most docile workers at the lowest cost. Domestically, despite union gains, miners, especially, worked in desperate conditions. By the time Zuma took office, although the 360,000-member NUM was the largest affiliate of COSATU, many workers saw the NUM leadership as unsympathetic. Expelled NUM leaders had founded a new union, the Association of Mineworkers and Construction Union (AMCU), which built on worker dissatisfaction with NUM's closeness to mine owners and their powerful Chamber of Mines. AMCU sought members in the worst shacks and shanties, places so miserable and crime-ridden that they were no-go areas for the police. For such people, the analyst Justice Malala suggested, what would happen in August and September 2012 was "a strike against the state and the haves, not just a union matter."[265]

Trouble began on August 10 at a Lonmin platinum mine called Marikana in Mafikeng in the northwest. Lonmin was the world's third-largest producer of platinum, and Cyril Ramaphosa, once head of NUM, was a board member. After Lonmin representatives refused to discuss their demands, drillers, encouraged by AMCU, began a wildcat strike, calling for a tripling of their salaries to R12,500 per month. The following day, as striking NUM workers marched on their offices, NUM leaders fired at them, killing two. Over the next three days, nine more people were killed, including two policemen and two security guards.[266] By then, the conflict had the world's attention.

On the scene were more than 500 armed officers and a police heli-copter. Violence soon erupted. On August 16, members of an elite SAPS unit fired on some of the strikers.[267] Thirty-four died, and at least 78 were wounded.[268] The shootings, immediately christened the Mari-kana Massacre, represented the most deadly encounter by South African security forces since Sharpeville in 1960. The following day, Zuma went to Marikana, declared a national week of mourning, and announced the creation of a commission of inquiry.[269] Known as the Farlam Commission for its head, former Supreme Court of Appeals judge Ian Farlam, the commission included cabinet ministers, raising questions of impartiality.

Meanwhile, accounts of the violence appeared worldwide. Images of protests by poor Africans being met by official force yielded com-parisons to the apartheid era. One commentator wondered whether the mine's ANC ties were "economic apartheid."[270] The *Sowetan* news-paper, the largest with a historically African readership, suggested that nothing had changed since the end of apartheid.[271] One journal-ist wrote that Marikana had forced the country to examine "its post-apartheid soul."[272]

Any such national reflection was subsumed by recrimination and ongoing strife. There were conflicting reports from eyewitnesses and the press. National Police Commissioner Mangashi Victoria Phiyega's official statement, released the day after the shooting, claimed that after peaceful negotiations by SAPS members failed, it was only when the miners attacked and the SAPS retreated to the point where their safety was in danger that they were permitted to use maximum force against the miners.[273] Rifts among trade unions were apparent. The opposition deplored the government's actions.[274]

Mediation efforts by the Ministry of Labor began on August 28, but only on September 18 was there a settlement of a 22 percent pay increase, a one-time payment of R2,000, and a return to work the next day.[275] By then, 47 people had died. The investment sector feared that Marikana would establish a national precedent.[276] It already had. The massacre had set off a rash of strikes and protests nation-wide. Police presence and, sometimes, violence accompanied them. By early October, some 75,000 gold and platinum miners were en-gaged in strikes, most of them illegal.[277] The important agricultural sector was also affected. Since the end of apartheid, poorly paid farmworkers had staged strikes for higher wages and improved living conditions. In November, workers in the Western Cape set fire to farms, overturned a police truck, and clashed with police in riot gear who fired tear gas. One man was killed, and at least five others were injured.[278] The year concluded with the distinction of being the one with the most labor protests since the ANC came to power.

The Farlam Commission continued the focus on police brutality into 2013.[279] There were widespread allegations of official evidence tampering. Photos of dead victims allegedly showed them unarmed and later with weapons presumably planted in a police cover-up. Many believed that the police had herded the miners into a small area and systematically shot them, as there was no evidence of a hail of bullets. There was also the claim that many of those killed had been shot in the back far from the line of demonstration.

Labor troubles also continued. In February and March 2013, there was a five-week coal miners' strike involving violence and police use of rubber bullets. It threatened to disrupt ESKOM's already much decried coal-dependent electricity service.[280] The country braced for more strikes and violence surrounding May's biennial mining sector wage talks. While workers viewed the settlement at Marikana as an AMCU victory, swelling its ranks to 105,000, a fifth of South Africa's mineworkers, talk was rife about marginal profitability at many gold mines and deficits at more than half of the platinum shafts. Closing mines, as Amplats, the world's largest platinum producer, threatened to do in order to restore profitability, would only further rankle their workforce of predominantly semiliterate rural men with many dependents and very few prospects for other employment.

The Quality of Life of the Majority of the People

It seemed that the real war on poverty was being fought by the poor in increasing numbers of protests over the lack of services. Official violence was common. At some demonstrations, the police relied on Casspirs, the heavily armored vehicles deployed throughout the country during the struggle against apartheid, and used live ammunition. One incident that riveted the nation was the death of Ficksburg activist Andries Tatane, who was brutally beaten by several policemen and shot twice in the chest with rubber bullets after he tried to block the passage of a water cannon vehicle that was targeting some elderly people.[281] The entire episode appeared on SABC-TV that evening. Perhaps a class war had replaced South Africa's race war, noted one commentator.

In 2009 there were 105 protests; the following year, 111.[282] The number dropped in 2011 to approximately 100, but there was a geographic shift toward urban areas, especially toward squatter camps; the 2011 municipal elections, which offered an outlet for dissatisfaction, may have been responsible for the decline. The decrease was only temporary. The number rose markedly in 2012 and by August had surpassed that for the entire previous year. The media described South Africa as the protest capital of the world.

There was a crisis of expectations not ameliorated by the ubiquity of the ANC slogan "a better life for all." As protesters relied on the apartheid-era tactic of refusing to pay taxes, a limited revenue base was partly responsible for inferior or nonexistent delivery of services. Skills deficits and corruption exacerbated the problem.[283] In the 2011 municipal elections, Zuma campaigned door to door in many of the most deprived communities. Claiming shock at what he found, Zuma issued a statement that he now understood the protests.[284] However, he seemed to have recovered his equanimity for his 2012 state of the nation address, which was silent on delivery issues.

Electricity

In order to address the crisis in electricity, in 2012 the government announced a "keeping the lights on" policy. Part of the strategy was to improve ESKOM's maintenance practices. It was not a success. The backlog was not cleared, and in 2013 repairs continued well beyond the South African summer, the time of their projected completion, as more equipment broke down. Consequently, the electrical grid typically operated dangerously close to its limits, and rolling blackouts were again likely in the winter.[285] The government's main hope lay in the building of two new power stations, Medupi in Lephalale, 160 miles northwest of Johannesburg, and Kusile in the Nkangala district of Mpumalanga. The two coal-fired plants were the first new such construction in more than twenty years. Part of a R350 billion plan to give South Africa enough power to support economic growth, they were already way behind schedule, largely because of frequent strikes at the sites and other construction delays.[286] The government talked tough about the problems, but ESKOM's longer-term viability was not assured.

Water

Just as the electricity supply was dubious, so, too, was the water supply. Blue Drop Program results were not encouraging. Private sector observers said a "strong spin element" surrounded the program; water quality was actually deteriorating nationally.[287] With respect to sanitation, progress was even slower. According to estimates by the WHO/UNICEF Global Joint Monitoring Program for Water Supply and Sanitation, the proportion of South Africans with improved sanitation rose slowly, from 71 percent in 1990 to 75 percent in 2000 and 79 percent in 2010.[288] While the 2011 census reported higher figures than WHO/UNICEF because of a looser definition of access, it found that approximately 11 million still used shared facilities (4 million), used buckets (3 million), or practiced open defecation (4 million).[289]

Wastewater also proved problematic. Fifty-five percent of treatment plants, particularly smaller ones, did not meet effluent standards, and some did not even measure effluent quality. As a counterpart to Blue Drop, the government initiated Green Drop, a certification program for municipal wastewater treatment, but few plants met regulatory compliance requirements.[290] By May 2011, only 7 of 159 water supply authorities and 32 of 1,237 wastewater treatment plants were Green Drop approved.[291] The adverse health impact of inadequate sanitation was evidenced by more than a million cases of diarrhea in children under five each year and the persistence of cholera, with more than 6,000 reported cases and more than 50 deaths in 2009 alone.

Beginning in 2011, the South African Human Rights Commission (SAHRC) began to investigate 144 water supply complaints, including cases from every province about no water or sanitation at all. In March 2013, after five months of public hearings, the commission released its findings during Water Week.[292] Most of the bulk water infrastructure was near the end of its life, resulting in uncontrolled, high levels of pollution, particularly in dams. Necessary infrastructure upgrades would require R670 billion over the next ten years, but the Department of Water Affairs reported it would be able to provide not even half that amount. An SAHRC spokesman blamed the problem on high levels of government inefficiency, lamenting, "We are two decades into democracy and some people have not tasted clean water."

Housing

The people wanted housing, too. Although official statistics for housing, as for other fields, were not entirely reliable, the government claimed to have provided some 2.7 million houses—usually small cinderblock structures—since 1996.[293] By September 2011, the Department of Human Settlements reported a backlog of some 2.3 million houses,[294] with more than 12 million people, approximately one quarter of the total population, still needing accommodation. While many government-built houses continued to collapse, the department announced a new policy aimed at reining in corruption and improving delivery, with a commitment to eradicate the backlog by 2030. In his 2012 state of the nation address, Zuma announced a new "gap market" subsidy for those whose income was above the cutoff level for free housing.[295]

There was growing concern that the government's efforts would not be enough, a fear highlighted by the clash of the haves and have-nots at Marikana and the ongoing labor problems. In 2013, a BBC journalist described the misery of millions of South Africans. At Marikana, he found that, "in the shadow of the mine, most of its migrant workers live in Wonderkop, a sprawling shanty settlement of 40,000 people with no running water, no proper electricity, no sewage—families in unspeakable poverty. I saw even more destitute circumstances 700 miles south near Mandela's birthplace in the Transkei, home to the widow of one murdered striker, their extended family income suddenly destroyed. It was hard to see how two decades of democracy had made any improvement to their living standards."[296]

Health Care and AIDS

Although some observers were disappointed when Zuma did not include Barbara Hogan in his cabinet, most were delighted with his December 2009 World AIDS Day speech.[297] After his much ridiculed testimony at his rape trial three years before, about showering to prevent AIDS, he now became the unlikely hero of South African AIDS activists. Zuma indicated that the government would distribute ARVs to many more infected people, including all HIV-positive children under one year old and pregnant women. The United States announced a $120 million two-year assistance package to coincide with the speech.[298]

Zuma likened the fight against HIV/AIDS to the struggle against apartheid. AIDS activists who had so vehemently opposed Mbeki's denialism now praised Zuma's "great leadership."[299] The government moved quickly. By the end of 2012, some 2 million people—more than twice as many as in 2009 and nearly ten times as many as in 2006—were taking ARVs in what had become the world's largest ARV program. According to a study in the British medical journal *Lancet,* the change caused a dramatic increase in life expectancy to 60 years. The lead researcher, Bongani Mayosi of the University of Cape Town, noted, however, that there was still a huge gap in access to health care between Africans and Whites. While the former made up 80 percent of the population, only 10.3 percent had health insurance, while 70.9 percent of Whites, who made up only 10 percent of the population, did.[300]

Inequality in insurance coverage was part of a much larger problem of lack of access to health care and of low-quality services. Children and pregnant women especially were affected. Although the government provided free primary health care to children under the age of six and pregnant women, mortality rates were not encouraging. Child mortality rates were virtually unchanged since the end of apartheid.[301] One in 15 died from preventable illnesses. Although by the end of Mbeki's presidency the District Health Information System reported that 84.2 percent of children under the age of one year had had their required vaccinations, subsequent surveys found that immunization rates were much lower than claimed and that there was poor delivery of vaccines. The quality of neonatal care also was unsatisfactory, with deaths in the first month of life accounting for 22 percent of deaths in children under five.

Maternal mortality, high and rising, added to the serious problem of orphans. The United Nations estimated that one of every 250 women died during pregnancy or childbirth. While AIDS-related illnesses were the major culprit, responsible for some 23 percent of all deaths, complications of pregnancy-related hypertension were next, even though reported rates of prenatal visits were high and 95 percent of women gave birth at hospitals and other types of clinics. After an estimate that better health services would prevent 38 percent of maternal deaths, the Department of Health introduced an improvement plan, which included a major community outreach component. Healthy children with at least one well parent would have better life chances. Nevertheless, given the burdens of poverty, including a disastrous education system, it was unlikely most would reach their potential.

Education

In education, apartheid's injustices endured while Zuma repeatedly insisted that improvement was his government's "priority number one."[302] In 2010, with government spending at 6.1 percent of GDP, more than most other nations, the World Economic Forum's Global Competitive Index ranked South Africa last of 133 countries in math and science.[303] This was no better than in 2003, when the Trends in International Mathematics and Science Study put it last of 48 countries,[304] or in 2006, when Progress in International Reading and Literacy Study placed it last of 40.[305] A Development Bank of Southern Africa analyst labeled the system a "national disaster."[306]

To increase enrollment and retention, the poorest families paid no school fees, but even so the situation was dismal. Of the approximately 87 percent of school age children who began primary school in 1999, only 42 percent finished secondary school; some 1.3 million from that cohort alone had dropped out.[307] By the time they reached the tertiary level, of the 14 percent of university age students enrolled, only 17 percent received a degree, a figure representing just 1.8 percent of those who entered the educational system in 1999.

Under apartheid the slogan "no education without liberation" regularly accompanied school boycotts, but the ANC government had failed to provide "education for liberation." Except for high-quality formerly white schools now racially integrated by the children of the new black middle class who had moved into previously white areas, the system was inept. The government admitted that 80 percent of state schools were failing.[308] As parents fled state schools, the independent school sector had grown by 75 percent since 2001. The very wealthy sent their children to a host of outstanding independent day and boarding schools. Those of modest means who were able to scrape together the tuition put their children into low-cost private schools that sprang up around the country.[309] Although the quality varied greatly, some 5,000 children had left state schools for such inexpensive alternatives. In many cases, the schools had very favorable matric results, but just a pass below a certain level was insufficient for university entrance.

In government schools, low teacher morale and poor pay often led to absenteeism. The Johannesburg-based Centre for Development and Enterprise claimed that data showed that low-paid teachers—drunk or moonlighting at other jobs—increasingly were not present on Mondays and Fridays.[310] Many schools had wretched facilities, with leaky roofs and broken or no windows and no running water or sanitation. In one case, students regularly entered the building via the windows because the broken door could not be opened.[311] By mid 2012, the deplorable conditions had prompted civil society groups to sue to enforce the constitutional right to education.[312] Despite overwhelming and very public evidence, the minister of basic education insisted that there was no crisis.

In 2012, University of the Free State Vice-Chancellor Jonathan Jansen claimed that the government's apartheid-era approach yielded poor performance, particularly in math. "Neither Hendrik Verwoerd nor the current minister of education," Jansen asserted, "believe that a black child can excel in mathematics."[313] The reference was to an infamous 1968 question by Verwoerd, then minister for native affairs: "What is the use of teaching a Bantu child mathematics when it cannot use it in practice?"[314] Now, black children received a dumbed-down math curriculum that would exclude them from university degree programs requiring math. Jansen decried the low international rankings and blamed the system's failure for the country's endemic violence. "Teachers sleep with pupils, here is rape, drugs, and pregnancies right in our schools. The violence we witness daily is because of the failure of the education system." Certainly, "a democracy should be concerned" about the results because "our democracy will implode if we do not."

Crime

Serious crime also threatened implosion. Zuma was no more successful than his predecessors in reducing it. The growing inequalities in South African society seemed to feed the incidence of crime, particularly violent crime. In 2011, the U.N. Office for Drugs and Crime reported that South Africa had the tenth-highest murder rate in the world.[315] Other studies placed it even higher. With regard to rape, the country ranked alongside conflict zones like Sierra Leone, Colombia, and Afghanistan. It also had among the highest rates of child and baby rape in the world; this was partly the consequence of the widespread myth that a cure for AIDS was to have sex with a child or a virgin. Particularly brutal rapes such as that of teenager Anene Booysen[316] were front-page news.[317] Many attacks were within the family.[318] Women's groups estimated that one rape occurred every 17 seconds and that one in nine rapes went unreported.[319]

Political killings by the apartheid state of its black rivals and by antiapartheid groups, notably the UDF and Inkatha, of each other's members were replaced by murders of local politicians by their political challengers.[320] In 2011 and 2012 there were more than 40 political assassinations in KwaZulu-Natal alone.[321] There also was increasing violence directed at white farmers, with many attacks racially motivated. Between 3,000 and 4,000 farmers had been killed since the end of apartheid.[322] Widely reported internationally was the 2010 murder of former right-wing AWB leader Eugene Terreblanche.

The government tried feebly to show that it was making inroads.[323] Police Minister Nathi Mthethwa characterized the statistics for the year ended April 2012 as a "mixed bag."[324] Criticism was immediate. The head of the crime and justice section of the Institute for Security Studies complained that trends over time were appalling. Moreover, there was no disaggregation of the statistics, so the numbers were not helpful. For example, the single appellation "sexual offences" encompassed nearly 50 different types of crime. Absent a breakdown, it was impossible to tell which offenses were rising, which were declining, and where certain types of offenses were most prevalent. The DA spokeswoman on police alleged the government used such broad categories to "hide the real situation on the ground."[325]

Underreporting was significant. The South African Institute of Race Relations estimated that in 2011, 3.3 million crimes were committed but only 48 percent were reported.[326] The annual Victims of Crime Survey for 2012 attributed the phenomenon of underreporting to a lack of confidence in the police, which led people to look to gangs, vigilante groups, and private security companies for help. Indeed, by 2013 there were more than 400,000 registered private security guards, a force bigger than the police and army combined.[327] Some of the deep distrust of police had its origins in apartheid, when the black masses viewed the police as instruments of state violence and oppression. The lack of respect for police created in that era survived despite majority rule and a police service so Africanized that by 2013 only 12 percent of the force was white.[328]

The culture of police corruption and brutality transcended any changes in racial composition. The police seemingly operated outside the legal institutions South Africans had fought so long to create. In 2008, South African journalist Jonny Steinberg, after hundreds of hours on patrol with the police, said there was only a pretense of apprehending criminals.[329] That year, Thabo Mbeki's National Police Commissioner Jackie Selebi was placed on special leave pending a court case on alleged corruption and obstruction of justice. He later received a fifteen-year prison sentence.[330] In July 2009, Zuma appointed as the new commissioner Bheki Cele, the minister for community and safety in Zuma's KwaZulu-Natal, who would, Zuma pledged, overhaul the criminal justice system and reduce crime.[331]

Zuma's aspirations were not realized. Three years later, Zuma fired Cele amid an inquiry into irregularities surrounding his signing of a lease worth some $100 million for new police headquarters. In his place, Zuma appointed Mangashi Victoria Phiyega, a woman with impeccable ANC credentials and considerable administrative experience but no familiarity with policing, thus making it unlikely that she easily would alter police culture.[332] By then, polls found two-thirds of South Africans thought the police were the most corrupt officials in the country.[333] Their view was not without justification. In 2009, Cele had said that police officers who dealt with the worst criminals should "shoot the bastards."[334] Since 2005, the number of deaths in police custody or through police action had risen annually, reaching 720 in 2012.[335]

Besides the shootings at Marikana, there were other shocking episodes, and some ANC leaders were loose-tongued with the language of authoritarianism. After the ANC held planning meetings in January 2013, Ngoako Ramathlodi, a deputy minister of prisons, claimed that the government would use an "iron fist" against the "seas of anarchy."[336] On February 14, Zuma announced a series of "tough" measures to deal with poor citizens protesting against a lack of services. That same day, South African star Olympian and Paralympian Oscar

Pistorius killed his girlfriend, an act he blamed on a mistake when he thought intruders, in South Africa a common phenomenon, had entered his home in the middle of the night. The incident prompted *Time* magazine to run a cover story about "South Africa's culture of violence."[337] Making matters worse, also in February, after a very public display of violence and perhaps xenophobia, nine policemen were jailed in the death of a 27-year-old Mozambican taxi driver, Mido Macia, who had aroused their ire by parking on the wrong side of the road in Daveyton, east of Johannesburg. The police manhandled Macia and handcuffed him to the back of their van, which then dragged him through the streets to the police station, where he was found dead in a cell two hours later.

Denounced by Zuma and other top officials, the Macia event drew worldwide condemnation. Former intelligence minister Ronnie Kasrils railed against "the menacing culture of police brutality" and the "descent into police state depravity."[338] Most damning was the criticism from Graça Machel, wife of Nelson Mandela and a former first lady of Mozambique. Her scathing remarks were thought to represent the voice of Mandela himself, although he was in failing health and no longer made public appearances or statements. Speaking at a memorial service, she decried the "increasing institutionalization of violence" that had yielded a police force "actively aggressive towards a defenceless public."[339] She continued, "South Africa is an angry nation. We are on the precipice of something very dangerous with the potential of not being able to stop the fall. The level of anger and aggression is rising. This is an expression of deeper trouble from the past that has not been addressed. We have to be more cautious about how we deal with a society that is bleeding and breathing pain."

Illegal Immigration

Regardless of whether the attack on Macia was inspired by xenophobia, illegal immigration, particularly from Zimbabwe and Mozambique, had continued to cause social unrest. Although the large-scale violence of the Mbeki years was not repeated, there were intermittent episodes.[340] In 2010 the country had anticipated a series of xenophobic attacks that would disrupt the soccer World Cup events, but nothing materialized and the games, which cost R40 billion to stage, were internationally acclaimed as a sporting success.

The message of the World Cup was one of international peace, with the host eager to showcase the glories of the harmonious and high-achieving Rainbow Nation. Much of the country reveled in a spirit of goodwill not felt since the 1994 election and inauguration of Mandela. For the month of the games, there was a drop in crime, a decline in road accidents, and a swelling of national pride. Mandela himself, in a rare public appearance, attended the final.[341] Joy and amity did not endure. In May 2011, residents in two Port Elizabeth townships attacked scores of Somali-owned shops, causing about 200 Somali immigrants to flee.[342] Two months later, the African Peer Review Mechanism gave South Africa the lowest possible rating for its handling of xenophobia.[343] In July 2012, there were violent incidents on the Cape Flats and in Botshabelo in the Free State. While no one was certain of the number of foreign nationals in South Africa, estimates ranged from two to seven million, including between one and three million Zimbabweans and the largest number of asylum seekers in the world; it was clear that the government had neither a comprehensive plan for dealing with illegal immigration nor any strategy for minimizing the angry perception of relative deprivation among the poorest members of society.

Even as South Africa's economic dominance in Africa made it a prime destination for impoverished people and organized crime from elsewhere on the continent, various factors contributed to a push by South Africans in the other direction. These included the epidemic of violent crime as well as a lack of faith in Zuma's presidency and the ANC's ability to bring to fruition the still unfulfilled promises of the first, heady days after apartheid. A huge brain drain threatened economic catastrophe if left unchecked; in 2011, one study estimated that the country had 829,900 unfilled jobs for highly skilled labor.[344] The South African Institute of Race Relations had reported in its 2007–8 annual survey that one-fifth of the white population, or 800,000 people, had emigrated since 1995, a scale consistent with "widespread disease, mass natural disasters or large-scale civil conflict."[345] It noted that most of the country's young Whites, those between 24 and 40, had already left and there were more white men over the age of 60 than young ones. Africans, Coloureds, and Indians also had gone. Although between 1996 and 2008 the number of Blacks obtaining advanced degrees had risen from 361,000 to 1.4 million per annum, the number of such degree holders strongly desiring to emigrate had doubled. In May 2008, a poll of 600 people of different ethnicities, ages, and sexes found that 20 percent were planning to emigrate, a phenomenon it described as "a new tipping point for an exodus . . . across-the-board in terms of race." More than 95 percent of those hoping to go indicated that their main reason for emigrating was crime. Their ranks included professionals and skilled farmers. Diminishing numbers of skilled farmers and a lack of corporate or black replacements portended an agricultural collapse of the sort experienced in Zimbabwe. The most highly skilled, the very people desperately needed to help South Africa overcome its past, were the ones leaving. While the opposition had tried and failed to have votes of no confidence against Zuma, it was these émigrés, voting with their feet, who had achieved them.

Clouds over the Rainbow Nation

In late 2009, the United Nations declared Mandela's birthday, July 18, Nelson Mandela Day, an annual event on which the citizens of the world were encouraged to do 67 minutes—one for each year of his political activism—of good deeds in honor of Mandela's struggle for peace and justice.[346] In 2013, Mandela's ninety-fifth birthday, many South Africans marked the event by doing charitable works.[347] Zuma, with high symbolism, went to a squatter camp inhabited by many poor Whites to inaugurate government housing for its denizens.[348] The day was part of a collective soul-searching about Mandela's legacy and the kind of nation postapartheid South Africa had become. That self-reflection had begun in earnest with Mandela's June 8 admission to a Pretoria hospital for a recurrent lung problem—his fourth hospitalization since December—where he remained on his birthday. Relatively little news about his condition appeared, fueling wild speculation. There were fears he was near the end, encouraged partly by court documents filed in a dispute among Mandela family members over the gravesites of three of his children, which alleged he was in a vegetative state. Later, there were reports he was making steady progress.[349]

Jockeying for the rights to Brand Mandela had already begun in earnest in April when the ANC and the DA got into a row over political pedigree. The DA, responding to ANC claims that the DA would bring back apartheid, launched a "Know your DA" campaign to counter this assertion and attract more, particularly African, members. The DA circulated material showing the late MP Helen Suzman, a party forebear, in an embrace with Mandela.[350] Suzman, who for years was the lone voice of opposition in the apartheid parliament and was widely credited with helping focus the attention of many, especially Western, governments on apartheid's evils, had previously been praised by Mandela. The ANC was mortified. It accused Suzman of not having been a revolutionary. Zuma visited Mandela at home in an apparent effort to bolster Zuma's credibility by association with the great man. Instead, the ANC was roundly criticized for invading Mandela's privacy because the released photos showed a smiling Zuma and a frail, blank-faced Mandela.[351] It was unclear whether the battling over this ancient history held any appeal to "born frees," the millions born after the end of apartheid, the oldest of whom were now young adults.[352] Many surveys and interviews portrayed them as a generation of pragmatists with little interest in the political struggles of their elders and no passion for politics or voting. Others, without deep allegiances born of the liberation struggle, might well, in time, move the nation toward new political terrain relatively untouched by old loyalties.

On December 5, Mandela died at his Johannesburg home where he had returned after his release from the hospital at the end of August. The days that followed until his funeral on December 15 in his beloved Qunu in the Eastern Cape were a period of national mourning. As the world honored an extraordinary life, South Africans, in a great display of unity, reflected on Mandela's achievements and their own. With the twentieth anniversary of the end of white rule fast approaching, there was cause for celebration and lamentation. The country had maintained its tradition of democratic elections, an independent judiciary, a vocal opposition, a vigorous press, and a vibrant civil society. In nearly two decades of ANC leadership, millions had received housing, however crude, and access to clean water, sanitation, electricity, and health care. Many had had a chance for an education, even a university education and its prize of a comfortable life. There was a new black elite and an expanding middle class. Measured by the size of its economy, the scope and sophistication of its infrastructure, the strength of its military, and its integration into the global economy, the country was without peer on the African continent.

At the same time, South Africa had many features that threatened its continued success and perhaps, ultimately, its very survival. Metastasizing antidemocratic biases and exploding corruption coupled with the giant, widening gap between rich and poor made it ever more difficult for many to achieve the South African dream of a decent living standard and equal opportunity. The country remained a de facto one-party state whose single party increasingly displayed antipathy toward dissent via attacks on the judiciary, the press, the political opposition, and even its own members. The ANC had a sense of entitlement that was reflected in Zuma's arrogant prediction that the party would "rule until Jesus comes back." It was a type of conceit common in a region where, by 2014, the dominant parties in the seven countries within the Southern African Development Community would have had political control for some 250 years combined. The fatuous but reflexive accusations of those in power that their critics, including black ones, were racist or, still more ludicrous, foreign spies or agents prevented mature examination of the government's many failings. The galloping culture of corruption left the government with fewer and fewer resources with which to expand employment and provide housing, basic services, health care, and education to millions of the still destitute; for them, the accommodation between white interests and black power that had yielded the Rainbow Nation had failed utterly to deliver the ANC's promised better life for all.

At least politically, there were small points of light. For many ANC supporters, there was the expectation that Ramaphosa would succeed Zuma and revive hope for a truly nonracial nation with universal affluence. With Zuma likely to win a second term, a Ramaphosa presidency was, at best, years away. More probable in the immediate future was an increasingly large and diverse opposition united in its goal of curtailing ANC power. With time, elements within it might even successfully challenge the ANC for control of the country. In that event, a graceful ANC exit from power would represent a true and unprecedented victory for democracy. After all, for nearly 50 years the NP had presided over a one-party state with authoritarian features. In that way, ANC rule represented continuity rather than a rupture with the past. In the end, despite everything, the NP government had gone gracefully. It could only be wished that if the time came, the ANC would follow that example, too.

APPENDIX:
STATISTICS

NOTE: South African statistics are particularly poor before World War II and at all times suspect concerning Africans. During the later apartheid years, inhabitants of "independent Homelands" were excluded from official statistics; however, they have been incorporated in these tables. Since the end of apartheid South Africa has conducted three censuses: 1996, 2001, and 2011. To illustrate South Africa's place in the contemporary world, tables are included comparing South Africa with other countries.

Table 1
Population of South Africa, in millions, 1911–2013

	1911 N	1911 (%)	1936 N	1936 (%)	1960 N	1960 (%)	1980 N	1980 (%)	1996 N	1996 (%)	2001 N	2001 (%)	2013 N	2013 (%)
African	4.0	(67)	6.6	(69)	10.9	(68)	20.8	(72)	31.1	(77)	35.4	(79.0)	42.3	(79.0)
Coloured	0.5	(9)	0.8	(8)	1.5	(9)	2.6	(9)	3.6	(9)	4.0	(8.9)	4.8	(8.9)
Indian	0.2	(3)	0.2	(2)	0.5	(3)	0.8	(3)	1.0	(0.3)	1.1	(2.5)	1.3	(2.5)
White	1.3	(21)	2.0	(21)	3.1	(19)	4.5	(19)	4.4	(10.9)	4.3	(9.6)	4.6	(9.6)
Total	6.0		9.6		16.0		28.7		40.6		44.8		53.0	

SOURCES: 1911, 1936, 1960, and 1980 census returns are from Merle Lipton, *Capitalism and Apartheid* (Totowa, N.J., 1985), 378; the 1996 data are derived from Statistics South Africa, *The People of South Africa Population Census, 1996: Primary Tables* (Pretoria, 1999), 38–39; the 2001 data are from Statistics South Africa, Census 2001, Census in Brief, Report no. 03-02-03 (2001), (2003), www.statssa.gov.za/census01/html/Cinbrief/CIB2001.pdf; and the 2013 data are from Statistics South Africa, Mid-year Population Estimates 2013, www.statssa.gov.za/publications/p0302/p03022013.pdf.

Table 2
Proportion of population estimated in urban areas

1904	1936	1960	1980	1990	1996	2001	2011
23%	31%	47%	47%	52%	53.7%	56.6%	62%

SOURCES: Francis Wilson and Mamphela Ramphele, *Uprooting Poverty: The South African Challenge* (New York, 1989), 26, for the years 1904, 1936, 1960, and 1980. The 1996 entry is derived from Statistics South Africa, *The People of South Africa Population Census, 1996, Primary Tables* (Pretoria, 1999), 38–39. The 1996 census was probably more accurate than its predecessors, though not without errors. The figures for 1990 and 2011 come from the South African Institute of Race Relations, Press Releases, January 22, 2013, referencing World Bank data, www.sairr.org.za. The figure for 2001 is from C. Vacchiani-Marcuzzo, Mondialisation et système de villes (Ph.D. diss.), Université de Paris (2005), referenced in International Institute for Environment and Development, United Stations Population Fund, Urbanization and Emerging Population Issues, Working Paper 8, Ivan Turok, Urbanisation and Development in South Africa: Economic Imperatives, Spatial Distortions and Strategic Responses, October 2012, www.delog.org.

Table 3
Corruption in South Africa, 1993–2012

	1995	1996	1997	1998	1999	2000
Rank/Number of Countries Ranked	21/41	23/54	33/52	32/85	34/99	34/90

	2001	2002	2003	2004	2005	2006
Rank/Number of Countries Ranked	38/91	36/106	48/133	44/145	46/158	51/163

	2007	2008	2009	2010	2011	2012
Rank/Number of Countries Ranked	43/179	54/180	55/180	54/178	64/182	69/176

SOURCE: Transparency International, Corruption Perception Index, published annually by year 1995–2012, www.transparency.org/researcch/cpi/overview.
NOTE: Transparency International is a German-based global civil society organization with more than 100 national chapters around the world. It partners with governments, businesses, and other civil society organizations to combat corruption. Its annual corruption perception index measures perceived levels of public sector corruption. The higher a country's ranking number, the more corrupt it is thought to be.

Table 4
Employment rate by race and gender for those aged 15–64

| | 2001 | | 2011 | |
	Women	Men	Women	Men
African	34.6%	45.6%	30.8%	42.8%
Coloured	46.3%	58.6%	43.2%	54.7%
Indian/Asian	38.4%	66.0%	40.2%	64.1%
White	54.8%	72.40%	56.1%	72.6%
Total	38.1%	50.7%	31.6%	47.4%

SOURCE: Statistics South Africa, www.statssa.gov.za/publications/Report
-03-10-05/Report 03-10-052011.pdf.
NOTE: Although official South African employment statistics are generally
more favorable than estimates by international organizations and other
governments, even the South African statistics show that the percentage of
employed Coloured and African women and Coloured, African, and Indian/
Asian men was lower in 2011 than it had been a decade earlier. Overall,
African women have remained the least likely to be employed.

Table 5

Levels of education by race, among those aged twenty years or more

	African (%)			Coloured (%)			Indian/Asian (%)			White (%)		
	1996	2001	2011	1996	2001	2011	1996	2001	2011	1996	2001	2011
Higher	3.6	5.2	8.3	4.9	4.9	7.4	11.6	14.9	21.6	26.8	29.8	36.5
Grade 12/ standard 10	12.0	16.8	26.9	12.3	18.5	25.2	29.9	34.9	40.0	39.3	40.9	39.5
Some secondary	32.6	30.4	35.5	42.2	40.1	42.0	39.3	33.0	26.1	31.6	25.9	21.4
Completed primary	8.3	6.9	4.9	11.1	9.8	7.4	4.9	4.2	2.8	0.5	0.8	0.7
Some primary	19.5	18.5	13.9	19.6	18.4	13.8	8.0	7.7	6.6	0.7	1.2	1.3
No schooling	24.0	22.3	10.5	10.0	8.3	4.2	6.3	5.3	29	1.1	1.3	0.6

SOURCE: Statistics South Africa, Statistical release (Revised), P03014, Census 2011 (2012), www.statssa.gov/publications/P03014/P030142011.pdf.

NOTE: These statistics do not illustrate the high levels of functional illiteracy, particularly among Africans, for those who have some schooling.

Table 6
The effects of AIDS *in South Africa*

HIV infection rates of women attending prenatal clinics, 1993–98					
1993	*1994*	*1995*	*1996*	*1997*	*1998*
4.0%	7.6%	10.4%	14.2%	16.0%	22.8%

SOURCE: *South African Survey, 1999–2000, 218–21.*

Knowledge of the HIV epidemic in South Africa is based largely on prevalence data gathered annually from pregnant women attending prenatal clinics since 1990. See above. The data yielded biased estimates of infection rates for the general population because of the limited sample. To remediate the problem, Statistics South Africa, the government's statistical bureau, changed its estimates by adjusting for relative attendance rates at prenatal clinics and for the difference in prevalence between pregnant women and the general adult population. See below.

HIV infection rates and the number of people living with HIV, 2002–13					
	Infection rate by percentage of population				
	Women 15–49	*Adults 15–49*	*Youth 15–24*	*Total population*	*by millions*
2002	15.9	15.1	13.6	8.7	4.00
2003	16.0	15.1	12.8	8.9	4.10
2004	16.1	15.1	12.0	8.9	4.18
2005	16.2	15.1	11.4	9.0	4.25
2006	16.4	15.2	10.9	9.1	4.34
2007	16.5	15.3	10.5	9.2	4.46
2008	16.7	15.4	10.1	9.3	4.59
2009	16.9	15.5	9.7	9.5	4.74
2010	17.1	15.6	9.3	9.6	4.88
2011	17.2	15.7	9.0	9.8	5.01
2012	17.3	15.8	8.7	9.9	5.13
2013	17.4	15.9	8.5	10.0	5.26

SOURCE: Statistics South Africa, Mid-Year Population Estimates, 2013, www.statssa.gov.za/publications/P0302/P03022013.pdf.

Table 7
South Africa's Human Development Index (HDI) trends, 1980–2012

	Life expectancy at birth	Expected years of schooling	Mean years of schooling	Gross National Income (GNI) per capita (U.S.$)	HDI value
1980	56.9	11.1	4.8	8,399	0.570
1985	59.8	11.1	4.8	7,892	0.581
1990	61.5	11.4	6.5	7,671	0.621
1995	59.9	13.1	8.2	7,350	0.650
2000	54.8	13.1	8.2	7,462	0.622
2005	51.1	13.1	8.2	8,420	0.604
2010	52.2	13.1	8.5	9,307	0.621
2011	52.8	13.1	8.5	9,463	0.625
2012	53.4	13.1	8.5	9,594	0.629

SOURCE: United Nations Development Program, *Human Development Report, 2013, the Rise of the South Human Progress in a Diverse World*, explanation notes on 2013 HDI composite indexes, South Africa (2013), hdrstats.undp.organization/images/explanations, ZAF.pdf.

NOTES: "The [Human Development Index] HDI is a summary measure for assessing long-term progress in three dimensions of human development—a long and healthy life, access to knowledge and a decent standard of living" (21). The HDI groups countries into four categories: very high human development, high human development, medium human development, and low human development. The 2013 Human Development Index covered 185 of the 193 member states of the United Nations as well as Hong Kong and the Palestinian territories. The closer a country's HDI value is to 1, the more developed it is. South Africa's value of 0.629 puts it among those countries in the medium human-development category. Between 1980 and 2012, life expectancy decreased. Years of schooling and expected years of schooling increased, as did the gross national income (GNI) per capita, using purchasing-power parity rates.

Table 8
South Africa's HDI indicators for 2012 in comparison with sub-Saharan Africa

	HDI value	*HDI rank*	*Life expectancy at birth*	*Mean years of schooling*	*Real years of schooling*	*GNI per capita (in U.S.$)*
South Africa	0.629	121	53.4	13.1	8.5	9,594
Republic of Congo	0.534	142	57.8	10.1	5.9	2,934
Namibia	0.608	128	62.6	11.3	6.2	5,973
Sub-Saharan Africa	0.475	—	54.9	9.3	4.7	2,010

SOURCE: UNDP, *Human Development Report, 2013.*
NOTE: South Africa's HDI is above the 0.475 average for sub-Saharan Africa. Like its neighbor Namibia, South Africa is in the medium human-development category. It ranks above many sub-Saharan African countries, which are included in the low human-development category. Of the 46 low human-development countries, 37 are in Sub-Saharan Africa, with Congo the most developed and Niger the least.

Table 9
South Africa's HDI *indicators for 2012 in comparison with* BRICS, IBSA, CIVETS, *and medium* HDI *countries*

	HDI value	HDI rank	Life expectancy at birth	Expected years of schooling	Mean years of schooling	GNI per capita (U.S.$)
South Africa	0.629	121	53.4	13.1	8.5	9,594
Brazil	0.730	85	73.8	14.2	7.2	10,152
Russia	0.788	55	69.1	14.3	11.7	14,461
India	0.554	136	65.8	10.7	4.4	3,285
China	0.699	101	73.7	11.7	7.5	7,945
BRICS	0.655	—	69.8	11.5	6.6	6,476
IBSA	0.588	—	66.4	11.2	5.0	4,401
Colombia	0.719	91	73.9	13.6	7.3	8,711
Indonesia	0.629	121	69.8	12.9	5.8	4,154
Vietnam	0.617	127	75.4	11.9	5.5	2,970
Egypt	0.662	112	73.5	12.1	6.4	5,401
Turkey	0.722	90	74.2	12.9	6.5	13,710
CIVETS	0.661	—	70.6	12.7	6.3	6,189
Medium HDI	0.640	—	69.9	11.4	6.3	5,428

SOURCE: UNDP, *Human Development Report, 2013.*

NOTE: South Africa is a member of the BRICS group of major emerging economies (Brazil, Russia, India, China, and South Africa) and its subgroup IBSA (India, Brazil, and South Africa). South Africa scores higher than the IBSA average but below the BRICS average. It also does worse than the average for the CIVETS group of emerging economies (Columbia, Indonesia, Vietnam, Egypt, Turkey, and South Africa) of which it is also a member. It scores below the other CIVETS members except Indonesia, with which it shares the HDI rank of 121, and Vietnam. South Africa also is below the average for the 47 countries and territories in the medium human-development group. However, it scores higher than the 7 other Sub-Saharan African countries in this group except for Gabon, which ranks 106, and Botswana, which ranks 119; the countries it outperforms are Namibia, Cape Verde, Ghana, Equatorial Guinea, and Swaziland.

NOTES

Chapter 1: The Africans

1. Peta Jones, "Mobility and Migration in Traditional African Farming and Iron Age Models," in *Frontiers: Southern African Archaeology Today,* ed. Martin Hall et al. (Cambridge, 1984), 289.

2. Most archaeologists of Southern Africa still adhere to this practice: e.g., Hall et al., *Frontiers;* Richard Klein, ed., *Southern African Prehistory and Paleoenvironments* (Rotterdam and Boston, 1984); Martin Hall, *The Changing Past: Farmers, Kings and Traders in Southern Africa, 200–1860* (Cape Town, 1987); and R. R. Inskeep, *The Peopling of Southern Africa* (Cape Town and London, 1978). David Phillipson, *African Archaeology* (Cambridge, 1985), however, abandons this terminology; so do John Parkington and Martin Hall in "Patterning Recent Radiocarbon Dates from Southern Africa as a Reflection of Prehistoric Settlement and Interaction," *Journal of African History* 28 (1987): 1–25.

3. Phillipson, *African Archaeology,* 60–65.

4. In the modern Republic of South Africa, I include the four "Homelands" that the South African government deems to be independent states but no other government recognizes as such.

5. William J. Burchell, *Travels in the Interior of Southern Africa,* 2 vols. (London, 1824; reprint, Cape Town, 1967), 1:291.

6. Inskeep, *Peopling,* 86–93; E. O. J. Westphal, "The Linguistic Prehistory of Southern Africa: Bush, Kwadi, Hottentot and Bantu Linguistic Relationships," *Africa* 33:3 (1963): 237–65; Christopher Ehret and Merrick Posnansky, eds.,

The Archaeological and Linguistic Reconstruction of African History (Berkeley and Los Angeles, 1982).

7. Inskeep, *Peopling*, 94.

8. P. Vinnicombe, *People of the Eland* (Pietermaritzbiurg, 1976); J. D. Lewis-Williams, "The Rock Art Workshop: Narrative or Metaphor?" in Hall et al., *Frontiers*, 323–27.

9. Inskeep, *Peopling*, 101–2.

10. Ibid.

11. Carmel Schrire, ed., *Past and Present in Hunter Gatherer Societies* (Orlando and London, 1984); R. B. Lee and I. DeVore, eds., *Man the Hunter* (Chicago, 1968).

12. Inskeep, *Peopling*, 112.

13. Marshall Sahlins, *Stone Age Economics* (New York, 1972). I thank Robert Harms for drawing my attention to Sahlins's book and clarifying his argument.

14. Ibid., 21, 23.

15. Ibid., 29.

16. Ibid., 14, 37.

17. Inskeep, *Peopling*, 114–15.

18. Khoisan is a coined word. Pastoralists called themselves Khoikhoi and called hunter-gatherers San. The Khoisan peoples were, of course, Africans; but I use the term African in the narrower sense to identify the mixed farming peoples who spoke Bantu languages and whose descendants are the vast majority of the inhabitants of modern Southern Africa.

19. This hypothesis was stated in its most extreme form in G. W. Stow, *The Native Races of South Africa* (London, 1905).

20. Richard Elphick, *Kraal and Castle: Khoikhoi and the Founding of White South Africa* (New Haven and London, 1977).

21. Richard Elphick, *Khoikhoi and the Founding of White South Africa* (Johannesburg, 1985), rev. ed. of *Kraal and Castle*; James Denbow, "A New Look at the Later Prehistory of the Kalahari," *Journal of African History* 27:1 (1986): 3–28; Nikolaas J. van der Merwe, "The Advent of Iron in Africa," in *The Coming of the Age of Iron*, ed. Theodore A. Wertime and James D. Muhly (New Haven and London, 1980), 463–506; John E. Yellen, "The Integration of Herding into Prehistoric Hunting and Gathering Economies," in Hall et al., *Frontiers*, 53–64.

22. Igor Kopytoff, ed., *The African Frontier: The Reproduction of Traditional African Societies* (Bloomington, Ind., 1987).

23. Phillipson, *African Archaeology*, 171. See also Tim Maggs, "The Iron Age South of the Zambezi," in Klein, *Southern African Prehistory*, 329–60.

24. Phillipson, *African Archaeology*, 171.

25. Peta Jones, "Mobility and Migration," 289–96.

26. J. B. Peires, *The House of Phalo* (Berkeley and Los Angeles, 1982), 19–22; Leonard Thompson, *Survival in Two Worlds: Moshoeshoe of Lesotho, 1786–1870* (Oxford, 1975), 21–22.

27. Maggs, "Iron Age."

28. Jones, "Mobility."

29. Denbow, "A New Look."

30. Phillipson says that in most of subequatorial Africa "the beginnings of food-production and of iron-working took place at the same time" (*African Archaeology,* 148); but Jones says, "There is no reason to suppose that iron-working and farming are congruent in space or time" ("Mobility," 296).

31. This section is based mainly on Elphick, "The Cape Khoikhoi Before the Arrival of Whites" (*Khoikhoi,* 3–68). See also Janette Deacon, "Later Stone Age People and Their Descendants in Southern Africa," in Klein, *Prehistory,* 221–324.

32. Robert Harms, personal communication, citing Sahlins, *Stone Age Economics.*

33. William F. Lye, ed., *Andrew Smith's Journal of His Expedition into the Interior of South Africa, 1834–36* (Cape Town, 1975), 25–26.

34. Phillipson, *African Archaeology,* 148–49; van der Merwe, "Iron Age," 489–90; Philip Curtin, Steven Feierman, Leonard Thompson, and Jan Vansina, *African History* (Boston, 1978), 20–25.

35. Eugène Casalis, *The Basutos; or, Twenty-Three Years in South Africa* (London, 1861; reprint, Cape Town, 1965), 131.

36. Ibid., 131–33. See also *Ludwig Alberti's Account of the Tribal Life and Customs of the Xhosa in 1807,* trans. William Fehr (Cape Town, 1968), 73–74 (hereafter, Alberti, *Xhosa*).

37. Eugenia W. Herbert, *Red Gold of Africa: Copper in Precolonial History and Culture* (Madison, Wis. 1984), 26–27.

38. Ibid., 210. See Burchell, *Travels,* 1:566–73, for an account of Tswana copper ornaments, with illustrations.

39. John Bird, *The Annals of Natal,* 2 vols. (Cape Town, 1888), 1:46.

40. Alberti, *Xhosa,* 54.

41. Monica Hunter (Wilson), *Reaction to Conquest,* 2d ed. (London, 1961), 70.

42. Samson Mbizo Guma, "The Forms, Contents and Techniques of Traditional Literature in Southern Africa" (D. Litt. et Phil. diss., University of South Africa, 1964), 130. Discussions in Hunter, *Conquest,* 65–71, and Hugh Ashton, *The Basuto* (London, 1952), 134–43.

43. Peires, *Phalo,* 9; Ashton, *Basuto,* 138.

44. Caslis, *Basuto,* 163–64; Alberti, *Xhosa,* 56. Discussions in Hunter, *Conquest,* 71–95, and Ashton, *Basuto,* 120–33.

45. Rev. John Brownlee, "Account of the Amakosae, or Southern Kaffers," in George Thompson, *Travels and Adventures in Southern Africa* (London, 1827; reprint, 2 vols., Cape Town, 1967, 1968), 2:209–10. Accounts of hunting also in Alberti, *Xhosa,* 74–78; Burchell, *Travels,* 2:420–21; and *Andrew Smith's Journal,* 121–23.

46. Brownlee, "Amakosae," 210–12.

47. Hall, *Changing Past,* 65–69.

48. Peires, *Phalo,* 95–98. For trade among the Tswana, see *William Somerville's Narrative of His Journeys to the Eastern Cape Frontier and to Lattakoe, 1799–1802,* ed. Edna and Frank Bradlow (Cape Town, 1979), 141.

49. Gerrit Harinck, "Interaction between Xhosa and Khoi: Emphasis on the Period 1620–1750," in *African Societies in Southern Africa: Historical Studies,* ed. Leonard Thompson (London, 1969), 145–70; Elphick, *Khoikhoi,* 63–67.

50. Lunguza ka Mpukane in *The James Stuart Archive of Recorded Oral Evidence Relating to the History of the Zulu and Neighboring Peoples,* vol. 1 (Pietermaritzburg, 1976), 342.

51. Alberti, *Xhosa,* 2, 21.

52. Ibid., 22–26; Bird, *Annals of Natal,* 1:47.

53. Amy Jacot-Guillarmod, *The Flora of Lesotho* (Lehrer, 1971); A. T. Bryant, *Zulu Medicine and Medicine-Men* (Cape Town, 1966).

54. Bird, *Annals of Natal,* 1:46.

55. Ralph Austen, *African Economic History* (Portsmouth, N.H., and London, 1987), 17.

56. Burchell, *Travels,* 2:512, 514. A fine amateur artist, Burchell published two illustrations of "Litakun": 2:360, 464.

57. Bird, *Annals,* 1:45–46.

58. Alberti, *Xhosa,* 57–59.

59. A. T. Bryant, *Olden Times in Zululand and Natal* (London, 1919), 74.

60. M. A. Boegner, ed., *Livre d'or de la mission au Lessouto* (Paris, 1912), 81–83. Hunter, *Conquest,* 87–92, describes Mpondo work parties in the 1930s.

61. Hunter, *Conquest,* 112–32.

62. Igor Kopytoff, "Introduction," in *African Frontier,* 47, 61. Jeff Guy claims that the married men or homestead heads formed a "dominant class" in Southern African precapitalist societies (Analyzing Pre-Capitalist Societies in Southern Africa," *Journal of Southern African Studies* 14:1 [October 1987]: 24). See also Claire Robertson and Iris Berger, eds., *Women and Class in Africa* (New York and London, 1986).

63. Thompson, *Survival,* 3–4.

64. Eugène Casalis, *Journal des missions évangéliques* 20 (1845): 283.

65. Prosper Lemue, ibid. 29 (1854): 209.

66. Kopytoff, "Introduction," 29.

67. Monica Wilson, "The Nguni People," in *The Oxford History of South Africa,* ed. Monica Wilson and Leonard Thompson, 2 vols. (Oxford, 1969, 1971), 1:120.

68. The information in this and the following two paragraphs is derived from my biography of Moshoeshoe, *Survival,* 14–16.

69. Guma, "Traditional Literature," 113, 124.

70. Robert Harms, "The Uncaptured Peasantry" (manuscript, 1986). See Goran Hyden, *Beyond Ujamaa in Tanzania: Underdevelopment and an Uncaptured Peasantry* (Berkeley and Los Angeles, 1980).

71. Alberti, *Xhosa,* 87. On Xhosa warfare, see also ibid., 87–93, and Henry Lichtenstein, *Travels in Southern Africa,* trans. Anne Plumtre, 2 vols. (London 1812, 1815; reprint, Cape Town, 1928, 1930), 1:341–44.

72. Keith Thomas, *Religion and the Decline of Magic* (New York, 1978).

73. Wilson, "Nguni People," 127–28.

74. On Mohlomi, see Thomas Arbousset and François Daumas, *Relation d'un voyage d'exploration au nord-est de la Colonie du Cap de Bonne Espérance en 1836* (Paris, 1842), trans. John C. Brown, *Narrative of an Exploratory Tour to the Cape of Good Hope* (Cape Town, 1846), 272–85; D. Frederic Ellenberger and J. C. Macgregor, *History of the Basuto: Ancient and Modern* (London, 1912), 90–97.

75. John Alexander and Peta Jones provide archaeologists' models of this process in Hall, *Frontiers,* 12–23, 289–96.

76. Thompson, *Survival,* 19.

77. Monica Wilson, "The Sotho, Venda, and Tsonga," in *Oxford History,* 1:148–49, 155–56, 165–66.

78. Alberti, *Xhosa,* 87.

79. Lichtenstein, *Travels,* 1:341.

80. Thompson, *Survival,* 13, 173.

81. Harinck, "Interaction."

82. Peires, *Phalo,* 19.

83. Ibid., 24. See also Philip Tobias, "The Biology of the Southern African Negro," in *The Bantu-Speaking Peoples of Southern Africa,* ed. W. D. Hammond-Tooke (London and Boston, 1974), 43–44, map on 26.

84. This is Kopytoff's core argument in *The African Frontier.*

Chapter 2: The White Invaders

1. Daniel J. Boorstin, *The Discoverers: A History of Man's Search to Know His World and Himself* (New York, 1983); J. H. Parry, *The Age of Reconnaissance* (New York, 1963).

2. Boorstin, *Discoverers,* 177.

3. C. R. Boxer, *The Dutch Seaborne Empire, 1600–1800* (London, 1965); Fernand Braudel, *The Perspective of the World,* trans. Sian Reynolds (New York, 1984), chap. 3; Philip Curtin, *Cross-Cultural Trade in World History* (Cambridge, 1984), chap. 7.

4. The annual publications of the Van Riebeeck Society (Cape Town, 1918ff.) include many documents that are primary sources for this chapter. The Van Riebeeck Society was also responsible for the publication of the *Journal of Jan van Riebeeck,* ed. H. B. Thom, 3 vols. (Cape Town and Amsterdam, 1952, 1954, 1958). The basic synthesis is Richard Elphick and Hermann Giliomee, eds., *The Shaping of South African Society, 1652–1820* (Cape Town and Middletown, Conn., 1989).

5. Gerrit Schutte, "Company and Colonists at the Cape, 1652–1795,"

Leonard Duelke, "Freehold Farmers and Frontier Settlers, 1652–1780," and Robert Ross, "The Cape of Good Hope and the World Economy, 1652–1835," in *Shaping*.

6. Nigel Worden, *Slavery in Dutch South Africa* (Cambridge, 1985); Robert Ross, *Cape of Torments: Slavery and Resistance in South Africa* (London, 1983); James C. Armstrong and Nigel Worden, "The Slaves, 1652–1834," in *Shaping*; R. L. Watson, *The Slave Question: Liberty and Property in South Africa* (Hanover, N.H., and London, 1990); Robert C.-H. Shell, *Children of Bondage: A Social History of the Slave Society at the Cape of Good Hope, 1652–1838* (Hanover, N.H., and London, 1994).

7. Richard Elphick, *Khoikhoi and the Founding of White South Africa* (Johannesburg, 1985); Richard Elphick and V. C. Malherbe, "The Khoisan to 1828," in *Shaping*.

8. Elphick, *Khoikhoi,* 237–38.

9. Ibid., 234.

10. Richard Elphick and Robert Shell, "Intergroup Relations: Khoikhoi, Settlers, Slaves and Free Blacks, 1652–1795," in *Shaping*, 231.

11. Abraham Bogaert in *Cape of Good Hope, 1652–1702: The First Fifty Years of Dutch Colonisation as Seen by Callers*, ed. R. Raven-Hart, 2 vols. (Cape Town, 1971), 2:479.

12. Ibid., 480.

13. Ibid., 480–81.

14. Henry Lichtenstein, *Travels in Southern Africa in the Years 1803, 1804, 1805, and 1806*, 2 vols. (London, 1812; reprint, Cape Town, 1928, 1930), 1:57–58.

15. F. Valentyn, *Description of the Cape of Good Hope with the Matters Concerning It*, 2 vols. (Cape Town, 1971, 1973), 2:259, cited in Worden, *Slavery,* 97.

16. Schutte in *Shaping,* 303–7; A. J. Boeseken, "The Settlement under the van der Stels," in *Five Hundred Years: A History of South Africa,* ed. C. F. J. Muller (Pretoria and Cape Town, 1969), 33–38.

17. Worden, *Slavery,* 115.

18. Carl Peter Thunberg, *Travels at the Cape of Good Hope,* ed. V. S. Forbes (Cape Town, 1986), 153.

19. Shell, *Children of Bondage,* 206–14; Worden, *Slavery,* 101–18.

20. Ross, *Cape of Torments*.

21. Robert Carl-Heinz Shell, "Slavery at the Cape of Good Hope, 1680 to 1731," 2 vols. (Ph.D. diss., Yale University, 1986), 1:292–93.

22. John Edwin Mason, "Paternalism under Siege: Slavery in Theory and Practice during the Era of Reform," in *Breaking the Chains: Slavery and Its Legacy in Nineteenth Century South Africa,* ed. Nigel Worden and Clifton Crais (Johannesburg, 1995). See also John Edwin Mason, *Fit for Trade: Slavery and Emancipation in South Africa* (Charlottesville, Va., 1995).

23. Worden, *Slavery,* 143–44.

24. Elphick and Shell, "Intergroup Relations," 204–24.

25. J. A. Heese, *Die herkoms van die Afrikaner, 1657–1867* (Cape Town, 1971), 17–20, cited in Worden, *Slavery,* 147.

26. Guelke, "Freehold Farmers," and Elphick and Malherbe, "Khoisan to 1828," in *Shaping;* Robert Ross, "The First Two Centuries of Colonial Agriculture in the Cape Colony: A Historiographical Review," *Social Dynamics* 9:1 (June 1983): 30–49; Pieter van Duin and Robert Ross, *The Economy of the Cape Colony in the Eighteenth Century* (Leiden, 1987).

27. Van Duin and Ross, *Economy,* 114–23.

28. Scholars have debated the question of the extent to which the trekboers were involved in the market economy. See Martin Legassick, "The Frontier Tradition in Pre-Industrial South Africa," in *Economy and Society in Pre-Industrial South Africa,* ed. Shula Marks and Anthony Atmore (London, 1980), 44–79; Guelke, "Freehold Farmers," 58–71; Ross, "First Two Centuries," 40–42.

29. Hendrik Swellengrebel to C. de Grijselaw, June 26, 1781, "A Few Considerations about the Cape," in *Briefwisseling van Hendrik Swellengrebel jr.oor Kaapse sake, 1778–1792* (Cape Town, 1982), 348.

30. Anders Sparrman, *A Voyage to the Cape of Good Hope . . . and to the Country of the Hottentots and the Caffres from the Year 1772–1776,* ed. V. S. Forbes, 2 vols. (Cape Town, 1975, 1977), 1:230.

31. Martin Legassick, "The Northern Frontier to c. 1840: The Rise and Decline of the Griqua People," in *Shaping;* Elizabeth Eldredge and Fred Morton, eds., *Slavery in South Africa: Captive Labor and the Dutch Frontier* (Boulder, Colo., 1994).

32. Hermann Giliomee, "The Eastern Frontier, 1770–1812," in *Shaping,* and "Processes in Development of the Southern African Frontier," in *The Frontier in History: North America and Southern Africa Compared,* ed. Howard Lamar and Leonard Thompson (New Haven and London, 1981), 76–119.

33. Giliomee, "Eastern Frontier."

34. John Barrow, *Travels in the Interior of Southern Africa in the Years 1797 and 1798,* 2 vols. (London, 1801, 1804; reprint, 2 vols. in 1, London, 1968), 2:372.

35. Sparrman, *Voyage,* 1:88.

36. There has been much controversy over the origins of racism among white South Africans, developing out of the pathbreaking work of the psychologist I. D. MacCrone, *Race Attitudes in South Africa* (London, 1937). See Legassick, "Frontier Tradition" and "Northern Frontier"; Giliomee, "Eastern Frontier"; Giliomee and Elphick, "Structure of European Domination"; and Leonard Thompson, *The Political Mythology of Apartheid* (New Haven and London, 1985).

37. K. Jordaan, "The Origins of the Afrikaners and Their Language, 1652–1720: A Study in Miscegenation and Creole," *Race* 15:4 (1974): 461–95; M. F. Valkoff, *New Light on Afrikaans and "Malayo-Portuguese"* (Louvain, 1972),

and *Studies in Portuguese and Creole, with Special Reference to South Africa* (Johannesburg, 1966).

38. Jeffrey Peires, "The British and the Cape, 1814–1834," in *Shaping*.

39. C. G. W. Schumann, *Structural Changes and Business Cycles in South Africa, 1806–1936* (Westminster, 1938), pt. 1.

40. W. M. Macmillan, *The Cape Colour Question* (London, 1927); Andrew Ross, *John Philip (1775–1851): Missions, Race, and Politics in South Africa* (Aberdeen, 1986).

41. J. S. Galbraith, *Reluctant Empire* (Berkeley and Los Angeles, 1963); A. G. L. Shaw, ed., *Great Britain and the Colonies, 1815–1865* (London, 1970).

42. Daniel R. Headrick, *The Tools of Empire: Technology and European Imperialism in the Nineteenth Century* (New York, 1981).

43. Peires, "British and Cape," in *Shaping*.

44. William Freund, "The Cape under the Transitional Governments, 1795–1814," in *Shaping*.

45. *The Record: or, A Series of Papers Relative to the Condition and Treatment of the Native Tribes of South Africa,* ed. Donald Moodie (reprint, Amsterdam, 1960), pt. 5:17–19.

46. Donald Maclennan, *A Proper Degree of Terror* (Johannesburg, 1986), frontispiece.

47. Ibid., chap. 3.

48. Peires, "British and Cape," 474.

49. M. D. Nash, *Bailie's Party of 1820 Settlers* (Cape Town, 1982).

50. G. E. Cory, *The Rise of South Africa,* vol. 2 (London, 1913); Thomas Pringle, *Narrative of a Residence in South Africa* (London, 1835); *The Chronicle of Jeremiah Goldswain,* ed. Una Long, 2 vols. (Cape Town, 1946, 1949).

51. For example, see John Mitford Bowker, *Speeches, Letters and Selections from Important Papers* (Grahamstown, 1864; reprint, Cape Town, 1962), and R. Godlonton, *A Narrative of the Irruption of the Kaffir Hordes . . . 1834–1835* (Graham's Town, 1855; reprint, Cape Town, 1965).

52. Bill Freund, *The Making of Contemporary Africa* (Bloomington, 1984), chap. 4; Galbraith, *Reluctant Empire;* B. Semmel, *The Rise of Free Trade Imperialism* (Cambridge, 1970).

53. Armstrong and Worden, "The Slaves"; Mary Isobel Rayner, "Wine and Slaves: The Failure of an Export Economy and the Ending of Slavery in the Cape Colony, South Africa, 1806–1834" (Ph.D. diss., Duke University, 1986).

54. R. Ross, *Cape of Torments,* 109.

55. J. S. Marais, *The Cape Coloured People, 1652–1937,* 2d ed. (Johannesburg, 1957); Macmillan, *Cape Colour Question;* Susan Newton-King, "The Labour Market of the Cape Colony, 1807–28," in *Economy and Society,* 171–207.

56. A. Ross, *Philip,* chaps. 1–2. Philip is a controversial figure in South African historiography. As Ross's biography demonstrates, he has been underrated both by conservative white South African historians and by Marxist historians.

57. Ibid., chaps. 3–4.

58. John Philip, *Researches in South Africa,* 2 vols. (London, 1828; reprint, New York, 1969), 1:xxv, xxvi.

59. A. Ross, *Philip,* 109.

60. Marais, *Cape Coloured People,* chap. 5.

61. Ibid., 131–34; Maclennan, *Terror,* chap. 4.

62. Elphick and Malherbe, "Khoisan."

63. Maclennan, *Terror,* 52–53.

64. Marais, *Cape Coloured People,* 223.

65. Ibid., 229.

66. Ibid., 233.

67. Ibid., 231–45; Tony Kirk, "The Cape Economy and the Expropriation of the Kat River Settlement, 1846–53," in *Economy and Society,* 226–46.

68. Peter Burroughs, "Colonial Self-Government," in *British Imperialism in the Nineteenth Century,* ed. C. C. Eldridge (London, 1984), 58. See also Bernard Porter, *The Lion's Share: A Short History of British Imperialism, 1850–1970* (London, 1975), 1–26.

69. Stanley Trapido, "The Origins of the Cape Franchise Qualifications of 1853," *Journal of African History* 5:1 (1964): 37–54; Marais, *Cape Coloured People,* 208–15.

70. Marais, *Cape Coloured People,* 199–208.

71. A. Ross, *Philip,* 215–28.

72. Union of South Africa, *Report of Commission of Inquiry regarding the Cape Coloured Population of the Union,* U.G. 54–1937 (Pretoria, 1937).

73. D. Hobart Houghton and Jenifer Dagut, *Source Material on the South African Economy: 1860–1970,* vol. 1: *1860–1899* (Cape Town, 1972), 32.

74. Van Duin and Ross, *Economy of the Cape Colony,* 88.

75. Houghton and Dagut, *Source Material,* 1:14–19, 133.

76. Leonard Thompson, "The Strange Career of Slagtersnek," in *Political Mythology of Apartheid,* 105–43.

77. Eric A. Walker, *The Great Trek,* 5th ed. (London, 1965).

78. Leslie C. Duly, *British Land Policy at the Cape, 1795–1844* (Durham, N.C., 1968).

79. C. F. J. Muller, *Die oorsprong van die Groot Trek* (Cape Town and Johannesburg, 1974).

80. G. W. Eybers, *Select Constitutional Documents Illustrating South African History, 1795–1910* (London, 1918), 143–45.

Chapter 3: African Wars and White Invaders

1. Daniel R. Headrick, *The Tools of Empire: Technology and European Imperialism in the Nineteenth Century* (New York, 1981), pt. 2, "Guns and Conquests."

2. Howard Lamar and Leonard Thompson, *The Frontier in History: North America and Southern Africa Compared* (New Haven, 1981); Leonard Thomp-

son, "The Southern African Frontier in Comparative Perspective," in *Essays on Frontiers in World History,* ed. George Wolfskill and Stanley Palmer (College Station, Tex., 1983).

3. J. B. Peires, *The House of Phalo: A History of the Xhosa People in the Days of Their Independence* (Berkeley and Los Angeles, 1981); Monica Wilson, "Cooperation and Conflict: The Eastern Cape Frontier," *The Oxford History of South Africa,* ed. Monica Wilson and Leonard Thompson, 2 vols. (Oxford, 1969, 1971), 1:233–71; W. M. Macmillan, *Bantu, Boer and Briton: The Making of the South African Native Problem* (London, 1929), 2d ed. (Oxford, 1963); J. S. Galbraith, *Reluctant Empire: British Policy on the South African Frontier, 1834–1854* (Berkeley and Los Angeles, 1963); John Henderson Soga, *The Ama-Xosa: Life and Customs* (London, 1931); Colin Bundy, *The Rise and Fall of the South African Peasantry* (Berkeley and Los Angeles, 1979), 1–64; David Hammond-Tooke, "The 'Other Side' of Frontier History: A Model of Cape Nguni Political Process," *African Societies in Southern Africa: Historical Studies,* ed. Leonard Thompson (London, 1969), 230–58. Les Switzer, *Power and Resistance in an African Society: The Ciskei Xhosa and the Making of South Africa* (Madison, Wis., 1993); Noel Mostert, *Frontiers: The Epic of South Africa's Creation and the Tragedy of the Xhosa People* (New York, 1992).

4. Donald Maclennan, *A Proper Degree of Terror* (Johannesburg, 1986); Hermann Giliomee, "The Eastern Frontier, 1770–1812," in *The Shaping of South African Society, 1652–1840,* ed. Richard Elphick and Hermann Giliomee (Cape Town and Middletown, Conn., 1989), 421–71.

5. Peires, *House of Phalo,* 58–63, 135–45.

6. Richard A. Moyer, "The Mfengu, Self-Defense and the Cape Frontier," in *Beyond the Cape Frontier,* ed. Christopher Saunders and Robin Derricourt (London, 1974), 101–26; Bundy, *Rise and Fall,* 32–44. It has been argued that the Mfengu were not refugees from the Zulu kingdom, but impoverished Xhosa; the evidence is not convincing. See Switzer, *Power and Resistance,* 58–60.

7. Peires, *House of Phalo,* 145–50; Macmillan, *Bantu, Boer and Briton,* 106–53; Galbraith, *Reluctant Empire,* 98–122. R. Godlonton, *A Narrative of the Irruption of the Kaffir Hordes into the Eastern Province of the Cape of Good Hope, 1834–1835* (Graham's Town, 1835; reprint, Cape Town, 1965), is a contemporary settler account.

8. Macmillan, *Bantu, Boer and Briton,* 154–93.

9. Peires, *House of Phalo,* 109–34; Macmillan, *Bantu, Boer and Briton,* 239–305; Galbraith, *Reluctant Empire,* 123–50.

10. Peires, *House of Phalo,* 150–58.

11. George McCall Theal, *History of South Africa from 1795 to 1872,* 4th ed., 5 vols. (London, 1927), 3:62. This anecdote may not be accurate.

12. Johannes Meintjes, *Sandile: The Fall of the Xhosa Nation* (Cape Town, 1971), 205.

13. Ibid., 202–30.

14. J. Rutherford, *Sir George Grey: A Study in Colonial Government* (London, 1961).

15. J. B. Peires, " 'Soft' Believers and 'Hard' Unbelievers in the Xhosa Cattle-Killing," *Journal of African History* 27:3 (1986): 443–61, and "The Central Beliefs of the Xhosa Cattle-Killing," *Journal of African History* 28:1 (1987): 43–63. Also Switzer, *Power and Resistance*, 65–75, and J. B. Peires, *The Dead Will Arise: Nongqawuse and the Great Xhosa Cattle-Killing Movement of 1856–57* (Johannesburg, Bloomington, Ind., and London, 1989).

16. Peires, "Central Beliefs," 56. On the cattle-killing see also Wilson, "Co-operation and Conflict," 256–60; Meintjes, *Sandile*, 240–63; and Charles Pacalt Brownlee, *Reminiscences of Kafir Life and History*, 2d ed. (Lovedale, 1916; reprint with Introduction by Christopher Saunders, Pietermaritzburg, 1977). Brownlee, the son of a missionary, was British commissioner to the Ngqika Xhosa at the time of the cattle-killing.

17. William W. Gqoba, "The Cause of the Cattle-Killing at the Nongqawuse Period," in A. C. Jordan, *Towards an African Literature* (Berkeley and Los Angeles, 1973), 70–71. This is the most authentic African version we have; Gqoba, a Xhosa, was living at the time.

18. Ibid., 73.

19. Peires, " 'Soft' Believers."

20. Brownlee, "Reminiscences," 140.

21. Peires, " 'Soft' Believers," 454, 456, 460.

22. Peires, "Central Beliefs," 43; Rutherford, *Grey*, 368.

23. Rutherford, *Grey*, 360–70.

24. John A. Chalmers, *Tiyo Soga: A Page of South African Mission Work* (Edinburgh, 1878), 249.

25. J. D. Omer-Cooper, *The Zulu Aftermath* (Evanston, Ill., 1966); Leonard Thompson, "The Zulu Kingdom" and "The Difaqane and Its Aftermath, 1822–36," in *The Oxford History of South Africa*, 1:336–64, 391–405; Donald R. Morris, *The Washing of the Spears: A History of the Rise of the Zulu Kingdom under Shaka and Its Fall in the Zulu War of 1879* (New York, 1965); Paul Maylam, *A History of the African People of South Africa* (New York, 1986), 54–63. See also n. 6, above.

26. J. B. Mcl. Daniel, "A Geographical Study of Pre-Shakan Zululand," *South African Geographical Journal* 55:1 (1973): 23–31; Jeff Guy, "Ecological Factors in the Rise of Shaka and the Zulu Kingdom," in *Economy and Society in Pre-Industrial South Africa*, ed. S. Marks and A. Atmore (London, 1980), 102–19; Martin Hall, *The Changing Past: Farmers, Kings, and Traders in Southern Africa, 200–1860* (Cape Town, 1987), 124–28, and "Settlement Patterns in the Iron Age of Zululand," *Cambridge Monographs in African Archaeology 5* (1981): 139–78.

27. Charles Ballard, "Economic Distress, Social Transformation and the Drought Factor in South African History, 1800–1830: With Particular Reference to the Societies of Natal and Zululand" (manuscript, 1986).

28. Guy, "Ecological Factors."

29. Lugunza, in *The James Stuart Archive of Recorded Oral Evidence Relating to the History of the Zulu and Neighboring Peoples*, ed. C. de B. Webb and J. B. Wright, 3 vols. (Pietermaritzburg, 1976, 1979, 1981), 1:342.

30. Baleka, in *Stuart Archive*, 1:8.

31. Two white traders wrote accounts of their visits to Shaka: Nathaniel Isaacs, *Travels and Adventure in Eastern Africa,* 2 vols. (London, 1836; new ed., Cape Town, 1935–36), and Henry Francis Fynn, *The Diary of Henry Francis Fynn,* ed. J. Stuart and D. Mck. Malcolm (Pietermaritzburg, 1950). Isaacs stressed the sensational, brutal aspects of Shaka's behavior; Fynn was more reliable, but his original manuscript was lost, and he wrote the surviving manuscript from memory many years later. There are additional documents in John Bird, *The Annals of Natal: 1495 to 1845,* 2 vols. (Pietermaritzburg, 1888) 1:60–71, 73–93, 95–124. The oral evidence collected by James Stuart, a Natal civil servant, in the late nineteenth and early twentieth centuries has been skillfully edited in *The James Stuart Archive.*

32. Alan Smith, "The Trade of Delagoa Bay as a Factor in Nguni Politics, 1780–1835," in *African Societies in Southern Africa,* 171–90; P. L. Bonner, "The Dynamics of Late Eighteenth Century Northern Nguni Society: Some Hypotheses," in *Before and After Shaka: Papers in Nguni History,* ed. J. Peires (Grahamstown, 1981), 74–81.

33. Julian Cobbing expounded his thesis in "The Mfecane as Alibi: Thoughts on Dithakong and Mblompo," *Journal of African History* 29:3 (1988): 487–519, and in a series of unpublished seminar papers, including "The Case against the Mfecane" (University of the Witwatersrand, 1984), "Grasping the Nettle: The Slave Trade and the Early Zulu" (University of Natal, Pietermaritzburg, 1990), and "Ousting the Mfecane" (colloquium on the Mfecane aftermath, University of the Witwatersrand, September 6–9, 1991). Published responses include Elizabeth A. Eldredge, "Sources of Conflict in Southern Africa, ca. 1800–1830: The 'Mfecane' Reconsidered," *Journal of African History* 33:1 (1992): 1–35; Carolyn Anne Hamilton, " 'The Character and Objects of Chaka': A Reconsideration of the Making of Shaka as 'Mfecane' Motor," ibid., 37–63; J. D. Omer-Cooper, "Has the Mfecane a Future? A Response to the Cobbing Critique," *Journal of Southern African Studies* 19:2 (1993), 273–94; J. B. Peires, "Paradigm Deleted: The Materialist Interpretation of the Mfecane," ibid., 295–313; Elizabeth A. Eldredge, "Slaving across the Cape Frontier," and "Delagoa Bay and the Hinterland in the Early Nineteenth Century: Politics, Trade, Slaves, and Slave Raiding," in *Slavery in South Africa: Captive Labor on the Dutch Frontier,* ed. Elizabeth Eldredge and Fred Morton (Madison, Wis., 1994), 93–166.

34. Hamilton, " 'Character and Objects of Chaka,' " 59. Besides the works listed in note 31, see A. F. Gardiner, *Narrative of a Journey to the Zoolu Country in South Africa* (London, 1836), and *The Diary of the Rev. Francis Owen, M.A., Missionary with Dingaan in 1837–38* (Cape Town, 1926).

35. Thomas Arbousset, *Missionary Excursion,* ed. and trans. David Ambrose and Albert Brutsch (Morija, Lesotho, 1991), 68–69. Also, Thomas Arbousset and F. Daumas, *Narrative of an Exploratory Tour to the North-East of the Colony of the Cape of Good Hope* (Cape Town, 1846; new ed., Cape Town, 1948); William F. Lye, ed., *Andrew Smith's Journal of His Expedition into the Interior of South Africa, 1834–36* (Cape Town, 1975).

36. R. Kent Rasmussen, *Migrant Kingdom* (London, 1978), and Omer-Cooper, *Zulu Aftermath,* 129–55.

37. Omer-Cooper, *Zulu Aftermath,* 49–85, 115–28.

38. Leonard Thompson, *Survival in Two Worlds: Moshoeshoe of Lesotho, 1786–1868* (Oxford, 1975), quotation on 161. See also Elizabeth Eldredge, *A South African Kingdom: The Pursuit of Security in Nineteenth-Century Lesotho* (New York, 1993).

39. Thomas Mokopu Mofolo (1875–1948), *Chaka* (Morija, Lesotho, 1925); Solomon Tshekisho Plaatje (1876–1932), *Mhudi* (Lovedale, 1930); Mazisi Kunene, *Emperor Shaka the Great* (London, 1979). There are many later editions of Mofolo and Plaatje. Kunene, writing in the shadow of apartheid, dedicated his poem "to all the heroes and heroines of the African continent and all her children who shall make her name great."

40. C. F. J. Muller, "The Period of the Great Trek, 1834–1854," in *Five Hundred Years: A History of South Africa,* ed. C. F. J. Muller (Pretoria and Cape Town, 1969), 122–56; Leonard Thompson in *Oxford History of South Africa,* 1:352–64, 405–34; Eric A. Walker, *The Great Trek* (London, 1938).

41. G. W. Eybers, *Select Constitutional Documents Illustrating South African History, 1795–1910* (London, 1918), 144–45.

42. Bird, *Annals of Natal,* 1:459.

43. Rasmussen, *Migrant Kingdom.*

44. Walker, *Trek,* 133–47.

45. Ibid., 147–65. Francis Owen, an Anglican missionary, was at Dingane's headquarters when the Retief party was massacred (*The Diary of the Rev. Francis Owen,* ed. G. Cory [Cape Town, 1926]). It is possible that no such treaty existed.

46. Official reports of the battle by Pretorius and his secretary, *South African Archival Records: Notule van die Natalse Volksraad, 1838–45,* ed. J. H. Breytenbach (Cape Town, n.d. [ca. 1958]), 270–73, 282–85, 290, 293–94, with inaccurate translations in Bird, *Annals of Natal,* 1:453–58. Critique in Leonard Thompson, *The Political Mythology of Apartheid* (New Haven and London, 1985), 144–54.

47. The emigrants considered they spoke Dutch. In fact, their spoken language was already closer to modern Afrikaans.

48. A. J. du Plessis, "Die Republiek Natalia," in *Archives Year Book for South African History* (1942): 1; Walker, *Great Trek,* 206–33.

49. Du Plessis, "Republiek Natalia"; J. A. I. Agar-Hamilton, *The Native Policy of the Voortrekkers, 1836–1858* (Cape Town, 1928).

50. On British policy toward the emigrants, see Galbraith, *Reluctant Empire,* and W. P. Morrell, *British Colonial Policy in the Age of Peel and Russell* (Oxford, 1930).

51. Bird, 2:146.

52. F. J. Potgieter, "Die vestiging van die Blanke in Transvaal, 1837–66," in *Archives Year Book* (1958): 2; Roger Wagner, "Zoutpansberg: The Dynamics of a Hunting Frontier, 1848–67," in *Economy and Society in Pre-Industrial South Africa,* 313–49.

53. Robert Ross, *Adam Kok's Griquas* (Cambridge, 1976); William Lye, "The Distribution of the Sotho Peoples after the Difaqane," in *African Societies in Southern Africa,* 190–206; Thompson, *Moshoeshoe.* See also Elizabeth Eldredge, "Slave Raiding across the Cape Frontier," in *Slavery in South Africa,* 93–126.

54. J. du Plessis, *A History of Christian Missions in South Africa* (reprint, Cape Town, 1965).

55. Galbraith, *Reluctant Empire,* 176–241.

56. J. F. Midgley, "The Orange River Sovereignty," in *Archives Year Book* (1949): 2; Thompson, *Moshoeshoe,* 140–54.

57. Thompson, *Moshoeshoe,* 163.

58. Eybers, *Select Constitutional Documents,* 359.

59. Ibid., 282–83.

60. Galbraith, *Reluctant Empire,* 242–76.

61. Leonard Thompson, in *Oxford History of South Africa,* 1:373–90; Maylam, *History of the African People,* 83–90; E. H. Brookes and C. de B. Webb, *A History of Natal* (Pietermaritzburg, 1965).

62. A. F. Hattersley, *Portrait of a Colony* (Cambridge, 1940), and *The British Settlement of Natal* (Cambridge, 1950).

63. David Welsh, *The Roots of Segregation: Native Policy in Colonial Natal, 1845–1910* (Cape Town, 1971); Bundy, *Peasantry,* 165–74; Henry Slater, "The Changing Pattern of Economic Relationships in Rural Natal, 1838–1914," in *Economy and Society,* 148–70.

64. Report of Natal Native Affairs Commission, 1854; Public Record Office, Confidential Print, C.O. 879/1, 15, 20.

65. Thompson, in *Oxford History of South Africa,* 1:382–86.

66. N. Etherington, *Preachers, Peasants and Politics in Southeast Africa, 1835–1880* (London, 1978), 47–59, 87–96. Edwin W. Smith, *The Life and Times of Daniel Lindley (1801–80)* (London, 1949), is a biography of one of the most influential of the American missionaries; Patrick Harries, "Plantations, Passes, and Proletarians: Labour and the Colonial State in Nineteenth-Century Natal," *Journal of Southern African Studies* 13:3 (1978): 372–99.

67. Hugh Tinker, *A New System of Slavery: The Export of Indian Labour Overseas, 1830–1920* (Oxford, 1974); Leonard Thompson, "Indian Immigration into Natal, 1860–1872," *Archives Year Book for South African History* (1952), vol. 2; Surendra Bhana and Bridglal Pachai, eds., *A Documentary History of Indian South Africans* (Cape Town and Stanford, Calif., 1984).

68. Leonard Thompson, in *Oxford History of South Africa*, 1:424–46; Maylam, *History of the African People*, 113–33.

69. Stanley Trapido, "Reflections on Land, Office and Wealth in the South African Republic, 1850–1900," in *Economy and Society*, 350–68.

70. Leonard Thompson, "Constitutionalism in the South African Republics," *Butterworths South African Law Review* (1954): 54–72; Eybers, *Select Constitutional Documents*, 288–96.

71. Thompson, "Constitutionalism"; Eybers, *Select Constitutional Documents*, 362–410.

72. Joseph Millerd Orpen, *Reminiscences of Life in South Africa* (Cape Town, 1964), 302–24; Fred Morton, "Captive Labor in the Western Transvaal after the Sand River Convention"; and Jan C. A. Boeyens, " 'Black Ivory': The Indenture System and Slavery in Zoutpansberg, 1848–1869," in *Slavery in South Africa*, 167–214.

73. F. A. van Jaarsveld, "Die veldkornet en sy aandeel in die opbou van die Suid-Afrikaanse Republiek tot 1870," in *Archives Year Book for South African History* (1950), vol. 2.

74. David Livingstone, *Missionary Travels and Researches* (London, 1857), and *Missionary Correspondence, 1841–56,* ed. I. Schapera (London, 1961).

75. Orpen, *Reminiscences*, 288–97.

76. Peter Delius, "Migrant Labour and the Pedi, 1840–80," in *Economy and Society*, 293–312.

77. Neil Parsons, *A New History of South Africa* (London, 1982).

78. Thompson, *Oxford History*, 1:440–41.

79. Peter Delius, *The Land Belongs to Us* (Johannesburg, 1983).

80. Thompson, *Survival in Two Worlds,* 219–311, and *Oxford History of South Africa*, 1:442–46.

81. C. W. de Kiewiet, *British Colonial Policy and the South African Republics* (London, 1929).

82. Ibid., 311–29; Thompson, *Oxford History of South Africa*, 1:446.

Chapter 4: Diamonds, Gold, and British Imperialism

1. William Beinart, Peter Delius, and Stanley Trapido, eds., *Putting a Plough to the Ground: Accumulation and Dispossession in Rural South Africa, 1850–1930* (Johannesburg, 1986); William Beinart and Colin Bundy, *Hidden Struggles in Rural South Africa* (Berkeley and Los Angeles, 1987); Colin Bundy, *The Rise and Fall of the South African Peasantry* (London, 1979).

2. William H. Worger, *South Africa's City of Diamonds: Mine Workers and Monopoly Capitalism in Kimberley, 1867–1895* (New Haven and London, 1987); Rob Turrell, *Capital and Labour on the Kimberley Diamond Fields, 1871–1890* (Cambridge, 1987).

3. Charles van Onselen, *Studies in the Social and Economic History of the Witwatersrand, 1886–1914,* 2 vols. (London, 1982).

4. Maureen Swan, *Gandhi: The South African Experience* (Johannesburg, 1985).

5. Eric Hobsbawm, *The Age of Empire, 1875–1914* (New York, 1987); Paul Kennedy, *The Rise and Fall of the Great Powers* (New York, 1987).

6. Leonard Thompson, "The Subjection of the African Chiefdoms," "Great Britain and the Afrikaner Republics," and "The Compromise of Union," in *The Oxford History of South Africa,* ed. Monica Wilson and Leonard Thompson, 2 vols. (Oxford, 1969, 1971), 2:245–364.

7. Worger, *City of Diamonds,* 191.

8. Geoffrey Wheatcroft, *The Randlords: The Exploits and Exploitations of South Africa's Mining Magnates* (New York, 1986), 47.

9. John Flint, *Cecil Rhodes* (Boston, 1974); Apollon Davidson, *Cecil Rhodes and His Time* (Moscow, 1988); Robert Rotberg, *Cecil Rhodes* (London, 1988).

10. C. W. de Kiewiet, *British Colonial Policy and the South African Republics, 1848–1872* (London, 1929); C. F. Goodfellow, *Great Britain and South African Confederation, 1870–1881* (Cape Town, 1966).

11. Worger, *City of Diamonds,* 114–15.

12. Ibid., 116.

13. Peter Richardson and Jean Jacques Van-Helten, "The Gold Mining Industry in the Transvaal, 1886–99," in *The South African War,* ed. Peter Warwick (Harlow, England, 1980), 18–36, and "Labour in the South African Gold Mining Industry, 1886–1914," in *Industrialization and Social Change in South Africa,* ed. Shula Marks and Richard Rathbone (New York, 1982); Sheila van der Horst, *Native Labour in South Africa* (London, 1942); Patrick Harries, *Work, Culture, and Identity: Migrant Laborers in Mozambique and South Africa, c. 1860–1910* (Portsmouth, N.H., and London, 1994).

14. Van Onselen, *Social and Economic History,* 1:xvi.

15. Paul Maylam, *A History of the African People of South Africa* (New York, 1986); Thompson, "Subjection."

16. Charles van Onselen, "Reactions to Rinderpest in Southern Africa, 1896–97," *Journal of African History* 13 (1972).

17. Jeff Guy, *The Destruction of the Zulu Kingdom* (London, 1979), and "The Destruction and Reconstruction of Zulu Society," in *Industrialization and Social Change;* C. W. de Kiewiet, *The Imperial Factor in South Africa* (Cambridge, 1937); D. M. Schreuder, *The Scramble for Southern Africa, 1877–1895* (Cambridge, 1980).

18. D. R. Morris, *The Washing of the Spears* (New York, 1964).

19. Thompson, "Subjection," 266.

20. Christopher Saunders, *The Annexation of the Transkeian Territories* (Archives Year Book for South African History, Pretoria, 1976), and "The Annexation of the Transkei," in *Beyond the Cape Frontier,* ed. Christopher Saunders and Robin Derricourt (London, 1974); William Beinart, *The Political Economy of Pondoland, 1860–1930* (Cambridge, 1982).

21. Beinart and Delius, "Introduction," in *Putting a Plough to the Ground.*

22. David Welsh, *The Roots of Segregation: Native Policy in Natal, 1845–1910* (Cape Town, 1971); W. R. Guest, *Langalibalele: The Crisis in Natal, 1873–1875* (Durban, 1976).

23. Neil Parsons, *A New History of Southern Africa* (London, 1982); William F. Lye and Colin Murray, *Transformations on the Highveld: The Tswana and Southern Sotho* (Cape Town, 1980); I. Schapera, *Tribal Innovators: Tswana Chiefs and Social Change, 1795–1940* (London, 1970).

24. Lye and Murray, *Transformations*, 73.

25. S. B. Burman, *Chiefdom Politics and Alien Law: Basutoland under Cape Rule, 1871–1884* (London, 1981); *Transformations on the Highveld.*

26. Peter Delius, *The Land Belongs to Us: The Pedi Polity, the Boers and the British in the Nineteenth-Century Transvaal* (Berkeley and Los Angeles, 1983).

27. P. Bonner, *Kings, Commoners and Concessionaires* (Cambridge, 1983).

28. The interesting history of the Bavenda and their resistance to conquest has not been adequately told.

29. Colin Murray, *Families Divided: The Impact of Migrant Labour in Lesotho* (Cambridge, 1981); Eldredge, *South African Kingdoms.*

30. Timothy Keegan, *Rural Transformations in Industrializing South Africa: The Southern Highveld to 1914* (Braamfontein, S.A., 1986); Bundy, *South African Peasantry;* Beinart, Delius, and Trapido, eds., *Putting a Plough to the Ground.*

31. De Kiewiet, *Imperial Factor;* Schreuder, *Scramble;* Thompson, "Great Britain and the Afrikaner Republics."

32. F. A. van Jaarsveld, *The Awakening of Afrikaner Nationalism, 1868–1881,* trans. F. R. Metrowich (Cape Town, 1961), and *The Afrikaner's Interpretation of South African History* (Cape Town, 1964); T. Dunbar Moodie, *The Rise of Afrikanerdom* (Berkeley and Los Angeles, 1975); Leonard Thompson, *The Political Mythology of Apartheid* (New Haven and London, 1985).

33. T. R. H. Davenport, *The Afrikaner Bond, 1880–1911* (Cape Town, 1966).

34. J. P. Fitzpatrick, *The Transvaal from Within* (London, 1900), is a contemporary and Boer polemic. Modern scholarly works on the Uitlanders include van Onselen, *Studies,* chap. 1; Wheatcroft, *Randlords;* and G. Blainey, "Lost Causes of the Jameson Raid," *Economic History Review,* 2d ser., 18 (1965): 350–66.

35. D. W. Kruger, *Paul Kruger,* 2 vols. (Johannesburg, 1961, 1963). Quotation from Thompson, *Political Mythology,* 32.

36. See n. 34; also Maryna Fraser and Alan Jeeves, ed., *All That Glittered: Selected Correspondence of Lionel Phillips, 1890–1924* (Cape Town, 1977); A. H. Duminy and W. R. Guest, *Fitzpatrick, South African Politician: Selected Papers, 1888–1906* (Johannesburg, 1976). Quotation from Shula Marks, "Scrambling for South Africa," *Journal of African History* 23:1 (1982): 109.

37. P. Mason, *The Birth of a Dilemma: The Conquest of Settlement of Rhodesia* (London, 1958); T. O. Ranger, *Revolt in Southern Rhodesia, 1896–7* (London, 1967); Davidson, *Cecil Rhodes;* Rotberg, *Cecil Rhodes.*

38. N. G. Garson, "The Swaziland Question and the Road to the Sea (1887–1895)," *Archives Year Book for South African History* (1957), vol. 2.

39. Jeffrey Butler, "The German Factor in Anglo-Transvaal Relations," and Wm. Roger Louis, "Great Britain and German Expansion in Africa, 1884–1919," in *Britain and Germany in Africa,* ed. Prosser Gifford and Wm. Roger Louis (New Haven and London, 1967).

40. J. L. Garvin, *The Life of Joseph Chamberlain,* vols. 1–3 (London, 1933–34); Andrew Porter, "In Memoriam Joseph Chamberlain," *Journal of Imperial and Commonwealth History* 3:2 (1986): 291–97.

41. Jean van der Poel, *The Jameson Raid* (Cape Town, 1951); Jeffrey Butler, *The Liberal Party and the Jameson Raid* (Oxford, 1968).

42. Lord Milner, *The Nation and the Empire* (London, 1913); C. Headlam, ed., *The Milner Papers,* 2 vols. (London, 1931, 1933); Eric Stokes, "'Milnerism,'" *Historical Journal* 5 (1962): 47–60; Shula Marks and Stanley Trapido, "Lord Milner and the South African State," *History Workshop Journal* 8 (1979): 50–80.

43. Phyllis Lewsen, *John X. Merriman: Paradoxical South African Statesman* (New Haven and London, 1982).

44. *Milner Papers,* 1:349–53.

45. W. K. Hancock, *Smuts: The Sanguine Years* (Cambridge, 1962); Kenneth Ingham, *Jan Christian Smuts* (London, 1986).

46. Debate on the origins of the war in 1899 started with the economic interpretation of Hobson and still continues. Besides works listed in previous footnotes, see: J. A. Hobson, *The War in South Africa: Its Causes and Effects* (London, 1900), and *Imperialism: A Study;* Ronald Robinson and Jack Gallagher, *Africa and the Victorians: The Official Mind of Imperialism* (London, 1961); J. S. Marais, *The Fall of Kruger's Republic* (Oxford, 1961); G. H. L. Le May, *British Supremacy in South Africa, 1899–1907* (Oxford, 1965); A. Atmore and S. Marks, "The Imperial Factor in South Africa: Toward a Reassessment," *Journal of Imperial and Commonwealth History* 3 (October 1974): 105–39; Robert V. Kubicek, *Economic Imperialism in Theory and Practice* (Durham, N.C., 1979); Andrew Porter, *The Origins of the South African War* (Manchester, 1980); and Bernard Porter, *Britain, Europe and the World, 1850–1982* (London, 1983).

47. Two works stand out from the mass of publications on the South African War: Thomas Pakenham, *The Boer War* (New York, 1979), and Peter Warwick, ed., *The South African War* (London, 1980).

48. Warwick, *Black People and the South African War, 1899–1902* (Cambridge, 1983), 4–5.

49. Milner, *Nation and Empire;* Marks and Trapido, "Lord Milner."

50. G. W. Eybers, *Select Constitutional Documents Illustrating South African History, 1795–1910* (London, 1918), 345–47.

51. Ibid.

52. Milner to Sir Percy Fitzpatrick, Nov. 28, 1899, *Milner Papers,* 2:35–36.

53. Warwick, *Black People,* 163–84; Peter Richardson, *Chinese Mind Labour in the Transvaal* (London, 1982); Jeremy Krikler, *Revolution from Above, Rebellion from Below: The Agrarian Transvaal at the Turn of the Century* (Oxford, 1993).

54. See note 32.

55. Bernard Porter, *The Lion's Share: A Short History of British Imperialism, 1850–1970* (London and New York, 1975), 206–7. On British policy toward South Africa in this period, see also Ronald Hyam, "The Myth of the 'Magnanimous gesture': The Liberal Government, Smuts and Conciliation, 1906," in *Reappraisals in British Imperial History,* ed. Ronald Hyam and Ged Martin (Toronto, 1975), 167–86, and A. E. Atmore, "The Extra-European Foundations of British Imperialism: Towards a Reassessment," in *British Imperialism in the Nineteenth Century,* ed. C. E. Eldridge (London, 1984), 106–25. On collaboration, see Ronald Robinson, "Non-European Foundations of European Imperialism: Sketch for a Theory of Collaboration," in *Theory of Imperialism,* ed. E. R. J. Owen and R. B. Sutcliffe (London, 1972).

56. Hyam, "Myth," 176.

57. Thompson, in *Oxford History of South Africa,* 2:339–43.

58. R. J. Hammond, *Portugal and Africa, 1815–1910* (Stanford, Calif., 1966); Jean van der Poel, *Railway and Customs Policies in South Africa, 1885–1910* (London, 1933).

59. Shula Marks, *Reluctant Rebellion: The 1906–1908 Disturbances in Natal* (Oxford, 1970).

60. *Parliamentary Papers,* Cd. 3564, *Papers relating to a Federation of the South African Colonies.*

61. Leonard Thompson, *The Unification of South Africa, 1902–1910* (Oxford, 1960).

62. Thompson, *Unification,* 109–10.

63. André Odendaal, *Vukani Bantu! The Beginnings of Black Protest Politics in South Africa to 1912* (Cape Town, 1984).

64. Parliamentary Debates (Commons), 5th ser. vol. 9 (1909), col. 1010.

Chapter 5: The Segregation Era

1. Union of South Africa, *Union Statistics for Fifty Years, 1910–1960* (Pretoria, 1960), G3, H23.

2. Merle Lipton, *Capitalism and Apartheid* (Totowa, N.J., 1985), 380.

3. Heribert Adam and Hermann Giliomee, *Ethnic Power Mobilized: Can South Africa Change?* (New Haven and London, 1979).

4. William Beinart, Peter Delius, and Stanley Trapido, *Putting a Plough to the Ground* (Johannesburg, 1986); John Cell, *The Highest Stage of White Supremacy: The Origins of Segregation in South Africa and the American South* (Cambridge, 1982); George Fredrickson, *White Supremacy: A Comparative Study in American and South African History* (New York, 1981).

5. Lipton, *Capitalism and Apartheid*, 387–88; Francis Wilson, *Labour in the South African Gold Mines* (Cambridge, 1972).

6. Adam and Giliomee, *Ethnic Power*, 173.

7. *Union Statistics for Fifty Years*, A27, A29; Richard Elphick, "Mission Christianity and Interwar Liberalism," in *Democratic Liberalism in South Africa: Its History and Prospect*, ed. Jeffrey Butler, Richard Elphick, and David Welsh (Middletown, Conn., 1987), 64–80.

8. André Odendaal, *Vukani Bantu! The Beginnings of Black Protest Politics in South Africa to 1912* (Cape Town, 1984); A. P. Walshe, *The Rise of African Nationalism in South Africa: The African National Congress, 1912–52* (London, 1970); Tom Lodge, *Black Politics in South Africa since 1945* (London and New York, 1983); George Fredrickson, *Black Liberation: A Comparative History of Black Ideologies in the United States and South Africa* (New York, 1995).

9. Helen Bradford, *A Taste of Freedom: The ICU in Rural South Africa, 1924–1930* (New Haven and London, 1987); William Beinart and Colin Bundy, *Hidden Struggles in Rural South Africa* (London, 1987).

10. Eddie Webster, ed., *Essays in Southern African Labour History* (Johannesburg, 1978).

11. Bengt Sundkler, *Bantu Prophets in South Africa*, 2d ed. (London, 1961).

12. T. R. H. Davenport, *South Africa: A Modern History*, 4th ed. (London, 1991), 293–324.

13. Davenport gives a full account of white politics in *South Africa*. See also Adam and Giliomee, *Ethnic Power*, and Hermann Giliomee, "Afrikaner Nationalism, 1870–2001," in *A Question of Survival*, ed. Alan Fischer and Michel Albeldas (Johannesburg, 1987).

14. W. K. Hancock, *Smuts: The Sanguine Years*, and *Smuts: The Fields of Force* (Cambridge, 1962, 1968); Kenneth Ingham, *Jan Christian Smuts: The Conscience of a South African* (London, 1986).

15. William Beinart provided substantial advice on this subject. Webster, ed., *Labour History*; Lipton, *Capitalism and Apartheid*; F. A. Johnstone, *Class, Race and Gold* (London, 1976).

16. G. Dekker, *Afrikaanse Literatuurgeskiedenis*, 7th ed. (Cape Town, 1963); E. C. Pienaar, *Die triomf van Afrikaans* (Cape Town, 1943).

17. In his autobiography, D. F. Malan devoted a 39-page chapter to the "Vlagstryd" (flag battle): *Afrikaner volkseenheid* (Johannesburg, 1959), 102–40.

18. K. C. Wheare, *The Statute of Westminster and Dominion Status*, 4th ed. (Oxford, 1949).

19. Margery Perham and Lionel Curtis, *The Protectorates of South Africa: The Question of Their Transfer to the Union* (London, 1935).

20. See note 14, above.

21. C. M. Tatz, *Shadow and Substance in South Africa* (Pietermaritzburg, 1962).

22. Phyllis Lewsen, "Liberals in Politics and Administration, 1936–1948," in *Democratic Liberalism in South Africa*, 98–115, and *Voices of Protest from Segregation to Apartheid, 1938–1948* (Craighall, S.A., 1988).

23. Leonard Thompson, *The Political Mythology of Apartheid* (New Haven and London, 1985), 186. See also J. H. P. Serfontein, *Brotherhood of Power* (London, 1979), and T. Dunbar Moodie, *The Rise of Afrikanerdom: Power, Apartheid, and the Afrikaner Civil Religion* (Berkeley and Los Angeles, 1975).

24. Note 14, above; also N. Mansergh, *Survey of Commonwealth Affairs, 1931–59: Problems of External Policy* (London, 1952).

25. Goran Hyden, *Beyond Ujamaa in Tanzania: Underdevelopment and an Uncaptured Peasantry* (Berkeley and Los Angeles, 1980), describes the phenomenon of an uncaptured peasantry in Tanzania.

26. There is a growing literature on rural history in South Africa. Besides Beinart et al., *Plough to the Ground* and *Hidden Struggles*, and Lipton, *Capitalism and Apartheid*, see Colin Bundy, *The Rise and Fall of South African Peasantry* (London, 1979); Monica Wilson, "The Growth of Peasant Communities," and Francis Wilson, "Farming, 1866–1966," in *The Oxford History of South Africa*, ed. Monica Wilson and Leonard Thompson, 2 vols. (Oxford, 1969, 1971), 2:49–171; Stanley Greenberg, *Race and State in Capitalist Development: Comparative Perspectives* (New Haven and London, 1980); Timothy J. Keegan, *Rural Transformations in Industrializing South Africa* (Braamfontein, S.A., 1986), which focuses on the Orange Free State area; Krikler, *Revolution from Above*, which focuses on the Transvaal; and Michael K. Robertson, "Segregation Land Law: A Socio-Legal Analysis," in *Essays on Law and Social Practice in South Africa*, ed. Hugh Corder (Cape Town, 1985), 285–317, which focuses on the Natives Land Act of 1913.

27. Union of South Africa, *Report of the Natives Land Commission, U.G. 22, 1916*, 2 vols. (Cape Town, 1916).

28. Union of South Africa, Social and Economic Planning Council, Report No. 9, *The Native Reserves and Their Place in the Economy of the Union of South Africa, U.G. 32, 1946* (Pretoria, 1946), 9.

29. Union of South Africa, *Report of the Native Economic Commission, 1930–1932, U.G. 22, 1932* (Pretoria, 1932), 224–28.

30. Bundy, *Rise and Fall*, chap. 8.

31. Muriel Horrell, *African Education: Some Origins, and Development until 1953* (Johannesburg, 1963).

32. Union of South Africa, *Commission for the Socio-Economic Development of the Bantu Areas within the Union of South Africa: Summary of the Report, U.G. 61, 1955* (Pretoria, 1955) (known as the Tomlinson Report), 53–55; Colin Murray, *Families Divided: The Impact of Migrant Labour in Lesotho* (Johannesburg, 1981); Les Switzer, *Power and Resistance in an African Society: The Ciskei Xhosa and the Making of South Africa* (Madison, Wis., 1993).

33. See notes 26, 28, above.

34. Sol. T. Plaatje, *Native Life in South Africa* (London, 1916; reprint, New York, 1969), 13–14. See also Brian Willan, *Sol Plaatje: South African Nationalist, 1876–1932* (Berkeley and Los Angeles, 1984).

35. Lipton, *Capitalism and Apartheid,* 85–92.

36. *Union Statistics for Fifty Years,* 122.

37. Lipton, *Capitalism and Apartheid,* 280; Union of South Africa, *Third Interim Report of the Industrial and Agricultural Requirements Commission, U.G. 40, 1941* (Pretoria, 1941), 35, 80.

38. Lipton, *Capitalism and Apartheid,* 379; Union of South Africa, *Report of the Native Laws Commission, 1946–48, U.G. 28, 1948* (Pretoria, 1948) (known as the Fagan Report), 10.

39. *Natives Land Commission, 1932,* 105–8, 228; *Native Laws Commission, 1948,* 25–33, 64–73; Francis Wilson, *Migrant Labour in South Africa* (Johannesburg, 1972), 233.

40. Sheila T. van der Horst, *Native Labour in South Africa* (London, 1942); Francis Wilson, *Labour in the South African Gold Mines, 1911–1969* (Cambridge, 1972); T. Dunbar Moodie with Vivienne Ndatshe, *Going for Gold: Men, Mines, and Migration* (Berkeley, 1994).

41. Wilson, *Labour in the Gold Mines,* 45–67.

42. Lipton, *Capitalism and Apartheid,* 256–364.

43. *Industrial and Agricultural Commission, 1941,* 42.

44. *Native Economic Commission, 1932,* 141–57.

45. Ibid., 80–103.

46. Lipton, *Capitalism and Apartheid,* 387.

47. *Industrial and Agricultural Commission, 1941,* 42.

48. Union of South Africa, *Report of the Industrial Legislation Commission, U.G. 37, 1935* (Pretoria, 1935), 141–57.

49. Ibid., 80–103.

50. Lipton, *Capitalism and Apartheid,* 387.

51. *Industrial and Agricultural Commission, 1941,* 42.

52. *Native Economic Commission, 1932,* 105–9, 228, 279–84.

53. Kenneth Grundy, *Soldiers without Politics: Blacks in the South African Armed Forces,* 48–62.

54. Fatima Meer, *Portrait of Indian South Africans* (Durban, 1969); Bridglal Pachai, ed., *South Africa's Indians: The Evolution of a Minority* (Washington, D.C., 1979); Surendra Bhana and Bridglal Pachai, eds., *A Documentary History of Indian South Africans* (Cape Town, 1984); Geoffrey Ashe, *Gandhi: A Study in Revolution* (New York, 1968); E. Erikson, *Gandhi's Truth: On the Origins of Militant Nonviolence* (London, 1970).

55. J. S. Marais, *The Cape Coloured People, 1652–1937* (Johannesburg, 1939; reprint, 1962); Union of South Africa, *Report of the Commission of Inquiry regarding the Cape Coloured Population of the Union, U.G. 54, 1937* (Pretoria, 1937); H. F. Dickie-Clark, *The Marginal Situation: A Sociological Study of a Coloured Group* (London, 1966); R. E. van der Ross, *The Rise and*

Decline of Apartheid: A Study of Political Movements among the Coloured People of South Africa, 1880–1985 (Cape Town, 1986); Roy H. Du Pre, *Separate but Unequal: The "Coloured People" of South Africa—A Political History* (Johannesburg, 1994).

56. Shula Marks, *The Ambiguities of Dependence in Southern Africa: Class, Nationalism, and the State in Twentieth-Century Natal* (Baltimore and London, 1986).

57. Richard Elphick, "Mission Christianity and Interwar Liberalism," in *Democratic Liberalism in South Africa*, 64–80.

58. Union of South Africa, *Report of the Interdepartmental Committee on Native Education, 1935–1936, U.G. 29, 1936* (Pretoria, 1936), 142. Standards 1 to 10 correspond with American grades 3 to 12.

59. Z. K. Matthews, *Freedom for My People* (London and Cape Town, 1981), quotation on 58–59. See also Thompson, *Political Mythology*.

60. Bradford, *Taste of Freedom*, 1.

61. Here I have adapted William Beinart and Colin Bundy's analysis in "Introduction: 'Away in the Locations,' " *Hidden Struggles*, 11–12.

62. Beinart and Bundy, *Hidden Struggles*, 35.

63. On black politics in this period, see notes 8, 9, 54, and 55, above, and *From Protest to Challenge: A Documentary History of African Politics in South Africa, 1882–1964*, ed. Thomas Karis and Gwendolen M. Carter, 4 vols. (Stanford, Calif., 1972–77); Edward Roux, *Time Longer than Rope: A History of the Black Man's Struggle for Freedom in South Africa* (London, 1948); H. J. and R. E. Simons, *Class and Colour in South Africa, 1850–1950* (Baltimore, 1969); I. B. Tabata, *The All African Convention: The Awakening of a People* (Johannesburg, 1950).

64. Odendaal, *Vukani Bantu!*, 273; Walshe, *African Nationalism*, 34.

65. Odendaal, *Vukani Bantu!*, 274–75.

66. Notes 54, 55, above.

67. Bradford, *Taste of Freedom*.

68. Ibid., 214–16.

69. Ibid., 273. But see Beinart and Bundy, *Hidden Struggles*, which puts less emphasis on betrayal by the leaders.

70. Bradford, *Taste of Freedom*, 274.

71. Simons, *Class and Colour*; Roux, *Time Longer than Rope*; Lerumo [Michael Harmel], *Fifty Fighting Years: The Communist Party of South Africa, 1921–1971* (London, 1971); Naboth Mokgatle, *The Autobiography of an Unknown South African* (Berkeley and Los Angeles, 1971).

72. Grundy, *Soldiers without Politics*, 63–89.

73. Raymond Dummett, "Africa's Strategic Minerals during the Second World War," *Journal of African History* 26:4 (1985); 381–408; Nancy L. Clark, *Manufacturing Apartheid: State Corporations in South Africa* (New Haven and London, 1994).

74. *Union Statistics for Fifty Years*, G5, K4, L10.

75. Ibid., G5, G11; Republic of South Africa, *South Africa, 1983: Official Yearbook of the Republic* (Johannesburg, 1983), 32.

76. Discussion in *Native Laws Commission, 1948,* 4–14.

77. A. W. Stadler, "Birds in the Cornfield: Squatter Movements in Johannesburg, 1944–1947," *Journal of Southern African Studies* 6:1 (1979): 93–123, quotation on 93.

78. Peter Abrahams, *Mine Boy* (1946; reprint, London, 1963), 75–76.

79. Union of South Africa, *The Economic and Social Conditions of the Racial Groups in South Africa: Social and Economic Planning Council Report No. 13, U.G. 53–1948* (Pretoria, 1948), 25.

80. Tom Lodge, *Black Politics in South Africa since 1945* (London and New York, 1983), 18.

81. Ibid., 13–16.

82. Ibid., 17–20; Wilson, *Labour in the Gold Mines,* 77–80, quotation on 79; T. Dunbar Moodie, "The Moral Economy of the Black Miners' Strike of 1946," *Journal of Southern African Studies* 13:1 (1986): 1–35.

83. E. S. Sachs, *Rebels' Daughters* (London, 1957); Iris Berger, "Solidarity Fragmented: Garment Workers of the Transvaal, 1930–1960," in *The Politics of Race, Class and Nationalism in Twentieth-Century South Africa,* ed. Shula Marks and Stanley Trapido (London, 1987), 124–55. See also John Lewis, *Industrialization and Trade Union Organization in South Africa, 1924–55: The Rise and Fall of the South African Trades and Labour Council* (Cambridge, 1984), and Webster, ed., *Labour History.*

84. Lipton, *Capitalism and Apartheid,* 21.

85. Phyllis Lewsen, "Liberals in Politics and Administration," in *Democratic Liberalism in South Africa,* 105.

86. *Native Reserves, 1946,* 47.

87. See note 76, above.

88. Lewsen, *Voices of Protest,* 15–62, and "Liberals in Politics and Administration."

89. Ingham, *Smuts,* 218. See also Hancock, *Smuts* (2 vols.).

90. Lewsen, *Voices of Protest,* 23. See also Alan Paton, *Hofmeyr* (London, 1964).

91. Walshe, *African Nationalism,* 271–76.

92. Ibid., 283.

93. Z. K. Matthews, *Freedom for My People* (London and Cape Town, 1981), 148.

94. Ibid., 150.

95. Dan O'Meara, *Volkskapitalisme: Class, Capital and Ideology in the Development of Afrikaner Nationalism, 1934–1948* (Cambridge, 1983), 221; Adam and Giliomee, *Ethnic Power,* 175.

96. J. Albert Coetzee, "Republikanisme in die Kaapkolonie," in *Ons republiek,* ed. J. Albert Coetzee, P. Meyer, and N. Diederichs (Bloemfontein, 1942), 104.

97. G. Eloff, *Rasse en rasvermenging* (Bloemfontein, 1941), 104.

98. Newell Stultz, *Afrikaner Politics in South Africa, 1934–1948* (Berkeley and Los Angeles, 1974); Patrick J. Furlong, *Between Crown and Swastika: The Impact of the Radical Right on the Afrikaner Nationalist Movement in the Fascist Era* (Hanover, N.H., 1991).

99. On the background to the election of 1948, see O'Meara, *Volkskapitalisme;* Adam and Giliomee, *Ethnic Power;* Stultz, *Afrikaner Politics;* Moodie, *Rise of Afrikanerdom.*

100. O'Meara, *Volkskapitalisme.*

101. G. Cronje, *'n Tuiste vir die nageslag* (Cape Town, 1945), 79.

102. Deborah Posel, "The Meaning of Apartheid before 1948: Conflicting Interests and Forces within the Afrikaner Nationalist Alliance," *Journal of Southern African Studies* 14:1 (1987): 123–39.

103. Davenport, *South Africa,* 323.

104. *National News,* May 19, 1948.

105. *Rand Daily Mail,* June 2, 1948.

Chapter 6: The Apartheid Era

1. White politics in the apartheid era are considered fully in T. R. H. Davenport, *South Africa: A Modern History,* 3d ed. (Toronto and Buffalo, N.Y., 1987). See also Philip Bonner, Peter Delius, and Deborah Posel, eds., *Apartheid's Genesis, 1935–1962* (Johannesburg, 1993); Hermann Giliomee and Lawrence Schlemmer, *From Apartheid to Nation-Building* (Cape Town, 1989), Part 1, "Apartheid and Its Reforms"; and Deborah Posel, *The Making of Apartheid, 1948–1961: Conflict and Compromise* (Oxford, 1991).

2. Heribert Adam and Hermann Giliomee, *Ethnic Power Mobilized: Can South Africa Change?* (New Haven and London, 1979), 174.

3. Jill Nattrass, *The South African Economy* (Cape Town, 1981), 25.

4. G. D. Scholtz, *Dr. Hendrik Frensch Verwoerd, 1901–66,* 2 vols. (Johannesburg, 1974); Henry Kenney, *Architect of Apartheid: H. F. Verwoerd—An appraisal* (Johannesburg, 1980).

5. Heribert Adam, *Modernizing Racial Domination* (Berkeley and Los Angeles, 1971); Roger Omond, *The Apartheid Handbook* (Harmondsworth, 1985); Study Commission on U.S. Policy toward South Africa, *South Africa: Time Running Out* (Berkeley and Los Angeles, 1981); Leonard Thompson and Andrew Prior, *South African Politics* (New Haven and London, 1982).

6. Thompson and Prior, *South African Politics,* 83–88.

7. Study Commission on U.S. Policy, *Time Running Out,* 147–67.

8. Roger Southall, "Buthelezi, Inkatha and the Politics of Compromise," *African Affairs* 80 (1981): 453–81.

9. Laurine Platzky and Cherryl Walker, *The Surplus People: Forced Removals in South Africa* (Johannesburg, 1985), 65.

10. Omond, *Apartheid Handbook,* 109.

11. Platzky and Walker, *Surplus People*, 17–18. See also Colin Murray, "Displaced Urbanization: South Africa's Rural Slums," *African Affairs* 86 (1987): 311–29.

12. Tom Lodge, *Black Politics in South Africa since 1945* (London, 1983), 91–113; *Time Running Out*, 57–59, 63–65.

13. Platzky and Walker, *Surplus People*, 128.

14. Ibid., 10.

15. See Appendix.

16. Ibid.

17. Study Commission on U.S. Policy, *Time Running Out*, 144.

18. Omond, *Apartheid Handbook*, 80.

19. South African Institute of Race Relations, *Survey of Race Relations in South Africa, 1980* (Johannesburg, 1981), 458–500; Mokubung Nkomo, ed., *Pedagogy of Domination: Toward a Democratic Education in South Africa* (Trenton, N.J., 1990).

20. Hendrik W. van der Merwe and David Welsh, eds., *The Future of the University in South Africa* (Cape Town, 1977).

21. South African Institute of Race Relations, *Survey of Race Relations in South Africa, 1978* (Johannesburg, 1979), 451.

22. J. Kane-Berman, *Sport: Multi-Nationalism versus Non-Racialism* (Johannesburg, 1972).

23. Alan Paton, *Apartheid and the Archbishop* (Cape Town, 1973).

24. John C. Laurence, *Race Propaganda and South Africa* (London, 1979); John M. Phelan, *Apartheid Media* (Westport, 1987); *Survey of Race Relations, 1978,* 128.

25. Leonard Thompson, *The Political Mythology of Apartheid* (New Haven and London, 1985).

26. Muriel Horrell, *Laws Affecting Race Relations in South Africa, 1948–1976* (Johannesburg, 1978); A. S. Mathews, *Law, Order, and Liberty in South Africa* (Berkeley and Los Angeles, 1972); Albie Sachs, *Justice in South Africa* (Berkeley and Los Angeles, 1973); John Dugard, *Human Rights and the South African Legal Order* (Princeton, 1978).

27. Adam and Giliomee, *Ethnic Power*, 166.

28. J. D. Brewer et al., *The Police, Public Order and the State* (London, 1988).

29. Kenneth W. Grundy, *Soldiers without Politics* (Berkeley and Los Angeles, 1983), and *The Militarization of South African Politics* (London, 1986); Gavin Cawthra, *Brutal Force: The Apartheid War Machine* (London, 1986); Lynn Berat, "Conscientious Objection in South Africa: Governmental Paranoia and the Law of Conscription," *Vanderbilt University Journal of Transnational Law* 22 (1989): 127–86.

30. Television started in South Africa in 1976. The 1977 annual report of the SABC stated that the television service "made the point of stressing the need for spiritual, economic and military preparedness" (*Survey of Race Relations, 1978,*

135). John M. Phelan, *Apartheid Media: Disinformation and Dissent in South Africa* (Westport, Conn., 1987).

31. On social conditions under apartheid in the African townships, see the works of African novelists, such as Ezekiel Mphahlele, *Down Second Avenue* (Johannesburg, 1959), Miriam Tlali, *Amandla* (Johannesburg, 1980), Mongane Serote, *To Every Birth Its Blood* (Johannesburg, 1981), Mbulelo Mzamane, *The Children of Soweto* (Johannesburg, 1982), and Njabulo Ndebele, *Fools and Other Stories* (Johannesburg, 1983). See also Joseph Lelyveld, *Move Your Shadow: South Africa, Black and White* (New York, 1985), and Robin Cohen et al., eds., *Repression and Resistance: Insider Accounts of Apartheid* (London and New York, 1990).

32. Helen Bernstein, *For Their Triumphs and Their Tears: Women in Apartheid South Africa* (London, 1983); Iris Berger, "Sources of Class Consciousness: South African Women in Recent Labour Struggles," *International Journal of African Historical Studies* 16:1 (1983): 49–66; Elaine Unterhalter, "Class, Race and Gender," in *South Africa in Question,* ed. John Lonsdale (Cambridge, 1988), 154–71; Diana E. H. Russell, *Lives of Courage: Women for a New South Africa* (New York, 1989); Lindiwe Guma, "Women, Wage Labour and National Liberation," in *Repression and Resistance,* 272–84.

33. Francis Wilson and Mamphela Ramphele, "Children in South Africa," in *Children on the Front Line* (New York, 1987), 52. See also Sandra Burman and Pamela Reynolds, eds., *Growing up in a Divided Society: The Contexts of Childhood in South Africa* (Johannesburg, 1986); Mamphela Ramphele, *A Bed Called Home: Life in the Migrant Labour Hostels of Cape Town* (Cape Town and Athens, Ohio, 1993); and Sean Jones, *Assaulting Childhood: Children's Experiences of Migrancy and Hostel Life in South Africa* (Johannesburg, 1993).

34. *Survey of Race Relations in South Africa, 1980,* 85.

35. Francis Wilson and Mamphela Ramphele, *Uprooting Poverty: The South African Challenge* (New York and London, 1989).

36. Wilson and Ramphele, "Hunger and Sickness," in *Uprooting Poverty,* 99–185; Aziza Seedat, *Crippling a Nation: Health in Apartheid South Africa* (London, 1984), 9, 87. See also S. R. Benatar, "Medicine and Health Care in South Africa," *New England Journal of Medicine* 315:8 (1986): 527–32; Mervyn Sussner and Violet Padayachi Cherry, "Health and Health Care under Apartheid," *Journal of Public Health Policy* 3:4 (1982): 455–75; Shula Marks and Neil Anderson, "Diseases of Apartheid," in *South Africa in Question,* 172–99; World Health Organization, *Health and Apartheid* (Geneva, 1983); H. M. Coovadia and C. C. Jinabhai, "The Pestilence of Health Care: Black Death and Suffering under White Rule," in *Repression and Resistance,* 86–116.

37. Seedat, *Crippling a Nation,* 9, 25–26. Official health statistics in South Africa, especially for Africans, are incomplete and often suspect. Wilson and Ramphele give the following average infant mortality rates for South Africa in 1978: White 23, Asian 41, Coloured 139, African 136 ("Children in South Africa," 43). Benatar gives the following infant mortality rates for South Africa in

an unspecified year: White 17, Asian 25, Coloured 65, African 95 (Benatar, "Medicine and Health Care," 530).

38. Seedat, *Crippling a Nation,* 31–48.

39. Ibid., 60.

40. Ibid., 10.

41. Thompson and Prior, *South African Politics,* 187–92.

42. John de Gruchy, *The Church Struggle in South Africa* (Grand Rapids, Mich., 1979).

43. "The Koinonia Declaration," *Journal of Theology for Southern Africa* (September 1978).

44. Van der Merwe and Welsh, *Future of the University; Survey of Race Relations, 1978.*

45. Cherry Michelson, *The Black Sash of South Africa: A Case Study in Liberalism* (London, 1975).

46. Paton, *The People Wept* (Kloof, Natal, 1958), 44.

47. Philip V. Tobias, *The Meaning of Race* (Johannesburg, 1961), 22.

48. Joanne Strangwayes-Booth, *A Cricket in the Thorn Tree: Helen Suzman and the Progressive Party in South Africa* (Bloomington, Ind., 1976).

49. William Minter, *King Solomon's Mines Revisited: Western Interests and the Burdened History of Southern Africa* (New York, 1986), is representative of the "blame capitalism" school; W. H. Hutt, *The Economics of the Colour Bar* (London, 1964), and Michael O'Dowd, "South Africa in the Light of the Stages of Economic Growth," in *South Africa: Economic Growth and Political Change,* ed. Adrian Leftwich (London, 1974), 29–43, represent the "Leave it to capitalism" school.

50. David Pallister, Sarah Stewart, and Ian Lepper, *South Africa, Inc.: The Oppenheimer Empire* (New Haven and London, 1987), 93.

51. Merle Lipton contends that the growth of the South African economy increased the costs of the constraints and inefficiencies inherent in apartheid, pushing businessmen toward reform (*Capitalism and Apartheid* [Totowa, N.J., 1985]). Stanley Greenberg argues that businessmen "managed to find the silver lining" in apartheid and reconciled themselves to its costs until "the African population has called the prevailing hegemony into question" (*Race and State in Capitalist Development* [New Haven and London, 1980] 208). Andrew Torchia reconciles the two positions ("The Business of Business: An Analysis of the Political Behavior of the South African Manufacturing Sector under the Nationalists," *Journal of Southern African Studies* 14:3 [1988]: 421–45).

52. Leo Kuper, *An African Bourgeoisie: Race, Class, and Politics in South Africa* (New Haven and London, 1965).

53. Tom Lodge, *Black Politics in South Africa since 1945* (New York, 1983); Peter Walshe, *The Rise of African Nationalism in South Africa: The African National Congress, 1912–1952* (Berkeley and Los Angeles, 1971); Thomas Karis and Gwendolen M. Carter, general eds., *From Protest to Challenge: A Documentary History of African Politics in South Africa, 1882–1964,* 4 vols., vol. 4:

Political Profiles, ed. Gail M. Gerhart and Thomas Karis (Stanford, Calif., 1977). In the rest of this section, I draw heavily on Thompson and Prior, *South African Politics,* 192–204.

54. Leo Kuper, *Passive Resistance in South Africa* (London, 1956).

55. Lodge, *Black Politics,* 68–74; Karis and Carter, eds., *From Protest to Challenge,* vol. 3: *Challenge and Violence, 1953–1964,* ed. Thomas Karis and Gail M. Gerhart (Stanford, Calif., 1977), 56–69.

56. Karis and Gerhart, eds., *Challenge and Violence,* 205–8.

57. Julia C. Wells, "Why Women Rebel: A Comparative Study of South African Women's Resistance in Bloemfontein (1913) and Johannesburg (1958)," *Journal of Southern African Studies* 10:1 (1983): 55–70; Debbie Budlender, Sheila Meintjes, and Jenny Schreiner, "Women and Resistance in South Africa: Review Article," ibid., 131–35.

58. Lodge, *Black Politics,* 83.

59. Gail M. Gerhart, *Black Power in South Africa: The Evolution of an Ideology* (Berkeley and Los Angeles, 1978), 124–72.

60. Lodge, *Black Politics,* 201–30; Gerhart, *Black Power,* 173–251.

61. Karis and Gerhart, eds., *Challenge and Violence,* 776–77.

62. Cited in John D. Brewer, *After Soweto: An Unfinished Journey* (Oxford, 1986), 305.

63. Brewer, *After Soweto,* 157–68; Lodge, *Black Politics,* 326–28.

64. Steve Biko, *I Write What I Like,* ed. Aelred Stubbs (London, 1979), 49. See also Gerhart, *Black Power,* 257–99, and Anthony W. Marx, *Lessons of Struggle: South African Internal Opposition, 1960–1990* (New York, 1992).

65. Baruch Hirson, *Year of Fire, Year of Ash: The Soweto Revolt: Roots of a Revolution?* (London, 1979); Lynn Berat, "Doctors, Detainees, and Torture: Medical Ethics v. the Law in South Africa," *Stanford Journal of International Law,* 25: 2 (1989): 501.

66. Minter, *King Solomon's Mines Revisited;* Thompson and Prior, *South African Politics;* Prosser Gifford and Wm. Roger Louis, eds., *The Transfer of Power in Africa: Decolonization, 1940–1960* (New Haven and London, 1982), and *Decolonization and African Independence: The Transfer of Power, 1960–1980* (New Haven and London, 1988).

67. Robert C. Good, *The International Politics of the Rhodesian Rebellion* (Princeton, 1973); Elaine Windrich, *Britain and the Politics of Rhodesian Independence* (London, 1978).

68. Lord Hailey, *The Republic of South Africa and the High Commission Territories* (Oxford, 1963); James Barber, *South African Foreign Policy, 1945–1970* (Oxford, 1973).

69. Kenneth Maxwell, "Portugal and Africa: The Last Empire," in Gifford and Louis, eds., *Transfer of Power,* 337–85.

70. Taiwan initially occupied the China seat; in 1971, it was transferred to the People's Republic of China.

71. John Dugard, *The South West Africa/Namibia Dispute* (Berkeley, 1973);

A. W. Singham and Shirley Hune, *Namibian Independence: A Global Responsibility* (Westport, Conn., 1985); Lynn Berat, *Walvis Bay: Decolonization and International Law* (New Haven and London, 1990).

72. Joseph Hanlon, *Beggar Your Neighbours: Apartheid Power in Southern Africa* (Bloomington, Ind., 1986).

73. Cited in Eric H. Louw, *The Case for South Africa* (New York, 1963), 147.

74. Louw, *Case for South Africa*, 62–76; Barber, *Foreign Policy*, 53–54, 57–59, 80–82.

75. James Barber and John Barratt, *South Africa's Foreign Policy: The Search for Status and Security, 1945–1988* (Cambridge, 1990), 2.

76. *Time Running Out*, 323–39; Thomas G. Karis, "South African Liberation: The Communist Factor," *Foreign Affairs* 65:2 (Winter 1986/1987): 267–87.

77. *Time Running Out*, 310–22.

78. Ibid., 134–35. See also Lipton, *Capitalism and Apartheid*; Nattrass, *The South African Economy*; Barbara Rogers, *White Wealth and Black Poverty: American Investments in Southern Africa* (Westport, Conn., 1976); Desaix Myers et al., *U.S. Business in South Africa* (Bloomington, Ind., 1980); Ann Seidman and Neva Seidman Makgetla, *Outposts of Monopoly Capitalism: Southern Africa in the Changing Global Economy* (Westport, Conn., 1980); and Duncan Innes, *Anglo American and the Rise of Modern South Africa* (New York, 1984).

79. *Time Running Out*, 141–43. See also Nancy L. Clark, *Manufacturing Apartheid: State Corporations in South Africa* (New Haven and London, 1994), 160–62.

80. *Time Running Out*, 302–3. See also Minter, *King Solomon's Mines Revisited*, for notes 79–83.

81. *Time Running Out*, 303–6.

82. Ibid., 340–62; William Foltz, "United States Policy toward Southern Africa: Economic and Strategic Constraints," *Political Science Quarterly* 92:1 (1977): 47–64; Rogers, *White Wealth and Black Poverty*; Ann and Neva Seidman, *South Africa and U.S. Multinational Corporations* (Westport, Conn., 1977); U.S. Department of State, *A U.S. Policy toward South Africa: The Report of the U.S. Advisory Committee on South Africa* (Washington, D.C., 1987).

83. Mohamed A. El-Khawas and Barry Cohen, ed., *The Kissinger Study of Southern Africa: National Security Study Memorandum 39* (Westport, Conn., 1978), 105–6.

84. *Time Running Out*, 353.

Chapter 7: Apartheid in Crisis

1. South African Institute of Race Relations, *Survey of Race Relations in South Africa, 1978* (Johannesburg, 1979) (annual hereafter cited as *Race Relations Survey, 1978*, etc.). See also Stephen Gelb, ed., *South Africa's Economic*

Crisis (Cape Town, London, and Atlantic Highlands, N.J., 1991); N. Nattrass and E. Arlington, eds., *The Political Economy of South Africa* (Oxford, 1990); Shaun Johnson, ed., *South Africa: No Turning Back* (Bloomington, Ind., 1989); Robert M. Price, *The Apartheid State in Crisis: Political Transformation in South Africa, 1975–1990* (New York, 1991); R. Hunt Davis, Jr., ed., *Apartheid Unravels* (Gainesville, Fla., 1991).

2. John D. Brewer, *After Soweto: An Unfinished Journey* (Oxford, 1986); Stephen M. Davis, *Apartheid's Rebels: Inside South Africa's Hidden War* (New Haven and London, 1987); Martin Murray, *South Africa: Time of Agony, Time of Destiny; the Upsurge of Popular Protest* (London, 1987); Heribert Adam, "Survival Politics: Afrikaners in Search of a New Ideology," *Journal of Modern African Studies* 16:4 (1978): 657–69.

3. Leonard Thompson and Andrew Prior, *South African Politics* (New Haven and London, 1982), 220–43.

4. George M. Houser, *No One Can Stop the Rain: Glimpses of Africa's Liberation Struggle* (New York, 1989); Mildred Fierce, "Black and White American Opinions towards South Africa," *Journal of Modern African Studies* 20:4 (1982): 669–87.

5. Leonard Thompson, "The Parting of the Ways in South Africa," in *The Transfer of Power in Africa: Decolonization, 1940–1960,* ed. Prosser Gifford and Wm. Roger Louis (New Haven and London, 1982), 417–44.

6. Heribert Adam and Hermann Giliomee, *Ethnic Power Mobilized: Can South Africa Change?* (New Haven and London, 1979), 145–76.

7. *Race Relations Survey, 1978,* 3–5.

8. Dirk and Johanna de Villiers, *PW* (Cape Town, 1984); Kenneth Grundy, *The Militarization of South African Politics* (Bloomington, Ind., 1986); Philip Frankel, *Pretoria's Praetorians* (Cambridge, 1984); Gavin Cawthra, *Brutal Force: The Apartheid War Machine* (London, 1986); Heribert Adam and Kogila Moodley, *South Africa without Apartheid* (Berkeley and Los Angeles, 1986).

9. *Race Relations Survey, 1979,* 202–20, 274–85, 391–97.

10. *Race Relations Survey, 1986,* 231–90.

11. *Race Relations Survey, 1983,* 71–98; Murray, *Time of Agony,* 107–18.

12. *Race Relations Survey, 1984,* 127–28.

13. Cited in Michael Savage, "The Imposition of Pass Laws on the African Population in South Africa, 1916–1984," *African Affairs* 85 (April 1986), 205. See also Hermann Giliomee and Lawrence Schlemmer, ed., *Up against the Fences: Poverty, Passes and Privilege in South Africa* (Claremont, S.A., 1985).

14. *Race Relations Survey, 1986,* 331–48.

15. Ibid., 97–109.

16. Ibid., xx.

17. Ibid., 417.

18. Josette Cole, *Crossroads: The Politics of Reform and Repression, 1976–1986* (Johannesburg, 1987).

19. Brewer, *After Soweto;* Davis, *Apartheid's Rebels;* Murray, *Time of Agony.*

20. *Race Relations Survey, 1983,* 57–61.

21. Brewer, *After Soweto,* 216–99; Murray, *Time of Agony,* 195–238.

22. Murray, *Time of Agony,* 239–352.

23. John D. Brewer, "Internal Black Protest," in *Can South Africa Survive?: Five Minutes to Midnight,* ed. J. D. Brewer (London and New York, 1988); Cole, *Crossroads.*

24. John D. Brewer, "From Ancient Rome to KwaZulu: Inkatha in South African Politics," in *South Africa: No Turning Back,* ed. S. Johnson (London, 1988), and *After Soweto,* pp. 338–406; Davis, *Apartheid's Rebels,* 106–12; Murray, *Time of Agony,* 315–24.

25. David Pallister, Sarah Stewart, and Ian Lepper, *South Africa, Inc.: The Oppenheimer Empire* (New Haven and London, 1988); Joseph Hanlon, *Beggar Your Neighbours: Apartheid Power in Southern Africa* (Bloomington, Ind., 1986); Ronald T. Libby, *The Politics of Economic Power in Southern Africa* (Princeton, 1987); William Minter, *King Solomon's Mines Revisited: Western Interests and the Burdened History of Southern Africa* (New York, 1986).

26. Hanlon, *Beggar Your Neighbours.*

27. Crocker enunciated his South African policy before he came into office in "South Africa: Strategy for Change," *Foreign Affairs* (Winter 1980–81): 323–51. See also Chester A. Crocker, *High Noon in Southern Africa: Making Peace in a Rough Neighborhood* (New York, 1992).

28. The Commonwealth Group of Eminent Persons, *Mission to South Africa: The Commonwealth Report* (Harmondsworth, 1986).

29. Anthony Sampson, *Black and Gold: Tycoons, Revolutionaries, and Apartheid* (New York, 1987); Pauline Baker, *The United States and South Africa: The Reagan Years* (New York, 1989).

30. Cited in Baker, *United States and South Africa,* 25.

31. *Race Relations Survey, 1986,* 139–40, 144–45, 146–48.

32. *Race Relations Survey, 1983,* 3; *1984,* xix; *1985,* xxviii; *1986,* xxi.

33. *Race Relations Survey, 1986,* 830–45.

34. Lynn Berat, "Doctors, Detainees, and Torture: Medical Ethics v. the Law in South Africa," *Stanford Journal of International Law; The Times* (London), February 13, 1987, February 25, 1988; *Race Relations Survey, 1987–88,* 509–604.

35. *Race Relations Survey, 1987–88,* 813–49.

36. *Guardian* (London), May 11, 1988.

37. Ibid., February 2, 1989.

38. *Race Relations Survey, 1987–88,* xxxi.

39. *The Times,* June 23, 1988.

40. *Independent* (London), August 19, 1988.

41. *The Times,* October 28, 1988.

42. *Race Relations Survey, 1987–88,* 103–5.

43. *The Times,* October 28, 1988.

44. *Daily Telegraph* (London), February 2, 1988.

45. *Financial Times* (London), October 21, 1988.

46. *Staffrider* (Johannesburg), 7:3, 4 (1988).

47. *Star* (Johannesburg), September 14, 1988.

48. *Race Relations Survey, 1987–88,* 667–84.

49. *The Times,* July 1, 1988. See also F. Chikane, *The Church's Prophetic Witness against the Apartheid System in South Africa* (Johannesburg, 1988); J. de Gruchy, *The Church Struggle in South Africa* (Cape Town, 1979); and C. Villa-Vicenicio, ed., *Theology and Violence: The South African Debate* (Johannesburg, 1987).

50. *New York Times,* December 15, 1988; *Daily Telegraph,* December 23, 1988; *Herald Tribune,* January 8, 1989; Lynn Berat, *Walvis Bay: Decolonization and International Law* (New Haven and London, 1990).

Chapter 8: The Political Transition

1. The political transition is dealt with in the autobiographies of the leading actors, Nelson Mandela, *Long Walk to Freedom* (Boston, 1994), and F. W. de Klerk, *The Last Trek: A New Beginning (London, 1998);* and in two excellent biographies, Martin Meredith, *Nelson Mandela: A Biography* (New York, 1997), and Anthony Sampson, *Mandela: The Authorized Biography* (New York, 1999); also in accounts by journalists—David Ottaway, *Chained Together: Mandela, de Klerk, and the Struggle to Remake South Africa* (New York, 1993); Marina Ottaway, *South Africa: The Struggle for a New Order* (Washington, D.C., 1993); Allister Sparks, *Tomorrow Is Another Country: The Inside Story of South Africa's Road to Change* (New York, 1995); and Patti Waldmeir, *Anatomy of a Miracle: The End of Apartheid and the Birth of a New South Africa* (New York, 1997). See also work by scholars—R. W. Johnson and Lawrence Schlemmer, "Introduction: The Transition to Democracy," and Mervyn Frost, "Preparing for Democracy in an Authoritarian State," in *Launching Democracy in South Africa,* ed. R. W. Johnson and Lawrence Schlemmer (New Haven, 1996), 1–34; Robert T. Mattes, "The Road to Democracy," *Election '94 South Africa,* ed. Andrew Reynolds (New York, 1994), 1–22; and Adrian Guelke, *South Africa in Transition* (New York, 1999).

2. South African Institute of Race Relations, *Survey of Race Relations in South Africa, 1987–88* (Johannesburg, 1989) (annual hereafter cited as *Race Relations Survey, 1987–88,* etc.), xxxiii, 10–14; W. P. Mostert and J. M. Lotter, eds., *South Africa's Demographic Future* (Pretoria, 1990). The annual *Surveys* by the South African Institute of Race Relations, renamed *South African Survey* in and after the 1994–95 volume, is an excellent detailed, objective source.

3. *Race Relations Survey, 1987–88,* lvii.

4. Ibid., 406, 409; Stephen Gelb, ed., *South Africa's Economic Crisis* (Atlantic Highlands, N.J., 1991); Sebastian Mallaby, *After Apartheid: The Future of South Africa* (New York, 1992), 42–69.

5. Readers are reminded that in this book the term "black" is used to include Coloureds and Indians as well as Africans.

6. *Race Relations Survey, 1987–88,* il.

7. Anthony Sampson, *Black and Gold: Tycoons, Revolutionaries, and Apartheid* (New York, 1987), 189–200; Sparks, *Tomorrow Is Another Country,* 68–75; *African Economic Digest,* July 17, 1987; *West Africa,* July 20, 1987.

8. *Race Relations Survey, 1989–90,* 688.

9. Mandela, *Long Walk to Freedom,* 254–78.

10. Meredith, *Nelson Mandela,* 388–90; Waldmeir, *Anatomy of a Miracle,* 104–5.

11. Waldmeir, *Anatomy of a Miracle,* 105.

12. Sparks, *Tomorrow Is Another Country,* 76–77.

13. Meredith, *Nelson Mandela,* 398.

14. Willem de Klerk, *F. W. de Klerk: The Man in His Time* (Johannesburg, 1991), 55.

15. F. W. de Klerk, *The Last Trek,* 159–72; Heribert Adam and Kogila Moodley, *The Opening of the Apartheid Mind* (Berkeley, Calif., 1993), 39–58; Robert Schrire, *Adapt or Die: The End of White Politics in South Africa* (New York, 1991); Sparks, *Tomorrow Is Another Country,* 91–108; Ottaway, *Chained Together,* 52–71; Guelke, *South Africa in Transition,* 23–44.

16. The complete speech is printed in Willem de Klerk, *F. W. de Klerk,* 34–46.

17. Sampson, *Mandela,* 406–13.

18. F. W. de Klerk (hereafter cited as de Klerk), *The Last Trek,* 183–85.

19. Mandela, *Long Walk to Freedom,* 494.

20. Ottaway, *Chained Together,* 104–5.

21. De Klerk, *The Last Trek,* 181–83; Mandela, *Long Walk to Freedom,* 504–5.

22. Ottaway, *Chained Together,* 105; Waldmeir, *Anatomy of a Miracle,* 156–66; Meredith, *Nelson Mandela,* 416–18.

23. De Klerk, *The Last Trek,* 200–202; Waldmeir, *Anatomy of a Miracle,* 81–82, 162, 164.

24. *Race Relations Survey, 1996–97,* 600.

25. De Klerk, *The Last Trek,* 202. In light of evidence given to the Truth and Reconciliation Commission by several people, including some of de Klerk's colleagues, it is probable that, as president, he knew much more than he has admitted. See also de Klerk's equivocal evidence given to the commission as described by Antjie Krog, *Country of My Skull: Guilt, Sorrow, and the Limit of Forgiveness in the New South Africa* (New York, 1999), 135–39.

26. For the Goldstone commission reports, see *Race Relations Survey, 1992–93,* 27–33, 124–26, and *Race Relations Survey 1993–94,* 652–72.

27. *Truth and Reconciliation Commission of South Africa Report* (hereafter cited as *TRC Report*), 5 vols. (Cape Town, 1998), 5:238. For a description of the work of the commission, see chapter 9.

28. However, unlike the rulers of the Ciskei, Bophuthatswana, and Venda

Homelands, Buthelezi had stopped short of accepting "independence" from the South African government.

29. Mzala, *Gatsha Buthelezi: Chief with a Double Agenda* (London, 1988); Jack Shepherd Smith, *Buthelezi: The Biography* (Melville, S.A., 1988); Georgina Hamilton and Gerhard Mate, "The Inkatha Freedom Party," *Election '94*, 73–87; Ottaway, *Chained Together*, 114–22; Meredith, *Nelson Mandela*, 419–33; Waldmeir, *Anatomy of a Miracle*, 168–88; Guelke, *South Africa in Transition*, 89–111.

30. See works cited in note 29 and *TRC Report*, 3:243–323.

31. *TRC Report*, 3:708; Waldmeir, *Anatomy of a Miracle*, 176–80; Meredith, *Nelson Mandela*, 425–31.

32. Mandela, *Long Walk to Freedom*, 514; Meredith, *Nelson Mandela*, 410–13.

33. Sampson, *Mandela*, 440–48; Meredith, *Nelson Mandela*, 458–65.

34. Mandela, *Long Walk to Freedom*, 515–17; Sampson, *Mandela*, 423–26; Meredith, *Nelson Mandela*, 445–57.

35. Ottaway, *Chained Together*, 166–68.

36. Meredith, *Nelson Mandela*, 444–57; Waldmeir, *Anatomy of a Miracle*, 191–95; Sampson, *Mandela*, 449–54.

37. *Race Relations Survey, 1991–92*, 557–58.

38. De Klerk, *The Last Trek*, 222–25; Mandela, *Long Walk to Freedom*, 519–21.

39. Hermann Giliomee, "The National Party's Campaign for a Liberation Election," *Election '94*, 43–71; Waldmeir, *Anatomy of a Miracle*, 193–94.

40. Tom Lodge, "The African National Congress and Its Allies," *Election '94*, 23–42.

41. Thus the title of David Ottaway's book, *Chained Together*.

42. De Klerk, *The Last Trek*, 232.

43. Sparks, *Tomorrow Is Another Country*, 141–46, is an eyewitness account of this event.

44. Ibid., 147–51; Meredith, *Nelson Mandela*, 471–73.

45. Meredith, *Nelson Mandela*, 476–77. De Klerk (*The Last Trek*, 252–57) gives a very different account of his September 26 meeting with Mandela. See also Sparks, *Tomorrow Is Another Country*, 179–84.

46. Joe Slovo, "Negotiations: What Room for Compromise?" *African Communist* (third quarter, 1992): 36–40; cited in Sparks, *Tomorrow Is Another Country*, 181–2.

47. Meredith, *Nelson Mandela*, 479–80.

48. Ibid., 481–84; Sparks, *Tomorrow Is Another Country*, 187–89.

49. Sparks, *Tomorrow Is Another Country*, 90–92.

50. Waldmeir, *Anatomy of a Miracle*, 225–32.

51. De Klerk, *The Last Trek*, 291.

52. Meredith, *Nelson Mandela*, 496.

53. Constitution of the Republic of South Africa, Act 200 of 1993.

54. Sparks, *Tomorrow Is Another Country,* 219–25; Mandela, *Long Walk to Freedom,* 535–37.

55. Mandela, *Long Walk to Freedom,* 536.

56. De Klerk, *The Last Trek,* 302–8.

57. Meredith, *Nelson Mandela,* 506–13.

58. De Klerk, *The Last Trek,* 313–16; Sparks, *Tomorrow Is Another Country,* 197–219; Waldmeir, *Anatomy of a Miracle,* 245–48; Guelke, *South Africa in Transition,* 67–88.

59. *Newsday,* March 27, 1994.

60. Meredith, *Nelson Mandela,* 513–14.

61. Ibid., 512–15; de Klerk, *The Last Trek,* 320–27; Sparks, *Tomorrow Is Another Country,* 219–25; Waldmeir, *Anatomy of a Miracle,* 248–50.

62. De Klerk, *The Last Trek,* 328–33; Giliomee, "The National Party's Campaign for a Liberation Election," 43–71.

63. Lodge, "The African National Congress and Its Allies," 23–42.

64. Benjamin Pogrund, "South Africa Goes to the Polls," *Election '94,* 159–81; Sparks, *Tomorrow Is Another Country,* 226–28; Guelke, *South Africa in Transition,* 112–35; Mandela, *Long Walk to Freedom,* 538–40; R. W. Johnson, "The Election, the Count, and the Drama in KwaZulu/Natal," in *Launching Democracy in South Africa,* 274–300. Meredith, *Nelson Mandela,* 515–17, is highly critical of the performance of the Independent Electoral Commission.

65. Andrew Reynolds, "The Results," *Election '94,* 182–220; R. W. Johnson, "The 1994 Election: Outcome and Analysis," and "How Free and Fair?" *in Launching Democracy in South Africa,* 301–52; John Jackson, "The 1994 Election: An Analysis," in *The New South Africa: Prospects for Domestic and International Security,* ed. T. H. Toase and E. J. Yorke (New York, 1998), 3–16; Guelke, *South Africa in Transition,* 112–35.

66. Mandela, *Long Walk to Freedom,* 541.

67. Mandela and de Klerk had shared the 1992 Nobel Peace Prize.

Chapter 9: The New South Africa

1. *Human Development Report, 1997* (New York, 1997), 150, based on 1994 data. "The human development index measures the average achievements in a country in three basic dimensions of human development—longevity, knowledge and a decent standard of living" (14).

2. *The People of South Africa Population Census, 1996: Primary Tables* (Pretoria, 1999). This was a far more elaborate South African census than its predecessors, especially in its collection of data on black South Africans. It found that the vast majority of white South Africans had full employment and lived in modern houses or apartments equipped with electricity, piped water, telephones, and flush toilets; by contrast, 42 percent of Africans of working age were unemployed, only 45 percent of the African population lived in modern

buildings, and only 30 percent of African households had electricity, 20 percent had piped water, 11 percent had telephones, and 19 percent had flush or chemical toilets in their homes. Conditions were far worse among rural Africans than among the 59 percent of the African population who lived in urban or peri-urban areas, even though many urban Africans occupied shacks.

3. Ibid.

4. *Race Relations Survey, 1993–94*, 623, 648, 677–751; *Economist,* May 20, Dec. 3, 1994.

5. Colin Bundy, "At War with the Future? Black South African Youth," in *South Africa: The Political Economy of Transformation,* ed. Stephen John Stedman (Boulder, Colo., 1994), 47–64; David Everett and Elinor Sisulu, eds., *Black Youth in Crisis* (Braamfontein, S.A., 1992).

6. *Race Relations Survey, 1993–94,* 300–301.

7. Ibid., 297.

8. *Weekly Mail and Guardian* (Johannesburg), Nov. 11, 1994; *Intermittent Newsletter* (Pretoria), Oct. 12, 1994, Dec. 5, 1994. The *Mail and Guardian* (Johannesburg) appears in two versions: the print edition, the *Weekly Mail and Guardian,* is published every Friday, and an electronic edition, the *Daily Mail and Guardian, ZA*Now,* has appeared since May 1996. For this daily electronic edition, and also for the electronic archive of the *Weekly Mail and Guardian* since 1994, see www.mg.co.za/mg/za/news.html.

9. *Intermittent Newsletter,* Dec. 5, 1994.

10. *This Week in South Africa,* Jan. 24–30, 1995. *This Week in South Africa* is a newsletter issued by the South African Consulate in New York.

11. *Economist,* Dec. 24, 1994; Tony Haskins, *The New South Africa: Business Prospects and Corporate Strategies* (London, 1994); *Race Relations Survey, 1993–94,* 372; Jesmond Blumenfeld, "The Post-Apartheid Economy: Achievements, Problems, and Prospects," in *After Mandela: The 1999 South African Elections,* ed. J. E. Spence (London, 1999), 33–48; Alan Ward, "Changes in the Political Economy of the New South Africa," in *The New South Africa: Prospects for Domestic and International Security,* ed. F. H. Toase and E. J. Yorke (New York, 1998), 37–56.

12. Thabo Mbeki, *Africa: The Time Has Come* (Johannesburg, 1998); Leonard Thompson, "Mbeki's Uphill Challenge," *Foreign Affairs* 78:6 (November–December 1999): 92.

13. Speech in the National Council of Provinces, Aug. 7, 1998, cited by David Welsh, "The State of the Polity," in *After Mandela,* 16.

14. *Constitution of the Republic of South Africa, Act 108 of 1996.* See also *South African Survey, 1996–97,* 517–44.

15. F. W. de Klerk, *The Last Trek: A New Beginning* (London, 1998), 342–55; Anthony Sampson, *Mandela: The Authorized Biography* (New York, 1999), 502, 526–27.

16. *South African Survey, 1997–98,* 513–14.

17. Ibid., 469–70.

18. Stanley Uys, "The ANC and Black Politics: The Buck Stops with Mbeki," in *After Mandela,* 28.

19. Welsh, "State of the Polity," 19. See also J. E. Spence, "Introduction," *After Mandela,* 1–6.

20. Welsh, "State of the Polity," 13.

21. *This Week in South Africa,* Aug. 9–25, Oct. 11–17, 1994. In 1996, one of the white judges of the Constitutional Court resigned and was succeeded by an Asian; and the Supreme Court, which formerly consisted of an Appellate Division and Provincial Divisions, was replaced by the Supreme Court of Appeals and Provincial High Courts.

22. *Business Day* (Johannesburg), Dec. 21, 1994.

23. For background, see Jacklyn Cock, *Colonels and Cadres: War and Gender in South Africa* (Cape Town, 1991); Herbert M. Howe, "National Reconciliation and a New South African Defence Force," and Jacklyn Cock, "The Dynamics of Transforming South Africa's Defense Forces," both in *South Africa,* 127–51.

24. *Weekly Mail and Guardian,* Nov. 11, 1994, Feb. 4, 1995.

25. Cited in Howe, "National Reconciliation," 134.

26. *South African Survey, 1997–98,* 77.

27. For background on the police, see John D. Brewer, *Black and Blue: Policing in South Africa* (Oxford, 1994), and Gavin Cawthra, *Policing South Africa: The South African Police and the Transition from Apartheid* (London, 1994).

28. *South African Survey, 1995–96,* 73–82; *South African Survey, 1996–97,* 90–97; *South African Survey, 1997–98,* 58–84.

29. *South African Survey, 1997–98,* 494; *Economist,* Feb. 28, 1998.

30. *South African Survey, 1997–98,* 496–97.

31. *South African Survey, 1996–97,* 540, 585; *South African Survey, 1997–98,* 481.

32. Sampson, *Mandela,* 512–16.

33. Martin Meredith, *Coming to Terms: South Africa's Search for Truth* (New York, 1999), 17–18.

34. *Truth and Reconciliation Commission Report* (hereafter cited as *TRC Report*), 5 vols. (Cape Town, 1998); Antjie Krog, *Country of My Skull: Guilt, Sorrow, and the Limit of Forgiveness in the New South Africa* (New York, 1998); Meredith, *Coming to Terms,* 17–18; Sampson, *Mandela,* 521–25.

35. Meredith, *Coming to Terms,* 17–18.

36. Chairperson's foreword in *TRC Report,* 1:1–23.

37. *TRC Report,* 2:182.

38. Meredith, *Coming to Terms,* 45–54.

39. Ibid., 181–87; Krog, *Country of My Skull,* 346–54.

40. Meredith, *Coming to Terms,* 187–99, 295–97. See also Krog, *Country of My Skull,* 135–39. De Klerk presented his own case in *The Last Trek,* 369–85.

41. *TRC Report,* 5:223–34.

42. *TRC Report,* 1:12–13, 2:325–99; Meredith, *Coming to Terms,* 203–19;

Krog, *Country of My Skull,* 150–61. The TRC also held extensive hearings that revealed that Winnie Madikizela-Mandela, who Nelson Mandela divorced in 1996, was morally and politically accountable for many gross violations of human rights (Meredith, *Coming to Terms,* 223–70; Krog, *Country of My Skull,* 318–40; *TRC report,* 2:581); and other hearings that revealed the extent to which big business, Christian churches, the legal profession, and the medical profession had cooperated with the apartheid state (*TRC Report,* vol. 4).

43. Krog, *Country of My Skull,* 275.

44. *TRC Report,* 5:436–56.

45. Meredith, *Coming to Terms,* 315–16, 318–19.

46. Ibid., 304.

47. Ibid., 306.

48. Nevertheless, Tina Rosenberg, in "Confronting the Past," in *Coming to Terms,* 325–70, considers that the South African TRC was an improvement on attempts to come to terms with the past in other countries.

49. On the South African economy during the Mandela presidency, see Blumenfeld, "The Post-Apartheid Economy: Achievements, Problems and Prospects," 33–48; Ward, "Changes in the Political Economy of the New South Africa," 37–56; Thomas A. Koelble, *The Global Economy and Democracy in South Africa* (New Brunswick, N.J., 1998).

50. Koelble, *Global Economy,* 103–17.

51. Ibid., 173–85.

52. *This Week in South Africa,* Oct. 4–10, 1994.

53. *South African Survey,* 1997–98, 222.

54. *Economist,* June 11, 1994, May 20, 1995; *New York Times,* June 7, July 27, Sept. 23, 1994.

55. *South African Survey,* 1996–97, 611–15.

56. Ibid., 41.

57. Ibid., 710–17; Blumenfeld, "Post-Apartheid Economy," 42–44.

58. Blumenfeld, "The Post-Apartheid Economy," 44–48; Thompson, "Mbeki's Uphill Challenge," 85; *Weekly Mail and Guardian,* July 23, 1999.

59. *South African Survey,* 1999–2000, 436–37.

60. Koelble, *Global Economy,* 167.

61. On the political consequences of GEAR see, besides Koelble, Gay W. Seidman, "Oppositional Identities in Brazil and South Africa," in *Comparative Perspectives on South Africa,* ed. Ran Greenstein (Houndsmills, U.K., 1998), 252–58; Heribert Adam, Frederik van Zyl Slabbert, and Kogila Moodley, *Comrades in Business* (Cape Town, 1997); and *South African Survey,* 1999–2000, 32, 395, 507, 508.

62. *This Week in South Africa,* Sept. 6–12, 1994, May 16–22, 1995.

63. *South African Survey,* 1999–2000, 152–55.

64. Ibid., 168.

65. Ibid., 173–76, 158–61.

66. Ibid., 188–89.

67. Ibid., 411.

68. "Up Bara Security," *Weekly Mail and Guardian,* Apr. 2, 1999, www.mg .co.za; "Gauteng Health Services Near Collapse," *Daily Mail and Guardian,* June 22, 1999, www.mg.co.za.

69. *South African Survey, 1999–2000,* 218–23; "AIDS Makes South African Living Standards Plummet," *Business Report,* July 20, 1999, www.iol.co.za; "AIDS the Top Killer in Africa," *Cape Times,* July 23, 1999, www.inc.co.za; "Africa Bears the Brunt of the World's AIDS Epidemic," *Daily Mail and Guardian,* Sept. 11, 1999, www.mg.co.za.

70. "AIDS Likely to Provoke a Rash of Crime," *Saturday Star,* July 30, 1999, www.inc.co.za/online/saturday_star.

71. "Black Picture Painted of Teacher Training Crisis," *Cape Argus,* Dec. 19, 1999, www.africanews.org.

72. South African Survey, 1999–2000, 109–13.

73. "South African Students are Scientifically Illiterate," *Daily Mail and Guardian,* Jan. 18, 2000, www.mg.co.za.

74. Thompson, "Mbeki's Uphill Challenge," 90–91; *South African Survey, 1999–2000,* 136–44; "Cash-strapped Universities Face Closure," *Daily Mail and Guardian,* July 31, 1999, www.africanews.org.

75. "Asmal Declares Education 'Emergency,' " *Cape Argus,* July 30, 1999, www.inc.co.za/online/cape_argus.

76. "Crime Stats Queried," *Saturday Star,* Feb. 14, 1998; *The Star,* May 5, 1999.

77. South African Survey, 1999–2000, 50.

78. *The Star,* May 5, 1999.

79. Tom Lodge, "Political Corruption in South Africa," *African Affairs* 97, no. 387 (1998): 157–87.

80. Lodge, "Political Corruption in South Africa," 187.

81. Adam, van Zyl Slabbert, and Moodley, *Comrades in Business,* 181, 205.

82. *South African Survey, 1999–2000,* 522.

83. Address by President Nelson Mandela to Parliament, National Assembly, Cape Town, Feb. 5, 1999. www.anc.org.za.

84. *South African Survey, 1999–2000,* 319–30.

85. United Nations Development Program, *Human Development Report 2000* (New York, 2000): 158–60.

Chapter 10: Beyond the New South Africa

1. Department of International Relations and Cooperation, Republic of South Africa, "The African Renaissance Statement of Deputy President, Thabo Mbeki, SABC, Gallagher Estate, Aug. 13, 1998, http://www.dfa.gov.za/docs/speeches/1998/mbeko813.htm.

2. "Thabo's Team from Asmal to Zuma," *Weekly Mail and Guardian,* June 25, 1999, www.mg.co.za.

3. Thabo Mbeki, Inaugural Speech as President of the Republic of South Africa, Pretoria, June 16, 1999, www.info.gov.za/speeches/1999/990617935a1002.htm.

4. Thabo Mbeki, State of the Nation Speech, National Assembly, Cape Town, June 25, 1999, http://www.dfa.gov.za/docs/speeches/1999/mbeko625.htm.

5. Thabo Mbeki, State of the Nation Address at the Opening of Parliament, National Assembly, Cape Town, Feb. 4, 2000, http://www.dfa.gov.za/docs/speeches/2000/mbeko204.htm.

6. *South African Survey, 1999–2000,* 342. On Mboweni's background and politics, see *Economist,* Feb. 5, 2000.

7. "Thabo Mbeki, Micro-manager," *Economist,* July 15, 2000.

8. "Mbeki's Lean, Mean Ruling Machine," *Weekly Mail and Guardian,* June 25, 1999.

9. Thabo Mbeki, Address at the Welcome Ceremony of the World Summit on Sustainable Development, Aug. 25, 2002, http://www.dfa.gov.za/docs/speeches/2002/mbeko825.htm.

10. Thabo Mbeki, Address of the President of the Republic of South Africa at the Opening of the World Summit for Sustainable Development, Johannesburg, Aug. 26, 2000, http://www.dfa.gov.za/docs/speeches/2002/mbeko826.htm.

11. Act No. 2 of 2000, Republic of South Africa, *Government Gazette,* Vol. 416, No. 20852, Cape Town, Feb. 3, 2000, http://www.info.gov.za/view/DownloadFileAction?id=68186.

12. R. Sorenson, "The Impact of South Africa's Promotion of Access to Information Act After Three and a Half Years: A Perspective," ESARBICA *Journal* 22 (2003).

13. Open Democracy Advice Centre, *Annual Report 2003.*

14. Tom Carter, "South Africa Probes Racism in Media," *Washington Times,* Mar. 9, 2000, http://www.highbeam.com/doc/1G1-60043579.html.

15. "Sheena Duncan Resigns over Racism Probe," *Weekly Mail and Guardian,* Feb. 25, 2000, www.mg.co.za.

16. *Soobramoney v. Minister of Health, KwaZulu-Natal,* 1998 (1) SA 765 (CC).

17. Thabo Mbeki, Remarks at Judicial Symposium, Aug. 1, 2003.

18. "Masses Desert the SACP in Droves," *Africa News Online,* May 17, 2000, www.africanews.org.

19. "Alliance of Concern to COSATU Chief," *Business Day,* July 14, 2000, www.africanews.org.

20. South African History Online, "The New South Africa and the New National Party (1993–2005)," http://www.sahistory.org.za.

21. Untitled article by Ed Stoddard, July 25, 2000, www.news.africa.com.

22. South African History Online, "Democratic Alliance (DA)," http://www.sahistory.org.za/organisations/democratic-alliance-da.

23. "South Africa: Sleeping with the Enemy. (Countryfile)." *Free Library,* http://www.thefreelibrary.com/South+Africa%3a+Sleeping+with+the+enemy.+(Countryfile).-a080757939.

24. "SA Apartheid Party Set to Disband," BBC *News,* Apr. 10, 2005, http://news.bbc.co.uk/2/hi/africa/4429307.stm.

25. "Patricia de Lille," *South African History Online,* http://www.sahistory.org.za/people/patricia-de-lille.

26. SA Web, http://www.saweb.co.za/elections/results.asp.

27. Thabo Mbeki, on the Occasion of his Inauguration and the 10th anniversary of Freedom, Pretoria, Apr. 27, 2004, polity.org.za, http://www.polity.org.za/article/mbeki-inauguration-and-10th-anniversary-of-freedom-27042004-2004-04-27.

28. South African Government Information, Address of the President of South Africa, Thabo Mbeki, at the Second Joint Sitting of the Third Democratic Parliament, Cape Town, Feb. 11, 2005, http://www.info.gov.za/speeches/2005/05021110501001.htm.

29. Open Democracy Advice Centre, http://www.opendemocracy.org.za/access-to-information/community-intervention/.

30. Protection of Constitutional Democracy against Terrorist and Related Activities Act, No. 33 of 2004, Republic of South Africa, *Government Gazette,* Vol. 476, No. 27266, Feb. 11, 2005.

31. Charlayne Hunter-Gault, "Graphic Cartoon Tests Press Freedom in South Africa," National Public Radio, Jan. 27, 2009, http://www.npr.org/templates/story/story.php?storyId=99339922.

32. "S. Africa's Zuma Cleared of Rape," *BBC News,* May 8, 2006, http://news.bbc.co.uk/2/hi/africa/4750731.stm.

33. "Zuma Sues SA Cartoonist," *BBC News,* Dec. 18, 2008, http://news.bbc.co.uk/2/hi/africa/7789272.stm.

34. Karima Brown, "South Africa: The Big Ones That Get Away Hurt War on Corruption," *allAfrica,* Aug. 1, 2006, http://allafrica.com/stories/200608010042.html; Adriaan Basson, "Extract: *Zuma* Exposed," *news24,* Nov. 15, 2012, http://www.news24.com/SouthAfrica/News/Extract-Zuma-Exposed-20121115.

35. Karyn Maughan, "'Shaik Did Bribe Zuma,'" *iolnews,* Feb. 27, 2008, http://www.iol.co.za/news/south-africa/shaik-did-bribe-zuma-1.391024#.UZZ7z7WmhzQ.

36. *S. v. Shaik and Others* (CCT 86/06) [2007] ZACC 19, 2008 (2) SA, http://www.saflii.org/za/cases/ZACC/2007/19.html.

37. SAPA, "Mbeki Fires Zuma," *Business Day,* June 14, 2005, http://www.armsdeal-vpo.co.za/articles08/mbeki_fires.html.

38. "Zuma Charged with Corruption," *Guardian,* Dec. 28, 2007, http://www.guardian.co.uk/world/2007/dec/28/southafrica.

39. African National Congress, *52nd National Conference—Polokwane,* last updated June 22, 2010, http://www.anc.org.za/events.php?t=52nd%20National%20Conference%20-%20Polokwane.

40. Ray Hartley, "Zuma Judgement: The Full Text," *Times Live,* Sept. 13, 2008, http://blogs.timeslive.co.za/hartley/2008/09/13/zuma-judgement-the-full-text/.

41. "Constitutional Court Dismisses Mbeki," *Mail and Guardian,* Nov. 12, 2008, http://mg.co.za/article/2008-11-12-constitutional-court-dismisses-mbeki-bid.

42. "Mbeki's Resignation to Take Effect on Thursday," *Mmegionline,* Sept. 23, 2008, http://www.mmegi.bw/index.php?sid=1&aid=33&dir=2008/September/Tuesday23.

43. Ray Hartley, "Zuma Charges Dropped by NPA—Full Text," Apr. 6, 2009, http://blogs.timeslive.co.za/hartley/2009/04/06/zuma-charges-dropped-by-npa-full-text/.

44. South African Government Information, Constitution of the Republic of South Africa, 1996, http://www.info.gov.za/documents/constitution/.

45. Sebastien Berger, "Kgalema Motlanthe to Be South African President as ANC Seeks to Reassure Voters," *Telegraph,* Sept. 22, 2008, http://www.telegraph.co.uk/news/worldnews/africaandindianocean/southafrica/3061193/Kgalema-Motlanthe-to-be-South-African-president-as-ANC-seeks-to-reassure-voters.html.

46. "Motlanthe: South Africa's Safe Hands," *BBC News,* Sept. 25, 2008, http://news.bbc.co.uk/2/hi/africa/7629239.stm.

47. *Jaftha v. Schoeman and Others, Van Rooyen v. Stoltz and Others* (CCT 74/03) ZACC 25; 2005 (2) SA 140 (CC), S005 (1) BCLR 78 (CC) (8 Oct. 2004).

48. Jackie Dugard and Stuart Wilson, "Taking Poverty Seriously: The South African Constitutional Court and Socio-economic Rights," 22 *Stellenbosch Law Review* 664 (2011).

49. Statement by the National Executive Committee of the ANC, 2005, www.anc.org.za.

50. Address of the President of South Africa, Thabo Mbeki, at the Ceremony to Mark the Retirement of Chief Justice Arthur Chaskalson and the Assumption of Office of Chief Justice Pius Langa and Deputy Chief Justice Dikgang Moseneke, Houses of Parliament, Cape Town, June 10, 2005, http://www.dfa.gov.za/docs/speeches/2005/mbek0610.htm.

51. Political staff, "Hearings on Hlophe's Conduct Delayed," *iolnews,* Apr. 15, 2007, http://www.iol.co.za/news/south-africa/hearings-on-hlophe-s-conduct-delayed-1.323129#.UYf_ubWmhzQ.

52. "Complaints Against Judge President Hlophe," *Legalbrief Today,* Oct. 18, 2007, http://www.legalbrief.co.za/article.php?story=20071023145931920.

53. Paul Halffman, "The Judge Hlophe Inquiry Papers," *Institute for Accountability in Southern Africa,* Jan. 2011, http://ifaisa.org/The_Hlophe_Inquiry_Papers.html.

54. Johann Kriegler, "Judge Hlophe Betrayed the Nation with His Greed," *Sunday Times,* Oct. 7, 2007.

55. "Public Statement by Senior Counsel Cape Bar," *Advocate,* Dec. 2007, p. 34, http://www.sabar.co.za/law-journals/2007/december/2007-december-vol020-no3-pp33-34.pdf.

56. Karen Breytenbach, "UCT Law Professors in Attack on Hlophe," *iolnews,* Oct. 11, 2007, http://www.iol.co.za/news/politics/uct-law-professors-in-attack-on-hlophe-1.374345#.UYfOSLWmhzQ.

57. Lenore Oliver, Siyabonga Mkhwanazi, and SAPA, "Hlophe May Have R2m Reasons to Ride out Storm," *iolnews,* Oct. 10. 2007, http://www.iol.co.za/

news/south-africa/hlophe-may-have-r2m-reasons-to-ride-out-storm-1.374251#
.UYfPdbWmhzQ.

58. SAPA, "Hlophe's 'Improper Attempt,'" *iolnews,* May 30, 2008, http://www
.iol.co.za/news/south-africa/hlophe-s-improper-attempt-1.402685#.UYfQor
WmhzQ.

59. Southern African Legal Information Institute, *Hlophe v. Constitutional
Court of South Africa and Others* (08/22932)[2008] ZAGPHC 289 (Sept. 25,
2008), http://www.saflii.org/za/cases/ZAGPHC/2008/289.html.

60. Address of the President of South Africa, Thabo Mbeki, at the Second
Joint Sitting of the Third Democratic Parliament, Cape Town, Feb. 11, 2005,
http://www.info.gov.za/speeches/2005/05021110501001.htm.

61. "New Pragmatism in South Africa's Foreign Policy Disappoints Some
Old Supporters," *New York Times,* June 19, 2000.

62. "Africa Ready for Rebirth," *Africa News Online,* Apr. 8, 2000, www
.africanews.org.

63. Gerrit Olivier, "Is Mbeki Africa's Saviour?" 79:4 *International Affairs*
(2003), http://www.chathamhouse.org/sites/default/files/public/International%20
Affairs/2003/inta_338.pdf.

64. International Democracy Watch, "Pan African Parliament," no date, http://
www.internationaldemocracywatch.org/index.php/pan-african-parliament.

65. Olivier, "Is Mbeki Africa's Saviour?"

66. "South Africa's Foreign Policy: Human Rights," *Economist,* Oct. 14,
2010, http://www.economist.com/node/17259138.

67. Peter Godwin, "Bloody Harvest," *New York Times Magazine,* June 25,
2000.

68. "Zimbabwe—the Untold Story," *Sowetan,* May 6, 2000 (edited version
of the address to the nation by Thabo Mbeki), www.africanews.org.

69. "Was Zimbabwe's Election Fair?" *BBC News,* Nov. 3 2003, http://news
.bbc.co.uk/2/hi/africa/3237327.stm.

70. "South Africa Mission Split over Zimbabwe," *Cape Times,* Apr. 4, 2005,
http://www.zimbabwesituation.com/apr4a_2005.html#link4.

71. Inter-Parliamentary Union, "Zimbabwe Senate," no date, http://www.ipu
.org/parline/reports/2383_E.htm.

72. "No Crisis in Zimbabwe," *Sunday Mail* (Zimbabwe), Apr. 13, 2008,
kubatana.net, http://kubatana.net/html/archive/elec/080413smail.asp?spec_code
=080121elecdex&sector=ELEC.

73. Mariette le Roux, "Mbeki Botched Legacy over Zim Analysts Say," *Mail
and Guardian,* Apr. 28, 2008, http://mg.co.za/article/2008-04-28-mbeki-botched
-legacy-over-zim-analysts-say.

74. "Rogue Democrat," *Washington Post,* Apr. 15, 2008, http://articles
.washingtonpost.com/2008-04-15/news/36899365_1_jacob-zuma-southern
-african-development-community-south-africa.

75. Cris Chinaka, "Zimbabwe Awaits Presidential Election Results," Reu-

ters, Apr. 28, 2008, http://www.reuters.com/article/2008/04/28/us-zimbabwe
-election-idUSL2871085720080428.

76. "Tsvangirai Withdraws from Zimbabwe Runoff, Seeks Refuge in Dutch
Embassy," PBS Newshour, June 23, 2013, http://www.pbs.org/newshour/updates/
africa/jan-june08/zimbabwe_06–23.html.

77. Reuters, "African Union Calls for unity government in Zimbabwe,"
Canada.com, July 1, 2008, http://www.canada.com/vancouversun/story.html?id
=ffd6130d-143f-4c2d-86ff-c62135b1270e.

78. Umar Ahmad At, "Proposed U.N. Sanctions on Zimbabwe Shot Down
at Security Council," Modern Intelligencer, July 12, 2008, http://www.canada
.com/vancouversun/story.html?id=ffd6130d-143f-4c2d-86ff-c62135b1270e.

79. "Zimbabwe Factions Reach Deal," Washington Post, Sept. 12, 2008,
http://articles.washingtonpost.com/2008-09-12/world/36897098_1_tsvangirai
-prime-minister-movement-for-democratic-change-president-robert-mugabe.

80. Economist, Feb. 12, 2000.

81. "Thousands March against Job Losses," Panafrican News Agency, May
11, 2000, www.africanews.org; untitled article by Ed Stoddard, Reuters (Johannesburg), May 11, 2000, www.newsafrica.com.

82. "ANC for Strike," Sowetan, May 4, 2000, www.africanews.org.

83. "Mbeki Fares Better Abroad," Daily Mail and Guardian, June 14, 2000,
www.mg.co.za.

84. Untitled Reuters report, July 2, 2000, www.news.africa.com.

85. South African Government Information, Address of the President of
South Africa Thabo Mbeki at the 2d Joint Sitting of the Third Democratic
Parliament, Cape Town, Feb. 11, 2005, http://www.info.gov.za/speeches/2005/
05021110501001.htm.

86. Patrick Bond, "South Africa Loses Its 'War on Poverty,'" Links: International Journal of Socialist Renewal, Aug. 6, 2010, http://links.org.au/node/1826.

87. South African Government Information, State of the Nation Address of
the President of South Africa, Thabo Mbeki: Joint Sitting of Parliament, Feb. 8,
2008, http://www.info.gov.za/speeches/2008/08020811021001.htm.

88. Global Poverty Research Group, "Unemployment and Wages in South
Africa" (2005), http://www.gprg.org/themes/t2-inc-ineq-poor/unem/unem-wage
.htm.

89. Republic of South Africa, Government Gazette, Vol. 463, No. 25899,
Jan. 9, 2004, Broad-Based Black Economic Empowerment Act, No. 53, of 2003,
http://www.info.gov.za/view/DownloadFileAction?id=68031.

90. Selaelo, "South Africa: From Black Economic Empowerment (BEE) to
Broad-Based Black Economic Empowerment (B-BBEE), Helium, Oct. 27, 2007,
http://www.helium.com/items/669208-south-africa-from-black-economic
-empowerment-bee-to-broad-based-black-economic.

91. United Nations, End Poverty 2015: Millennium Development Goals,
http://www.un.org/millenniumgoals/.

92. "South Africa: The Great Debate: Desmond Tutu v. Thabo Mbeki," *New African,* No. 436, Jan. 2005.

93. Thabo Mbeki, "The Sociology of the Public Discourse in Democratic South Africa: Part I—The Cloud with the Silver Lining," ANC *Today.*

94. Thabo Mbeki, "The Sociology of the Public Discourse in Democratic South Africa: Part II—Who Shall Set the National Agenda?" ANC *Today.*

95. Alan McIver, "Desmond Tutu's Moral Compass," *Quo Vadis Southern Africa,* no date, http://www.quovadis-southern-africa.co.za/content/11/4248/en/desmond-tutu-5-moral-compass.html.

96. *OECD Economic Surveys: South Arica 2009,* www.oecd-library.org.

97. "South Africa: Inequality Not so Black and White," IRIN, Feb. 8, 2010, http://www.irinnews.org/Report/88038/SOUTH-AFRICA-Inequality-not-so-black-and-white.

98. Kerri MacDonald, "Poverty, and Little Sympathy, in South Africa," *New York Times,* June 25, 2010, http://lens.blogs.nytimes.com/2010/06/25behind-45/.

99. Jocelyn Newmark, "Anatomy of a Catastrophe," *Mail and Guardian,* Feb. 11, 2008, http://articles.latimes.com/2008/feb/03/world/fg-power3.

100. Michael R. Mapa, "Eskom Impacts Gold Production and Platinum Prices," *Stockhouse,* June 11, 2008, http://www.stockhouse.com/columnists/2008/june/11/eskom-impacts-gold-production-and-platinum-prices.aspx.

101. ESKOM, *Annual Report 2008, Business and Sustainability Performance Review* (2008), http://financialresults.co.za/eskom_ar2008/ar_2008/index.htm.

102. State of the Nation Address, Thabo Mbeki, Feb. 8, 2008.

103. Terry Mackenzie-Hoy, "Eskom over the Last 30 Years: Why It Has Crashed," *Engineering News,* Feb. 1, 2008, http://www.engineeringnews.co.za/article/eskom-over-the-last-30-years-why-it-has-crashed-2008-02-01.

104. Brendan Ryan, "Coal Transport under Scrutiny," *Miningmx,* Sept. 8, 2009, http://www.miningmx.com/news/energy/coal-transport-under-scrutiny.htm.

105. "Electricity in South Africa," *libcom.org,* May 15, 2010, http://libcom.org/library/electricty-south-africa.

106. State of the Nation Address, Thabo Mbeki, Feb. 8, 2008.

107. "Chapter 3: The Constitutional Right to Water in South Africa," *ourwater commons.org,* http://ourwatercommons.org/water-solutions/case-3-constitutional-right-water-south-africa.

108. Ola Busari and Barry Jackson, "Reinforcing Water Sector Reform in South Africa," *Water Policy* 8:4 (2006).

109. South African Government Information, State of the Nation Address of the President of South Africa, Thabo Mbeki, Houses of Parliament, Cape Town, Feb. 6, 2004, http://www.info.gov.za/speeches/2004/04020610561002.htm.

110. Development Bank of Southern Africa, "The DBSA Infrastructure Barometer 3006: Economic and Municipal Infrastructure in South Africa," March 2006, http://www.dbsa.org/Research/Documents/Infrastructure%20Barometer.pdf?AspxAutoDetectCookieSupport=1.

111. Republic of South Africa, Department of Water Affairs, Introduction to the Blue Drop Programme & Handbook, version 1, http://www.dwa.gov.za/dir_ws/DWQR/Subscr/ViewNewsDoc.asp?FileID=262.

112. Admin, "'Blue Drop'" Water Quality Scheme Gains Momentum, but Critics Say More Is Needed, " *Rainharvest.co.za,* Nov. 21, 2010, http://www.rainharvest.co.za/2010/11/blue-drop-water-quality-scheme-gains-momentum-but-critics-say-more-is-needed/.

113. Kate Tissington, "A Review of Housing Policy and Development since 1994," *Socio-Economic Rights Institute of South Africa,* Sept. 2010, http://www.spii.org.za/agentfiles/434/file/Research/Review%20of%20the%20Right%20to%20Housing.pdf.

114. Department of Human Settlements, *National Housing Code* (2000), http://www.dhs.gov.za/content.php?pagename=National-Housing-Code.

115. *Government of the Republic of South Africa and Others v. Grootboom and Others,* 2001 (1) SA 46 (CC).

116. Republic of South Africa, Department of Human Settlements, "Housing Subsidies and Support Services," http://www.etu.org.za/toolbox/docs/government/housing.html.

117. Martin Zhuwakimyu, "New Deal Is Planned for Gauteng Housing," *Engineering News,* Oct. 19, 2001, http://www.engineeringnews.co.za/article/new-deal-is-planned-for-for-gauteng-housing-2001-10-19.

118. Lindsay Dentlinger, "Housing Backlog: South Africa Needs to Pick up the Pace," *iolnews,* Oct. 24, 2007, http://www.iol.co.za/news/south-africa/housing-backlog-sa-needs-to-pick-up-the-pace-1.376184#.UZaOe7WmhzQ.

119. Centre on Housing Rights and Evictions, Submission to the Office of the High Commissioner for Human Rights, 2008 http://lib.ohchr.org/HRBodies/UPR/Documents/Session1/ZA/COHRE_ZAF_UPR_S1_2008_CentreonHousing RightsandEvictions_uprsubmission.pdf.

120. Republic of South Africa, National Building Regulations and Building Standards Act, No. 103 of 1977.

121. IRIN, "South Africa: Poor Squatters Make Way for 2010 World Cup," *worldpress.org,* Apr. 16, 2007, http://www.worldpress.org/Africa/2755.cfm#down.

122. "South Africa: South African Government Urged to Stop Abusing Eviction Policy to Clean up Cities," *Afrika.no,* Aug. 7, 2005, http://www.afrika.no/Detailed/10113.html.

123. Thabo Mokgola, "Government's R160m housing project," *Southafrica.info,* Aug. 16, 2004, http://www.southafrica.info/news/socialhousing-project.htm.

124. "New Housing Policy Unveiled," *Southafrica.info,* Sept. 3, 2004, http://www.southafrica.info/news/housing-policy.htm.

125. "South African Government Information, Auditor-General's Performance Audit Highlights Irregular Awarding of More Than R10 Million in Housing Subsidies by the Free State Department of Housing," *SouthAfrica.info,* May 10, 2006, http://www.southafrica.info/news/housing-policy.htm.

126. Abigail Isaacs, "Serious Defects in Low Cost Housing: South Africa:

News: News24," July 8, 2008, http://lowcosthousing.blogspot.com/2008/07/serious-defects-in-low-cost-housing.htm.

127. Abigail Isaacs, "Serious Defects in Low-cost Housing," *News24,* May 9, 2008, http://www.news24.com/SouthAfrica/News/Serious-defects-in-low-cost-housing-20080508.

128. Pierre de Vos, "Irene Grootboom Died, Homeless, Forgotten, no C-class Mercedes in Sight," *Anti-Eviction: Western Cape,* Aug. 11, 2008, http://antieviction.org.za/2008/08/13/irene-grootboom-died-homeless-forgotten-no-c-class-mercedes-in-sight/.

129. Deputy President Thabo Mbeki, Address to the Seventh International Conference on People Living with HIV and AIDS, Cape Town, 1995.

130. "Evaluating Health Care: The Health of Nations," *Economist,* June 24, 2000.

131. Rachel, L. Swarns, "Drug Makers Drop South Africa Suit over AIDS Medicine," *New York Times,* Apr. 20, 2001, http://www.nytimes.com/2001/04/20/world/drug-makers-drop-south-africa-suit-over-aids-medicine.html.

132. *Minister of Health v. Treatment Action Campaign (TAC)* (2002) 5 SA 721 (CC).

133. "Dissent on AIDS by South Africa's President: Thoughtfulness or Folly?" *New York Times,* July 7, 2000.

134. Rachel L. Swarns and Lawrence K. Altman, "Amid Controversy, South Africa Opens World AIDS Forum," *New York Times,* July 10, 2000, http://partners.nytimes.com/library/world/africa/071000africa-aids.html.

135. Address by President Thabo Mbeki at the Inaugural Z. K. Mathews Memorial Lecture, Oct. 12, 2001, http://www.unisa.ac.za/contents/colleges/docs/2001/tm2001/tm101201.pdf

136. Chris McGreal, "Mbeki Admits He Is Still Aids Dissident Six Years On," *Guardian,* Nov. 5, 2007, http://www.guardian.co.uk/world/2007/nov/06/southafrica.aids.

137. "A History of Official Government HIV/AIDS Policy in South Africa," *South African History Online,* http://www.sahistory.org.za/topic/history-official-government-hivaids-policy-south-africa.

138. "Manto Tshabalala-Msimang dies," *Mail and Guardian,* Dec. 16, 2009, http://mg.co.za/article/2009-12-16-manto-tshabalalamsimang-dies.

139. "South Africa Aids Policy Attacked," BBC *News,* Aug. 19, 2006, http://news.bbc.co.uk/2/hi/africa/5265432.stm.

140. "Highly Qualified Doctor Who Ravaged South Africa's Health Service," *Sydney Morning Herald,* Jan. 13, 2010, http://www.smh.com.au/national/obituaries/highly-qualified-doctor-who-ravaged-south-africas-health-services-20100112-m4qm.html.

141. "Kader Asmal Vows to Fight Illiteracy," *Star* (Johannesburg), Feb. 14, 2000, in *This Week in South Africa,* Feb. 1–14, 2000.

142. "South African Pupils Are the Dunces of Africa," *Sunday Times* (Johannesburg), July 16, 2000, www.suntimes.co.za.

143. "Universities Face Major Revamp," *Sunday Times* (Johannesburg), July 9, 2000, July 9, 2000, www.suntimes.co.za.

144. "Pandor: Education Department Budget Vote 2007/08," *polity.org.za*, May 9, 2007, http://news.bbc.co.uk/2/hi/africa/5265432.stm.

145. South African Institute of Race Relations, Education, sairr.org.za, http://sairr.org.za/services/publications/south-africa-survey/south-africa-survey-online-2009–2010/education.

146. OECD, *Reviews of National Policies for Education: South Africa 2008* (2008).

147. "Gauteng Hospitals Rocked by Protests," *Independent Newspapers,* July 4, 2000, www.iol.co.za; "Pilot's Scam: Omar Was Told," *Sunday Times* (Johannesburg), July 4, 2000, www.suntimes.co.za.

148. Helen Epstein, "The Mystery of AIDS in South Arica," *New York Review of Books,* July 20, 2000, 51.

149. South African Police Service, Department of Police, Crime Statistics: Overview Republic of South Africa, 2003/2004, September 2004, www.saps.gov.za.

150. Charlene Smith, "Rape Has Become a Way of Life in South Africa," *iolnews,* Sept. 25, 2004, http://www.iol.co.za/news/south-africa/rape-has-become-a-way-of-life-in-south-africa-1.222663#.UZPUMLWmhzQ.

151. Angela Quintal, "Mbeki Attacks Writers for Their Crime Reports," *iolnews,* Dec. 3, 2004, http://www.iol.co.za/news/south-africa/mbeki-attacks-writers-for-their-crime-reports-1.223189#.UZPU_bWmhzQ.

152. "South Africa Rejects African Peer Review Mechanism Report," *Africa Files,* 2007, http://www.africafiles.org/article.asp?ID=15042.

153. Chris McGreal, "Report Attacks S African Crime and Corruption," *Guardian,* Jan. 28, 2007, http://www.theguardian.com/world/2007/jan/29/southafrica.chrismcgreal.

154. "Crime in South Africa—An Unassailable Problem?" *WorldNomads.com,* Feb. 12, 2007, http://journals.worldnomads.com/safetyhub/post/3282.aspx.

155. "Mbeki Critical of Crime Issues in APRM Report," *Mail and Guardian,* Dec. 6, 2007, www.mg.co.za.

156. "Special Report: Xenophobia" (2008), *Mail and Guardian,* www.mg.co.za.

157. Tererai Karimakwenda, "South Africa: Mbeki Blamed after 20 More Die in Xenophobic Attacks," *allAfrica,* May 19, 2008, http://allafrica.com/stories/200805191523.html and http://journals.worldnomads.com/safetyhub/post/3282.aspx.

158. Pierre de Vos, "Does Mbeki Think Corruption Is a Problem or Not?" *Constitutionally Speaking,* Dec. 8, 2006, http://constitutionallyspeaking.co.za/does-mbeki-think-corruption-is-a-problem-or-not/.

159. Address of the President of South Africa, Thabo Mbeki, at the Opening Ceremony of the United Nations Global Forum on Fighting Corruption and Safeguarding Integrity, Sandton Convention Centre, April 2, 2007, http://www.dfa.gov.za/docs/speeches/2007/mbek0402.htm.

160. Republic of South Africa, Department of International Relations and Cooperation, Newly-elected President Kgalema Motlanthe Addresses the National Assembly, Sept. 25, 2008, http://www.dfa.gov.za/docs/speeches/2008/motl0926.html.

161. Claire Suddath, "South Africa's AIDS Truthsayer," *Time*, Oct. 15, 2008, http://www.time.com/time/world/article/0,8599,1850886,00.html.

162. Celia W. Dugger, "Study Cites Toll of AIDS Policy in South Africa," *New York Times*, Nov. 25, 2008, http://www.nytimes.com/2008/11/26/world/africa/26aids.html?pagewanted=2&_r=0&em.

163. "The *Time* 100," *Time*, June 1, 2009, http://www.time.com/time/magazine/article/0,9171,1899834,00.html.

164. Ray Hartley, "Ginwala Commission Report—Conclusions and Recommendations—Full Text," *TimesLive*, Dec. 8, 2008, http://blogs.timeslive.co.za/hartley/2008/12/08/ginwala-commission-report-conclusions-and-recommendations-full-text/.

165. Stephen Grootes, "What's Next for Motlanthe?" *BDlive*, Dec. 19, 2012, http://www.bdlive.co.za/blogs/politics/2012/12/19/what-next-for-motlanthe.

166. Agence France Presse, "S. Africa Denies Dalai Lama Visa over World Cup Worries," Mar. 29, 2009, http://www.zimbio.com/Dalai+Lama/articles/654/Africa+denies+Dalai+Lama+visa+over+World+Cup.

167. Associated Press, "S. Africa Bars Dalai Lama from Peace Forum," Mar. 23, 2009, http://www.nbcnews.com/id/29841454/ns/world_news-africa/t/s-africa-bars-dalai-lama-peace-forum/#.uzwcuLWmhzQ.

168. "Lekota 'Serves Divorce Papers' on ANC," *iolnews*, Oct. 8, 2008, http://www.iol.co.za/news/politics/lekota-serves-divorce-papers-on-anc-1.419380#.uzp04rWmhzQ.

169. Ray Hartley, "Mosiuoa Lekota Announces Challenge to Zuma's ANC: Transcript," *TimesLive*, Oct. 8, 2008, http://blogs.timeslive.co.za/hartley/2008/10/08/mosiuoa-lekota-announces-challenge-to-zumas-anc-transcript/.

170. "'Shikota' Convention Oversubscribed," *iolnews*, Nov. 1, 2008, http://www.iol.co.za/news/politics/shikota-convention-oversubscribed-1.422704#.UZd7ebWmhzQ.

171. Clare Byrne, "Analysis: Can South Africa's ANC COPE with real opposition?" *m&c*, Dec. 16, 2008, http://news.monstersandcritics.com/africa/news/article_1448752.php/ANALYSIS_Can_South_Africa_s_ANC_COPE_with_real_opposition.

172. Congress of the People, "Official Constitution of the COPE," http://www.copesa.org.za/index.php/official-constitution-of-the-congress-of-the-people.

173. "ANC Breakaway Scores Poll Upset," *BBC News*, Dec. 11, 2008, http://news.bbc.co.uk/2/hi/africa/7777998.stm.

174. Election Resources on the Internet: Republic of South Africa General Election Results Lookup, Apr. 22, 2009, General Election Results—Republic of

South Africa Total: National Assembly, http://electionresources.org/za/provinces.php?election=2009.

175. "South Africa's Election Triumph," *SouthAfrica.info,* Apr. 28, 2009, http://www.southafrica.info/about/democracy/election-winner.htm#.uzwDkrWmhzQ.

176. SAPA, "National Assembly Elects Zuma as President," *polity.org.za,* May 6, 2009, http://electionresources.org/za/provinces.php?election=2009.

177. Republic of South Africa, South African Government News Agency, Address by His Excellency Mr. Jacob Zuma on the Occasion of his Inauguration as Fourth President of the Republic of South Africa, Union Buildings, Pretoria, May 9, 2009, http://www.sanews.gov.za/south-africa/full-text-president-zumas-inaugural-address.

178. IFEX, "Amendment Act a 'Grave Intrusion' on Freedom of Expression, says FXI," Sept. 9, 2009, http://www.ifex.org/south_africa/2009/09/09/films_and_publications_amendment_act/.

179. Republic of South Africa, *Government Gazette,* Vol. 530, No. 32534, Aug. 28, 2009, Act No. 3 of 2009, Films and Publications Amendment Act, 2009, http://www.unesco.org/new/fileadmin/MULTIMEDIA/HQ/CI/WPFD2009/pdf/Films%20and%20Publications%20Act%202009.pdf.

180. Mandy de Waal, "The New Age Launches; Underestimate It at Your Peril," *Daily Maverick,* July 23, 2010, http://www.dailymaverick.co.za/article/2010-07-23-the-new-age-launches-underestimate-it-at-your-peril#.UZnIcrWmhzQ.

181. "South Africa: City Press Publishes Maharaj Interview with Scorpions," *Africa—News and Analysis,* Nov. 28, 2011, http://africajournalismtheworld.com/2011/11/28/south-africa-city-press-publishes-maharaj-interview-with-scorpions/.

182. Stephen Grootes, "Analysis: Zuma v. Zapiro Is Possibly Much More Than Just Another Court Case," *Daily Maverick,* Dec. 15, 2010, http://www.dailymaverick.co.za/article/2010-12-15-analysis-zuma-vs-zapiro-is-possibly-much-more-than-just-another-court-case#.UZH5rWmhzQ.

183. "Zapiro and Zuma," June 13, 2011, http://whatishappeninginsouthafrica.blogspot.com/2011/06/zapiro-and-zuma.html.

184. "Goodman Gallery Removes Brett Murray's Painting of Jacob Zuma with His Private Parts Hanging Out," *OleAfrica,* no date, http://oleafrica.com/politics/goodman-gallery-removes-brett-murrays-painting-of-jacob-zuma-with-his-private-parts-hanging-out/4511.

185. Mioranda Andrew and Jenni Evans, "Cartoon Is a Serious Commentary: Zapiro," *Post,* July 6, 2012, http://www.thepost.co.za/cartoon-is-a-serious-commentary-zapiro-1.1336084#.UZRq-rWmhzQ.

186. Republic of South Africa, Minister of State Security, Protection of Information Bill, B6-2010, http://www.info.gov.za/view/DownloadFileAction?id=118894.

187. David Smith, "Proposed South African Secrecy Laws Widely Condemned," *Guardian*, Mar. 30, 2012, http://www.guardian.co.uk/world/2012/mar/30/south-africa-secrecy-laws-condemned.

188. "Excerpts from a Speech Delivered by Luwellyn Landers, MP During the Debate in the National Assembly: Protection of State Information Bill on Wednesday, Nov. 16, 2011," *Politicsweb*, Nov. 16, 2011, http://www.politicsweb.co.za/politicsweb/view/politicsweb/en/page71619?oid=267171&sn=Marketing web+detail.

189. "South Africa MPs Pass Controversial 'Secrecy Bill,'" BBC *News Africa*, Nov. 22, 2011, http://www.bbc.co.uk/news/world-africa-15822105.

190. Andisiwe Makinana, "Secrecy Bill Could Be Made Law by June," *Mail and Guardian*, Feb. 26, 2013, http://mg.co.za/article/2013-02-26-secrecy-bill-could-become-law-by-june/.

191. "Outrage as Secrecy Bill Is Passed," *Legalbrief Africa*, No. 52, Apr. 30, 2013, http://www.legalbrief.co.za/article.php?story=2013043011404331.

192. Sarah Evans, "MPs Acting Oddly? They Could Be Reading the Secrecy Bill," *Mail and Guardian*, May 5, 2013, http://mg.co.za/article/2013-05-05-mps-acting-oddly-they-could-be-reading-the-secrecy-bill.

193. Reporters Without Borders, *World Press Freedom Index 2013*, http://fr.rsf.org/IMG/pdf/classement_2013_gb-bd.pdf.

194. Delia Robertson, "South Africa's African National Congress Celebrates 100th Anniversary," *Voice of America*, Jan. 7, 2012, http://www.voanews.com/content/safricas-anc-celebrates-100th-anniversary-136901858/150444.html.

195. Ray Hartley, "Kgalema Motlanthe on 'the Sins' of Incumbency," *Times Live*, Oct. 13, 2009, http://blogs.timeslive.co.za/hartley/2009/10/13/kgalema-motlanthe-on-the-sins-of-incumbency/.

196. J. Brooks Spector, "The Agonies of Choice: Kgalema Motlanthe Contemplates the Future," *Daily Maverick*, Dec. 3, 2012, http://www.dailymaverick.co.za/article/2012-12-03-the-agonies-of-choice-kgalema-motlanthe-contemplates-the-future#.UZR1YrWmhzQ.

197. "Motlanthe Criticizes ANC Election Process," *Sowetan Live*, Dec. 3, 2012, http://www.sowetanlive.co.za/news/2012/12/03/motlanthe-criticises-anc-election-process.

198. Agence France Presse, "Ramaphosa Tapped as South Africa's New Leader," *News24*, Dec. 20, 2012, http://www.news24.com/SouthAfrica/Politics/Ramaphosa-tapped-as-SAs-new-leader-20121220.

199. Ranjeni Manusamy, "Mangaung Massacre and the Rise of the New ANC," *Daily Maverick*, Dec. 21, 2012, http://www.dailymaverick.co.za/article/2012-12-21-mangaung-massacre-and-the-rise-of-the-new-anc#.UYu7frWmhzQ.

200. African National Congress, "Statement of NEC Meeting on 15–17 March 2013," http://www.anc.org.za/show.php?id=10133.

201. ANC Kwazulu-Natal, "Address by President JG Zuma to KZN Provincial General Council University of KZN Durban Westville," Mar. 25, 2013, http://

www.anckzn.org.za/media/speeches/address-president-jg-zuma-kzn-provincial
-general-council-university-kzn-durban-westvi.

202. Robyn Dixon, "Power Struggle Paralyzes South Africa's Ruling ANC
Party," *Los Angeles Times,* Dec. 2, 2012, http://articles.latimes.com/2012/
dec/02/world/la-fg-south-africa-zuma-20121203.

203. Ibid.

204. Bianca Capazorio, "Cost of Nkandla Renovations Rises," *iolnews,*
March 23, 2013, http://www.iol.co.za/news/politics/cost-of-nkandla-renovations
-rises-1.1490601#.UZZMtrWmhzQ.

205. amaBhungane, "The Nkandla Files," *amaBhungane Centre for Investigative Journalism,* July 5, 2013, http://amabhungane.co.za/article/2013-07-05
-the-nkandla-files.

206. Craig McKune, "Project Railroaded from the Start," *amaBhungane
Centre for Investigative Journalism,* July 5, 2013, http://www.amabhungane
.co.za/article/2013-07-05-project-railroaded-from-the-start.

207. Phillip de Wet and Sam Sole, "Guptagate: Why Waterkloof Report
Won't Fly," *Mail and Guardian,* May 24, 2013, http://mg.co.za/article/2013-05
-24-00-guptagate-why-waterkloof-report-wont-fly.

208. "You Don't Understand Democracy, Zuma Told," *News24,* Sept. 14,
2012, http://www.iol.co.za/business/business-news/gordhan-corruption-a-social
-problem-1.1506499#.UXptmrWmhzQ.

209. Siyabonga Mkhwanazi, "'ANC to Rule Until Jesus Comes Back,'" *iolnews,*
May 5, 2008, http://www.iol.co.za/news/politics/anc-to-rule-until-jesus-comes
-back-1.398843#.UZnhm7WmhzQ.

210. "Zuma to Name New Chief Justice," *Times Live,* Oct. 1, 2009, www
.timeslive.co.za/news.

211. SAPA, "Sandile Ngcobo Appointed Chief Justice," *Polity.org.za,* Oct. 1,
2009, http://www.polity.org.za/article/ngcobo-is-the-new-chief-justice-2009-10-01.

212. "The Decision by President Jacob Zuma to Extend the Term of South
Africa's Top Judge Is Being Challenged in Court, a Legal Body and an NGO Said
on Wednesday," Reuters, Oct. 1, 2009, http://www.reuters.com/article/2011/
06/15/ozatp-safrica-judiciary-idAFJOE75E08D20110615.

213. "Ngcobo Withdraws Term Extension," *Polity.org.za,* July 27, 2011,
http://www.polity.org.za/article/ngcobo-withdraws-term-extension-2011-07-27.

214. Robyn Dixon, "South Africa's Zuma Names Controversial New Chief
Justice," *Los Angeles Times,* Sept. 9, 2011, http://articles.latimes.com/2011/
sep/09/world/la-fg-south-africa-jurist-20110909.

215. Richard Lee, "Stop Mogoeng from Being SA Chief Justice," *Open Society Initiative for Southern Africa,* Sept. 2, 2011, http://www.osisa.org/law/
south-africa/stop-mogoeng-being-sa-chief-justice.

216. Pierre de Vos, "Full Sowetan Interview with Gwede Mantashe," *Constitutionally Speaking,* Aug. 18, 2011, http://constitutionallyspeaking.co.za/full
-sowetan-interview-with-gwede-mantashe/.

217. Address by President Jacob Zuma on the Occasion of Bidding Farewell to Former Chief Justice Sandile Ngcobo, and Welcoming Chief Justice, Mogoeng Mogoeng, National Assembly, Cape Town, Nov. 1, 2011, www.anc.org.za.

218. President Jacob Zuma, Address on the Occasion of the 3rd Access to Justice Conference, Pretoria, July 8, 2011, www.info.gov.za.

219. Democratic Governance and Rights Unit, University of Cape Town, "Time to Break the Glass Ceiling," Oct. 15, 2012, www.dgru.uct.za.

220. Fatima Schroeder and Bianca Capazorio, "JSC Faces Crisis over Transformation," *iolnews,* Apr. 13, 2013.

221. "CLC Kicks off Amidst South Africa's Transformation Row," *This Day Live,* Apr. 23, 2013, http://www.thisdaylive.com/articles/clc-kicks-off-amidst-south-africa-s-transformation-row/145705/.

222. *Freedom Under Law v. The Judicial Service Commission and Others,* Applicant's Submission, Case 052/2010, http://www.freedomunderlaw.org/wp-content/files/FUL_v_JSC_-_Appellants_heads_of_argument_in_the_SCA.pdf.

223. Denise Williams, "Zuma Wants 'African' Justice," *Times Live,* Nov. 2, 2012, http://www.timeslive.co.za/thetimes/2012/11/02/zuma-wants-african-justice.

224. Dixon, "Power Struggle Paralyzes South Africa's Ruling ANC Party."

225. Bradley Dubbelman, "South Africa: Post-election Report, " *Polity.org.za,* Oct. 12, 2009, http://www.polity.org.za/article/south-africa-postelection-report-2009-10-12.

226. Newsguy, "DA and ID Unite Against ANC," *The Right Perspective,* Aug. 15, 2010, http://www.therightperspective.org/2010/08/15/da-and-id-unite-against-anc/#sthash.jDVyk9jK.dpbs.

227. Marianne Merten, "Mbeki Slates ANC's Lack of Leadership," *iolnews,* Oct. 21, 2012, http://www.iol.co.za/news/politics/mbeki-slates-anc-s-lack-of-leadership-1.1407509#.UYuhO7WmhzQ.

228. State of the Nation Address by His Excellency Jacob Zuma, President of the Republic of South Africa on the Occasion of the Joint Sitting of Parliament in Cape Town, Feb. 14, 2013, http://www.info.gov.za/speech/DynamicAction?pageid=461&sid=34250&tid=98676.

229. Liesl Peyper, "Opposition Parties Reject President Zuma's State of Nation Address," *finweek,* Feb. 15, 2013, http://finweek.com/2013/02/15/opposition-parties-reject-president-zumas-state-of-the-nation-address/.

230. Caiphus Kgosana, "United Opposition 'Bad for Democracy': Zuma," *TimesLive,* Feb. 22, 2013, http://www.timeslive.co.za/thetimes/2013/02/22/united-opposition-bad-for-democracy-zuma.

231. Faranaaz Parker, "Ramphele: Join Agang to Build the Country of Our Dreams," *Mail and Guardian,* Feb. 18, 2013, http://mg.co.za/article/2013-02-18-ramphele-join-agang-to-build-the-country-of-our-dreams.

232. Sipho Masondo, "Ramphele's Agang Worries ANC," *City Press,* Feb. 18, 2013, http://www.citypress.co.za/politics/rampheles-agang-worries-anc/.

233. "Malema: It's an EFF Revolution," SAPA, News24, July 11, 2013, http://www.news24.com/SouthAfrica/Politics/Malema-Its-an-EFF-revolution-20130711.

234. "Sudanese President to Skip Zuma's Inauguration," The Free Library, May 9, 2009, http://www.thefreelibrary.com/Sudanese+president+to+skip+Zuma%27s+inauguration.-a0199435046; "Sudan's Kiir Witnesses South Africa's Zuma Inauguration," The Free Library, May 9, 2009, http://www.thefree library.com/Sudan%27s+Kiir+witnesses+South+Africa%27s+Zuma+inaugurat ion.-a0199480220.

235. "SA: Department Foreign Affairs Renamed, Restructured," AllAfrica, May 10, 2009, http://allafrica.com/stories/200905100043.html.

236. Proceedings of the Seventeenth African Union Summit, www.au.int/en/sites/default/files/17th%20_SUMMIT_-_DECISIONS_DECLARATIONS_and_RESOLUTIONS_-_eng%20FINAL.pdf.

237. C. Molele, "SA Defends 'Ambivalent' Stance on Syria," Mail and Guardian, Oct. 7, 2011, http://mg.co.za/article/2011-10-07-sa-defends-ambivalent-stance-on-syria.

238. L. Redvers, "Lion's Share of Swazi Loan to Go to Construction," Mail and Guardian, Sept. 2, 2011, http://mg.co.za/article/2011-09-02-lions-share-of-swazi-loan-to-go-to-construction.

239. Office of the High Commissioner for Human Rights, United Nations Human Rights, South Africa Country Report, www.ohchr.org/EN/countries/Africa Region/Pages/ZAIndex.aspx.

240. www.unhcr.ch/tbs/doc.nsf/Newhv/VAIISPRByCountry?OpenView&Start=1&Count=250&Expand=162.8#162.8

241. David Smith, "Desmond Tutu Attacks South African Government over Dalai Lama ban," Guardian, Oct. 4, 2011, http://www.guardian.co.uk/world/2011/oct/04/tutu-attacks-anc-dalai-lama-visa.

242. "The SCA's Judgment on the Dalai Lama Visa delay," politicsweb, Nov. 29, 2012, reprint of judgment, http://www.politicsweb.co.za/politicsweb/view/politicsweb/en/page71656?oid=343918&sn=Detail.

243. SAPA, "Dalai Lama Can Visit for My 90th Says Tutu," www.news24.com, Nov. 29, 2012, http://www.news24.com/SouthAfrica/News/Dalai-Lama-can-visit-for-my-90th-says-Tutu-20121129.

244. Republic of South Africa, Building a Better World: The Diplomacy of Ubuntu, White Paper on South Africa's Foreign Policy, May 13, 2011, http://www.info.gov.za/view/DownloadFileAction?id=148482.

245. Address by His Excellency, President of the Republic of South Africa, Dr. Jacob Zuma on Aspects of South African Foreign Policy at the University of Pretoria, South African Government Information, Oct. 13, 2011, http://www.info.gov.za/speech/DynamicAction?pageid=461&tid=45990.

246. Franz Wild and Mike Cohen, "Zuma Ready to Redeploy Army to CAR," Bloomberg, Apr. 25, 2013, http://www.bloomberg.com/news/2013-04-24/s-africa-s-zuma-to-send-army-to-central-african-republic.html.

247. Ian Davidson, "Statement by Ian Davidson, MP DA Shadow Minister of International Relations and Co-Operation, July 22, 2013, *politicsweb.co.za,* http://www.politicsweb.co.za/politicsweb/view/politicsweb/en/page72308?oid =393261&sn=Marketingweb+detail&pid=90389.

248. Angus Shaw, "South Africa Rebukes Its Officials over Zimbabwe," ABC *News,* July 22, 2013, http://abcnews.go.com/International/wireStory/south -africa-rebukes-officials-zimbabwe-19737029.

249. "Foreign Direct Investment Drops in South Africa," *Bizcommunity.com,* July 27 2011, http://www.bizcommunity.com/Article/196/516/62283.html.

250. Bond, "South Africa Loses Its 'War on Poverty.'"

251. United Nations Development Programme, "Assessing Progress in Africa Toward the Millenium Development Goals—Country MDG Report—South Africa" (2010), http://web.undp.org/africa/mdg2010.shtml.

252. United Nations Development Programme, *Human Development Index 2010,* http://hdr.undp.org/en/media/Lets-Talk-HD-HDI_2010.pdf.

253. Organisation for Economic Cooperation and Development, *Economic Survey of South Africa 2010: Trends in South African Income Distribution and Poverty since the Fall of Apartheid,* http://www.oecd.org/southafrica/southafrica 2010.htm.

254. "Black Economic Empowerment: The President Says It Has Failed," *Economist,* Mar. 31, 2010, http://www.economist.com/node/15824024.

255. "South Africa: Inequality not so Black and White," IRIN, Feb. 8, 2010, http://www.irinnews.org/printreport.aspx?reportid=88038.

256. Erin Conway-Smith, "Black South Africans Moving Up the Wealth Ladder," *Globe and Mail* (Canada), Sept. 17, 2011, http://www.theglobeandmail .com/report-on-business/economy/economy-lab/daily-mix/black-south-africans -moving-up-the-wealth-ladder/article2203192/.

257. Euromonitor International, "South Africa—The Most Unequal Income Distribution in the World," June 13, 2012, http://blog.euromonitor.com/2012/ 06/south-africa-the-most-unequal-income-distribution-in-the-world.html.

258. "Report: Corruption in South Africa Worsens, Harms Citizens," *NewsMaxWorld,* May 3, 2013, http://www.newsmaxworld.com/Africa/safrica -corruption-citizens-worse/2013/05/03/id/502668.

259. SAPA, "Gordhan: Corruption a Social Problem," *Business Report,* Apr. 25, 2013, http://www.iol.co.za/business/business-news/gordhan-corruption-a -social-problem-1.1506499#.UXptmrWmhzQ.

260. Moody's, "Rating Action: Moody's Downgrades South Africa's Government Bond Rating to Baa1; Outlook Remains Negative," Sept. 27, 2012, http://www.moodys.com/research/Moodys-downgrades-South-Africas -government-bond-rating-to-Baa1-outlook--PR_256159.

261. Nicholas Kotch, "Equitable Balance of Trade Needed between South Africa, China—Zuma," *BDlive,* 3/26/13, http://za.news.yahoo.com/equitable -balance-trade-needed-between-sa-china-zuma-142010134--finance.html.

262. "South Africa Joins BRIC Nations at China's Request," *2point6billion*

.com, Dec. 29, 2010, http://www.2point6billion.com/news/2010/12/29/south
-africa-joins-bric-nations-at-chinas-request-8291.html.

263. David Smith, "Brics Eye Infrastructure Funding through New Development Bank, *Guardian,* Mar. 28, 2013, http://www.guardian.co.uk/global-devel
opment/2013/mar/28/brics-countries-infrastructure-spending-development-bank.

264. T. J. Strydom, "Business Confidence Drops," *Times Live,* Apr. 4, 2013,
http://www.timeslive.co.za/thetimes/2013/04/04/business-confidence-drops.

265. Justice Malala, "The Marikana Action Is a Strike by the Poor against
the State and the Haves," *Guardian,* Aug. 17, 2012, www.webcitation.org/
6A2cAXPZn).

266. "Miners Killed Like Possessed Vermin," *Mail and Guardian,* Oct. 23,
2012, www.mg.co.za.

267. "Lonmin Death Toll at 34, 78 Injured," *Moneyweb,* Aug. 16, 2012,
www.moneyweb.co.za/mw/content/en/moneyweb-mining?oid=593753&sn
=2009+Detail.

268. Henry D. Gombya, "At Least 34 Dead, 78 Wounded in Marikana Massacre," *London Evening Post,* Aug. 17, 2012, http://www.thelondoneveningpost
.com/at-least-34-dead-78-wounded-in-marikana-massacre/.

269. "South African Mine Killings: Jacob Zuma Announces Inquiry," BBC
News, Aug. 17, 2012, www.bbc.co.uk/news/world-africa-19301690.

270. "Inside Story: South Africa's Economic Apartheid," *Al Jazeera,* Sept. 12,
2012, www.aljazeera.com.

271. Reuters, "Police Kill 34 Striking Miners in South Africa," *Jerusalem Post,*
Aug. 17, 2012, www.jpost.com.

272. Jon Herskovitz, "Mine 'Bloodbath' Shocks Post-apartheid South Africa," *Independent,* Aug. 17, 2012, http://www.independent.co.uk/news/world/
africa/mine-bloodbath-shocks-postapartheid-south-africa-8056663.html.

273. "South African Official Defends Police Killing of 34, *New York Times,*
Aug. 19, 2012, www.nytmes.com.

274. "Anger Mounts over South African Miners' Fate—Africa," *Al Jazeera
English,* Aug. 20, 2012, www.Aljazeera.com/news/Africa.

275. Matthew Hill, "Lonmin Workers Agree to 22% Pay Rise, to Return
Sept. 20," Bloomberg News, www.bloomberg.com/news/2012–09–18/lonmin
-workers-agree-to-22-pay-rise-to-return-sept-20.html.

276. Mandy de Waal, "Marikana: The Strike Might Be Over, but the Struggle Continues," *Daily Maverick,* May 7, 2013, http://www.dailymaverick.co.za/
article/2012-09-19-marikana-the-strike-might-be-over-but-the-struggle-continues#
.UYlDyLWmhzQ.

277. "Amplats Fires 12,000 South African Platinum Miners," BBC *News,*
Oct. 5, 2012, www.bbc.co.uk/news/world-africa-19848915.

278. "South Africa Vineyard Clashes Leave One Dead," BBC *News Africa,*
Nov. 14, 2012, http://www.bbc.co.uk/news/world-africa-20328701.

279. "Marikana Inquiry Updates," *Times Live,* Oct. 23, 2012, www.timeslive
.co.za.

280. Admin, "Exxaro Strike Ends," *All ZA News,* Mar. 23, 2013, http://www
.allzanews.com/2013/03/23/exxaro-strike-ends/.

281. "Police under Fire after Ficksburg Protester's Death," *Mail and Guardian,* Apr. 18, 2011, http://mg.co.za/article/2011–04–18-police-under-fire-after
-ficksburg.

282. Multi-Level Government Initiatives, "Service Delivery Protests Barometer 1: Frequency and Fluctuation by Year and Season," Aug. 2012, http://www
.mlgi.org.za/barometers/service-delivery-protest-barometer/service-delivery
-protests-barometer-1-frequency-and-fluctuation-by-year-and-season.

283. Auditor-General South Africa, Annual Report 2010–11, Centenary
Edition, www.agsa.co.za.

284. Moipane Malefane and Sibusiso Ngalwa, "Now I Understand the Service Delivery Protests, Says Zuma," *Times Live,* May 15, 2011, http://www
.timeslive.co.za/local/article1067580.ece/Now-I-understand-the-service
-delivery-protests-says-Zuma.

285. Sherilee Lakmidas, "Update2—S. Africa's Eskom May Resort to Blackouts This Winter," Reuters, May 22, 2013, http://www.reuters.com/places/africa/
article/2013/04/22/safrica-eskom-idUSL5NoD9oRS20130422.

286. SAPA, "Medupi Delays Disturb Minister," *City Press,* July 10, 2013,
http://www.citypress.co.za/news/medupi-delays-disturb-minister/.

287. Admin, "Water Rhapsody: Blue Drop Water Quality Scheme Gains Momentum but Critics Say More Is Needed, " Nov. 21, 2010, *Rainharvest.co.za,*
http://www.rainharvest.co.za/2010/11/blue-drop-water-quality-scheme-gains
-momentum-but-critics-say-more-is-needed/.

288. WHO/UNICEF Joint Monitoring Programme for Water Supply and Sanitation Data Table South Africa 2010.

289. Statistics South Africa, Census 2011: Statistical Release (October 2012),
pp. 52–53, http://www.statssa.gov.za/Publications/P03014/P030142011.pdf.

290. Republic of South Africa, Department of Water Affairs, Green Drop
Assessment, http://www.dwaf.gov.za/dir_ws/gds/DefaultAssessmentOverview
.aspx?ProvCode=SA.

291. Global Water Intelligence, "Bluewater Bio's South African Safari," Nov.
2009, http://www.globalwaterintel.com/about/.

292. Diane Hawker, "Plea for State to Kick the Bucket System," *iolnews,* Mar.
24, 2013, http://www.iol.co.za/news/politics/plea-for-state-to-kick-the-bucket
-system-1.1490802#.UZSD8LWmhzQ.

293. Statistics South Africa, General Household Survey 2009 (May 2020),
Polity.org.za, http://www.polity.org.za/article/general-household-survey-2009
-may-2010-2010-05-07.

294. Laurie Prinsloo, "Sexwale Calls on All South Africans to Help with
Housing Backlog," *Polity.org.za,* Sept. 29, 2011, http://www.polity.org.za/article/
sexwale-calls-on-all-south-africans-to-help-with-housing-backlog-2011-09-29.

295. South African Government Information, State of the Nation Address
by His Excellency Jacob G. Zuma, President of the Republic of South Africa, at

the Joint Sitting of Parliament, Cape Town, Feb. 10, 2011, http://www.info.gov
.za/speech/DynamicAction?pageid=461&tid=27985.

296. Peter Hain, "South Africa: A Crisis for Business over Social Reform,"
Guardian, Apr. 22, 2013, http://www.guardian.co.uk/commentisfree/2013/
apr/22/south-africa-crisis-business/print.

297. South African Information, Address by President Jacob Zuma on the
Occasion of World AIDS day, Pretoria Showgrounds, Dec. 1, 2009, http://www
.info.gov.za/speeches/2009/09120112151001.htm.

298. Peroshini Govender, "South Africa to Expand AIDS Treatment: Zuma,"
Reuters, Dec. 1, 2009, http://www.reuters.com/article/2009/12/01/us-aids-safrica
-idUSTRE5B021420091201.

299. David Smith, "South Africa's Jacob Zuma Promises to Take HIV Test in
Aids Policy Reversal," *Guardian,* Dec. 1, 2009, http://www.guardian.co.uk/world/
2009/dec/01/jacob-zuma-hiv-test.

300. Tosin Sulaiman, "AIDS Drug Roll-out Boosts South African Life Expectancy," Reuters, Feb. 29, 2012, http://in.reuters.com/article/2012/11/29/safrica
-aids-idINDEE8AS0DC20121129. Not all researchers shared this view. See
Appendix, Table 7.

301. UNICEF, "South Africa: Women and Children in South Africa," Nov. 11,
2009, http://www.unicef.org/southafrica/children.html.

302. South African Government Information, State of the Nation Address
by His Excellency JG Zuma, President of the Republic of South Africa, at the
Joint Sitting of Parliament, Cape Town, Feb. 11, 2010, http://www.info.gov.za/
speeches/2010/10021119051001.htm.

303. World Economic Forum, *Global Competitiveness Index 2010,* www
.wef.org.

304. *Trends in International Mathematics and Science Study 2003,* http://
timss.bc.edu/timss2003.html.

305. *Progress in International Reading and Literacy Study 2006,* http://timss.
bc.edu/pirls2006/index.html.

306. "Our Diagnosis of SA's Problems—Trevor Manuel," *Politicsweb,* June 9,
2011, http://www.politicsweb.co.za/politicsweb/view/politicsweb/en/page71656
?oid=240405&sn=Detail.

307. Aldero Education, "South African Education Statistics—Parts 1–3,"
Sept. 2011, http://www.youtube.com/watch?v=s5CVjorySCw.

308. Deon de Lange, "80% of Public Schools Dysfunctional—Report," *iolnews,* Apr. 7, 2008, http://www.iol.co.za/news/south-africa/80-of-public-schools
-dysfunctional-report-1.395456#.uzwPgrWmhzQ.

309. Celia Dugger, "New Schools in South Arica Serve the Underserved,"
Sept. 9, 2011, http://www.nytimes.com/2010/09/09/world/africa/09safrica.html
?pagewanted=1&_r=0.

310. "South Africa Has too Few Good Teachers—Study," *News24,* Sept. 21,
2011, http://www.news24.com/SouthAfrica/News/SA-has-too-few-good-teachers
-study-20110921.

311. "South Africa's Education System Crumbling," *Voice of America,* June 1, 2010, http://www.voanews.com/content/south-africas-education-system-crumbling--95459494/160415.html.

312. "EE Sues the Minister for Failure to Set Education Standards," *Skills Portal,* Mar. 8, 2012, http://www.skillsportal.co.za/page/education/1196960-EE-sues-ministers-for-failure-to-set-education-standards#.UYgc4LWmhzR.

313. Jonathan Jansen, Helen Suzman Foundation Memorial Lecture, Nov. 22, 2012, http://hsf.org.za/resource-centre/lectures/Helen%20Suzman%20Memorial%20Lecture_The%20mathematics%20of%20democracy_Jonathan%20Jansen.pdf/view.

314. Hermann Giliomee, "Reconsidering Verwoerd and Bantu Education," *politicsweb,* Sept. 13, 2012, http://www.politicsweb.co.za/politicsweb/view/politicsweb/en/page71619?oid=326297&sn=Detail.

315. United Nations Office on Drugs and Crime, *The 2011 United Nations Survey of Crime Trends and Operations of Criminal Justice Systems,* http://www.unodc.org/unodc/en/data-and-analysis/United-Nations-Surveys-on-Crime-Trends-and-the-Operations-of-Criminal-Justice-Systems.html.

316. "Anene Booysen: Doctor Reveals Bredasdorp Rape Victim's Injury Details," *South Africa News,* Feb. 7, 2013, http://southafricanews.wordpress.com/tag/anene-booysen/.

317. Maria Hengeveld, "South Africa Finally Wakes up to Sexual Violence," *Guardian Africa Network,* Feb. 15, 2013, http://www.guardian.co.uk/world/2013/feb/15/south-africa-sexual-violence-women.

318. "Child Rape in South Africa," *Women in Society,* Aug. 8, 2011, http://womenandsocietyinworld.blogspot.ca/2011/08/child-rape-in-south-africa.html.

319. Lebogang Seale, "He Said Sex with a Virgin Could Cure HIV," *iolnews,* Apr. 25, 2013, http://www.iol.co.za/news/crime-courts/he-said-sex-with-a-virgin-could-cure-hiv-1.1505971#.UXkxB7WmhzQ.

320. Sipho Hlongwane, "Analysis: The ANC's Provincial Criminal Enterprises Problem," *Daily Maverick,* July 31, 2012, http://www.dailymaverick.co.za/article/2012-07-23-analysis-the-ancs-provincial-criminal-enterprises-problem#.UZS_TrWmhzQ.

321. "S Africa: KwaZulu-Natal Sees Return to Bloody Political Fighting and Taxi Wars," *Mail and Guardian,* Oct. 19, 2012, http://africajournalismtheworld.com/tag/political-murders-in-s-africa/.

322. Olivia Kumwenda, "Farm Murders Highlight Apartheid's Toxic Legacy in South Africa," Reuters, Nov. 28, 2012, http://www.reuters.com/article/2012/11/29/us-safrica-farming-crime-idUSBRE8AS02120121129.

323. South African Police Service, Department of Police, Crime Statistics Overview RSA, 2011/2012, http://cdn.mg.co.za/content/documents/2012/09/20/2012_Crime_Statistics.pdf.

324. Farnaaz Parker, "Crime Statistics Show Marginal Improvement," *Mail*

and Guardian, Sept. 20, 2012, http://mg.co.za/article/2012-09-20-marginal
-improvement-in-crime-stats/.

325. SAPA, "Crime Stats 'Cold Comfort': DA," *iolnews,* Sept. 20, 2012, http://
www.iol.co.za/news/crime-courts/crime-stats-cold-comfort-da-1.1387571#
.uztCr7WmhzQ.

326. South African Institute of Race Relations, "2010/2010—Crime and Security," in *South Africa Survey 2010/2011,* http://www.sairr.org.za/services/
publications/south-africa-survey/south-africa-survey-online-2010–2011/
crime-and-security.

327. Victoria Eastwood, "Bigger Than the Army: South Africa's Private Security Forces," CNN, Feb. 8, 2013, http://www.cnn.com/2013/02/08/business/
south-africa-private-security/index.html?sr=sharebar_facebook.

328. Araminta Wordsworth, "South African Police in the Headlines Again
for All the Wrong Reasons," *National Post,* Mar. 12, 2013, http://fullcomment
.nationalpost.com/2013/03/12/south-african-police-in-the-headlines-again
-for-all-the-wrong-reasons/.

329. Jonny Steinberg, *Thin Blue: The Unwritten Rules of South African Policing* (Jeppestown [Johannesburg], 2009).

330. "Selebi Gets 15 years," *iafrica.com,* http://news.iafrica.com/sa/650288
.html.

331. Jacob Zuma, "Why I Chose Bheki Cele—Jacob Zuma," *Politicsweb,*
Sept. 29, 2009, http://politicsweb.co.za/politicsweb/view/politicsweb/en/page
71619?oid=138018&sn=Detail.

332. "President Zuma Axes Cele, Appoints First Female National Police
Commissioner," *SAcommercialprop.News,* Dec. 6, 2012, http://www.sacom
mercialpropnews.co.za/business-specialties/commercial-property-leasing/4938
-president-zuma-axes-cele-appoints-first-female-national-police-commissioner
.html.

333. "SA Sees SAPS as Most Corrupt within the State—Survey," *corruption-
watch,* June 27, 2012, http://www.corruptionwatch.org.za/content/sa-sees-saps
-most-corrupt-within-state-survey.

334. Piet Coetzer, "Police Brutality: Statistics over 10 Years Tell a Horror
Story," *Leadership,* Mar. 5, 2013, http://www.leadershiponline.co.za/articles/
police-brutality.

335. Jonathan Miller, "South Africa: Man Dragged by Police Van Dies in
Custody," *4news,* Feb. 28, 2013, http://www.channel4.com/news/south-africa
-man-dragged-by-police-van-dies-in-custody.

336. Carien du Plessis, "'Iron Fist" to Deal with Lawlessness during Protests," *City Press,* Feb. 14, 2013, http://www.citypress.co.za/news/iron-fist-to
-deal-with-lawlessness-during-protests/.

337. Alex Perry, "Pistorius and South Africa's Culture of Violence," *Time,*
Mar. 11, 2013, http://www.time.com/time/magazine/article/0,9171,2137420,00
.html.

338. Ronnie Kasrils, "Letter: Zuma Should Dismiss Police Chiefs," *BDlive*, Mar. 6, 2013, http://www.bdlive.co.za/opinion/letters/2013/03/05/letter-zuma-should-dismiss-police-chiefs.

339. Scott Johnson, "Those Who Love South Africa Ask If It's Existentially Violent," IHT *Rendezvous*, Mar. 11, 2013, http://rendezvous.blogs.nytimes.com/2013/03/11/those-who-love-south-africa-ask-if-its-existentially-violent/.

340. Francis Hweshi, "Media: Tension Brewing in Townships over Foreigners," *Anti-Eviction Campaign, Western Cape*, June 1, 2009, http://antieviction.org.za/2009/06/02/media-tension-brewing-in-townships-over-foreigners/.

341. David Smith, "Nelson Mandela Gives World Cup a Dream Finale with a Wave and a Smile," *Guardian*, July 11, 2010, http://www.guardian.co.uk/football/2010/jul/11/world-cup-final-nelson-mandela/print.

342. "Somali Shops Looted, Burnt in PE," News 24, May 26, 2011, http://www.news24.com/SouthAfrica/News/Somali-shops-looted-burnt-in-PE-20110526.

343. "South Africa: Government Gets Lowest Rating on Xenophobia," IRIN, July 4, 2011, http://www.youtube.com/watch?v=s5CVjorySCw.

344. "South Africa's Extraordinary Skills Shortage—Adcorp," *politicsweb*, May 1, 2011, http://www.politicsweb.co.za/politicsweb/view/politicsweb/en/page71619?oid=235542&sn=Marketingweb+detail.

345. Scott C. Johnson, "Fleeing from South Africa," *Newsweek*, Feb. 13, 2009, http://www.thedailybeast.com/newsweek/2009/02/13/fleeing-from-south-africa.html.

346. "UN Declares 18 July Mandela Day," *SouthAfrica.info*, Nov. 12, 2009, http://www.dailymail.co.uk/news/article-2368573/Nelson-Mandela-celebrations-South-Africa-95th-birthday-confirmed-health-improving.html.

347. Anthony Bond, "Celebrations across South Africa for Mandela's 95th Birthday as It Is Confirmed His Health Is Improving . . . as Granddaughters Launch L20 'Legend' T-shirts," *Mail Online*, July 18, 2013, http://www.dailymail.co.uk/news/article-2368573/Nelson-Mandela-celebrations-South-Africa-95th-birthday-confirmed-health-improving.html.

348. "Zuma Thought Poor Whites Were Doing Well," *News24*, July 18, 2013, http://www.news24.com/SouthAfrica/News/Zuma-on-poor-whites-I-thought-they-were-all-doing-so-well-20130718.

349. Wandoo Makurdi, "Nelson Mandela Showing Sustained Improvement, Says South Africa President, Jacob Zuma," *Huffington Post*, July 22, 2013, http://www.huffingtonpost.com/2013/07/22/nelson-mandela-sustained-improvement-south-africa-president-jacob-zuma_n_3634771.html.

350. SAPA, "DA Pamphlet Showing Madiba, Suzman Embracing Angers ANC," *City Press*, Apr. 8, 2013, http://www.citypress.co.za/politics/da-pamphlet-showing-madiba-suzman-embracing-angers-anc/.

351. AP, "Nelson Mandela Looking Frail in News Video at Anti-apartheid Hero's Home," *Guardian*, Apr. 29, 2013, http://www.guardian.co.uk/world/2013/apr/29/nelson-mandela-frail-video-zuma-visit.

352. Jon Herskovitz, "Analysis: ANC Risks Losing South Africa's 'Born Free' Voters," Reuters, Jan. 1, 2013, http://www.reuters.com/article/2013/01/28/us -safrica-anc-idUSBRE90R0GH20130128; Luke Waters, "South Africa's 'Born-free' Generation," *World News Australia,* July 2, 2013, http://www.sbs.com.au/ news/article/1784720/South-Africas-born-free-generation.

INDEX

421

Missionaries, 16–17, 19, 22, 24; in
  pre-1870 Cape Colony, 50, 53,
  58–59, 61, 68–69; in Natal and
  Afrikaner republics, 71, 75, 78,
  93–94, 99–101, 104; *post-1870*,
  122–24, 126–33, 156, 164, 171–73,
  191
Mixed farmers: economy of, 15–21;
  society of, 21–30
Mlambo-Ngcuka, Phumzile, 302
Modise, Joe, 269, 272
Mofolo, Thomas, 87
Mogoeng, Mogoeng, 322, 323
Monongoaha, Oriel, 178
Montsioa, George, 175
Moody's, 330
Moseneke, Dikgang, 322
Moshoeshoe, 86, 94–95, 106–7
Mosquitoes, 20, 93, 104
Motlana, Dr. Ntatho, 273
Motlanthe, Kgalema, 290, 296–97,
  313–15, 318–19
Motsepe, Patrice, 329
Movement for Democratic Change,
  300
Mozambique: *pre-1870*, 3, 16, 32, 36,
  45, 84; *post-1870*, 214, 216,
  231–32, 236, 257, 269, 299, 342
Mpande, 91
Mpondo, 18, 72
Mpumalanga province, 334
Msimang, Richard, 174–75
Mswati, 86
Mthethwa, Nathi, 313, 340
Mthimkulu, Oupa Thando, 238
Mufamadi, Sidney, 273
Mugabe, Robert, 216, 300–301, 328
Multiparty Forum, 325
Multiparty Negotiating Forum, 325
Muslims, 36, 65
Myanmar, 209
Mzilikazi, 86–87, 91, 93, 138

Namibia: *pre-1948*, 4–5, 8, 70, 159,
  187; *post-1948*, 214, 222, 230–32,
  236, 239–40, 243, 300

Natal: precolonial, 4, 7, 12, 18, 21–22;
  pre-1870, 65, 72, 75, 85, 90–92,
  96–100; *post-1870*, 158, 208, 230,
  249–50, 260
National Assembly, 269, 273
National Building Regulations, 306
National Council of Provinces, 269
National Executive Committee (of the
  ANC), 296, 297, 320
National Housing Code (2000), 305
National Income Dynamics Study, 329
Nationalism. *See* Afrikaner nationalism
National party: *1910–48*, 162;
  1948–78, 187–88, 190, 198, 207;
  1978–89, 223–26, 234, 237;
  post-1989, 247–50, 255, 269–70,
  271, 272, 288, 294, 346
National Prosecuting Authority, 295
National Security Study Memorandum
  39, 219, 232
National Union of Mineworkers, 331
National Union of South African
  Students (NUSAS), 205, 212
Nation-building, 290
Native Laws Amendment Act (*1937*),
  180
Natives Land Act (*1913*), 163–64, 245
Natives Representative Council, 182,
  185
Native Trust and Land Act (*1936*),
  180, 245
Naudé, C. F. Beyers, 204–5, 239
Ndebele, 86–90, 93, 102
Ndlambe, 73, 80
NEC. *See* National Executive Committee
Negotiating Forum, 249, 250
NEPAD. *See* New Partnership for
  Africa's Development
New Age, 316
New National Party, 294
New Partnership for Africa's Develop-
  ment, 299
Ngcobo, Sandile, 322
Ngoyi, Lilian, 209
Ngqika, 73, 75, 77, 80
Nicholson, Chris, 296